Maurice Gilbert, S.J.

THE PONTIFICAL BIBLICAL INSTITUTE

A Century of History (1909-2009)

Translated by Leo Arnold, S.J.

EDITRICE PONTIFICIO ISTITUTO BIBLICO

Imprimi potest
Romae, die 21 mensis Januarii anno MMIX

J.M. ABREGO, S.J.
Rector
Pontificii Instituti Biblici

Cover: Serena Aureli
Editing: Carlo Valentino
Printing: Consorzio AGE – Roma

Printed in Italy: February 2009

First reprint

ISBN: 978-88-7653-**643**-4

FOREWORD

In May 1909 Pius X founded the Pontifical Biblical Institute in Rome which he entrusted to the Society of Jesus. It seemed fitting, on the occasion of the centenary of that academic institution, to tell its story from its origins.

Since, at the request of the rector of the Institute, Fr. Stephen F. Pisano, S.J., whom I here thank for his confidence, it is a matter of establishing the facts in their historical truth, as far as that is possible, the archives of the Institute, in Rome (APIBR) and Jerusalem (APIBJ) have been largely drawn upon, as well as some other sources.

In Rome and Jerusalem, for the Institute has two centres, the main one being in Rome and the one in Jerusalem, opened in 1927, being only a branch. The account that follows contains two parts, one concerning the Roman centre and the other, the Jerusalem one. Their history is linked, of course, but the situation of the two houses and the problems that have cropped up in them favour the separate treatment of what happened in each of them.

The historical account deals only with the Institute, omitting what properly concerns the two Jesuit communities, in Rome and Jerusalem, in charge of the two centres. The history of those religious communities would require an enquiry based on other criteria and that will be left aside in this book.

Lastly, in the second part of this work the analysis of specifically academic matters, of which earlier chapters explain the meaning and development, has been relegated to a final chapter.

The century the Biblical Institute has come through has had its difficult, even hard, times, and other, happier ones, but it has always wanted to serve the Church and the Bible, whatever direction it may have taken at this or that time.

Written originally in French, this book is appearing simultaneously in other languages. Mr. Carlo Valentino has seen to the Italian and Fr. Leo Arnold, S.J., has done the English version. I wish to thank them sincerely for this. I also thank archivists of other sources who have allowed me to publish certain documents here.

Finally, my sincere gratitude goes to Cardinal Carlo Maria Martini, S. J., to Fr. Jean-Michel Poffet, O. P., and to my fellow Jesuits Jean-Noël Aletti, William J. Fulco, Bernard J. McGuckian, Karl Plötz and Francesco Rossi de Gasperis; each of them came to my assistance with their valuable co-operation at specific times when the book was being written.

I dedicate this book to our two founders, Fathers Leopold Fonck and Alexis Mallon, as well as to our benefactors, in particular the Coëtlosquet family, without whom the Institute would not exist.

Rome, January 20th, 2009

PART ONE

THE PONTIFICAL BIBLICAL INSTITUTE IN ROME

In the course of this century the Biblical Institute has been governed as a whole, that is to say, both in Rome and Jerusalem, by thirteen successive rectors, all Jesuits, whose names are as follows:

Leopold FONCK, German, from 1909-1918, died in 1930; refugee in Switzerland during the Great War, his place was taken from 1915 by the vice-rector, Andrés FERNÁNDEZ TRUYOLS,

– Andrés FERNÁNDEZ TRUYOLS, Spanish, from 1918 to 1924, died in 1961,

– John J. O'ROURKE, American, from 1924 to 1930, died in 1958,

– Augustin BEA, German, from 1930-1949, Cardinal in 1959, died in 1968.

– Ernst VOGT, Swiss, from 1949-1963, died in 1984,

– Roderick A. F. MACKENZIE, Canadian, from 1963-1969, died in 1994,

– Carlo Maria MARTINI, Italian, from 1969-1978, Cardinal in 1983,

– Maurice GILBERT, Belgian, from 1978-1984,

– Albert VANHOYE, French, from 1984-1990, Cardinal in 2006,

– Klemens STOCK, German, from 1990-1996,

– Robert F. O'TOOLE, American, from 1996-2002,

– Stephen F. PISANO, American, from 2002 to 2008,

– José María ABREGO DE LACY, Spanish, from 2008-.

The list of the Directors of the Institute in Jerusalem will be found at the beginning of the second part of this book.

CHAPTER I

The preliminaries of the foundation
1885-1909

Bibliography

Jean CALÈS, *Un Maître de l'exégèse contemporaine. Le P. Ferdinand PRAT, S.J.*, Paris, Beauchesne, 1942, esp. pp. 61-80. – Francesco TURVASI, *Giovanni Genocchi e la controversia modernista*, Uomini e dottrine, 20, Roma, Ed. di Storia e Letteratura, 1974, 502 p. – Ernst VOGT, "San Pio X fondatore del Pontificio Istituto Biblico", in *San Pio X promotore degli studi biblici, fondatore del Pontificio Istituto Biblico*, Roma, PIB, 1955, pp. 23-42. – Le Père LAGRANGE, *Au service de la Bible. Souvenirs personnels*, Chrétiens de tous les temps, 22, Paris, Cerf, 1967, esp. pp. 119-138.

I. Under Leo XIII: from 1885-1903

The foundation of the Biblical Institute was the outcome of a long process aimed at restoring the fortunes of Catholic exegesis after two centuries of stagnation. In 1680 the victory of Bossuet over Richard Simon had indeed sounded the triumph of traditional exegesis over modern criticism.

1. A difficult setting

Towards the end of the 19th century, several factors questioned that traditional exegesis.

From the time that Champollion, from 1822 on, discovered the principles governing the deciphering of the hieroglyphics of the ancient Egyptian language until the discoveries of Sumerian and Akkadian monuments and literatures in Mesopotamia, the cultural and religious setting in which the Bible was rooted gradually appeared. In palaeontology, too, successive discoveries were made that revealed the great antiquity of prehistoric man: the Neanderthal skull had been found in 1856, and the *homo sapiens* at Cro-Magnon in 1868. As regards the natural sciences, Darwin's book on the *Origin of the*

Species by way of Natural Selection that appeared in 1859 gave credit to the thesis of transformism or the evolution of the species in the course of time.

Moreover, in non-Catholic exegetical circles, rationalism was *de rigueur*. It rejected any kind of revelation and the supernatural. To take just one famous example, the *Vie de Jésus* by Ernest Renan, which appeared in 1863, enjoyed enormous success in the bookshops. These same circles were putting forth several theses on the composition of the Pentateuch, for example, and, on the synoptic gospels, the theory of the two sources was beginning to clarify their prehistory.

All these works were questioning the traditional theses on the Bible, the history of its composition and its chronology of the origins, the attribution of the Pentateuch to Moses, and the figure of Jesus, in the eyes of rationalists, was losing its divine character, with his miracles and resurrection being rejected. Besides, comparison between the religion and culture of the Bible and those of the neighbouring countries of the ancient Near East was remeasuring the originality of the former, when it was not purely and simply being put on the same level as mythology.

In the face of these questionings, Catholic exegesis vegetated in a state of torpor, inventing fragile solutions like concordism until the German Jesuit, Rudolf Cornely (1830-1909) who had become professor of exegesis at the Gregorian University in 1879, published, over the period 1885-1886, his *Historica et critica introductio in utriusque Testamenti libros sacros* that comprised three stout volumes of real scholarship and sound theology.

The movement therefore started off in Rome. It was to continue there, even if the arrival of Fr. Lagrange, O. P., in Jerusalem and the opening of the École biblique at the end of 1890, then the appearance of the first issue of the *Revue biblique* at the end of 1891, were going to serve as points of reference a little later – in 1892 Leo XIII had approved those undertakings – before giving rise to concern and contention.

In 1893, Leo XIII issued his encyclical "*Providentissimus Deus*", the first important document from the Roman teaching office in modern times on the interpretation of Scripture. The guidelines given by the Pope, who was aware of what was at stake at the time, were all remarkable for their openness, common sense and encouragement.

2. *Two Roman efforts: from 1889-1898*

In 1889 the "Società per gli studi biblici" had been founded. It was also called "Accademia". It had the support of Cardinal Parocchi, the Vicar of Rome, and even of Leo XIII (cf. Turvasi, pp. 52 ff.). It included some big names, Italian and foreign, who, in the course of their public sessions set out the results of their work. Lagrange spoke there in 1890 about the Nabatean inscription he had just discovered. But when in 1898 Giovanni Genocchi spoke on the Pentateuch in contemporary research (cf. Turvasi, pp. 64-77) he actually fell into step with Fr. Lagrange, whose lecture given at Fribourg and published at the beginning of the *Revue biblique* for 1898 set fire to the powder-keg: that Moses was the author of the Pentateuch is not an article of faith was Lagrange's conclusion. The storm broke out and the Society had to put an end to its activities.

Meanwhile, Genocchi had nevertheless, with the support of Leo XIII, been appointed professor of Holy Scripture at the Pontifical University of the Apollinare in Rome. That institution, to be moved to the Lateran in 1913, would also open a special programme in Holy Scripture with an introductory course, a course in exegesis and a course in Assyriology (Turvasi, pp. 77-82). Genocchi dealt with the two books of Samuel in it. But there again his critical attitudes led to the revoking of his mandate in June 1898 and Leo XIII confirmed his removal (Turvasi, pp. 89-93).

On November 25th, 1898, in a letter to the Master General of the Friars Minor, Leo XIII called for greater prudence in accepting new theories coming from non-Catholic circles (cf. Lagrange, *Souvenirs*, p. 94). Same warning bell in the letter *"Depuis le jour"* that Leo XIII addressed to the clergy of France on September 8th, 1899 (cf. MONTAGNES, *Marie-Joseph Lagrange. Une biographie critique*, Paris, Cerf, 2004, pp. 172-173). These were obviously putting the brakes on. It was thought at the time that the Pope was influenced in this domain by Cardinal Camillo Mazzella, S.J. (1833-1900), very hostile to exegetical novelties.

3. *The Pontifical Biblical Commission: 1901-1903*

The Pontifical Biblical Commission was established by Leo XIII with his letter *"Vigilantiae"* of October 30th, 1902 (*EB*, 137-148). A preparatory commission actually met on January 23rd, 1902. It was made up of three Cardinals, Parocchi, Segna and Vives y Tuto and twelve consultors. At this session (Turvasi, pp. 218-219) it was decided, among other things, to ask the Pope to set up a "Biblical Library" in Rome, in which the books would be at the disposal of the members of the commission. In the early months of 1903 the list of Cardinals and consultors was drawn up. The Pope added Cardinals Satolli and Rampolla, the Secretary of State who, on the death of Cardinal Parocchi in January 1903, became president of this commission; the consultors were forty-one in number; among them were Fr. Ferdinand Prat, Fr. Lagrange and Fr. Genocchi!

Now when he was summoned to Rome on February 1st, 1903, Fr. Lagrange was given to understand by Cardinal Rampolla that Leo XIII wished the *Revue biblique* to become the official organ of the Biblical Commission (Lagrange, *Souvenirs*, p. 122): "But that was not all, adds Lagrange. The Pope had resolved to found a Biblical Institute in Rome, widely open to the capabilities of the different orders, inviting seculars and regulars, and I was to have a place in it, while keeping the directorship of the *Revue*". He also notes in this month of February 1903 (*Souvenirs*, p.125): "If the spirit of the *Revue biblique* and the method used at the Jerusalem School seem to the Holy See to be of use, the speculative part of the biblical School along with the *Revue* could easily be moved to Rome. Three or four professorships could be set up at Easter. The Jerusalem School would be kept especially as a school for applied studies. When the courses are finished in Rome, a year would be spent in Jerusalem doing geography, topography and archaeology on the spot and making contact with the customs and languages of the country".

Some weeks later Leo XIII received Fr. Lagrange who relates the interview: "Yes, he said to me kindly, go to Jerusalem for Easter, then you will come back, I shall have you working with Us" (*Souvenirs*, p. 133). But, suffering as he was from erysipelas, Lagrange was not back before the spring of 1905. On June 22nd, 1903, answering a letter from Lagrange, Cardinal Rampolla points out to him: "As regards what concerns the Institute of Higher Biblical Studies, it is clear that your Reverence is not aware of the facts in detail. I can assure you in advance that your Reverence will be fully satisfied once you have fully understood the steps taken by the Holy Father in this matter" (*Souvenirs*, p. 134).

What had happened? Some notes by Fr. Prat published by Fr. Calès in 1942 tell us. The original manuscript has not been found. On January 31st, 1903, Prat had been appointed a consultor to the Biblical Commission and remained one until 1907. In his notes, under the date of February 19th, 1903, we read as follows: "The Review, however fanciful it may seem, has been decided upon in principle and, for the moment, no attempt is to be made to stop it. It is the most cherished of the projects. Why? It is hard to say. Be that as it may, they are sticking to it. The Cardinals are taking their stand behind the Pope's wish, and he is prepared to make any sacrifice. Then there will be the Institute. They are looking for teachers. The Holy Father is reported as saying he would do anything to bring about the success of this undertaking, the last one in his life" (Calès, *Prat*, p. 68).

Later on, probably after Easter in 1903, Fr. Prat was given the task of drawing up a plan for the Biblical Institute which was first discussed in a sub-committee. When he presented it to the commission itself he explained that the plan did not completely reflect his thinking because he had had to take into account the opinions expressed at the sub-committee stage. However that may be, a decision had to be taken about what kind of institute they wanted: "Is it an ordinary school, aimed at making a lot of people with doctorates, filling the world with teachers who are not quite so ignorant, in short, to popularize the Bible? The thing is easy, even useful, but it is not to be trumpeted forth *urbi et orbi* in that form. It is not worth the trouble. Do we really want to start up a proper higher school that can rival the famous special schools, or at least bear comparison not too unfavourably with them? If that is what is wanted, the plan is worthy of the Pope and Rome, supremely useful, for it is better to train two real scholars than ten mediocre teachers. (That) seems necessary to raise the standard of Catholic scholarship and put an end to our inferior standing. But this concept has its consequences in terms of time for studies, which should last at least three years, and in terms of the entrance (test), examinations, etc. Everyone is of this opinion. An Institute of truly higher studies is necessary, whatever the consequences may be ...". Finally, quoting a passage from a letter he had written to Fr. General Luis Martín the date of which is not known but which may be June, 1903, Prat concludes: "I can say, without betraying any secrets, that everything I have suggested so far has been unanimously agreed upon both by the Consultors and the Cardinals, and approved by the Pope himself" (Calès, *Prat*, pp. 73-74).

We are fortunate in having a printed copy of the plan proposed by Fr. Prat to the commission (cf. Doc. R. I,1) in the Roman archives of the Institute. This plan, without any notes, written in French, covers seven pages and takes the form of an organic statute of the envisioned biblical Institute. It contains six chapters. 1. The purpose of the Institute is a high scholarly standard. 2. The teaching staff, which will at first comprise six professors, covers the main parts of the field (exegesis, biblical languages, archaeology, etc.), and long-term provision is made for other chairs to be set up, especially in oriental languages; the titular professors make up the Council and the Rector is chosen from among them; provision is also made for a chancellor to see to the good administration of the Institute. 3. Students are divided into those registering for the doctorate and those taking courses; students must already be doctors in theology, and the Institute offers but one diploma, the doctorate. 4. The programme contains courses in special subjects – they are not all compulsory and each professor gives two a week – and "conferences", corresponding to what are called seminars or practical exercises today. 5. There will be an entrance examination in Hebrew, Greek and biblical culture; provision is made for an oral and written examination in each course. 6. The Institute will have a good specialized library.

Fr. Prat obviously aimed high. The only point on which there was no agreement in the sub-committee was the length of the studies preparatory to the doctorate; the majority preferred three rather than two years, with the candidate starting on the thesis only in the third year. In addition, the level of competence of the teaching body must be high and this must be maintained by producing learned publications. That provision be made for a specialized library in the building of the Institute is also a good sign. We are already a far cry from the "Biblical Library" that the preparatory commission wanted in 1902.

But what is most striking when one reads this plan is, on the one hand, the serene way it is presented, with no allusion to the tensions in 1898-1899, and, on the other, the implied principle *non multa sed multum* with, furthermore, something coming from the pedagogical tradition of the Society, those "conferences" which must stimulate the students, and the willingness to help on the part of the professors.

Finally, the academic curriculum did not allow for any particular diploma at the end of the ordinary classroom work, and, if we understand it correctly, it was going to take about six or seven years from the time the student enrolled until he was declared a doctor (in what?; it does not say).

This plan was never carried out. This was because on July 20th, 1903, Leo XIII passed away at the age of ninety-three. Turvasi published (p. 220) an undated note by J.-B. Frey, a consultor of the Biblical Commission since 1910, summarizing the situation that other documents have explained in the preceding pages. This note also reveals serious tensions arising after the death of Leo XIII. Here is the text:

> At the end of Leo XIII's pontificate, the creation of a biblical institute in Rome had been decided on. Fr. Lagrange was to be its director and the "Revue biblique" was to be its official organ. Fr. Lagrange had laid it down as a condition that he would reside in Rome for only six months each year so as to be able to devote the rest of his time to the École Biblique in Jerusalem (I was told this by Fr. Hugueny, O.P., who added that Fr. Louis [O.P.] was going to be socius to Fr. Lagrange). Fr. Fleming OFM, the secretary of the Commission, would be Vice-director of the Institute. Poels, Minocchi, Genocchi, Prat were to be professors. If Leo XIII had lived two months longer this Institute would have been created; it would have been a plague upon the Church (a remark made by M. Vigouroux to Fr. Fonck). What stopped it from becoming a reality is that they had not been able to find premises suitable for it.

As Vigouroux died in 1915 and Fonck came to Rome and joined the Commission only at the end of 1908, it may be considered that this note dates from the years 1910-1915.

II. Under Pius X: from 1903-1909

Pius X was elected on August 4th, 1903. Once again it is from Fr. Prat that comes the earliest information concerning the plan for a biblical institute in Rome. On November 27th Prat is received by Pius X and notes: "The Institute will not be founded, at least not for the moment. The project has been suspended but not abandoned. Only lack of funds is putting it off. Unforeseen gifts may remove the obstacle. Meanwhile, thought should be given to building up biblical studies in the various establishments in Rome" (Calès, *Prat*, p. 77). This is just what Pius X repeats, on February 23rd, 1904, in his letter

"*Sacrae Scripturae*" which creates academic degrees in Holy Scripture at the Biblical Commission. Here is a translation of the passage in question:

> To prepare a good number of teachers who, being recommended by the soundness and purity of their teaching, interpret the sacred Books in Catholic schools, it would surely be very advantageous, and we know that this was also the wish of Leo XIII, to found a special Athenaeum in Rome, with professorships of higher education and all the equipment for biblical erudition, to which properly chosen young people from everywhere could come to receive training in biblical learning. But, since at present We lack the means, as did our predecessor, to make the thing a reality, We have the good and sure hope that one day these means will come from the generosity of Catholics ... (cf. *EB*, 150).

1. *A very tense situation*

The modernist crisis breaks out and the Roman authorities step in.

The situation, difficult as it already was, in which biblical exegesis found itself at the end of the 19th century has been pointed out above, as has been the uproar caused in 1897-1898 by Fr. Lagrange's stance on the Mosaic authorship of the Pentateuch. The crisis deepened during the early years of Pius X's pontificate. Without going into the details of the controverted exegetical positions and the reactions of the Roman teaching office, a certain number of well-known facts are recalled here which, from 1903-1908, clouded things over, especially among Catholic exegetes.

At the end of 1902, Alfred Loisy simultaneously published his "little red book" *L'Évangile et l'Église* and his *Études évangéliques*. Lagrange (cf. *RB* 12 [1903], pp. 292-313) and others saw the poison in them. On December 23rd, 1903, five of Loisy's books, including the two just mentioned, are placed on the Index. But the other little book that Fr. Lagrange published at the beginning of 1903, *La méthode historique,* aroused the conservative reaction of Fr. Alphonse Delattre, a Belgian Jesuit conversant rather with orientalism who, in May 1904, published *Autour de la question biblique*. This riposte was so effective that at the request of Pius X Delattre was called to teach at the Gregorian University, and then appointed a consultor of the Biblical Commission.

Meanwhile, the General of the Society of Jesus, Fr. Luis Martín, on the 4th of November, 1904, had sent a letter to the provincial Superiors in which he warned about a "methodum, quam appellant historicam" that had the same impious purpose as Strauss had: to undermine the foundations of revealed religion (cf. *Epistolae selectae Praepositorum Generalium ad Superiores Societatis*, Romae, 1911, p. 258). In 1905 Fr. Leopold Fonck in his turn took Fr. Lagrange to task in his study on "the struggle for the truth of Holy Scripture over the last twenty-five years" (cf. *infra*).

Changes in the Biblical Commission are observed. Besides Fr. Delattre in 1905, other consultors are appointed: the Jesuits Lucien Méchineau (cf. *infra*) in 1906 and Fonck in 1908, whereas Fr. Prat is not a consultor as from 1907.

In 1905 this same Commission also starts upon the series of its decrees aimed at calming things down but which were to hamper Catholic exegesis for several decades. These decrees deal successively with "implicit quotations" (February 13th, 1905), "what appears to be historical" (June 23rd, 1905), the Mosaic authorship of the Pentateuch (June 26th, 1906), the fourth gospel (May 29th, 1907), the book of Isaiah (June 28th, 1908) and Genesis 1–3 (June 30th, 1909). This series of decrees was to go on, as is known, in the following years.

But papal disapproval is going to make itself more explicit. At the end of May 1907, Pius X forbade the publication of Fr. Lagrange's manuscript on the book of Genesis and the one by Fr. Albert Condamin, a French Jesuit, on the book of Isaiah. On July 3rd the decree *"Lamentabili"* from the Holy Office appeared and, on September 8th the encyclical *"Pascendi"* by Pius X. Modernism was formally condemned by these two documents from the Church's teaching office.

On January 18th, 1908, the new General of the Society, Fr. Fr.-X. Wernz, sent another letter to the provincial Superiors asking that books written by religious, even if they are members of the Biblical Commission, be excluded if they smacked of modernism (cf. *Epistolae selectae*, p. 265).

Lastly, on March 8th, 1908, Loisy was excommunicated by the Holy Office.

It is important to remember, however, that during this period the Jesuits are not all in the same camp. If some, such as Delattre, Fonck and Méchineau show themselves opposed to anything questioning the traditional exegesis – and they had the support of the Vatican – others, such as Prat, Condamin or Léonce de Grandmaison are clearly more open, while loyally submitting to the directives from the Church's teaching office and from their Superiors.

2. An Institute? Two precursory signs in 1907 and 1908

In 1955 Fr. Vogt, in his article on "San Pio X", pp. 27-28, points to two episodes that prove that Pius X still clung to the hope of founding a biblical institute in Rome.

The first was recounted to Fr. Vogt by Cardinal Eugène Tisserant, who gave him further details in a letter dated February 26th, 1955 (APIBR B-XVIII,3 [XX,1/07/2]). On March 19th, 1907, Fulcran Vigouroux, the secretary of the Biblical Commission, had called Tisserant, the young seminarian, to the Rue Notre-Dame des Champs in Paris, to tell him that "the Holy Father Pius X intended to carry out a project of Leo XIII, namely the creation of a Biblical Institute. He added that the Pope, not having the necessary funds available, wished to organize that Institute gradually, starting with the professorship in Assyrian, because there was no one in Rome teaching that language in the ecclesiastical colleges. He therefore suggested that I should become the first teacher of Assyrian in Rome." But Tisserant asked to put off his coming to Rome until the end of the academic year 1907-1908 so that he could finish his studies of Semitic languages at the Institut Catholique in Paris.

When he got to Rome at the end of October, 1908, Tisserant was introduced to Cardinals Rampolla and Merry del Val, the secretary of State, and then to Pius X by Vigouroux. It was then decided that Tisserant would teach at the Athenaeum at the Apollinare and would also work at the Vatican Library. "Fu deciso che sarei stato pagato dalla cassetta personale di S. Pio X". So Tisserant taught Assyrian at the Apollinare until the beginning of the academic year 1912-1913, when the Apollinare was moved to the Lateran. He still remained at the Vatican Library, about which he gives the following details:

> When I got to Rome, the Rev. Father Ehrle [S. J., Librarian at the Vatican] had made a special section with biblical books in the room that is between the reference room and the present manuscript room. A certain number of those books were later placed at the disposal of the P. Biblical Institute, first in its premises in the Via Pompeo Magno [in the Leonine College], and then in its final premises. When I arrived there, because the projected Biblical Institute did not yet exist, the biblical section was supposed to help the Consultors of the P. Commission with biblical studies.

The request from the preparatory committee at the Biblical Commission (cf. *supra)* had been agreed to and acted upon.

The second episode was described in 1950 by Fr. Fr. Rensing, S. J., in the bulletin of the Jesuits in Cologne *Canisius* (fasc. 2, p. 7), a copy of which is kept in the APIBR (B-XVIII,3 [XX,1/07/1]). When he was a young secular priest at Münster, Rensing accompanied Fr. Fonck, his former professor of exegesis at Innsbruck, on a voyage to Palestine in the February of 1907. At Jerusalem Fonck drew up the plan for a biblical institute similar to the Dominicans' École Biblique (Rensing mistakenly speaks of the White Fathers). Did he find out about the details from the Dominicans and even from Fr. Lagrange who was actually in Jerusalem in May, 1907? In an unpleasant article that appeared on September 7th, 1912, in the *Journal des Débats*, Maurice Pernot says so, although he says it happened in 1908, which is also wrong. Still, on their return Fonck and his companion were received by Pius X on June 18th, 1907, to whom Fonck explained his plan. While listening the Pope repeated: "Va bene", then he asked Fr. Fonck to put his plan in writing so that it could be submitted to the cardinals of the Biblical Commission, or so it seems, because Rensing writes: "die Kardinalscongregation".

Nothing more is known about this matter, as Fonck did not keep the plan in question. It may also be wondered whether he was thinking of an institute in the Eternal City or whether he was thinking rather of setting up one in Innsbruck where he had already founded a biblico-patristic seminary in 1906 with a library on which Pius X had congratulated him in a letter dated July 30th, 1906 (APIBR B-XVIII,3 [XX,1/06/2]). Anyway, there is every reason to believe that Fonck knew nothing about the plan prepared by Fr. Prat in 1903.

3. Fr. Leopold Fonck, S.J. (1865-1930)

Born at Wissen, near Düsseldorf, he did brilliantly in humanities at Kempen, initiating himself into Hebrew at the same time. From 1883 to 1890 he was at the Germanicum in Rome and followed the curriculum in philosophy and theology at the Gregorian University where he gained the doctorate in both branches; he had Fr. R. Cornely as professor of exegesis. He was ordained priest in 1889. After theology he taught for two years in his own diocese, Münster, then, in 1892 he entered the Society of Jesus. When the noviceship was over, he went to England for a year to brush up his theology and exegesis. Then he visited the Near East in 1895 and 1896, getting to know Syriac and Arabic as well; in 1896 he met Fr. Lagrange (cf. Lagrange, *Souvenirs*, p. 71). Back in Europe, from 1896 to 1899 he specialized in Assyriology and Egyptology at the universities of Berlin and Munich. In 1901 he was appointed professor of New Testament exegesis at Innsbruck, a post he kept until 1908.

In 1900 he published his first book; it was on biblical flora; in 1902 his second one appeared, on the gospel parables; in 1903 his third, on Jesus' miracles; in 1905 his fourth, on *Der Kampf um die Wahrheit der Heiligen Schrift seit 25 Jahren*, of which Fr. Lagrange, who had been taken to task in it, wrote a long review in the *Revue biblique* 15 (1906), pp. 48-60. Lastly, in 1906, his fifth appeared, on method in scholarly work. To these books should be added several articles that appeared in the journal *Zeitschrift für katholische Theologie*, in the first two volumes of the *Lexicon Biblicum*, edited by M. Hagen in 1905 and 1906, as well as some unsigned articles on questions of biblical hermeneutics that appeared in 1901 in *La Civiltà Cattolica* (cf. Lagrange, *Souvenirs*, p. 110, note 42).

At Innsbruck Fr. Fonck had shown himself an excellent organizer, but also a vigorous polemicist, a stout defender of exegetical tradition and increasingly opposed to Fr. Lagrange whom he accused of following Protestant exegetes too much.

4. *A first step: the "Cursus superior Scripturae Sacrae", 1908-1909*

During the academic year 1908-1909 the Gregorian University, which at that time was located in the Borromeo palace at no. 120, Via del Seminario, offered a "Higher course in Holy Scripture". The wish to see such a programme set up had been expressed by Cardinal Merry del Val to Fr. Méchineau when, in the final months of 1906, the latter, who had just been appointed a consultor of the Biblical Commission, went to visit him: "A school of Holy Scripture", the Cardinal said, "ought to be established at the Gregorian University to spearhead the movement" (cf. Doc R. I,2, p. 5). Fr. Lucien Méchineau took up the idea in September 1907.

Fr. Lucien Méchineau (1849-1919), a professor of Holy Scripture in the Jesuit theological school at Chieri, near Turin, had been called to the Gregorian University in the autumn of 1906, not in 1907 as is often written, to replace Fr. Delattre, whose teaching was a disaster among the students. Méchineau thus entered upon the last stage of his long career as teacher of the Bible. He had made himself known in the past especially with an article that appeared on November 5th, 1898, in the journal *Études* in which he treated Lagrange as a deserter because of his article on the "Sources of the Pentateuch".

During his first two academic years, 1906-1907 and 1907-1908, Méchineau on his own gave the courses on the exegesis of the two Testaments at the rate of five hours a week. His courses were intended for students in the third and fourth year of theology. Because of his age, such a load was tiring for him.

However, he realized that his teaching was not really preparing the students for the examinations that Pius X, in his letter *"Scripturae Sacrae"* of February 23rd, 1904, had entrusted to the Biblical Commission. To ensure success in these examinations leading to the academic degree of the licentiate something else was needed.

On September 16th, 1907, Méchineau took the initiative in the letter he sent to Fr. General Wernz (cf. Doc. R. I,2), but one of the conditions for opening a "higher course in Holy Scripture" at the Gregorian was, in his eyes, to have an extra professor "of criticism and exegesis". On being consulted by Fr. General, Fr. Hermann van Laak, who was then at the Gregorian, teaching the dogma of Revelation and the inspiration of Scripture in the first year of theology, showed himself favourable, except for two details, but in particular he proposed Fr. Fonck as extra professor: that is the opinion he expressed in a letter to Fr. General on October 18th, 1907 (ARSI PIB-1001-III,3, pp. 5-6).

Some months later, Fr. General asked Fr. Méchineau to prepare a plan for this "higher Course" for him, and the latter, in a letter of April 18th, 1908, submitted it to him, first of all proposing that Fr. Fonck be brought to Rome as professor, not without noting that the latter could sometimes be too lively in polemics (cf. Doc. R. I,3).

On being consulted, in his turn, by Fr. General, Fr. Schwärzler, the Austrian provincial, gave his consent and informed Fr. Fonck about it by letter on July 31st, 1908. Finally, on August 5th, Fr. General called Fr. Fonck to Rome to take part in this new "higher Course". Once the decisions were taken, Fr. Méchineau wrote to Fr. Fonck on August 16th to explain to him the content of the programme and how it was to work (Doc. R. I,4).

For the academic year 1908-1909 then, Méchineau would take on the lectures in Old Testament and Fonck those on the New. Both would, of course, each have to teach the students in theology two hours a week. For the "higher Course", each would also have two hours, except that Fr. Fonck might have to take three, which had not yet been decided in August 1908. This was done when classes were resumed, since Fonck also had to give the course in biblical Greek.

As regards the details of the programme of the "higher Course", it was up to each of the two professors to prepare the students for the examinations at the Biblical Commission, which had precisely fixed the subjects, as he thought fit. But, at all events, in Méchineau's opinion, one year of preparation would not be enough; it was already necessary to start thinking of two academic years.

On the choice of Fr. Fonck, Méchineau had to make certain things clear to him which, after the lapse of a century, are not without their humorous side: "Fr. Rector [of the Gregorian, Fr. L. Querini]", writes Méchineau to Fonck on September 1st, 1908, "has told me that as regards the choice of the new professor, from the Vatican came three requests, which come to the same thing: 1. that he be conservative, 2. that he have the reputation of being so, 3. that he give every assurance that he will not change. This is exactly what they wanted two years ago when I was called here." (APIBR B-XVIII,3 XVIII,3 [XX, 1/08/7]).

As ill-luck would have it, if Fr. Fonck is to be believed (cf. *Primum Quinquennium Pontificii Instituti Biblici*, Rome, 1915, p. 7), Fr. Méchineau's health could hold out no longer against this regime. The "higher Course", that had just been set up, was in trouble, probably as from February, 1909, for, on January 10th Pius X, while receiving Fr. Fonck, had been pleased with the success achieved until then (APIBR B-XVIII,3 [XX,1/09/1]).

5. *The real plan for a Pontifical Biblical Institute: February-May 1909*

This real plan, drawn up in this context, covers two pages which Fr. Fonck, having spoken about it to Fr. General, submitted to Pius X at a private audience on February 14th, 1909. Fonck noted the fact on the copy he kept (cf. Doc. R. I,5) adding, still in German: "He [Pius X] took the sheets and read them aloud, then he said «Sì, lo facciamo», [Yes, let us do it!]. He gives his approval. Sent on to the V. R. Fr. General on February 15th, 1909". This text, which in Latin has as title: "De Pontificia Academia Biblica erigenda", marks the beginning of the process which was to lead, in May, to the creation of the Pontifical Biblical Institute. Here is a summary of the three chapters that make it up:

I. The reasons for setting up an Academy: 1. the "tristissima" present situation as regards the Bible, confusion and trouble, 2. furthering biblical studies among Catholics, putting an end to unbecoming and dangerous dependence on heterodox authors, 3. the will of the Holy See expressed by Pius X in his letter "*Scripturae Sacrae*".

II. The purposes of the Academy: to promote biblical scholarship as the Church understands it and in accordance with the norms of the Holy See, 2. to train young people from every nation and religious order who, later on, being commended by the soundness and purity of their teaching, defend the dignity of the sacred Books, 3. to help the members of the Academy and anyone wishing to do specialized studies in exegesis by placing the appropriate means at their disposal, 4. to defend, publish and promote sound exegesis according to the norms of the Holy See, especially against some recent "false, erroneous, rash, heretical" opinions.

III. Means suited to the aims of the Academy: 1. courses and exercises preparing the young people for the examinations at the Biblical Commission by giving them a methodical training, 2. a biblical library, including the works of ancient authors – the Fathers of the Church – and those of modern ones, Catholic or not, encyclopaedias, periodicals, critical editions, 3. publications by the Academy to defend the Catholic truth concerning the sacred Books and spread sound doctrine everywhere in biblical matters. 4. One may add: a biblical museum, public lectures, some funds for travel, and others for the maintenance of the members of the Academy in Rome.

The main advantage of this text is its brevity. In a few sentences it goes to the essential point. Still, several particular matters can be noted. It speaks of a Pontifical Academy in Rome but without saying whether it would be independent or attached to an institution. Next, the tone is distinctly one of a confrontational period; there is talk of confusion, trouble, danger, recent opinions described with adjectives reserved for condemnations from above. On the other hand, continual stress is laid upon sound doctrine and fidelity to the directives from the Holy See and by this is meant the decrees from the Biblical Commission, the decree *"Lamentabili"* and the encyclical *"Pascendi"*. Finally, on the means to be taken, once again the essential point is made: examinations will be taken at the Biblical Commission, as was the case for the "higher course in Scripture"; the Academy would therefore not be totally autonomous. A biblical library, publications by the Academy itself, a museum, are added, but nothing is said about where the money for all this is coming from.

Compared to the plan prepared by Fr. Prat in 1903 and approved then, Fr. Fonck's text is still vague and the atmosphere has changed; a crisis is on.

In 1929 (APIBR B-XVII,3 [XX,1/09/37, p.2]), Fr. Fonck was to point out that in February, 1909, he was giving the "higher Course" at the Gregorian, that he did not know Leo XIII's plan and that, in his plan proposed to Pius X, he had drawn inspiration from the biblico-patristic Seminary he had founded in Innsbruck in 1906.

The unresolved problem was that of financing the operation. The Holy See had exhausted its reserves in helping the victims of the terrible earthquake that had destroyed the city of Messina on December 28th, 1908. "I have not got a penny", Pius X said to Fr. Fonck, "but I give you the Sacred Heart as patron of the Institute and we shall see that the Lord will fulfil his promise to bless anything consecrated to his Sacred Heart". In addition, the Pope undertook to say three Our Fathers and three Hail Marys in honour of the Sacred Heart every day, in the hope of obtaining the funds for creating the institute (cf. Vogt, "San Pio X", p. 32).

In the meantime, he suggested to Fr. Fonck to contact the retired bishop of Olmütz, Olomouc today, in the Czech Republic. Theodor Kohn, whose generosity towards the Vatican's financial needs was well known (cf. R. Aubert in DHGE 29, 2006, col. 474-475). On this same day, February 14th, Fr. Fonck therefore passed on Pius X's request, probably along with the two pages the Pope had approved at that morning's audience, by way of *aide-mémoire* (APIBR, B-XVIII,3 [XX,1/09/3]). What was the archbishop's answer? Certain indications (cf. *infra*) point to its being positive.

The next day, February 15th, Fr, Fonck submits what he calls, in the margin and in pencil, a "first sketch", *Erst Entwurf*, to Fr. General (APIBR B-XVIII,3 [XX,1/09/4]). Now here the title is different: "De Pontificio Instituto Biblico in Universitate Gregoriana erigendo". The text, also in Latin, takes up the three chapters of the one that had been submitted the previous day to Pius X and adds a fourth. This is a summary of it:

I. The reasons for setting up an Institute like this. Here the text covers two and a half pages. Modernism and its misdeeds are mentioned and the encyclical *"Pascendi"* is quoted, then a passage from the Letter *"Scripturae Sacrae"* in which Pius X expressed his desire to create an Athenaeum specializing in the Bible in Rome is reproduced; finally, given the number of its students, its past and even the recent "higher Course in Scripture", the Gregorian is the place to set up this biblical Institute.

II. The aims of the Institute are those given to Pius X the day before.

III. The means to be put in place are also the same, except that it should be pointed out that the funds envisaged for journeys concern, among others, those to be made "in regiones biblicas".

IV. Constitution and regulation of the Institute. This new chapter contains four points: 1. the president of the Institute will be appointed by the Fr. General of the Society, 2. the professors will be the biblical scholars at the Gregorian, 3. a Secretary will have charge of the administration, including that of the library, 4. fidelity to the directives from the Holy See in biblical matters is again insisted upon.

Fr. Fonck is obviously not wasting time. You have to strike while the iron is hot! But, apart from inserting the projected Institute into the Gregorian University and the Society's responsibility – it would thus lose its autonomy – the text is still somewhat vague when compared with Fr. Prat's text. There is still an air of crisis about it.

But the comparison between the two documents, the one Fonck gave to Pius X and the one he submitted to Fr. General the next day, raises a question. Let us remember that the title of the first one is: "Biblical Academy" and the second "Pontifical Biblical Institute to be set up at the Gregorian University". It is hard to believe that the change was made without the Pope knowing about it.

However, the budget that Fonck drew up and submitted to the Pope on February 25th, and then to the Fr. General on March 6th (APIBR B-XVIII,3 [XX,1/09/5]) speaks only of a Biblical Academy. The budget amounts to half a million Italian liras, about three million euros at the end of 2008, say. The academy would be installed on the first floor of the building recently acquired by the Holy See in the Via della Pigna and Fonck had allowed for about one hundred people there. Is there still any question of setting up at the Gregorian?

Yes, because on March 30th Fonck lays before Pius X a preliminary plan for what was to become the apostolic letter "*Vinea electa*" in May. Now this plan, which repeats almost word for word the ends and means that Fonck set before the Pope in February, adds a paragraph III that says: "Institutum cum Pontificia nostra Universitate Gregoriana ita coniunctum erit, ut eius cura ac regimen specialiter et immediate ad Praepositum Generalem Societatis Iesu spectet" (APIBR B-XVIII,3 [XX,1/09/7, p. 3]). The publication of the apostolic letter was arranged for April 2nd, 1909.

But there seems to have been some disagreement between the Vatican and the Fr. General in the April of that very same year, 1909. On April 16th, Fonck actually wrote a letter intended for the Pope but which he never sent to him (APIBR B-XVIII,3 [XX,1/09/8]). In this document, that at least reveals the writer's thinking, knowing that some of Fr. Lagrange's students were going to teach in Rome in the academic year 1909-1910, Fonck considers that the future "biblical Institute" – that is what it is now called – ought to be put under the authority of the Society. In this way he excludes one of the preliminaries in Fr. Prat's plan at the time of Leo XIII. But then the intentions of the donor, the "Reverendissimo Benefattore e Fondatore" – probably Mgr. Kohn – would not be complied with. To get out of the impasse, "mentioning the Society could be omitted in the Brief, while informing the Father General in a private letter of the intentions of Your Holiness" (p. 2, translated from the Italian). As regards the library, which also posed a problem, to oblige members of the Institute to go to the Vatican, where Fr. Ehrle had already got together a stock of biblical books (cf. *supra*), would be very inconvenient and, if one did not want students from the Institute to go to the one that the "modernists in Rome" had created in the centre of the city (this refers to the library opened by Fr. Genocchi: cf. Turvasi, *Genocchi*, p. 94, note 2), it would be better if the Institute had its own, especially if the transfer of the Vatican library's stock of books on the Bible to the Institute could be considered.

Such were the problems being discussed. The result was that in the second draft of the apostolic letter "*Vinea electa*", approved by Pius X on May 5th, 1909, every mention of the Society was suppressed and the date fixed for the publication of the document is now May 7th. Of this second plan we have the manuscript draft by Fr. Fonck (APIBR B-XVIII,3 [20,1/09/9-10]).

On May 6th Fr. Fonck submitted his sketch for the "Statutum organicum Pontificii Instituti Biblici" to Cardinal Merry del Val, the Secretary of State. We have Fr. Fonck's manuscript draft of this, too (APIBR B-XVIII,3 [XX,1/09/10]). Now in this draft it is made clear in paragraph II,8, that the president of the Institute is to be appointed by the Pope on the basis of a list of three names that the General of the Society shall put before him and, in paragraph III,13, that the professors shall be appointed by the Fr. General, with the agreement of the Holy See. These two arrangements were to remain in the final text of the "*Leges*" of the Institute. On the problem of the library it is agreed that the Institute is to have its own (paragraph V).

But not everything was finished and time was passing. One last decision was made about the appointment of full-time professors. The Holy See intended them to be appointed for only one year. Fr. Fonck, after consulting the Fr. General and one of his Assistants, wrote to the Secretary of State on May 26th, asking him to leave out that awkward restriction (APIBR B-XVIII,3 [XX,1/09/12]), which in fact disappeared in the final text of the Institute's "*Leges*".

Finally the apostolic letter "*Vinea electa*" was published on the front page of *L'Osservatore Romano* for May 30th, 1909, Whitsunday, and it bears the date May 7th. It is followed by an introduction that is unsigned but was written by Fr. Fonck. On June 1st the pontifical document was published in the *Acta Apostolicae Sedis*.

On May 29th Cardinal Merry del Val had written to Fr. General Wernz to assure him "come d'intesa", "as agreed", that the Biblical Institute was entrusted to the Society (cf. *Acta Romana Societatis Jesu* 1 [1906-1909], p. 32). On June 11th a note from the Secretariat of State indicated that the Pope had appointed Fr. Fonck President of the Institute (cf. *AAS* 1 [1909], p. 571).

Thus the foundation of the biblical Institute was essentially the joint work of Pius X and Fr. Fonck. Cardinal Merry del Val and Fr. General Wernz cooperated in it but at one remove, both being in regular contact with Fr. Fonck. The Cardinal and Fr. General probably met several times but without leaving any written document. On the other hand, it seems that the Biblical Commission did not intervene.

Fr. Fonck worked so well, right from February 1909, that the first suggestions he then submitted, either to the Pope or to Fr. General, are almost word for word to be found in the final document "*Vinea electa*" (*EB* 282-298), including its most polemical sentences. As for the "*Leges*" of the Institute (*EB* 299-323), it is clear that Fr. Fonck had at hand the plan prepared by Fr. Prat for the Biblical Commission and approved by Leo XIII in June 1903. To be sure of this it is enough to compare the following two texts where the similarity is the most striking:

– in 1903, in paragraph IV,2 (cf. Doc. R.I,1):

  In addition to their ordinary teaching, professors must help and direct students in their essays. They will strive to make the Institute known and appreciated with their scholarly publications. This is why it is good that, as far as possible, they remain in their special field, without taking on a number of courses that would be contrary to the traditions and dignity of higher education, harmful to their personal work and bad for the intellectual training of the students".

– in 1909 the "*Leges*" of the Institute stipulate, in paragraph III, 15 (cf. *EB* 313):

  Magistri omnes etiam extra lectiones atque exercitationes practicas alumnis praesto erunt eosque in disciplinae biblicae studiis adiuvabunt ac dirigent. Scriptis quoque suis propositum Instituto finem assequendum curabunt, illudque maxime cavebunt, ne in varias ac dissitas doctrinae investigationes abstracti, maturo laborum suorum fructu destituantur.

Lastly, it will be noted that in the 1903 plan the examinations are the responsibility of the Institute whereas, according to the "*Leges*" in 1909, they take place before the Biblical Commission. The "*Leges*" in 1909 also leave out the entrance examination, which was part of the 1903 plan (paragraph V,2).

A long period of gestation thus came to an end; during it the problems posed by the Bible got worse. From now on the Pontifical Biblical Institute has its credentials. It remains for them to be put to work in a concrete way since, with the exception of the papal document that creates it, the Institute does not exist yet. There is therefore a lot to be done.

6. *Setting up the Institute: June-October 1909*

In the months following the papal decisions the concrete problems had to be faced, before any academic year could start. Where would the Institute be located? How would its teaching body be constituted? What funds would it have, especially for the library and furniture? What about the students? Here again Fr. Fonck put everything he had into it, except during the month of August, during which he probably went on holiday. With his attention turned to everything, he once again showed his talents as an organizer.

Where would the Institute be sited? It has been said above that on March 6th, 1909, there was talk of installing it in the Via della Pigna, between the Largo Argentina and the Pantheon. The Marescotti palace, or the palace "of the bank", had been acquired there by the Vatican for setting up the offices of the Vicariate there, and it still occupies it today. But in the summer of 1909 it was not yet available. So, for the immediate future, the Vatican suggested establishing the biblical Institute in the Leonine College in the Via Pompeo Magno in the district called "Prati" about five hundred metres to the north of the Castel Sant'Angelo. Yet the installation of the Institute at the Leonine College was likely to last over a year before it could settle in at the Via della Pigna; Pius X told Fr. Fonck this on September 17th. The latter was very unhappy with this and said so in writing two days later to the Secretary of State, even threatening to resign (APIBR B-XVIII,3 [XX,1/09/27, p.2])! Nothing availed and on September 30th Fonck told the professors at a conference that the activities of the Institute would take place in the mornings at the Gregorian, in the Via del Seminario, and at the Leonine, of which it would occupy the ground floor, in the afternoons (APIBR B-XVIII,3 [XX,1/09/28]). And when, on October 17th, Pius X received the teaching staff (cf. Doc. R. I,6), there was still talk of moving the Institute as soon as possible to the Marescotti, leaving open the possibility of getting another building for the Vicariate. In October, 1909, there was still no definite solution and the one that had to be adopted was distinctly shaky.

The composition of the teaching staff was officially drawn up on October 15th when it was published in the *Acta Pontificii Instituti Biblici*, 1 n° 2, pp. 11-12. Papal approval had been requested by Fr. General, for whom Fr. Fonck had prepared the draft of a letter on September 19th (APIBR B-XVIII,3 [XX,1/09/26]). To establish this list of professors a survey was made of all the biblical scholars in the Society, province by province. In the end ten were selected. Six were appointed regular professors: A. Fernández, L. Murillo, L. Fonck, E. Gismondi, H. van Laak and L. Méchineau; the other four, A. Deimel, L. Szcszepański, E. Rosa and M. Chaîne became associate professors. In fact, only four professors arrived in Rome for the Institute: A. Fernández, from Tortosa in Catalonia, A. Deimel, from the seminary at Anagni, L. Szcszepański, from Innsbruck, and L. Murillo, from Madrid; the others were already teaching at the Gregorian and would continue to do so. Finally, on October 27th, at the second meeting of the professors, Fr. Fonck announced that Fr. Méchineau was appointed Vice-president of the Institute (APIBR B-XVIII,3 [XX,1/09/31]).

On July 2nd the first issue of the *Acta Pontificii Instituti Biblici* came from the press. In eight pages it described the Institute, conditions of admission, the academic programme extending over two years, plans for lectures and publications. This issue must have been widely distributed, for, on the 6th, Fr. Fonck gave a copy of it to the very active bishop of Brooklyn, Mgr. Charles E. McDonnell who, on a visit to Rome, thanked him for it the following day, adding that he would try to interest Mr Carnegie in the library (APIBR B-XVIII,3 [XX,1/09/20]). But it is not known whether there was any outcome to this move.

It was from the Secretary of State that Fr. Fonck actually received three successive payments, each of 10,000, on June 5th, June 26th and October 1st, 1909. This money had to go first of all into the purchase of furniture. Thus it is, for example, that on August 31st the bill for eight long double sets of shelves for the library, to be assembled at the Leonine, was sent from Strasburg (APIBR B-X,3) and, when the Institute was installed in the Piazza della Pilotta, they were to be found in the great hall of the library (cf. L. Fonck, *Primum Quinquennium*, Tab. I and VIII). As regards books, on October 25th, Fr. Fonck had already bought some to the value of 17,923 liras, the equivalent of 100,000 euros at the end of 2008. These books were bought in various places scattered throughout Europe, but especially from the M. Bretschneider bookshop in the Via del Tritone in Rome (APIBR B-X,2). During this period Migne's patrologies, fifty-two volumes of the *Corpus Scriptorum Ecclesiasticorum Latinorum*, the commentaries on the Old and New Testaments by Keil and Delitzsch were acquired in this way, as well as hundreds of volumes, especially in German. It is good to recall these details, for Fr. Fonck was without any doubt the well-informed and very dedicated creator of the Institute's library.

What about the students? On September 19th, 1909, Fr. Fonck wrote to the Secretary of State (APIBR B-XVIII,3 [XX,1/09/27]) to ask him, among other things, to insist that the German and Austrian bishops send students to the Institute. At that time there were in fact already about thirty students enrolled but none from Germany and only one from Austria. On October 27th, at the second consultation or meeting of the professors (APIBR B-XVIII,3 [XX,1/09/31]), Fr. Fonck announced that he counted between 30 and 35 *alumni*, about ten *auditores* and about 25 *hospites*, that is to say an approximate total of seventy people enrolled. It should be noted that the Institute's *Leges*, like Fr. Prat's plan in 1903, distinguished between three categories of students and only the *alumni* would follow the full programme with a view to taking examinations at the Biblical Commission. At all events, it was already a great success.

So during this period Fr. Fonck proved that he had worked hard to see to it that the academic opening of the Institute was well prepared. This was to take place at the Leonine on November 5th, 1909.

Doc. R. I,1

APIBR B-XVII,1

On the fly-leaf, in pencil in Fr. Fonck's handwriting in the top right-hand corner:
Inst. bibl. (sub secreto Pontificio); *in the bottom right-hand corner:* Programma
Instituti Biblici a Leone XIII a. 1903 deliberatum. *Translated from the French.*

(printer's proofs)

BIBLICAL INSTITUTE

I.
Purpose of the Institute.

1. The Biblical Institute, which owes its existence to the generous initiative and munificence of His Holiness Pope Leo XIII, has as its purpose the establishment, in the very centre of Catholicism, of a permanent centre of higher biblical studies in contact with the needs of today's apologetics and with the enormous developments that have taken place these days in scriptural matters.

2. Its special purpose is to prepare competent professors for our seminaries and Catholic Universities and to train writers, aware of the results and methods of modern learning, in the various domains of biblical scholarship.

3. It also sets out to promote biblical studies among the members of the young clergy by making available to them, in addition to everything needed for work, a full education, sound guidance from, and reassuring contact with, teachers and fellow-students dedicated to the same studies.

[2] II.
Teaching staff

1. The Institute can start with six professors:
    1.° A professor of Old Testament exegesis,
    2.° A professor of New Testament exegesis,
    3.° A professor of introductory matters, history or archaeology,
    4.° A professor of Hebrew and oriental languages,
    5.° A professor of Greek, biblical criticism and palaeography,
    6.° A professor of Assyriology.

2. As the Institute goes through its normal development, certain professorships will be doubled and it will be possible to add courses in Semitic epigraphy, Egyptology, biblical theology, Aramaic, Arabic, Ethiopic, Coptic, comparative Semitic languages, etc., according to the specializations of the scholars whose co-operation will be enlis-

ted, and according to the wishes expressed by groups of students. – Modern languages will not be taught at the Institute, but knowing them will have real advantages when it comes to examinations.

3. Apart from titular professors, there will be lecturers and teachers offering revision periods. Professors who have not already shown proficiency in teaching will only be admitted as titular professors after com[3]pleting a period of two or three years as lecturers.

4. Titular professors – from whom the Rector and Chancellor are chosen – form the Council of the Institute.

5. The Council decides with a majority vote questions concerning admission of students, studies, programmes, examinations, maintenance and development of the library, as well as matters submitted to it by higher authority.

6. The rector normally presides at proceedings, public sessions and when theses are being defended; he is the recognized intermediary between higher authority and the Institute and represents the Institute to persons outside.

7. The Chancellor watches over the observance of the programmes and the Statutes, makes sure that all the conditions of residence, attendance and examinations are fulfilled according to regulations by the students and, lastly, takes the place of the Rector in case of absence or incapacity.

III.
Students.

1. The Institute comprises: 1.° Students in the full sense; 2.° people enrolled and attending lectures; 3.° people attending lectures without any commitment who may attend classes without completing any formalities.

2. Students are those who take courses with a view to reaching the doctorate conferred by the Institute. They are [4] bound by certain conditions of residence, attendance and examinations.

3. People enrolled and attending lectures are those who, without aspiring to diplomas, regularly follow one or several branches of the teaching given at the Institute. They have access to the library, but on condition that they attend the courses for which they are enrolled.

4. Students are only admitted as pupils after passing an entrance examination.

5. Students in the full sense are those who have doctorates in theology. In exceptional cases and with the express consent of the Council of the Institute, students without the doctorate may be admitted as pupils provided they have finished their theology and can furnish proof of special studies and specialized knowledge.

6. Young people who have not done theology but have taken courses in languages at the Institute and passed an examination in those languages will later be exempt from examinations in those languages.

7. The sub-committee did not reach agreement on the minimum amount of time required for studies for the doctorate. Two members think that two years are enough; the other four are of the opinion that three years are necessary.

8. During these two or three years of actual residence, students will not be able to get ready for any examination other than those at the Institute under pain of *ipso facto* losing the benefit of the residence completed in these conditions.

[5]IV.

Courses and conferences.

1. Courses at the Institute are real courses and not classes. They give students the result of study at first hand, and they initiate them into personal work, the direct use of the sources and into scholarly method and spirit.

2. Besides their regular teaching, the professors must help and direct the students in their essays. They will strive to make the Institute known and appreciated with their learned publications. That is why it is good that they should stay, as far as possible, within their special field, without taking on a large number of courses which would be contrary to the traditions and dignity of higher education, harmful to their personal work and fatal to the intellectual training of the students.

3. Professors, other than those teaching languages, will give two lectures a week, plus a conference every fortnight.

4. The purpose of the conference is to tackle the students' passivity, stimulate their rivalry, get them used to expounding their ideas in speech and in writing, to bring out their academic ability, to develop their pedagogical qualities and lastly to keep them in suspense and prepare them properly for the examinations.

5. It may take various forms according to the nature of the courses. It may consist: 1.° In written assignments judged [6] and corrected in public by the professors; 2.° in lessons given by the students, designated by choice or by drawing lots; 3.° in debates among students on a given subject; 4.° in tests set by the professor on the subject of his course; 5.° in practical exercises in criticism, palaeography, etc.

6. A further regulation will indicate the obligatory courses. It is good not to fit all the students into the same mould and to allow for the tastes of each one and for individual preferences. Overloading the students with classes should also be avoided, to get them used to working on their own, allow them to assimilate the teaching and leave them time to do written work.

V.

Examinations.

1. The examination must be at once a gauge of attendance at classes, an attestation of serious work and a means of assessing the candidate's worth.

2. The *entrance examination* covers Greek and Hebrew as well as ordinary seminary teaching: introductory notions, contents of the Sacred books, history of both Testaments. A syllabus will be published. Nevertheless candidates may be received without a knowledge of Hebrew, but then during the first year they will have to take the elementary course in that language.

3. To be admitted to take the examinations at the end of the year it will be necessary: 1.° to prove one's attendance [7] at classes and conferences; 2.° to have obtained a satisfactory average in the various tests during the year.

4. The examination at the end of the year will consist of one written examination and one oral examination in each of the courses taken by the candidate. However, in the last year, the oral examination will be the only obligatory one; the doctoral thesis that the candidate is beginning to start on will take the place of the written examination.

5. It is understood that the doctoral thesis can be presented after leaving the school.

6. The most brilliant laureates at the Institute may be granted scholarships or partial scholarships. Those who are to benefit from them will have to send the Institute reports or written statements testifying to their serious work.

VI.

Library.

1. A well-stocked and easily accessible library will be installed on the premises of the Institute itself. It will contain works of reference and the main literature on biblical sciences, as well as the most important periodicals. This library is necessary for the professors to prepare their classes seriously and for the students to spend their time usefully before and after classes. Special regulations will describe how it is to be used and what its function is.

[*on the back of p. 7*:] VATICAN PRESS

*   *   *   *   *

Doc. R. I,2

Archivum Romanum Societatis Iesu (ARSI)
PIB-1001-III,2
Letter from Fr. Lucien Méchineau to Fr. General Wernz (extract)
Translated from the French

Very Reverend Father General

I am asking permission to submit some considerations to you that concern the studies and the prosperity of our Gregorian University […]

[4] III. A Higher school leading to degrees in Holy Scripture
The *Biblical Commission* confers the degrees of licentiate and doctorate in Holy Scripture on those who, being doctors in theology, successfully take the tests indicated by the Commission's programmes. The number of young doctors in theology who come to do the licentiate in Holy Scripture is getting greater and greater. In general they are young priests whom their bishops destine to occupy a teaching post in exegesis. Last June 14 came to do the licentiate; 12 were admitted. [5] Out of these 12 there were five doctors in theology from the Gregorian Univ., 2 from la Sapienza, two from the Institut Catholique in Paris, 3 from the École Biblique of the Dominicans in Jerusalem,
To prepare for this licentiate not more than one year is necessary for doctors in theology who have given some attention to their Scripture studies, and to the study of Hebrew and Greek; if not, they take two years. As regards the doctorate, much more time is needed because there is a written thesis on a new subject, of a technical nature and approved by the Commission, to be given in. Over and above this there is nothing to be laid down here concerning the doctorate, which is done elsewhere, slowly and at length (so far there has not been any doctor), while at the same time performing the functions of ministry in parishes or of professor in a seminary. Only candidates for the licentiate, therefore, need to be guided. Yet they are in a difficult situation. In Rome there is no advanced course in biblical languages, biblical criticism or exegesis which

might be of use to them; no school preparing people for these degrees. The candidates' only resource is to go occasionally to see, and ask advice from, the consultors of the Biblical Commission who will be their examiners, and if they ask about higher courses they can only be referred to Paris, Beirut or elsewhere. Is that not a matter of regret for the very honour of the Roman faculties?

Leo XIII wanted to found a higher school for Holy Scripture; the idea could not be put into effect for many reasons; it has not, however, been completely abandoned, but it has taken another form. When, after my appointment as consultor, I paid a visit to the cardinals on the Commission, Cardinal Merry del Val told me: "A school for Holy Scripture should be set up at the Gregorian Univ. which would spearhead the movement." On the other hand, the Fathers at the French Seminary, who have successfully presented many candidates, seeing that there is no preparatory school for the degrees, have themselves begun to give their students supplementary classes and repetitions, and have already got one of their young fathers to do special studies for that purpose.

Now this is what I am saying: If the Gregorian University had a second professor of biblical languages and, besides the two professors of Holy Scripture needed for classes for our theologians, a third professor of biblical criticism and exegesis, it would be possible to have a higher school of Holy Scripture here, preparing people for the degrees at the Biblical Commission and training future professors. This would be a great honour for Rome, our University and a great achievement indeed. I am simply submitting this idea to your Paternity. [...]

[8] Rome, September 16th, 1907
L. Méchineau s.j.

* * * * *

Doc. R. I,3

ARSI: PIB-1001-III,4

Letter from Fr. Lucien Méchineau to Fr. General Wernz (extract)
Translated from the French

Very Reverend Fr. General

I am sending your Paternity the result of my first reflections on the subject which you kindly discussed with me: the steps to be taken with a view to organizing a higher course on Holy Scripture, leading to the degrees from the Biblical Commission, and in a certain sense being the seed of a biblical faculty.

I. The appointment of a second professor of Holy Scripture for the year 1908-1909

In conformity with the wishes expressed by Your Paternity in your letter of March 25th, 1908, to our Rev. Fr. Rector, Fr. Querini, I have discussed the matter of the choice of a second professor to teach Holy Scripture with him. I naturally proposed the name of Fr. Fonck, the only one I had thought about until then. When the Rev. Fr. Rector expressed to me the desire to have several names I listed a certain number of others whom I know, pointing out, however, that if those Fathers had the necessary learning, none of them had the qualities required for stimulating and directing ideas, which Fr. Querini did not seem to doubt any more than I did. Finally, the name of Fr. Jubaru, prof. of Holy Script. at Anagni last year, and Enghien this year, came to mind. I think he would be ready for the New Testament and would have the right ideas along with the energy required not to flinch in the face of opposing influences. This would be at least a matter to be gone into in case Fr. Fonck, for one reason or another, could not come to Rome.

On the subject of Fr. Fonck, here are some small details perhaps useful to note. Men who have come out against biblical modernism are being sought for the Biblical Commission, with a view to getting them to join it and even having them in Rome. The first Secretary *ab Actis*, M. Vigouroux, questioned me about this and asked me if I could not point out some people of perfectly sound doctrine among those of our Fathers who are familiar with biblical studies. I asked for time to think about it. Some weeks later I had to reply that I could not indicate anyone. In fact the only name I had found, that of Fr. Fonck, as fulfilling all the conditions, I could not give to M. Vigouroux without reminding him of a very unpleasant recollection. About twelve [2] years ago Fr. Fonck made an extremely forceful attack upon something published by M. Vigouroux who, for the first and only time in his life, if I am not mistaken, thought he ought to defend himself and did so by means of the newspaper "L'Univers". That attack was that much more distasteful to him, coming as it did from a Father of our Society, with which he has always had good relations. I saw him weep when he told me about it at the time. You will see why, Very Reverend Father General, I could not give M. Vigouroux himself Fr. Fonck's name; but I have made known all his qualities, both to Cardinal Merry del Val who has spoken to me about him and to the second Secretary *ab Actis*, Rev. Fr. Janssens. Cardinal Merry del Val holds Fr. Fonck in very high esteem; Fr. Janssens finds him a bit too lively in polemics [...].

[10] Rome, Gregorian University, April 18th, 1908.

L. Méchineau, S.J.

* * * * *

Doc. R. I,4

APIBR B-XVIII,3 (XX,1/08/6)

Letter from Fr. Méchineau to Fr. Leopold Fonck. Translated from the French

Rome, August 16th, 1908

Rev. and dear Father
P.C.

I had been foreseeing for a long time that we would be colleagues here in teaching Holy Scripture; now it is definitively settled, and allow me to say that I am very pleased about it. Very Rev. Fr. General came into my room on Friday morning and said: Everything is now settled, you can get into touch with Fr. Fonck and arrange the division of the subjects with him.

As you know, it is already understood that we are in charge of the ordinary teaching of Holy Scripture to our students in the third and fourth years and of a preparatory practical course for degrees at the Biblical Commission for doctors in theology who wish to take those degrees. You have everything concerning the New Testament, and I what concerns the Old Testament, for [2] the two courses, each of us remaining free to arrange the subjects as he intends. This is the combined timetable for the two courses which I had suggested to the Very Rev. Fr. General. You will notice that the ordinary course and the higher course take place at different times so as to give the biblical students the opportunity to follow the ordinary course as well, if they think fit:

Monday and Tuesday at 10.00 a.m. ordinary course in O. T.
Wednesday and Friday at 10.00 a.m. ordinary course in N. T.
Monday and Tuesday at 9.00 a.m. special course in New Test.
Wednesday and Friday at 9.00 a.m. special course in O. T.

There remains the Saturday class for the ordinary course which was the fifth class; I suppressed it, or rather I asked Very Rev. Fr. General to change it to a course in patrology but this point has not yet been definitely settled and it is quite possible that you will be asked to take a 3rd class in the ordinary course, you who are young and full of strength and verve. For my part, in the [3] two years that have just elapsed I have always found it very hard to give our large audiences five hours of exegesis a week. This will therefore be a matter to be settled, and if one of us has to give three classes of exegesis in the ordinary course, I really think that it will fall on the shoulders of the valiant Fr. Fonck.

As regards the special course, we give our students two hours of each, which comes to four hours a week. All are agreed that the degree candidates must not be burdened with many courses and that they should above all devote themselves to personal work and find more of a guide to the study of their programme here with us, with practical lessons where they will have to reply to questions put by us. This is what, I think, you call a seminar in Germany, and what we in Paris are used to calling a practical course in higher studies. The student is made to work, he is spared the eloquent tirades of the professor who gets carried away; a twofold advantage, what do you think?

[4] If now we are allotting the subjects of the programme for the *licentiate*, the only one we have to deal with – putting, on the one side, everything which essentially or more closely has to do with the Old Test. and, on the other, what has to do with the New, this is what we get (See loose sheet [*absent from dossier, it is probably about the syllabus for the examinations at the Biblical Commission*]).

As you can see, the syllabus is a full one, everyone, even at the Commission, says it is too full. It is impossible for us to get through it with four classes a week even in two years. I think it should be clearly understood that our students, without the exception which is always possible, will therefore have two years of preparation. Most of them will certainly need it and besides, if we were to put them forward after a year we would be leaving ourselves open to failures which would compromise the good reputation our school wants to earn. It is up to each of us, consequently, to cover his subject in two years. You will note that in the part about the New Testament, apart from introductions, you do not really go beyond the Gospels and the Acts; the Old Testament is a much wider field, and if it suits you [5] to take on nos 11 and 12 of the V as well [*it seems to concern the following subjects in the oral examination for the licentiate*: "11. De kalendario et praecipuis ritibus sacris Hebraeorum. 12. De ponderibus, mesuris et nummis in Sancta Scriptura"], I shall let you have them without any difficulty; for those two nos. have just as much, or almost as much relevance to the New Testament, and that would to that extent reduce my extensive programme.

Now this is how things go in the examinations:

Monday, lasting six hours, a written exegesis essay on a passage from the Gospels or the Acts in the Greek text. This essay counts double, that is to say if, for example, the candidate earns 15 marks, he gets thirty.

Tuesday morning lasting 3 hours: A written essay on a historical subject, either Old or New Testament, chosen from the programme.

Tuesday evening for again three hours: A written essay on a subject of an introductory nature, either general or special, according to the programme.

On Thursday the *oral* exams start. Each candidate is examined:

1° for half an hour by one examiner on the Hebrew text of the four books of Kings, which he must translate fluently. The result counts *double*.

2° same test and under the same conditions on the Greek text of the Gospels and the Acts.

[6] 3° before a board of three examiners they are examined for

20 minutes on the history of the O. and N. Test.

20 minutes on the special introd.

20 minutes on some questions from the general Intro.

Everything of course being taken from the programme.

I think, R[ev] and dear Father, that these various explanations will give you a clear idea of what we are asking for and will enable you to make all the observations you think useful on the way our classes, subjects etc. are apportioned. It would be good if, as soon as possible, we could be clear about what each of us will have to do, so that we can get ready immediately. I shall therefore be very grateful to you if you can let me have all your comments and I think it will be quite easy for us to agree on apportioning the work as we have agreed for a long time on the good and sound doctrines that we propose to teach. Oremus pro invicem.

[7] Inf. in Xto servus et frater

L. Méchineau S.J.

P.S. You can reply to me in French or Italian. If you prefer German, I would ask you to write in your most beautiful handwriting; it will be a pleasure to read it.

* * * * *

Doc. R. I,5

APIBR B-XVII,3 (XX,1/09/2)

In pencil, in Fr. Fonck's handwriting, on the right: Copia; *on the left*: Secretum Mit ARP General mündlich besprochen, dann in d. Privat-Audienz[.] Dem Hlg Vater vorleget am 14.2.1909: Er nahm den Bogen u. las ihn mit lauter Stimme, und sagte dann: Sì, lo facciamo. Approbiert. Dem ARP General übergeben 15.2.09.

Translated from the Latin.

Setting up the Pontifical Biblical Academy

I. Reasons for setting up the Academy

1. The very sad state of biblical matters at present and the great confusion and upheaval of minds about these matters that is to be seen everywhere.

2. Greater progress in biblical studies among Catholics whereby the unbecoming and dangerous dependence of our people on heterodox persons in biblical matters may gradually be removed.

3. The wish of the Holy See that has already been expressed in the Apostolic Letter of our Holy Father Pius X "Scripturae Sanctae", February 23rd, 1904

II. The Purpose of the Academy

1. The purpose of the Pontifical Biblical Academy is, with high hopes, to promote biblical scholarship and all studies connected with it as the Church understands them and in accordance with the norms established, or to be established, by the Apostolic See.

2. For this purpose it is in the first place important that young people be chosen from among various nations and religious orders and instructed and exercised in studies pertaining to the Sacred Books so that thereafter, in public and in private, by writing and teaching, they may be able to profess them and, being recommended by the seriousness and sincerity of their teaching, defend their dignity.

3. It then pertains to the same purpose that both the members of the Academy and others, who wish to make progress in biblical studies outside the ordinary course of study, be helped in every way suited to this purpose and with everything needed for biblical learning.

4. Lastly, it is in keeping with the purpose of the Academy that it should defend, promulgate and promote sound scholarship concerning the Sacred Books and doctrine in conformity with the norms established, or to be established, by the Holy See, especially against false, erroneous, rash, and heretical opinions expressed by some people recently.

III. Means suited to the purpose of the Academy

1. For the Academy to achieve its purpose it must first and foremost include lectures and practical work in everything to do with the Bible. And in the first place those subjects will have to be dealt with in which the young people are got ready for exams to be taken at the Biblical Commission. But they are also to be led in a methodical way to a more profound knowledge of Holy Scripture and trained to deal with biblical questions in a scholarly way.

2. A second extremely necessary means is a biblical library that includes all ancient and modern works that are really necessary and useful for making real progress in biblical studies. Among these, apart from the writings of the Holy Fathers and other Catholic interpreters and more outstanding non-Catholic ones, special provision will be made for those large encyclopaedic works, more recent periodicals and critical editions of texts which can hardly ever be available to private individuals at their own expense.

3. A third means will be a series of various writings, to be published under the name, and with the authority, of the Academy, some of which will help learned research, some will help to defend Catholic truth about the Sacred Books, and some will help to spread sound doctrine everywhere concerning biblical matters.

4. To these may be added: a) a biblical museum with everything which may be useful in illustrating the sacred text; b) public lectures on biblical matters; c) financial provision for making journeys; d) financial provision for members of the Academy so that they can board freely in a College in the city during study periods.

A. M. D. G.

Doc. R. I,6

APIBR B-XVIII,3 (XX,1/09/30)
Papal audience on October 17th, 1909. Translated from the Latin

+

Pontifical
Biblical Institute
in Rome

Audience with H. H.
17.10.1909

As the Pope himself, at an earlier audience (17 Sept.), had expressed a desire to see all the professors of the Institute, immediately after Fr. Murillo's arrival (13 Oct.) on the following day (14.), I asked for a private audience for the teaching staff of the Institute through the good offices of the Rev. Mgr. Bisleti. I received an answer on the 16th: "His Holiness will receive the Very Rev. Fr. Fonck S. J. along with the teaching staff of the Biblical Institute in audience on the 17th of this month at 10.45. I immediately sent invitations to Frs. Franc. Ehrle (who sent his apologies), L. Murillo, A. Fernández, A. Deimel, H. Rosa, L. Méchineau, H. Gismondi (who sent his apologies because he was "indisposed"), H. van Laak, M. Chaîne, L. Szcszepański.

We were all at the door at 10.30 and went up together to the papal antechamber where we were soon kindly greeted by the Very Rev. Mgr. Caccia dei Dominioni and taken to the Holy Father's own room. Fr. Gismondi also came there, almost at the last minute. Shortly afterwards, V. R. Fr. General Wernz (who, unbeknown to us, also had an audience), came out of the Holy Father's room. We then went immediately into the Holy Father's room.

I introduced each one as they genuflected, and the Holy Father spoke to each one in quite an amusing way. In particular he said that two Spaniards had to leave the City for two reasons, one being that they were Jesuits, and the other because they were Spaniards. He then invited us to be seated at the places prepared for us around his own table on which stood a statue of Bl. John Vianney at one place and one of Bl. Joan of Arc at another. Speaking in the name of all I said roughly this: "Holy Father, the professors of the Biblical Institute have come to pay homage to Your Holiness and to ask your blessing before starting work. This is like the beginning of a great new day, and we come like workers called to the vineyard. We come to express to Your Holiness our gratitude at the honourable invitation, our readiness for the work entrusted to us, and our sincere dedication to serving Holy Church and obeying every order from Your Holiness (the Holy Father kindly nodded at this and said: "I am quite convinced of that"). But in the master of the vineyard we also find a real father of a household with a paternal heart full of benevolence and charity in which we have our comfort and help". The Holy Father thereupon added: "Yes, I want that, and I shall do what I can. And I thank all who came and, in the first place, the Rector Magnificus – for that is what he should be called, as Fr. General told me – and I wish the great work of the Institute every success. And it is an undertaking more than ever necessary these days to be able get the carriage – to use a very ordinary metaphor – back on track so that it can reach its destination. Courage and trust in Providence". Then, in an informal way, he went on to tell us a lot about the Institute's first benefactor [Mgr. Kohn?], and about its temporary and, in a year's time, permanent premises in the Marescotti palace: "Yesterday evening the Monsignor Secretary of the Vicariate was with me and I asked him: But are you unhappy at the Vicariate's palace being given in part to other people? Well, I want the Biblical Institute to have its premises there first of all, and if there is not enough for the Vicariate, we shall buy another building for it". Then he mentioned a central seminary to be built at Assisi in Umbria, at Posilippo in Campania and at Cattanzaro in Calabria and showed us a sketch of this and an outline of the buildings and explained them to us. Then, when I had said: "You see, Holy Father, with the development of the Biblical Institute we, too, can therefore hope one day to have a new building like that", he answered: "Look! What a Rector Magnificus you have!" He then very kindly gave the apostolic blessing to us, our work and enterprises and dismissed us, after spending about half an hour with us.

Then for a short while we greeted His Eminence Card. Secretary Merry del Val who likewise welcomed us very cordially.

L. Fonck sj

CHAPTER II

Settling in and first decisions
1909-1934

Bibliography

L. Gonzaga DA FONSECA, "*Fasti* Pontificii Instituti Biblici", in *Verbum Domini* 14 (1934) 193-210. – A. BEA, *Pontificii Instituti Biblici de Urbe prima quinque lustra. 1909 – VII Maii – 1934.* Roma, Pont. Ist. Biblico, 1934, 79 p.

The first twenty-five years of the Biblical Institute, until the beginning of the rectorate of Fr. Bea, saw its organization, activities and achievements gradually set up. This long period starts with the *Leges Pontificio Instituto Biblico regendo* of May 7th, 1909 and ends with the *Statuta Pontificii Instituti Biblici*, approved by the Holy See on August 7th, 1934, and published in 1935. It can, however, be divided into three stages

I. Under Pius X, the first steps: 1909-1914

Bibliography

Leopoldus FONCK, *Primum quinquennium Pontificii Instituti Biblici, cum XII tabulis phototypicis.* Scripta Pontificii Instituti Biblici, Romae, Pont. Inst. Bibl., 1915, 41 p. – Ernst VOGT, "San Pio X fondatore del Pontificio Istituto Biblico", in *San Pio X, promotore degli studi biblici, fondatore del Pontificio Istituto Biblico*, Roma, PIB, 1955, especially pp. 35-42.

1. The first year: 1909-1910

a) Academic activity

On Friday, November 5th, 1909, the inauguration of the first academic year took place *privatim et modeste* (*Acta PIB* 1, p. 17) at the Leonine College. No outside authority had been invited. The Eucharist was celebrated, after which, in the presence of the students, the professors together made the Tridentine profession of faith.

Then, in the main lecture hall of the college, Fr. Fonck made a short speech in Latin of which he left the outline (APIBR B-XVIII,3 [XX,1/09/32]). He suggested a reading, adapted to the circumstances, of the parable of the labourers in the vineyard, in particular of the verse in Matt 21,33 according to the Vulgate: "A new day is dawning", he said, "in which the Father of the household is sending labourers into his vine. The vineyard chosen for us is Holy Scripture. We are all called to work in it. It will be helpful to consider briefly what our part in it is". The President of the Institute then develops three points. 1. The work done by other people whom the Father of the household did not send into his vineyard has, like passers-by, only gleaned the vineyard (cf. Ps 79 [80], 13): with their method and discoveries they have only touched the bark. 2. For us, the need to work is urgent, because some harmful principles of interpretation are prevalent; many people pass judgment and cast doubt, which is a natural tendency; yet it is not enough to cling to the Ancients; new ideas have to be added to them. 3. The work in the vineyard that has been allotted to us may be described with the terms used in Matt 21,33: the enclosure, the tower, the winepress, which the speaker does not develop in his outline. Henceforth, to avoid a series of errors, he explains what our method of working will be. In conclusion, he goes back to Ps 79 [80],15: "Powerful God, come back!"

On one side of the main lecture hall where Fr, Fonck gave his *lectio brevis* was the library, containing 6,000 books and 314 periodicals, all divided into various sections. The biblical museum was laid out in six cupboards, they, too, being in the same space as the library (cf. *Acta PIB* 1, pp. 26-30).

The professors, as already stated, were ten in number. The task of each of them was marked out, on October 15th, in the *Acta PIB* 1, pp. 11-12:

- Lucien Méchineau would do the introduction to the Old Testament,
- Andrés Fernández would also concern himself with the Old Testament: textual criticism, exegesis and theology,
- Leopold Fonck would teach the introduction to scholarly work, to the New Testament and the history of the gospels,
- Lino Murillo would give the exegesis of the gospels,
- Hermann van Laak would deal with the inspiration and inerrancy of Scripture.
- Ladislas Szczepański would look after biblical geography and archaeology.

As regards ancient oriental languages, they were distributed as follows:

- Aramaic and Arabic: Enrico Gismondi,
- Assyrian and Assyriology: Anton Deimel,
- Coptic: Marius Chaîne,
- Hebrew: Ladislas Szczepański,
- Biblical Greek: Enrico Rosa.

Besides this, Fr. Franz Ehrle, S. J., at the time Prefect of the Vatican Library and future Cardinal, would give some classes in palaeography.

All, or almost all, the subjects were thus covered right from the beginning of the Institute. But the exiguity of the premises provided by the Leonine College meant giving classes in the morning at the Gregorian University, at 120 Via del Seminario, while the "seminars" would be held in the afternoon at the Leonine College which placed two rooms at the disposal of the Institute for that purpose. Such a situation did not facilitate contacts between professors and students, and professors who lived in different houses must have found it difficult to work together properly.

As regards the students, it had been announced on July 2nd, 1909 (cf. *Acta PIB* 1, p. 1) that their registration, attendance at classes and use of the library were free. When the deadline for registration was past the number of people registered came to 117, divided into three categories:

- 47 *alumni*, doctors in theology, were studying for the licentiate and the doctorate in Holy Scripture from the Pontifical Biblical Commission,
- 18 *auditores* had not finished their theological studies and could not lay claim to those degrees,
- 52 *hospites* would be following only such and such courses; they were the biggest group.

The geographical origin of the *alumni* was confined to western Europe, with the exception of one Mexican. Italy, France and Belgium were the best-represented countries (cf. *Acta PIB* 1, pp. 18-19).

According to the catalogue of the professors and students at the Gregorian University in 1908-1909 the Higher Course in Holy Scripture had been taken by 21 students. In 1909-1910, with that course dropped, 12 of those students enrolled at the Biblical Institute, 6 as *alumni*, 1 as *auditor*, 3 as *hospites* and 2 in an unknown capacity.

Among the very first students, some made a name for themselves later on, but none of them had followed the Higher Course offered at the Gregorian. Here they are in alphabetical order:

- Joseph Bonsirven (1880-1958), from the diocese of Albi, *auditor*, later joined the Society of Jesus and was professor at the Biblical Institute from 1948 to 1954 (cf. *Bib* 39 [1958] 262-268).
- Paul Capelle (1884-1961), from the diocese of Namur, *hospes*; became a Benedictine with the name of Bernard in the Abbey of Mont-César at Louvain and was one of the initiators of the liturgical renewal (cf. *RHE* 56 [1961] 1024-1025).
- Felice Cappello (1879-1962), from the diocese of Belluno, *hospes*; later joined the Society of Jesus and became professor of canon law at the Gregorian. Venerable.

- Lucien Cerfaux (1883-1968), from the diocese of Tournai, *hospes*; professor at the Catholic University of Louvain and specialist in the Pauline writings.
- Achille Liénart (1884-1973), from the diocese of Cambrai; bishop of Lille and Cardinal; he was one of the presidents at the Vatican II council and became famous for his speech on the first day of the council.
- Alexis Médebielle (1877-1953), a Betharam priest, *alumnus*; his 1910 thesis was republished in 1923 in the "Scripta PIB" collection under the title *L'expiation dans l'Ancien et le Nouveau Testament*; he died at Nazareth.
- Athanasius Miller, O. S. B., *alumnus*; he was the secretary of the Pontifical Biblical Commission from 1949-1962.
- Alphonse Tricot (1884-1971), from the diocese of Poitiers, *alumnus*; he was a professor at the Institut Catholique de Paris and, along with A. Robert, edited the volume entitled *Initiation biblique*, Paris, 1939.
- Primo Vannutelli (1885-1945), of the diocese of Palestrina, *alumnus*; he is known above all for his two synopses, the one of the gospels and the one on the historical books of the Old Testament; the latter appeared in 1931 in the "Scripta PIB".

At the end of this first academic year, in June, 1910, thirteen students from the Institute obtained the licentiate in Holy Scripture at the Pontifical Biblical Commission, as provided for in the *Leges*. Four received it with honours. Among the others were Achille Liénart and Alphonse Tricot. Also in June 1910, five other students passed the exams set by the Biblical Institute which prepared them for the ones at the Biblical Commission; they did not yet fulfil the conditions for admission to the latter (cf. *Acta PIB* 1, pp. 24-25).

b) The purchase of the Muti Papazzurri palace

Bibliography

Giuseppe MARINELLI, *L'architettura palaziale romana tra Seicento e Settecento. Problemi di linguaggio.* Un approccio filologico: la testimonianza delle incisioni dello "Studio d'Architettura Civile"; una verifica sistematica; il palazzo Muti Papazzurri alla Pilotta. A thesis presented to the faculty of architecture of the La Sapienza University, Rome, 1991, esp. pp. 141-338. – D. BATORSKA, "Grimaldi and the Galleria Muti Papazzurri", in *Antologia di Belle Arti* 2 (1978) 204-215. – G. FUSCONI et al., "Note in margine ad una schedatura: i disegni del Fondo Nazionale delle Stampe", in *Bolletino d'arte* 17 (1982) 105-107.

On July 1st, 1910, at the end of many a long search for a suitable place for the Institute, the Holy See acquired the Muti Papazzurri palace, situated between the Piazza della Pilotta and the Via dell'Archetto. The history of this palace and the family that gave its name to it has been minutely studied by G. Marinelli, on whom we draw in the following pages.

The patrician family of the *Rione Trevi* has been known from the 11th c. and its history has been well documented since the 16th. Bearing first the name *de' Papazzurri* it added that of *Muti* in remembrance of Zannetto de' Papazzurri who lived in the 15th c.: he was dumb.

The history of the family and its property is complex. The owner was normally one descendant of the family. Until 1626, the family already possessed part of the land that today goes from the Via dell'Archetto to – and only that far – the part occupied at present by the Aula Pio X with its two wings to the right and left. In 1626, Gerolamo Muti Papazzurri acquired some adjacent land to the east: the garden or courtyard to the north of the plot and the small de' Branchis house to the south. The property was thus extended towards the present Piazza della Pilotta. In 1665, Pope Alexander VII granted some public land still further to the east: in trapezoidal form (cf. the spot where the Via del Vaccaro opens out on to the square), this last acquisition made Pompeo Muti Papazzurri the sole owner of the whole area.

On becoming a marquis in 1674 and, in 1678, *Mastro delle Strade*, he took it upon himself to reorganize his property. The architect chosen was Mattia De Rossi (1637-1695), Bernini's favourite pupil: the fact is now certain. Work began in 1678, but its main phase comes between 1687 and 1695, the finishing touches being made in 1703.

Keeping the existing walls, as far as possible, Rossi's plan opened up the palace to the square: a portal, flanked by double columns, gave access to an inner courtyard between two buildings forming wings. In 1910 that was still the overall aspect of the palace seen from the square (cf. *Acta PIB* 1, on the left of p. 33). De Rossi also redid the great façade to the north which today faces on to the North American College; with a very fine appearance, on the third floor it had square windows giving light to rooms with low ceilings. A classic roof covered everything. On the ground floor De Rossi had divided the property using a north-south passage accessible to coaches; the present entrance to the Institute was its starting point. Finally, between this passage and the Via dell'Archetto, De Rossi had placed a small inner courtyard that is still there. It will be noted that the idea of double columns at the portal was taken up by De Rossi above the northern entrance of the transverse passage, as well as at the foot of the big staircase where they are still in place.

On the first floor of the north wing of the main courtyard giving on to the square there was, and still is, a gallery with frescos. These are the work, not of Nicolas Poussin and Claude Lorrain, as was thought (cf. *Acta PIB* 1 p. 33), but of Giovanni Francesco Grimaldi, *il Bolognese*, and of Giacinto Calandrucci. Grimaldi painted the walls, starting in 1679, then Calandrucci the vault (cf. Batorska and Fusconi).

The time of Pompeo Muti Papazzurri, who died in 1713, marked the apogee of the family and the palace. Shortly after the death in December 1750 of his son Gerolamo who, in 1713 had been made mayor of Rome and who, in his lifetime, had occupied the first floor, four of Gerolamo's sons – a fifth was a Jesuit – shared the occupation of the palace; in January, 1750, they stipulated that the first floor would be common to all of them and that the second would be divided into four parts, each one occupying his own (cf. Marinelli, pp. 262-263).[1] Later on, in spite of a sharp recovery at the time of Curzio Muti Papazzurri who, as from about 1778, managed to restore the fortunes of his house, the family's decline and financial problems got the better of the palace. The last owner was Curzio's grandson, Rafaele Muti Papazzurri, a bachelor. About 1824 he was only occupying the second floor, the rest being rented out as apartments. In 1854, without any offspring and crippled with debts, he sold the palace to the brothers Giovan Battista and Gaetano Trucci, his creditors who, in 1875, sold it to the Bruschi-Falgari family and they, in turn, sold it to Count Carlo Tomba.

Tomba then proceeded to make changes in the palace: for reasons of hygiene he heightened the third floor so that the square windows overlooking the square became rectangular; he also replaced the roof with a terrace. Going bankrupt in 1901, Tomba had to hand over the palace to the *Credito Fondiario* which was dissolved shortly afterwards to the benefit of the *Banca d'Italia* and, in 1906, the latter sold the palace to Giovanni Gianini from Milan.

---

[1] Actually, in the introduction to the joint volume of which he is the editor, *The Stuart Court in Rome: The Legacy of Exile*. Ashgate Publishing, 2003, Edward CORP puts forward the hypothesis that our Muti Papazzurri palace would have been occupied from 1719 and for about forty years by James Stuart (1688-1766), banished from the throne of England, and his family. In 1747 the cardinalate of his son Henry would have been celebrated there. A painting dating to that period and recently acquired by the Scottish National Portrait Gallery in Edinburgh, actually represents the façade of our palace seen from the Piazza della Pilotta. However, in the absence of any documents from the period, the hypothesis may be doubted. In the first place, an authentic document, summarized above, proves that at the time, the first and second floors of our palace were occupied by Gerolamo Muti Papazzurri and his family (cf. the reference given by Marinelli, p. 279, note 59). Next, the documents adduced by Corp mention the Muti palace(s), today called Balestra, giving on to the square of the Holy Apostles, but never the name of the Muti Papazzurri palace, the two families being of different origin. G. Marinelli, p. 152, has pointed out this confusion in other authors. Moreover, the painting in question, with its theatrical decoration of the façade facing the Piazza della Pilotta, depicts that façade too inaccurately for it to be considered authentic. In particular, the portal, designed by De Rossi and completely hidden on the picture, was distinctly higher and the two side entrances visible on the picture are unrealistic; the vaults that can be discerned on the picture inside the two side entrances not only never actually existed like that but, for anyone who knows the inside of the building, they are quite impossible. Whatever may be said about the defects in the picture, if the painter really wanted to give an idea of the feast organized in honour of Prince Henry Stuart's cardinalate, one could imagine that, for the occasion, Gerolamo Muti Papazzurri would have lent his salons on the first floor which surrounded his palace's courtyard.

In 1907, Gianini, who lived in part of the third floor, had some rooms built on the terrace for his use; the other floors were let out as apartments to eight separate parties and access was in the Via dell'Archetto, while the ground floor was divided up among five tenants (cf. Marinelli, pp. 334-335).

Then it was that, unexpectedly, Fr. Fonck intervened. After many a fruitless attempt to find a building for the Institute, on the first Friday of February, 1910, he was with Mgr. Thomas F. Kennedy, the Rector of the North American College. Fr. Fonck had come to ask him for information about a possible place he had heard about. The Monsignor, who had his office right in front of the Palazzo Papazzurri, thought that Fr. Fonck was coming to find out about that palace next door, which was not the case. The misunderstanding was removed by the conversation recorded by Fr. Fonck himself. "But which building are you talking about?", asked Fr. Fonck. "This one, of course", replied the Monsignor, pointing at the Muti Papazzurri palace through the window. "Is it for sale?", Fr. Fonck then enquired. "Yes", replied the Monsignor, "immediately and on the best terms" (cf. Vogt, p. 38).

On February 11th Mgr. Kennedy told Fr. Fonck by letter (Doc. R. II,1) that Gianini was selling at 525 thousand lire, that the Il Messaggero newspaper was already involved in discussions, that one could build in the big courtyard of the palace and that its correspondent that very evening would already have the plans of the palace. It was therefore a matter of urgency.

On March 15th, two days after receiving the professors and students of the Biblical Institute (cf. Acta PIB 1, pp. 21-24) the Pope signed the authorization to purchase this Muti Papazzurri palace, which would become part of the Patrimony of the Holy See for the Biblical Institute. Carlo Patriarca, the lawyer, was given charge of the negotiations. On the 16th the contract of sale was signed in the presence of the notary Tito Firrao (cf. Marinelli, after p. 313). The agreement was made for 400 thousand lire. However, the contract was held over until the palace was completely free of all its tenants. In the price was also included the mortgage which, since Carlo Tomba, had lain heavily upon the palace and its owners, namely a bit more than 185 thousand lire.

To support his offer to buy, Fr. Fonck got a sketch of the changes he had in mind for the palace drawn by the engineer Giuseppe Astorri. This sketch was attached to the contract dated March 16th.

On July 1st, 1910, with the conditions already fulfilled, the final deed of sale was signed and the Holy See provided the rest of the price to be paid, namely a little over 213 thousand lire. The Muti Papazzurri palace was acquired for the Biblical Institute.

c) The gift made by the du Coëtlosquet family

On December 17th, 1909, Fr. Charles du Coëtlosquet, S. J., a missioner in Madagascar, brought from France, where he had returned for a rest, the sum of twenty thousand lire of which he made a gift to Pius X in his family's name for the Biblical Institute. In fact, though knowing nothing about the Biblical Institute, he had learnt about its foundation and need of money from a newspaper. He had spoken about it to his family and the latter decided to help with financing the Institute. Thus it was that in the spring of 1910, to cover the cost of purchasing the Muti Papazzurri palace, Caroline du Coëtlosquet and her mother Marie-Renée made a gift of 500 thousand lire to Pius X. That is what Fr. Fonck states when writing on May 12th, 1911, to Fr. General Wernz (APIBR B-XVIII,3 [XX,1/11/11]). The Pope thanked Caroline for it in an autographed letter dated July 1st, 1910, the very day on which the final deed of sale was signed (cf. Vogt, pp. 37-38 + Tab. V).

Sole heir of the family and sick for a long time, Caroline was to die on February 1911, at the age of 35. It is said that she herself had taken the decision to give the Pope her share of the inheritance for the Biblical Institute.

This family, of Breton origin, having settled in Metz and then, after 1870, in Nancy, was of the old nobility. Baron Jean-Baptiste Gilles du Coëtlosquet (1751-1813) had had three sons by Charlotte-Eugénie de la Salle, two of whom were: Charles (1794-1852) who died in Jerusalem during a pilgrimage (at Nancy in 1854 his family published the letters he had sent to his people during his travels in the Near East), and Jean-Baptiste Maurice, a viscount (1808-1893). The latter, by a first marriage with Anne de Wendel, had a son, Joseph-Charles Maurice, a viscount (1836-1904), who married Marie-Renée de Guerre (died in 1931), and they had only one daughter, Caroline (1875-1911). By a second marriage, with Marie-Sophie de Maillier, Jean-Baptiste Maurice du Coëtlosquet had six children: Jeanne (1848-1915), spinster; Charles (1850-1944), a Jesuit; Édouard (1851-1940), a Benedictine; Georgette (1852-?), a Little Sister of the Poor; Jean (1860-?), a Benedictine; and Marie (1862-?), spinster. On the death of Caroline in 1911 the family therefore had no one in the direct line.

Fr. Fonck left only two references to the gift of the du Coëtlosquet family. The first has just been mentioned; the second comes in one of his letters, dated June 4th, 1919 (cf. Doc. J. I,11), in which he points out that Jeanne du Coëtlosquet gave a million gold francs for the Institute in Jerusalem.

So on July 20th, 1931, Fr. Bea, then rector of the Institute, asked Fr. Édouard du Coëtlosquet, then living at Clervaux Abbey in Luxemburg, to provide him with further information. The latter replied to him on August 2nd that, if his recollection was correct, his sister-in-law, Marie-Renée, like her daughter Caroline, "contributed a sum that could be from one to two million, if not more, to the foundation of the Institute". He adds that at his instigation his sister Jeanne "made provision for the installation of the library in the palace in the piazza Pilotta and gave a million for the Jerusalem foundation". When he raised the subject with his sister Mary, he had "no difficulty in obtaining a similar contribution from her" (APIBR B-XVIII,1). On September 17th he further informs Fr. Bea (ibid.) that Marie du Coëtlosquet's contribution "was twelve hundred thousand francs".

Two and a half years later, answering another letter from Fr. Bea on March 23rd, 1934, Fr. Édouard gave these particulars on the first gift made by his family (ibid.):

> Fr. Fonck has been asked first of all to mention a *French family* as founder of the Biblical Institute, without revealing its name [cf. Doc. R. II,3, p. 14]. A little later, as a result of various considerations, of which I shall be able to give you the details, secrecy was no longer required, and Fr. Fonck himself, in a Latin publication on the origins of the Institute, mentioned the name of my elder brother Fr. Charles S. J. [*Primum quinquennium*, p. 32] who brought to Pope Pius X in Rome, on behalf of his niece Caroline du C., the amount necessary for the purchase of the palace in the piazza della Pilotta. In the same article, he alludes to the acts of generosity, made by the family, that followed this first gift. [...] Pius X received Fr. Charles in audience and sent a letter of thanks to the first of the four foundresses.

And on March 26th, in another letter addressed to Fr. Bea (*ibid.*), Fr. Édouard du Coëtlosquet went on to give the following details:

> If you wish to be precise and in accordance with historic truth, it must be said that Fr. Charles brought the amount necessary for the purchase of the palace in the piazza della Pilotta. But he had not been given any charge to make any promise and did not have the right to commit his people in the future in this way.
> I came to Rome some time after him [on March 16th, 1911, he was received by Pius X: APIBR B-XVIII,3 (XX,1/11/7)], and I enthusiastically got my people, by word of mouth and in writing, not to limit themselves to that first gesture and to continue their liberal giving, according to the needs of the Biblical Institute. My niece had died in the meantime. My sisters and my sister-in-law, having seen Fr. Fonck in Lorraine, came to Rome in 1912 and made new gifts to the Institute. I was with them and can vouch for the reality of the facts.

Thus Caroline du Coëtlosquet made the first gift of about 500 thousand golden francs. Her mother gave one or two million, if not more. Jeanne du Coëtlosquet gave a million for the Institute in Jerusalem and covered the cost of installing the library at the Institute at Rome. Lastly, Marie du Coëtlosquet made a gift of one million 200 thousand gold francs. All that between December, 1909, and throughout 1912. The total does not seem to have been less than five million gold francs, which would correspond to about thirty million euros at the end of 2008. That really is gigantic. It must be remembered.

Let us, lastly, recall Fr, Fonck's conclusion in a *mémoire* he sent to the Cardinal Secretary of State on September 23rd, 1914 (APIBR B-XVIII,3 [XX,1/14/15, p. 7]):

> Indeed, the generosity of this noble French family has, in the space of three years, made provision for all the needs of the Biblical Institute in such a generous and

complete way that the Holy See has not had to give the slightest help to the Institute so far and the latter's future, if the Lord wishes to preserve it, is already assured with a paid-up capital endowment of which the interest is enough in normal times for the maintenance of the community of professors, aid to students, library and museum costs, the Institute's publications and the branch in Jerusalem.

2. *The next four years; from 1910 to 1914*

a) Academic life

In 1909 a two-year curriculum had been planned at the end of which the students would take the examinations for the degree of licentiate at the Pontifical Biblical Commission. The programme for this *biennium* was already drawn up. A third year was also planned which would be preparatory to the doctorate at the same Commission, and special courses, in methology, among others, would then be offered to students (cf. *Acta PIB* 1, pp. 2-5).

When the 1910-1911 academic year opened, the programme, which does not distinguish what concerns the first or second years, had to be partially modified in relation to the 1909 plan (*Acta PIB* 1, pp. 34-35). For the following year, 1911-1912, a beginning was made to distinguish between the programme of each of the three years, but in a very schematic way (cf. *Acta PIB* 1, pp. 49-50). Thus we learn that the third year will still include courses in exegesis and a third oriental language (besides Hebrew and biblical Aramaic) but a course in archaeology and another in the history of exegesis are added. On August 2nd, 1912, the *Acta PIB* 1, p. 78, announce that to obtain the Institute's diploma (cf. *infra*), third year students still have to produce a dissertation amounting to at least 32 printed pages. Lastly, for the years 1912-1913 and 1913-1914, a table clearly sets out the programme for each year separately (*Acta PIB* 1, pp. 92-93 and 120-121). In 1912, for the first time, an entrance examination in Greek and Hebrew is established (*Acta PIB* 1, p. 76) which, however, Fr. Prat had envisioned back in 1903! From now on the Institute had reached cruising speed.

The teaching staff grew. If this or that person withdrew, as, for instance, L. Méchineau who went back for good to the Gregorian, new faces appeared and some stayed for a long time: A. Mallon was to teach Coptic and Egyptian from 1910 to 1913 before being put in charge of the foundation of the branch in Jerusalem; Henri Lammens was to teach Arabic from 1910 to 1914; A. Vaccari comes on the scene in 1912 for Old Testament exegesis and the history of exegesis in which he was to become a past master; finally, J. J. O'Rourke arrives in 1913 for biblical Greek and is to become rector eleven years later.

But it is at the level of the students that the pinch was felt. The number of *alumni* is gradually and dangerously dropping: from 49 in 1910-1911, there are only 29 in 1913-1914. It is now two years since France sent any, for the Institute does not offer an official diploma (cf. *infra*).

As regards the Institute's publications, on February 12th, 1911, the professors' Council had begun to envisage a periodical with a bibliography on biblical subjects, but on June 13th, 1912, the Fr. General told Fr. Fonck that he was not in favour of it: once the periodical was started, could it keep going? (cf. APIBR B-XVIII,3 [XX,1/12/26]). On the other hand, until the summer of 1914, the series "Scripta Pontificii Instituti Biblici" had published about fifteen books. Several of them had been very seriously reviewed in the *Revue Biblique* for 1914. Five were reviewed by Fr. Lagrange; their authors were the very conservative L. Murillo ("Le Cid Campeador ou don Quijote?", the reviewer asks himself, p. 294) on the book of Genesis, A. Hudal on the book of Proverbs, which he dated to before the Babylonian exile, G. Mezzacasa on the Greek version of the book of Proverbs, L. Pirot, whose thesis it was, having been presented at the Biblical Commission and being about Theodore of Mopsuestia's exegesis, and H. Schuhmacher on Phil 2,5-8. Two others were reviewed by Fr. Dhorme: they were the first volumes, coming out in 1912, by Fr. Deimel for use by his students in Assyriology.

As at the end of the first academic year, the *alumni* could take the examinations for the licentiate in Holy Scripture in June, 1911, at the Biblical Commission, but the *Acta PIB* do not say how many took them. Discretion reigns! On March 12th, 1911, Pius X, in his letter "*Iucunda sane*" (cf. *Acta PIB* 1, pp. 43-44), actually granted the Institute the right to validate internal examinations taken by its *alumni* and *auditores*, which would be awarded with a diploma. On June 2nd, 1912, the Pope, in his letter "*Ad Pontificium Institutum Biblicum*" fixed the wording of this diploma, and its bearer would have the title "lecturer or professor of Holy Scripture" (*Acta PIB* 1, pp. 63-64). Eight days later, on the 10th, he pointed out in a note (cf. Doc. R. II,4) that those who had the diploma from the Institute, if they wanted the doctorate in Holy Scripture, would only have to present their thesis at the Biblical Commission, the degree of the licentiate conferred by the latter being no longer required for those with these diplomas from the Biblical Institute.

However, these solutions were not entirely satisfactory. In a letter dated June 21st, 1914, addressed, it seems, to the Cardinal Secretary of State (cf. APIBR B-XVIII,3 [XX,1/14/9]), Fr. Fonck, who had certainly had a hand in drawing up the earlier documents – as the archives of the Institute prove – explained the problem and offered a solution. The title given at the Institute is not canonical and, in many countries, including France and Spain, is not recognized by the civil authorities. How, then, would graduates from the Biblical Institute be able to have access to university teaching posts? The solution would be that the Biblical Institute should be able to grant the degrees of baccalaureate, licentiate and doctorate! But it was too late to get approval: on August 20th, 1914, Pius X passed away. It was going to be Benedict XV to agree to Fr. Fonck's request, at least in part (cf. *infra*).

b) Fitting out the Muti Papazzurri palace

At the end of December, 1910, the professors of the Institute were able to settle in at the new building, 6, Via dell'Archetto; that was their official address just for the year 1911, as is clear from the S. J. Catalogue for the Roman Province. As from February, 1911, classes were held at 35, Piazza della Pilotta, the Institute's new address, and in the summer of 1911 the books from the library at the Leonine College were brought to the Institute's new premises (cf. Vogt, p. 39). This means that the work of adapting the Muti Papazzurri palace to the needs of the Institute was quickly done. But the official inauguration of the Institute took place only on February 25th, 1912. In fact, the Roman engineer Giuseppe Astorri, who gave his detailed account (APIBR A-24-25), notes at the end of his second volume (pp. 1341 seq.) that work started on September 4th, 1910 and ended on January 16th, 1912, for a total cost of 294 thousand lire, i. e. just over one million eight hundred thousand euros at the end of 2008.

Let us come to the details of this work. On August 10th, 1910, forty days after the definitive purchase of the palace, Fr. Fonck, who had already taken up residence at 6, Via dell'Archetto, signs a contract with the Vitali firm (APIBR K-1-A). The latter undertakes to complete the bulk of the work by October 25th, including the ossature of the main lecture hall, which henceforth occupies the courtyard of the palace, and the raising of the façade overlooking the Piazza della Pilotta, as well as about twenty rooms and public places for the Jesuit community, but with the exception of the library. The Vitali firm also undertakes to hand over within six months, i. e. by February, 1911, the other parts of the building, along with the Institute's new central staircase (which was demolished in 1981), with the exception of the library, heating, lighting and finishing touches.

As for the library, which could contain a hundred thousand books (cf. APIBR B-XVII,4), on July 25th, 1910, the Wolf Netter & Jacobi firm, from Strasburg (cf. *supra*, ch.1) made a first estimate, comparing its prices with those it had got for the library of the house of theological studies of the German Jesuits at Valkenburg in the Netherlands. On December 21st, 1910, it sent its final offer, amounting to 60 thousand five hundred DM. In the meantime, Fr. Fonck, through the rector of Valkenburg, had contacted the architect Mr Jos. Hürth, Aachen. The latter laid down the plan for the library on October 8th, 1910, and, on January 4th, 1911, indicated his approval of the offer from the Netter & Jacobi firm. The last letter from this firm to Hürth the architect is dated April 25th, 1911. And on August 27th, 1911, as he was about to leave for the Near East, Fr. Fonck wrote a letter of thanks to Hürth the architect.

In March 1911, the Berlin firm Panzer had provided the furniture for the Museum, the essential part of which was in the fresco gallery on the first floor.

Clearly, thanks to Fr. Fonck, who was completely taken up with this enterprise, everything went very quickly. Still, the changes in the Muti Papazzurri palace were important.

The key to them was a clear separation between the part of the building reserved for the Institute and the one to be occupied by the teaching staff. On October 14th, Astorri had made his plans floor by floor for everything not concerning the library.

The teaching staff would occupy the western part of the building. On the ground floor there would be the kitchen, heating equipment etc., the entrance being at 6, via dell'Archetto. On the first floor were the refectory and recreation room (where the library depot is today), as well as a chapel, still in use in our time. On the second, in the space now occupied by the Aula orientalis in the library, Astorri had placed seven rooms for professors and the President-Rector had his office in the north-western corner. On the third, there were about twenty rooms for professors and other members of the Jesuit community. On the terrace, lastly, there were the linen-room, laundry, but to get to them Astorri had added a flight to the great staircase built by De Rossi.

For its part, the Institute was to have its own staircase, too, going up two floors in the middle of the north-south passage that De Rossi had built at the centre of the palace. This staircase would lead to the first floor, to the classrooms, to the Museum, as well as to the new Main Lecture Hall. On the second floor, the staircase gave access to the library. This latter also took in the large entrance-hall, as well as the rooms, to left and right, in the wings of the former palace. The librarian had his office in the room in the south-east corner, today occupied by the reserve for valuable items. The first two floors of the eastern part of the building were therefore to serve the Institute.

This plan was to last almost unchanged until 1949.

The official and solemn inauguration of the Institute took place on February 25th, 1912. Everything was ready for the ceremony that started at 15.30 hours. Thirteen Cardinals attended, including Merry del Val, Secretary of State, Rampolla, President of the Biblical Commission, Billot, from the Gregorian, and Gasparri, the future Secretary of State to Benedict XV. A good number of bishops and abbots also attended. Two speeches were made, with some singing in between, including that of the Canticle of the Sun by St. Francis of Assisi. Fr. Fonck gave the speech inaugurating the Institute, recalling its origins and purpose and thanking all the people who had contributed to fitting out the new building (cf. Doc. R. II,3). Then Fr. H. Lammens gave a lecture on "an Arab adaptation of biblical monotheism", which appeared in *RSR* 7 (1917), pp. 161-186. *L'Osservatore Romano* for February 26th gave the celebration wide coverage.

To mark the fulfilment of his wishes, Pius X then offered a statue of the Sacred Heart and had a medal struck. The statue, which was the work of Ignaz Weirich, stood enthroned in the Aula Magna (in 1950 it moved to the community chapel of the Jesuits at the Institute and was replaced with a statue of Pius X, offered by Pius XII); on its plinth, and carved on a bronze plaque were three fleurs-de-lis in homage to the French du Coëtlosquet family; they can also still be seen in the Pius X Hall below the present statue of Pius X. The medal, carved by Francesco Bianchi, was presented to Pius X on June 15th, 1912; it represents the Pope on the obverse side and, on the reverse side, the new façade of the Institute with, in the foreground, Moses and the apostle Peter looking straight at each other; the inscription *Studiis Scripturae Sacrae provehendis* and the date of 1912 surrounded the scene (cf. *Acta PIB* 1, fascicule 7, the photos inserted between pp. 62 and 77).

3. *Achievements in the five-year period 1909-1914*

In 1915, Fr. Fonck took stock of this *Primum quinquennium* (cf. the bibliography *supra*). At the end of the enquiry undertaken here, that generally positive statement can indeed be confirmed. The Institute is formally firmly established. It possesses its own building that has been well fitted to the needs of the time. Financially, everything is covered and, it was thought, the future was assured.

Among the successes, the impressive growth of the library in so few years should also be mentioned.

Although Fr. J. Schellauf (1861-1929) became librarian of the Biblical Institute in 1911, Fr. Fonck continued to be interested in new acquisitions of books. Thus it was that he obtained a document from the Cardinal Secretary of State, signed on December 29th, 1910, whereby the Vatican Library lent the Biblical Institute the books on the Bible and orientalism that it had acquired for the members of the Biblical Commission at the time of Leo XIII (cf. *supra*, ch. 1 and Doc. R. II,2). At that time the work of setting up the library was not finished but Fr. Fonck went ahead.

In March, 1914, Fr. Joseph Lémann, from Lyons, offered Pius X seven crates of books for the Biblical Institute, amounting to about eighty volumes collected by himself and his deceased brother Augustin; it was mainly a matter of biblical and Talmudic literature (cf. APIBR B-XVIII,3 [XX,1/14/3-4], and *Acta PIB* 1, pp. 107 and 147). The Pope in person wrote to thank the donor.

In short, in September, 1914, the library possessed about 50 thousand volumes and 350 periodicals (cf. APIBR B-XVIII,3 [XX,1/14/15], p. 7).

Yet, alongside the patches of light, some spots of darkness are also to be seen. The number of students has gone down and only 35 of them have followed the three-year curriculum; among them not one Frenchman or Belgian (cf. Fonck, *Primum quinquennium*, p. 32). The question of academic degrees has not been settled and it is an important one for attracting new *alumni*. The quality of the publications is very variable; even allowing for the fact that we are not yet completely out of the modernist crisis, the few publications in biblical exegesis feel its effects.

To this evaluation should also be added the fact that, since 1911, Fr. Fonck had committed himself fully to the plan to create a branch of the Institute in the Holy Land. The documented history of this enterprise, which was to run into many difficulties and was not one of the most felicitous, is being reserved for the second part of this book (ch. I). It will also be seen there how the Biblical Institute's first "caravan" in the Middle East took place in 1913.

There was something more serious. Fr. Fonck's enterprising and authoritarian character was gradually going to alienate the trust his brethren at the Institute had in him. Giacomo Martina, the Jesuit historian of the Gregorian, has published some documents from May and June, 1914 – a note from Pius X to Fr. Fonck and an exchange of letters between the Pope and Fr. General Wernz – some of which, the exchange of letters, prove the seriousness of the crisis. Moreover, on March 4th, Fr. Fonck had presented his resignation, which was not accepted, however ("A novant'anni della fondazione del Pontificio Istituto Biblico", in *AHP* 37 [1999] 129-160, esp. pp. 136-137 and 155-159). However, the very paternal note sent to Fr. Fonck by Pius X on May 19th, 1914, is part of quite a different story: on May 7th, 1914, the date of the anniversary of the creation of the Institute, Fr. Fonck had sent the Pope a long letter in which he mentions a radical criticism of the Institute made by the Prefect of the Congregation for Studies; according to Cardinal Lorenzelli, the teaching at the Biblical Institute ought to be reformed in the light of the teaching of St. Thomas Aquinas; in this very fine letter, which was also indicative of his state of mind, Fr. Fonck shows how such a reform would have no meaning in the present state of biblical studies: the critical problems posed by the Bible are not solved with systematic theology (cf. Doc. R. II,5). All things considered, Fr. Fonck may rightly be considered the indefatigable founder of the Roman Institute.

II. Under Benedict XV, the time of clarifications: 1914-1922

1. *During the First World War from 1914 to 1918*

First of all let us recall some historical facts.

The Great War was caused by the assassination of the Austrian Archduke Francis Ferdinand on June 28th, 1914, at Sarajevo. The outbreak of hostilities occurred in the period of August 1st to the 4th. The belligerents are, on the one hand, Germany and, on the other, mainly Russia, France and Britain. Italy declared war on Austria only, on May 28th, 1915. The war came to an end, on the one hand, with the armistice signed at Padua between Austria and Italy on

November 3rd, 1918 and, on the other, by the one signed by Germany and the Allies on the 11th in Foch's railway carriage at Rethondes, in the forest of Compiègne.

Fr. Wernz, whose relations with Pius X had been more and more tense for several years, died in Rome on August 19th, 1914. His successor, Fr. Wl. Ledókowski, was to be elected in Rome only on February 11th, 1915, but from the month of May onwards he resided in a neutral country, Switzerland, at Zizers; Fr. Francesco di Paola Nalbone, whom Wernz had summoned to Rome in July, 1914, as Italian Assistant, kept up the contact in Rome between the Vatican and Fr. General. Fr. Ledókowski was to return to Rome only in December 1918.

Pius X died in the Vatican on August 20th, 1914, two hours after Fr. Wernz. Benedict XV was elected on September 3rd, 1914 and was to die on January 22nd, 1922. On his election, he chose Cardinal Domenico Ferrata as Secretary of State, but the latter died thirty-six days later and his successor was Cardinal Pietro Gasparri, who was also to serve Pius XI until 1930.

a) Academic Life

The effect of going to war was such that the number of students, which had already dropped in the preceding years, was almost halved in 1914-1915: in 1913-1914 there were 99 in all and there were no more than 55 in 1914-1915. They were to fall again in the following years:
– in 1915-1916, 29 students, including 8 *alumni*,
– in 1916-1917, 22 students, including 15 *alumni*,
– in 1917-1918, 18 students, including 13 *alumni*.

The *auditores* group tends to disappear: from 1916-1917 to 1918-1919 there was not a single one of them; the *hospites* hold firm, whatever that may be worth, in any case better than the *auditores*. The worst year was the last year of the war, 1917-1918.

As regards the teaching staff, the situation is just as serious: at the beginning of the war the Frenchmen J. Neyrand and M. Chaîne, then L. Ronzevalle were called up. At the end of the academic year 1914-1915 the situation is complicated by the entry into the war of Italy against Austria: professors of German origin or subjects of the Austro-Hungarian empire had to leave Rome and Italian territory; this was the case with Fathers Deimel, Ehrle, Fonck, van Laak and Szczepański. Hence the end of the academic year had to be brought forward by a month, with the examinations starting on May 31st, 1915, instead of June 22nd as planned.

The Institute only managed to save the essentials by sharing out the work of the absent people among other people and by bringing in new professors: in January 1915, Fr. Paul Joüon, expelled from Beirut in December, 1914, by the Turks who had joined the war on Germany's side, took on the Hebrew and

Aramaic courses; Fr. Edmond Power was given Syriac and Arabic (cf. *Acta PIB* 1, p. 174).

The most damaging thing was the exile of the President of the Institute. Fr. Fernández, who had succeeded Fr. Méchineau in 1910-1911 as Vice-President, found himself henceforth at the head of the institution. Still, Fr. Fonck, even when exiled in Switzerland, in Zurich, kept a firm hand on the Institute's affairs until, on December 9th, 1918, Fr. Fernández was appointed President of the Institute by the Pope.

So it was still Fr. Fonck who introduced the Institute, professors and students, at the audience granted by Benedict XV on February 25th, 1915 (cf. *Acta PIB* 1, pp. 175-177).

Lastly, in a letter from Fr. General to Fr. Fernández dated November 29th, 1916 (APIBR K-11-A [II-1 Fernández]), we learn that the Pope asked the Institute to prepare a new translation of the Bible into Italian; it would be for the use of the general public and would contain short notes; some professors and former students of the Institute accepted the plan which was to lead to the publication of *La Sacra Bibbia tradotta dai testi originali con note a cura del Pontificio Istituto Biblico*; the Pentateuch appeared in 1922 and the poetical books in 1925; its main contriver was Fr. Vaccari.

b) The unsolved question of academic degrees

The death of Pius X had left the request made by Fr. Fonck about the granting of degrees to students at the Institute (cf. *supra*) in abeyance. After the election of Benedict XV, Fr. Fonck took up the matter again with the new Secretary of State, Cardinal Ferrata. In fact, he had presented him first of all with the first version of a memorandum about it, but the Cardinal had suggested some adjustments to him. The text that he sends to him on September 23rd, 1914, contains 18 pages (APIBR B-XVIII,3 [XX,1/14/15]). In his first twelve pages, Fr. Fonck recalls the origin and development of the Institute, including the plan for the branch in Jerusalem. The Cardinal would thus be aware of the ins and outs of the Biblical Institute's affairs. Then Fr. Fonck expounds the "questions in abeyance concerning the Institute" (pp. 13-18), that is to say, essentially, the question of academic degrees. Actually, he is taking up the line of argument he had already developed in his letter of June 21st to the previous Secretary of State. However, he adds the following elements. 1) During the first two years of the Institute, the students had to take examinations at the Biblical Commission at one session; since then, this excessive requirement on the part of the Biblical Commission, despite Fr. Fonck's representations, had been still further reinforced by an increase in the subjects to be taken. 2) After Pius X's three interventions in 1911 and 1912, it was suggested (by the Commission?) that a return be made to the earlier situation where only the Commission granted the licentiate, but such a return backwards would be unseemly for more than one reason. 3) If the Institute obtained the right to grant academic degrees, it could not be objected that other institutions – meaning the École Biblique at Jerusalem – will ask for the same right, for the disparity between the Institute and those other institutions is *grandissima*. 4) Moreover, Fr. Wernz always considered that, for its very existence, the Institute ought to give academic degrees. 5) Fr. Fonck's concrete proposal is that the baccalaureate ratifies examinations in the first year, and the licenciate those of the second; those of the third year give access to the title of *lector et professor S. Scripturae* with diploma. 6) The Commission would keep its prerogatives as regards those not following the curriculum at the Biblical Institute.

Without any reply, as far as we know, on April 21ˢᵗ, 1915, Fr. Fonck wrote a new memorandum on the question. In it he takes up the same line of argument, in Latin (APIBR B-XVIII,3 [XX,1/15/2]). He explains that neither the examinations taken at the Biblical Commission nor the title and diploma granted by Pius X to students finishing the curriculum at the Institute are suitable, and for the same reasons. However, Fr. Fonck now adds the following points: 1) Purity of doctrine is not guaranteed either in those who get the licentiate from the Commission – the facts prove that – nor even in some of their examiners (he must have Fr. Lagrange in mind). 2) He asks that the Institute be able to give all the degrees, including the doctorate; he thereby goes back to his proposal on June 21ˢᵗ, 1914. He closes with these words, translated from Latin: "But whether it is fitting or not to let the Biblical Commission grant the degrees, other than those the Biblical Institute would confer, it is up to the Holy See, in its wisdom, to decide". Such an idea, put forward at the end of the document, was not going to settle matters.

The line taken in this new memorandum by Fr. Fonck was different this time, judging from the sequence of events. In March, 1916, Fr. Fonck had to send from Zurich an Italian version of it to Fr. General Ledókowski, and then discuss it with him at Zizers. The latter sent the memorandum to the Pope, with an accompanying personal letter. We know this thanks to a long letter sent by the Fr. General to Fr. Fernández on April 23ʳᵈ (cf. Doc. R. II,6). In it he sets out the content of Fr. Fonck's memorandum, which he wholeheartedly supports, for the benefit of the Vice-President of the Institute who had stayed in Rome. In particular, he explains to his correspondent (p. 5) that the Society is not looking for anything for itself and that it is ready to withdraw from the Institute if that was necessary for the Institute to have the right to grant academic degrees, including the doctorate.

Still, on April 25ᵗʰ, 1916, Fr. Nalbone, who was coming for another matter, was received by the Pope and in fact the conversation revolved entirely around the question of the academic degrees requested by Fr. Fonck. The Assistant for Italy later sent Fr. General and Fr. Fonck a detailed account of the audience (APIBR B-XVVIII-8). Here is a summary of it. Fr. General would have liked to deal with the matter of degrees by word of mouth with the Pope, but there was little likelihood that the war would end so soon. So Fr. Nalbone was given the task of taking to the Pope the clarifications he would wish. On receipt of Fr. Fonck's document, the Pope passed it on to the Biblical Commission for their opinion, adding that he would perhaps have the reply from Cardinal van Rossum, its president, in the coming days. Despite everything, the conversation gets underway but the Pope is reticent. For instance, he tells Fr. Nalbone: "I think we could get on with Fr. General, but I do not hope to do so with Fr. Fonck, in view of his memorandum". Fr. Nalbone then explains that a foreigner does not completely manage Italian; Fr. General grants that Fr. Fonck's text could have been improved but he did not want to keep the Pope waiting any more. At all events, Fr. Fonck is a model of obedience. Agreed, replied the Pope, but, with his firm and resolute character, Fr. Fonck, if he is not satisfied, might withdraw, causing a scandal and others might follow him (let us note in passing that the Pope was mistaken on the point that the Society could withdraw if that was a condition for granting degrees at the Institute). I do not think so, replied Fr. Nalbone, who added that Fr. Fonck's request did not come from the Society but is fully in line with the decisions of previous Popes; it is a natural consequence from them because the Biblical Institute has all the characteristics of a Faculty and it would be decapitating it to deny it the right to grant the doctorate, continued Fr. Nalbone. On the other hand, for Benedict XV the normal solution is for the Institute to offer the courses and for the Commission to offer examinations and degrees. "But", he added "much more is requested and not everything can be granted". Besides, he said further, the Commission will not want to give up its rights; that Fr. Nalbone can confirm, because Fr. Fernández told him so.

So the matter seems stuck there. In spite of another letter from Fr. General to Cardinal van Rossum dated June 30th (cf. APIBR K-11a [II-1 Fernández]) in which there is still talk of the doctorate, among other things, the letter "*Cum Biblia Sacra*" by Benedict XV, dated August 15th, 1916 (cf. *Acta PIB* 1, pp. 201-204), has all the appearances of a judgment by Solomon. These are its main decisions. 1) The academic degree of baccalaureate will be given to students at the Biblical Institute at the end of their second year; at the end of their third year they will receive the licentiate degree, but in the name of the Pontifical Biblical Commission. 2) The jury which, at the Institute, examines the candidate for the licentiate will include a consultor from the Biblical Commission, chosen by the Cardinals on the Commission, and that consultor will have the same rights to judge the candidate as the other members of the jury. 3) The right to confer the doctorate is reserved to the Biblical Commission. 4) Every year the Biblical Institute will send the Biblical Commission a written report on its activities and matters of greater importance.

The Pope was obviously giving priority to the Biblical Commission, but without denying the Institute the granting of any degree. For the doctorate it still has to wait.

The Pope's decisions were to be applied immediately, so that in June, 1917, four *alumni* received the licentiate in Holy Scripture and six others in June, 1918.

On June 20th, 1918, for some unknown reason, Benedict XV all the same sent a note in Latin to the Institute; it was reproduced in A. BEA, *P.I.B. de Urbe prima quinque lustra*, p.19. Here is the translation of this handwritten note (APIBR K-1-A):

> In our desire to show the Pontifical Biblical Institute the same goodwill as our predecessor, its founder, did, and in gratitude for the services it is giving to the Church and to Holy Writ, we express our special benevolence towards its authorities, masters and students, and we grant them, in token of our very great affection, the apostolic blessing.

2. *After the war: from 1918-1922*

a) Academic Life

The next four academic years saw students gradually coming back to the Institute, but without ever reaching pre-war figures:
- in 1918-1919 the number came to 21 students, including 12 *alumni*,
- in 1919-1920, 35 students, including 15 *alumni*,
- in 1920-1921, 43 students, including 16 *alumni*,
- in 1921-1922, 45 students, including 26 *alumni*.

As regards professors, there were still only eight in 1918-1919, whereas in 1919-1920 four others, back from the war, joined them: Frs. Fonck, van Laak, Neyrand and Deimel, but it was no longer possible to count on Fr. Joüon who, for reasons of health, retired from teaching, while staying in Rome until 1925; Fr. Ehrle returned only in 1921-1922, and Fr. Szczepański did not come back to Rome. Marius Chaîne (1873-1960), a renowned specialist in Coptic and Ethiopic who had stayed in France after the war, left the Society and was incardinated in the diocese of Perpignan in 1922.

Once peace was restored, on November 24th, 1918, the Institute organized a solemn session to commemorate the encyclical *"Providentissimus Deus"* which Leo XIII had published twenty-five years earlier. In a letter bearing the same date, Benedict XV wished to be associated with this tribute (APIBR K-1-A and *Acta PIB* 2, pp. 2-3): Frs. da Fonseca and Jean-Baptiste Frey, a consultor of the Biblical Commission, recalled the content and consequences of the encyclical; their addresses, clearly taking the anti-modernist line, appeared in *La Scuola Cattolica* 47 (1919), pp. 8-27 and 28-45.

b) Elephantine and Jerusalem

In 1918 the Institute started on archaeological excavations on the island of Elephantine on the Nile, but it is preferable to postpone that story to the second part of this book (ch. III), in which the excavations at Teleilat Ghassul are also dealt with. Likewise to be recounted in the second part of this volume (ch. I) are the reasons that led Benedict XV on June 29th, 1919, to send Fr. Fernández a letter in which he stated the part that the branch that the Institute planned to establish in Jerusalem should play (ABPIR K-1-A). The second "caravan" in the Middle-East, organized by the Institute from September 7th to October 23rd, 1921, will also be mentioned in it (ch. III).

c) New publications from the Institute

It will be recalled that in 1911 the Institute had envisaged the publication of a periodical but Fr. General Wernz had advised against it. The plan came up for discussion again in 1919. The matter was referred to the Council of professors on February 20th. We know this thanks to the minutes of the meetings of this Council that are kept in the Registrar's office at the Institute. Fr. Fonck took part in them only as from November 23rd. During the consultation on February 20th, everyone was invited to submit topics for articles for March and, as publishing two periodicals, *Biblica* and *Semitica*, straight away had been given up, so as to keep just the former, the articles requested were to deal only with biblical matters. On November 23rd, putting a Preface to the first number of *Biblica* was dropped and the question of a second periodical came up again, the title of which would be either *Semitica* or *Orientalia*. On December 14th several titles for this second publication were suggested; the rector, Fr. Fernández, was in favour of *Orientalia* which, because of the shortage of time to get it ready, would not be a periodical but a series of fascicules and it was hoped it would be possible to publish the first one during the 1919-1920 academic year; lastly, during that same meeting the creation of a third periodical was discussed, not a scholarly one this time but one for popular consumption: in 1921 it was to be *Verbum Domini*.

So the first fascicule of *Biblica* appeared on January 15th, 1920; the next three, on April 15th, July 1st and September 30th. On the first page the title stated: *Commentarii editi a Pontificio Instituto Biblico*. The layout of each fascicule was fixed for a long time: first of all the *Commentationes*, then the *Animadversiones*, the *Res bibliographicae*, followed by some news items or current events. Each fascicule also included part of an *Elenchus bibliographicus* compiled by Fr. Fonck. The authors and reviewers were for the most part professors at the Institute.

The third fascicule was dedicated to St. Jerome and its subtitle was: *In centenariam memoriam obitus S. Hieronymi doctoris maximi XXX Sept. CDXX –*

XXX Sept. MCMXX and pp. 431-517 were devoted to this tribute. The idea of a publication of this kind went back to the consultation of professors held on October 22nd, 1917, and January 16th, 1918.

Concerning *Orientalia*, the series subtitle was: *Commentaria de rebus Assyro-Babylonicis, Arabicis, Aegyptiacis etc. editi a Pontificio Instituto Biblico (Supplementum ad "Biblica")*. The first two fascicules appeared in 1920; they brought together, each in 64 pages, articles by Fr. Deimel. The third, which appeared in 1921, was the work of Fr. A. Mallon, *Les Hébreux en Égypte*, 215p.

Finally, as from January, 1921, the twelve fascicules of the periodical *Verbum Domini. Commentarii de Re Biblica omnibus Sacerdotibus accommodati a Pontificio Instituto Biblico singulis mensibus editi* came out, amounting to 384 pages in all. On receiving the first fascicule, Benedict XV, with his Secretary of State as intermediary, thanked the President of the Institute for it, asking that later issues be sent to him (*Acta PIB* 2, pp. 34-35). This periodical had obviously got off to a good start: the articles were many and varied, intelligible to non-specialists; the homiletic section was done by Fr. Fonck, who had probably been at the origin of this publication.

3. *Evaluation of seven and a half years: from 1914 to 1922*

The war and its consequences had nearly cost the Institute its life; professors and students really were too few. Financially, just after the war, the treasury was almost empty and the standard of living was poor. But the Institute survived the crisis that almost ruined it.

Benedict XV's interventions were at once encouraging and disappointing. On the question of academic degrees the Pope had only taken a half-measure, somewhat vexatious for the Institute, and the question was going to need reviewing. On the other hand, as regards Jerusalem, as will be seen, he settled once and for all a problem that was dividing the Jesuits at the Institute.

And when, just after the war, it was decided to produce new publications at the Institute, a long-term enterprise was successfully launched.

III. At the beginning of Pius XI's pontificate: 1922-1934

1. *Four years living together: the Oriental Institute at the Biblical Institute from 1922 to 1926*

Bibliography

Vincenzo POGGI, *Per la storia del Pontificio Istituto Orientale. Saggi sull'istituzione, i suoi uomini e l'Oriente Cristiano* (OCA 263), Rome, Pont. Ist. Orientale, 2000, esp. pp. 22-24, 52-56, 98-101, 119-121, 360-369.

Benedict XV died of pneumonia on January 22nd, 1922, and Pius XI was elected on February 6th. On June 24th, for the first time the new Pope received the Biblical Institute in audience (cf. *Acta PIB* 2, fascicule 4, pp. 3-4), but his first letter concerning the Biblical Institute dates from September 14th; it was addressed to Fr. Ledókowski. Pius XI decided to place the Pontifical Oriental Institute, set up in 1917 by Benedict XV, in the palace that housed the Biblical Institute in the Piazza della Pilotta; he also gave the Society of Jesus the task of ensuring the future of the Oriental Institute (cf. *Acta PIB* 2, fasc. 4, pp. 14-15; from November 1st, 1922, to November 1st, 1924, the title of fascicules 4-6 was *Acta Pontificii Instituti Biblici et Orientalis*).

Until then the Oriental Institute was housed in the "Casa Raffaelo", which was knocked down in the 'thirties to make room for the Via della Conciliazione. Since 1919 Dom Ildefonso Schuster, abbot of St. Paul's Outside the Walls and future archbishop of Milan, was its president. In 1920 Benedict XV had already granted this Institute the right of conferring academic degrees, including the doctorate.

On June 23rd, 1922, Dom Schuster met Fr. Fonck at St Paul's Outside the Walls and the Jesuit suggested to him that the two institutions, the Biblical Institute and the Oriental Institute, be united. That same day, Fonck drew up a memorandum to that effect which the abbot passed on to the Pope on the 28th. On July 3rd Pius XI gave his approval and so it was that, until the end of August, Fr. Fonck was the mainspring of the plan; it was he again who sketched out the papal letter of September 14th, but he was held to absolute secrecy in the whole of this matter, even as regards his superiors.

On October 20th, Fr. Michel d'Herbigny was appointed president of the Oriental Institute and some professors at the Biblical Institute were on the teaching staff of the Oriental: Frs. Ehrle, made a Cardinal on December 11th, Fonck, Hofmann, Neyrand, O'Rourke, Pelster, Power and Vaccari.

With Pius XI's approval, the *Orientalia* series at the Biblical Institute became the organ of the Oriental, but to mark the distinction between the two institutions, the Oriental called its first fascicule *Orientalia Anno IV Series II, Christiana Num. 1 Pasqua 1923*, but as from fascicule 3 for June, 1923, the title became more simply *Orientalia Christiana*. Parallel to this, the *Orientalia* series at the Biblical Institute went on its way.

This life together came to an end in 1926, at the instigation of Fr. d'Herbigny who wanted to free himself from the Biblical Institute. Pius XI bought some land near the Basilica of St. Mary Major on which, among other things, was the ancient hospice of St. Anthony the Abbot, which he had fitted up and which was to house the Oriental Institute to this day, and the inauguration, in which Mgr. Angelo Roncalli, the Nuncio in Bulgaria, took part, was held on November 14th, 1926.

a) Still the question of academic degrees

The school years 1922-1923 and 1923-1924 saw the number of students still similar to that of previous years: in 1922-1923 there was a total of 54 students, including 23 *alumni*, and in 1923-1924, 21 *alumni* out of 41 students.

The situation changed radically as from the next year. The reason was the *Motu proprio* "Bibliorum scientiam" *de disciplinarum biblicarum Magisteriis* which Pius XI signed on April 27th, 1924 (cf. *Acta PIB* 2, fasc. 6, pp. 5-7). The Pope stated that the degrees conferred by the Biblical Commission or by the Biblical Institute bestowed the same rights and had the same effects as degrees in theology or canon law. But the main point of the papal document was this: to teach Holy Scripture in seminaries it would be necessary to have at least the baccalaureate that the Biblical Institute could give its students after the first two years of the Institute's curriculum, while leaving unaffected the right to give preference to those with the licentiate or the doctorate. It should be understood that if the licentiate could in fact be granted at the end of the third year of the Institute's curriculum, that degree was always conferred in the name of the Biblical Commission (cf. *Acta PIB* 2, fasc. 7, p. 9); as regards the doctorate, the Institute still did not have the right to grant it. Lastly, Pius XI calls upon religious Superiors and Bishops to send their more suitable subjects to the Institute.

To complete this new legislation, on December 19th, 1924, Pius XI declared that those who, from 1912-1916, had received the diploma and title of "*lector et professor Sacrae Scripturae*" were henceforth on the same footing as those with licentiates. Cardinal van Rossum, president of the Biblical Commission, put this officially in writing on December 26th (cf. *Acta PIB* 2, fasc. 7, p. 4, and APIBR K-6-B [1-2]).

What we do not know is the origin of the *Motu proprio* and how it was put together. Whose initiative was it? It may be doubted whether the authorities of the Institute had anything to do with this matter which still did not correspond with their wishes, although the thrust of the document was in the Institute's favour. Be that as it may, the immediate consequence of Pius XI's *Motu proprio* was the sharp increase in the number of students: from 46 in 1923-1924, there were 76 the next year, including 38 *alumni*, and that growth was to be maintained during the following ten years, as will be seen.

b) A new Rector and teaching staff

On July 5th, 1924, Fr. John J. O'Rourke was appointed rector of the College of professors by Fr. General and, on November 4th the Pope appointed him President of the Institute. Fr. O'Rourke was going to tackle the question of degrees with vigour, with Fr. General's support, and finally to carry out the plan for the branch in Jerusalem (cf. Part Two, ch. I).

The teaching staff underwent hardly any changes during this period, except that from the academic year 1924-1925, Fr. Augustin Bea was given the Introduction to the books of the Old Testament to teach and Fr. Ludwik Semkowski took the courses in biblical Hebrew and Aramaic as from the school year 1925-1926. The former of these two took the place of Fr. Murillo, one of the veterans of the first hour, who retired to Oña in Spain, while the latter took the place of Fr. Neyrand who went back to Jersey.

Since August 23rd, 1924, Fr. Bea – one of the most outstanding figures in the history of the Institute – had been, and was still, rector of the Jesuit "biennists" at 45, Piazza del Gesù. Born in 1881 at Riedböhringen, on the outskirts of the Black Forest, and only child of parents already advanced in years – his father was at once carpenter, contractor and farmer – Augustin was in weak health. From 1900 to 1902, with his father unwilling that he should join the Society, he begins a cycle of theological studies at Freiburg im Breisgau and finally he meets up with the Society in the Low Countries, for, since 1872, the Jesuits had been banned in Germany. After the novitiate he spent three years studying philosophy at Valkenburg and one year teaching in a secondary school and, in 1910, he did a semester of classical philology at the University of Innsbruck. Then, back at Valkenburg, he completes the theology cycle, in particular with Frs. Pesch, Merk and Knabenbauer. After being ordained priest in 1912 he spends a semester at Berlin University in 1913 where, with masters like Ed. Meyer and H. L. Strack, he is introduced to oriental philology. That same year there is talk of his coming to Rome, perhaps to the Biblical Institute, but an attack of pleurisy holds up the plan. During the war we find him at Aachen where he is superior of the young German Jesuits who, being in the army, need rest. In 1917 he starts teaching Old Testament at Valkenburg but, in 1921, he is appointed Provincial of the Jesuits in Munich; it is there that he makes the acquaintance of the Nuncio, Mgr. Eugenio Pacelli. At the end of his term of office, Fr. General calls him to Rome in 1924. Thus Fr. Bea has followed the normal Jesuit training, at two different periods he took some courses in philology but he has not had any really biblical training; yet he is a peerless superior. This is the man who is soon to take over the reins of the Biblical Institute.

Among the publications by professors at the Institute, to be noted especially is the *Grammaire de l'hébreu biblique* that Paul Joüon published in 1923 and for which he received the "Volney" prize from the Académie des Inscriptions et Belles-Lettres in Paris; the book, which has now been translated and brought up to date in English by T. Muraoka, still stands out as one of the best on the subject. One could also mention the fact that in 1925 Fr. A. Deimel published the first volume, consisting of 189 pages, of his *Šumerisches Lexikon*, a pioneer work that was to keep him busy until 1950.

2. *The big manœuvres: from 1926 to 1930:*

a) The Commission and the Institute: the great crisis and its resolution

In September or at the beginning of October, 1926, Fr. Frey, the secretary of the Biblical Commission, in the name of Cardinal van Rossum, gave Fr. O'Rourke a one-page document coming from the Commission but without date or signature. At that time, the Commission, apart from its president, consisted of Cardinals Merry del Val, Gasquet, O.S.B., Ehrle, S. J., and, until his resignation in 1927, Billot, S.J. Now this document, registered at the Commission as N° 65/26 (APIBR K-6-B [I.-3a]), set out the conditions for the admission of students to the Institute. This was indeed proof that the Commission wanted to rule the Institute. It therefore intended to insist on the need to have the ecclesiastical doctorate in theology in order to be admitted as *alumnus* at the Institute. Anyone who did not have it, because the theological school from which that student came did not have the power to grant it, should, in order to obtain it, follow at least two years of classes in a pontifical faculty. Those who did not have the chance to obtain this doctorate in a pontifical faculty in which they followed the whole progamme should pass a special examination in doctrine before the Commission. The *auditores* should have successfully completed the full courses in philosophy and theology (without the doctorate, as far as one can tell). The same goes for the *hospites*, but with the added condition that they be willing to study biblical subjects.

In comparison with the rules then in force at the Institute (cf. *Acta PIB* 2, fasc. 7, p. 10), this made entry more difficult for students. The matter was referred by the rector to the Council of professors on October 26th, 1926, and it had a long discussion about it on November 16th, Fr. Bea being absent. On the first restriction concerning the *alumni* the Council considered it detrimental to the students and the Institute, harmful to non-pontifical institutions, and that the problem really concerned the Congregation for Seminaries and universities. About the second restriction, Fr. Vaccari, then vice-president of the Institute, explained that it ought to be a matter of just one oral examination in dogmatic theology and the majority of the Council seems to have been in favour of the text envisaged by the Commission. On the other hand the proposition concerning the *hospites* met with strong opposition from the Council which asked that nothing be changed in what had been the tradition in all universities and in the Institute from its inception.

A very strongly-worded document, undated and unsigned, but corrected by Fr. O'Rourke (APIBR K-6-B [I-3a]) sets out, over four pages, the Council's opinion and it is likely that it was sent to the Biblical Commission after being tidied up.

Be that as it may, on February 26th, 1927, the Biblical Commission published its final document, approved by Pius XI. This *Declaratio de laurea in theologia ad gradus academicos in Sacra Scriptura obtinendos requisita* appeared in the *AAS* 19 (1927), p. 160. The Institute's observations had obviously been taken into account, but not entirely. First of all, the text makes no further mention of the Biblical Institute and hence is just as valid, at least in principle (cf. *infra*), for those who take examinations at the Biblical Commission. Then another consequence is that there is henceforth no question of *auditores* or *hospites*. Yet the first restriction remained, the one that the Council of professors had severely criticized.

The Institute did not stop there. There was then a veritable immediate and long-lasting clash. From Pius XI the rector got permission to give him a written statement explaining the difficulties the Institute had with the Biblical Commission so that the Pontiff could make a judgment. At the end of March, 1927, the dossier, drawn up in Latin, was ready. Along with a letter from the rector, it comprised two parts (APIBR B-XVII-5). The first, of which the one-page initial Summary had been written by Fr. General himself, came to nineteen pages. It gave a historical account up to the latest decisions from the Biblical Commission, showing how unfavourable they were to the Institute (pp. 1-8). Then it went into precise details about four differences in what was the practice, on the one hand, at the Commission and, on the other, at the Institute (pp. 9-19); these differences concerned:

1. the time at which examinations were licitly held: at the Commission the licentiate could be obtained just after the doctorate in theology and the doctorate two years later, while at the Institute the licentiate was conferred three years after the doctorate in theology and the doctorate, reserved to the Commission, was conferred two years after the licentiate at the Institute;

2. the examination syllabus in the two institutions: at the Commission there were only six subjects to be taken for the licentiate, while at the Institute three years of lectures had to be followed, also including a third oriental language and a thesis; for the doctorate the Commission required what the Institute gave in the 2nd and 3rd years for the licentiate and the thesis required was in fact the equivalent of the one for the licentiate at the Institute;

3. the diversity between the degrees and the inequality in the value of the same degree: the Commission's doctorate corresponded to the licentiate at the Institute and the Institute's baccalaureate corresponded to the Commission's licentiate;

4. the recent conditions imposed on the admission of the *alumni* at the Institute, conditions, which, as far as is known, the document pointed out, do not apply to candidates for examination at the Commission.

The second part of the dossier brings together the documents, pontifical and internal, which governed the Commission (pp. 1-18) and the Institute (pp. 19-

47). The whole dossier was then sent to the Pope by the Rector on April 1st, 1927.

That does not seem to have been enough. Fourteen months later, on June 13th, 1928, Fr. General was received by Pius XI and the conversation centred on some remarks made by the Pope which Fr. General was to pass on to the rector of the Biblical Institute concerning Fr. Fonck's leaving Rome and the Biblical Institute's independence in accordance with the letter "*Vinea electa*" by Pius X. To clarify his thinking Fr. General, on June 20th, sent Pius XI a letter in which he takes up these questions (cf. Doc. R. II,7). As regards the Institute, on the one hand, it was under pressure from Cardinal van Rossum that in 1916 Benedict XV placed it under the Biblical Commission and, on the other, the rector of the Institute asks the Pope to take into consideration the adverse effects that the Commission's Declaration on the doctorate in theology had on the Institute; the document that the rector had sent the Pope on April 1st of the previous year had therefore been of no avail.

There is every reason for thinking that this letter from Fr. Ledókowski brought about the settlement of the question of degrees and the independence of the Biblical Institute. It was at this time, apparently, that Fr. General drew up a new document in Italian and that a fascicule containing all the Holy See's documents about the Institute was printed, starting with the 1909 apostolic letter "*Vinea electa*" and ending with the latest Declaration by the Commission in February 1927; this 32-page fascicule was entitled *Documenta Pontificium Institutum Biblicum spectantia.*

The dossier that Fr. General sent directly to the Pope was entitled *Promemoria circa il Pontificio Istituto Biblico di Roma*; it came to seven pages, to which were added eight supporting documents amounting to twenty-five pages. Fr. General's *Pro-memoria* (APIBR B-XVII-5) repeated the grievances expressed in the previous dossier about the four inequalities between the Commission and the Institute. He added a note on a new *Cursus Biblicus* in preparation for Biblical Commission examinations that the Angelicum College run by the Dominicans in Rome was organizing during the school year 1927-1928; a privately-run Biblical Institute like that, through the advantages it offered, was also harmful to the Pontifical Biblical Institute. Lastly Fr. General asked 1. that the licentiate and the doctorate be the same at the Commission and at the Institute, 2. and, even if the Institute had to stay dependent on the Commission, that the humiliations following upon that dependence should cease, especially as regards the final examination for the licentiate at the Institute where a consultor from the Commission was on the jury, 3. lastly, that there should be only one Biblical Institute at Rome; Fr. General ended by adding that, if the Pope considered it fitting, the Society was prepared to withdraw in favour of others.

This time the Holy See acted. With his *Motu proprio* "Quod maxime" of September 30th, 1928 (cf. *Acta PIB* 3, fasc. 2, pp. 3-12 and fasc. 3, pp. 6-12), Pius XI set up the consortium of the academic institutions of the Society of Jesus in Rome, the Gregorian University, the Biblical Institute and the Oriental Institute. Now this papal document certainly went through the hands of the Society before its publication. The Institute's Roman archives (B-XVII-5) in fact possess some documents that prepared the papal *Motu proprio*. In the course of an audience on an unknown date the Pope gave Fr. Ledókowsi a four-page draft document – a handwritten note in the margin says so: *Draft document handed by His Holiness Pius XI in person to the Very Rev. Fr. General* – and the latter was to pass it on to the rector of the Biblical Institute; in it these words, in a mixture of Latin and Italian, can be read: "The Bibl. Institute biblical and accessory sciences with the power to grant degrees, including the Doctorate, according to a programme to be approved by Us; although it will always be open to the students to apply to the Pont. Biblical Commission. However, the Institute, in this new system, stays dependent solely upon the Holy See". Our archives also contain the first inkling of the *Motu proprio*; on pp.14-15 it is stated that the Biblical Institute is henceforth independent of the Biblical Commission and has the right to confer academic degrees, including the doctorate. Fr. General stayed at the Villa Rufinella, above Frascati and Mondragone, in August 1928 and worked there with Fr. Vidal, the canon lawyer at the Gregorian, on matters concerning the Biblical Institute; a letter of his, dated the 3rd or 4th of August, 1928, shows this (APIB B-XVII-5). He certainly looked over this first draft, because a note in the margin is in his hand. At that time, the publication of the *Motu proprio* was intended for September 8th; in fact, Pius XI signed it on the 30th but, on October 3rd, the rector of the Biblical Institute received some more final proofs of it to be corrected. The decisions already taken were confirmed: henceforth the Biblical Institute no longer depended on the Commission and could grant all academic degrees.

Once the *Motu proprio* had appeared in the *AAS* 20 (1928), pp. 309-315, there were several matters still to be settled. On October 2nd Fr. O'Rourke was received by Cardinal Bisleti, the prefect of the Congregation for Seminaries and Universities, under which the Institute now came, and he left an account of the interview (cf. Doc. R. II,8). In it there was question of students who did not have the doctorate in theology and of the number of years to obtain the doctorate at the Institute. On these points the Prefect was very open. Still, on the first point the rector returned to the charge because Benedict XV's letter *"Cum Biblia Sacra"* spoke of a doctorate "or a similar title"; on November 27th, 1928, Pius XI decided that recourse should be had in each case to the Congregation (APIBR K-1-A). At the Institute, on October 7th, 1928, the same day as the rector was received by Cardinal Bisleti, the Council of professors also turned its attention to the practical consequences of the *Motu proprio*: when ought the baccalaureate, if it was kept, the licentiate and the doctorate be conferred? A dossier was prepared, along with a letter addressed to the Pope, but nothing was sent because, in the meantime, Fr. General, to whom the matter had been referred, drew up a short document (cf. Doc. R II,9) which was reproduced in extenso in the volume of the minutes of the Council of professors. On October 10th Fr. General submitted this new document to the Pope, who signified his agreement but asked that it be also submitted to Cardinal Bisleti for approval; on October 12th the rector of the Biblical Institute saw the cardinal and the latter considered that Fr. General's concrete proposal was becoming the norm for the Institute, namely:

– only doctors in theology are admitted to the Institute;
– the curriculum at the Institute lasts three years;
– the degree of licentiate is conferred after two years of study at the Institute;
– for the doctorate, it is necessary to do a third year of lectures, take a fourth year of study in private, get a thesis ready and pass the final examination.

In this way, Fr. General concluded, in four years after the doctorate in theology students will be able, apparently, to reach the doctorate in Holy Scripture in a suitable and sound way.

Lastly, at Fr. O'Rourke's request, Pius XI officially accepted the following points: 1. the baccalaureate will be conferred after the first year of study at the Institute; 2. the licentiate, conferred after the second year, and not the baccalaureate any more, gave the right to teach Holy Scripture; 3. the doctorate is to be conferred two years after the licentiate; 4. those who, since 1924, received the baccalaureate will be able to receive the licentiate provided they do a thesis approved by the Council of professors. The document that sets out these decisions is dated April 10th, 1929 (APIBR K-1-A) and was published in the *Acta PIB* 3, fasc. 3, pp.13-14.

Thus a long crisis came to an end. The tenacity of Fr.O'Rourke, as well as that of Fr. General, made it possible for the Institute to come out of it freer than ever, now in possession of everything that constitutes a university institution worthy of the name. It took almost fifteen years, starting with Fr. Fonck's first request in June, 1914, for the Biblical Institute to obtain its total independence and its academic titles. It was only possible thanks to the practically unfailing perseverance of Fr. Fonck and, later, of Fr. O'Rourke, but also thanks to the support of Fr. General Wernz, who was no longer able to go directly to Pius X, and especially of Fr. General Ledókowski who threw his weight into the balance and spared no effort. Only Fr. Fernández did not insist, for he knew about the resistance put up by the Commission and Benedict XV had to yield to pressure from it. The opposition came mainly from Cardinal van Rossum, from 1916 on, and Pius XI was probably going to have to use all his authority to get him to give way in 1928. Could it be that, to do so, the Pope or Fr. General imagined the association of the Biblical Institute with the Gregorian and the Oriental Institute? In any case, nothing transpired in this matter (but cf. *infra*).

What we can say is that the Biblical Institute's most important concerns were settled only slowly. The tricky project for a branch of the Institute in the Holy Land was only carried out in 1925 after almost fifteen years of tergiversation. The second part of this book (ch. I) will explain this. Here again it is from Fr. O'Rourke and Fr. General that the concrete solution came.

b) The departure of Fr. Fonck in September 1929

Fr. Fonck left the Institute and Rome on September 30th, 1929. However unpleasant it may be, it is important to shed light on this departure. Its origin goes back to 1925 and the main items in the dossier are in the Institute's Roman archives (B-XVII-5, II-III). Fr. O'Rourke gave a summary of the sequence of events (Doc. R. II,10).

In 1924 the second edition of the *Praelectiones biblicae ad usum scholarum. Novum Testamentum. I: Introductio et commentarius in quattuor Iesu Christi Evangelia*, by Adriano Simón, C.SS.R. was published by Marietti in Turin. The volume contained XXXII-652 pages and Cardinal van Rossum had written a commendatory letter which appeared on pages VII-VIII of the book. A. Simón had been an *auditor* at the Institute in 1913-1914 and died on September 27th, 1924, at the age of 36.

The work was reviewed at length by Fr. Lagrange who questioned many points in it, while appreciating its overall worth (cf. *RB* 34 [1925], pp. 132-139). But the book did not please Fr. Fonck, then director of *Biblica*, who prepared an eighteen-page criticism that he planned to publish in the journal.

Since Cardinal van Rossum had praised the book, the rector, O'Rourke, asked Fr. Fonck to let him have his review and having received it, had it read by Frs. Vaccari and Power. The latter then wrote an eighty-page assessment in which he criticized Fr. Fonck and vindicated Fr. Simón. Whereupon the rector forbade Fr. Fonck to publish his pages in *Biblica*. In his irritation Fr. Fonck replied that he was going to refer the matter to the Holy Office. But after several months, not having received any reply from the Holy Office, he told the rector that he would go directly to the Pope, for he could not bear that his competence be questioned. Up to this point all this is known from a report to Fr. General made by Fr. O'Rourke (APIBR B- XVII-5 [II-A, pp. 1-2]). Fr. Fonck actually wrote a letter to the Pope; our Roman archives have the copy, dated December 10th, 1925, by Fr. Fonck himself (APIBR B-XVII-6 [1-3a]). In nine brief points covering two pages in it he mentions the essential part of the criticism he made in the article he had wanted to publish in *Biblica* but he expressed himself in the form of questions. Here are two examples:

3. Notwithstanding the differences between the Matthean story of the appearance of the risen Christ to the holy women (Matt 28,9ss) and the story in John of the appearance to Mary Magdalen (John 20,14-18), would it be permissible to explain the text of the two evangelists as referring to the same appearance?

8. About the words that John 1,49 attributes to Nathanael ["Rabbi, you are the Son of God, the king of Israel"], is it permissible to doubt that Nathanael really used them ?

These questions certainly were serious from the exegetical point of view and can be answered either in the affirmative or in the negative, but Fr. Fonck obviously expected negative answers from the Pope, the same as his own and opposed to those of Fr. Simón. It is well known that Fr. Fonck had a rigid conception of the literal meaning of the texts and their historical truth. It was soon to be known that Fr. Fonck handed his letter personally to the Pope.

In 1926, things got complicated because Fr. Fonck thought fit to give Fr. Frey, the secretary of the Biblical Commission, Fr. Power's long report, which was favourable to Fr. Simón. In his turn, Cardinal van Rossum asked Fr. O'Rourke for a copy of it, which he gave him. The result was that on April 25th, 1926, the cardinal sent Fr. General, in confidence – Fr. Ledókowski puts that in writing in his own hand at the top of the document – a statement covering four pages in Latin, without date or signature, in which, considering Fr. Power's assertions, which were approved by his colleagues Bea, O'Rourke and Vaccari, the cardinals of the Commission sharply criticized the Institute and reminded it of its obligations of fidelity to the decrees of the Holy See and the Biblical Commission. The Commission in fact repeated most of Fr. Fonck's objections: the refusal to consider that the evangelists give the *ipsissima loquentis verba*, opposition to the faith of old and the tradition of the Fathers, lastly, the inspiration and inerrancy of the gospels placed in great jeopardy. The Institute, which had received a copy of this document from Fr. General, then began to prepare its defence.

On June 4th, 1926, Fr. O'Rourke was summoned by Pius XI, who kept him for a hour. On the 7th, he gave Fr. General a detailed account of the audience (ARSI, PIB-1002-III,8); the text is in Latin and some extracts will be quoted in translation. The reception was informal and fatherly. The Pope wanted to talk with the rector about the Biblical Commission's document. Guessing he would, Fr. O'Rourke had brought it with him. Together they read it through and carefully examined the points for which the Institute had been reproached. "His Holiness openly admitted the injustice of the accusations", writes the rector, "and spoke with great affection for the Society and of his confidence in the professors at the Biblical Institute". He wanted to know who wrote the document from the Commission, but the rector knew nothing about it; the Pope also asked the rector to question Fr. General on this subject of great importance, adding that the reply the Biblical Institute was preparing should describe the real situation, indicating the errors committed by *the others* (probably meaning the authors of the document). Continuing his letter, the rector then indicates some urgent points to Fr. General:

1. "His Holines requires that Fr. Fonck be removed and sent back to his province; the Pope believes that Fr. Fonck is not quite mentally sound (*non esse omnino mentis compotem*) and, notes Fr. O'Rourke, he described the conversation he had with him when Fr. Fonck brought him one of his papers (*aliquam suam elucubra-tionem* [it must be the letter of December 1925]). Furthermore, Fr. O'Rourke continued, His Holiness has very little esteem for Fr. Fonck's learning; he considers that he can write 'popular' books but that he is lacking in real learning and scientific method; the Pope has been convinced of this for many years. The fact that certain cardinals may perhaps be unwilling to accept Fr. Fonck's removal does not really constitute an obstacle because the danger would be to put it off; with the trouble getting worse from day to day, the remedy must be applied immediately".

2. The Pope also wanted the departure of Fr. Fernández, whose relations with Ernesto Buonaiuti, a notorious modernist excommunicated in January 1926, made the Father "*a bit of a leftist*". But the rector had defended the orthodoxy of Fr. Fernández. Be that as it may, the Pope went on, the General should apply the remedies "*cum omni suavitate*". From this resulted, Fr. O'Rourke went on, addressing the General, the question of new professors of exegesis; he is thinking of Fr. Galdos to replace Fr. Fernández and Fr. A. Merk to take the place of Fr. Fonck. At the close of the audience the Pope asked the rector to come and see him every time there was something to tell him: "by listening to only one side his judgment might well be wrong".

This letter explains why Fr. Merk came to the Biblical Institute in 1927, why Fr. Fernández was moved to the Jerusalem branch in 1929 and especially why Fr. Fonck had to be removed. It also becomes clear why, in 1927, Fr. Fonck had to hand over the direction of *Biblica* to Fr. O'Rourke who, in turn, entrusted it the following year to Fr. Power actually. Finally, it is worth noting the following conclusion by Fr. O'Rourke, summarizing his conversation with Pius XI: "It opened the way for us to receive the right to confer the doctorate" (Doc R. II,10).

Meanwhile Fr. Fonck was still in Rome where he continued to teach. On June 20th, 1928, in a letter addressed to the Pope (cf. Doc. R. II,7) Fr. General had to come back to the question of Fr. Fernández's move and especially Fr. Fonck's return to his province; the Pope would have to intervene so that the Biblical Commission would agree to release one of its Consultors. A year later, on July 15th, 1929, while Fr. Fonck was still in place, Fr. O'Rourke, in a letter addressed to Fr. General (ARSI, PIB-1002-IV, 19), again expressed a negative judgment on Fr. Fonck. The latter, on July 7th, had handed him a manuscript for inclusion in the volume *Institutiones Biblicae* which the Institute was preparing. In it Fr. Fonck sets out what he calls his principles, and those of tradition, in the interpretation of the Bible, adding that if they are accepted by the censors he would stay in Rome, whereas if they are rejected, he would go! Now those principles, about which he had not the slightest doubt, would lead, according to Fr. O'Rourke, to accusing anyone who did not accept them of heresy, and the reputation of the Biblical Institute would suffer. To this grievance Fr. O'Rourke added some others, the ones which the Pope had formulated in June 1926, the impossibility for Fr. Fonck to collaborate with his colleagues, as well as the fact that he is always contrasting Pius XI unfavourably with his predecessors, finding him too influenced by liberals such as Mgr. Mercati, Dom Quentin or Mgr. Tisserant; besides, Fr. O'Rourke goes on to say, Fr. Fonck is fully aware of the crisis he is going through.

Things must have finally have been settled: Fr. Fonck ceased being a consultor of the Biblical Commission and Fr. Urban Holtzmeister came from Innsbruck to replace the one who was leaving. On September 29th, 1929, Fr. Fonck took the train for Prague at Rome railway station. At Prague and later at Vienna the following year he devoted himself to the spiritual ministry but at the beginning of October 1930 he suffered from what was discovered some days later to be cancer of the rectum. While he was giving a retreat to the Servants of the Divine Heart of Jesus in Vienna he was taken by them to their Rudolfspital where he underwent two operations on the 14th and the 15th, but on the 17th the heart began to give out and the following day Fr. General was informed. Lucid until the end and entrusting himself to the Lord, Fr. Fonck died on October 19th, 1930, comforted by a papal blessing which Fr. Provincial brought him on the very morning of his death. These and many other details are known from a letter that Fr. F. X. Jungmann, a Jesuit at Vienna, wrote on October 28th for a nun in Rome (APIBR M-Fonck, 3).

c) Academic life from 1926-1930

In accordance with the earliest traditions, students had free access to the Institute but, and this is revealing, from 1927-1930, they were explicitly asked to take care of everything placed at their disposal (*Acta PIB* 3, pp. 14 and 126). Was vandalism already rampant?

During Fr. O'Rourke's last four years as rector the second generation of professors arrived. In 1926, Fr. Alfredo Vitti for Ethiopic which he taught until 1943. In 1927 Fr. Augustinus Merk for New Testament until his death in 1945. In 1928 there were four: Giuseppe Messina for Sanskrit, Iranian languages and the history of religions; he had studied at Berlin under the direction of Joseph Markwart who bequeathed his library to the Institute (cf. *Acta PIB* 3, pp. 107-108); he died in 1951; Alfred Pohl for Assyriology which he resumed after his doctorate and continued until his death in 1961; Émile Suys for Egyptology, but he died unexpectedly in 1935; and Franz Zorell for

Armenian and Georgian which he taught until 1944, while working on his Hebrew-Latin dictionary. In 1929 Urban Holzmeister succeeded Fr. Fonck for the New Testament until 1950.

After Pius XI's *Motu proprio* "Quam maxime" and the complementary decisions of the Holy See, the *Acta PIB* 3, fasc. 3, published the new academic rules for the Institute on June 1st, 1929; the Congregation for studies had approved them for six years on June 7th, 1929 (APIBR K-4-C [I – O'Rourke 1929]). It is pointed out in particular that the doctoral thesis must cover at least one hundred octavo pages. In addition, before the defence of his thesis the candidate must give a lesson lasting one hour on a subject to be given to him one hour earlier (*Acta PIB* 3, fasc. 3, p. 22); that spartan regime was to last until January 1948 (cf. *ARSI*, 11, pp. 404-405).

Finally, on July 6th, 1930, Fr. Augustin Bea succeeded Fr. O'Rourke as President of the Institute. His predecessor left him a situation that had been definitely clarified and augured well for the future. Fr. Bea, who had been a professor at the Institute since 1924, was teaching Old Testament and in 1927, taking over from Fr. Fonck, he had started a course, then a seminar in methodology, which was a task he was to keep until his elevation to the cardinalate in 1959! This spell of clear and very pedagogical teaching was one of the most famous in the whole history of the Institute.

3. *To the Statutes of 1934*

Fr. Bea had already been a Superior three times, but never for more than four years. No one could imagine that he would be rector of the Biblical Institute for nineteen years.

a) Fr. Bea and the Constitution *"Deus scientiarum Dominus"*

Bibliography on Fr. Bea's rectorate

Stjepan SCHMIDT, *Agostino Bea il cardinale dell'unità*, Roma, Città Nuova, 1987, esp. pp. 89-130 = *Augustin Bea the cardinal of Unity*, New York, New City Press, 1992, esp. pp. 90-128 (a somewhat hagiographic biography). – Stanislas LYONNET, "Le Cardinal Bea et le développement des études bibliques, in *RivBib* 16 (1968) 371-392. – ID., "L'orientamento dato dal P. Bea agli studi biblici: un contributo all'ecumenismo", in *CC* 132 (1981/2) 550-556. – Max ZERWICK, "Am Päpstlichen Bibelinstitut in Rom", in Maria BUCHMÜLLER (ed.), *Augustin Kardinal Bea. Wegbereiter der Einheit*, Augsburg, Winfried-Werk, 1972, pp. 70-84. – Norbert LOHFINK, "Augustin Bea und die Freiheit der biblischen Forschung", in *Orientierung* 45 (1981) 129-134. – ID., "Augustin Bea und die moderne Bibelwissenschaft" in Dietmar BADER (ed.), *Kardinal Augustin Bea. Die Hinwendung der Kirche zur Bibelwissenschaft und Ökumene*. Munich, Schnell & S., 1981, pp. 56-70. – M. GILBERT, "Le Cardinal Augustin Bea. 1881-1968. La Bible, rencontre des Chrétiens et des Juifs", in *NRT* 105 (1983) 369-383.

On being relieved of the office of superior at the Gesù on October 12, 1928, Fr. Bea came to live at the Biblical Institute. However, he had to be away from June to November, 1929: Fr. General sent him to Tokyo to decide on the future of the Jesuit "Sophia" University after the earthquake in 1923. In common agreement with the Fathers at the University, Fr. Bea decided that it would stay in the centre of the city. That had only been an interlude, for he was already on the pontifical Commission charged with preparing the constitution "*Deus scientiarum Dominus*" on ecclesiastical Universities and Faculties which Pius XI signed on May 24th, 1931.

The Commission worked for more than two years and Fr. Bea co-operated very actively with it; the dossier which he left in the Roman archives proves it (B-XVII-3-4). Even if his official appointment as member of that Commission dates from March 1929 (cf. Pius XI's letter to Cardinal Bisleti, February 6th, 1930, note), Bea had already proposed a *votum* to the Commission dated February 28th, 1929. In it he analysed the disparities between universities as regards the doctorate in theology: at the Gregorian, for example, to be a doctor it was enough to pass the examination in dogmatic theology after four years of study, whereas in Louvain four years of theology gave only the baccalaureate, the doctorate being conferred only after six years and on the basis of a thesis of scholarly worth. It is probably from this that the saying arose: *"Doctor romanus, asinus lovaniensis"*. It was quite obviously becoming necessary to lay down common rules. Then again, the plan meant to define rules equally valid for specialized institutions like the Biblical Institute. Fr. Bea's views carried great weight here, especially because he had been rector of that Institute since the summer of 1930. The decisions in favour of the Biblical Institute taken by Pius XI in 1928 and 1929 were upheld, except that henceforth, to get into the Biblical Institute, the licentiate in theology, obtained after four years would be enough. As regards the method to be adopted in teaching, Bea, whose great concern this was, took the opportunity to promote his ideas. In the matter of courses, the Commission distinguished between the "main" subjects, those which were "auxiliary" and those concerned with the "speciality"; in the case of the Biblical Institute, it would therefore be necessary to revise the curriculum published in 1929. Lastly, the academic institutions were authorized to ask their students to cover tuition costs; the great financial crisis of 1929 was not yet over.

Once promulgated, the Constitution was analyzed by Fr. Bea in *Biblica* 12 (1931), pp. 385-394. In that article he dealt with everything concerning biblical studies, both in faculties of theology and in the Institute.

b) The creation of the Oriental Faculty at the Biblical Institute and the Statutes

While the Constitution *"Deus scientiarum Dominus"* was being written, Fr. Bea was received by Pius XI. On March 8th, 1931, he spoke about that audience at the Council of professors and the minutes of the session give the substance of his remarks which we translate from the Latin:

> The Holy Father exhorts us to study oriental languages carefully. He desires that, in our Institute, an 'Oriental Section' with its degrees be set up, so that there may be in a sense two integral parts at the Institute, one exegetico-dogmatic and the other for the Ancient East.

This note requires some explanation. On January 26th Fr. Bea came to thank Pius XI for having appointed him a consultor of the Biblical Commission on January 16th (APIBR K-1-A). On the same day he reported to Fr. General on how the interview went (APIBR K-23-[II-1]). The rector informed the Pope about the first results of the excavations at Teleilat Ghassul (cf. Part Two, ch. II), then the Pope inquired about the situation at the Institute. Fr, Bea took the opportunity to explain to the Pope that the Institute would have to revise its programme after the appearance of the Constitution. The Pope's encouraging remarks stirred the rector to raise the question of studies in orientalism and to expound to him his intention to place these studies at the Institute on the same level as in the universities and thus make going to Protestant universities unnecessary.

> The Pope, he went on, strongly approved of this idea and thought that we ought, however, to start immediately, first with Assyriology or something like that, then, gradually, add on the rest. I could see that he was not fully informed about what we had already and I briefly explained the important parts of it to him; I then added that we could first of all separate off studies in orientalism into a distinct section, then we could draw conclusions later about whether we ought to go further. The idea pleased him greatly: 'Yes, Yes, do that; and then we shall see how things develop'. I then hinted that, starting with one section, a faculty in the full sense of the word might gradually be set up, perhaps with its own degrees. Thereupon the Holy Father: 'That is exactly what I meant. We must make that our aim' (translated from the German).

The audience came to an end. Fr. Bea also mentioned preparations being made for the journal *Orientalia* and the launching of the series *Analecta Orientalia*.

The result was that during the 1931-1932 academic year on an experimental basis the Institute offered an "Assyriological section" (*Acta PIB* 3, p. 187). Frs. Deimel and Pohl were put in charge of it, along with Fr. Maurus Witzel, O.F.M. (1882-1968). The latter was the first non-Jesuit long-term professor working at the Institute; he taught Sumerian and Hittite there until 1957 (cf. *Acta PIB* 7, pp. 223-225). This Assyriological section was in fact a first step towards a faculty; as from November 1st the Council of professors showed that it was well aware of this.

On April 28th the following year the same Council decided, with a strong majority in favour, that the Congregation for Seminaries and Universities should be asked to create an oriental faculty at the Institute immediately. On June 21st, Fr. Bea drew up a petition along these lines which he addressed to the Pope and, on the 27th, Fr. General sent it with an accompanying letter (APIBR K-31 [III-7]). To be on the safe side, Fr. Bea wrote to Cardinal Bisleti on July 6th, passing on to him the Institute's opinions on some objections that might be raised against the plan at the Congregation (Doc. R. II,11); here is a summary of them:

1. a faculty is better because a simple oriental section would not make it possible to do Bible studies and oriental studies together in three years;
2. Bible study requires the study of orientalism; that was the case at the very beginning of the Institute; by the same token, orientalism belongs to those studies that can be called ecclesiastical;
3. no competition with the Oriental Institute because that concerns itself with the Christian East, whereas the Biblical Institute's oriental faculty is interested in the Ancient East;
4. the study of the Bible will not be harmed by the creation of this oriental faculty; the authorities will be stimulated by it to strengthen the biblical faculty even more.

On August 7th, 1932, the Congregation gave its approval (APIBR K-1-A and *Acta PIB* 3, p. 231).

Once that was settled – it was an important decision – the Institute put the finishing touches to its Statutes, in conformity with Pius XI's Constitution and already dealing with the "Faculty of studies of the Ancient East", in brief: oriental faculty, which the Constitution had evidently not provided for. The first rough draft of these Statutes, dated 1932, contained 48 octavo pages (APIBR K-31 [III-3a]). The Congregation approved it on a temporary basis on September 6th, 1932, and authorized its application during the academic year 1932-1933, postponing definite approval to a later date (cf. *Acta PIB* 3, p. 232). A fascicule entitled *Facultas studiorum Orientis antiqui. Excerpta ex Statutis Pontificii Instituti Biblici* was published at the same time.

Revising these Statutes took a long time. The professors were consulted, of course, and they often replied in writing (APIBR A-11 [III-2]). On February 23rd, 1933, the rector, at the Council of professors, reported on how the work was going. As regards the biblical faculty, progress was slow because of the Institute's links with the other members of the Consortium, the Gregorian and the Oriental Institute; at all events, the Council of that faculty, that is to say the ordinary professors and the rector, were working at it. In the oriental faculty not everything had yet been discussed; once the work was finished the rector assembled the changes to be made to these Statutes of the faculty and they were incorporated into the definitive edition (APIBR K-31 [III-3a]).

The Statutes of the Institute were finally presented to the Congregation, which approved them on August 7th, 1934, at the same time as those of the

Gregorian University and the Oriental Institute. A photo of the Congregation's decree was printed at the beginning of 1935 in the official booklet of the *Statuta Pontificii Instituti Biblici*, just after the *Praenotio historica*.

In connection with these Statutes, it can be noted that they do not contain any *"Ordinatio"*. As regards the biblical faculty, the essential matters have been mentioned above, only three revealing points are to be made: 1. the history of exegesis, which Fr. Vaccari had been teaching since 1912, became a "special" subject; 2. the study of the Mishna and the Talmud appears as a "special" subject and Fr. Semkowski is the first to deal with it; 3. third year students will be able to spend that year in Jerusalem (*Appendix A*). The oriental faculty, for its part, is open to anyone who has a diploma in classical studies at secondary level, comprising Latin and Greek, that is to say, a diploma which at that time gave access to a university.

c) The Institute's publications

On December 7th, 1930, Fr. Bea proposed changing the series *Orientalia* into a regular journal to the Council of professors. A lapse of one year was necessary to achieve the task, so that the first fascicule appeared at the beginning of 1932. For three years the new journal consisted of only three fascicules. Fr. Bea took on the editorship of it.

In 1931 the new series *Analecta Orientalia* was started, edited by Fr. Deimel. Three volumes appeared that year; no. 9 appeared in 1934. So it was a success.

The journal *Biblica*, for its part, went on its way under the editorship of Fr. Bea with Fr. Power being the new editor of the *Elenchus Bibliographicus*.

Among the Institute's other publications some were to have a great future:

- A. MERK, *Novum Testamentum graece et latine*, Rome, 1933 (11th ed. in 1992);
- Fr. ZORELL, *Lexicon graecum Novi Testamenti*, 2nd ed., Paris, Lethielleux, 1931 (5th ed. in 1999);
- Fr. ZORELL, *Grammatik zur altgeorgischen Bibelübersetzung*, Rome, 1930.

In 1933 Fr. Bea published the second, reworked edition of his *De Pentateucho*. Fr. Marcel Lobignac, in the review he wrote of it in *RSR* 24 (1934), pp. 229-234, pointed out the differences from the 1928 edition and that did not, unfortunately, please Fr. Bea (cf. Gilbert, pp. 373-374), who, however, did not hold it against him because, in the same year, he sent him to Jerusalem as director of the branch of the Institute. Fr. Lobignac wrote: "in the face of the theories of criticism there is always the same rejection, but it is sometimes more nuanced", (p. 230); and his conclusion: "If we may be allowed to state our opinion frankly, we do not believe that all the difficulties of a certain number of readers will be met by an attentive and conscientious examination of this book" (p. 234), for the problems are so complex that it is not possible to arrive at a solution all at once.

d) The first "Biblical Weeks" for seminary professors

In September 1930 the first "Biblical Week" for professors in Italian seminaries was held at the Institute. Fr. Vaccari was in overall charge and it was also he who published its *Atti della settimana biblica tenutasi nel Pontificio Istituto Biblico dal 22 al 29 Settembre 1930*, Roma, PIB, 1931, xxx-116 p. It should be noted immediately that such sessions, which today are held in many countries, were at that time unheard of.

The idea did not come from Fr. Vaccari but from seminary professors who, in 1922, had contacted him about this by letter. The Council of professors at the Institute had discussed it on June 7th, 1922, and again on January 8th, 1924; at that time there was talk of a "summer course" but the plan was put off until later, there being no means to carry it out. Finally, in April 1930, Fr. Vaccari sent a circular letter to the seminary professors, setting out the plan and asking their opinion. He received about fifty positive replies. On September 12th the programme was sent through the post to those who had shown interest in the project. So it was that, from the 22nd until the 29th of September, the first "Biblical Week" was held at the Institute. At the rate of two lectures in the morning and two others in the late afternoon, the programme was not overloaded, except for Fr. Vaccari, who spoke every day, especially on methodological and practical matters; Fr. Vitti gave four lectures in which he reported on some recent research, on Saint Paul, for example; Fr. Messina, in the course of two lectures, spoke of comparativism in biblical exegesis; among other speakers we note the presence of Don G. Ricciotti. On the last day of the session those attending were received by Pius XI.

The acts of this congress first of all give the events that took place each day and the content of the lectures (pp. XII-XXV), then (pp.1-116) give the text of eight of the lectures, but none of Fr. Vaccari's.

The fourth "Biblical Week" was also held at the Institute, as every year, from September 25th to September 30th 1933. The twelve lectures delivered at it were also published by Fr. Vaccari in a book entitled *La Redenzione. Conferenze bibliche tenute nell'anno giubilare 1933 al Pont. Istituto Biblico (IV Settimana Biblica)*, Rome, PIB, 1934, IV-323 p. This collection, to which Frs. Vaccari and Vitti had also greatly contributed, was of the quality and exegetical worth that honoured the jubilee that was being celebrated (*VD* 14 [1934] 23-25, 57-62).

e) The 1933 Holy Year and the twenty-five years of the Institute in 1934

The origin of the celebration of a Holy Year in 1933 is common knowledge (cf. Schmidt, p. 95) and only some details will be added here. A few days before Christmas Fr. Bea went to give the Pope his best wishes and present him with the Institute's main publications for the year that was closing. Pius

XI asked him point-blank what year Jesus died in. The rector, in his embarrassment, excused himself by saying that he was not competent to give an answer. However, the Pope replied, it is something you ought to know! He gave him twenty-four or forty-eight hours, we are not sure, to bring him a clear answer.

Back at the Institute, Fr. Bea asked Fr. Holzmeister to compile a short dossier on the matter for him. Actually, in 1930, the Father had published a *Chronologia vitae Christi*, the last twenty pages of which discuss the problem and the conclusion was that, without excluding the year 33, "all things considered, it seems necessary to conclude that the year 30 must be preferred" (p. 64, translated from the Latin). So he gave Fr. Bea some pages on the subject which most often summarize his 1930 study. Fr. Bea set himself to translate into Italian what Fr. Holzmeister had written probably in German or Latin; still, the references to the authors mentioned in the rector's note could only be checked in Holzmeister's book. Most of all, Bea's conclusion full of nuances and without too much commitment differed from that of the professor he had consulted because, for the rector (Doc. R. II,12), "The statement that the Lord died between the years 29 and 33 is *certain*. It is *probable* that the year of his death is either the year 30 or the year 33.This could be sufficient reason for celebrating the centenary of the Lord's death '*in the last of the years generally assigned by the authors as the most probable date for the death of the divine Saviour*'".

At half past eleven on December 23rd the rector gave the Pope, who was getting worried, his hastily-written five pages. Pius XI was satisfied with them, since, on the following day, while addressing the Cardinals of the Curia coming to offer their best wishes, he announced a Holy Year for 1933. In 1983 John Paul II fell into step with him.

This did not stop Fr. Holzmeister resuming his work and publishing, in 1933 to be sure, a fuller edition of it comprising 246 pages, at the end of which he upheld his preference for the year 30. Fr. Power, for his part, without ever quoting his colleague, defended the position in favour of the year 33 in the journal *Verbum Domini* 13 (1933), pp. 129-137, 173-181 and 199-208.

On May 7th, 1934, the Institute celebrated the twenty-fifth anniversary of its foundation. On February 23rd the previous year the Council of professors proposed that for the occasion, the Institute publish a double and special fascicule of *Biblica*. In addition to scholarly studies by resident professors, but also by some former students of the Institute, an outline of the history of the Institute would be given. The opportunity would also be taken to establish the list of all former students since 1909.

That list was in fact drawn up and a total of 911 former students was reckoned, including the academic year 1933-1934. In each case the following particulars are given: nationality, membership of this or that diocese or religious order, years spent at the Institute and degrees obtained, and lastly present occupation or address. This dossier was never published but it must have helped to make this anniversary known (APIBR B-III-B).

On the other hand, the special number of *Biblica* 15 (1934) appeared in time for May 7th. It covered fascicules 2 and 3 of the journal, on pages 121-450. But that was only half of the articles received for the Institute's anniversary. So this double fascicule was published separately along with a second volume comprising the articles that *Biblica* had not included; a strange procedure was in fact followed: articles were arranged in alphabetical order of the authors' names and, in *Biblica*, they stopped with the letter K! The two volumes, therefore, also published in 1934, were entitled *Miscellanea Biblica edita a Pontificio Instituto Biblico ad celebrandum annum XXV ex quo conditum est Institutum 1909 – VII Maii – 1934*; the first volume comprised 316 pages and the second 406; there were thirty studies in them, thirteen of which were written by professors of the Institute. The historical sketch had been written in Latin by Fr. Bea; in *Biblica* it came on pages 121-172, in the *Miscellanea* on pages 1-52, but that was not enough; it was published again the same year as a 79-page separate fascicule, nineteen pages being illustrations, and its title was *Pontificii Instituti Biblici de Urbe prima quinque lustra 1909–VII Maii–1934*.

So the Institute's twenty-fifth anniversary was worthily celebrated. On May 3rd Pius XI sent Fr, Bea a letter of congratulations and encouragement for the Institute (APIBR K-1-A), reproduced in the *Acta PIB* 3, pp. 289-290. On the 7th a pontifical Mass was celebrated in the morning in the church of St. Ignatius by Bishop Jan Smit, a Canon of the Vatican basilica, who had been a student at the Institute in 1909. The solemn session was held in the afternoon in the Main Lecture Hall of the Institute; in the middle were placed the two volumes of the *Miscellanea Biblica* as well as the first volume, just published, of the report on the excavations at *Teleilat Ghassul* (see Part Two, ch. III). Finally, on May 12th, in the Hall of Blessings, Pius XI received the two thousand persons making up the three institutions in the Consortium, the Gregorian, the Biblical Institute and the Oriental Institute, but it was the Biblical Institute that was celebrating. After a tribute paid by Fr. Bea and a speech recalling the work of recent Popes for biblical studies – a speech made by G. Stano, O.F.M.Conv., a student at the Institute – Pius XI addressed the assembly and spoke of the scholarly apostolate (cf. *VD* 14 [1934] 161-177).

f) From 1930 to 1934, students, professors and academic authorities

The number of students had already increased since 1924; there was a definite increase during the last two years of this period: in 1932-1933 there were 96, including 78 *alumni* and in 1933-1934, 93, including 72 *alumni*. Almost all of them must have been in the biblical faculty. Figures are lacking for the oriental faculty, unfortunately; all we know is that Pancratius Keilbach, O.F.M., of German origin, received the licentiate in orientalism in 1934; as that degree was conferred after three years of study, it may be supposed that he started in the "Assyriological Section" which only existed in 1931-1932.

The first doctors in biblical studies were: Ricardo Arconada, S.J., a Spaniard, in 1931 – his thesis on Messianism in the Psalms appeared in 1937; William L. Newton, from Cleveland in the United States, in 1932; José Gonzalez Brown, from Mexico, and Johannes Pohl from Cologne, in 1933; Vincenzo Iacono, from Agrigento, and Johannes Schildenberger, O.S.B. from Beuron, in 1934. Unfortunately, J. Pohl soon began to collaborate with Nazism (cf. Maria KÜHN-LUDEWIG, *Johannes Pohl (1904-1960)*, Hannover, Laurentius Verlag 2000, 334 p.).

Two new professors arrived at the oriental faculty: Fr. Witzel (cf. *supra*), then, in 1932, Fr. Jean Simon, a Belgian Jesuit who taught Coptic, mainly, until 1964; he died tragically in 1968.

As regards the authorities at the Institute, on June 21st, 1932, Pius XI appointed the Cardinal Prefect of the Congregation for Seminaries and Universities Grand Chancellor of the Consortium's three institutions, the Gregorian, the Biblical Institute and the Oriental Institute (*Acta PIB* 3, pp. 183-184). The Father General of the Society of Jesus became Vice-Grand Chancellor. Frs. Vaccari and Deimel were promoted dean of the biblical faculty and dean of the oriental faculty respectively (*Acta PIB* 3, p. 233).

How can we forget such a discreet and efficient character? From the end of 1930 until 1968, Brother Bernhard Hageman (1890-1972), a German, was secretary to the rector of the Institute. He it was who typed Fr. Bea's letters, then those of Frs. Vogt and MacKenzie. Having joined the noviceship in 1913 he was called up at the beginning of the war in August 1914. At the end of that month, on the 24th, he had witnessed the massacre of almost four hundred civilians, men, women and children, in the square at Tamines, on the banks of the Sambre in Belgium. The German soldiery committed that crime, but he did not fire, as he emotionally explained to the writer of these lines one December evening in 1967. Br. Hagemann, an upright and reserved person, possessed the level-headedness of the wise and he was happy to live in Rome (cf. *Acta PIB* 7, p. 634).

Lastly, on November 6th, 1930, the Piazza della Pilotta was the scene of a unique event. On the morning of that day the new building of the Gregorian University was inaugurated. The official procession left the Main Lecture Hall of the Biblical Institute, now the Pius X Hall, and, with the great bronze door wide open, crossed the square in the pouring rain (cf. *Pontificia Università Gregoriana. L'inaugurazione della nuova sede*, Rome, 1930, 20-23).

4. *Assessing the twelve years 1922-1934*

The reader may be surprised that no reference has been made in the preceding pages to the rise of Fascism in Italy and National Socialism in Germany. How can one overlook the "March on Rome" organized by Mussolini in Italy in 1922 up to the period when he took complete control in 1925? How can one overlook Hitler's inflammatory book *Mein Kampf* (1924-1928), and the events leading up to his assuming full power in 1934? It is because these events which would lead to the tragedy did not directly affect the Biblical Institute, at least not during the period that concerns us.

And yet. On September 26th, 1980, at the close of the Second international congress of Coptic studies, of which the last sessions were held at the Biblical Institute – Fr. Hans Quecke was a good specialist in the subject – a reception was held in the courtyard at 25 via della Pilotta in honour of Professor H.J. Polotsky (1905-1991), a linguist with a world-wide reputation (cf. *Acta PIB* 8, p. 523). He made a speech. He was celebrating his seventy-fifth birthday and, being at the Biblical Institute, he wanted to pay a moving and unexpected tribute to Fr. A Pohl. In 1933 Polotsky, who was then at the University of Berlin, had published an article in *Orientalia* 2, pp. 269-274. But that same year the Nazis, on coming to power, had removed the Jews from teaching at universities. Fr. Pohl, who assisted Fr. Bea in the editorship of the journal, informed the Jewish orientalists in Germany that *Orientalia* remained open to them. In 1935, when he had emigrated to Jerusalem, Polotsky actually published an article in the journal. The writer of these lines was present at that reception in his capacity as rector of the Institute.

The political event that directly concerned the Institute was the signing of the "Lateran Agreements" between Italy and the Holy See on February 11th, 1929; the Institute, which took no part in any of the negotiations, was simply mentioned in article 16 and in an attached document (*All. III Tav 2*) among places belonging to the Holy See exempt from tax in Italy.

What marks this period as regards the Institute is first of all the courage and tenacity of Fr. O'Rourke in dealing successfully with situations that became acrimonious either with the Pontifical Biblical Commission or with Fr. Fonck. Then there were the creativity and the organizational gifts of Bea the rector.

In 1934, with its Statutes, the Biblical Institute is not only very different from what it was at the death of Benedict XV but it henceforth possessed a structure and the wherewithal which were to last.

Furthermore, the attentive concern of Pius XI, a real scholar, made it possible for the Institute to enter the scholarly world at last. Probably smarting from what happened over F. Vigouroux's *Manuel biblique*, republished by A. Brassac in 1920, which the Holy Office had placed on the Index in 1923, the Pope, in the face of the scandal caused by that condemnation, had to act. The

Biblical Commission's negative attitude to A. Simón's manual, which appeared in 1924, elicited a healthy reaction on the part of Pius XI, to whom, incidentally, the following remark is ascribed: "One Galileo case is enough for me" (quoted by Schmidt, p. 105). The Commission lost some of its power and serious scholarship could develop at the Institute where less conservative exegetes were appearing, Holzmeister and Merk, with the Old Testament being held up by Vaccari and especially Bea, both being not so well trained in the subject. We would still have to wait.

Meanwhile, thanks to Pius XI's Constitution, students began to flock to the biblical faculty since, to enter it, only a licentiate in theology, obtained after four years of study, was required. In addition, the efforts made in orientalism since the foundation of the Institute bore their fruit: the oriental faculty made a name for itself, thanks especially to its publications.

Lastly, in 1934, according to Fr. Bea's estimate given in his offprint on the story of the Institute (p. 60), the library possessed a hundred thousand volumes, double what it had in 1914.

Conclusion

It took twenty-five years for the Institute to set itself up with two faculties, each conferring all academic degrees. This would not have been possible without the foresight and tenacity of Fr. Fonck. He really was the founder of the Institute, not only on the material level – and what a success he made of it! – but also because by calling upon professors of oriental languages as early as 1909 he was unwittingly preparing for the creation of the oriental faculty in 1932 and because in 1914 he had clearly seen that the Institute had to grant academic degrees, which he finally obtained in 1928.

Pressure from the Pontifical Biblical Commission over a long period prevented the Institute from enjoying full autonomy. Pius XI accorded this to it because that Commission had gone wrong in 1926. The anti-modernist attitudes impeding real scholarly work had to be stopped. The professors who, since 1909, belonged to this ultraconservative group gradually disappeared, as did Fr. Fonck himself in 1929, he who had been putting a spoke in the wheel for ten years.

Among the rectors to succeed Fr. Fonck, if Fr. Fernández was somewhat uninspiring, except for the planned sister house in Jerusalem (cf. Part Two, ch. I), Fr. O'Rourke was a man of extraordinary courage and without his work – getting academic degrees, opening the house at Jerusalem, the arrival of a new generation of professors and the removal of Fr. Fonck – Fr. Bea would not have found a situation favourable to the latest developments at the Institute.

When this first period in the history of the Institute was over, everything was henceforth in place for the future. Of the professors there from the start, only Fr. Deimel was left. Three others had arrived at the Institute a little later.

Fr. Vaccari in 1912, having studied biblical exegesis and orientalism at the oriental faculty of St. Joseph's University in Beirut from 1907-1908; a specialist in the history of exegesis by training, he was full of activity; as from 1912 he acted as secretary to the Council of professors, in 1924 we find him practically vice-rector, before combining these functions with being dean of the biblical faculty. Fr. O'Rourke, with an Oxford doctorate in classical philology, arrived in 1913 to teach Greek, but his gifts led to his being entrusted with the presidency of the Institute for six years. Fr. Edm. Power arrived in 1914; he, too, had studied at the oriental faculty in Beirut from 1902 to 1906 and came away with a doctorate in oriental languages.

The disappearance of the first generation of professors of exegesis, along with the arrival of new faces, meant that a less rigid and more serious study of texts, especially New Testament ones, was possible. Fr. Merk had received an advanced training, first at Valkenburg from 1900 to 1902, then at Munich from 1903 to 1906. Fr. Holzmeister had also studied at the oriental faculty in Beirut from 1904 to 1906 and was a doctor of theology from Innsbruck. Yet it was exegesis of the Old Testament that left the most to be desired, as everywhere in the Catholic world. If one looks at the Institute's publications, exegetical works in the strict sense do not shine forth particularly well, with anti-modernist pressure being still so strong. Even in the journal *Biblica*. Until when? The best books and articles published by the Institute, those that have not lost all their value, deal with the grammar of ancient languages, textual criticism, orientalism or the history of exegesis.

In 1934 Fr. Vaccari was already making a name for himself in the history of the Vulgate and of early exegesis; when, in 1952 and 1958, his best *Scritti di erudizione e di filologia* were brought together in Rome, more than a third of them had been published before 1934. Fr. Joüon's *Grammaire de l'hébreu biblique*, as we have seen, is still considered to be excellent and its updating proves it; midway between elementary and the most monumental grammars, it is noted, among other things, for clarity of exposition and the attention given to the syntax of the language. The critical edition of the manual *Novum Testamentum graece et latine* by Fr. Merk, later revised by Fr. C. M. Martini in 1964, and then by Fr. J. O'Callaghan in 1991 still holds its place among the best by reason of the research done on a large number of papyri and ancient manuscripts; since exegesis comments on the biblical text, it is of prime importance to be sure of the quality of that text, and as there are many hand editions it is preferable, in order to make a personal judgment, not to keep to just one edition; hence the importance of the one by Merk, whose choices are sometimes different from others; besides, his edition of the Latin Vulgate is a necessary complement to the early understanding of the Greek text, as well as for the exegesis of the Latin Fathers. As regards orientalism, Fr. Deimel's many works on Sumerian were those of a pioneer, as we have seen; this ancient

Mesopotamian language was different from Accadian, but showed many unknown features; Fr. Deimel's work certainly contributed to furthering knowledge of this non-Semitic language; the seventeen volumes of the *Materialen zum sumerischen Lexikon*, which came out over the period 1937-1986 at the Biblical Institute, continue the work by Fr. Deimel who, in 1934, had got to only the second of his five volumes comprising the *Šumerisches Lexikon*.

The *Elenchus Bibliographicus Biblicus*, which had been started in 1920 by Fr. Fonck and carried on by Fr. Power from 1925 to 1938 soon became one of the most basic tools for all exegetes. In 1920 this bibliography for matters concerning the Bible numbered 81 pages; in 1934 it had already reached 116 pages.

Bibliographers were greatly helped by the Institute's library of which the development during this period has been remarked upon. In fact, every year from 1913 to 1918 (cf. *Acta PIB* 1, pp. 107-109 and 254-255), then from 1924-1934 (cf. *Acta PIB* 2, fascicule 6, pp. 3-4; 3, pp. 302-303), gifts flowed in and we were grateful to the benefactors. Apart from purchases, many are the books that arrive for review in *Biblica*, as well as in *Orientalia*, which are journals which are exchanged for others. The Institute's library was probably the most important in the world as far as the Bible is concerned as early as 1934, so that on May 7th, Fr. G. Messina, who had been the librarian since 1929, put his signature to the *Foreword* to the 93-page edition of his *Elenco alfabetico delle pubblicazioni periodiche esistenti nella biblioteca del Pontificio Istituto Biblico* (APIBR K-29-B).

As regards the museum, Fr. Fonck, who was so concerned with it, had already put together its first collection in 1907 at the time of his stay in the Levant. Three batches were later added. The first, from Ancient Egypt, came from Flinders Petrie (1853-1942) with the Belgian Egyptologist Jean Capart (1877-1947) as intermediary; (cf. *Acta PIB* 1, pp. 109-110). The second came from Fr. Mallon in 1925; it was a collection of ancient coins from the land of Israel in the 1st and 2nd centuries A. D. (*Acta PIB* 2, fascicule 7, p. 6). Later on, with research carried out by Frs. P. Bovier-Lapierre, A. Mallon, R. Koeppel and Mr Neuville (cf. Part Two, ch. III), a rich prehistoric section could be set up. In the Assyriological section the museum possessed a certain number of tablets covered with texts in cuneiform writing; Fr. Deimel edited them and commented on them in the *Orientalia* series from 1924 to 1927. Thus in 1934, in his *Prima quinque lustra*, pp. 61-65, Fr. Bea could offer a good summary of what was in this museum, in which it seems no interest is being taken any more.

In short, during the first quarter of a century of its existence, the Biblical Institute did not act in a blameworthy manner. To be sure, it was born at the height of the Modernist crisis and had been set up as an anti-Modernist bastion. It was biblical exegesis in the full sense, especially exegesis of the Old

Testament, that suffered most from it even if, as from 1926, Pius XI implicitly called for more openness and scholarship. What saved the Biblical Institute throughout all this period was high-level work in fields connected with biblical exegesis, which included orientalism. This is why no one will be surprised to find that, in spite of the consequences of the crisis at the beginning of the century, the Institute could provide first-class working tools.

DOCUMENTS FOR CHAPTER II

Doc. R. II,1

APIBR B-XVIII,3 (XX,1/10/3)
Translated from the Italian

Rome, 11-2-10
North American College
Via dell'Umiltà 30

Very Rev. Fr. Fonck

As per news reaching me, they are asking 525,000 lire for the land; they are now in negotiations with newspaper Il Messag[g]ero for £500,000 and it may perhaps get it at that price.

The matter is extremely urgent, and as regards the big salon it would be possible to have it out of a garden which is there at present.

With kind regards,

+ Thomas F. Kennedy

The walls for the big salon are already there a covering is enough as you will be able to see if you look at the building from the della Pilotta square where there is an iron gate.

You will be able to have the plans sometime this evening.

* * * * *

Doc. R. II,2

APIBR K-1-A
Handwritten document with genuine signature. Translated from the Italian

SECRETARY OF STATE
OF HIS HOLINESS

.FROM THE VATICAN, 29 December 1910

No. 47.886

(*at the bottom of the first page*:)
Very Rev. Fr. Leopold Fonck, S.J.
President of the Pontifical Biblical Institute
        Leonine College

Our Lord His Holiness
Pope Pius X,

wishing to provide the new Biblical Institute with a library in keeping with its importance, has arranged that some books from the Apostolic Vatican Library be lent to the said Institute.

However, in order to safeguard, as far as possible, laws sanctioned by so many of His predecessors concerning the keeping and conservation of the above-mentioned Vatican Library and the special obligations concerning some parts of it and at the same time and in the most effective way to secure for the Holy See the right of ownership of the library of the Biblical Institute, the Holy Father has deigned to approve and prescribe the following norms for the [2] loan of books to the above-mentioned Biblical Institute by the Vatican Library.

I. All the books that are transferred to the Biblical Institute from the Apostolic Vatican Library remain the full and absolute property of the same Vatican Library and, consequently, of the Holy See; hence any book transferred, as above, shall be considered as lent;

II. Likewise, all books bought with the special funds granted to the Biblical Institute shall be assigned to the Vatican Library so that the latter possesses absolute and full ownership over them; such books shall therefore be marked with the stamp of the aforesaid Library and be likewise entered into its [3] catalogues and inventories;

III. First and foremost, books bought with the special funds granted by His Holiness Leo XIII, of blessed memory, for the foundation of a biblical library in the Vatican Library itself, shall be lent to the Biblical Institute, namely the books on excavations and on archaeological studies on Palestine and Assyria, as well as exegetical and oriental Journals;

In second place, duplicates in the Vatican Library on biblical subjects may be transferred to the Biblical Institute, to the extent that no special obligations or considerations prevent this;

IV. Neither manuscripts nor books necessary for the study of manuscripts shall be lent;

V. On the books to be lent, the Prefect of [4] the Vatican Library and the President of the Biblical Institute shall come to an agreement; in the case of any difference of opinion between the one and the other, the decision shall be deferred and referred to the Most Eminent Cardinal Librarian of the H. R. C. and to His Eminence the Cardinal Secretary of State to His Holiness.

Lists of books to be transferred to the Biblical Institute shall first be submitted, for the relevant approval, to the judgment of the Most Eminent Cardinal Librarian, just mentioned;

VI. The Prefect of the Vatican Library must, every year, either himself or through a person he can trust, make an accurate check of all the books in the Biblical Institute and submit a written report on them to the same Most Eminent Cardinal Librarian.

R. Card. Merry del Val

* * * * *

Doc. R. II,3

APIBR B-XVIII,3 (XX,1/12/8)
In Fr. Fonck's handwriting; 17 pages; Italian corrected in another hand.
Translated from the Italian

For the 25.2[19]12

The Pontifical Biblical Institute
Inaugural Address

Your Eminences, Your Excellencies
Most Reverend Gentlemen and Brothers in Christ

A general law requires that in every living organism in which, due to some shock or other, harmony and order are disturbed, the repercussion of vital energy soon begins to act and seeks to re-establish the full equilibrium of the organic forces. If, for example, the hand has been injured, nature immediately starts to act around the wound and brings to it in greater abundance the elements necessary to keep forming new cells successively until the harm is removed. Similarly, if in a small tree, a fir-tree, for example, the top has been damaged, the nearest small branch at the top soon bends to take its place and make up for the injured part. This rule in the physical order is also met with in the moral order. The story of our Church shows us always new examples of this on almost every page. Not to go outside our field, let it be enough to recall the two great periods of greatest prosperity in biblical study in the 4th and 5th centuries, as well as in the sixteenth and seventeenth centuries; those periods had been caused and in a sense prepared by the very serious blows inflicted on the organic unity and life of the Church.

It seems, Gentlemen, that in the context of the same biblical studies, our time and the present day [2] offer us further confirmation of that great truth. Please allow me to declare my thought to you with a short reference to the conditions of our time and the history and programme of this Pontifical Biblical Institute in which all of you, Gentlemen, by your illustrious presence at this function of its solemn inauguration, recognize an outstanding enterprise in the indefatigable work of restoration by His Holiness Pope Pius X.

I

The conditions of the present time

As we consider the last decades of the history of these biblical studies, we cannot not notice a double fact: on the one hand *great progress*, on the other *a great mistake*.

The progress shows itself in the unexpected development of the *means* at the disposal of scholarly work. To the zealous worker in any field of learning there can hardly be anything more welcome than to see *the sources*, from which flow a new and limpid vein of hitherto unknown documents, increase in number. In the domain of biblical and oriental studies the last fifty years have supplied an unparalleled abundance of this kind of new sources. The great discoveries of unknown monuments and texts in Palestine, Asia Minor, Mesopotamia, Egypt and other parts of the ancient East succeeded [3] each other. Fields of learning that, towards the middle of the last century, had barely had the right to exist, have not only taken their first steps already but have also rendered great and valuable service to the study of Holy Scripture. Thousands upon thousands of cuneiform tablets have enriched the collections in museums and the treasuries of scholarship, showing us the life of the Ancient East in a new and unhoped-for light. Inscriptions, papyri and potsherds have done their part in contributing to knowledge about many facts and details of ancient history. The number of manuscripts containing the biblical text or fragments of it is increasing year by year, giving us ever more ample means for knowing the sacred text and the story of its past.

So we cannot be surprised that the new discoveries have given rise to new enthusiasm for these studies and have brought about such an abundance of literary, bibliographic, philological, historical and archaeological *aids* that they could somehow even be considered excessive. A glance at the periodicals in the room set aside for them in a library will be enough to convince us of that.

[4] Where new sources and new literary aids are plentiful great progress cannot fail. But that is only progress in means; it is *material* progress which, on its own, is not enough for the real progress in a field of knowledge. For such progress the *formal* element is also required, I mean the more perfect, fuller, deeper, surer knowledge of the truth in a particular field of work. Thus in biblical studies, which have the inspired word of God as their object, true progress will be made when we reach a more perfect knowledge of the sacred text in the full setting of its human-divine dignity and of its complete sense according to the norms that that dignity requires and of all the circumstances that refer to its origin and history.

If we consider the last decades in this light we cannot say that we are really in the presence of great progress. We readily acknowledge the praiseworthy efforts that have been made in many countries. The merit of those who have contributed their share in achieving a [5] full and more perfect knowledge of Holy Scripture by duly using the new sources and literary aids acquired in our day is also beyond doubt. But although we do not wish to refuse to acknowledge that, we cannot forget the other unfortunately characteristic fact in the tendencies in the latest period of contemporary history. If profound aversion to the supernatural was one of the distinctive marks of intellectual and scholarly work as from the time of the Deists and Encyclopaedists in the 17th and 18th centuries, that naturalistic tendency was more particularly turned upon the study of Holy Scripture in the 19th century in the schools of Paulus, Strauss and Baur. In the second half of that century the critics almost all abandoned the essential principles of the schools of Heidelberg and Tübingen. But repugnance to the supernatural element remained and the implacable war that is waged in the name of scholarship against faith and miracles, mysteries and dogmas that it [Holy Scripture] teaches gets even more bitter.

This rationalist spirit, which is quite opposed to the supernatural, reigned and reigns in the great centres of intellectual life in our time. I am not afraid of being accused of exaggeration; those who know those centres [6] and the flood of more or less learned books that come from them every year are not unaware of how rare the exceptions to the general rule are. They also know that the Supreme Pontiff Leo XIII was not exaggerating when he described these "*portenta errorum*" in his encyclical *Providentissimus Deus*.

But can we then be surprised if the atmosphere of those centres and the flood of those books should have been contagious, even for the very defenders of the faith against the attacks of science that has no faith? The infection must needs have been dangerous to the extent to which the material means provided by the new sources and the new aids available in modern times were used in greater abundance, with greater skill and assiduity by the adversary

And so in fact we see in many countries in recent decades, especially in the biblical field, various grave errors being spread concerning the concept of inspiration, the infallibility of God's word, the historical character of the biblical narratives, not even excepting the Gospel accounts, and on the very person of Our Lord Jesus Christ. There is no need to insist; for it is unfortunately a lamentable fact which we [7] all know and deplore, especially when we look at the very sad facts, mentioned just now, that have appeared in almost all countries. What we deplore with greater feeling is seeing that the very defenders of the city of God "were working", as Leo XIII said in another letter to the French clergy [on] 8 September, 1899, "with their own hands to open a breach in the walls of their city".

In this way the organism of the Church was touched at its most vital point. It was actually a matter of the very heart of its doctrine and discipline. *Its doctrine*: because the soul of all our theology is Holy Scripture, which does not rest assured with the new theories; the other source of life for our doctrine is the Church's tradition, and now a break with the tradition of the past is being openly proclaimed necessary so as to be able to satisfy the needs of the present time. *Its discipline*: because it is clear to all that the Church's supreme authority is firmly upholding, and must uphold the deposit entrusted to it and require submission to its decrees, whereas the new theories reject any such submission and thus cause obvious discord between the members and the head.

* * *

[8] II
The history of the Institute

The organic life of the Church was thus threatened with grave danger. What will follow from this? If the organism no longer reacts to the blow, if the vital energy has no more strength to strike back, if the new cells do not form around the wound, there is no more hope that the harm will go away and life will flourish again.

In the Church's organism the principle of life which the Lord its Founder passed on to it is still vigorous. This principle, being quite supernatural, is also active in a higher way on the limits and forces of nature. However, in accordance with the proper mode of all actions of this order, it presupposes and uses the means and capabilities already in place in the normal order so as to use all of them for the benefit of its highest purposes.

This principle of life has been shown to be effective in our case, too, by preparing a new remedy for the grave and dangerous error. It will suffice to recall briefly the events of recent years.

The remedy for the trouble had to contain two elements. The first concerns the Church's magisterium. It must declare the true doctrine against false, dangerous and rash opinions and it must [9] give directive norms for teaching in Catholic schools. The first great authoritative act coming from this supreme teaching office in biblical matters after the Vatican Council was the above-mentioned Encyclical "*Providentissimus Deus*" of November 18th, 1893, on the study of Holy Scripture. This was the first energetic and effective reaction to the blow caused by the erroneous doctrines of the liberal school.

Another similarly effective move was the apostolic letter from the same Supreme Pontiff Leo XIII *"Vigilantiae"* of October 30th, 1902, whereby the Pontifical Commission for biblical studies was established and organized; this was to be practically the organ for the ordinary exercise of the Church's magisterium in biblical matters. The decrees of this Commission, approved by the Supreme Pontiff constitute the authoritative declarations of Catholic doctrine and give directive norms for Church teaching on biblical questions. These acts and decrees are not the work of some school or institute but are part of the exercise of the supreme magisterium in the Church.

The third solemn exercise of the same magisterium was the condemnation of the errors of the modernists with the decree *"Lamentabili"* of July 5th, 1907 and the Encyclical *"Pascendi"* of September 8th in the same year.

[10] Thus we see the ecclesiastical magisterium with its supreme authority opposing the evil and the various causes of disorder in the very extensive field of doctrines. But for the remedy to be effective, apart from these acts by the supreme authority, the creation of a vital centre for the practical exercise of biblical studies was needed in the same place as the magisterium itself. Such a school or academy or Institute ought to form practically the necessary complement to the Biblical Commission and make the action and control of the ecclesiastical magisterium more effective.

The plan for such an Institute was not new. You have, for instance, the famous school of Alexandria, which is usually called a catechetical school; it was a real biblical academy and the great works of criticism and interpretation of the text of the Bible by the most famous of the rulers of that school, Origen, would even today honour our great Universities and their professors. In our times, after the foundation of the biblical school of the Dominican Fathers in Jerusalem, Leo XIII, in his great Encyclical on biblical studies, in a particular way recommends that selected students, once they have finished the ordinary course in theology, be left free to dedicate themselves exclusively to studies [11] in the sacred books for three years. The plan already referred to in this document took on more concrete forms in the later years of Leo XIII's pontificate. A scheme for the constitution to be provided and the rules to be prescribed for the new Institute were already prepared and printed on a provisional basis. But the moment chosen by the Lord had not yet come. For a number of reasons, among which the place to be assigned to the new foundation was one, the plan could not be carried out and Leo XIII departed this life without being able to do more than recommend the future happy outcome of his project to the Lord.

And his prayer was heard. Pope Pius X, gloriously reigning, just a few months after his elevation to the See of Peter, manifested his desire to carry out the wishes of his predecessor, at the same time expressing his regret at not being able to do so in the immediate future and hoping for help from the generous charity of Catholics in the future: *"For this reason"*, these are the words of the Holy Father in the apostolic letter *Scripturae Sanctae* of February 23rd, 1904, *"it would be altogether very fitting, which we know was also among the wishes of Leo, to set up in the City of Rome a proper Athenaeum, endowed with higher teaching facilities and everything needed for biblical erudition [12] to which young people chosen for the purpose may come together from everywhere to emerge later as outstanding in the knowledge of the divine utterances. At the moment, however, the ability to carry out this plan is beyond Us, as it was to Our Predecessor, but which we have a good and sure hope will be forthcoming through the liberality of some Catholics"*. This good and sure hope could not be vain; and quite soon the hour of the Lord was coming.

To respond in some way to the urgent needs in the field of biblical studies, a higher course in Holy Scripture, apart from ordinary teaching, was initiated in the autumn of the year 1908 at the Pontifical Gregorian University. On being informed of the successful outcome of this modest attempt, the Holy Father thought fit to develop it further by transforming it into a Pontifical Biblical Institute and traced out the general lines it was to follow in his apostolic letter *"Vinea electa"* of May 7th, 1909, the first Friday of the month of Mary.

* * *

Thus the Institute was erected. The first steps had to be taken, both in getting good teachers and in finding suitable premises. In keeping with the Supreme Pontiff's intentions, the teaching staff were brought together in the first months after the letter of foundation and right from the first year comprised [13] ten professors for the various subjects, general and special introduction, interpretation of the Old and New Testaments, history, geography, palaeography and various biblical and oriental languages. As regards suitable premises, the paternal goodness of the Holy Father first assigned the Institute's lectures and library a temporary home in the Apostolic Leonine College where, for almost two years, we found most cordial hospitality.

So in the autumn of 1909 everything was ready for the opening of school and the library. But will any students come? [14] Not many students could be expected, of course, since to be admitted a necessary condition was that the ordinary studies in the philosophy and theology courses be completed. Hence it was being said among the teachers that we could be content if from the start we managed to get twenty or thirty pupils. It really was a pleasant surprise for everyone when, at the end of November, when the deadline for registering was over, it was noticed that the number of registered students reached 117.

* * *

There was still another important question, but a difficult one as well, on the answer to which the future of the Institute largely depended. I am referring to the question of finance.

[14] The Supreme Pontiff was certainly not lacking in benevolence or generous liberality in helping his foundation. But having to think of the very many needs there are in all parts of the Church, he found himself obliged to place his hopes in the generosity of Catholics when it came to providing the necessary means to meet the needs of his new Institute, as he had already said in the words just quoted from the letter *Scripturae Sanctae*. *"Hope does not disappoint"*, in this case, too, the Apostle's great saying found its confirmation. Several benefactors were remarkable from the beginning for the help they offered the Institute, and among them is the Most Eminent Archbishop of Boston. To his very great consolation the Holy Father then saw the Institute set up as regards finances almost entirely by one single family of very noble stock, and even more noble by reason of its merit in a living and generous faith. It has wished, and still wishes, to remain anonymous. It has allowed me to say simply that this outstanding benefaction, too, has been made to the Holy See from France's generous charity. A permanent record and a plaque to honour the noble French nation will be the ensign with the lilies of Saint Louis and France at the foot of the statue of

the Sacred Heart in this noble Hall. – That same statue, the work of the illustrious professor *Ignatius Weirich*, will remind future generations that the Holy Father Pius X recognizes the happy success of the Biblical Institute's first steps as an outstanding benefaction on the part of the Divine Redeemer.

[15] Having thus made provision for the foundation of the Institute, it was also possible to look for a stable and permanent home for it. After long and difficult searches, Providence, through the mediation of our neighbour here present, the Most Illustrious and Reverend Mgr. Thomas Kennedy, Rector of the Pontifical North American College, on the first Friday of February 1910, almost unexpectedly found me the building that has now become our house.

The difficult problem of adapting the old building to its new function, after much work over a long period has been solved in a way that met with general approval. It is a great pleasure for me to recall here with due gratitude the names of the three engineers to whom the merit of the success of the work belongs: they are Father *Camillo Armellini*, who helped me particularly with the early prospects and the first steps; the engineer *Giuseppe Astorri* to whom goes the all the merit for the planning and the final designs, and the engineer *Domenico Giordano Apostoli*, who, with indefatigable zeal, directed the execution of the work entrusted to the *Domenico Vitali* firm. The solution applied to the difficult problem seems to me almost to confirm the outstanding privilege that ought to be recognized as proper to *engineers*, namely that even their *name* is derived from *genius*.

* * *

[16] III
The programme

The story of the foundation of the Institute already shows how the principle of life in the Church acts against the danger threatening the doctrine and discipline of the clergy and faithful. The programme of the new [Institute] as it was traced out for it by the Supreme Pontiff Pius X states even better how that principle prepares the effective remedy for the Church's present needs in the biblical field.

A short reference to this programme will suffice. Considering it in the way the Holy Father proposed it to us, it seems fully in conformity with the Divine Redeemer's great programme: *restoring all things in Christ* still remains his great motto.

In the last conversations with the disciples, among the other moving words, Jesus Christ explained this programme of his with the well-known sentence: *I am the way, the truth and the life*. It seems to me that in these words the three essential points of our programme can easily be met with.

The Biblical Institute is to be first of all an Institute for teaching; and so it must show its students the *way*. In higher education, more than the material widening of knowledge, the formal development of the faculties is important, and so our teaching must insist primarily on the *method* to be followed in a threefold perspective: the *method of knowing* [17] biblical science through personal study; the method of *communicating* that knowledge in the position of professor; the method of *propagating, defending and promoting* that same knowledge through our own writings and publications.

The Institute's programme thus includes the *way* to be taught.

It also includes the *truth*, I mean promoting the knowledge of the truth by means of positive scholarly work in the biblical field: all the means that can serve that purpose:

a library with collections of sources and all kinds of literary aids, periodicals, bibliographies, texts, journeys, research, etc.

Lastly, it includes the *life*: putting knowledge at the disposal of the clergy and the faithful; making the ancient patrimony known, appreciated and loved; communicating new facts and documents; solving recent difficulties.

The way the truth and the life.

Such is the Holy Father's intention for the programme of the Institute. It is clear how the vital energy of the organism of the Church reacts but it reacts with *positive work* and by preserving the *organic unity*.

The word of God remains forever.

* * * * *

Doc. R. II,4

APIBR K-1-A

With Pius X's signature. Translated from the Latin

The words of the letter "Ad Pontificium Institutum Biblicum", dated 2nd June, 1912, with which it is said of the students at the Institute "in order that those who have a diploma may, by teaching or writing, work towards academic degrees to confer which we reserve the right and power solely to the Pontifical Commission" do not mean that the said students with the diploma, apart from the last examination called the doctorate have also to do a first examination for the licentiate in order to obtain the doctorate in Holy Scripture, but they are to be understood as meaning that those at the Institute who have been examined in the triple doctrine experiment and have received the diploma have only one last examination to pass for the doctorate in Holy Scripture at the Pontifical Biblical Commission.

Rome, at the Vatican, June 10th, 1912.

Pope Pius X

* * * * *

Doc. R. II,5

APIBR B-XVIII,3 (XX,1/14/7)

Handwritten draft of a letter from Fr. Fonck to Pius X.
Translated from the Latin

Copy

Pontifical Biblical Institute
Piazza Pilotta
  Rome

Most Blessed Father

The truly paternal charity which Your Holiness has always and with such outstanding proof shown towards this Your least Biblical Institute encourages me today, on the fifth anniversary of the foundation of the Institute, to speak to Your Holiness about a serious case with the simplicity and frankness that the youngest son can and must use with his most beloved Father.

Holy Father, I am seriously worried about the future of the Institute for a reason which I humbly bring to the attention of Your Holiness.

I have it from an authoritative and absolutely certain source that His Eminence Cardinal Lorenzelli, the Prefect of the Congregation for Studies and a Member of the Biblical Commission, recently and in the hearing of some persons from outside said: "The Biblical Institute is also a big fiasco. The Holy Father himself is not happy with it. They only do philological studies there, but they do not do what was expected. Biblical studies and the Institute will have to be completely reformed according to the teaching of St. Thomas".

There is no need to say what impression these words must make on the mind of the unworthy but faithful servant of Your Holiness. With the best will possible and all physical and moral strength, and with most fervent and assiduous prayers, in the midst of countless difficulties, calumnies and contrarieties, with continual and grave sacrifices, for five years I have tried to carry out the task [2] that the paternal charity and trust of your Holiness saw fit to commit to me. The thought that my hard work was not in vain, that I could hope to meet with the approval of Your Holiness and that the Lord himself seemed to approve of my work with the most abundant blessings of his Sacred Heart strengthened me, with God's grace,

And now I hear it said to me by a person in authority: The whole Institute is one great fiasco! The Holy Father is not at all happy, either!

If that were true, there would be nothing else left for me to do than to ask Your Holiness humbly to see fit to relieve me of my task and leave me free to go either to the place from which my superiors called me against all my wishes or to where I have ardently desired to go from the first moment of my religious vocation, to the foreign missions, since in my present position I cannot hope to achieve better results in the future, where in the past I have used all my best will and all the strength the Lord has given me.

If it were true! But it cannot be true, because Your Holiness in person has repeated, so often to me and others, in private and at solemn public functions, that you are content with Your Institute and that Your heart takes real comfort from seeing the heavenly blessing in the very satisfactory development of Your work.

Yet there is still a very serious case here; the Prefect of the Congregation for Studies declares the Institute a great fiasco and the people who heard him say that aloud are going around spreading that sinister judgment to the great detriment of the Institute. And how the adversaries, who are many and powerful, will exult if they hear judgment so authoritatively passed on an institution that was expected and thought by many to be the great bulwark of orthodoxy and sound doctrine on Holy Scripture! More than one person, including some influential people in this City, will be easily disposed not only to believe this verdict but also to co-operate in such a reform in biblical studies and the Institute according to the teaching of St. Thomas.

[3] But who are these reformers and what will be gained from such a reform? I say this without bitterness and without wishing to judge eminent people, but necessity and truth force me to say so: none of these reformers have ever done any serious biblical studies, none have any idea of the weapons that are needed these days by anyone wanting to fight the enemies of tradition and sound doctrine in the biblical field, inside and outside the Church. They may well be eminent in philosophical and theological speculation, but speculation is not enough in positive studies. And a reform of these studies according to the teaching of St. Thomas! That a solid training in that

teaching is required is all well and good; the Institute requires it as well and supposes it to be necessary in all its students. And the theological part of our teaching in the treatise on the inspiration and inerrancy of Holy Scripture and in the doctrinal inter-pretation of the sacred text also reverently follows [the] doctrine of Aquinas. But to train professors and writers in the biblical field according to the needs of our time, St. Thomas alone cannot really be enough. We need absolutely all the modern philologi-cal baggage and all the positive erudition our adversaries boast of so as to train our students in a *modern*, not *modernist* way, as Your Holiness put it to me in one of my first audiences.

To tell the truth, such a reform by such reformers would simply be the complete ruin of the Institute. And in this sentiment I am confirmed by the Eminent President of the Biblical Commission and the Very Rev. Father Presid. of the Comm. for the Revision of the Vulgate, to whom I wanted to submit this grave accusation against the Institute.

No doubt much remains to be reformed at the Institute, and I am the first to admit it and to co-operate effectively in that reform. But with those reformers who are unac-quainted with biblical studies and with that reform programme no other effect will be had than the ruin of the work so happily begun and exposing the Holy See and our Church to the derision of unbelievers and modernists.

[4] Your Holiness will excuse my frankness and may You deign to consider the gravity of the case and again confirm Your charity and paternal benevolence on me by bestowing the Apostolic Blessing on the Institute.

Prostrate in kissing the Feet of Your Holiness, I humbly profess myself

Your Holiness's

most lowly servant in Christ
L.Fonck sj

7 May 1914

* * * * *

Doc. R. II,6

APIBR K-11a (II-1: Fernández)

Translated from the Italian

Zizers, 23 April 1916

(at the bottom of the first page)
R. Fr. Fernández S.J.
Vice-rector of the Biblical Institute Rome

Reverend Father in Christ
P.C.

I thank you for the letter sent to me on the 4th of this month and for the copy of the points sent to Your Reverence by His Eminence Card. Van Rossum on the subject of degrees at the Biblical Institute.

On the one hand I admired the very refined spirit of conformity to the directives received whereby, for fear of in any way going against my wish and that of Fr. Rector that the question be put off until our return to Rome, you abstained from being too polite towards the person who gave them to you and in your heart of hearts would have preferred not to send me anything. But on the other hand it was quite evident that you ought to have sent me the Cardinal's observations, as you did, and that many thanks were due to His Eminence for having communicated them to us. It was just a humble wish and fervent prayer on my part, and nothing more, knowing that the Institute's documents are locked there in the College. So it is quite clear that we have no right that our request be answered. A day before Your Reverence's letter I sent Fr. Assistant a memorandum from the Rector about the new arrangement for degrees which by now will have been presented to the Supreme Pontiff and of which Fr. Assistant informed Your Reverence.

In keeping with what is said in the memorandum it seems to us that the most natural solution is that both the Biblical Commission [2] and the Institute should have the faculty to grant the degrees at the same time, each one in its own right. In that way the Biblical Commission would not lack such a faculty; and the Institute as a higher *school* for *teaching* would in suitable cases confer its academic degrees on those whom it makes professors of Holy Scripture. The reasons are neither few in number nor inconsiderable.

In the first place, that is in accordance with the intention of Leo XIII, the one who thought up the Institute, according to which it was to be a *completely autonomous and entirely independent* academy for higher education, as the third great undertaking later entrusted to the Benedictine Fathers for the correction of the Vulgate would be independent. Its purpose was the systematic, orderly and perfect training of teachers of Holy Scripture. This emerges from the plan which he had drawn up and printed (1903) and which is in the Secretariat of State. This intention was inherited by his Successor, the founder of the Institute. Pius X explicitly manifested it many times, actually, and went on maturing it step by step, first by providing a way of grappling with the serious inconvenience of preparing people with courses at the Institute for degree exams to be taken at the Biblical Commission, then by granting the Institute the right to confer a diploma of its own, then by stating the meaning of this and exempting students who were awarded it from the examination for the licentiate at the Commission. The last step towards the goal was missing, but the death of the Holy Father stopped that.

Secondly, the right is required by the very nature of the Institute. Having been set up for the purpose of training readers in Holy Scripture and spreading them worldwide, it does not come up to the expectations of Bishops who, if they see good professors coming back to the [3] Dioceses still cannot, they say, put them to teach for the simple reason that they do not have a canonical document authorizing them. Hence it comes about that the Institute in their eyes is an incomplete institution. Not possessing that lustre it will never be able to attract the number of students which the Pontiffs expected when they founded it as a centre for the whole world of higher biblical studies. Such a privation in fact halves its authority and truncates the course of aspirants in this way, unless they resign themselves to prolonging it in another way. Moreover, once the Institute is set up thanks to a college of professors held by all to be competent in every biblical and related subject, with a library of the highest quality, with a biblical museum unique in its kind and with every other scholarly activity, whether it be in print or in public lecture halls, on the same footing as any University, it really does represent the Higher Athenaeum for the teaching of biblical studies that Leo XIII yearned to put in the heart of Christianity. Like all the other study centres with the same facilities, therefore, it is also fitting that it should have its natural complement in the right to confer academic degrees.

Account should also be taken of the pedagogical reason that the necessary prestige of professors in higher studies requires the complete range of professorial power and the incontestable psychological fact is joined to this, namely that studies are not entered upon with due diligence by students under masters who have to be left at the best and most difficult time, namely at examinations set by other people. It is a fact: the long yearning for the doctorate, which is the key to their future [4], separated from the course the students have to follow at the Institute keeps them there unwillingly and to their annoyance, and yet while preparing for the former they neglect the hard, methodical and formative study at the latter.

Lastly, the different nature of the two institutions. The Commission, which is the organ of the authentic teaching office admits men of different methods and different ways of thinking among its Consultors, so that, having weighed up the diversity of opinions, the true meaning and the true doctrine to be declared to the church that is being taught may appear more clearly to that supreme tribunal. The Institute, which has to teach that meaning and doctrine, stated to be the only true and authentic one cannot, without ruining its work and the soundness and worth of that doctrine, tolerate those divergences of opinion among those who must constitute its students who are to teach the declared truth. But this fusion (if only for examinations) of the Institute with the Commission is harmful to the aim of the Institute for this reason also that the examinations at the former, almost of necessity, are involved in such great erudition that they rather amount to an exercize in memory, very different from the proof which, in examinations at the Institute, has to be given of possessing the profound doctrine which the Popes require in future professors for the real good of the Church and the sure, victorious defence of divine inspiration.

To these reasons may be added some serious difficulties of a practical nature, such as the doctorate to be prepared after the third year at the Institute. Such an arrangement would mean an overall length of 5 or 6 or more years of study after the ordinary period of philosophy and theology, which is quite intolerable and unheard of elsewhere [5] and hence not durable. Likewise, the exclusion, unjust in itself because quite unnatural, from the doctorate of not a few *uditori* students who come to the Institute well-equipped with intelligence and theological knowledge but who have not been able to get doctorates in theology in ordinary diocesan schools, often for lack of financial resources; they would be forever deprived of the highest canonical honour that crowns readers in Holy Scripture and which, by adding authority, more and more enkindles the desire for this divine study. Unknown candidates, whose morals or non-Catholic faith do not qualify them to be inscribed on the roll of masters of the Word of God can apply to the Commission, too. There is no danger of that at the Institute.

Now as we carefully reflect upon these reasons, it seems to us so important for the good of the Church to have the power to grant degrees at the Institute itself that if to have this it were necessary for us to withdraw from the Institute, we would be very ready to do so. If the Commission thinks that a doctorate given only after a few years teaching would bear more authority it could act accordingly, leaving us free to give a doctorate after three years of serious special studies. Experience will soon show which doctorate is held in higher esteem. – We do not seek ourselves but only the good of the Church.

As we have already expounded our reasons to the Supreme Pontiff, it seems we should be very prudent in speaking with Cardinals. For the rest I ask you always to take advice from the Father Assistant for Italy.

The advice given by His Very Reverend Eminence, Card. Merry-[6] Del Val also to invite other Eminences not belonging to the Biblical Commission was very good, since we are in such difficult conditions and with not a few opponents.

What you tell me about Br. Theodore [Zaepffel's] return to France is good, and I was very pleased that some public lectures were held for students in the Roman colleges.

Lastly, I thank you for the care taken to avoid unnecessary expense and for what you did to make my first circular known and put into practice.

I have also passed on the good news about Frs. Chaîne and Neyrand to Fr. Fine [the French Assistant] and we are praying the Lord to preserve them for us.

Finally, I send you my paternal blessing, which Your Reverence will pass on to all the Fathers and brothers.

I commend myself earnestly to your Holy Sacrifices.

Your Reverence's
Servant in Christ
W. Ledókowski SJ.

* * * * *

Doc. R. II,7

APIBR B-XVII-5

Translated from the Italian

(Copy)

Most Blessed Father

I have passed on to the Fr. Rector of the Biblical Institute the remarks that concern him which Your Holiness deigned to make to me in the audience granted to me on the 13th of this June and, now that it has been decided to move Fr. Fernández to Jerusalem, we have given immediate attention to the other more urgent matter, namely the return of Fr. Fonck to his province, which, since I had not fully perceived what Your Holiness had in mind, was, unfortunately, not effected earlier. We seem to have found a successor for his teaching post but we do not know how to put the matter to His Eminence Cardinal Van Rossum.

According to paragraph 10 in Benedict XV's Apostolic Letter "Cum Biblia Sacra", dated August 15th, 1916, the Father General of the Society of Jesus chooses the professors, but has to propose them for approval by the Biblical Commission, so I shall have to propose the name of Fr. Fonck's successor to His Eminence. Moreover, since Fr. Fonck is a Consultor of the Biblical Commission, according to the normal practice of the Roman Curia he cannot be removed from Rome without the approval of the Biblical Commission itself. I must therefore in any case place the matter before the said Most Eminent Cardinal. I am, of course, quite prepared to do everything in my own name, but I am afraid that in that way I shall receive a negative answer from His Eminence.

I humbly therefore make so bold as to ask Your Holiness to allow me to be able to write to the Most Eminent Cardinal Van Rossum that Your Holiness himself wants this change, or at least that You consider it fitting and opportune.

I next take leave to add something that in my inadequacy [2] I was unable to explain properly in the last audience, namely that according to the Apostolic Letter "Vinea Electa" of May 7th, 1909, whereby the Biblical Institute was founded, although the students in those early days had to take all their examinations at the Biblical Commission ("All students must regularly complete the course of study at the Institute so as to prepare themselves to take the examination at the Pontifical Biblical Commission": Laws of the Bibl. Inst., par. 4, n. 17), the Institute, however, depended directly upon the Holy See, as stated in the first paragraph of the part laying down the enacting terms of the same Apostolic Letter "Vinea Electa" ("1. The Pontifical Biblical Institute is to depend directly on the Apostolic See"). Thus also appointments of Professors were dealt with by the Fr. General directly with the Holy Father until 1916, that is to say until, at Cardinal Van Rossum's suggestion, the Biblical Institute was placed under the Biblical Commission.

Furthermore, the Fr. Rector of the Biblical Institute asks me humbly to draw the attention of Your Holiness to the fact that, with the new regulation that came last year from the Biblical Commission concerning the prerequisite doctorate in theology, all those who, having completed a good course in theology, are getting ready privately for examinations at the Commission, even if they come under paragraph 2 of the same regulation, can, in just two years, prepare for the doctorate in theology as well as the examination for the Commission's Licentiate, which they can do immediately after the aforesaid doctorate, and after two more years can get the Doctorate in Holy Scripture; whereas those who wish to study at the Institute have to spend two years just in preparing for the doctorate in theology, then three years of regular course work before being able to take the examination [3] for the Licentiate and wait another two years before being able to do the examination for the Doctorate at the Commission; this means that there would be a difference of three years. In this way, normally speaking, with this regulation a considerable number of students, mainly from those regions in which ecclesiastical Institutes that have the faculty of conferring the doctorate are rare, are practically excluded from the Biblical Institute.

, Prostrate in embracing the holy Foot, I humbly beg the Apostolic Blessing, and with deepest veneration I willingly proclaim myself again

Your Holiness's
lowliest son
Wl. Ledókowski
Superior General of the S. of Jesus

Rome, 20 June 1928

* * * * *

Doc. R. II,8

APIBR K-1-A
Account by Fr. O'Rourke of his interview with Card. Bisleti.
Typewritten text with corrections in handwriting, noted here in italics

Oct. 7 *1928*   *viva voce*

Card. Bisleti holds that the regulations of the Biblical Commission, now that we are free from *the Commission* are not binding on us. Hence he holds that students who had made their studies in a seminary that has not got the faculty of conferring the doctorate may take that degree at any seminary that has that faculty. This does away with two years additional study. (Therefore all laurea degrees of seminaries approved by the Congregation of studies are to be accepted.)

Further he believes that those who come to the Institute without the theological laurea may if they have made their studies in a seminary or university approved by the Holy See be examined for admission by the professors; this examination includes one in theology *by the professors of the Gregorian* especially on points that will indicate the theological position of the student. In this case it will depend on us whether we shall admit him or not.

If the students are strong in their theology and are anxious to have the laurea in theology His Eminence thinks they should be allowed to try the Gregorian examination although he is aware, he says, that Rev. Fr. General is against *this plan*. The argument is that as we are now a part of the general University it should all be within our own walls for our own students. (However, this apart, the Lateran examination would always be open for them.)

His Eminence also believes that we should keep our present course and approves of the doctorate after *four* years and also of the permission to be granted to those who come well prepared in the languages to have a chance of obtaining the baccalaureate after one year and the licenza (*sic*) after two and consequently the laurea after three. *(In this His Eminence holds we are free.)*

* * * * *

Doc. R. II,9

APIBR B-XVII-5
Three handwritten sheets by Fr. Ledókowski. Translated from the Latin

Only those who are doctors in Sacred Theology are admitted as ordinary students.

———

The ordinary course of lectures takes three years during which they must attend the lectures and exercises according to the method of study approved by the Holy See and usage.

[2] After the second year, having duly passed the examinations, they are admitted to the licentiate degree.

Those who wish to go on to the doctorate must attend lectures for a third year and devote themselves to private study for a fourth year and prepare a thesis for the doctorate and at the end take a final examination.

[3] In this way the students, thanks to well-organized studies extending over *four* years after the doctorate in theology, seem to be duly and soundly prepared to receive the doctorate in Holy Scripture.

* * * * *

Doc. R. II,10

APIBR B-XVII-5

Two handwritten pages by Fr. O'Rourke
on the stir caused by the book by A. Simón, *Praelectiones biblicae, 1, 1924*

+

Order of events

1. Book of Fr. A. P. Simon C.SS.R. reviewed by Fr. Fonck for Biblica

2. "Censores" Frs Vaccari and Power rejected Fr. Fonck's recension

3. Fr. Power as censor made a detailed recension of Fr. Fonck's recension. Fr. Fonck in his own article for Biblica brought in all his own rigid opinions condemning those who disagreed with him.

4. Fr. Power's recension of Fr. Fonck's article was carried by Fr. Fonck to the Secretary of the Biblical Commission Fr. Frey.

5. The Cardinals of the Commission condemned Fr. Power's recension of Fr. Fonck's recension of Fr. Simon's book, and sent an unsigned and undated document to Fr. General, specifying as false opinions Fr. Power had written in his recension. At the end of their restrictions they condemned the teaching of the Institute as a whole.

6. Rev. Fr. General called me and gave me a copy of the document. He was much worried and asked me to write a mollifying letter to the Cardinals admitting there were certain errors in Fr. Power's recension owing to improper expression[s] etc. I told Fr. General this could not be done as Fr. Power's expressions were clear and sound.

7. Fr. General appointed three of the Professors to review carefully Fr. Power's recension together, and make a report to his Paternity. The censors were Frs. Bea, Vaccari and myself. Fr. General excluded Fr. Power "because it is his case that is being discussed". I objected to Fr. Power's complete exclusion as thus he would be deprived of his right to defend himself. Then Fr. Power was allowed to make his own private defence.

8. The censors found nothing in Fr. Power's recension that was in any way "advanced". In fact in no case did he give *his own* opinion on the points specified by the Cardinals, but cited the opinions of "approved authors" including the Holy Fathers of the Church and members of the Biblical Commission.

[2] 9. I then presented Fr. Power's private answer to the restrictions of the Cardinals to the Rev. Fr. General adding a letter of mine, with a synopsis of Fr. Power's answer, and a defence of the Fathers of the Institute.

10. His Holiness Pius XI had received words whether directly or indirectly I do not know. He called me to his room and asked about the document. I suspected I was called for a discussion and had carried the document of the Cardinals with me. His Holiness placed me at his side and we went over the document together. He condemned the document as it was neither signed or dated, and agreed totally with Fr. Power's answers.

This opened the way to our obtaining the right to confer the doctorate.

[*The list of the four documents inserted in the dossier follows.*]

* * * * *

Doc. R. II,11

APIBR K-4-C (I-2: 1932)
Copy of a document by Fr. Bea in favour of the Oriental Faculty at the Institute
Translated from the Italian

REF. NO. 444 I/2
Rome, 6 July 1932

Most Reverend Eminence

With the approach of the day for the Sacred Congregation's deliberation on the Oriental Faculty proposed by this Institute, I think I am doing something your Eminence will welcome by setting out some considerations referring to objections that could be raised against the erection of that faculty in a brief Memorandum, along with the relevant answers which, in my humble opinion, could be given to those questions. In the course of our consultations we have, as was our duty, also considered these questions, and what I take leave to set before Your Most Reverend Eminence is indeed the result of those deliberations. Should Your Most Reverend Eminence require further explanations I shall be pleased to give you them.

I bow to embrace the Holy Purple and have the honour to state that, with a feeling of most religious veneration, I am,

Your Most Eminent Reverence's
most devoted servant

His Most Reverend Eminence
Cardinal Gaetano BISLETI
Prefect of the Sacred Cong.
for Seminaries and Universities
R o m e

Memorandum

on the plan for an *"Oriental Faculty"* to be erected at the Pontifical Biblical Institute with the right to confer academic degrees "in Ancient Eastern studies".

1. – Granted the usefulness of oriental studies for the purpose assigned to the Institute by the Papal Letters, it might be thought that it is enough to have *two "sections"*, *one "biblical" and one "oriental"* and to give those who study in the "oriental section" the degrees "in biblical studies" (perhaps with the addition of: "in the oriental section").

This solution was taken into serious consideration by the Professors of the Institute before proposing the plan for a proper faculty, but it was thought it should be rejected because it was considered that such a combination *would not be useful either to biblical studies or oriental studies.*

On this supposition, those students who would devote themselves primarily to oriental studies *would have to* omit, it should be noted, either the biblical or the oriental part of the studies since it is not possible to do both parts properly in only three years. Those who omit the biblical part would graduate "in biblical studies", with the rights reserved to graduates in biblical studies but without having a solid formation in Bible and exegesis; the others, however, who would devote themselves [3] more to biblical studies, would never be able to attain a solid formation in the oriental part which is, as the proposed programme and the experience of those who have done oriental studies show, have [: *omitted*] such a wide field that three whole years are barely enough to cover it in. Yet the Church, in the present problems arising in the biblical field out of oriental questions, needs *capable* specialists, not half-trained scholars.

For that reason our humble opinion was *not to touch* the structure of the biblical part in favour of the oriental part but rather to reinforce the strictly exegetical and biblical training still more, and yet to give the orientalists a proper, sound training in oriental studies accompanied, however, with the kind of biblical training that is necessary and sufficient to give them a sound orientation in biblical questions. The programme of both Faculties has been worked out with these criteria.

Hence in our view *the Church is better served by a complete separation between the two parts than by any half measures.*

2. – It could further be objected that an Oriental Faculty *lies outside the scope of the Biblical Institute*, and even from that of the ecclesiastical studies envisioned in the Apostolic Const.

[3] Such an objection does not seem to be well founded, since:

a) According to that same foundation letter ("Vinea electa") the studies that help biblical scholarship are necessarily part of the Institute, and the history of the Institute over almost 25 years confirms this interpretation. Right from the beginning the Institute has, under the eyes of the Holy See and with the most authoritative encouragement, developed this part of its activity and has drawn great benefit for biblical studies and its own influence from it. To deny that this field pertains to the Institute would be to challenge those very people who drew up its first programme and had charge of the Institute throughout that period.

b) The modern state of biblical studies clearly shows the *need for oriental studies* for Catholic biblical scholarship; from them come the strongest attacks, as well as the most valuable support.

c) From this it results that oriental studies are "connected with sacred subjects" (Ap. Const. art. 2) just as philosophy or Christian archaeology or the study of "both laws" are connected with theology. Nothing, therefore, seems to stand in the way of granting degrees of ecclesiastical standing in oriental studies as well.

3. – It might be said that an "Oriental Faculty" at the Biblical Institute is *in competition with the Pontifical Oriental Institute*, and that the degrees from the two Institutes are indistinguishable.

[4] This objection, too, was carefully considered and discussed with the Authorities of the Oriental Institute who have no objection to the Oriental Faculty of the Biblical Institute. In our humble opinion

a) the Oriental Institute concerns itself with sacred (*theological*) studies that deal with the *Christian* East, whereas the Biblical Institute deals with studies of the *ancient* (non-Christian) East in so far as they are useful for biblical studies. Both Institute [*meaning*: Institutes] have peacefully *coexisted* so far, although the Biblical Institute has already, as explained in the request, carried out the full programme which is now being proposed more systemically by way of a Faculty.

b) The Oriental Institute confers degrees "*in ecclesiastical studies dealing with the Christian East*" (Statutes of the Orient. Inst., n. 5), whereas the Oriental Faculty of the Biblical Institute "*in studies dealing with the Ancient East*". The very title given to the degrees shows the difference both between the scope and between the degrees.

4. – Finally, it is clear from what is being said here that even a possible fear that the Oriental Faculty might *be harmful to the study of biblical subjects* at the Institute would not be well founded:

a) Setting up the Oriental Faculty in no way diminishes the number and commitment of the *Professors of biblical subjects* that have been taught so far [5]; on the contrary, the separation will be a new incentive for the Authorities at the Institute to strengthen the Biblical Faculty still more and to further its development, according to the needs of the times.

b) *Students in the Biblical Faculty* will have to concentrate more on the subjects in their *own* Faculty and will not be able, without special permission, to engage in subjects belonging to the collateral Faculty.

c) *Students in the Oriental Faculty* will also benefit from biblical studies because in quite a number of subjects they have to take courses in the Biblical Faculty. In this way a sound exegetico-biblical training will be brought into the ranks of the Orientalists themselves, too.

d) Thus the creation of the new faculty will actually favour studies in both Faculties of the Institute, and can we hope that the new Faculty will greatly contribute to carrying out, ever more fully and better, the noble intentions of the venerable Founder, the Holy Father Pius X and of the Holy Father Pius XI, now gloriously reigning?

Rome, 6 July 1932

* * * * *

Doc. R. II,12

APIBR K-1-E (I-1: 1934-1928)
Copy of the document by Fr. Bea on the date of the death of Jesus
Translated from the Italian

REF. NO. 568 I/1

Most Blessed Father

In pursuance of the revered charge that Your Holiness deigned to give me I have the honour humbly to submit to Your Holiness the memorandum on the date of the death of the Lord, hoping to have in some way complied with the sublime wish of Your Holiness.

Prostrating to kiss the Holy Foot and beseeching the Apostolic blessing I have the honour of reaffirming myself to be

Your Holiness's

Rome,
23 December 1932

Rector of the Pont.Biblical Inst.

The date of the Lord's death

A. *The various theories*

I. – Among the years given by the authors for the death of Christ the *main ones are the years 29, 30, 33* of our era.

1) *The year 29*: in Tertullian, Lactantius, Sulpicius Severus, and (sometimes) St. Augustine the Lord's death is assigned to the year of the consulate of the "two twins", i. e. 29. In the Greek church (except for one version of the "Acta Pilati["] and a text by Cedrenus) this date is unknown, just as among the Latins it is unknown to St. Cyprian, St. Hilary, St. A[m]brose and St. Jerome. The opinion was revived by San-clemente (Rome, 1793) and was recently adopted by Patrizi, Cornely, Méchineau, Pasquier, Mangenot, Prat, Rinieri, Ruffini and Villoslada.

2) *The year 30* = "in the 16th year of Tiberius". In the *early Church*: the followers of Basilides, Julius Africanus, Hilarion and (implicitly) some other authors:

in *recent times*: a) all authors defending the theory of only *one* year of the Lord's public life: e. g. van Bebber, Belser, Hontheim, Cladder, Mader, Olivieri;

[2] b) those defending *two* years of public life: e. g. Zellinger, Lagrange, Reatz, Meinertz;

c) among authors defending three years [of] public life: Grimm, Schanz, Jak. Schäfer, P. Marco Sales, J. Bover.

3) *The year 33*. In the *early Church* some speak of the "year 19 of Tiberius" (e. g. the Armenian text of the Chronicle of Eusebius, the Latin text of the Acts of Pilate) or the "year 4 of the 202nd Olympiad", e. g. Eus., Chron.; St. Bede and (once) St. Augustine.

In *later times*: Roger Bacon, Alf. Tostate, Tillemont, Laury.

In *our day*: e. g. Fl. Riess, Ladeuze, Homanner, Peserico, Merk. Power.

II. *Years 25, 26, 31, 34* have few supporters:

31: J. Kepler, Dion. Petavius, Bucherius;

"*31 and 32*": J. Sickenberg;

34: Baronius, Bellarmine (no one today);

III. *The Protestants*, like the Catholics, favour the years 29, 30, 33, but with a preference for years 29 and 30, because they often overlook the gospel of St. John, from which alone it is possible to deduce [a] length of 2 or 3 years for the Lord's public life. Lewin ("Fasti Sacri") and Headlam, for instance, prefer the year 33.

Among the *astronomers* two (Fotheringham and Schoch) come out in favour of the year 30.

[3] B. *The root of the controversy*

In discussing the year of the Lord's death, these points are to be considered:

1) The tradition of the Holy Fathers, which is not always unanimous, however;

2) The interpretation of Luke 3,1: St. John the Bapt. began his activity "in the 15th year of the reign of Tiberius Caesar" (= 19 Aug. 28 – 18 Aug. 29);

3) *Luke 3,23*: Jesus, when he began the public life, "was about thirty years old".

4) The Lord died on a *Friday* that was either the 14 or 15 of the month of Nisan. Hence all the years in which the 14 or 15 of Nisan is not a Friday are excluded, and *astronomy* seems to show that only the years *30* and *33* remain.

The positive answers are inconclusive: rather, the line of argument is negative: some years are excluded for astronomical reasons (29, 31, 32). Of the two remaining (*30 and 33*) preference is given to one or the other according to the various ways of arguing the case, especially as regards Luke 3,1 and 3,23 and the length of the public life.

C. *Assessment of the main theories*

I. *The year 29* seems excluded: the *tradition* is not of a conclusive nature; according to astronomy there is no Friday that fits the biblical texts. A special difficulty crops up in the theory of *3 years* [4] *of public life*: the mission of St. John the Bapt. would start as early as 25, before Pontius Pilate (whose term as procurator was from 26-36). Cf. Luke 3,1 ("when Pontius Pilate was procurator of Judea").

II. *The year 30*: 1) *in favour* of the year 30: it corresponds to Luke 3,23: in the year 27 (beginning of public life) the Lord was 32-33 years of age.

2) *arguments against*: the year 30 would fit in with the theory of a *one year* public life, but it is difficult to defend this theory. In the theory of a *two year* public life Luke 3,1 would have to be explained in a way that is possible, but improbable. In the *three year* theory (which is the commonest among Catholic authors) the year 30 can only be defended on the supposition of the "Crownprince period" which is not sufficiently proved.

The "Crownprince period" is the hypothesis that in the years of the reign of Tiberius the years of his "co-reign" with Augustus (Mommsen) were also included.

III. *The year 33*: this theory avoids the "Crownprince period", but has difficulty in justifying, according to Luke 3,1, the start of the public life in the year 30. Besides, the Lord, born in the year 7 or 8 before our era, would have been (at the start of the year 30) 35 or 36, a supposition which, to some people, does not seem to fit in with the "about thirty years" in Luke 3,23.

[5] *Conclusion*

1) *Excluded* are
- a) all years before 29 (year 15 of the reign of Tiberius Caesar = 28/29[)];
- b) all the years after 33 (because the public life would have lasted at least four years);
- c) the years 31 and 32 (for astronomical reasons);
- d) the year 29 (for lack of sound arguments).

2) There remains *a sound probability for the years 30 and 33 only*. Authors have come down in favour of one or the other but the arguments put forward do not seem to be of the kind that justifies a *sure* decision one way or the other.

3) There are no *theological arguments*: the tradition is not unanimous; the interpretation of Luke 3,23 is controverted.

Hence the statement that the Lord died between 29 and 33 is *certain*; it is *probable* that the year of death is 30 or 33. This foundation could be enough for celebrating the centenary of the Lord's death "*in the last of the years generally assigned by the authors as the most probable date for the death of the divine Saviour*".

* * * * *

CHAPTER III

The Bible finds its place at last
1934-1968

Thirty-four years passed before the Statutes of the Biblical Institute were revised in the wake of the Second Vatican Council, when Paul VI promulgated the *Normae quaedam* on May 20th, 1968. These new norms prescribed bringing the rules governing the Institute's functioning up to date.

As for the preceding period, which had covered twenty-five years, this one can be divided into several stages, in which there were many dramatic events, but also in the course of which some important times in the life of the Church succeeded each other to place the Bible in its true place and exegesis in full light.

I. The last years of Pius XI: 1934-1939

These five years, until the death of Pius XI on February 10th, 1939, were apparently without any history, and yet . . .

Students continued to come to the Institute in ever greater numbers. This was the outcome of the new Statutes in 1934 which applied the constitution "*Deus scientiarum Dominus*" of 1932. In 1934-1935 there were 92 all told, 76 of whom were *alumni*; in 1938-1939 there were 118 all told, but the *alumni* surpassed the hundred figure; there were 105 of them. Growth had been steady.

The teaching body acquired three new specialists. Fr. Robert A. Dyson (1895-1959), an English emigrant to the United States, had studied at the Biblical Institute from 1929-1932 and went back there in 1936 mainly to teach Old Testament theology and the basic course in Egyptian; on the one hand he took over from Fr. Vaccari and, on the other, he replaced Fr. Suys who had died the previous year. Prevented from coming back to Rome, he spent the war years at Stonyhurst, in England, and from 1945 to 1958, resumed his classes at the Institute; he was a born professor (cf. *Bib* 41 [1960]

76-77). Fr. Max Zerwick (1901-1975), a Bavarian, had obtained doctorates in theology at Innsbruck and in classical philology at Vienna when he, too, arrived at the Institute in 1936. As from 1937, in place of Fr. O'Rourke who returned to New York for ten years, he taught biblical Greek, a task which he fulfilled until his death. It was in 1937 and at the Institute that he published his Vienna thesis *Untersuchungen zum Markusstil* (cf. *Bib* 56 [1975] 444-445). Fr. Raimund Köbert (1903-1987) had done studies in Arabic and Semitic philology in various university centres in Germany; at the Institute this very mild-mannered, meticulous and somewhat complicated scholar taught Arabic and Syriac from 1938 to 1983, thus succeeding Fr. Power (cf. *Acta PIB* 9, 316).

Another notable figure arrived at the Institute in 1935: Fr. Jean Ruwet (1876-1956), from Verviers, in Belgium, had received the diploma from the Institute in 1914 with high honours; after that, he had taught at the Jesuit theological college in Louvain until he was summoned in 1924 to the Gregorian University to be academic secretary, a post he was to leave in 1935 so as to take on the same, but lighter, function at the Institute, and that until 1952 (cf. *Bib* 37 [1956] 384-385).

As a result of the new Statutes, Fr. Luis Gonzaga da Fonseca became dean of the biblical faculty in 1934 and, in 1937, Fr. Ludwik Semkowski succeeded him to remain in that office until 1945. In the oriental faculty in 1934 Fr. Giuseppe Messina succeeded Fr. Deimel as dean and he, too, remained so until 1945.

1. *The Old Testament congress at Göttingen: 1935*

On December 31st, 1934, Professor Friedrich Stummer, of the Catholic faculty of theology at Würzburg, sent Fr. Bea a letter in which he invited him to take part in the 2nd international Congress for the Old Testament to be held at Göttingen from the 4th until the 10th of September, 1935.

Such an invitation was a novelty. Professor Stummer was communicating with Fr. Bea on behalf of the organizing committee of which the two other members were professors Paul Voltz and Johannes Hempel, big names in Protestant exegesis in Germany. The planned congress thus took on an ecumenical dimension ahead of its time.

Stummer was known to Fr. Bea because he had already published three articles on Jerome and the Vulgate in *Biblica*. He asked the rector for a reply by January 15th. On the 14th Bea very amiably replied that he could not give an answer at such short notice because a congress like that would have to touch upon questions of theology and the Biblical Institute, being directly dependent upon the Holy See, could not decide on its own.

In agreement with the Fr. General, Bea sent Cardinal Bisleti, the Grand Chancellor of the Institute, a document in which he asked the Pope to decide himself whether the invitation should be accepted or not. Three reasons were put forward for accepting and three others for declining. In favour of accepting, Bea noted a change of mentality towards Catholics on the part of Protestants and those prevailing good attitudes deserved to be welcomed; moreover, Catholic presence at the congress could favour a return to sounder exegetical principles; finally, such a congress would create personal contacts between exegetes of different backgrounds. However, the theological bearing of such a congress could not be undervalued; the Biblical Institute delegation might find itself in an embarrassing situation when faced with certain theories defended by non-Catholics; worse still if those theses were defended by Catholics (Doc. R. III,1).

On this last point, Bea gives no names; perhaps he was thinking of Friedrich Schmidtke, whose book on the Pentateuch had been censured the year before by the Pontifical Biblical Commission (cf. *EB* 515-519); however that may be, Schmidtke does not seem to have come to the congress.

On January 21st, Pius XI, replying by word of mouth to Cardinal Bisleti, said that the Biblical Institute should go to this congress and that he trusted the scholarly competence of its representatives, even when it comes to disowning Catholic professors who go astray. The Pope also suggested that care should be taken to see that only doctrinally sound Catholics should speak at the congress. Finally, he asked that his decision be transmitted to Roman colleagues who would be invited to this congress. The Cardinal immediately and in writing passed this papal judgment on to Fr. Bea (Doc. R. III,2).

On January 23rd, Bea told Professor Stummer the good news and suggested that during the congress he speak about the excavations undertaken by the Institute at Teleilat Ghassul (cf. Part Two, chaps. II and III). Stummer thanked him on the 26th, as did Hempel himself on the 27th (cf. APIBR B-XI-2).

When the congress was over, Bea sent an account of it to Pius XI (Doc. R. III,3) in which one senses the rector's somewhat triumphalist satisfaction. Fr. St. Schmidt (*Agostino Bea*, p. 98) even cites an unpublished piece by Bea according to which he overturned the thesis of a speaker for whom the Old Testament knew nothing of belief in life after death; as is known, the question is still debated today, at least for the Hebrew Bible, except for Daniel 12,1-3. The fact remains that, according to Bea's report, the congress passed off without incident, the Catholic exegetes were listened to with great attention, and that he himself was invited to make the closing speech.

Today, now that ecumenism has made such progress, one can only be struck by the courtesy of the Protestant exegetes who had taken the initiative at this congress and who maintained good form throughout it. This first step in the right direction was to be followed by others, but it was important to point out this first opening in 1935.

The acts of the Göttingen congress came out in 1936 in the series *Beihefte zur Zeitschrift für die alttestamentliche Wissenschaft*, no. 66, with the title *Werden und Wesen des Alten Testaments*, and Fr. Bea's lecture comes on pages 1-12 in it.

In the same report that Bea sent the Pope, mention is made of two other congresses in which the Institute took part. In particular, of the 19th International Congress of Orientalists which was held in Rome from the 23rd until the 28th of September of the same year, 1935 (cf. also *Acta PIB* 4, pp. 58-59). On the evening of the 27th, seventy of those attending this congress came to the Biblical Institute to offer Fr. Deimel, who was celebrating his seventieth birthday, a volume of *Miscellanea Orientalia* in which were articles that had been written by thirty-four specialists in Assyriology. This volume was published as no. 12 in the *Analecta Orientalia* series and numbered 349 p. The Acts of the congress appeared in fascicules 3 and 4 of the periodical *Orientalia* 4 (1935), pp. 257-501; articles by Fathers Messina and Simon, professors at the Institute, appear in them. These publications and this tribute had given proof that the Biblical Institute was fully part of the international world of orientalists.

2. The "Cursus Sacrae Scripturae" at the Biblical Institute: 1936

On June 19th, 1936, with the approval of the Provincial Superiors of Germany, Fr. General transferred responsibility for the "*Cursus Sacrae Scripturae*" to the professors at the Biblical Institute (cf. *ARSI* 8, pp 543-545).

This collection had been planned by Fr. Rudolf Cornely when he was teaching at the Gregorian University and had started it off in 1885-1886 with his excellent historical and critical introduction to the books of both Testaments (cf. *supra* ch. I, § I,1). His main collaborators were Fathers Josef Knabenbauer and Franz von Hummerlauer. Most of the biblical books were thus commented on in Latin by these three German exegetes. Some other people working with them also published aids for study, concordances, lexicons, etc. The Paris firm Lethielleux saw to the publication. But the first world war interrupted the continuation of this monumental work (cf. *DHCJ*, I, p. 441).

The sequel to the history of this series, from 1917 to 1957, can be traced with the aid of the archives of the Biblical Institute (APIBR B-XI and XI-1). Only the essential points, which make it possible to understand Fr. Ledókowski's decisions and its consequences, will be noted here.

Carrying on the series was first of all envisaged by Fr. Fonck. In his *Bemerkungen* on what was to be done with this undertaking, he wrote, on December 30th, 1917, that an agreement – a *Kollusion* – was necessary with the professors of the Biblical Institute, not with the Institute; this particular point was going to be made until the end of this matter. This was followed in 1918 by an exchange of letters between Fonck and Bea, a young professor at

Valkenburg, and Fr. General was kept informed of the matter by Fr. Fonck, who sent him a report on it on July 12th, 1918. Evidently, it was necessary to wait until the end of the war.

On November 11th, 1920, Fr. Franz Zorell who, while not yet teaching at the Biblical Institute, already belonged to its Jesuit community as a *scriptor*, asked Benedict XV to bless the resumption of the work. A small team was actually assembling. On December 28th the Pope encouraged him (*ARSI* 3, p. 211), so that on February 11th, 1921, Fr. General promulgated the *Leges et normae* to be followed in resuming the *Cursus*. Some years later, then, some new volumes appeared. In 1927 Fr. Merk, still at Valkenburg, published a completely reworked version of Fr. Cornely's introduction; in 1931 Fr. Zorell put out a second edition of his New Testament Greek dictionary; the first was dated 1911. On July 31st, 1933, Fr. General promulgated some new *Leges et normae* in which he asked that an agreement now be reached with the authorities of the Biblical Institute. Actually, Fr. Bea, in a ten-page, undated report, could see no other future for the collection than simply handing it over to the Institute.

Then, at the end of a long exchange of letters between Fr. Bea and the one in charge of the series at Valkenburg, Fr. General, in 1936, reached the decision that has been mentioned. Under Fr. Bea's direction there then appeared three new commentaries: the one by Fr. Holzmeister on 1 Peter in 1937, the one by Fr. Fernández on the book of Joshua in 1938 and the one by Fr. Joseph Linder on Daniel in 1939. In 1940 Fr. Merk produced the last edition of his introduction. The second world war stopped the enterprise.

Once again the resumption of the *Cursus* was on the agenda in March, 1955. Fr. Bea, who was its director, was favourable to starting this large-scale work up again; according to him, everything was to be done in Latin again, with the help of former students of the Institute. In April a meeting of professors gave its approval, except that Fr. Lyonnet was not in favour of Latin, and on May 24th, 1955, Fr. General Janssens acquiesced. Whereupon Fr. Bea proposed new statutes for this new *Cursus* and, in February, 1957, Fr. General approved them: Fr. Bea stayed as director, Fr. Vaccari was in charge of the Old Testament and Fr. Lyonnet of the New. A pious wish! By 1940 everything had already come to an end.

3. *Pius XI intervenes directly: 1937-1938*

Here begins a long story that reached a conclusion only with Pius XII.

Since 1930 a Neapolitan priest by the name of Dolindo Ruotolo (1882-1970) had been publishing, under the pseudonym of Dain Cohenel, a huge commentary on the books of the Old Testament. In 1930 he had brought out three volumes on the Pentateuch and, in 1931, three others on the books that follow, from Joshua to 2 Kings. The general title of these commentaries was in fact his program: *La Sacra Scrittura. Psicologia – Commento – Meditazione*. These volumes were published at Gravina di Puglia. According to what Fr. Schmidt says (*Agostino Bea*, p. 98), Pius XI had received one or other of them and was astonished at their contents. The author, relying on the Vulgate, more often than not neglected the literal meaning of the texts so as to propose his own pious lucubrations. These volumes had already obtained the warm approval of several bishops. Very early on, however, Fr. Vaccari had done a short, very critical review of them, considering them not to be recommended (*VD* 13 [1933] 160); these first volumes had reached the Biblical Institute thanks to Cardinal Ehrle who had received them (cf. Doc. R. III,4). Still, the author did not stop. Despite early difficulties with the censorship over his book on Job, in 1936, he got to thirteen volumes on the Old Testament in 1939; there only remained the commentaries on the prophets and the two books of Maccabees.

In the meantime, Cardinal Bisleti died on August 31st, 1937, and rather than replacing him, Pius XI himself took on the charge of Prefect of the Congregation for Seminaries and Universities, including that of Grand Chancellor of the Biblical Institute, and that until his death on February 10th, 1939.

In September 1937 the 7th "Biblical Week", held at the Institute, as usual, was marked by some odd events.

On the first day, September 20th, there was, to start with, a lecture by Natale Bussi on "the Pastoral orientation of biblical studies in diocesan seminaries". The speaker advised against critical introductions and discussions and favoured a truly theological exegesis. Quite a lively debate had followed the too one-sided exposition (cf. *VD* 17 [1937] 369), which did not stop the author from publishing his lecture the same year.

The following day the people attending the event were received by Pius XI at Castel Gandolfo and Frs. Bea and Vaccari, in the presence of the Pope, gave their opinion on two questions about the Pentateuch. Fr. Bea dealt with "the Prehistory and interpretation of the book of Genesis". His lecture was later published in *VD* in 1937 and 1938. As could be expected, his views were very prudent. Without denying the antiquity of the hominids already discovered, he stressed the lack of agreement among scientists on dating them; he thus rejected the theory of the evolution of animal into man; on the flood related in Gen 4–11, one should not look for a historical foundation for it during the neolithic period, since the biblical account only proves the existence of a tradition going back to that same period and of which parallels are found in Babylonia and elsewhere.

Fr. Vaccari's lecture was about "the Question of Moses and philology". The complete text was not published but, as in the case of Fr. Bea's, Fr. Vaccari published a summary of it in *VD* 17 (1937), pp. 371-373; on October 27th the Paris newspaper *La Croix*, had already given one. Fr. Vaccari, keeping to the 1906 decree of the Pontifical Biblical Commission (cf. *EB* 181-184), claimed the Mosaic authenticity of the Pentateuch. In his opinion, comparison between the text of the Hebrew Bible and the Samaritan Pentateuch made it necessary to date the final form of the text, including, therefore, the Priestly Writings, to the 7th century. On the other hand, the alternation of the divine name, YHWH or Elohim, is found, for example in Psalms 13 (14) and 53 (52); it is, then, a matter of variations in the transmission and it must have been the same for the Pentateuch in which the same variations are found.

Pius XI, who had been closely following the two lecturers, showed himself satisfied. Fr. Lagrange, who was resuming his work on the book of Genesis, was less so. His last article appeared shortly after his death on March 10th, 1938, in *Revue Biblique* 47 (1938), pp. 169-183, and had as title "the Mosaic Authenticity of Genesis and the theory of documents". On pp. 169-174, Lagrange there discusses Fr. Vaccari's new theory; he had heard about it from *La Croix*, and faithfully quotes the summary given there. He can only find an accumulation of hypotheses in it, "each of which is improbable" (p. 174). It can be seen that Fr. Vaccari's construction had no effect, no more, to tell the truth, than did Lagrange's. Will that come as a surprise to anyone? For Catholic exegesis, held back by the decrees of the Biblical Commission that appeared at the beginning of the century, the hour had not yet come.

Still, at the end of the audience, Pius XI had expressed the wish that, especially in seminaries, biblical sciences should be fostered and that the Institute, which he had so much at heart, should develop them still more and make them valued (cf. *Acta PIB* 4, 146). At all events, that morning of September 21st, 1937, clearly indicated which kind of exegesis the Pope was in favour of.

He proved it again when, on May 19th, 1938, in his full capacity as Grand Chancellor of the Institute, he wished to preside in person at the defence of the doctoral thesis by Giorgio Castellino, a Salesian from Turin, which took place at Castel Gandolfo. The subject of the thesis was: *Individual lamentations and hymns in Babylonia and in Israel, compared as regards form and content*. This work of scholarly research, which was to be published in 1940, had been written in Italian under the direction of Frs. Vaccari and Pohl. At the end of the defence, the candidate received a distinction (*cum laude*) and – something just as important – Pius XI made a long speech, given in Latin in *VD* 18 (1938), pp. 187-191. The Pope concluded by wishing "that in all dioceses there should be at least someone who has academic degrees in biblical studies, including the doctorate".

Such a wish was soon thwarted. On June 2nd a letter written by some Italian bishops who did not have the courage to give their names, was sent to the Pope (APIBR B-XVII-7). These bishops asked Pius XI for "another word of life for souls". They had not attended the session on May the 19th and they had read the Pope's position in the *Osservatore Romano* for May 21st. They attacked the praise given to the Institute as well as Castellino's thesis; for them, critical exegesis smacked of Protestant rationalism and modernism; comparison with Near Eastern literatures was an insult to the Word of God and served no purpose, "to say the least"; their priests who had received the doctorate at the Institute came back to their diocese "completely disorientated, pitiless and a hundred per cent presumptuous"; in their eyes, "it was therefore indispensable for the Institute to become a school of holy living, nourished by the Word of God, and not a school for hypercritics"; so they called upon Pius XI to read N. Bussi's lecture (cf. *supra*) of which they gave him a copy; in fact, they added, their young priests who were being trained along the lines of Cohenel's work "are renewed, change their lives, become zealous", etc., so much so that that work ought to be recommended; lastly, they called upon Pius XI to crown his pontificate with an act that would really give new life to biblical studies in the sense they indicated and then, they wrote "we will willingly send our young men to the Institute in order to see them come back, not pretending to know everything (*saputelli*), but wise, not critics of the divine Word, but of their heart".

This letter, which bears witness to unease among some Italian bishops, was insolent and provocative. The Pope would not have answered it; you do not answer an anonymous letter. However, on November 24th, he summoned the whole Biblical Institute to the Vatican, to the great hall of Benedictions, for another thesis defence he wanted to preside at. The candidate was Fr. Benjamin Wambacq, a Premonstratensian from Tongerloo in Belgium, and his thesis was on *the divine Epithet Seba'ôt. A philological, historical and exegetical study*. It had been composed under the direction of Frs. Bea and Vaccari and received the distinction of *magna cum laude*; because of the war it was only published in 1947. During the session, which was attended by more than twelve hundred people, Pius XI spoke twice, at the beginning and at the end, to repeat all the high opinion he had of the Biblical Institute and to encourage it to continue along the same lines (cf. *Acta PIB* 4, 177-178).

Meanwhile, on December 28th, Mgr. G. B. Montini, by now Substitute to the Secretariat of State, sent Fr. Bea the anonymous letter of the previous June 2nd, asking his advice. On January 8th, 1939, Fr. Bea replied (APIBR B-XVII-7) that the authors of that letter formed only a small group attached to Cohenel's commentaries, whereas many were the bishops and religious superiors who thanked the Institute for the solid formation given to their young men; besides, the Institute did not fail to point out to the latter that, in the seminary, the pastoral dimension of exegesis ought to be predominant, since it was not possible simply to repeat there the teaching received at the Institute; Fr. Bea also mentioned that Fr. Vaccari, in consequence of his critical note in 1933, had at the time received (APIBR M-Vaccari-1) a letter similar to the one that had been sent to the Pope and the rector sent it to him; lastly, the

Pope was thanked for having presided at the two thesis defences mentioned above.

The matter did not have any sequel in the immediate future because, on February 10th, 1939, Pius XI expired. Throughout his pontificate he had been a defender of the Biblical Institute: the speeches he made in 1937 and 1938 were final proof of it.

II. Pius XII promotes exegesis: 1939-1949

Pius XII was elected on March 2nd, 1939. On the 14th he appointed Cardinal Giuseppe Pizzardo Prefect of the Congregation for Seminaries and Universities. The latter became *ipso facto* Grand Chancellor of the Biblical Institute (*Acta PIB* 4, 172).

1. Consequences of the Cohenel affair

Bibliography

St. LYONNET, "Les études scripturaires" in G. M. GARRONE et al., *La vie de l'Église sous Pie XII* (Recherches et Débats, 27) Paris, Fayard, 1959, 120-137, esp. 123-126. – A. VACCARI, *Lo studio della Sacra Scrittura. Lettera della PONTIFICIA COMMISSIONE BIBLICA con Introduzione e commento*, Roma, La Civiltà Cattolica, 1943, 152 p. (reprint of articles appearing in *La Civiltà Cattolica* between December 1941 and October 1942). – L. H. VINCENT, "Bulletin. Biblica", *Vivre et penser* 3 = *Revue Biblique* 52 (1943-1944) 162-164

Fr. Ruotolo continued imperturbably to publish new books, so much so that during the 8th "Biblical Week" at the end of September 1939 Fr. Vaccari once again spoke out. A summary of his lecture on "la Sacra Scrittura dalla cattedra, sul pulpito e nella stampa" ("Holy Scripture in class, in the pulpit and in the press") appeared in the *Osservatore Romano* for October 1st 1939. In the first part Fr. Vaccari recalls that in 1920 the Congregation for Seminaries had put out a document asking that in Italy professors of Holy Scripture should not omit either the critical introduction or controversial questions. N. Bussi's booklet did not follow these norms. Fr. Vaccari then turned again to Cohenel's volumes, repeating his 1933 criticisms and furthermore pointing out the numerous places in which faith and morals were badly handled.

Some weeks later, on December 8th, two bishops, one from Gravina and the other from Campania, published a defence of Cohenel and called upon Fr. Vaccari to retract publicly; there is a copy in the APIBR K-10-I-6 (cf. *Palestra del Clero* 19 [1940] 76). Fr. Bea, in his turn, took up Fr. Vaccari's defence in two letters he sent to the bishop of Gravina, Mgr. Sanna, on December 20th 1939 and January 8th 1940; they are to be found in the same place in the archives at the Institute. According to Fr. Bea (cf. Doc. R. III,4), Fr. Vaccari appealed to the Holy Office and this latter imposed silence on both parties, pending its decision. This came on November 14th, 1940: all Cohenel's books were placed on the Index "until correction" and the author "humbly submitted" (*AAS* 32 [1940] 553-554). The publication of his commentaries therefore ceased at that point. Still, he went on writing others, about ten, which were published after his death, from 1975 to 1987! His submission was quite relative, especially as, on May 24th, 1941, he published an anonymous 48-page booklet with the title: *A very serious danger for the Church and for souls. The critico-scientific system in the study and interpretation of Holy Scripture, its harmful deviations and its aberrations.* This booklet was addressed to the Italian bishops. Taking the historian Giuseppe Ricciotti and Fr. Vaccari as main targets, the author reproached scholarly exegesis for studying ancient languages and neglecting the Vulgate, doing textual criticism and archaeology, looking for the literal meaning of texts and rejecting any allegorical meaning. In his eyes, on the contrary, it was meditation on the Word of God that counted.

Such an attitude and the impact it might have on the Italian episcopate was not to remain unanswered. On August 20th, 1941, despite the Roman heat Cardinal E. Tisserant, the president, and Fr. J. M. Vosté, O. P., the secretary, with Pius XII's approval published a long letter from the Pontifical Biblical Commission, also addressed to the Italian episcopate (*EB* 522-533).

This letter roundly condemns the anonymous booklet by Ruotolo-Cohenel, of which the main attacks are repulsed, with arguments in support. Four questions are thus broached. The search for the literal meaning has been necessary since St. Jerome and St. Thomas Aquinas, as Leo XIII and Benedict XV have mentioned. According to the Council of Trent, the Vulgate is "authentic" in the juridical sense, which does not exclude variations from the original texts. There is need of textual criticism: the critical edition of the Vulgate, as wished for by Popes, is proof of that, as is the decision of the Holy Office which, in 1927, allowed discussion of the more than doubtful authenticity of the *Comma Ioanneum* in 1 John 5,7. The study of oriental languages and related sciences is not, of course, an end in itself for biblical exegesis but it helps in the understanding of sacred texts. The Commission's letter ends with praise for the Biblical Institute and the "Biblical Weeks" it sponsors and from which so many Italians benefit (in 1940-1941, out of 74 enrolled at the Institute, 34 Italians were numbered).

In the months that followed the appearance of the letter from the Biblical Commission, Fr. Vaccari published a full commentary on it in two Roman periodicals run by the Society of Jesus, *Periodica de re morali canonica et liturgica* and *La Civiltà Cattolica*; in March 1943 he brought this commentary out again in the form of a book called: *The Study of Holy Scripture.*

There is still one question: did Frs. Bea and Vaccari have any part in writing the Commission's document? Both were consultors to it, Vaccari since

1929 and Bea since 1931. At the time, the Commission comprised Cardinals Tisserant, its president, von Faulhaber of Munich, Liénard, of Lille, Villeneuve, of Quebec, Maglione, the Secretary of State, Pizzardo, the Prefect of the Congregation for Seminaries and Universities, and Mercati, the Prefect of the Vatican Library. Because the Biblical Institute was being called to account, it may be imagined that the Commission's reply was made without it; one cannot be judge and party to a dispute at the same time. Moreover, the Commission with its other Consultors and especially its secretary, Fr. Vosté, could quite easily draw up the letter without having recourse to the Biblical Institute. Finally, after the appearance of the document, Fr. Bea, in the name of the Institute, thanked Fr. Vosté for it on September 10th and Cardinals Tisserant and Pizzardo on the 11th; his letter to Cardinal Tisserant does not give any reason for thinking, no more than does any other document in the archives at the Institute, that the Institute was involved in drawing up this document (APIBR K-10-I-5); on the contrary, when writing to Fr. General on September 17th Fr. Bea notes that "both Cardinal Tisserant and Fr. Vosté really have taken great pains in this matter" (APIBR K-23 [II-1]).

2. *The encyclical* Divino afflante Spiritu*: 1943*

On December 13th, 1942, Fr. Ledókowski died in Rome. Throughout his time as General he had closely followed and supported the Institute's initiatives. He had shown himself particularly effective when there was question of allowing the Institute to grant academic degrees (cf. *supra*, ch. II). Frs. A. A. Magni (1942-1944) and N. de Boynes (1944-1946) substituted for him as Vicars General until, on September 15th, 1946, the 29th General congregation of the Society of Jesus elected Fr. John Baptist Janssens as Superior General, who remained so until his death in 1964.

On the occasion of the fiftieth anniversary of Leo XIII's encyclical *Providentissimus Deus*, Pius XII, on September 30th, 1943, the feast of St. Jerome, published his encyclical *Divino afflante Spiritu*. After giving the history of papal pronouncements since 1893, the Pope went over the positions adopted by the Biblical Commission in 1941, before coming round to the "particular tasks of the exegetes of our day" and it is there that he calls upon them to study the "literary genres" used by the sacred authors (*EB* 558-560).

Bibliography

H. Höpfl, "Critique biblique", *DBS* 2 (1932), esp. 202-212: "V. B. Les genres littéraires". – A. Bea, *De Scripturae Sacrae Inspiratione*, Rome, PIB, ²1935, esp. 101-114. – A. Robert, "L'inerrance et les genres littéraires", in A. Robert – A. Tricot, *Initiation biblique. Introduction à l'étude des Saintes Écritures*, Paris – Tournai – Rome, Desclée & Cie, 1939 (²1948), 24-26. – J. Levie, "L'encyclique sur les études bibliques", *NRT* 68 (1946), esp. 780-789, reproduced in his book *La Bible parole humaine et message de Dieu* (Museum Lessianum, Section biblique, 1) Paris-Louvain, Desclée De Brouwer, 1958, 188-198, English translation in *The Bible, Voice of God, Words of Man*, London, Chapman, 1961, chap. VII, § 3. – E. GALBIATI, "I generi letterari secondo il P. Lagrange e la 'Divino afflante Spiritu'", *ScC* 75 (1947) 177-186, 282-292. – St. SCHMIDT, *Agostino Bea*, 105-110. – Fr. LAPLANCHE, *La crise de l'origine. La science catholique des Évangiles et l'histoire au XXᵉ siècle* (L'évolution de l'humanité), Paris, Albin Michel, 2006, esp. 320-329.

No Pope had ever committed himself up to this point on this question. However, Pius XII recognized that research in this domain had progressed notably "in these recent decades" (*EB* 558). In 1932 H. Höpfl had already given an account of how the matter stood and in 1935 Fr. Bea had come back to it, so that in 1938 A. Robert, who had studied under Fr. Lagrange in 1931-1932, traced it in outline, which the encyclical did not contradict (cf. his 1948 second edition).

The archives of the Holy See not yet being accessible for the period of Pius XII's pontificate, it cannot be known for certain who wrote that part of the encyclical devoted to literary genres. For the Biblical Institute, the question comes to this: did Fr. Bea set his hand to those paragraphs?

In 1946 Fr. Levie, S. J., noted in it (p. 782 or p. 190) the echo of a view taken by Fr. Lagrange, whose student he had been in 1922. The following year, E. Galbiati, who had been trained at the Institute from 1938 to 1941, at the risk of misrepresenting Fr. Lagrange's teaching, tried to show that Fr. Bea had been the author of those paragraphs on the literary genres and, in 1987, Fr. Schmidt followed in his footsteps, adding statements from both sides, and in particular stressing the relationship of confidence between Fr. Bea and Fr. Vosté, O. P., a disciple of Fr. Lagrange. In 2006 Fr. Laplanche inclined "to think that Vosté was the original author and that the text was revised and amended by Bea" (p. 329). Would we therefore simply have here a matter of petty rivalries? Not necessarily, because the encyclical clearly pointed out that the question of literary genres had been the object of research during the decades preceding its publication and Fr. Lagrange's writings on the subject go back to at least 1896 (*RB* 5, 496-518); he would even have been the first Catholic to see that this question was necessary for the defence of the truth of Scripture. Fr. Bea only entered the lists much later. As regards knowing what part Fr. Bea took in the composition of the encyclical, the Roman archives of the Institute possess only the rough draft of a letter addressed to Pius XII, written by Fr. Bea, who dates it April 19th, 1943 (APIBR K-1-E [I-1]); here it is:

Most Blessed Father,
I have the honour to enclose my humble opinion on the new draft of the encyclical, hoping to have in some way satisfied Your Holiness's august wishes, thus contributing a little to this important work of the commemorative Encyclical. [...]

Fr. Bea therefore intervened quite early on and at the Pope's request in a new draft of the encyclical. This is what can be gathered from this document, but it confirms that Fr. Bea had a hand in the encyclical, without it being possible to state exactly where and in what paragraph. One can also gather from this letter that the new draft in question would not have been written by Fr. Bea. The theory put forward by Fr. Laplanche (pp. 327-329) must be right.

3. *The Institute during the Second World War: 1939-1945*

As from September 1939, Western Europe was a scene of blood and fire. At the beginning of the school year at the Institute on November 3rd the effect was immediate: from 118 in 1938-1939, the number of students drops to 90; the French go from 18 to 2 and the Poles from 9 to none! The following year only 74 are numbered, but in 1941-1942 there are three Poles and the Italians come back in force: 47. Then the decrease is inexorable: from 76 in 1942-1943, there is a drop to 63 the following year and to 57 in 1944-1945, the year of the great battles, the defeat of the Nazis and the end of Italian fascism. When the war ends in the West, students return to the Institute in small numbers: in 1945-1946 they are still only 77.

The war years were hard at the Institute. On April 19th, 1942, for example, at a meeting of the council of the biblical faculty it was pointed out that "some students are without sufficient nourishment" and the rector states his readiness to make provision for this.

Is there any need to recall the drama that the Eternal City went through? The Nazis occupied Rome as from September 10th, 1943; at last declared an "open city", Rome was going to be liberated only on June 4th, 1944, but in the meantime, on October 16th, 1943, the Nazis proceeded to round up Jews in Rome, of whom more than a thousand were taken off to Auschwitz on the 18th.

In the German edition of his biography of *Augustin Bea. Der Kardinal der Einheit* (Graz, Styria, 1989, 165-166), Fr. St. Schmidt recounted the following episode which has been supplemented from the Roman Archives of the Institute. That October 16th, shortly before midday, five Nazi policemen, accompanied by an SS officer, came to the Biblical Institute; they were looking for a certain Salvatore di Capua, whose name appeared on the lists of the Jewish community in Rome; on September 29th the Nazis laid hands on those lists (cf. G. RIGANO, *Il caso Zolli*, Milano, Guerini, 2006, 222). The man being sought, aged 50 years, as the Register of residents at the Institute for 1942 mentions (APIBR A-20), was of Jewish origin but had become a Catholic twenty-five years earlier and had worked at the Institute as assistant cook since May 14th, 1942, but he had left in the September of the same year and Fr. Bea therefore answered the policemen that he was no longer at the Institute, adding, with some insistence, that the German police were not to enter the building which belonged to the Holy See. An official document, bearing the name of the German General Stahel, forbade them from doing so (cf. Doc. R. III,5-6). The same day he told Cardinal L. Maglione, the Secretary of State, about the incident (Doc. R. III,7). Fr. Bea would not yet have known what the Nazis were perpetrating that morning. Generally speaking, while the Holy See had called upon convents of men and women religious to open their doors to persecuted Jews, it seems that in fact the Institute did not hide any during that dramatic period. The reason may have been that at that time the Institute occupied a completely isolated building, offering no chance of escape through adjacent buildings. The Oriental Institute, however, which is linked with the Russian College and the Lombard Seminary was searched two months later by the Nazi police still looking for Jews (cf. P. BLET, *Pie XII et la Seconde Guerre Mondiale d'après les archives du Vatican,* Paris, Perrin, 1997, p. 246; p. 285 in the Italian translation and p. 217 in the English translation).

At the end of 1941, Fr. Zorell, whose eyesight was failing, had to give up teaching. On January 21st, 1942, Fr. Stanislas Lyonnet (1902-1986; cf. *Bib* 68 [1987] 141-142) arrived from Lyons and occupied the chairs of Armenian and Georgian in the oriental faculty. He had received the diploma at the École Pratique des Hautes Études in Paris for his work on *The perfect in classical Armenian*, (Paris, Champion, 1933), and had already written about the Armenian and Georgian versions of the gospels for Fr. Lagrange's book on *La critique textuelle* (Paris, Gabalda, 1935; cf. *Bib* 71 [1990] 280-298). From 1936 to 1938 he had studied in the biblical faculty at the Institute and his licentiate paper had been published in *Biblica* 20 (1939), pp. 131-141; it was on the angel's greeting (Luke 1,28: "Rejoice . . .") and is still a work of reference in exegesis. In June 1943 he brilliantly defended his doctoral thesis in the biblical faculty; its title was: *La première version arménienne des Évangiles et le Diatessaron* (cf. *Acta PIB* 4, 334), – the *Diatessaron* is a compilation of the four gospels into one and is ascribed to Tatian (2nd cent.). From then on, Fr. Lyonnet, who had been the last pupil of A. Meillet at Paris and, in his turn, in 1942-1943, had initiated the future teacher at Louvain, Gérard Garitte, in Georgian, began his teaching with the letters of Paul, while keeping his classes in the oriental faculty. His co-operation was greatly valued, especially when, on April 3rd, 1945, Fr. A. Merk died. Whereas, during the First World War, the teaching staff at the Institute had been considerably reduced, during the Second it remained in place and was able to continue its activities.

In spite of the war, the Institute went on publishing. In 1940 there was much hesitation about continuing with the periodicals in particular. It was then decided to reduce the number of pages in *Biblica*, and that was especially noticeable for the year 1945.

Among the few books from the Institute that appeared during the war, only those that made their mark will be mentioned here. Three in 1940. The second final report of the excavations carried out by the Institute at *Teleilat Ghassul* was published in 1940 by Fr. R. Köppel (See Part Two, chaps. II and III). That same year, Professor Cyrus H. Gordon published *Ugaritic Grammar*, no. 20 in *Analecta Orientalia*, which he reworked in 1965 (AnOr, 38); the Ugaritic language had been deciphered in 1930 on cuneiform tablets discovered at Ras Shamra in Western Syria. Still in 1940, Fr. Pohl started the *Keilschriftbibliographie* in *Orientalia*, which still continues publishing it annually. From 1941 to 1943 Pohl was aided by C. H. Gordon and, from 1944 to 1946, by P. W. Skehan.

In 1943, Fr. Messina published a *Notizia su un Diatessaron persiano tradotto dal siriaco*, no. 10 in *Biblica et Orientalia*, which he reworked more fully in 1951 (BibOr, 14); we have seen that Fr. Lyonnet, too, had worked on the Diatessaron and it was in 1950 (BibOr, 13) that he published his thesis on it. Before them, however, in 1938, Fr. Vaccari, in collaboration with two other people, had published *Il Diatessaron in volgare italiano* (Studi e Testi, 81, Vatican City) going back to the Middle Ages. The Biblical Institute obviously took an interest in the *Diatessaron*! In 1944, Fr. Zerwick published his *Graecitas biblica*, a grammar that has been updated several times, translated into English in 1963 and still in use.

Lastly, in 1945, among the "Scripta Pontificii Instituti Biblici", at no. 93, there came from the press the *Liber Psalmorum cum Canticis Breviarii Romani*, xxxi-350 p.

4. *The new Latin Psalter: 1945*

Bibliography

Antecedents: M.-J. LAGRANGE, "La revision de la Vulgate", *RB* 17 (1908) 102-113. – Fr. ZORELL, *Psalterium ex hebraeo latinum* (Scripta PIB, 53), Rome, PIB, 1928, xxi-311 p.; [2]1939, xxxii-434 p. (pocket edition on missal-style paper). – J. CALÈS, *Le Livre des Psaumes traduit et commenté*, 2 vols., Paris, Beauchesne, 1936, 699 and 687 p. – J. COPPENS, "Pour une nouvelle version latine du Psautier", *ETL* 15 (1938) 5-33.

Editions: *Liber Psalmorum cum Canticis Breviarii Romani. Nova e textibus primigeniis interpretatio latina cum notis criticis et exegeticis cura professorum Pontificii Instituti Biblici edita*, Rome, PIB, 1945, xxxi-349 p.; [2]1945, xxiv-350 p. – S. ELY, *Le Psautier romain, traduction et commentaire du* Liber Psalmorum *édité par l'Institut Biblique Pontifical à Rome le 15 août 1945*, St-Maurice, Œuvre St-Augustin, 1948, 465 p. – P. GALETTO, *I salmi e i cantici del Breviario Romano. Traduzione italiana dei testi originali secondo la nuova versione latina del Pontificio Istituto Biblico*, Rome, PIB, 1949, xxxvi-720 p.

Reactions: A. BEA, "La nuova traduzione latina del Salterio", *Bib* 26 (1945) 203-237. – ID., *Il nuovo Salterio latino. Chiarimenti sull'origine e lo spirito della traduzione* (Scripta PIB 95), Rome, 1946, iv-180 p. = *Le nouveau Psautier latin. Éclaircis-*

sements sur l'origine et l'esprit de la traduction. Paris, Desclée De Brouwer, 1947, 210 p. – "Le nouveau psautier", *MD* 5 (1946) 60-106. – Chr. MOHRMANN, "Quelques observations linguistiques à propos de la nouvelle version du Psautier", *VigChr* 1 (1947) 114-128, 168-182. – T. E. BIERD, "Some Queries on the New Psalter", *CBQ* 11 (1949) 76-81, 179-187, 296-307; 12 (1950) 34-47, 213-220, 301-310. – B. STEIERT, "Das Psalterium Pianum in seiner sprachlichen Neuheit gegenüber der Vulgate", *Analecta Sacri Ordinis Cisterciensis* 6 (1950) 166-180; "Einführung in die neue römische Psalmenversion", *ibid.*, 7 (1951) 91-166. – A. BEA, "I primi dieci anni del nuovo Salterio latino", *Bib* 36 (1955) 161-181.

This new Latin translation of the Psalter, which was soon to be called the "Pian Psalter" from the name of Pius XII who had ordered it to be done by the Biblical Institute, appeared in 1945 in two successive editions: the first was printed at the Vatican and the preface bears the date of October 29th, 1944, while the second, a corrected one, was printed on bad paper at the Pius X Press and its preface is dated March 24th, 1945; that was the day Pius XII signed his Motu proprio "*In cotidianis precibus*".

a) Antecedents

On the occasion of the establishment by Pius X of the commission entrusted with the critical edition of the Vulgate in 1907, Fr. Lagrange (p. 109) had expressed the wish that it be corrected in places where it was obviously wrong. Now, as from 1920, Fr. Zorell published a series of articles on the Psalms in *Verbum Domini*. In them he gave a new translation of them that was more in conformity with the Hebrew text. It is generally known that the Psalter in the Vulgate, called the Gallican Psalter, is a translation of the Greek Septuagint version. In 1928, and later in 1939, Fr. Zorell published his translation from the Hebrew in one volume; this was the fruit of his earlier work. In 1936 Fr. Jean Calès, too, offered his Latin translation of each Psalm based on the original Hebrew. In 1938 Joseph Coppens took the opportunity to ask for "a new Latin version of the Psalms". The sequence of events is known thanks to documents kept in the Roman archives of the Institute (B-XIII-1 and 3). Shortly after the appearance of his article, the young professor at Louvain, writing to Fr. Calès, suggested that he might interest the Society of Jesus in this reform of the Psalter, with the ecclesiastical authorities at that time being easier to convince.

Professor Coppens could not have known that the 18th General Congregation of the Society, which met from March to May, 1938, without making it the object of a decree, had given its approval to a request that a *Roman Psalter for the Use of Ours* be compiled to nourish the piety of young Jesuits, for it could be hoped, the request said, that the Church might undertake a reform of the Latin Vulgate Psalter. On August 2nd Fr. Bea informed Fr. Calès of this by letter. In the ensuing months the latter was entrusted with drawing up a plan.

For health reasons it was only on November 1st, 1939, that he was able to send Fr. Bea what he called an *Enchiridion ad psallendum sapienter*. On the 16th Bea presented it to the Fr. General (cf. Doc. R. III,8) who submitted it to the opinion of his Vicar General, Fr. M. Schurmans and some other personalities of his Curia. Their observations, on the whole positive, were passed on to Fr. Bea who reworked the translation of the first three Psalms selected for translation by Fr. Calès, Psalms 94 (95); 2 and 18 (19). On March 29th, 1940, the rector of the Institute sent Fr. General his printed *Specimen*, along with some explanations. The reception on the part of the persons consulted, including the Vicar General, was even more positive. Then there was a long silence, probably due to the war that was breaking out in Western Europe. However, on September 29th, 1940, Fr. Bea told the Fr. General that he had spoken to Fr. Vosté and some consultors of the Pontifical Biblical Commission about the project, adding that Fr. Vosté thought that Cardinal Tisserant would not be opposed to it; Bea himself thought that the Pope might be favourable to it (APIBR K-23 [II.1]). At that time the plan left the Society and passed into the hands of the Holy See.

b) Immediate preparation

To make it easier to follow the work to be done, let us briefly recall, by way of example, what the proposed translations of Ps 94 (95),1 were. The Vulgate, translating the Septuagint, had:

> *Venite, exultemus Domino / iubilemus Deo salutari nostro.*

Saint Jerome, in his translation from the Hebrew, had, in his own style, given:

> *Venite laudemus Dominum / iubilemus petrae Iesu nostro.*

Those who, in the twentieth century, had proposed a new Latin translation kept to the Hebrew. Thus Zorell: *Venite, exultemus Dño / iubilemus Petrae salutis nostrae*. Or Calès in 1936: *Venite exultemus Yahweh / Jubilemus petrae salutis nostrae*, and in 1939: *Venite exultemus Yahweh / jubilemus rupi salutis nostrae*. In 1940 Bea left the choice:

> *Venite exultemus DOMINO*
> *iubilemus Deo salutari nostrae* or *Petrae salutari nostrae.*

The main point was to know whether one wanted to keep to the Latin tradition that came from the Greek version of the Septuagint or whether one advocated a return to the Hebrew text. Priority was given to the Hebrew.

It was on January 19th, 1941, that, thanks to Fr. Bea's influence (APIBR M-Bea-4), the Biblical Institute was entrusted by Pius XII with the task of producing a new Latin version of the Psalter. The committee, sworn to secrecy, was made up of Frs. Bea, Köbert, Merk, Semkowski, Vaccari and Zorell (cf. *Bib* 36 [1955] 161, note 3). It met for the first time on January 22nd, 1941, in a room next-door to that of the rector; the latter had prepared a document for discussion about the rules to be followed and the procedure to be adopted (Doc. R. III,9). This committee held 139 sessions, until the end of July, 1944. The agenda for each session was preserved, as were all the manuscripts proposed and reworked for each Psalm, following their numerical order as it appears in the Vulgate (APIBR B-XIII and XIII,1-3). At each session the result of the previous session was first gone over, then work was done on the plan for three other Psalms. The principal editors were Frs. Bea, Köbert and Semkowski; the others gave their opinion. On August 10th, 1941, Fr. Bea sent Pius XII, to have his opinion, Psalms 1-20 in the new translation, along with four pages of explanation (cf. Doc. R. III,10). On November 17th, 1943, when the committee was about to start the revision of its work, Fr. Bea informed it of the opinion expressed by the Pope to Fr. Merk a few days before about what ought to be kept from the Vulgate and the Latin to be used in the new translation: not the classical Latin of papal documents, nor that of late ecclesiastical Latin style, which was too faulty, but just *good* Latin; on this occasion Fr. Merk was designated *advocate of the Vulgate* (Doc. R. III,11). Finally, on February 9th, 1944, Fr. Zorell, not being able to see any more, withdrew from the committee and was not replaced.

At the Pope's request, the Motu proprio "*In cotidianis precibus*" was drawn up by Fr. Bea. An earlier version was sent to the Pope on August 16th, 1944, and its publication, along with the Psalter, was at that time scheduled for September 30th. But the text had to be revised on a fundamental point: the use of the new Psalter was to be optional, whereas in the first version it was obligatory. The Motu proprio, thus modified, finally appeared on March 24th, 1945 (APIBR B-XIII-2).

c) Outcome and consequences

To grasp the impact of this new version of the Psalter, let us first of all recall that it is a matter of correcting the Vulgate where it did not correctly give the meaning of the original Hebrew. Thus in the case of Psalm 94 (95),1, this Pius XII Psalter translated:

> *Venite, exultemus Domino / acclamemus Petrae salutis nostrae.*

What was not known at that time was that several decades later Latin would give way to modern languages. In the case of this verse it would then be translated as the Pius XII Psalter translated it. Thus for this same verse the *Traduction œcuménique liturgique du Psautier* has this in French:

> *Venez, crions de joie pour le Seigneur*
> *acclamons notre Rocher, notre salut!*

The New Revised Standard Version has:

> *O come, let us sing to the Lord*
> *Let us make a joyful noise to the rock of our salvation!*

It was the same in the other languages. The Pius XII Psalter had opened the way.

Yet, following the opinion of specialists in the Vulgate, the Second Vatican Council asked that the revision of the Latin Psalter be "completed as soon as possible, with an eye to Christian Latin style, ... as well as to the whole tradition of the Latin Church" (*Constitution on the liturgy*, 91). So that when the Neo-Vulgate appeared in 1979, the text of Ps 95 (94),1 was still that of the Vulgate translating from the Septuagint:

> *Venite, exultemus Domino;*
> *iubilemus Deo salutari nostro.*

The Pian Psalter had another consequence. On April 7th, 1945, Fr. Bea notified Fr. N. de Boynes, Vicar General of the Society of Jesus, in a letter that "the Holy Father who has already given me the task of continuing the work on the translation of other books as well will not hear of calling on others for this work" (APIBR K-23 [II-1]). The Roman Archives of the Institute actually possess the sketches of this task that ended in 1956 (APIBR A-20; B-21; M-Bea-3 and 4). According to Fr. Bea's notes (APIBR M-Bea 4), the new task that Pius XII had just entrusted to the Institute consisted in retranslating the whole Bible according to the principles that had governed the work on the new Latin Psalter. The Pope suggested starting with the Book of Genesis, but Bea suggested rather the Wisdom Books or the epistles of Paul. The Pope answered: "Give me some proposals". After an early meeting of the committee held on April 11th, 1945, Bea wrote on the 12th to Pius XII who answered him by word of mouth on the 14th: a start could be made with the Wisdom Books and the reason was that Fr. Vaccari could offer his help; later on a translation of the pericopes contained in the Breviary would be retranslated. Thus it was that on June 6th the plan passed to the Congregation of Rites and it was that that would henceforth be in charge; as Fr. Bea remarks, work in co-operation with the Congregation was needed and the Institute was no longer independent in this matter, especially as regards the distribution of the pericopes.

The committee at the Institute began with the pericopes from the Wisdom Books selected by the Congregation of Rites and that work occupied it from April 11th, 1945, until December 7th, 1949, at the time of its 123rd weekly session. But at that moment Fr. Bea was no longer rector of the Institute. So what was to become of this long-term project? That will be told in the following part of this chapter.

5. Eugenio Zolli, Professor at the Institute

Bibliography

Ernst VOGT, "In memoriam Eugenii Zolli", *Bib* 37 (1956) 261-262. – Paolo DEZZA, "Eugenio Zolli: da Gran Rabbino a testimone di Cristo (1881-1956)", *CC* 132 (1981,1) 340-349. – Eugenio ZOLLI, *Prima dell'alba*, a cura di Alberto Latorre, Cinisello Balsamo (MI), San Paolo, 2004, 284 p. – Gabriele RIGANO, *Il «caso Zolli». L'itinerario di un intellettuale in bilico tra fede, cultura e nazioni* (Contemporanea, Civiltà e transizioni, 15), Milano, Guerini, 2006, 447 p.

The first known contact of the chief rabbi of Trieste with the Biblical Institute goes back to 1935. Israel Zolli (1881-1956), from his real name Israel Zoller, was born at Brody in Galicia, at that time an Austrian province and today in the Ukraine, to the north-east of Lviv. At the beginning of the 20th cent., he had studied at Florence and from then on attached himself to Italy. Once his studies were completed he became vice-rabbi of Trieste in 1911, then chief rabbi in 1920. Since 1934 he had taught courses in Hebrew and comparative Semitic languages at the University of Padua and it was there that he had the young Jesuit, Pietro Boccaccio, the future professor of Hebrew at the Institute, among his students.

In September 1935 Zolli took part in the congress of orientalists held in Rome (cf. *supra*) and read two short papers at it. The second dealt with the meaning of the word *Nazarene* used in the gospels. At the end of December he offered the manuscript to Fr. Bea for the periodical *Biblica* (cf. Doc. R. III,12), but the article was not accepted. On April 9th, 1936, Zolli thanked Fr. Bea, however, and still more so Fr. Ruwet "for his valuable observations of a critical nature". When he resumed his study in 1938, at the beginning of his book on *The Nazarene*, Zolli, on page 4, again thanks Fr. Ruwet for his observations.

On becoming chief rabbi of Rome in 1939 Zolli, who published a lot, gave *Biblica* five articles on philology that appeared before 1945. Drawn by the figure of Jesus since his youth, Zolli had himself baptized in Rome on February 13th, 1945; Fr. Bea was his godfather. According to Fr. Dezza (p. 347) it was on the initiative of Pius XII, whose Christian name Zolli had taken, that the latter taught courses at the Biblical Institute in the languages and texts of post-biblical Jewish tradition from 1945 to 1955 (cf. *Acta PIB* 5, 31 and 42). As we have seen, these courses were not a novelty at the Institute, but this time they were given by a scholar specialized in the field. Not being compulsory, but at choice, these courses were taken by only some students; Mgr. Gianfranco Nolli has spoken of the master's teaching (cf. Rigano, pp. 340-341). Professor Zolli, who lived in the city, also taught from 1946-1951 at the La Sapienza University in Rome.

The stir caused by his move to Catholicism is well known. He kept up a faithful friendship with Fr. Boccaccio, so much so that the latter had in his keeping the first typewritten manuscript of Zolli's autobiography, dated Good Friday 1950 (APIBR M-Zolli); this was fully published only in 2004, based on another copy.

6. *Should the Institute's programme be changed?*
   A debate lasting from 1945 to 1948

The registrar's office at the Institute, in the record it keeps of the meetings held by the council of all the professors of the Institute, has a discussion vital for the future of the Institute, dated March 8th, 1945. Fr. Lyonnet pointed out that in the biblical faculty "many students do not have the necessary training for successfully following truly scholarly courses". The rector went further: the students should be divided into two groups, on the basis of an entrance examination, for instance, with each group being assigned the courses suited to them. But, he added, in that case the 1934 Statutes would have to be changed and there would have to be more professors. Fr. Messina then summarized what had been said on this question (Doc. R. III,13): 1. Pius X's aim was twofold: training professors for seminaries and training researchers who could promote biblical studies. If the first aim has been achieved, thanks to the Institute, the second has not been sufficiently accomplished. 2. Only 10% of the students are capable of following scholarly instruction; a further 20% might do so if they got the preparation; but there is still the 70% who will never be able to do it; add to this the fact that the programme contains too many diverse subjects, so that the professor cannot treat the subjects in depth and the student cannot study in a personal way nor train himself for research. 3. To meet these difficulties, which have been so often noted, it would then be necessary to choose students really able to be trained seriously for research; they would be given a programme at high university level. The other students would follow the present programme. 4. The rector should therefore speak to the Pope about it, pointing out that apart from biblical exegesis, oriental subjects would play a great part in this special programme, in conformity with what the 1943 encyclical required.

In spite of the common opinion among the professors the rector had expressed his objections and he probably spoke of them with Fr. de Boynes, then Vicar General of the Society, but in any case the proposals resumed by Fr. Messina did not have any outcome in the immediate future. They were only spoken of again after the election of Fr. Janssens as General of the Society in September 1946. He soon appointed Fr. de Boynes as his delegate for the Society's Roman institutions. In that capacity the latter came to the council of professors of the Institute on March 16th, 1947. The same record of the deliberations of these councils shows that the Delegate took the initiative of reopening the debate in March 1945 that had not been followed up. The summary of the remarks made by the professors that it had called forth amounts to what Fr. Messina had proposed two years earlier. However, the rector granted only two points: 1. students with a diploma from elsewhere could be dispensed from the course and examination in the subjects already taken; 2. those students could even take third-year courses in advance so as to be freer for some private study during that last year.

Fr. Bea then had a conversation with Fr. de Boynes who, as he had promised, on March 26th gave him some directives in a letter for getting things going again (Doc. R. III,14). The Delegate of the Fr. General, with the latter's permission, made the professors' analysis his own and asked that the courses in exegesis be doubled, a higher course being reserved for students capable of following it. Pending the reinforcement of the teaching staff, the rector, along with the professors, would have to study what could already be started up. Another difficulty, noted by the Delegate, was a certain rigidity in applying the Statutes of the Institute. In his opinion, the rector should use all the powers the Statutes conferred on him, leaving open the possibility of asking for more. Together with the more competent professors the rector should think over how to improve the programmes; then, with the General's permission, he should discuss them with the Congregation for Seminaries and Universities which, Fr. de Boynes points out, is really favourably disposed. If need be, the rector should talk directly to the Pope about it.

The next day, March 27th, on receipt of that letter from the Delegate, Fr. Bea, taking up first of all the actual terms used by Fr. de Boynes, wrote to all the professors of the Institute and called upon them to let him have in writing before April 13th their proposals on: 1. the means to be adopted in training competent exegetes; 2. what to do with students who have already received further training and, consequently, the necessary powers for the rector and deans to regulate it; 3. changes to be made to the Statutes to promote the personal work of students in the 1st and 2nd years; 4. lastly, other points arising. On April 3rd, Fr. de Boynes thanked the rector for getting things started in this way (Doc. R. III,15).

The Roman archives of the Institute (K-26-F [101]), which preserve the dossier on this matter, possess the opinions set out by Frs. Lyonnet, Messina, Dyson, Follet, Holzmeister, Köbert, R. T. O'Callaghan, O'Rourke, Pohl, Semkowski, Vaccari and Zerwick.

Fr. Bea then drew up a first draught which he sent to the professors, after the summer, on October 17th. Their observations were then discussed at the academic senate of the Institute; this was composed of the rector, vice-rector Vaccari, the two deans Lyonnet and Pohl, and the two previous deans Semkowski and Messina. On November 4th they drew up the text of the draught to be presented to the Father General; this text contained only seven points: the first two dealt with the recognition of studies done elsewhere by certain students; the next three favoured the exegetical training of the best of them by offering courses in exegesis proper, exempting them from courses in secondary subjects and letting them write up some research work instead of following this or that course; the last two allowed these same students to specialize, thanks to advanced courses and practical work, in one secondary field or another and in an oriental language of their choice.

One point had not been dealt with; it was taken up on January 11th, 1948, at the council of the biblical faculty, of which the registrar's office of the Institute keeps the record of the deliberations. At that time, the rector had already obtained endorsement in principal from the Cardinal prefect of the Congregation. It will be recalled that the 1934 Statutes leave the candidate for the doctorate only one hour in which to prepare his exegetical lesson (cf. *supra*); no serious professor would be content with so short a time in which to prepare his own classes. It was therefore proposed to give the candidate, early on in the morning, the subject he would have to deal with for an hour later in the day.

Completed at the last minute in this way, the eight proposals for change in the Statutes were transmitted to the Fr. General on January 13th, with three pages of explanations (Doc. R. III,16). On the 20th the Fr. General sent all of it to the Pope and on the 26th the Congregation gave its unqualified approval (*ARSI* 11 [1948] 402-405, where there is the letter from the prefect of the Congregation, along with the text of the amendments obtained). The odd thing is that the *Acta PIB* made no mention of this agreement or of its content. It was all printed on a sheet apart.

Stranger still is the fact that even before this agreement, Albert Descamps, the future bishop and secretary of the Biblical Commission, already a doctor in theology, got the licentiate in biblical studies in just one year, 1946-1947. Others, arriving after the agreement, also got the same licentiate in a year: 1948-1949, Charles Matagne, S.J., who had a licentiate in orientalism from Louvain and was soon to be director of the *Nouvelle Revue Théologique*; in 1949-1950, Édouard Massaux, the future rector of Louvain University (UCL) and the French exegete Henri Cazelles, also a future secretary of the Biblical Commission; then in 1950-1951, the American exegete Joseph A. Fitzmyer, S.J.

As regards a higher course in exegesis for the better prepared students, there was no sign of it for a long time. Still, a wider choice was gradually offered them.

7. Students and professors: 1945-1949

Just before the Second World War the number of *alumni* at the Institute was over one hundred; during the last year of Fr. Bea's rectorate there were to be 156 out of a total of 184 signed up. Their number rose swiftly: 58 in 1945-

1946, 82 in 1946-1947, 125 in 1947-1948. The Italians were always the most numerous, but the French and the Americans came back in force.

There is a reason for this. With the war over, it was possible to get interested in studies again, especially as the 1943 encyclical had opened up bright prospects: biblicists were no longer a priori suspects. Mgr. Philippe Delhaye, who was the secretary of the International Theology Commission told the writer of these lines that in 1937 his bishop suggested to him that he take up biblical studies but he had declined the offer, maintaining that he did not have a calling to be a martyr. In 1945 the climate had therefore changed in two ways.

The teaching staff at the Institute also had to be renewed as well and that was a task to which the rector tenaciously set his hand; provincial superiors had to be persuaded to give up men of greatest promise and see them go off for good to the Institute. In these negotiations Fr. Bea was supported by the Fr. General. Thus it was that from 1946 to 1949 nine young Jesuit professors arrived at the Institute.

In 1946 there were two. Roger T. O'Callaghan (1912-1954), from New York, was a first-class linguist. From 1942 to 1945 he had studied under the direction of W. F. Albright at Johns Hopkins University in Baltimore. He gave the courses in archaeology, geography and history of the Old Testament, then he taught Ugaritic. Unfortunately, he died in a car accident in Baghdad in 1954. His main publication was *Aram Naharaim, A Contribution to the History of Upper Mesopotamia in the Second Millennium B.C.* (AnOr 26), Rome 1948, xvi-164 p. (cf. *Bib* 35 [1954] 258-259). – René Follet (1902-1956), a Frenchman, had studied orientalism at Paris; he taught Akkadian and then Ugaritic at the Institute (cf. *Bib* 37 [1956] 258-261).

In 1947 Gioacchino Patti (1903-1980), from Favara in Sicily, arrived; he had been a pupil of Fr. Messina from 1935 to 1937, then later studied Sanscrit, Pali and the ancient languages of Persia in Berlin. He taught until 1978 at the Institute, but from 1964 to 1975 he also taught courses at Messina University (cf. *Acta PIB* 8, 458-459).

In 1948 four new people arrived. Joseph Bonsirven (1880-1958); he was at first a priest of the diocese of Albi; in 1910 be presented a doctoral thesis at the Pontifical Biblical Commission on *Eschatologie rabbinique d'après les Targums, Talmuds, Midrachs. Ses éléments communs avec le Nouveau Testament*, but it was rejected, for external reasons, it seems: in the *Bulletin de littérature ecclésiastique* 71 (1970), pp. 262 *et seqq.* M. Becamel published the correspondence between the unfortunate candidate and his bishop at the time. In 1919 Bonsirven joined the Society of Jesus; he taught New Testament, mainly at Enghien in Belgium, to the French Jesuits who had been expelled from their country. At the Institute he taught the same courses, but some courses or seminars on the theology of ancient Judaism as well. Before his arrival in Rome he had published, among other things, the following books, which came from Beauchesne in Paris: *Le judaïsme palestinien au temps de Jésus-Christ. Sa théologie*, 2 volumes, 1934-1935 (part of the first volume resumed his rejected thesis); *Exégèse rabbinique et exégèse paulinienne*, 1939; *Les enseignements de Jésus-Christ*, 1946. He resented teaching in Rome as being a kind of reparation and withdrew in 1953 (cf. *Bib* 39 [1958] 262-268). – Édouard Barbou des Places (23 July 1900 – 19 January, 2000), a Frenchman hailing from Berry, a pupil in Paris of Paul Mazon, the famous Hellenist, received the doctorate with a thesis on *Études de quelques particules de liaison chez Platon* (Paris, Les Belles Lettres, 1929, x-382 p.); after that he was professor of Greek at the house of studies for young Jesuits at Yzeure in the department of Allier; in 1946 he was called to the Institut Catholique in Paris and it was there that he published his study on *Le Pronom chez Pindare* (Paris, Klincksieck, 1947, 114 p.) and that he began to work on his other study on *Pindare et Platon* (Paris, Beauchesne, 1949, 194 p.). As a first-class philologist and being well versed in Greek thought, he concerned himself with the links between Greece and the Bible; he did so as a member of the biblical faculty until 1983; from 1948 to 1966 he was also librarian at the Institute and it is to him that we owe the enrichment of the Greek and Latin literature section of our library. – Adhémar Massart (1906-1985), born at Spy, near Namur in Belgium, had studied Egyptology from 1939 to 1942 and again from 1946 to 1948 at the University of Oxford where he became a friend of Alan Gardiner; he therefore taught Egyptology at the Biblical Institute until 1980 ("Egyptian without tears", he used to say); in 1953 he finally got the doctorate at Oxford and the following year published *The Leiden Magical Papyrus I 343 + I 345* (Leiden, Brill, xv-143 p. Cf. *Acta PIB* 9, 67-68). – Ernst Vogt (1903-1984) was born in Basle; his brother Emil was a famous archaeologist; in 1939 he obtained the doctorate in biblical studies at the Institute with great success; his thesis was on *Der Erwählungsglaube im Alten Testament (Acta PIB* 4, 186), of which he only published extracts from 1939 to 1948. He taught Old Testament exegesis at the school of theology for Jesuits at São Leopoldo in Brazil and it was from there that he was summoned to the Institute to teach mainly the prophetic books but also to succeed Fr. Bea in 1949 (cf. *Bib* 65 [1984] 438-439 = *Acta PIB* 8, 780-781).

Two new people also arrived in 1949. Pietro Boccaccio (1910-2006), born in Turin, had obtained the doctorate in Letters at the University of Padua at the end of classical studies from 1935 to 1938 and it was then that he took I. Zolli's Hebrew course (cf. *supra*); from 1943 to 1946 he did the curriculum at the Biblical Institute so brilliantly that in 1949 he was called upon to take the chair of biblical Hebrew and Aramaic when Fr. Semkowski left for Jerusalem (cf. Part Two, ch. II), and it was like that until 1985. During the early years of his teaching and along with his friend Don Guido Berardi, from Faro, he

compiled what he called "the little Zorell", an abridged Hebrew-Latin dictionary, but the enterprise stopped at p. 416, with the verb *ṣâdaq*, owing to the
death in 1973 of the printer who worked with him; he had published several
booklets of biblical and Qumranic texts with him which were much sought
after by the students (cf. *Bib* 87 [2006] 581). – Karl Prümm (1890-1981) came
from the Saarland and was at first a priest of the diocese of Trier; he entered
the Society of Jesus in 1918; from 1922 he studied the history of religions
firstly and then classical philology at Münster where he obtained a doctorate
in philosophy in 1930; then, from 1931 to 1938, he taught New Testament at
the school of theology for German Jesuits at Valkenburg in the Netherlands;
after this, from 1938-1949, he taught the same subject at the faculty of theology at the University of Innsbruck when he was summoned to the Biblical
Institute to occupy the chair of Pauline writings and the history of Hellenistic
religions; with a very cultivated, inquiring and encyclopaedic mind, clarity
was not his strong point and it used to be said of him that he did "zigzag"
exegesis; that did not prevent his stout volumes from already having an impact, in particular his *Religionsgeschichtliches Handbuch für den Raum der
altchristlichen Umwelt* (Freiburg i. Br., Herder, 1943, xvi-921 p.). He taught
at the Biblical Institute until 1966 (cf. *Acta PIB* 8, 610-612).

Lastly, let us note that as from the academic year 1948-1949 the date for
the start of classes was not to be set for November 3rd any more, as had been
the case since 1909, but for October 15th (*Acta PIB* 5, 136). This decision
came from the rectors of ecclesiastical institutions in Rome and on June 18th,
1947, it had obtained the approval of Cardinal Pizzardo, the prefect of the
Congregation for Seminaries and Universities (APIBR K-4-C).

8. *The Biblical Commission's letter to Cardinal Suhard: 1948*

Bibliography

A. BEA, "Il problema del Pentateuco e della storia primordiale. A proposito della
recente lettera della Pontificia Commissione Biblica", *CC* 101 (1948, 2) 116-127. –
St. SCHMIDT, *Agostino Bea il cardinale dell'unità*, pp. 119-124. – Fr. LAPLANCHE, *La
crise de l'origine*, pp. 338-342.

On January 16th, 1948, with Pius XII's approval, Fr. Vosté, as secretary to
the Pontifical Biblical Commission, signed a letter addressed to Cardinal
Suhard, archbishop of Paris. It dealt with the dating of the documents that are
at the basis of the Pentateuch and the literary genre of the first eleven chapters
of Genesis (*EB* 577-581).

The background to this letter was given by Fr. Laplanche (pp. 338-340),
who consulted the archives at the Institut Catholique of Toulouse and those of
the diocese of Paris. Here we summarize the essential points, adding here and
there some details from the archives of the Institute.

It was the rector of the Institut Catholique of Toulouse, Mgr. Bruno de Solages, who took the initiative on October 26th, 1946; he had a letter sent to
Mgr. Montini which the latter passed on to Pius XII, who passed it on to the
Biblical Commission. To remove obstacles to the exegesis of the Pentateuch
despite the 1943 encyclical, Mgr. de Solages suggests that the Biblical Commission publish two new decrees, one on the date of the composition of the
documents of the Pentateuch, the other on the literary genres of Genesis 1-11.
In his opinion the time was ripe and he asked that exegetes be able to work
freely on these two questions.

The Commission went into the matter during the year 1947 and at the end
of November Cardinal Tisserant sent the proofs of the Commission's document to Cardinal Suhard, because the archbishop of Toulouse, Cardinal
Saliège, was not in favour in Rome at the time. But on December 22nd Mgr.
Grano, from the Secretariat of State, phoned to Fr. Vosté to inform him that
the letter would not be published. In a spirit of faith Fr. Vosté deferred and, on
the following day, told Fr. Bea about the decision taken. Now, on January 3rd,
1948, Bea had the unscheduled opportunity to talk to the Pope about this
matter (Doc. R. III,17) and the Pope explained to him that one item in the
Commission's project caused him a problem; this project, which satisfied
Mgr. de Solages' wishes, actually stated that the Commission also wanted to
promote biblical studies "allowing them the fullest liberty, within the limits of
revealed doctrines". The Pope was afraid of the abuse that such a formula
might give rise to and considered that Catholic tradition and the norms established by competent ecclesiastical authority should also be taken into account.
Fr. Bea then suggested to the Pope that the Commission could revise its copy
and formulate the phrase in question better. The Pope agreed and told Fr. Bea
to explain the difficulty to Fr. Vosté, asking him for a wording less open to
wrong interpretations. On January 8th Vosté thanked Bea on behalf of Cardinal Tisserant. The Commission's letter finally appeared in the *AAS* 40 (1948),
pp. 45-48, with new wording to the phrase in question: "allowing them the
fullest freedom within the limits of the Church's traditional teaching" (*EB*
578).

Fr. Bea intervened, therefore. As for the content of the letter, the hand of
the rector of the Institute is easily detected in it, even if he was not the only
one to have a hand in it. As far back as 1935 (*Bib* 16, 179-185 and 195-198)
he was opposed to the documentary hypothesis about the Pentateuch and,
commenting on the Commission's letter in 1948, he returned to the charge.
On the other hand he was sensitive to the psychological approach to the ancient texts (cf. *Bib* 25 [1944] 253; *EB* 580). However, that did not prevent H.
Cazelles from taking up the documentary hypothesis again in 1964 (in *DBS* 7,
768-855) in a last effort of any importance before the doubts cast on it in its
classical form in 1975.

On the other hand, Fr. Bea had published an article in 1944 (*Bib* 25, 70-87) about "new problems and work on primordial biblical history". Being a consultor of the Commission, he comes across in it full of the competence he had acquired, so that when the Commission wrote that: "all the material from palaeontological and historical, epigraphic and literary sciences must be brought together, without any prejudices" (*EB* 581), one can here again detect an attitude dear to Fr. Bea.

Finally, Fr. Schmidt (p. 123) reports what Fr. Duncker, O.P., states; according to him, at the time of this affair, Bea dissuaded Pius XII from abolishing the decrees of the Commission published at the beginning of the 20th century. At all events, in 1955 Fr. Athanasius Miller, O.S.B., then secretary of the Biblical Commission, published a note in which one reads:

> To the extent to which the decrees maintain ways of thinking that have no relation, mediate or immediate, with truths of faith and morals, it goes without saying that the exegete may in all freedom pursue his researches and put their results to good use, allowance always being made, of course, for the authority of the ecclesiastical teaching office.

This vital and liberating text was commented on by Fr. Jacques Dupont, O.S.B., in *Revue Biblique* 62 (1955), pp. 417-418.

9. Enlarging the premises of the Institute in Rome: 1949

Above the door of the present main lecture hall a marble plaque recalls that it was Pius XII who had it built and the date is precise: 1949. Now that main lecture hall is not in the original building of the Institute any more, the former Muti Papazurri palace, but in what had been St. Bonaventure's College, established by Sixtus V in 1587 and forced to close its doors in 1873. This extension of the Institute was the end of a long story (cf. APIBR A-18 and K-23).

Bibliography on the former College of St. Bonaventure

Lorenzo Di Fonzo, "Lo studio del Dottore Serafico nel «Collegio di San Bonaventura» in Roma (1587-1873)", *Miscellanea Francescana* 40 (1940), pp. 153-186. – Id., "Nel quarto centenario di fondazione del Romano «Collegio di San Bonaventura» OFMConv (1587-1987)", *Miscellanea Francescana* 87 (2007), pp. 3-31.

It all starts with a decision by the government of the city of Rome which had to be put into effect as from October 28th 1938. It concerned the demolition of all the buildings, including the Balestra palace, situated between the Via San Marcello and the Via dell'Archetto, with the North American College not being entirely untouched. The city wanted to lengthen the Piazza SS.

Apostoli and construct a new twenty-metre wide road as far as the Via dell'Umiltà. The Biblical Institute, momentarily threatened with destruction, too, was finally to be spared.

But the Institute felt more and more straightened. Let us recall that for the school year 1938-1939 it numbered 118 registered students. For Fr. Bea, drawing up a ten-page *Promemoria* on August 4th, 1938, the only solution would be to add a storey to the building the Institute had occupied since 1910, but to do that the Holy See, which owned the property, would have to be involved. On August 6th the rector sent that *Promemoria* to Fr. General Ledó-kowski, with an accompanying letter.

On August 21st Fr. Bea again sends Fr. General two *Promemorias* he had written the day before. The first envisaged installing the Institute at no. 120 in the Via del Seminario, the former premises of the Gregorian, in the Borromeo palace. In that case the former Muti Papazzuri palace that had become the Biblical Institute would take in the sixty-or-so Jesuit biennists hitherto residing either at the Gesù or at the Gregorian. As for the people living in the Borromeo palace, about a hundred young Jesuits studying theology or philosophy, they would take the place of the biennists at the Gesù, at least from what one understands. But this game of musical chairs has serious disadvantages: not only the cost of the operation, but also distancing the Institute from the Gregorian and the fact that the huge Borromeo palace would not be fully occupied by the Institute, to say nothing about the other fact that the Muti Papazzuri palace could not take the sixty-or-so biennists. This plan, which does not seem to have come from Fr. Bea, should, in his opinion, be abandoned.

The second *Promemoria* of August 21st, 1938, returns to the raising of the building hitherto occupied by the Institute. But, writing also on August 21st to Fr. Pedro Basterra, Fr. General's advisor on building matters, – he had supervised the building of the Gregorian – Fr. Bea points out that the engineer G. Astorri, who had fitted up the building for the Institute in the past, always maintained that the walls could not support an extra storey.

And everything stopped there, for the simple reason that the city did not carry out its plan. But for the Institute, cramped within its walls, the problem remained.

It came to the surface again in January 1943 and from then on it was to be a question of the former College of St. Bonaventure. In the 1929 Lateran Treaty, in article 14, it is agreed by Italy and the Holy See that all the buildings of the former convent of the Conventual Franciscan Fathers adjoining the Basilica of the Holy Apostles become the property of the Holy See, in particular, therefore, the former College of St. Bonaventure. In 1960, Fr. Bea, now a cardinal, stated (*Bib* 41,15) that back in 1929 Pius XI was thinking of giving that former college to the Institute. However, the complex of the former convent of the Conventual Fathers had been leased to the Italian War Ministry who had made a barracks out of it.

In a note he sent on January 28th, 1943, to Fr. A. A. Magni, Vicar General of the Society, Fr. Bea points out that he has not been able to write the *Promemoria* he had promised "about the house and the military barracks" with the plans of those barracks but that he hopes to do so before their meeting on February 7th. In the course of the following days but, it seems, before that February 7th, the Vicar General in his turn, sends Fr. Bea a handwritten undated note:

> Many thanks for the plans you sent me so solicitously; they give me quite a precise idea of the whole background and confirm the quality of the plan we have studied together.
>
> Let us pray the Lord that all goes well and that the Holy Father approves.

On the 8th, the Fr. Vicar further adds, in a more official letter in Latin, dated February 8th: "About the lack of space you complain of, something is being done; in fact there is already some certainty in the matter, of which I have informed you" (APIBR K-23 [II-1]). This *Promemoria* from Fr. Bea, along with the plans he himself was to pass on, two years later, on December 5th, 1944, to Mgr. Domenico Tardini, from the Secretariat of State, for the attention of Prince Carlo Pacelli, councillor general of the Vatican City State.

After the liberation of Rome by the Allies in June 1944, the former College was occupied by the British military command, who did not know that it was a question of property belonging to the Holy See! At the end of difficult negotiations the British finally vacated the place on November 5th, 1945, but the Italian War Ministry still had to restore the building in question officially to the Holy See and that was done only in September 1946; in a letter he addressed to Pius XII on October 17th, 1946, Fr. Bea confirms this (APIBR K-1-E).

However, on February 9th, 1945, to show clearly who would occupy the building from now on, Fr. P. Boccaccio, Fr. St. Schmidt and a third young Jesuit, all three students at the Institute, lodged there on the second floor. Work on fitting the place up started on September 19th, 1946, and, on the 24th, preparations for building the bridge spanning the Via del Vaccaro began. This bridge was to connect the two buildings, the old and the new ones (APIBR B-XVIII-10: *Historia domus 1935-1960*, pp. 67 and 79). The new one would be occupied by the Jesuit community in charge of the Institute, except that on the western side of the courtyard of the new building a chapel was built on the ground floor and, on the second, resting on the columns of the courtyard and on the walls of the chapel the Institute's main lecture hall. In July 1948 Fr. Bea asked Mgr. Antonio Bacci, secretary of the briefs to princes and a good Latinist, to put the text that was going to be carved on a marble plaque into form; the plaque was to be placed at the entrance to the main lecture hall. On the 30th, Mgr. Bacci sent back the corrected draft; it was adhered to as it was, except that it bore the date 1948 (APIBR K-11-A [1-7]). Now the construction of this main lecture hall took longer than expected and it only came into use in October 1949. The date on the commemorative plaque was therefore changed. At that time the rector's office was situated on the second floor of the new building, over a period of more than thirty years, with the window overlooking the Via della Pilotta. The *Acta PIB* 5, p. 171, notes the end of the work, of which Pius XII had covered the cost.

Besides Mgr. Tardini and Prince Pacelli, Count Enrico P. Galeazzi, director general of technical services at the Vatican, also contributed to the enterprise, as did the engineer G. Astorri, who had transformed the Muti Papazzuri palace between the years 1910 and 1912, and the architect Mario Leonardi, who was to be involved with the Institute for another thirty years or so. The Conventual Fathers, for their part, were not enthusiastic about the operation (APIBR A-18: letter from Bea to Galeazzi dated July 7th, 1947).

To finish with this story, the handwritten document that Pius XII sent to Fr. Bea's successor, Fr. Ernst Vogt, on May 30th, 1954, the day after Pius X's canonization, must be mentioned; the text was published in *ARSI* 12, pp. 489-490. The original document was accompanied by cadastral data concerning the two buildings of the Institute, as well as by floor-by-floor plans of its new premises, and each page is signed by the Vatican's architect, Enrico P. Galeazzi and Mgr. G. B. Montini who, in November, was to become archbishop of Milan. This papal document (APIBR K-1-A), among the clearest when it comes to justifying the occupation of premises by the Institute, had been asked for by Fr. Vogt on May 5th. On May 1st he had informed the house consult of the situation: the Institute did not actually possess any official document from the Holy See attesting the legitimacy of its presence in the new building, and for two years every attempt to get one had failed: the Pope would have to be approached, and that was successfully done (Doc. R. III,18). Such a document had in fact been suggested by Fr. Vogt for a long time. Following an outburst from Fr. Beda Hess, the Minister General of the Conventual Fathers, the rector had asked Fr. Janssens on June 2nd, 1950, to see to it that the Institute quickly had an authentic document proving the transfer of the building in question to the Institute (APIBR K-7-C [II-1]).

Assessment of Fr. Bea's rectorate

Without wishing to centre the history of the Institute around the person of the rector, one cannot deny that without Fr. Bea, as in the case of Fr. Fonck in former times, the Institute would not have been as well known as it is. To be sure, Fr. Bea was not alone; he had some eminent specialists around him, Frs. Vaccari, Pohl, Messina, Merk, Zorell and Lyonnet, to start with and to mention only some of the best-known. But more so than his distant predecessor, he knew how to work with other people. Thanks to the 1934 Statutes he henceforth had two faculty deans and the councils of both faculties were functioning; the council of all the professors was also functioning and, sometimes despite his reservations, as in 1947 on a question of the Statutes, the rector played the game properly. To serve the Church Fr. Bea put together a trustworthy team to draw up the new Latin Psalter and, in 1946, another commission for writing the Institute's *votum* on Pius XII's plan to define the dogma of the Assumption of Mary (APIBR K-1-E [I-1]).

For the rector, working with others also meant defending the reputation of his own people when they were accused in an underhand and dangerous way, as he did in the Cohenel case.

Yet, while being clever at working with others, Fr. Bea was always a leader, a refined politician, tenacious and able to adapt to circumstances. He proved it when it came to giving the Institute more room.

With the passing of the years he felt the weight of his charge. In April, 1947, it was at the request of Fr. de Boynes that he agreed to carry on until the conclusion of the work on the extension of the Institute (Doc. R. III,15). Unless one has to understand the episode as follows. At the time of Fr. Prešeren's visit in March 1945 Fr. Bea had succeeded in blocking any change in the biblical faculty's programme such as the professors, including Fr. Messina who had become their spokesman, wished. But when, two years later, in March, 1947, Fr. de Boynes himself restarts the debate that had fallen through, Fr. Bea was caught out and became evasive. After the meeting the conversation between the two men could not have been easy. The Fr. Delegate who, a little later on, was going to insist, with authority, that the professors' opinion be taken into account, was going to find the rector so put out that he envisaged resigning. The Fr. Delegate spoke to the Fr. General about it and together they urged Fr. Bea to stay in office and at the same time get the reform of the Statutes along the lines suggested by the professors under way. The rector obeyed on the spot.

The rector also had ways into the Vatican and when he became confessor to Pius XII after the death of Fr. Merk in 1945 he was even quite bold, as in 1948 when he got the letter from the Biblical Commission released. It was not only with the Pope that Fr. Bea kept up loyal and devoted relations but also with Superiors General of the Society of Jesus and with their Vicars or delegates. His concrete relations with the latter are admirable: with Fr. Magni in 1943 he opened the way to the enlargement of the Institute; in 1947 he submitted loyally to the authorized opinion of Fr. de Boynes who asked him for a revision of the Statutes, as stated above.

There was also a certain rigidity about Fr. Bea, for which Fr. de Boynes discreetly reproached him. The rector really wanted to be faithful to the decisions of the Holy See. For him the earlier decrees of the Biblical Commission were still in force and, as we shall see in the Guillet affair, with what consequences. However, it should then clearly be seen that the rector had no illusions about the dangers that, in the eyes of the Vatican, Catholic exegesis had continued to run since the beginning of the century; it was at all costs necessary to make sure that the Institute had the confidence of the Pope and to keep it free from any blame that might ruin its work. In this matter, Fr. Bea, while possessing an astonishing capacity for information in exegesis, had not had a high-level university training in his youth. He must have felt this, but his gifts were not of that kind. He did not leave behind anything of worth in exegesis, but he was a great leader of intelligent men totally dedicated to their task in the Church.

At all events, when he handed over to Fr. Vogt on July 2nd, 1949 (*Acta PIB* 5, 174 and APIBR K-1-A), Fr. Bea left him with a clear and promising situation, as Fr. O'Rourke had done in times past. Catholic exegesis was opening a new, hopeful chapter this time. The Institute was in full expansion; the number of students had more than doubled in nineteen years, the teaching staff had been renewed and several new professors were in place for about thirty years and, lastly, people were no longer cramped within the walls of the former Muti Papazzuri palace. Fr. Bea really had laid the foundations for hopes for the future.

III. The last years of Pius XII: 1949-1958

1. The project to retranslate the whole Bible into Latin, continued

Fr. E. Vogt had become rector in 1949, but the project to retranslate the whole of the Bible into Latin remained in the hands of Fr. Bea who continued to preside over the committee and to deal with the Holy See in the matter (APIBR M-Bea-3).

After the Wisdom Books of the Old Testament they went on to translate passages of the prophetic books still used in the Roman Breviary. That work occupied the committee until November 23rd, 1955, i. e. from the 124th until the 283rd session. They then went on to the books of Tobit, Judith and Esther until the 299th session on April 18th, 1956.

However, Pius XII kept firmly to the idea that the Biblical Institute should retranslate all the Bible into Latin, as it had already done for the Psalter. On May 10th, 1950, Mgr. Montini, from the Secretariat of State, confirmed this by letter (226962) to the archbishop of São Paulo. As the committee at the Institute had begun with the Old Testament, Fr. Bea wrote a six-page typed "Memorandum on the revision of the Latin Vulgate of the New Testament". He envisaged keeping any changes to be made to a minimum and the norms he proposed in this document were approved by the Pope so that on November 19th, 1952, Fr. Bea let the members of the renovated committee have them. The latter were to meet in December to make definitive plans for their future work.

Meanwhile, on November 26th, 1946, Fr. Bea had already asked the committee the following question: was it not fitting to prepare the publication of a whole book, for example Qohelet, with the permission of the Supreme Pontiff? The answer had been positive but since the committee was keeping to the extracts in the Breviary it had to complete its work; Fr. Bea took charge of it so that the first fruit of the committee appeared in the following fascicule:

> *Liber Ecclesiastae qui ab Hebraeis appellatur Qohelet. Nova interpretatio Latina cum notis criticis et exegeticis edita a curis* Augustini BEA, Romae, Pont. Inst. Bibl., 1950, xiv-30 p.

The passages from the book of Isaiah were retranslated over the period from December 7th, 1949, to May 30th, 1951, i. e. from the 123rd until the 173rd session. Frs. Bea, Vogt, Vaccari, Lyonnet, Boccaccio, Dyson and Köbert were members of the committee at the time. When the work was completed Fr. Bea had the ninety-eight typed pages of this new translation bound in one volume and the title was: *Liber Isaiae Prophetae. Pericopae selectae. Nova e textu primigenio interpretatio Latina*, Romae 1951. Some other important passages from the theological and spiritual point of view had been added to the extracts for the Breviary.

Finally, a second product of the committee's work came out:

> *Canticum Canticorum Salomonis quod hebraice dicitur Šir Haššîrîm. Nova e textu primigenio interpretatio latina cum textu massoretico ac notis criticis et exegeticis edita curis* Augustini BEA, Romae, Pont. Inst. Bibl., 1953, 68 p.

In this last publication, as in that of the book of Qohelet, the introduction and the exegetical notes are evidently from the hand of Fr. Bea, as is the translation of the passages not in the Breviary; in the case of the latter Fr. Bea was able to make wide use of the texts worked out by the committee that had been engaged upon those two books from February to June 1946. These were the only two publications that appeared, at least in part, from the committee at the Institute

Lastly, it seems that the committee, of which Fr. M. Zerwick was now a member, went on, after its work on the Old Testament, to some first attempts at the New Testament, as from the end of April 1956. On the basis of the norms approved in 1952 it thus retranslated three Pauline epistles, those addressed to the Philippians, Colossians and the 2nd to the Corinthians.

That, in outline, was the situation when Pius XII died on October 9th, 1958. To save the reader from being faced with the dispersal of information about this new translation of the Bible, what can be known about the rest of the enterprise is given here.

On October 28th, 1958, John XXIII was elected. On December 11th Fr. Bea met Cardinal Gaetano Cicognani, Prefect of the Congregation of Rites and on the next day he wrote a "Memorandum on a new translation of the passages from Holy Scripture to be put in the reformed Breviary" for the Cardinal. This six-page typewritten text, supplemented by some annexed documents, was really meant for the new Pope whom Fr. Bea asked: 1. whether he confirmed the charge, entrusted to the Biblical Institute by Pius XII, of retranslating the whole Bible into Latin; 2. whether, in the Breviary, the translation of the passages from the Bible was to be the one prepared by the Institute; 3. whether, in the event of an affirmative answer to the second question, the Institute can continue to apply the norms that Pius XII approved for the translation of the New Testament; 4. whether the Pope wishes the Pius XII Psalter to be reviewed in accordance with the norms approved for the translation of the New Testament.

At the beginning of March 1959 Cardinal Cicognani gave John XXIII Fr. Bea's "Memorandum" and, on the 16th Cardinal Tardini, who had become Secretary of State, handed Cardinal Cicognani the Pope's answers: 1. the Institute remains entrusted with retranslating the whole Bible on the basis of the original Hebrew, Aramaic and Greek texts; 2. in this new translation the Institute is to follow the rules approved by Pius XII for the New Testament; 3. the Roman Breviary will use that new translation; 4. lastly, as regards the Pius XII Psalter, John XXIII does not wish to give the impression of going back on what his predecessor laid down, which does not mean that some "suitable alterations" may not be made to that translation. On March 22nd Fr. Bea, who had received from Cardinal Tardini a copy of the reply sent to Cardinal Cicognani, thanked the Secretary of State and undertook to carry on with the work.

The situation changed completely when, on December 14th of that same year 1959, Fr, Bea was made a cardinal. However, people got back to work at the Institute. From March to May 1960 the committee, now comprising Fr. Vogt, the rector, and Frs. A. Vaccari, P. Boccaccio, L. Alonso Schökel and W. L. Moran, started on the revision of the Pius XII Psalter, following John XXIII's indications, so that on June 23rd Fr. Vogt sent Fr. Bea the annotated translation of Psalms 1-7 in which some "suitable alterations" had been made (APIBR A-20).

Wasted effort, for, on June 5th, while preparations for Vatican II were going on, the Pope had set up the Secretariat for the Unity of Christians and Cardinal Bea became its president, who would have other matters to attend to. The plan to have the whole Bible translated by the Biblical Institute stopped there. When at the end of November, 1965, Paul VI decided that the whole of the

Vulgate was to be corrected, and not just the Psalter, as the Council had de-cided (*Sacrosanctum concilium*, 91), the texts prepared by the Institute just went down the drain. All the same, Paul VI was fully in line with Pius XII in his decision, from which John XXIII did not wish to dissociate himself. Hav-ing been a useless servant for two decades, still the Institute was not to have worked in vain for, if the Neo-Vulgate owes nothing to it, it showed that in the Latin Church, as regards its liturgy, it was possible to translate the Bible from the original texts and its example was followed in the main languages of the west.

2. Reorganizing the "Old House" – Budget deficit and partial letting: 1949-1954

So when, in October 1949, during the rectorate of Fr. Vogt the Jesuit com-munity could move into the former College of St. Bonaventure, there was a reorganization of the use to which the premises of the "Old House", as the Jesuits still call it, were put. It had housed the Institute since 1909.

The western part of the ground floor was, and still is, almost entirely occu-pied by the management of the Institute's publications, with its offices and depots. On this it should be observed that the publications, periodicals and books bearing the name of the Institute are the property of the teaching staff and not of the Institute. The former main lecture hall, to the east, became Hall IV, today's Pius X Hall.

On the first floor the western part was cleared, apart from the chapel, since the Jesuits' dining room and recreation or reading room were moved into the new building. The fine walnut panelling that covered the dining room walls was also moved into the new recreation room and to the end of the dining room. The room used for meetings was made into two small classrooms, but what was to become of the others in the south-western corner?

On the second floor, to the west, it was also possible to put some rooms for classes or seminars by knocking down the walls of some rooms now empty. In the north-weastern corner the rector still kept an office for a while. The registrar of the Institute, Fr. Ruwet, had his nextdoor to the rector's, and the librarian, Fr. des Places, had his next to the registrar's at the entrance to the library; likewise, the librarian's former office, situated in the south-eastern corner of the floor, became the first embryo of the *Aula orientalis* (it is today the place where rare books are kept).

On the third floor several Jesuits still lived or had an office; however, two classrooms were opened in the north-west of the floor. When work was com-pleted the Institute certainly had enough rooms for classes or seminars.

Yet the surprising thing is that with the new building the old one seemed not only sufficient but too big for immediate needs. On January 25th, 1949, when he was still rector, Fr. Bea was already telling the council (APIBR B-XIII-2) that the Bank of Rome wanted to hire the former refectory for its staff, along with the room next to it and the kitchen and its pantry just beneath the ground floor. Despite the councillors' approval the plan came to nought.

The problem came back in a more serious form in February 1950, Fr. Vogt then being rector. The work of reorganizing the "Old House" had cost some sixty thousand dollars, a sum which, in buying power at the end of 2008, would be worth about five hundred thousand dollars, so that the Institute's available funds were being drawn upon too much and lacked ready cash with which to pay bills. Rather than have recourse again to the Holy See, the Institute began to let some of its premises. At the beginning of February 1950, as the council meeting on March 15th mentions, two rooms on the ground floor and one on the first floor in the south-east corner of the building, at no. 6A of the Via del Vaccaro, were rented out to the layperson who was bookbinder to the Conventual Fathers. However, on February 15th, 1950, Fr. Feldhaus, in charge of the running of the Institute and its finances as minister and bursar, explained to the council that it would also be necessary to let the former main lecture hall. A year later, on March 15th 1951, the same council gave its approval to the following proposal: The Nobles' Sodality of Our Lady, whose headquarters was at the Gesù, would rent this former main lecture hall annually, along with the premises the bookbinder had had on lease for a year. This new rent was to have brought in two hundred thousand lire a month, i. e. more than twenty thousand 2008 euros. Fr. Feldhaus pointed out that this Sodality was setting up an institute for the training of trade union leaders. In view of the fact that no great increase in the number of students at the Institute in the coming years was foreseen, the council gave its consent.

Fr. Paul Feldhaus, who was in charge of this matter, was born at Mülheim in the Ruhr in 1901. From 1938 to 1943 he had been sub-minister at the Pio Latino College in Rome; he then taught German at the Jesuit college of Mondragone, on the Frascati heights. He arrived at the Biblical Institute on July 29th, 1946, and according to the house diary (APIBR A-11) was officially installed on the following 1st of November. A reserved but efficient man, he succeeded Fr. Gozzolino Birolo, who had died on June 19th, 1945 (cf. *Acta PIB* 5, p. 16); Fr. Zerwick had generously taken on the task during the interval. Unfortunately, Fr. Feldhaus died unexpectedly on September 30th, 1965, in the swimming pool at the Villa San Pastore at Gallicano, near Palestrina in Lazio. In its century of history the Institute never enjoyed the services of minister-bursars like Frs. Birolo (from 1930 to 1945) and Feldhaus (from 1946 to 1965) for so long.

On October 1st, 1951, the said Sodality actually rented the premises mentioned above, but with another adjacent room, in short the former main lecture hall, the ground floor of 6A in the Via del Vaccaro (a garage today) and all the first floor of the south-east wing of the former Muti Papazzuri palace. For this purpose a contract was finally signed by Fr. Feldhaus, for the Institute, and Fr. Giuseppe Castellani, S. J., the director of that Sodality, in the presence of the lawyer Luigi Filippo Re, acting as notary on behalf of the Vatican City State. The whole dossier on this matter is in the archives of the Institute (APIBR K-A). On Fr. G. Castellani (1886-1976) , cf. *Notizie dei Gesuiti Italiani* 9 (1975-1976), pp. 271-273.

The Biblical Institute thought it could solve part of its financial problems with this contract. Not so, because it was just a series of *pasticci*, as the Italians say, a series of quite bizarre misadventures of which the following gives the essentials. The contract with the Sodality of Our Lady had gone through in April 1952 and was valid until October 1st, 1954. But the Sodality which, in the space rented from the Institute, had set up a *Centre of trade union and labour studies* which it had created, did not regularly pay the rent agreed upon. The Institute therefore rescinded the contract on September 15th 1953 and asked to have the keys of the premises back, but to no avail. In fact the Sodality, without telling the Institute, had gone ahead with a subletting in April 1953 to a *Civic Roman Committee*, mainly under the wing of *Catholic Action* of which L. Gedda was director. However, this subletting, without previous notice, was ruled out by the April 1952 contract. At the time, the election campaign of June 7th, 1953, was at its height. So much so that from September 15th 1953 on, this Committee continued to occupy the premises without any contract and hence without any right. Finally, they left at the beginning of December 1953. In future the Institute would think twice before taking on any more renting out.

3. *Students, professors and publications: 1949-1958*

The increase in the number of students that was noticed since 1946 occurred again in the academic Year 1949-1950; at that time the *alumni* numbered 183 out of a total of 207 registered students. The Institute had never had such large numbers, which were not noted for another ten years. In fact, from the school year 1950-1951 until 1957-1958 the number of *alumni* varied between 136 and 152 and the number of registered students between 162 and 182. What had happened? It is not impossible that the encyclical *"Humani generis"* which Pius XII signed on August 12th, 1950, had something to do with this sudden decrease. After a decade marked with openness in biblical exegesis Pius XII put the brakes on and the last four years of his pontificate, after the long attack of hiccups he had in 1954 and Mgr. Montini's departure for Milan, are often considered as a period of tightening up, especially within the Holy Office.

Here we must speak of Fr. Jacques Guillet (1910-2001), the well-known exegete from Lyons.

Bibliography

Jacques GUILLET, *Habiter les Écritures. Entretiens avec Charles Ehlinger* (Les interviews), Paris, Centurion, 1993, 351 p. esp. pp. 88-94 and 160-171.

When he arrived in Rome on October 14th, 1949, Fr. Guillet had already been designated a future professor at the Institute and when he left to go back to Fourvière, on the heights above Lyons, in June 1951, there is no longer any question of it. Fr. Bea had known him for over ten years; from September 1936 to June 1938 the young Guillet had stayed at the Institute in Jerusalem; there he had started to learn Hebrew, exegesis and biblical theology; he had visited the country, except for Galilee because of the troubles, and had sometimes taken part in the excavations at Ghassul. On returning to Fourvière to start his theology he only spent a year there because from September 1939 on he had been in the forces; he was made prisoner of war, then escaped and joined the Free French in London. He only got back to Fourvière in September 1945 to finish his theology. It was there that, in June 1947, he learned that the Fr. General destined him to teach at the Biblical Institute where he was to succeed Fr. Vaccari. But the Superiors allowed him two years to complete his manuscript on biblical themes (Doc. R. III,19). This book, inspired by Fr. Victor Fontoynont, was already with Aubier the publishers, of Paris, when Guillet arrived in Rome. Six months later, on April 7th, 1950, Fr. Vogt wrote to Fr. de Boynes that at the latter's request he had explained to Fr. Guillet that his manuscript would have to be censored by the Institute, not because of any suspicion about his doctrine, but to save him from possible difficulties (APIBR K-12-B [II-2]). There were several censures between March and August; the matter went up to the General; the last censure, the one by Fr. Bea was severe and carping: too many concessions to recent, especially Protestant, exegesis, in particular on Second Isaiah and original sin (APIBR P-Guillet). The rest was related by Fr. Guillet himself: after the appearance of the encyclical *"Humani generis"* on August 12th, his manuscript finally came back to him and he submissively started on the requested corrections. Then a check by Fr. Lyonnet and finally approval by Fr. de Boynes for the publication of these *Thèmes bibliques* in the spring of 1951. It was perfectly clear that Fr. Guillet was no longer destined to be a professor at the Institute.

With Fr. Guillet excluded, the teaching staff of the Institute was none the less enriched with seven new people during this period from 1949-1958. The first was Fr. Joseph P. Smith (1912-1964) an Englishman from Lancashire. He had studied classics at London from 1938-1941. He arrived at the Biblical Institute in 1947 to do the licentiate in orientalism and obtained it in 1950. From 1951 until 1962 he not only taught the course in textual criticism, thus relieving Fr. Vogt, but also the courses in Armenian and Georgian languages and literatures. In fact, being a perfectionist by temperament, he took on too many courses, to such an extent that when his health gave way he left the Institute in March 1962 to go and live near Évian in Switzerland; he died in a Parisian clinic on March 18th, 1964. His chief publications were, firstly, ST. IRENAEUS, *Proof of the Apostolic Teaching* (Ancient Christian Writers, 16), Westminster Md – London 1952, which gave the translation of, and a commentary on, the Armenian text and, secondly, *Biblical Greek*, which was published at the Institute and was a reworked translation of Fr. Zerwick's grammar of New Testament Greek (cf. *Bib* 45 [1964] 605-606). – In 1954, just after defending his thesis on the reform of Ezra, Fr. Viliam Pavlovský, a Slovak, began teaching at the Institute. His field was mainly biblical history and, more precisely, the chronology of the kings of Israel and Juda; in conjunction with Fr. Vogt he published the principles and details of it in *Biblica* 45 (1964), pp. 321-354, but he used to say that his fellow-author unfortunately changed some of the data! At different times he taught Aramaic (1954-1959), Syriac (1960-1982) and Arabic (1961-1968). Though suffering from a weak heart he still went on with his task until 1982. A reserved and nervous person, he was not without a sense of humour (cf. *Bib* 65 [1984] 440-441). – Fr. Robert G. North (1916-2007), born in Iowa City in the United States, started the full curriculum of biblical studies at the Institute in 1946 and published his doctoral thesis in 1954; it dealt with the *Sociology of the Biblical Jubilee* (AnBib, 4). Having defended his thesis in 1951 he began a long career as professor of biblical archaeology and history at the Institute in Rome. In February and March 1952, and again in 1953, he took part in the excavations that Miss Kathleen M. Kenyon directed at Tell es-Sultan, Jericho, and gave an account of the first season of those excavations in *Biblica* 34 (1953, pp. 1-12). Fr. North went on with his career at the Institute in Rome until 1986, apart from a spell in Jerusalem (1956-1960; cf. Part Two), then in the United States (1960-1964). Cf. *Acta PIB* 9, pp. 645-647. – in 1955, Eugen Bergmann (1907-1965), of Berlin origin, began his teaching of Sumerian, Akkadian and Hittite in the oriental faculty of the Institute. From 1942 to 1949 he had served his country and ended up in a Russian prison camp. On being released he resumed his studies in orientalism at Heidelberg under the direction of Professor Adam Falkenstein. He taught at the Institute only during the academic year 1955-1956 and again from 1958-1960; then he withdrew for health reasons (cf. *Orientalia* 34 [1965] 455-456). – From 1948-1950 Fr. Francis J. McCool (1913- 1996) had got the licentiate in biblical studies at the Institute and finished the preparatory year for the doctorate. He was born at Londonderry in Northern Ireland but, while still young, had emigrated with the family to the United States. From 1955 to 1985 he taught a special introduction to the New Testament at the Institute (cf. *Acta PIB* 10, 220-221). – In 1956 Fr. Mitchell

Dahood (1922-1982) arrived; he succeeded Fr. Follet who had died in the January of that year. Hailing from Anaconda in Montana in the United States he had studied the influence of the Ugaritic language on the Hebrew text of Qohelet under the direction of W. F. Albright in Baltimore. He published the essentials of his thesis in *Biblica* 33 (1952), pp. 30-52 and 191-221. He was an enthusiastic and interesting professor and was to prove himself to be a leading light when it came to relations between Ugaritic and biblical Hebrew. – Lastly, in 1957, Fr. Luis Alonso Schökel (1920-1998) began his teaching at the Institute. Born in Madrid of an Austrian mother, he had arrived at the Institute in 1951 to follow the curriculum of the biblical faculty in it. In 1957 he had defended his doctoral thesis on the poetic style of Isaiah 1-35, but had only received the qualification of *cum laude*, with his promoter, Fr. Dyson, reproaching him for setting little value on historico-critical exegesis, as is noted in the register of the deliberations of the biblical faculty. Although breaking new ground, this thesis was not published until 1963, and in Barcelona (cf. *NRT* 86 [1964] 420-421). In 1957 Fr. Alonso Schökel was already known in Spain for his books on poetic style; in Rome he became a master of Hebrew stylistics and their hermeneutic consequences (cf. *Acta PIB* 10, 569-574).

Side by side with the professors as a research partner, a title he was to receive officially in 1970, Fr. Peter Nober (1912-1980) put together the *Elenchus Bibliographicus Biblicus*, Volumes 30 to 60, over the period from 1949 to 1979. He succeeded Fr. Emilio Bürgi (cf. *Acta PIB* 7, 300-301) who had compiled it from 1941 to 1948. Fr. Nober, a German born at Murville in the French department of Meurthe et Moselle, had arrived at the Institute in 1946 and obtained the licentiate in biblical studies in 1949. To his main work he added an *Elenchus suppletorius* in *Verbum Domini* from 1960 to 1966, which was more pastoral. To celebrate his twenty-five years of hard work in 1974 the Fr. General, and Professors M. H. Goshen-Gottstein, from Jerusalem, W. Zimmerli, from Göttingen, B. Rigaux, from Louvain, and Fr. M. Dykmans, from the Gregorian University, paid him a warm tribute which was entered in Volume 53 of that *Elenchus* (cf. *Biblica* 61 [1980] 396-397).

During that same period that saw some new professors arriving, six members of the Institute died, two of them when they were fully active. Fr. G. Messina died on June 28th, 1951 (cf. *Acta PIB* 5 264-269). Fr. U. Holzmeister on November 15th, 1953 (cf. *Bib* 35 [1954] 126-130). Fr. R. O'Callaghan met his death in a car accident in Baghdad on March 3rd, 1954 (cf. *Bib* 35 [1954] 258-259). An emeritus since 1945, Fr. A. Deimel, the last survivor of the early days – he had been among the first team of professors at the Institute in 1909 – died at the age of 89 on August 7th, 1954. On January 29th, 1956, Fr. R. Follet died suddenly (cf. *Bib* 37 [1956] 258-261). Lastly, on May 19th, 1956, Fr. J. Ruwet passed away. Right to the end he assisted his successors Fr. Leo

Studer (1952-1953), then Fr. St. Schmidt (1953-1959) in the office of the registrar at the Institute (cf. *Bib* 37 [1956] 385-386).

To these deaths that hit the Institute hard were added those of three former professors, Fr. Ed. Power died in Dublin on August 2nd, 1953 (cf. *Bib* 35 [1954] 122-126). Fr. J. Bonsirven, at Toulouse on February 12th, 1958 (cf. *Bib* 39 [1958] 265-268). And Fr. J. J. O'Rourke in New York on March 27th, 1958 (cf. *Acta PIB* 6, 195-196).

On February 16th, 1955, Br. Ignacio Padró also died (cf. *infra*).

Since 1930 Mr Michele Calbucci had helped successive librarians, Frs. Messina, Bürgi, des Places; this highly educated layman passed away on December 19th, 1954, at the age of fifty-three years (cf. *Acta PIB* 6, 31).

With all these deaths an era in the Institute's history came to an end.

The Institute's publications continued to increase. In 1926 the Catalan Brother Ignacio Padró (Manresa 1879 – Rome 1955) had come to Rome to be manager (cf. *Acta PIB* 6, 30). However, from 1930 to 1955 responsibility for that department was assumed by Fr. Birolo, then, for an interim period, by Fr. Zerwick and finally by Fr. Feldhaus; Br. Padró simply became their assistant, in charge of sending off the post. From 1956 to 1963 responsibility for this department came back to Fr. Vogt, the rector. In the meantime, Br. Rafael Sampedro, from Aragon, arrived at the Institute; he was twenty-three. At first he was assistant to Br. Padró, then he played an increasingly greater part in this department; as from 1951 his correspondence with Fr. Vogt proves the point (APIBR K-75-B). In 1956 an organization chart for the *Publication Management* was actually established, according to which there were quite a lot of lay employees.

It was with this logistic support that the first two volumes of a new series appeared: *Analecta Biblica. Investigationes scientificae in res biblicas.* We do not know at whose initiative the series was started: Fr. Vogt, who was certainly concerned with raising the level of exegesis at the Institute, or Fr. Lyonnet, who became its director in 1954 and remained so until 1982? At all events, the decision must have been taken in 1950 because the prefaces to the first two volumes are dated April 30th and June 29th 1951 respectively. The fact is that from 1952 to 1958, the period we are concerned with here, the following Volumes were published:

vol. 1: S. ZEDDA, S. J., *L'adozione a figli di Dio e lo Spirito Santo*, 1952, XXIII-190 p.

vol. 2: A. KERRIGAN, O. F. M., *St. Cyril of Alexandria Interpreter of the Old Testament*, 1952, XXIX-489 p.

vol. 3: J. DE FRAINE, S. J., *L'aspect religieux de la royauté israélite*, 1954, XL-425 p.

vol. 4: R. NORTH, *Sociology of the Biblical Jubilee*, 1954, XLVI-245 p.

vol. 5: L. MORALDI, I. M. C., *Espiazione sacrificale e riti espiatori*, 1956, XXXI-304 p.

vol. 6: J. MEHLMANN, *Natura Filii Irae. Historia interpretationis Eph. 2,3 eiusque cum doctrina Peccati Originalis nexus*, 1957, XIX-137 p.

vol. 7: J. SCHREINER, *Septuaginta-Massora des Buches der Richter*, 1957, XI-137 p.
vol. 8: St. PORÚBČAN, *Il patto nuovo in Is. 40-66*, 1958, XVI-334 p.
vol. 9: G. BOUWMAN, *Des Julian von Aeclanum Kommentar zu den Propheten Osee, Joel und Amos*, 1958, XX-154 p. + 1 pl.

Among the publications of the professors at the Institute, between 1949 and 1958 the following will be noted in particular:

– on the Bible and the Fathers:

A. VACCARI, *Scritti di erudizione e di filologia. 1. Filologia biblica e patristica*; II. *Per la storia del testo e dell'esegesi biblica.* Rome, Ed. di Storia e di Letteratura, 1952 and 1958, 396 and 518 p.

– on the Old Testament:

E. VOGT, *Os Salmos traduzidos e explicados*, São Paulo, Liga dos Estudos Biblicos, 1951, 375 p.
F. ZORELL – L. SEMKOWSKI, *Lexicon hebraicum et aramaicum Veteris Testamenti. Fasc. 9*, Roma, PIB, 1954, pp. 809-912 [this was the last fascicule of the Hebrew part].

– on the New Testament:

J. BONSIRVEN, *Théologie du Nouveau Testament* (Théologie), Paris, Aubier, 1951, 470 p.
St. LYONNET, *Les épîtres de Saint Paul aux Galates et aux Romains* (La Sainte Bible en français sous la direction de l'École Biblique de Jérusalem), Paris, Cerf, 1953, 136 p.
M. ZERWICK, *Analysis philologica Novi Testamenti graeci*, Roma, PIB, 1954, XV-608 p.
St. LYONNET, Nouvelle édition de J. HUBY, *Saint Paul. Épître aux Romains* (Verbum salutis, 10), Paris, Beauchesne, 1957, 644 p. [the appendices, pp. 513-636, are by Fr. Lyonnet].

– on orientalism:

G. MESSINA, *Diatessaron Persiano. Introduzione, testo e traduzione* (Biblica et Orientalia, 14), Roma, PIB, 1951, CXIV-389 p.
J. SMITH, *ST. IRENAEUS, Proof of the Apostolic Teaching* (Ancient Christian Writers, 16). Westminster, Md – London, 1952, 233p.
E. BERGMANN, *Codex Hammurabi. Textus primigenius* (Scripta PIB, 51), Rome, 1953, 4-52 p. [improved version of the edition by A. DEIMEL].
Ad. MASSART, *The Leiden Magical Papyrus I 343 + I 345*, Leiden, Brill, 1954, XVI-143 p. + 13 pl.
G. PATTI, *Der Samavaya im Nyaya-Vaiçesika-System. Ein Beitrag zur Erkenntnis der indischen Metaphysik und Erlösungslehre* (Scripta PIB, 109), Roma, 1955, XII-162 p.
R. KÖBERT, *Vocabularium syriacum*, Roma, PIB, 1956, VIII-216 p.

– on Greek literature:

Éd. DES PLACES, *PLATON, Œuvres complètes*, t. 10: *Lois I-VI, texte établi et traduit* (Collection des Universités de France), 2 vol., Paris, Les Belles Lettres, 1951, CCXXI-70 and 154 double pages.

Éd. DES PLACES, *DIADOQUE DE PHOTICE, Œuvres spirituelles. Introduction, texte critique. traduction et notes* (Sources chrétiennes, 5bis), Paris, Cerf, 1955, 306 p.

This list gives only a sample of the learned work of the professors at the Institute. To be more complete, one has to refer to the *Acta PIB* which draw up the list of each one's publications every year. The following facts deserve at least a special mention: 1. Fr. Messina had dedicated his *Diatessaron Persiano* to Pius XII, who thanked him for it in a handwritten reply (Doc. R. III,20). – 2. Fr. Prümm produced his *Religionsgeschichtliches Handbuch für den Raum der altchristlichen Umwelt* at the Institute in 1954 and the translation of his 1939 book *Il Cristianesimo come novità di vita*, which was done by P. Rossano, came out in Brescia in 1955. – 3. In addition to many articles, Fr. Lyonnet published the content of several courses on the Letter to the Romans for the use of his students; these notes, regularly updated and filled out, were going to have an ecumenical impact after the council. – 4. The Qumran discoveries that started in 1947 gave rise to many articles by Fr. Bea as from 1948, then by Fr. Boccaccio as from 1951, then by Fr. Vogt as from 1953, and lastly by Fr. North as from 1954. Moreover, to help students directly to get to know the texts that had been discovered, Fr. Boccaccio, in co-operation with G. Berardi, published in fascicule form the Hebrew text, along with a Latin translation, of the *Manual of Discipline* (1953), *Commentary on Habakkuk* (1955), the *War Scroll* (1956), the *Rule of the Community* (1956), the *Commentary on Nahum* (1958) and the *Commentary on Psalm 37* (1958). These fascicules were republished several times.

As can be seen, the period from 1949 to 1958 produced a lot of good work. Fr. Vogt had obviously brought in some new life into a context not always all that reassuring.

4. *The Biblical Institute celebrates the canonization of Pius X:1954.*

Bibliography

S. SCHMIDT (ed.), *San Pio X, promotore degli studi biblici, fondatore del Pontificio Istituto Biblico, a cura della direzione del Pontificio Istituto Biblico*, Rome PIB, 1955. 59 p. – Thomas BARROSSE, C. S. C., "The Unity of the Two Charities in Greek Patristic Exegesis", *Theological Studies* 15 (1954) 355-388. – Jean-Louis D'ARAGON, S. J., "Saggio di storia dell'esegesi sul testo «In tutti i modi vi mostrai che, faticando così, bisogna sostenere i deboli» (Atti 20,35)", *Scuola Cattolica* 83 (1955) 225-240. – Id., "«Il faut soutenir les faibles» (Actes 20:35)", *Sciences ecclésiastiques* 7 (1955)

5-23, 172-203. – Prosper GRECH, O.S.A., "2 Corinthians 3,17 and the Pauline Doctrine of Conversion to the Holy Spirit", *CBQ* 17 (1955) 420-437.

On June 3rd, 1951 Pius XII had beatified his predecessor Pius X and on June 29th, 1954, he canonized him. On that day the Institute, wholly associating itself with the feast, was not able to organize anything to commemorate its founder because the academic year was coming to an end, with all its examinations in June. The academic session in honour of the new saint was therefore postponed until December 1954.

On being informed of the plan Pius XII sent a handwritten letter to Fr. Vogt, the rector of the Institute (APIBR K-1-A). In it the Pope stressed the fidelity of the Institute to the Church's teaching office, as well as the need to permeate the whole of theology with the use of Scripture, so that it "may be, as it were, its soul", he wrote, following Leo XIII who had taken up the idea in his 1893 encyclical. Pius XII thus called upon the Institute to keep steadily on that course, despite the fact that among Catholics there were some who did not avoid the "novelties" nor the objections coming from a false science (cf. 1 Timothy 6,20 Vulgate) well enough; those who gainsay should therefore be exhorted and abashed "*in sound doctrine*" (Titus 1,9). The Latin text of this letter appeared in the *Acta PIB* 6, pp. 7-8, and in the booklet *San Pio X*, pp. 11-12 (cf. Bibliography, *supra*).

The commemoration of Saint Pius X took place in the main lecture hall of Institute. The morning was devoted to scholarly works showing how the Institute trained its students in the spirit of the letter *Vinea electa* whereby Pius X had founded it, and what fruit could be expected from it. Fr. Lyonnet, dean of the biblical faculty, introduced three students whose recent work, done at the Institute in the course of their studies, was then going to be read to the assembly by the authors.

The first speaker was Fr. Prosper Grech, a Maltese Augustinian. He spoke of the Pauline doctrine of conversion to the Holy Spirit, according to 2 Corinthians 3,17; it was a paper he had presented in May 1954 of which Fr. Prümm had been sponsor (cf. Bibliography, *supra*). The second was the Canadian Jesuit Jean-Louis D'Aragon, from Montreal. He summarized in Italian (cf. Bibliography, *supra*) the paper he had written the previous year, likewise, under the direction of Fr. Lyonnet; in this way he completed his preparation for the doctorate which, however, he did not start upon. He traced the early and modern exegesis of Acts 20,35 and showed that the obligation to help the "weak" in fact meant coming to the aid of the sick. Lastly, Fr. Thomas Barrosse, of the Congregation of the Holy Cross and born in New Orleans, went over the *little thesis* he had presented with a view to the licentiate in biblical studies and which Fr. Lyonnet had directed. He explained how the Greek Fathers had understood the unity of the two precepts of love of God and love of neighbour (Matt 22,37-39; cf. Bibliography, *supra*).

The solemn academic session was held in the afternoon. A number of Cardinals and prelates attended it. Fr. Janssens sat discreetly at the end of the second row. Fr. Vogt went over the history of the Institute and the part that Pius X took in it. To do so the rector had gone through the Institute's archives and, for the period going from 1899 to 1920, he had arranged them in a precise and thorough way (APIBR B-XVIII-3). That dossier has again been used by the author of this book (cf. chapters I and II). Fr. Vogt's lecture appeared in the booklet *San Pio X*, pp. 23-42. A talk by Cardinal Giacomo Lercaro (1891-1976), archbishop of Bologna, then followed. He had been at the Institute for the one year 1914-1915, and succeeded brilliantly when his bishop then recalled him to the diocese of Genoa; Italy had just declared war on Austria. Already a leading figure in the Italian episcopate, he recalled Pius X's work in favour of Scripture during the early years of his pontificate (*San Pio X*, pp. 13-22).

When the commemorative booklet *San Pio X* appeared in May 1955, the conferences given by the cardinal and the rector were accompanied by an article by Fr. Bea entitled "Blessed Pius X, biblical studies and the Biblical Institute" (pp. 43-57); this text had been read by Fr. Bea on January 16th, 1952, when the Institute had organized a solemn session on the occasion of the beatification of Pius X, a session which, however, the *Acta PIB* had not even mentioned.

5. Renewed attacks on the Institute and advice from Fr. Janssens: 1954-1958

At the end of the meeting of all the professors of the Institute on January 28th, 1955, Fr. Prešeren, Fr. General's delegate, had read some passages from the letter Pius XII had sent to Fr. Vogt on December 14th, 1954; he then insisted on fidelity to the Church's teaching office and called upon each one to be prudent in lectures and in private conversation. Now why this discreet call to order?

In a confidential note of February 14th, 1961 (APIBR L-130-A), Fr. Vogt explained that at the end of 1954 rumours against the Biblical Institute were circulating in Rome but the rector really became aware of the danger only when Cardinal Pizzardo, the prefect of the Congregation for Seminaries and Universities and Grand Chancellor of the Institute gave him, on January 27th, 1955, to be precise, a memorandum in which serious accusations against the Institute were made, in particular against Frs. Dyson and North (cf. Doc. R. III,22). This pamphlet reproached the Institute for propagating some avant-garde (*avanzate*) ideas from modern liberal Protestant criticism and placing faith in God in doubt as well as faith in future retribution in the Old Testament.

The author was Mgr. Antonino Romeo (1902-1979), *Aiutante di studio*, that is to say secretary in charge of drawing up the reports of the Congregation in question. In October, 1927, he had with difficulty obtained the licentiate from the Institute.

On March 3rd, 1955, Fr. Vogt wrote a refutation of the accusations brought against the Institute which was intended for Cardinal Pizzardo. That was not to Mgr. Romeo's liking who, on the 11th, went to complain to Fr. Bea about the disclosure of his pamphlet which he had reserved for the cardinal and the Holy Office.

On May 4th the rector went to see the cardinal again, for he had heard that Mgr. Romeo and, this time, Mgr. Igino Cecchetti, undersecretary of the Congregation, were trying to remove the two professors in question from the Institute. But the cardinal calmed him down; he had seen Pius XII the day before or the day before that and the Pope, who was aware of the rector's reply, showed himself satisfied with the Institute. The cardinal promised to silence the two "fundamentalists", as he put it, in the Congregation.

That is the context of the letter Fr. General sent to the professors of the Institute on October 3rd (Doc. R. III,21), a fatherly letter, full of encouraging sentiments and good advice, in which he urged the professors to be prudent and explained to them how he understood that: "True prudence summons us to appreciate the importance of [traditional] authorities loyally and objectively ...; for prudence must be courageous" ... And first of all, for the good Jesuit, it is a question of "*thinking with the Church*", as the *Spiritual Excercises* of St. Ignatius call it. "We do not want to be, a priori, people with avant-garde solutions, nor those with old solutions; rather, we try to love only the truth; ... at the cost of strenuous effort we acquire knowledge that has the advantage of being up to date without sacrificing soundness to being up to date. We never lose sight of the fact that scientific techniques have their limits and that they – however valuable and indispensable they may be – do not take the place of that light that comes from union with Christ and secretly puts the mind in tune with the message of the Scriptures". He ends by urging the professors to show this prudence outwardly, especially towards the students.

Still, two years later, Mgr. Romeo took up the cudgels again. In a letter of December 23rd, 1957, he accused the Institute of being responsible for a book he considered dangerous. It was the first edition of the *Introduction à la Bible*, Vol. 1, edited by André Robert and André Feuillet. It came out in 1957 and had a preface by Mgr. Jean-Julien Weber, bishop of Strasburg, who drew attention to the "novelty" of it (since "*Humani generis*" the word frightened some people). Mgr. Romeo, who had only read one hundred and thirty pages of this big book, wrote: "I know perfectly well that two pious religious at the

Pontifical Biblical Institute are responsible for this incredible volume which is stupidity of the kind that has not hitherto been forthcoming in the field of Catholic exegesis".

On January 15th, 1958, Fr. Vogt, who had got to know about this new diatribe, sent Cardinal Pizzardo a seven-page letter in which he took up the defence of the Institute as well as of the book criticized by Mgr. Romeo (APIBR L-130-A).

All the same, on February 27th, the Holy Office warned bishops and superiors of religious orders that the book, not for doctrinal but methodological and pedagogical reasons, was not suitable for teaching. But on April 21st the Congregation for Seminaries and Universities added "and for other reasons" ("*tum aliis de causis*"). Still worse, when with the help of Fr. Bea and Fr. Miller, secretary of the Biblical Commission, a second edition of this *Introduction* was being got ready, the *Osservatore Romano* of July 2nd on its front page published a fundamentalist diatribe against the 1957 edition. Scandalized and worried, a cardinal (Mgr. Ernest-Joseph van Roey of Malines?) warned the Pope in a letter of the danger that fundamentalism was causing Catholic exegetes who were following the directives of the encyclical "*Divino afflante Spiritu*". Pius XII acted on the spot by sending, on July 28th, a fine letter of support to the International Catholic Biblical Congress to be held at the Brussels International Exhibition from August 25th to the 30th (cf. *Sacra Pagina* [BETL, 12], Gembloux, Duculot, 1959, pp. 14-16).

So, right to the end, Pius XII was to be coherent, whereas certain circles at the Roman Curia were still threatening. Mgr. Romeo was still getting himself talked about.

IV. During the Pontificate of John XXIII: 1958-1963

1. The controversy about the Biblical Institute continues: 1958-1962

Attacks on the Biblical Institute started again in December 1960 with an accusation by Antonino Romeo. They brought about the exclusion of Frs. Lyonnet and Zerwick from teaching exegesis at the Institute in June 1962; this exclusion was withdrawn only in May, 1964, in Paul VI's pontificate, John XXIII having died on June 3rd, 1963. The controversy was centred on the historico-critical exegesis of the Old Testament and still more so on that of the gospels. The Biblical Commission was to take up a stance on April 21st, 1964 (*Sancta Mater Ecclesia*) and the council was to follow in its footsteps (*Dei Verbum*, 19). The dossier kept at the Institute (L-130-A-C) will be used here as source.

Bibliography

– Publications by the Institute:

Stanislas LYONNET, "Il racconto dell'Annunciazione e la maternità della Madonna", in *La Scuola cattolica* 82 (1954) 411-446 = "Le récit de l'Annonciation et la maternité Divine de la Sainte Vierge", in *L'Ami du Clergé* 66 (1956) 33-46. – Luis ALONSO SCHÖKEL, Review of: Bonaventura MARIANI, *Introductio in Libros Sacros Veteris Testamenti*, Romae, Herder, 1958, xvi-646 p., in *Biblica* 39 (1958) 499-502 and *VD* 36 (1958) 116-117. – Max ZERWICK, *Critica letteraria del N. T. nell'esegesi cattolica dei Vangeli. Conferenze tenute al Convegno Biblico di Padova 15-17 Settembre 1959*, S. Giorgio Canavese (Torino), 1959, an 18-page cyclostyled booklet. – ID., "I limiti della storicità dei Vangeli", in *Notizie della Provincia Torinese* [the Jesuit one] 2,24 (Dicembre 1959) 410-416 [summary of the lecture given at Chieri, Turin, September 29th, 1959]. – ID., "In difesa della storicità dei Vangeli" in *Bollettino della Diocesi di Treviso* 49 (1960) 362-388 – Stanislas LYONNET, "Le péché originel en Rom 5,12. L'exégèse des Pères grecs et les décrets du concile de Trente" in *Bib* 41 (1960) 325-355. – Luis ALONSO SCHÖKEL, "Dove va l'esegesi cattolica?", in *CC* 111 (1960, III) 449-460 = "Où va l'exégèse catholique?", in *L'Ami du Clergé* 71 (1961) 17-22. – [Max ZERWICK], "Pontificium Institutum Biblicum et recens libellus R.mi D.ni. A. Romeo", in *VD* 39 (1961) 3-17. – Ernesto VOGT, *Pro-memoria sugli attacchi contro il Pontificio Istituto Biblico*, [Roma, 3 January 1962], a 29-page cyclostyled booklet. – INSTITUT BIBLIQUE PONTIFICAL, *Une nouvelle attaque contre l'exégèse catholique et l'Institut Biblique Pontifical*, [Rome, 25 October 1962], a 15-page cyclostyled booklet = *Un nuovo attacco contro l'esegesi cattolica e il Pontificio Istituto Biblico*, 15 p. = *A New Attack against Catholic Exegesis and against the Pontifical Biblical Institute*, 15 p. [Other translations into German and Spanish]. – Jean-Julien WEBER, *Orientations actuelles des études exégétiques sur la vie du Christ*, Rome, Institut Biblique Pontifical, 13 November 1962, a 23-page cyclostyled booklet, reproduced in *DC* 60 (3 February 1963) 203-212 and in *Choisir* 4,39 (January 1963) 18-23. = *Present-Day Tendencies in Exegetical Studies on the Life of Christ: A Bishop's Reflections*, 21 p. [There is at least a Spanish translation of this also].

– Publications by Cardinal Bea:

Agostino Card. BEA, "Discorso" delivered on February 17th, 1960, in the presence of John XXIII on the occasion of the 50th anniversary of the Pontifical Biblical Institute, in *Bib* 41 (1960) 9-16. – ID., "Parole di chiusura del card. Agostino Bea alla Settimana biblica italiana. Roma, Pont. Istituto Biblico, 24 September 1960" in *CC* 111 (1960, IV) 291-295. – ID., *L'historicité des Évangiles* [Rome, end of November] 1962, a 59-page cyclostyled booklet = *La storicità dei Vangeli*, 59 p. = *The Historicity of the Gospels*, 69 p.

– Publications by the presidency of the Associazione Biblica Italiana:

Silverio ZEDDA, *Chiarificazioni sul convegno di Padova (a proposito di un recente articolo [di A. Romeo]*, Roma, [March] 1961, 36 p. [on the remarks made by M.

Zerwick, quoted at length, on "I limiti della storicità dei Vangeli", pp. 10-15, and "L'episodio di Cesarea di Filippo", pp. 17-19]. – ID., *Osservazioni sull'articolo «Un documento notevolissimo per l'esegesi cattolica» a firma di Francesco Spadafora in* Palestra del Clero *15 sett. 1961, pp. 969-981*, Roma, 18 October, 1961, 10 p.

– Publications criticizing the Biblical Institute:

Nicholas ASSOUAD, *Enormità scientifico-esegetiche (con Appendice)*, Napoli - S. Chiara, 1957, 24 p. [against Stanislas Lyonnet's article on the Annunciation]. – Bonaventura MARIANI, "La persona di Adamo e il suo peccato originale secondo San Paolo, Rom. 5,12", in *Divinitas* 2 (1958) 486-519. – ID., "L'Introduzione al Vecchio Testamento e le recensioni. Risposta ai RR. PP. G. Duncker O.P. e A. Schökel S.J.", in *Palestro del Clero* (1959-1960), republished in fascicule form at Rovigo, Istituto Padano di Arti Grafiche, [1960], 56 p. – Francesco SPADAFORA, "Rom. 5,12: Esegesi e riflessi dogmatici", in *Divinitas* 4 (1960) 289-298. – Antonino ROMEO, "L'enciclica «Divino afflante Spiritu» e le «opiniones novae», in *Divinitas* 4 (1960) 387-456. – Ernesto card. RUFFINI, "Literary Genres and Working Hypotheses in Recent Biblical Studies", in *The American Ecclesiastical Review* 145,6 (Dec. 1961) 362-365 [translation of the article "Generi letterari e *ipotesi di lavoro* nei recenti studi biblici" which appeared in *L'Osservatore Romano* for August 24th, 1961, p. 1]. – Fr. SPADAFORA, *Razionalismo, Esegesi Cattolica e Magistero*, Rovigo, Istituto Padano di Arti Grafiche, [1962], 36 p. – ID., *«Razionalismo, Esegesi Cattolica e Magistero» di Francesco Spadafora e «Un nuovo attacco contro l'esegesi cattolica e il Pontificio Istituto Biblico» del Pontificio Istituto Biblico*, Roma, Armellini, 1962, 15 p. – [Anonymous], *De quibusdam periculis in statu hodierno exegeseos catholicae*, Roma, Rocchi-Galeffi, Novembre 1962, 5 p.

– Reports on this controversy (cf. also Peter NOBER, *Elenchus Bibliographicus Biblicus* 43 [1962] 18*, no. 236):

Joseph A. FITZMYER. "A Recent Roman Scriptural Controversy", in *Theological Studies* 22 (1961) 426-444. – Raymond BRÉCHET, "L'affaire du «Biblique»", in *Choisir* 4,39 (January 1963) 16-18. – Giuseppe SEGALLA, "Un caso recente di comunicazione perturbata (a proposito di alcune questioni bibliche)", in *Credere oggi* 3,1 (1983) 45-48. – Angelo TAFI, *Mezzo secolo a servizio della Chiesa in Italia. Note storiche sull'Associazione Biblica Italiana*, Treviso, S. Vito, 1985, especially pp. 55-82. – Riccardo BURIGANA, *La Bibbia nel concilio. La redazione della costituzione «Dei Verbum» del Vaticano II*, Bologna, Mulino, 1998, *passim*. – François LAPLANCHE, *La crise de l'origine*, pp. 460-464.

a) Waiting for Vatican Council II to start

At the end of Pius XII's pontificate, as we have said, ultra-conservative positions held firm. As regards the Old Testament, they appeared in an introduction to it, published in 1958, by the Franciscan Bonaventura Mariani, for whom Moses was indeed the main author of the Pentateuch, and similarly for the other books. His big book in Latin was critically reviewed in December

1958 by Fr. Luis Alonso Schökel in *Bib* and by Fr. Duncker, O. P., in the periodical *Angelicum* 36 (1959), pp. 51-62. Fr. Mariani replied in 1959 and at the beginning of 1960 in the periodical *Palestra del Clero*, then gathered his replies together in a booklet of 56 p. The difficulties arose mainly out of the decrees of the Biblical Commission issued at the beginning of the 20th century, concerning which, however, Fr. A. Miller had explained in 1955 that on the level of critical exegesis, they could be considered as no longer binding.

In 1958 Fr. Santino Raponi, a Redemptorist and a former student of the Biblical Institute, had published an article entitled "Rom. 5,12-21 e il peccato originale" in the Lateran review *Divinitas* 2, pp. 520-559, in which he was especially influenced by Fr. Lyonnet's work. This provided the opportunity for Fr. Mariani in 1958 and Mgr. Francesco Spadafora in 1960 to publish some strong criticisms of Fr. Lyonnet in the same review. By way of reply, the latter took up the subject again in December 1960 in *Biblica*. Contrary to what his detractors claimed, Fr. Lyonnet had spelt it out back in 1955 that the exegesis of Rom 5,12 was not freely open to interpretation, since the council of Trent had given the dogmatic interpretation of it: the verse concerned original sin; moreover, all Fr. Lyonnet's efforts were aimed at refuting the exegesis offered by Pelagius; to do so, in line with the councils of Carthage and Trent, he showed that the Greek and Latin Fathers, despite different approaches, actually saw the doctrine of original sin in this verse.

Meanwhile, on August 27th of the same year, Fr. Alonso Schökel had published twelve pages in *La Civiltà Cattolica* entitled "Dove va l'esegesi cattolica?". Fr. Vaccari had approved them but quickly regretted it. The author of the article showed how, since the beginning of the the 20th century, exegesis had been on the move and how, despite some excesses the Church's teaching office had not failed to point out, the Popes, especially Pius XII, had encouraged biblical scholars to go ahead; with time, thanks to new studies, there was a move away from a rigid position to an attitude that was more open to scholarly research.

It was then that A. Romeo took up his pen again in December 1960. He had Fr. Alonso Schökel's article chiefly in mind, accusing him in polemical language of paying little attention to Tradition. Romeo was trying to set the author of the article at variance with Cardinal Bea and even with the teaching of Pius XII; he also openly criticized Fr. Jean Levie for his book that had become a classic; it was on *La Bible parole humaine et message de Dieu* (Louvain, 1958; English translation: *The Bible, Word of God in Words* of *Men*, New York, 1962), he then reserved the same fate for Fr. Zerwick. In September 1959, the latter had given a series of lectures at Padua in the course of which he had expounded the interpretation of Matt 16,16-18 proposed by A. Vögtle: compared with Mark's text, Matthew's adds a beatitude (16,17) and especially the promise of the primacy of Peter (16,18-19); it does not seem that that promise can be linked with the episode at Caesarea Philippi, which does not mean that it does not keep its historical value, even if the pre-Matthean tradition has kept it without a precise context. In any case, Fr. Zerwick wrote at the bottom of page 7 in his manuscript that: "the promise itself regains all the probability, or rather the certainty, of being historical". But for Romeo the Vögtle-Zerwick reading denied the historicity of the promise of the primacy of Peter!

The Biblical Institute reacted with an article that appeared in June 1961 in its periodical *Verbum Domini*, on pp. 3-17, in which it refuted Romeo's accusations point by point. Fr. Vogt immediately sent an offprint to John XXIII's private secretary, Mgr. Loris Capovilla, who thanked him for it on February 24th. At the beginning of that same month of February, Fr. Vogt made contact by letter with Mgr. Antonio Piolanti, the director of the review *Divinitas*, to ask if he could exercise the right to reply. When faced with a refusal from Mgr. Piolanti, Fr. Vogt circulated a double typewritten document on February 6th: "The Pontifical Biblical Institute and a recent article by Mgr. Romeo. Memorandum", with two pages introducing a "Detailed exposition of the defamatory statements against the Pontifical Biblical Institute", covering eight pages. Still in February 1961, Fr. Lyonnet, for his part, wrote thirteen pages for internal use on "Mgr. Romeo's article and its historical context" in which he recalled the earlier events that have been mentioned here in previous pages. Finally, on February 11th, Fr. Zedda, the president of the Italian Biblical Association, sent professors of Holy Scripture in Italy a 35-page refutation of Mgr. Romeo's article, especially to defend Fr. Zerwick against the accusations brought against him for what he said at the meeting in Padua; to make things clear, Fr. Zedda reproduced in full the very terms Fr. Zerwick had used at Padua. Was the affair going to calm down, then? One might have thought so, because, on February 23rd, 1961, John XXIII appointed Fr. Vogt a consultor of the Theological Commission in preparation for the council (*AAS* 53 [1961] 183): this was manifestly a mark of the pontiff's trust in the Biblical Institute and its working methods. On July 12th, 1960, Fr. Vaccari had already been made a consultor to the central Commission and in September 1962 he was to be named as an expert at the council (*AAS* 52 [1960] 797; 54 [1962] 784).

On June 20th, 1961, in agreement with the Cardinals of the Biblical Commission, the Holy Office issued a "Monitum" calling for prudence in the matter of the historicity of the words and deeds of Christ according to the New Testament (*AAS* 51 [1961] 507). Whom did this text have in mind? Perhaps Jean Steinmann, from Paris, for his *Vie de Jésus* which was placed on the Index on June 26th (*ibid.*, 506-507). This book had, in fact, so scandalized Cardinal Ernesto Ruffini (1888-1967) that he reported it to Cardinal Ottaviani, the secretary to the Holy Office, in a letter dated May 9th, 1961 (published by F. M. Stabile in *Cristianesimo nella storia* 11,1 [1990] 115). At all events, it is certain that, on August 24th, 1961, Cardinal Ruffini published an article on the front page of *L'Osservatore Romano* entitled "Literary genres and *working hypotheses* in recent biblical studies", which was later translated into English and Spanish. Now, the Cardinal wrote:

> Parlare di ipotesi di lavoro, che nel caso nostro sono palliate negazioni della storicità, a riguardo per es. dell'Annunciazione dell'Arcangelo Gabriele a Maria Santissima (*Luc.* 1,26-38) e della promessa del primato a San Pietro (*Matt.* 16,17-19) fatte derivare da imitazioni di precedenti esemplari o da maturazioni posteriori del pensiero cristiano, è capovolgere l'esegesi cattolica e un attentato eretical contro verità ritenute sempre – a cominciare dai Primi Padri della Chiesa – corrispondenti a realtà storiche.

> [To talk about working hypotheses, which in our case are watered-down denials of historicity, concerning, for example, the Archangel Gabriel's Annunciation to Most Holy Mary (*Luke* 1,26-38) and the promise of the primacy made to Saint Peter (*Matt* 16,17-19) as deriving from imitations of earlier patterns or from later developments of Christian thought, is to overturn Catholic exegesis and is a heretical attack on truths always considered – starting with the first Fathers of the Church – to correspond to historical reality.]

Cardinal Tardini, the Secretary of State, had died on July 30th and Cardinal Cicognani had succeeded him. Cardinal Ruffini wrote to the latter on September 7th: he reported to him that his predecessor, a few days before dying, had told him that, in September, two or three professors from the Biblical Institute were to be replaced because of the trouble they were causing (*CrSt* 11,1 [1990] 116)! Be that as it may, in his article of August 24th, Cardinal Ruffini, without the slightest doubt, had Fr. Lyonnet and Fr. Zerwick in mind. We have just seen what the latter's position was, while Fr. Lyonnet was being criticized for a lecture he had given at the Biblical Institute on January 10th, 1954!

To celebrate the centenary of the dogmatic definition of the Immaculate Conception, Pius XII had decreed that 1954 would be a "Marian year". The Biblical Institute associated itself with this by holding three lectures (*Acta PIB* 5, 398). Fr. Lyonnet had given the first in French on "the divine motherhood of the H. Virgin according to the story of the Annunciation". This brilliant study was so appreciated that the speaker was invited to give it again at the Mariological congress held in Rome, at the Lateran in October-November; it was published twice in French and in two different versions in Italian. So what did Fr. Lyonnet say? Despite the cautious opinions of Juan Maldonado, the "prince of exegetes" (1597) and Fr. Lagrange (1921), he had shown that the title "son of God" given by the angel in Luke 1,35 must really indicate the divinity of Jesus; this verse actually starts by stating that Mary will become the place of the divine Presence, which Lyonnet explained in the light of the Old Testament Texts that speak of the cloud "covering" the sacred Tent (cf.

the notes in the *Traduction Œcuménique de la Bible*). Now this lecture, which had greatly pleased Fr. Bea, was criticized in 1957 by the Franciscan Nicolas Assouad who had read only the references to Maldonado and Lagrange in it! And here in 1961 Cardinal Ruffini attacked Lyonnet's argument (*"made to derive from earlier models"*). Yet it was only in October 1961 that Frs. Lyonnet and Zerwick learnt that the Holy Office was requiring their removal (Doc. R. III,23).

Meanwhile, on September 15th, Fr. Spadafora published a virulent and slanderous article in the *Palestro del Clero* entitled "Un documento notevolissimo per l'esegesi cattolica" in which, misusing the "Monitum" from the Holy Office which was issued in June, he hit out against anything that smacked of novelty in exegesis, especially the lecture Fr. Zerwick had given at Padua in 1959 on Matthew 16,16-19 (no. 4), nor did he fail to praise the diatribe from Mgr. Romeo that appeared in 1960. One month later, on October 18th, Fr. Zedda answered him with a refutation extending over ten pages addressed to professors of Holy Scripture in Italy. This reply, precise and correct as it was, did not prevent Spadafora from republishing his defamatory pages in December in the *Monitor Ecclesiasticus*, the semi-official organ of the Vatican Curia.

No more than that was needed for Fr. Vogt, on January 3rd, 1962, to put out a 29-page booklet entitled "Memorandum on the attacks against the Pontifical Biblical Institute", the first pages of which have been quoted above (Doc. R. III,22). This booklet carefully retraces the attacks of which the Biblical Institute had been the target from 1954 until December 1961; five supplements dealt essentially with Mgr. Romeo's pages that had appeared in December 1960: Fr. Miller, on behalf of the Consultors of the Biblical Commission, and Cardinal Achille Liénart, from Lille, restated their support for the Institute; then the rector took up the defence of Frs. Levie, Zerwick and Alonso Schökel, showing how lacking in objectivity Romeo's accusations were; he then pointed out similarity of ideas between Romeo and the famous Cohenel in 1941 and ended with some quotations from documents by Pius XII and John XXIII that encourage learned research in exegesis, joined to fidelity to the Church's teaching office.

This is the context in which the beginning of the Lyonnet – Zerwick affair is set: these two professors at the Biblical Institute were banned from teaching exegesis at it. Two reports of the events, one by Fr. Lyonnet, the other by Fr. Vogt, are kept in the Institute's archives (Doc. R. III,23-24); they date from September 1963 and seem to be written for Fr. Roderick A. F. MacKenzie who, as rector, had succeeded Fr. Vogt on May 31st, 1963, three days before the death of John XXIII (*Acta PIB* 6, 479).

It will be recalled that, on August 24th, 1961, Cardinal Ruffini had implicitly criticized Frs. Lyonnet and Zerwick in his article in *L'Osservatore*

Romano. At the beginning of October 1961, Fr. General Janssens, through his Vicar, Fr. John L. Swain, informed Fr. Vogt that the Holy Office required that Frs. Lyonnet and Zerwick should no longer teach exegesis at the Institute. But Fr. General declined to suspend the two professors without knowing the reasons why; in his opinion, it was up to the Holy Office to fulfil its responsibilities; furthermore, Fr. General suggests to Fr. Vogt that the two Fathers should not start their classes before receiving an answer from the Pope to whom he had sent a "memorandum". Fr. Lyonnet was due to continue his exegesis of the letter to the Romans (chap. 8 *et seqq.*) and Fr. Zerwick was offering a course on the first two chapters of John's gospel (*Acta PIB* 6, 383 and 386). A pretext was therefore found for delaying the start of these two courses: Fr. Lyonnet was declared unwell and went "to convalesce" at Fiuggi! On October 23rd, Fr. General suggested that these two exegetes should declare in class that they had never held the doctrines they were accused of and about which they had not received any details. The suggestion was accepted and carried out, but to no avail. Finally, on November 23rd, Fr. General passed on a new decision from the Holy Office to Fr. Vogt: Lyonnet and Zerwick could start teaching during the current academic year 1961-1962, but would have to be replaced in the course of the year.

At the beginning of January 1962 Fr. Lyonnet had a long interview with the Fr. General, who concluded by saying: "Father, I have nothing to reproach you with". Neither one nor the other knew exactly what the complaints of the Holy Office were. A month later, Fr. Janssens was received by John XXIII, but this matter, it seems, was not dealt with on that occasion. The Pope, in fact, like a refined diplomat, let things take their course and did not want to change anything in the Holy Office's decision; as Fr. Lyonnet was to write to Cardinal Marella on January 15th, 1964, when he was still suspended: "I am quite convinced that the Holy Father intended in this way mainly to satisfy certain persons and thereby to prevent them from opposing other, far more important measures".

However, in mid-May 1962, people at the Holy Office and the Secretariat of State were surprised that the two persons accused had not been replaced and the Fr. General mentioned this to Fr. Vogt, who pointed out to him that the school year was coming to an end and a change would not have much sense. Then again, on May 23rd, Fr. Janssens heard that the matter was now in the hands of the Biblical Commission. But the latter had other fish to fry, because it had been entrusted with drawing up a text on the whole question of the Bible in the Church.

In fact, in May 1962, John XXIII wanted to get this Biblical Commission going again (cf. GIOVANNI XXIII, *Lettere 1958-1963*, L. F. Capovilla (ed.), Roma, Storia e Letteratura, 1978, pp. 536-537); so in May and July he goes ahead with new appointments, but no one from the Biblical Institute (*Bib* 43 [1962] 110 and 553). It seems that the basic ideas of the text that was to become the Instruction *"Sancta Mater Ecclesia"* in April 1964 came from Mgr. Lucien Cerfaux, from Louvain, that their first being put into shape is due to Fr. Béda Rigaux, O.F.M., also from Louvain, and that very soon Professor Rudolf Schnackenburg, from Würzburg, and Fr. Xavier Léon-Dufour, S.J., from Fourvière, Lyons, had worked together on successive drafts of the document (cf. F. LAPLANCHE, *La crise de l'origine*, p. 476; Xavier LÉON-DUFOUR, *Dieu se laisse chercher. Dialogue d'un bibliste avec Jean-Maurice de Montremy*, Paris, Plon, 1995, p. 90).

Finally, on June 2nd, 1962, Fr. Vogt asked Fr. General if Fathers Lyonnet and Zerwick could teach exegesis during the next academic year, 1962-1963, but Fr. Janssens replied in the negative. So Fr. Zerwick taught only New Testament Greek, while Fr. Lyonnet, still remaining dean of the biblical faculty, continued to publish in the field of exegesis, but did not teach anything during the first semester; during the second, he left Rome on March 14th, 1963, and returned there on June 10th, according to the house diary (APIBR A-11); in Jerusalem he visited the country and gave a minor course on the *Codex Neofiti I* from the Vatican Library, about which Professor A. Díez Macho, from Barcelona, had discovered seven years earlier that it contained a complete Palestinian Targum of the Pentateuch (cf. *Acta PIB* 6, 464).

b) At the beginning of the council: October-November 1962

The council opened on October 11th, 1962. The discussion on the schema on the liturgy started on the 22nd. On November 14th, they moved on to the schema *"de fontibus revelationis"*, but, in the face of sharp criticism, it was withdrawn on the 20th by John XXIII, following a significant vote by the council Fathers. However, as from before the council and during its early weeks, bishops and experts from various quarters got down to preparing some counter-projects, which also concerned the question of biblical exegesis (cf. Burigana, *La Bibbia nel concilio*, pp. 88-97, 105-128). On November 8th there was a meeting, held at the Biblical Institute itself, of Belgian, French and Swiss experts seeking to formulate how to oppose this schema *"de fontibus"*, the discussion of which was about to start (Burigana, p. 120). This, then, is the climate of tension and feverish activity in which the following documents and events have to be placed.

1. On October 14th, Fr. Spadafora was authorized to distribute to the Italian episcopate his printed booklet called *Razionalismo, Esegesi cattolica e Magistero* (Burigana, p. 106); he introduced it with these sentences:

Dalla fine del 1960 [cioè dall'articolo di Mons. Romeo], il campo biblico ha manifestato in publico il malessere che lo affliggeva da circa una quindicina di anni.
Si tratta della tentata immissione nella Chiesa (o 'semplice accettazione') del «criticismo» razionalista: evoluzionismo wellhauseniano e sistema del Gunkel per il Vecchio Testamento e *Formgeschichte* per il Nuovo.

Tentativo – prescindo dalle intenzioni – preparato tramite la formazione culturale dei giovani, nell'Istituto ufficiale a ciò destinato.

[From the end of 1960 [i. e. from the article by Mgr. Romeo], the biblical field has shown in public the malaise it had been suffering from for about fifteen years.

It is a matter of trying to introduce into the Church (or 'simply accepting') rationalist «criticism»: Wellhausenian evolutionism and Gunkel's system for the Old Testament and *Formgeschichte* for the New.

An attempt – I prescind from intentions – prepared by the cultural training of the young, in the official Institute destined for that purpose.]

At the bottom of the page the author asks: 1. that the system of *Formgeschichte* explicitly receive an express condemnation, 2. that "all the necessary steps be taken *so that the young priests who come to study* [in Rome] *Holy Scripture do not lose everything they have learnt in theology*, but be trained according to the directives of the Holy See".

The booklet contained three articles. The first reproduced what the author had published on September 15th, 1961, concerning the "Monitum" issued by the Holy Office the previous month of June (cf. *supra*). The second attacked an article by the Italian biblical scholar Francesco Festorazzi that had appeared in 1961 in the periodical *Rivista Biblica* on Genesis 2-3: Spadafora refused to see in it, as Festorazzi did, "a story of a mythical literary genre of a sapiential type"; the reason was that then the historicity of the story would be placed in doubt. The third, "Criticism and the gospels" outspokenly explained what, in the eyes of the author, *Formgeschichte* was: Spadafora singled out the initiators Dibelius and Bultmann and their theories, then he accused Fr. Léon-Dufour of following them without any qualification.

2. On October 25th, the Biblical Institute distributed a 15-page reply to Spadafora among the council Fathers: "A new attack against Catholic exegesis and against the Pontifical Biblical Institute". In it were mentioned the calumnies against Frs. Zerwick and Léon-Dufour, the latter having just been appointed a consultor of the Biblical Commission. What the calumniator refused to see is that, like Thomas Aquinas using Aristotle, one can use *Formgeschichte* without assuming its unacceptable philosophical and sociological presuppositions. Let us note that Fr. Lagrange had already felt this (*RB* 43 [1934] 303) and Fr. Pierre Benoit, O.P, had shown it in 1946 in the same periodical; now, Fr. Léon-Dufour was explicit about these reservations.

3. Spadafora retorted in a 15-page pamphlet distributed at the council at the beginning of November. In it he went over some gossip, about Fr. Dyson, for example, alluded, at the bottom of p. 8, to the ban placed by the Holy Office on Frs. Lyonnet and Zerwick, and asked why the Biblical Institute did not indicate a monograph that exposed *Formgeschichte* in an acceptable sense (p. 12),

4. The Biblical Institute took him at his word; on November 13th it republished for the council Fathers an article by Mgr. Jean-Julien Weber (1888-1981), a Sulpician and former student of the Institute in 1913-1914 and bishop of Strasburg at the time. Mgr. Weber had first of all published it at the beginning of October in the *Bulletin ecclésiastique du diocèse de Strasbourg*. With the title "Orientations actuelles des études exégétiques", the article introduced *Formgeschichte*, and then showed what was acceptable in it, on the one hand, and, on the other, what it should be criticized for. Without rejecting it, the bishop called for discernment and modesty since, like any method, it is always perfectible and does not answer all the questions.

5. The Biblical Institute still wanted to cause a sensation. This was on November 22nd with the defence of the thesis by Fr. Norbert Lohfink, S.J. On that day the council had not held a general congregation in the morning and, the day before, notice had been given to the council Fathers that the Pope was withdrawing the schema *"de fontibus revelationis"*. Fr. Lohfink's doctoral thesis was on "the great commandment" in Deuteronomy 5–11. The council of the biblical faculty had met on October 28th to hear the opinion of the promoter, Fr. William L. Moran, and of the second reader, Fr. Alonso Schökel. The minutes of this council's deliberations mention their very positive reactions. The defence was scheduled for November 8th, but *"propter adiuncta specialia"*, as the minutes note, it took place on Thursday the 22nd in the late afternoon. The council Fathers were invited to attend this solemn academic act which, in the circumstances, would be held in the atrium of the Gregorian University. Several cardinals apologized for absence, including Cardinal Montini. However, twelve cardinals were present, among whom were B. Alfrink, A. Bea, J. Döpfner, J. Frings, P.-E. Léger and E. Tisserant. About four hundred bishops and many well-wishers were also seen; among the latter was the young professor Joseph Ratzinger, an expert at the council; he recalled it on November 3rd, 2006, on the visit he paid as pontiff to the University. The board, presided over by Cardinal Pizzardo, the Grand Chancellor of the Institute, consisted of Frs. Vogt, the rector, Moran, Alonso Schökel, Ignace de la Potterie and Pavlovský. Fr. Lohfink first gave a summary of the contents of the thesis in Latin (cf. *VD* 41 [1963] 73-77). Then came the discussion with the members of the board. At the end of the session the candidate received the highest honours. Some photos, which were to immortalize the event, are kept in the Institute's archives; three of them were published recently in the periodical *Vinea electa*, a bulletin for former students at the Institute (6 [2006] 20-21). The thesis itself was published in its entirety in 1963 in the series *Analecta Biblica*, no. 20, with the title: *Das Hauptgebot. Eine Untersuchung literarischer Einleitungsfragen zu Dtn 5–11*.

6. Lastly, in the closing days of November, perhaps on the 26th (cf. Burigana, p. 276, note 48), Cardinal Bea distributed a brochure he had written on "the Historicity of the Gospels" at the council. The text, available in several languages, was in answer to a request by many council Fathers. But it was really published only in 1964 in *La Civiltà Cattolica*, by way of explanation of the Instruction "*Sancta Mater Ecclesia*" that had been published a little earlier by the Biblical Commission. Other editions in various languages also appeared in the years to follow.

Right from the start, but discreetly, in a note, the cardinal wrote, concerning the recent arguments: "it is known that certain people were seriously lacking in justice and charity". What he says in the brochure was meant to be objective and calm. It contained two chapters written in a simple and very intelligible style. The first one showed that, contrary to what the initiators of *Formgeschichte* stated, early Christian communities had a sense of history and were concerned to transmit in all its truth what had happened during the life of Jesus: they invented nothing nor did they go in for syncretism with pagan myths; for them, faith and history were not opposed to each other. The second article dealt with difficulties arising out of differences between the synoptic gospels, as in the case of the Our Father, the beatitudes and Jesus' words about the eucharist. The cardinal reduces these difficulties with some remarks of a psychological nature, all from common sense: each one has his way of recounting an event, yet without lying or going wrong. What must be determined, therefore, is what was the intention of the evangelist, his point of view and the literary genre he is using. That, along with the conviction that the charism of inspiration was shielding him from all error.

The last three steps taken by the Biblical Institute and Cardinal Bea, as well as the withdrawal of the controversial schema, had the effect of calming things down. There was indeed a last pamphlet printed in November in bad Latin, probably by Spadafora: "*De quibusdam periculis in statu hodierno exegeseos catholicae*", then, in the same tone, a letter addressed to the Pope on November 24th by nineteen cardinals, published by Stabile (pp. 124-126). The first session of the council ended peacefully on December 8th. On the 20th, Fr. Vogt wrote to Fr. Giovanni Canfora (1920-2003), O.M.I., the secretary of the Italian Biblical Association, concerning Spadafora:

With his attacks he has contributed a lot to arousing new sympathetic reactions and even getting bishops, who before now had not had time or opportunity to do so, interested in studying biblical questions. ... On the whole we can thank God for what happened at the council. Perhaps it is clearly and irrevocably the beginning of a new era in the history of the Church, an era of Catholicity and universality (quoted by Tafi, pp. 81-82).

Still, the fact remains that Frs. Lyonnet and Zerwick had not got their teaching posts in exegesis back.

2. *What the Biblical Institute did for the council: 1960-1962*

a) The Biblical Institute's "*votum*": April 24th, 1960

Bibliography

"Pontificium Institutum Biblicum", in Acta et documenta concilio oecumenico Vaticano II apparanda. Series I (Antepraeparatoria). Volumen IV. Studia et vota Universitatum et facultatum ecclesiasticarum et catholicarum. Pars I. Universitates et facultates in Urbe, 1. Typis polyglottis vaticanis, 1961, pp. 121-136.

While the controversy against the Biblical Institute was going on, the latter was taking up a position on some of the problems the council had to tackle.

The most important position taken up was the "*votum*" or proposal that Fr. Vogt sent to Cardinal Tardini on April 24th, 1960, in the name of practically all the professors at the Institute. This fourteen-page typed document had been asked for from the Institute, on July 18th, 1959, as it had been from all ecclesiastical or Catholic universities and faculties throughout the world, including Rome. Cardinal Tardini, who presided over the pre-preparatory council Commission, had asked in particular that answers or proposals should reach the Commission by April 1960. On April 27th Mgr. Pericle Felici, the Commission's secretary, sent Fr. Vogt an acknowledgement of receipt (APIBR K-7-B). The Biblical Institute's text was published at the Vatican in 1961.

This "*votum*" had been worked out on a collegial basis and the signatories were Frs. Vogt, the rector, Vaccari, the vice-rector, Lyonnet, the dean of the biblical faculty, Pohl, the dean of the oriental faculty, as well as Frs. Alonso Schökel, Boccaccio, Dahood, de la Potterie, Köbert, Martin, McCool, Moran, Novotný, the registrar at the Institute, Patti, Pavlovský, des Places, Simon, Smith and Zerwick. Both faculties had therefore worked together on the composition of the document. Only the absence of Fr. Prümm's name among the signatories comes as a surprise.

This document comprises a preliminary "*votum*", followed by five doctrinal proposals (pp. 1-10) and four disciplinary proposals (pp. 11-14). The whole is signed by Fr. Vogt in his capacity as rector.

Here is the translation of that preliminary proposal:

Since the Sovereign Pontiff John XXIII, in announcing the ecumenical council, also wished to promote the unity of all Christians, and since, moreover, the study and reading of the Sacred Books greatly contributes to concord and unity among Christians, given that Holy Scripture is recognized in common by all Christians as the word of God [*verbum Dei*], *it is requested* that the Council again and with all its power recommend the study and use of Holy Scripture.

To this end the Institute puts forward five doctrinal proposals:

1ˢᵗ proposal. Show that, far from constituting two sources of revelation, Scripture and Tradition have as common source the Gospel proclaimed by Christ and preached by the apostles. The text also puts forward some items concerning the reciprocal relations of priority between them both: being inspired, scripture is read "in the Church".

2ⁿᵈ proposal. The importance of faith in the work of salvation: this doctrine, neglected these days, is worth restating: according to St. Paul, justification and justice imply the infused gift of faith.

3ʳᵈ proposal. The efficacy of God's word: this doctrine, frequent in the New Testament (cf. for example, 1 Tim 3,16-17), has been blurred since the council of Trent because of controversies with Protestants.

4ᵗʰ proposal. The historicity of the Gospels. Here is the translation of this *"Votum"*:

1. That the council recall those truths of the Catholic faith that must govern the interpretation of the gospels and the defence of their historical reliability [*fidei historicae*], namely:
   a. Christian faith, as it is manifested in the creeds themselves, is based on divine facts that took place in history, especially on the mysteries of the incarnation, the life, death and resurrection of Jesus.
      Hence any exegesis that would deny or cast doubt on the historicity of these facts cannot be accepted by a Catholic.
   b. Revelation was not complete before the end of the apostolic age.
      Hence it would be rash to state that the Gospels must be excluded from the activity of the Holy Spirit through which he explained Christian revelation more clearly and more explicitly than did Jesus and applied it to the needs of the Church.
   c. Our four gospels, being inspired, are endowed with inerrancy, which has to be reconciled with the above mentioned historicity.
      That is why any conception of historicity that, either by excess or default, makes that reconciliation impossible is necessarily wrong.
2. That the council declare, after recommending these principles, that it is the function of Catholic exegetes, under the guidance of the Church's teaching office, to determine further what kind of history must be ascribed to both the Gospels as a whole or every particular passage.

Some long explanations of these proposals follow:

1. Even if today we know better how the Gospels were born, the council should not go into details but recall the immutable principles of Church doctrine indicated in paragraphs a, b and c. About a, we recall that, in the Gospels, the historical genre is not what it is today and that it has many forms. About b, it is to be noted that a less rigid understanding of historical genre makes it possible to see, even in the Gospels, a deeper and more explicit

interpretation of the words and deeds of Jesus, corresponding to the needs of the Church. About c, it is shown that the required reconciliation is possible if account is taken of the sacred writer's intention: no one can be accused of error, except in what he actually states, and to know what he states, the literary genres he uses have to be analyzed. That goes for the evangelists, too.

2. In these matters, let the council have confidence in the exegetes, as Pius XII requested in 1943 (cf. *EB* 565).

5th proposal. Antisemitism must be avoided. In 1959, the Vatican had already modified some liturgical texts along these lines. The Institute not only disapproves of any expression that accuses or condemns the Jewish people for the death of Jesus, among other things, but it also recalls St. Paul's hope in Romans 11.

The four disciplinary proposals are as follows:

1st proposal. That the council confirm the norms given by Pius XII in his encyclical "*Divino afflante Spiritu*" for research into, and the interpretation of, Scripture.

2nd proposal. That the council declare that the decrees of the Biblical Commission at the beginning of the 20th century leave exegetes a healthy freedom of research, under the vigilance of the Church's teaching office, in those matters that are not, either immediately or mediately, connected with faith or morals. This was asking that Fr. Miller's letter of 1955 be made official.

3rd proposal. That no Roman Congregation publish anything about the Bible without previously asking the opinion of the Biblical Commission.

4th proposal. Before impugning the reputation of an author of whom a book has been censured for its doctrine, the indications given by Benedict XIV in 1753 in his constitution "*Sollicita et provida*" should be followed, that is to say: the author should be able to defend himself, the Bishop who allowed the publication should be heard and the author should know the precise reasons, not just the general ones, for the ban imposed on him. This was alluding to the methods of the Holy Office. Let us note that in 1960 Frs. Lyonnet and Zerwick were not yet being investigated, but, when they were, they did not know why and were not to have the chance to defend themselves!

These proposals from the Institute are impressive on account of the seriousness and serenity of their content and explanations. Many of them were to find an echo at the council. They also show what the state of mind of the teaching staff at the Biblical Institute was like just before the council, as well as its concept of exegetical research. The openness brought by the council is already there in those proposals.

b) During the council's first session: October-December 1962

The professors at the Biblical Institute were very discreet in their dealings with the council Fathers. The Institute's archives provide only three cyclostyled documents and only one typewritten one. All are in Latin.

Fr. Giovanni Caprile, in his survey of *Il concilio Vaticano II. Il primo periodo 1962-1963*, Rome, La Civiltà Cattolica, 1968, mentions two of them (p. 162, note 6), which, coming from the Biblical Institute, were distributed at the council and on which further remarks can be provided here. The first, of which the author is unknown, is called "*Iudicium generale de schemate I de fontibus revelationis*"; it covers three pages and a note in pencil added in the margin of the first: "Opinion of the Indonesian Bishops. Nov. 1962"; this note, probably by Fr. Vogt, corresponds in fact to the agreed statement of those bishops which was delivered in a speech by Mgr. G. Manek, SVD (Caprile, pp. 159-160: 14 November); the judgement is negative, but some positive proposals are put forward for a new schema. The second document mentioned by Caprile has as title: "*De Fide Historica Evangeliorum*" and is two pages long; in the margin the same hand added "de la Pott[erie]"; the author wants to show this: "Christian faith is based essentially on historical facts which are recorded in the four gospels and, besides, the gospel account of those events was worked out in the Church, under the guidance of the Holy Spirit, so as to manifest their true meaning"; this was the position the Institute had defended in its "*votum*"

The Roman archives of the Institute (L-130-A) contain two other documents. The first of them is called: "*De Historicitate Evangeliorum*" and contains seven pages; a marginal note similar to the others says: "Fr. Zerwick Eppis. [sic] SVD. Nov. 1962"; ascribing it to this author must be correct, because the contents of this document goes over some analyses Fr. Zerwick had done in 1959, especially on the death of Judas according to the gospels; the author shows the subtleties of all literary analysis, then, excluding any attempt to reconcile the gospel account with historical fact, insists on the importance of knowing what was the evangelists' intention. The last text is entitled: "*De schemate de Fontibus (praes. cap. 2 et 5) et doctrina Pii XII*"; this time the marginal note is by the author of these three pages: "(Fr. Lyonnet) for Card. Liénart and Léger"; in Fr. Lyonnet's opinion the schema must be rewritten in another spirit; referring to the encyclicals "*Divino afflante Spiritu*" and "*Humani generis*", the Father stresses in his first paragraph that the sacred writer's intention must be kept clearly in sight; now, he adds, despite the repeated objections of some rare biblical scholars present, including Fr. Vogt, the preparatory Commission deliberately rejected this doctrine, finding it "very dangerous"; it was only the central Commission (of which Fr. Vaccari was a member) that made a passing allusion to it. Fr. Lyonnet's second paragraph deals with literary genres; there again the proposed text (no.

13 in it) misrepresents Pius XII's teaching and just keeps to commonplaces used in the past (history, poetry, instruction, law etc.), without realizing that it is precisely when it comes to history that several literary genres have to be distinguished. In its fifth chapter the schema deals with the Vulgate (no. 25) in such a way that recourse to the original texts of the Bible seems secondary. Lastly, with regard to exegetes, the schema has nothing but suspicion, whereas Pius XII encouraged scholarly research.

These documents show how the Institute was not content with refuting the accusations brought against it but also worked to enlighten the council Fathers about what was at stake in the debate that was to lead to the dogmatic constitution "*Dei Verbum*".

3. *A jubilee, a congress and a double* Festschrift: *1959-1962*

In the meantime, the Institute took advantage of three opportunities that occurred for making known what genuine Catholic exegesis was.

1. In May, 1959, the Biblical Institute celebrated the fiftieth anniversary of its foundation. It did so in two ways. First of all, as in 1934 for its twenty-fifth anniversary, the periodical *Biblica* 40 (1949) published a series of articles on the Old Testament (pp.133-567) and on the New (pp. 569-983). These articles were later reproduced in the collection *Analecta Biblica* in volumes 10 and 11, and to them was added volume 12 devoted to the ancient East. This combined work, which came out in the course of the jubilee year, bore the title *Studia Biblica et Orientalia*. As Fr. Lyonnet had suggested at a meeting of professors held on November 10th, 1957, the main Catholic exegetes of renown, including many former students of the Institute, wrote articles for the first two volumes. These volumes were arranged in different ways. For the Old Testament, the thirty-two articles were divided into five chapters: textual criticism, literary questions, hermeneutics, biblical exegesis and theology, lastly, archaeology and institutions. For the New Testament, twenty-nine articles were divided according to the order of the canon, from Matthew's gospel to the Apocalypse. In the volume devoted to the ancient East, the alphabetical order of the names of the thirty authors was followed. Fourteen professors from the Institute, the majority, contributed a study to this vast publication. However, it had no index of quotations.

There was therefore no congress to celebrate the jubilee of the Biblical Institute. After the one at Brussels, held in the August of the previous year, it would have been difficult to convoke another in such a short space of time.

Oddly enough, the date of May 7th passed almost unnoticed. That day was the feast of the Ascension and the jubilee celebrations were postponed until the following academic year. People were satisfied with taking a photograph of the teaching staff at the Biblical Institute on May 6th.

It was only on Wednesday, February 17th, 1960, that the Institute's jubilee was solemnly celebrated at the Vatican. At 8.30 a. m. a pontifical Mass was celebrated by Mgr. van Lierde, an alumnus of the Institute (1933-1936), in St. Peter's basilica at the altar below which lies the body of Pius X. Then at 5.00 p. m., John XXIII received the whole Institute and its 2,000 guests in the hall of Blessings. Those are the data recorded by the house diary (APIBR A-11).

But the periodical *Biblica* opens its 41st volume, the one for 1960, (pp. 1-16) with a short account of the event, followed by the publication of the speeches delivered on the occasion. After paying homage to Cardinal Pizzardo, the Grand Chancellor, Cardinal Bea retraced the history and work of the Institute, not without first having recalled that his elevation to the cardinalate in November 1959 had been desired by the Pope during that jubilee (cf. *Acta PIB* 6, 312-313). Then came the Pope's address. Looking over the past, he ended with these words: "Like any human undertaking, not everything has been achieved nor have all the difficulties been overcome, or rather new ones may arise, but have confidence in Him who protects you: 'I am with you' (Haggai 1,12), says the Lord, with you who study and search the depths of his Word. Go on then, beloved sons, 'in nomine Domini'!" (p.3). The essential part of the speech then revolved around two points: the Institute's mission is at the service of truth, which means "earnestness, soundness, scholarly loyalty in study and teaching and, at the same time, absolute fidelity to the sacred deposit of faith and the Church's infallible teaching office" (p. 4). To carry out this task, concluded the pontiff, "the comforting light of the Holy Spirit must be invoked" (p. 7).

2. From the 25th until the 30th of September 1961 an international Catholic congress of Pauline studies was held in Rome. Three years had passed since the Brussels biblical congress. To celebrate the nineteenth century of the arrival of the apostle Paul in Rome, John XXIII had charged Mgr. Cesare D'Amato, O.S.B., the abbot-bishop of St. Paul's Outside the Walls, with preparing the festivities. To the Biblical Institute, already caught up in the turmoil, was entrusted the task of putting on this congress. Seven public lectures, including one by Fr. Lyonnet on "the gratuitousness of justification and the gratuitousness of salvation", were given at the Apostolic Chancellery, in the Corso Vittorio Emanuele II, while the ninety-six papers were given in the various classrooms at the Gregorian University. This congress provided the opportunity to show where the exegesis of Paul's letters stood just before the council or thereabouts; above all it showed the scholarly and theological value of Catholic exegetes. But, unlike Pius XII, John XXIII did not send any message to those at the congress.

In June, 1963, all the papers were published in two volumes in the *Analecta Biblica* collection, nos. 17-18, in which the canonical order of Paul's writings was followed. The title was: *Studiorum paulinorum congressus internation-*

alis catholicus de re biblica completo undevicesimo saeculo post s. Pauli in Urbem adventum. This time the indices of biblical quotations and Greek words analyzed were added.

3. The Biblical Institute still wanted to show quite clearly how it went about biblical exegesis. In *Biblica*, volume 43 for 1962, it dedicated the third fascicule (pp. 253-476), which appeared in December, to two of its masters, Cardinal Bea and Fr. Vaccari; the former completed sixty years in the Society of Jesus that year and fifty years of priesthood, while the latter completed half a century of teaching at the Institute and seventy years in the Society.

Cardinal Bernard Alfrink, from Utrecht, who had obtained a brilliant licentiate from the Institute in 1926, signed his *Dedication* on November 25th, 1962, that is to say at the end of the heated debates on the schema *"de fontibus revelationis"*: in a few pages, without mincing his words, he gave a perfect illustration of the much-discussed use of *Formgeschichte* once it is stripped of its unacceptable presuppositions and took the opportunity to show that the thesis defended by Fr. Zerwick on Matt 16,17-19 was perfectly Catholic (pp. 258-259).

Then the bibliography of the two masters was given: Cardinal Bea's was done by Fr. St. Schmidt and Fr. Vaccari's by Fr. Nober.

The bulk of the collection consisted of studies carried out solely by professors at the Biblical Institute: Frs. Alonso Schökel (his article on "Motivos sapienciales y de alianza en Gn 2–3" is famous), Moran, Vogt, Köbert, Dahood (on "Qohelet and Northwest Semitic Philology"), de la Potterie (his pages on "L'emploi dynamique de *eis* dans Saint Jean et ses incidences théologiques" are also well known), des Places (who took a study by Fr. Zerwick on Acts 17,28 further), Prümm, Lyonnet and, lastly, Albert Vanhoye, a young professor at the Institute.

This rich festive fascicule thus made the voice of the masters at the Biblical Institute heard at a time when the controversy of which they had been the object was beginning to die down. Their way of doing exegesis could be seen from what they wrote.

So from 1959 to 1963 the Institute was not content with replying to attacks of which it was victim or with letting council Fathers know what it thought about the subjects being discussed on Scripture and the methods of interpreting it. It called upon the best Catholic exegetes of the time to show, in writing or orally, how they did biblical exegesis and oriental studies in the concrete, and took the good opportunity to do the same thing itself.

4. *Life within the Institute in the time of John XXIII*

From 1958 to 1963 there was a new increase in the number of students: they went from 193 to 242, with the number of *alumni* going from 161 to 209, a figure never reached before. During this five-year period, the Spanish students went from 37 to 46, more than the Italians, and the students from the United States from 19 to 30.

The teaching staff continues to be renewed, while two legendary figures at the Institute passed away. Fr. Pohl died on October 23rd, 1961, and Fr. da Fonseca on May 21st, 1963; with them we turn over a new page: the first mentioned, who arrived at the Biblical Institute in 1924, had been the mainspring of the oriental faculty (cf. *Or* 31 [1962] 1-6), the second had been at the Biblical Institute since 1916 (cf. *Bib* 44 [1963] 395-396)! Both taught right up to the utmost limit of their strength. Of the first generation only Fr. Vaccari was left; at the ripe old age of eighty-three he held his last seminar during the first semester of the school year 1958-1959; he kept publishing, however.

When Fr. Bea was made a cardinal in December 1959 he was still teaching hermeneutics and the treatise on inspiration at the Institute; he still kept his seminar in methodology, in particular on how to teach biblical subjects. It was Fr. Alonso Schökel who took his place.

A new generation of professors came to take over. Fr. Ignace van Pottelsberghe de la Potterie (1914-2003), hailing from Waregem in western Flanders, had followed the curriculum in biblical studies from 1947-1950 at the Institute, then taught at the Jesuits' theological college at Louvain. Although not yet having obtained the doctorate, he was summoned to the Biblical Institute at the beginning of 1960 to teach New Testament exegesis there for one semester a year until in October 1963 he became a permanent professor, while still preparing his thesis. He soon proved himself to be unusually competent in the exegesis of the Johannine writings. He ceased teaching in 1989 (cf. *Acta PIB* 10, 1211-1212; *ETL* 79 [2003] 516-517). – Fr. Pierre Proulx, born at Nicolet in Quebec, had also studied at Johns Hopkins University under the direction of W. F. Albright, but without ever managing to publish his thesis; it was on *The Ugaritic Verse Structure and the Poetic Syntax of Proverbs* (1956). He then did a doctorate in theology in Innsbruck (1967) with a thesis written under the direction of Fr. Hugo Rahner; it was entitled *Paradigme de kérygme baptismal. Les 'Homélies Catéchétiques' de Théodore de Mopsueste*; this thesis of about 250 pages was never published either. He first taught Akkadian at the Biblical Institute from 1961 to 1964, taking Fr. E. Bergmann's place; then, succeeding Fr. Vaccari, he was given patristic exegesis to teach, which he did until December 1990 (*Acta PIB* 9, 962-963). – Fr. Albert Vanhoye was born at Hazebrouck in 1923 in French Flanders. Being a brilliant Hellenist, trained when he was a young Jesuit in the school of Fr. des Places, he had made a brilliant defence of his doctoral thesis which appeared only in April 1963: it dealt with "La structure littéraire de l'épître aux Hébreux". In January 1963 he left the Jesuits' theological college at Chantilly to come to the Biblical Institute to take the place of Fr. Lyonnet, as requested by the Holy Office. First a professor, then dean, and finally rector of the Institute (1984-1990), he became emeritus in 1998. In 2006 Benedict XVI made him a cardinal. – Fr. Carlo Maria Martini, born at Turin in 1927, was already a doctor in theology at the Gregorian University when, in 1962 he was summoned to the Biblical Institute. From 1954 to 1956 he had followed the curriculum just for the licentiate in biblical studies at the Institute, then prepared and defended a thesis in theology at the Gregorian on *Il problema storico della Risurrezione negli studi recenti* (AnGr 104) which was published in 1959; since 1958 he had been working at the Jesuits' theological college at Chieri, just outside Turin. Back in Rome in August 1962, he at first confined himself to the preparatory programme for the doctorate in biblical studies, while teaching textual criticism in the second semester. He obtained his second doctorate, this time in biblical studies, in June 1966 (cf. *infra*). He, too, after being a professor, then dean and finally rector of the Institute (1969-1978), then went to the Gregorian as rector until John Paul II appointed him archbishop of Milan in December 1979, before making him a cardinal in 1983. In 2002 he retired to the Biblical Institute in Jerusalem.

Fr. Paul Beauchamp (1924-2001), a French Jesuit born at Tours, had followed the licentiate curriculum at the Institute from 1957 to 1959; while he was preparing his doctorate on Genesis 1, he gave a one-semester course from 1962 to 1964; in particular, his course *De libro Sapientiae Salomonis* (1963-1964), cyclostyled in Latin, marked the renewal in the exegesis of this book: his thesis, which was defended in 1966, was published in Paris in 1969 with the title of *Création et séparation* (cf. *Acta PIB* 10, 870-871).

Two other professors were also taken on at the Institute, but they only stayed there a few years and left the Society. William J. Moran (1921-2000), hailing from Chicago, had been one of the most brilliant pupils of W. F. Albright, under whose guidance he had obtained the doctorate in 1950. At the Institute he occupied the post of teaching the Pentateuch and directed some doctoral theses, including those of Nobert Lohfink, Paul Beauchamp, Julien Harvey and Edward Lipiński. In 1966 he left the Biblical Institute for the University of Harvard where he taught until 1990. He is best known for his work on the Amarna Letters. – Malachi F. Martin (1921-1999), an Irishman, was a doctor in orientalism from Louvain with a thesis on *The Scribal Character of the Dead Sea Scrolls*, 2 vols. (BMus, 44), Louvain, 1958-1959. At the Biblical Institute he taught Semitic palaeography from February 1959 until January 1964, and rabbinic theology from 1961; after the death of Fr. Pohl he was also chief editor of the periodical *Orientalia*. He left the Institute without any fuss in June 1964. Having settled down in New York some years later, he published, among other things, an outrageous book on *The Jesuits. The Society of Jesus and the Betrayal of the Roman Catholic Church*.

Among the professors' publications, apart from many articles mentioned in the *Acta PIB*, to start with we shall recall three big books by Fr. Prümm: *Die Botschaft des Römerbriefes*, Fribourg in Br., Herder, 1960, 238 p.; *Diakonia Pneumatos. Der zweite Korintherbrief als Zugang zur Apostolischen Botschaft*, II, 1-2, Rome, Herder, 1960, 630 p., and 1962, vii-788 p. (tome I was to come out only in 1967). The doctoral theses of Frs. Alonso Schökel, *Estudios de poética hebrea*, Barcelona, Juan Flors, 1963, xii-550 p. and A. Vanhoye, *La structure de l'épître aux Hébreux* (SN), Paris-Bruges, DDB, 1963, 285 p. also appeared; these two works started off the renewal of literary studies at the Institute.

Finally, on the death of Fr. Pohl, Fr. Jean Simon became dean of the oriental faculty for two years.

Assessment of Fr. Vogt's rectorate: 1949-1963

The rector's actions were entirely along the lines of the encyclical "*Divino afflante Spiritu*" and that is how he furthered an unprecedented development in scholarship at the Institute, especially in biblical exegesis. He himself undertook some important tasks with this in mind. Throughout his time as rector, he directed the periodical *Biblica*, as had Fr. Bea, but the openness was soon felt. He was also in charge of the new series of monographs *Analecta Biblica*, which was quickly going to establish itself with works of high quality. Fr. Vogt taught textual criticism and the exegesis of the prophets, especially Isaiah, Jeremiah and Ezekiel, using historico-critical methods; he also taught the exegesis of the Psalms, pointing out their literary genres, as H. Gunkel had done (cf. Pius DRIJVERS, *Over de Psalmen*, Utrecht, Spectrum, 1956 = *Les Psaumes* [LeDiv 21], Paris, Cerf, 1958, which takes its inspiration from Fr. Vogt). He directed only one doctorate, the one by Fr. Paul Lamarche, in 1960, because he devoted himself entirely to his office and his classes. In fourteen years he published more than sixty notes in *Biblica*, often informative ones, but always of a high scholarly standard; during his rectorate in fact, apart from his 1951 Brazilian Psalter, he wrote only seven fully worked out studies which still hold their own: all were on history and historico-critical exegesis; to be sure of this, it is enough to read his 1954 study on Pius X; a work at first hand, based on the archives (cf. *supra*, ch. I-II).

Fr. Vogt raised the level of studies at the Institute. During his rectorate Fr. Lyonnet did his best work on the Pauline letters. It was Fr. Vogt who brought to the Institute the masters who were to leave their mark on exegesis for a long time to come: M. Dahood, L. Alonso Schökel, W. L. Moran, I. de la Potterie, C. M. Martini and A. Vanhoye, to mention only the best known.

He took two other initiatives which were to raise the level of studies in the biblical faculty. In 1925 the Institute had actually provided for an assessment of knowledge of Hebrew and Greek at the time students entered the Institute (cf. *Acta PIB* 2,7,7, 10-11), but that assessment had lapsed. So, in November and December 1951, the rector suggested to the biblical faculty that a real, compulsory, "qualifying examination" be set up in those two biblical languages, then, with the same exacting standards, an examination in knowledge of the three modern languages most used in biblical exegesis, German, English and French; every student would have to take an examination in each of them as they went along with their curriculum. With the backing of the professors, the rector, on February 8th, 1953, received the approval of the Congregation of Seminaries and Universities (*Acta PIB* 5, 366-367) and saw to it that, on April 27th, the Fr. General told all the Fathers Provincial of the Society about it (*ARSI* 12, 382-383): a word to the wise! In December 1960 Fr. Alonso Schökel suggested to the faculty that the examination in Hebrew should henceforth not just be on the book of Ruth but on the first eleven chapters of Deuteronomy; this was to become effective only in 1966. Meanwhile, in 1956, Fr. McCool started up a rapid reading course in New Testament Greek in the second semester and the following year Fr. Alonso Schökel established one in the Hebrew Bible, lasting the whole year. In January 1961 the idea of having a preparatory course for the "qualifying examinations" began to develop; the proposal was to offer it in September, but three years later, the Institute was creating the propaedeutic year devoted essentially to the study of biblical Hebrew and Greek.

That is the overall context in which the Institute, from 1954 to 1962, confronted opposition from outside which could have done away with it. It had to defend itself and Fr. Vogt did that just as vigorously as Fr. Bea did in the Cohenel affair. It was a serious moment, especially when the criticisms became known to the bishops at the council. In 1960 the Biblical Institute had already given its opinion in its "*votum*" for the council and the latter was not to disappoint it. Lastly, when peace was restored, the Biblical Institute was not disturbed again, not even in its recent choices. But when, on May 31st, 1963, Fr. Vogt handed over to Fr. Roderick A. F. MacKenzie, Frs. Lyonnet and Zerwick were still on the sidelines.

V. The early years of Paul VI's pontificate: 1963-1968

1. The solution of the Lyonnet-Zerwick case: 1963-1964

The papal decree appointing Fr. Roderick A. F. MacKenzie rector of the Biblical Institute is dated May 13th, 1963 (*ARSI* 12, 294) and the new rector was officially installed on the 31st; the matter was urgent because the Pope was dying. MacKenzie had been asked to come as soon as possible from Toronto to Rome; the death of the Pope before his installation would have meant suspending the whole process of his appointment. On June 16th the new rector went back to Toronto for the summer and came back to stay at the Biblical Institute only in September. Meanwhile, Paul VI had been elected on June 21ˢᵗ. Fr. MacKenzie (1911-1994) was born at Grassendale near Liverpool, but in 1924 had emigrated with his family to Canada. At the end of the usual Jesuit training he had gone in for Semitic studies at Toronto University. From 1946 to 1949 he went through the full cycle of studies at the Biblical Institute. His doctoral thesis in biblical studies was on "The Forms of Israelite Law. A Comparative Study of Some Word-Patterns in the Pentateuch"; it covered 172 typewritten pages and dealt with "apodictic" and "casuistic" formulas of biblical law which Albrecht Alt had brought to light in 1934. The defence took place on November 10ᵗʰ, 1949, before a board composed of Frs. Dyson, Vaccari, O'Callaghan, Bea and Boccaccio. Fr. MacKenzie had been quick, thanks to his earlier studies at Toronto: one year over the baccalaureate, one semester over the licentiate, another over preparation for the doctorate and the thesis written in just over a year. It only got a "*bene*".

Still, being taken up with work in Toronto, the Father did not publish his thesis, except for an extract consisting of 47 pages, which came out in Toronto in 1961, called: "Two Forms of Israelite Law". Why was this? On page 5 of this extract the author explains, not without a touch of humour, that his unpublished thesis was already known because it had helped Walter Kornfeld (1917-1988) with the first part of the latter's book *Studien zum Heiligkeitsgesetz (Lev 17–26)*, Vienna, Herder, 1952, 158 p., esp. pp. 13-68. Kornfeld, who had followed the curriculum at the Biblical Institute from 1947 to 1949, almost at the same time as MacKenzie, explained at the beginning of his preface, dated March 1952, that he had just finished a two-year stay at the Biblical Institute at Rome, i. e. during the years 1950 and 1951, and that he had benefited from the help of Frs. Bea and Follet. The latter had not been on MacKenzie's thesis board and the review of the book by Kornfeld that he had published in *Biblica* 35 (1954), pp. 95-97, says nothing about the act of plagiarism, although Kornfeld mentions the source of his pages 13-68 more than once but without putting in the inverted commas. Be that as it may, thanks to the publication of the extract from his thesis, Fr. MacKenzie certainly was a doctor in biblical studies.

He was a real gentleman; he was tactful and humanized relations within the Institute. Being discreet and courageous, in less than a year he managed to solve the case involving Frs. Lyonnet and Zerwick. Having been general editor of *Biblica* during the first year of his rectorate, he handed over to Fr. McCool the following year. The rector was no high-flying exegete: apart from the extract from his thesis he had so far only published five or six articles which mainly show an interest in biblical theology. In six years as rector he gave only four one-semester courses, either on Job or the book of Genesis.

After his death the Biblical Institute paid tribute to him in the *Acta PIB* 9, pp. 963-968 and in *Biblica* 75 (1994), pp. 447-448.

But let us see how the ban on teaching placed on Frs. Lyonnet and Zerwick was lifted. Fr. Robert Rouquette has mentioned, probably based on a remark by Fr. Lyonnet, that "Fr. Janssens revealed that he had asked Paul VI, immediately after his election, to wait for a while before rehabilitating Frs. Lyonnet and Zerwick, so as not to seem to be disowning John XXIII" (*La fin d'une chrétienté*, tome 2 [Unam Sanctam, 69b], Paris, Cerf, 1968, p. 475).

On his return to Rome in September 1963, Fr. MacKenzie, while seeking to get information on this dossier received some short reports from Fr. Vogt on September 21st and then from Fr. Lyonnet concerning the chronology of events leading up to the ban (Doc. R. III,23-24). While the Father was reflecting on how to proceed, Paul VI took up a public stance at the conclusion of a speech he made on October 31st at the opening of the academic year at the Lateran University from which had come the recent attacks on the Biblical Institute. Here, according to *L'Osservatore Romano* for 2-3 of November, are the pontiff's words:

> And our wishes are so fervent that, on the one hand, they hope that regularity of function, a rigorous, serious attitude to study, a persevering effort at improvement involve everyone, Masters and Pupils, to give this University virtue and merit in keeping with the excellence of its name; and, on the other, that its attitude within the concert of the great, famous and meritorious Roman institutes of great ecclesiastical culture be one of sincere gratitude, fraternal co-operation, loyal emulation, mutual respect and friendly concord, never of jealous rivalry, or tedious polemics; never!

A bolt from the blue like that did not go unnoticed in exegetical circles throughout the world.

In the weeks that followed, Fr. MacKenzie decided to ask Cardinal Ottaviani, the all-powerful secretary at the Holy Office, for an audience. In all probability this meeting could take place only after the second session of the council (September 29th – December 4th 1963). To get ready for it, the rector had a two-page *aide-mémoire* drawn up in English for himself, filled out with some annotations in his own hand; this exercize, worthy of a good diplomat, indicated the gaffes to be avoided during the audience: the main thing is to keep in mind the fact that the cardinal: "is the source of power. He can or cannot allow these men to teach again". Then the rector envisaged how the meeting might go; to do this he had studied the dossier with those concerned. Lastly, he thought up some replies to possible reactions by the cardinal. Prepared in this way, Fr. MacKenzie was received on December 16th.

On January 22nd, 1964, the rector then wrote to Cardinal Ottaviani to thank him for the reception he had been met with and to put in writing the main points of what he had said to him on December 16th (Doc. R. III,25).

Fr. MacKenzie had thought this letter over for a long time; he left two successive drafts of it in English. Then came a first sketch of a letter in Italian, with handwritten corrections. He then sent that sketch to Cardinal Bea who sent it back to him on January 21st with a page of changes which the cardinal, who knew a lot about the practice of the Roman Curia and had been a member of the Holy Office since October 1st, 1963, suggested to the rector. In particular, one had to avoid writing anything that might seem to be a defence of the two Fathers. Fr. MacKenzie took this into account in the letter he sent to Cardinal Ottaviani on the 22nd. Hoping the ban would be lifted, the rector undertook to be vigilant in matters of prudence and the fidelity of the professors to the Roman teaching office. Things stayed like that, as far as is known.

In the meantime, Fr. Lyonnet, who had been doing a lot for the council Fathers and experts, was received at the beginning of this month of January 1964 by Cardinal Paolo Marella, a member of the Consistorial Congregation in charge of the dioceses and episcopal appointments in the Latin Church. Cardinal Marella had been nuncio in Paris from 1953-1959, after Mgr. Roncalli, the future Pope John XXIII, and played an important role in the council as regards bishops. On January 15th Fr. Lyonnet sent him a letter of thanks to which he attached an eleven-page Memorandum in which he went over the history of the matter that had concerned him as well as Fr. Zerwick. I. Thus he explained to Mgr. Marella: 1. the accusation that Mgr. Romeo had made against him in the periodical *Divinitas* in December 1960, on p. 243, of wanting to destroy the New Testament, having succeeded in destroying the Old! 2. Then he explained his theological position concerning Romans 5,12 and original sin (cf. *supra*). 3. lastly, he defended his exegesis of the account of the Annunciation, of which he obviously maintained the historicity. II. He then got round to the defence of Fr. Zerwick, who held to the historicity of Matthew 16,17-19 (cf. *supra*). III. Finally, he explained that the argument was aimed directly at the teaching of Pius XII: 1. what Fr. Spadafora had published against the Biblical Institute as well as 2. the schema "*de fontibus revelationis*" or 3. Cardinal Ruffini's article in *L'Osservatore Romano* for August 24th, 1961, rejected any exegesis that looks for the sacred writers' intention and the literary genres they use, especially in historical matters. IV. This Memorandum ends with a reminder of some polemical episodes in the time of Pius XI and Pius XII (cf. *supra*), so similar to what happened at the beginning of John XXIII's pontificate.

That was how things stood when, on February 24th, Paul VI, who was to visit the Gregorian on March 12th, received Fr. MacKenzie in a private audience; the precise date is known from the "Historia domus" of 1963-1964, kept by Fr. G. Novotný (APIBR B-XVIII,10). The rector often recounted how the audience went. After giving a report on the state of the Biblical Institute in general, while the Pope was concluding the interview, Fr. MacKenzie, against all the rules of propriety, still wanted to bring up the Lyonnet-Zerwick affair. The Pope agreed, listened, took notes without wincing and said he was going to see to the problem (cf. Gerald P. Fogarty, *American Catholic Biblical Scholarship. A History from the Early Republic to Vatican II*, San Francisco, Harper, 1989, p. 331).

Paul VI quickly got Cardinal Bea to elucidate the question. The latter contacted Fr. MacKenzie and the rector invited the two professors to let the cardinal have in writing the criticisms made against them which had motivated the steps taken by the Holy Office. We have only one copy of Fr. Lyonnet's reply, dated March 17th, 1964: it covers three pages in French. Because the complaints of the Holy Office had not been communicated either to the Fr. General or to himself, Fr. Lyonnet could only confine himself to the "rumours circulating about me", he writes, "within the milieux of the Roman Curia", that is to say, the exegesis of Romans 5,12 and original sin he was proposing, as well as the 1954 conference on the story of the Annunciation. He explained himself once again, therefore, on these two points. At the end of his letter he comes back again to the accusation of wanting to destroy the New Testament, which Mgr. Romeo had formulated in his article in the periodical *Divinitas*, in 1960, on p. 443, note 128. In conclusion, Fr. Lyonnet leaves it up to the cardinal: "May your Eminence please excuse the length of these pages. May you find in them what you seek and, in any case, the expression of my deepest gratitude".

The Holy Office lifted the ban on May 13th and informed the Fr. General by letter about it on the 25th. He, in turn, told Fr. MacKenzie about it in a letter on the 31st, adding that he wished that the rehabilitation of Fathers Lyonnet and Zerwick be done "sine clamore aut, ut patet, gloriatione", without any fuss or, of course, boasting about it".

Throughout this story we have kept mainly to the dossier in the Institute's Roman archives (L-130-A). In October 1964, as if nothing had happened, Fr. Lyonnet resumed his course on the epistle to the Romans, and Fr. Zerwick his on Luke's gospel (*Acta PIB* 6,552 and 554). Is there any need to say that Fr. Lyonnet had gone through the trial with serenity whereas Fr. Zerwick had been deeply affected by it? After their rehabilitation both of them were surprisingly discreet over this unfortunate adventure.

2. New proposals from the Biblical Institute to the council: September 1964, January and September 1965

Bibliography

"Observations sur le schéma de constitution *De divina revelatione*, rédigées par plusieurs professeurs de l'Institut biblique pontifical à l'intention des évêques du Brésil (Rome 27 septembre 1964)", in B.-D. DUPUY (éd.), *La Révélation divine*, t. 2 (Unam Sanctam, 70b), Paris, Cerf, 1968, p. 623-629. – *Documenta Concilii Vaticani*

II de divina revelatione, ad usum privatum, no date or place [Romae, 1966?], quarto, 187 p. – Ignace DE LA POTTERIE, "L'interprétation de la Sainte Écriture dans l'Esprit où elle a été écrite (DV 12,3), in R. LATOURELLE (éd.), *Vatican II. Bilan et perspectives vingt-cinq ans après (1962-1987)*, t. 1, Montréal, Bellarmin – Paris, Cerf, 1988, pp. 235-276 – Riccardo BURIGANA, *La Bibbia nel concilio*, Bologna, Mulino, 1998, pp. 305-307, 342 note 163 and 372-374.

A. On September 27th, 1964, when the third session of the council had started on the 14th, some professors of the Biblical Institute circulated a three-page document entitled "*Observationes aliquae in schemate Constitutionis De divina revelatione ab aliquibus professorum Instituti Biblici factae ad usum Ex.morum et Rev.morum DD. Episcoporum Brasiliae*". The Roman archives of the Institute possess neither the original nor a copy of it, but the document, examined by Burigana (pp. 305-307), was translated into French and published in 1968 in the second volume of the collection of studies devoted to *la Révélation divine* (pp. 623-625). Fr. Henri de Lubac (his *Memento du concile*, ad loc.) noted that on October 1st he received a copy of it from the hands of Fr. Zerwick. On September 30th the council had started on the presentation and discussion of the third schema that had been prepared during the previous months. These *Observationes* from the Biblical Institute were then deposited with the Secretariat for the council by Mgr. Da Mota e Albuquerque, archbishop of Vitoria in Brazil, with several complementary remarks mainly concerning nos. 11 and 12 of this third schema (cf. *La Révélation divine*, 2, pp. 626-629).

These professors from the Biblical Institute straightaway showed their satisfaction:

> We approve the reworked schema and have no doubt that it now corresponds to the spirit and desires of the majority of council Fathers. [...] Nothing of substance seems to us to need to be withdrawn or added. However, some changes [...] seem opportune to us and we put them forward here.

On no. 3, the proposed reading of Gen 3,15 (the redemption promised to our first parents after their fall) is, of course, Christian, but cannot be ascribed to the inspired author. – In the fourth schema (1965), the conciliar Commission mitigated the sentence that was called into question (cf. *Documenta*, p. 108).

On no. 5, defining the obedience of faith as a "voluntary assent to revealed truth" is a scholastic formula: better leave it out. – The same Commission refused to suppress the formula, but it toned it down (*Documenta* p. 110). The final text replaced "revealed truth" with "revelation".

On no. 8, to the sentence "Through this same Tradition, the Holy Scriptures become known to the Church with absolute certainty" the mention of the canon should be added for clarity. Moreover, the expression "with absolute certainty" ought to be omitted because until the council of Trent the limits of the canon were uncertain; as for the verb "become known", if it has the understanding of the biblical text in mind, it would mean that scholarly research would become useless. The Commission accepted these remarks (cf. *Documenta*, p. 115) and changed the passage as follows: "Through this same Tradition, the complete canon of the Holy Scriptures becomes known to the Church".

On no.10, in the sentence "The task of authentically interpreting the word of God, written or handed down, has been entrusted solely to the living and infallible teaching office of the Church", the words "authentically" and "infallible" are, in the first case, ambiguous and, in the second, exaggerated.– The Commission clarified the sentence by omitting "infallible".

At the end of no.11, on inerrancy, some council Fathers wanted it to be written that "the books of Scripture *manifest* the truth without any error". The Biblical Institute asked that the verb *"teach"* be kept, because there are many errors in the Bible, in cosmology, for example, but the Bible does not teach them. – The Commission therefore kept this verb *"teach"* (cf. *Documenta*, p. 120).

On no. 19, on the gospels, the Biblical Institute asked that the sentence in the recent instruction *Sancta Mater Ecclesia* from the Pontifical Biblical Commission be quoted correctly, namely: "...or *explaining* others while paying attention to the situation of the Church ...". – The Commission admitted the mistake (cf. *Documenta*, p. 127).

Finally, at the end of no. 23, the encouragement given to exegetes, although taken from the encyclical *Divino afflante Spititu* by Pius XII (*EB* 569), was restrictive to the point of casting suspicion on them, and non-Catholic exegetes might feel offended by these restrictions. The Commission took no action (cf. *Documenta*, p. 134), but the fourth schema finally answered the Biblical Institute's request and omitted those restrictions (cf. *Documenta*, p. 178). Times had changed!

Without exaggerating the importance of these requests from the Biblical Institute, among hundreds of others from the council Fathers, one cannot fail to notice the openness they show and the approval they obtained.

B. Once again at the request of the Brazilian bishops the Biblical Institute circulated a new document among the council Fathers. Covering thirteen pages it was introduced both by Fr. Lyonnet, in his capacity of dean of the Institute's biblical faculty, and dated January 25th, 1965, and by an official letter from the rector of the Biblical Institute, Fr. MacKenzie, dated January 30th. The title was *"Modi"*, *qui proponuntur pro schemate "De divina revelatione"* (cf. Doc. R. III,26; cf. Burigana, p. 372, note 17). The text came after the third session of the council which closed on November 21st, 1964. In the meantime, the third schema on Revelation had been revised by the doctrinal

Commission and a fourth one had been issued to the council Fathers on November 20th. So it is on this fourth schema that the Biblical Institute had something to say in January 1965. R. Burigana (pp. 372-374) mentions some of the more significant "*modi*" proposed by the Biblical Institute.

The fourth session of the council opened on September 14th 1965. From the 20th until the 22nd, voting took place on the successive chapters of this fourth schema on Revelation. The votes showed that a very large majority accepted the new text, but the votes "*placet iuxta modum*" were numerous. One month later the doctrinal Commission submitted to the council its report on the changes requested and it is in that report that it can be seen what happened to the Biblical Institute's proposals which had been passed on by the council Fathers.

On the last paragraph of no.11, about what the third schema still called the "inerrancy" of Scripture, the fourth preferred to speak of "truth" and in the last paragraph the more precise expression "saving truth", which the Biblical Institute approved and justified. – At the request of Paul VI, this passage was revised at the last minute and changed as follows: "the truth which, for our salvation [*salutis nostrae causa*], God willed be set down in Holy Scripture" (cf. *Documenta*, pp. 159-160, no. 8).

On no.12, about seeking the intention of the inspired author, the Biblical Institute suggested distinguishing between literary genres and the ways of expressing oneself in interpersonal exchanges. – The Commission accepted the distinction without, however, adopting the proposal word for word (cf. *Documenta*, 162, no. 25).

On the beginning of the third paragraph of no. 12, the Biblical Institute suggested inserting the proposition: "*cum Sacra Scriptura eodem Spiritu quo scripta est etiam legenda et interpretanda sit*". – The Commission accepted this addition (cf. *Documenta*, p. 162, no. 27), a fact which Burigana did not mention (cf. de la Potterie, p. 257, note 66).

On the end of no. 12, about the role of exegetes, the Biblical Institute feared that the conciliar text confined their work to only the obscure "passages [*locos*]" of the Bible, which is in fact what some council Fathers had asked. – With the support of others, of whom there were more, the Biblical Institute's request was granted in the sense that exegetes were asked "to understand *and expound the meaning* of Holy Scripture more profoundly" (cf. *Documenta*, p. 163, no.31).

Lastly, the Biblical Institute expressed its unreserved admiration for chapter 5, devoted to the New Testament; in its opinion this difficult chapter wisely expounded how things stand as regards the authenticity and historicity of the Gospels.

Let us conclude by pointing out that no professor from the Biblical Institute was an expert at the doctrinal Commission.

C. The Biblical Institute, it seems, intervened for the last time at the end of September 1965. The one-page document was called: "*Animadversiones ad ea quae Subcommissio doctrinalis respondit circa modos a Patribus propositis relate ad cap. II Schematis De divina revelatione*" (cf. Burigana, p. 398, note 79). It dealt mainly with the request from a hundred and eleven council Fathers to insert a sentence in no. 9 saying that the Church cannot draw all Catholic doctrine directly from Scripture alone. The Biblical Institute was opposed to that addition, as was Fr. Karl Rahner (cf. Burigana, p. 398, note 79). – The point was hotly debated at the doctrinal Commission on October 4th. But, at the request of Paul VI, the matter was referred back to the Commission on October 19th and it finished up by proposing, in its report of October 22nd, the insertion of the following sentence, suggested by Cardinal Bea, about the relation between Tradition and Scripture: "Consequently, it is not from Scripture alone that the Church draws its certainty on all points of Revelation" (cf. *Documenta*, pp. 153-154, no. 40, D and *Ad D*, and pp. 183-184, II, 2). On October 29th, the council accepted this addition by a very large majority.

3. *The teaching staff*

On December 7th, when Paul VI was at St. Peter's, bringing the work of the council to a close, the Institute performed the funeral rites for Fr. Alberto Vaccari. He had died the previous morning at the age of ninety-one. He had spent fifty-three of them at the Biblical Institute. Though growing weak in his last months, he had kept the post of vice-rector to the end.

The post remained unoccupied until, on February 8th, 1968, with the Pope's approval, it was filled by Fr. Lyonnet. He had already been replaced as dean of the biblical faculty by Fr. C. M. Martini on December 10th, 1967. In 1966, Fr. Adhémar Massart had become dean of the oriental faculty. That same year, Fr. Johannes Lessel (Breslau 1905-Rome 1999) had succeeded Fr. G. Novotný as Registrar of the Institute and remained so until 1972.

As regards the higher authorities of the Institute, Fr. Pedro Arrupe was elected General of the Society of Jesus on May 22nd, 1965, and, in that capacity, became Vice-Grand Chancellor of the Biblical Institute; his delegate was firstly Fr. Paolo Dezza who, since July 31st, 1964, had held that function, after Fr. René Arnou; on July 2nd, 1966, Fr. Francis McCool, a professor at the Biblical Institute, succeeded Fr. Dezza.

Between 1963 and 1968 nine new professors were taken on at the Institute, five in the biblical faculty and four others in the oriental faculty.

To join the biblical faculty there came: Fr. James H. Swetnam, a Jesuit born in 1928 in St. Louis, in the United States; with a licentiate in biblical studies gained at the Institute in 1962, he was preparing for the doctorate when, in 1963, he was called upon to give a course in Greek to some students who did not know that language; this was the beginning of the propaedeutic year that was to be set up the following year (cf. Doc. R. III,27). – Fr. Léopold Sabourin (1919-2001), a Jesuit hailing from the Canadian province of Manitoba; with a doctorate in theology from Montreal with a thesis on *Rédemption sacrificielle. Une enquête exégétique* (Bruges-Paris, 1961), he was a member of the Institute at Jerusalem from 1964 to 1967 (cf. Part Two, ch. II) before being called to the Roman centre to teach biblical theology there until 1978. In 1971 he started up the periodical *Bulletin de théologie biblique*, which also came out in English: *Biblical Theology Bulletin* (cf. *Acta PIB* 10, 977-978). – Roger Le Déaut (1923-2000), a Holy Ghost Father of Breton origin; he obtained the doctorate at the Biblical Institute in 1963 with a thesis on *La Nuit pascale. Essai sur la signification de la Pâque juive à partir du Targum d'Exode XI,42* (AnBib, 22), which he had written under the direction of Fr. Lyonnet; from 1964 to 1994 he taught Targumic language and literature; he had full mastery of the subject; among his publications the *Targum du Pentateuque* is to be mentioned first; it is in four volumes that appeared from 1978 to 1981 in the collection Sources chrétiennes, in collaboration with Jacques Robert; along with that he also published the *Targum des Chroniques (Cod. Vat. Urb. Ebr. 1)* in 1971 in the collection Analecta Biblica, 51; lastly, his posthumous masterpiece on the "Targum" in the *Supplément au Dictionnaire de la Bible* (cf. *Acta PIB* 10, 868-870). – Norbert Lohfink, S. J., succeeded W. Moran in 1966; his teaching on the Pentateuch was outstanding, but, for reasons of health, he retired to Frankfurt 1969; however, from 1983 to 1994, he was seen at the Biblical Institute every other year for a semester of teaching the Old Testament. – Petrus Duncker, O. P. (1898-1990), from the Netherlands; while being professor at the Angelicum he taught the propaedeutic biblical Hebrew course from 1966 to 1974; he succeeded Fr. G. Novotný, who had started that course the year before (cf. *infra*).

To join the oriental faculty there came: Mr Karlheinz Deller (1927-2003), a native of Nuremberg; as a token of gratitude to the Society to which he owed some of his training he taught Akkadian from 1963 to 1967 (cf. R. Borger in *AfO* 50 [2003-2004] 498-499). – Hans Quecke (1928-1998) a German Jesuit from Duisburg on the Rhine; he had specialized in the languages of the ancient Christian East; he came to Rome in 1965 to succeed Fr. J. Simon; in 1970 he obtained the doctorate in orientalism with a thesis on *Untersuchungen zum koptischen Stundegebet*; in poor health, he was considered one of the best scholars in Coptic (cf. *Acta PIB* 10, 715-720; *Or* 69 [2000] 189-208). – Richard I. Caplice, a Jesuit from the New York Province; he came to the Biblical Institute in 1966; he was thirty-five; he took over from K. Deller, teaching Akkadian from 1966-1973 and then from 1978 to 1989; he was the first general editor of the collection Studia Pohl, started in 1967. – Fr. Jan J. A. van Dijk (1915-1996), born near The Hague, in the Netherlands; he was already a Sumerologist of long standing – since 1961 he had been teaching at the University of Copenhagen – when he arrived at the Biblical Institute in 1968; his doctoral thesis, presented at Leiden in 1953, dealt with *La sagesse suméro-akkadienne*; at the Biblical Institute he taught until 1987 (cf. *Acta PIB* 10, 333-336).

Among the professors' publications, the full list of which can be read every year in the *Acta PIB*, let us here recall the main books:

Éd. DES PLACES, *Syngeneia. La parenté de l'homme avec Dieu d'Homère à la patristique* (Études et commentaries, 51), Paris, Klincksieck, 1964, 225 p.; *Jamblique. Les mystères d'Égypte*. Notice, texte critique, traduction et notes (Collection des Universités de France), Paris, Les Belles Lettres, 1966, 400 p.

I. DE LA POTTERIE – St. LYONNET, *La Vie selon l'Esprit condition du chrétien* (Unam Sanctam, 55), Paris, Cerf, 1965, 285 p.

L. ALONSO SCHÖKEL, *La palabra inspirata. La Biblia a la luz de la ciencia del lenguaje* (Biblioteca Herder, Sagrada Escritura, 75), Barcelona, Herder, 1966, 388 p.

M. DAHOOD, *Psalms I: 1-50* and *Psalms II: 51-100. Translated with an Introduction and Notes* (AncB, 16, 17), Garden City, N. Y., Doubleday, 1966, XLVI-329 p. and 1968, XXX-399 p.

St. LYONNET, *La storia della salvezza nella lettera ai Romani*, Napoli, D'Auria, 1966, VIII-270 p.

C. M. MARTINI, *Il problema della recensionalità del codice B alla luce del papiro Bodmer XIV* (AnBib, 26), Roma, PIB, 1966, XXIV-192 p.; *Epistulae Beati Petri Apostoli ex Papiro Bodmeriana VIII transcriptae atque apparatu critico instructae*, Città del Vaticano, 1968.

4. *Students and the propaedeutic course*

To judge from the figures given every year by the *Acta PIB*, the number of students during this period extending from 1963 to 1968 grew considerably; this was to continue until the academic year 1969 to 1970, only to fall slowly from then on (cf. *infra*). In fact, for the year 1963-1964, the total came to 252 students, including 213 *full-time students*. The first record was reached in 1965-1966 with 305 registered students including 253 *full-time students*. The number of the latter dropped in the next two years, although in 1967-1968 the total was 334 registered students, of whom only 223 were *full-time*.

The council and the reputation of the Institute probably had something to do with this increase, as well as a clearer awareness of the universality of the Church. Thus it was that the studies at the Biblical Institute were no longer the prerogative of western clerics. Lay people entered the biblical faculty: in 1963-1964 there were only five, but in 1967-1968 there were sixteen laymen and eight ladies. More important was the opening up to the other continents: in 1963-1964 Latin America was represented by nineteen registered students and in 1967-1968 by twenty-five; in 1963-1964 Asia had twenty, including ten from India, while in 1967-1968 it had thirty-four, including fourteen from India; Africa numbered six in 1963-1964 and thirteen in 1967-1968.

However, another reason must be noted. The number of *guest students* is actually seen to rise astonishingly during this period: from thirty-six in 1963-1964 it reaches one hundred and eight in 1967-1968, whereas for decades the number of *part-time students* had been dropping until it reached single figures. If one consults the register of the *Inscriptiones Alumnorum ab anno 1954-1955 ad annum 1970-1971* in the Registrar's Office at the Institute, the following facts can be observed.

1. The oriental faculty had only two *guest students* in 1963-1964 and 1964-1965; the following year, one *guest* and one *full-time student*; in 1966-1967, three *guests* and one *full-time student* (Kevin J. Cathcart, from Ireland); finally, in the following year seven *guests* and two *full-time students* (Fr. Alviero Niccacci, O.F.M., from Italy, and Mrs Michiko Ishida, from Japan).

2. As from the year 1964-1965 the register lists the men and women students registering as *hosp. praep.*, guests for a preparatory year that the Institute was organizing (*Acta PIB* 6, 541; cf. Doc. R. III,26) and which it was to implement fully the following year (*Acta PIB* 7, 42). This new programme now offered a basic course in biblical Greek and another in biblical Hebrew. In 1964-1965, eight students signed up, among them the future archbishop of Kisangani, now of Kinshasa in Congo Kinshasa, Laurent Monsengwo Pasinya. The following year there were thirty-six, including five from black Africa. (Let us note that the first black African student was, it seems, Fr. Peter Butelezi, O.M.I., from South Africa; registered as a *full-time student* in 1958, he got the licenciate in biblical studies in 1960; he died in 1997). In 1966-1967 there were no more than twenty-seven people signed up for that preparatory course, but the year after there were sixty-three of them!

3. Lastly, a sign of the new times, in 1965-1966, three Italian ladies registered at the Biblical Institute for this preparatory year: Maria Luisa Rigato who, while continuing to teach in a secondary school, only got the licentiate in 1974 – she began to be known affectionately as Miss Biblicum (cf. what she says in the *Acta PIB* 10, 492-493, note 1); Anna Maria Bellia, who completed the course for the licentiate in 1969 as a *special student*; there was another one, lastly, who did not continue with studies at the Institute.

Fr. James H. Swetnam has kindly written up his memories of the new enterprise to which he has devoted his best efforts over thirty-six years (Doc. R. III,27). In December 1967 he was even given charge of that programme in his capacity as vice-dean of the biblical faculty (*Acta PIB* 7, 193). In 1965 Fr. Swetnam was helped with the teaching of Hebrew by Fr. Novotný; the latter was succeeded by Fr. Duncker in 1966.

As from the school year 1968-1969, this programme definitively assumed the title of propaedeutic Course (*Acta PIB* 7, 237). Such an initiative had become necessary due to the fact that a great number of candidates at the Biblical Institute had no longer done secondary Graeco-Latin studies. Besides, this propaedeutic year prepared students for the qualifying examination in Greek and Hebrew, being successful in which was the necessary condition for admission to the programmes geared to academic degrees in biblical studies. Not being compulsory in itself, this year did not enter into the academic curriculum; it was a facility which proved ever more necessary.

5. *A start at reforming the Statutes, while waiting for the "Normae quaedam" of May 20th 1968*

In no. 11 of its declaration on Catholic Education, October 28th, 1965, the council had asked for the revision of the statutes of ecclesiastical faculties. There then began a long journey of almost two decades for the Biblical Institute. Let us be content here with the first stage.

On March 13th, 1966, Fr. Dezza, Fr. General's delegate, had a long meeting with the professors at the Institute, as the diary kept at the time shows (APIBR A-11). Two days later, Frs. Alonso, de la Potterie, Martini and McCool, who had been formed into a committee, sent a letter to all the professors at the Institute. Following on the "decisions taken during Rev. Fr. Delegate's visit about the reform and *aggiornamento* of studies and statutes at the Institute", they asked their colleagues' views on two general problems: 1. How to specify the purpose of the Institute: purely scholarly or pastoral as well, with "a stronger accent placed on the historico-salvation and theological aspect in exegesis"? 2. Must the Biblical Institute still be unique in its kind or could other institutions confer academic degrees in Holy Scripture? (APIBR K-26-H: Revising Statutes 3). Before the end of the month, eleven professors answered these questions.

On April 30th the committee presented a four-page document; it recalled in the first place what the official documents of the Holy See said about the purpose of the Biblical Institute; then it summarized the opinions received; lastly, it made an overall assessment of the matter; the conclusion points out that it sent present students and former students over the past five years a questionnaire "on the various aspects of activity at the Institute" (and their replies were numerous: APIBR K-26-I: 8).

Here, in brief, are the contents of the overall assessment (cf. Doc. R. III,28):

A. The fundamental purpose of the Biblical Institute is to promote higher studies of the Bible. More specifically: 1. Personal research at a scholarly level and publications, especially at that level, are expected from the professors. 2. The training of teachers must be kept at the same scholarly level. 3.

Scholarly work by the students must be promoted, and those who are suitable must be got ready for a scholarly career. A note makes it clear that these three purposes are closely linked: teaching on a scholarly level calls for research of that order; moreover, this teaching and this research sow the seeds of scholarly careers among the students.

B. Our teaching cannot separate work in the positive sciences, such as philology and history, from the theological orientation. In the present context and in the spirit of Vatican II, "we must give our exegesis a biblico-theological and 'heilsgeschichtlich' orientation". It means "directing interpretation towards a deeper understanding of God's plan". In doing so, exegesis will in fact always be pastoral and priestly, as John XXIII said.

C. The Biblical Institute is unanimous in considering that its monopoly must not be maintained, to the extent that other institutions will favour a serious approach to biblical studies in the Church.

This last option must be stressed. In April 1939, right at the beginning of Pius XII's pontificate Fr. Bea had written a memorandum for the Pope in which he opposed the idea that other academic institutions should confer the same degrees as the Institute. He was thinking primarily of the École Biblique in Jerusalem, but also of some renowned Catholic university centres, such as the ones at Louvain, Paris, Fribourg or Washington. His objection was of a doctrinal order: in those institutions, the tendency was likely to be more liberal, even "very broadminded", and the laudatory reactions to the death of Fr. Lagrange on March 10th, 1938, were already giving a foretaste of this (APIBR B-XVII-7).

However, in 1966, the question arose in a different way, not only because scholarly exegesis henceforth had its rightful place within the Church, but especially, as some professors were suggesting, because for many students, a faculty which was not so insistent on language requirements could concentrate more on the pastoral side. We shall see that the idea was to make headway.

In the autumn of 1966 two steps were taken by official bodies.

On November 15th, the 31st General Congregation of the Society of Jesus, in its 31st decree, dealt with the "interprovincial houses in Rome", including the Biblical Institute. Among the recommendations it made to the Fr. General, we read the following text (§ 4, d: no. 566):

> The General Congregation recommends that the Fr. General, with the cooperation of the teaching staff, have the statutes of the Society's university institutions in Rome revised; an enquiry should be made at the same time into whether, in guiding academic activity, it would not be suitable to give the teaching staff, with a view to giving it a more important role in this domain, a consultative, and even, for certain decisions, a deliberative vote.

Meanwhile, on October 7th, The Sacred Congregation for seminaries and universities sent a list of five questions with a view to revising their statutes to the rectors of all these institutions. These questions touch in particular on faculty structure and academic degrees (APIBR K-26-H: Revising Statutes 3).

At the end of January 1967 the Biblical Institute sent its reply (APIBR K-26-H: Revising Statutes 3), in which, as a handwritten note by Fr. Martini shows, the orientation of the faculty on several points appears. Let us bring them out. The Biblical Institute wishes (no.1) that in theological studies Scripture should be as it were the soul, according to the wish of the council (*Optatam totius*, 16). "Several specialized institutions [...] should be able to grant degrees in biblical studies" (no. 5). Academic life should normally be governed collegiately by the rector and the academic councils, in conformity with each faculty's statutes, mainly as regards the appointment of professors and setting up the programme (no. 6); hence, wider autonomy should be granted to faculties (no. 9). Research is insisted upon (no. 10) and, for that purpose, a sabbatical year should be granted occasionally to permanent professors for pursuing their research (no. 11). On degrees, the Biblical Institute finds it necessary that, in various nations or regions, institutions be set up in which a pastoral licentiate in biblical studies may be conferred (no. 16). To prepare candidates for this kind of licentiate, as for the one that prepares people to teach in seminaries and faculties, it would be necessary to develop practical group work under the direction of a professor, both in quantity and quality, "and consequently lighten the obligation to attend classes" (no. 17). A licentiate in pastoral theology, should continue to be a requisite for going on to degrees in biblical studies, and it should be available to lay people, men and women (no. 18). Lastly, the language of teaching should be chosen freely according to the place (no. 19: Latin has had its day!)

The sequence of events is also given in the same handwritten note by Fr. Martini: in December 1967 a project for new rules was examined by the biblical faculty, of which he had just been appointed dean, then, from January to May 1968, the draft of a new curriculum was drawn up which included several points from the statutes.

Next, in the course of March 1968, Fr. Martini asked Fr. Maurice Gilbert, a first-year student in the curriculum for the licentiate, to organize a delegation of students who could henceforth take part in the work of the council of professors and thus in reforming the statutes. On contacting some fellow-students and meeting a large number of students from the Biblical Institute in their respective colleges, Fr. Gilbert explained to them what was at stake in the new move; he managed to persuade them to organize themselves into language groups, rather than national ones, and hold elections in which each group would chose its delegate. Forging ahead, despite the Easter holidays in mid-

April, the plan worked and the delegates were elected for the immediate future and for the following year, 1968-1969 (cf. *Acta PIB* 7, 265-266).

On April 26th, Fr. Martini met with those delegates and asked them to choose one of them to attend the council of professors that same evening; Fr. Gilbert was chosen. Fr. Martini also asked the delegates to let the one representing them have their opinions on the points on the council's agenda; for that purpose two documents were distributed to the delegates.

In the course of the council's meeting, three points were discussed and put to the vote: 1. the baccalaureate degree was to be either dropped or changed in accordance with future directives from the Holy See. 2. The final examination *ad licentiam* was to be overhauled: to be taken before a board of two professors at each examination session it would not, according to the wish of the students' delegate, cover so many subjects as the project had in mind. 3. While not being obliged to do so, students were recommended, when exercising their free choice of exegesis courses, to take one in each corpus of both Testaments.

Other points from the reform project were to take effect right from the resumption of classes in October 1968: 1. Semesters were to be independent and, for each course, the student could take the examination during one of the three examination sessions that followed. 2. Each exegesis course would be given at the rate of only two hours a week. 3. In the exegetico-theological section the courses are interchangeable in the sense that a course in exegesis could be taken as a course in biblical theology, and conversely. 4. In the introductory and history-geography sections, some less exacting courses, either "informative" or "monographic" will be set up. 5. In the first year, an *exercitatio* or group exercise will be arranged under the guidance of a professor, but without requiring writing up any research. 6. The pro-seminar, introduced in 1967 and aimed at preparing new students for scholarly work in the *exercitationes*, is to be kept (Doc. R. III,29).

That is how things were when, on May 20th, 1968, the Congregation for Catholic Education – that is its new title – published the "*Normae quaedam*", updating the 1932 constitution "*Deus scientiarum Dominus*". At the Biblical Institute the reform had been up and going for two years already.

6. *The Council for the administration of the three institutions in the Consortium is set up: 1966-1968.*

On November 15th, 1966, in its decree, already quoted above, on the interprovincial houses of the Society in Rome (4, a-b; nos. 563-564), the 31st General Congregation had also recommended that Fr. General: 1. provide the Fathers Provincial with a list of the professors and other Jesuits who would be needed in Rome in the coming three, five and ten years; 2. set up a permanent administrative Council to help in the administration of those institutions which the Holy See had entrusted to its care. This Council would include, in addition to the rectors of those institutions, Provincials working in various regions.

The implementation of these decisions was soon got ready (cf. the whole dossier in the APIBR K-9-A: 11). On December 1st a meeting was held at the Villa Cavalletti, above Frascati, under the presidency of Fr. McCool, Fr. General's Delegate; Fr. MacKenzie, rector of the Biblical Institute, was there. The purpose was to work out concrete ways of doing what the General Congregation had decreed. Then there was a period of waiting until October 10th, 1967, so that Fr. McCool could get started on the plan to draw up a list of the staffing needs of the Biblical Institute, as well of the Gregorian and the Oriental Institute; he asked each house to compile the list by December 15th. Things were then to move quickly. On December 27th, Fr. General set up this Council of administration (cf. *ARSI* 15, 134-136). Apart from the Fr. Delegate and the rectors of the Gregorian, the Biblical Institute and the Oriental Institute, four Provincials would belong to it, those of France, Chicago, the Philippines and Toledo.

At the Biblical Institute preparations had therefore been made for the first meeting of this Council by drawing up the required list.

Finally, from February 27th to the 29th, 1968, the Council of administration met in Rome at Fr. General's residence. On April 7th Fr. General gave an account of the debates to all the Provincials of the Society (cf. *ARSI* 15, 275-276), to whom he also sent a list, along with explanations, of tasks, both in teaching and administration, and, with the unanimous agreement of the Council, asked that Jesuits arrive in Rome before October 1968. The Biblical Institute was hoping for six Jesuits, for Rome and Jerusalem. It did not get any straightaway!

Conclusion

At the end of this long chapter, some general conclusions will suffice.

1. The 1934 statutes had a long lifetime, because they were still in force in 1968. However, in 1945 the first cracks appeared that were to lead to some adjustments in 1948. After the Vatican II council and under its influence their reform was the order of the day and the Biblical Institute began to set about it. One thing never failed, and that was the frequently expressed wish to pursue really scholarly work at the Institute, especially at the research level. And what was in keeping with the spirit of the council was that new insistence on the theological dimension of exegesis, as well as the part played by students in the reform project.

2. Trouble that always kept coming back characterized this long period. Undisguised opposition to scholarly exegesis showed itself first of all with the

Ruotolo-Cohenel affair, with the support of several Italian bishops at the time of Pius XI and at the beginning of Pius XII's pontificate. Despite official pronouncements by the Holy See, the attacks on the method and orientation of exegesis at the Biblical Institute resumed in 1954. With the announcement of the council, which was the wish of John XXIII, and during its first session, those attacks became virulent and the Biblical Institute ran real risks for its survival, because the trouble-makers had support in very high places. This opposition resulted in Frs. Lyonnet and Zerwick being forced to withdraw from teaching exegesis for the period from 1962-1964; their rehabilitation was due to Paul VI and Fr. MacKenzie.

3. Still, the Institute was able to surmount the difficulties, thanks to the unfailing trust on the part of the Holy See, the authorities of the Society of Jesus and, during the council, the majority of the bishops. Pius XI's last public pronouncements in favour of the Institute and then, under Pius XII, the three major texts from the magisterium on exegesis, in 1941, 1943 and 1948, were at once an authoritative answer to the objections and an obvious encouragement of serious exegesis. Lastly, Vatican II's constitution *"Dei Verbum"*, in the composition of which the Biblical Institute collaborated from the outside, especially through the work of Frs. Lyonnet, Alonso Schökel, de la Potterie and Zerwick, not only put an end to all controversy, but was also a renewed source of energy and desire to serve better.

4. Life inside the Institute was facilitated in 1949 by the enlargement of its premises. The gradual increase in the number of students, especially just after the council, reached its peak. This, of course, was one of the first fruits of the council and of the place it gave to Scripture in all sectors of theology and the Church's life. To answer these needs the Biblical Institute, whose exegesis had been gradually freed from the anti-modernist yoke and which, since 1945, had been aware of the inadequacy of the preparedness of many students, finally opened, during the council, a propaedeutic course in Greek and Hebrew for candidates who knew nothing of those two biblical languages.

As for the teaching staff, the Society always successfully saw to its renewal. The qualities of the teachers were recognized in scholarly exegetical circles and by the Holy See, then by the council Fathers. The serious approach and dedication, the uprightness and courtesy of those professors played a large part in safeguarding the Institute and in expanding its commitments.

In brief, without forgetting that May '68, mainly in France and Italy, experienced the cultural revolution everyone knows about, the Biblical Institute at that time went through a springtime of promise in which, as professor or student, people felt they were taking an active and responsible part in the future.

Doc. R. III,1

APIBR B -XI-2

From Fr. Bea, unsigned and undated, but probably mid-January 1935.
Translated from the Italian

In September an *"International Congress for Old Testament Studies"* will be held at Göttingen (Germany). Mr. Stummer, who is one of the Committee and a professor of exegesis in the (Catholic) Theological Faculty of Würzburg writes to Fr. Rector to say that the Committee intends to send an official invitation also to the Biblical Institute to the said Congress and to ask Fr. Rector himself to give one of the lectures. In addition, the Committee is also thinking of inviting other Old Testament professors living in Rome, as, for instance, Fr. Frey, Fr. Vosté, Abbot Quentin.

The question now arises whether the Institute can accept this invitation or should decline it. There are reasons for and against.

I. In favour of acceptance:

1) The very fact that a Committee in large part non-Catholic feels the need to invite Catholic Exegetes and especially the Biblical Institute reveals a completely changed mentality in comparison with the contempt with which until a short time ago non-Catholic exegetes were wont to treat Catholic scholarship. Perhaps it would not be right to reject these good dispositions.

2) These good dispositions give rise to hope that Catholic exegetes may have also a healthy influence on the Congress itself, as has been the case at other similar Congresses (e. g. of philosophy, archaeology). As in other fields many non-Catholics are seeking support in the Church, which alone stands firm amidst all the upheaval, in present-day difficulties, even in biblical matters a certain return to good sense has already been observed, and it could be a work of the apostolate to favour this return to sane principles.

3) In the case of the Professors at the Biblical Institute there would be a certain advantage in making the personal acquaintance of the more influential people in biblical studies who belong to the other side and thus to establish relations that could be useful to the study of the Bible and the prestige of the Catholic Church.

II. Against acceptance:

1) Unlike other congresses at which the Institute is usually represented, e. g. oriental and prehistoric studies, etc., the subject being dealt with is a formally theological

one, to be discussed with non-Catholics as well. Working together in this field undoubtedly calls for more serious motives than in other fields.

2) The situation could be very awkward for the Institute's representatives if theories that cannot be allowed to go unchallenged are proposed by non-Catholic members of the Congress.

3) Indeed, given the mentality of some Catholic professors of Holy Scripture, quite well known from their publications, it could be that doctrines and theories may be put forward even by them which cannot be approved of, and that would make the position of the Institute's professors and those representing sound doctrine even more awkward.

The Professors of the Pont. Biblical Institute humbly submit these reasons for and against acceptance of the invitation and devoutly request that His Holiness kindly decide what answer should be given. Whatever the decision may be, they will strive effectively to promote the interests of the Holy See.

* * * * *

Doc. R. III,2

APIBR B-XI-2
Handwritten. Translated from the Italian

JMS-

(Copy)
Audience held on January 21st, 1935

I have read the *Statement* I had been given by Fr. Bea to the Holy Father, the Rev. Fr. General being aware of this, concerning the intention of the Committee for an *International Congress of Old Testament studies* to invite the Biblical Institute officially and to ask the Director to give a lecture at it and also to invite other resident professors, etc. –

His Holiness replied by giving His august opinion in the following words: –

"Although We have not examined the program, which may contain an opinion or something similar that is quite unacceptable, and trusting that the Biblical Institute, and not it alone among our Institutes, have people capable of dealing professionally with all foreseeable difficulties, the Holy Father is of opinion that (or rather firmly believes) that the Congress in question should be attended. ./.

To the difficulty raised in no. 3 of the second part of the Statement (against acceptance), His Holiness replied that it seemed to Him that the said Congress might provide a suitable opportunity to disown those Catholic Professors who have shown mistaken ideas about Holy Scripture in their publications. – But he added that addresses by orthodox Catholic Professors only should be delivered. – Of which notice should be given to other Institutes *of ours* and to *our* Professors who have been invited."

Rome 22nd January 1935

Gaetano Card. Bisleti

* * * * *

Doc. R. III,3

APIBR K-1-E

Report attached to a letter from Fr. Bea to Pius XI dated October 10th, 1935.
Translated from the Italian

C o p y

Statement
on the part played by the Pont. Biblical Institute at learned congresses
in the year 1934 [*corr.*: 1935]

I

At the "*2nd international congress of Old Testament Professors* ", held at Göttingen from 4th –10th of September, the Institute was represented by the Fr. Rector A. BEA and by Fr. Alfred POHL, Professor of Assyriology and History of the Old Testament. There were 64 voting members, 24 of whom were Catholics, the rest being German Protestants and Anglicans. The presidents were the Protestant prof. Volz (Tübingen) and the Catholic prof. Stummer (Würzburg). The part played by the Catholics, and particularly by the Biblical Institute, was greeted by all with joy, and as from the first address the line taken was that there was no question of hiding the principles and premises proper to each one (the time of "Voraussetzungslosigkeit der Wissenschaft" being already over), but rather of illustrating the problems from various angles and different points of view. And in fact the Catholics often spoke to expound the Catholic point of view and also to show the weakness of theories and explanations put forward by others and were always listened to with great attention and sometimes, e. g. in an explanation of the Catholic concept of prophetic inspiration, with particular interest and gratitude. The whole congress took place in full harmony and without the slightest incident.

The Catholics were represented by 4 papers, one of which was by the Rector of the Institute on the Institute's excavations in Transjordan and had been placed first at the first session by Prof. Hempel to mark it out; it met with keen attention and applause. All the papers given by Catholics were distinguished by the absolute seriousness of their study and methods, and could not but give others the impression that in the Catholic field work is being done with zeal and success. The superiority of Catholics was noticeable in particular in fields allied to exegesis, in the subsidiary sciences and in philosophico-theological fields.

The direction taken by the congress was quite different from the earlier one. The older generation of the followers of "literary criticism" was, even among the Protestants, poorly represented and no longer met with serious interest. The prevalent tendency was religious rather: Old Testament exegesis is a theological and religious understanding of the O.T.; the religion of the O. T. is quite a special phenomenon in the ancient world, based on the particular nature of the idea of God, different from all the others in antiquity.

Thoughtful attention was given to the Pontifical Biblical Institute because, at the end of the congress the Rector of the Institute was asked to give the farewell address and to give a short synthesis of the congress. With applause from all sides he was able to describe the congress as a meeting for working together and research in depth ("Vereinigung" and Vertiefung").

It is undeniable that the presence of Catholics marked this congress out in a special way and greatly stressed the tendency that many already had towards a return to more solid principles and sounder methods.

[We omit the points that follow, II and III.]

* * * * *

Doc. R. III,4

APIBR B-XII-2: S
Fr. Bea's reply to Fr. Gioachino Scattolon. Translated from the Italian

March 21st 1940

Reverend and very dear Professor

[...] I thank you also for that lively interest in the good of the Institute and of our good Fr. Vaccari, and very gladly will I give you some news about them, especially as it seems to me that this regrettable matter is being taken too much to heart. This is how things are at present. Fr. Vaccari has himself appealed to the ecclesiastical authority (to the Holy Office) which is examining the matter and in the meantime has imposed silence on both parties. That is the reason why Fr. Vaccari has not published the promised article. And I think the other party is also keeping to the directive; at least I am not aware of any publication that has come out after the beginning of this year 1940. Or do you know of any? (I am not speaking about the short article that appeared in the "Palestro del Clero", which was not written by a follower of Cohenel and called forth a reply that Fr. Vaccari quite welcomed, actually pointing out certain things to the Director of the journal). We here know that the highest authorities at the Roman Curia are on our side and that the behaviour of the two signatories of the booklet has been greatly disapproved of. One of them who came to Rome must have heard some words that were certainly not pleasant, as a very Em. Cardinal Prefect of a S. Congregation has told me, assuring me that he completely disapproves of the way in which Cohenel treats Holy Scripture.

As regards the Institute against which the booklet seems to bring some serious accusations, I approached Mgr. Sanna, bishop of Gravina, officially with the request to state whether the insinuation about rationalist- and modernist-based teaching is aimed at the Institute and, if so, to lay the proof before the S. Congregation for Seminaries. A few days later I had the formal reply that those accusations are not directed against "the venerable Pontifical Institute". I did not fail to pass on this declaration to the S. Congregation for Seminaries, of which the Very Emin. Cardinal Prefect actually is prepared to take energetic steps if the propaganda against Fr. Vaccari were to continue in the Seminaries.

You yourself have already guessed how much the authoritative approval of so many Cardinals or Prelates is worth. A Cardinal told me: "Every week we receive a pile of books, and of course it would be literally impossible to read them. Not to be discourteous, we send a word of thanks for the book". And the Cardinal was very indignant that use had been made of his words. Another Cardinal told me that he had sent a simple mark of gratitude along with the price of the book – and, lo and behold, his name is there among those who highly approve of the book. Cardinal Ehrle, of holy memory, answered that he was grateful for the book sent to him and had sent it to the Biblical Institute – he, too, is among those who approve of it. Not only that, but a bishop tells of having sent his visiting card with "w. t." ("with thanks") on it and of being among the "authoritative approvers" as well! That will be enough to give an idea of the propaganda that goes on in favour of Cohenel's work. It is obvious that involving the Cardinals and Bishops in the matter is also an embarrassment to the Roman authorities who, with due regard for the hierarchy, have to proceed very cautiously. That is the reason why the matter is going slowly, slowly . . .

This much is for your information. For the rest, if any propaganda literature in favour of Cohenel should come to hand I would be grateful if you could let me know; you should be aware of the fact that neither the first nor second booklet of the two bishops, nor the book by Cohenel himself nor any writings in his favour have been sent to the Institute. Only just now, after a long time, has Fr. Vaccari received the two booklets. That way of proceeding, too, is significant.

Let that be enough for today. Should you require any more information on one or other concrete point, please be sure that I am always at your disposal.

With renewed thanks and best wishes for a Happy Easter, I give you a heartfelt greeting.

Yours most devotedly in the Lord

* * * * *

Doc. R. III,5

APIBR K-6-B (I-3)

A placard supplied by the German authorities between October 10th and 25th, 1943

BEKANNTMACHUNG !

Dieses Gebäude diebt religiösen Zwecken un gehört dem V a t i k a n s t a a t. Haussuchungen und Beschlagnahmungen sind verboten.

Der Deutsche Kommandant
General STAHEL
(ink stamp)

===========

N O T I C E

Translated from the Italian

This building serves religious purposes and depends on the Vatican City State. Any searches or requisitioning are forbidden.

Der Deutsche Kommandant
General STAHEL
(with ink stamp)

* * * * *

Doc. R. III,6

APIBR K-6-B (I-3)

Translated from the Italian

SECRETARIAT OF STATE
OF HIS HOLINESS

From the Vatican. 25 October 1943

N. 72694

His Holiness's Secretariat of State is sending the one notice to be posted at the entrance to your building, but only after "the state of emergency" has been declared.

At the same time it prescribes that written or printed notices (such as "Property of the Holy See", "Diplomatic Protection of the Holy See", etc.) and declarations forbidding searches and requisitions that may be issued by the German Military Command in Rome or by the German Embassy to the Holy See be withdrawn from the front door or from the outside of the building to which they refer and kept, with due diligence, within the buildings themselves, close to the entrance.

Only those printed notices must be kept posted outside which indicate the extraterritorial character of buildings belonging to the Holy See which enjoy that prerogative.

His Holiness's Secretariat of State also expresses the hope that those in charge of extraterritorial buildings, or of buildings exempt from sequestration and taxes, as well as Superiors of Institutes or Religious Houses, for which the attached notice is issued, will be moved to the diligent observance of the arrangements and instructions from the Holy See and to that discreet and prudent upright behaviour which is always, but now more than ever, necessary.

(with ink stamp)

VATICAN CITY STATE

Vatican City, 25 September, 1943

GOVERNMENT OFFICE

_____

The Government Office of the Vatican City State, by order of the Most Emin. Cardinal Luigi Maglione, Secretary of State to the Reigning Supreme Pontiff Pope Pius XII, states that

the Pontifical Biblical Institute, Piazza della Pilotta, 35

is the property of the Holy See and as such is exempt from any search or requisition.

STAAT DER VATIKANSTADT

_____

Der Gouverneur des Staates der Vatikanstadt bescheinigt im Auftrag Seiner Eminenz des Herrn Kardinals Aloisius Maglione, Staatssekretärs des Regierenden Papstes Pius XII, dass

das Päpstliche Bibelinstitut, Piazza della Pilotta, 35

Eigentum des Heiligen Stuhles ist und somit frei ist von jedweder Haussuchung und Beschlagnahme.

THE GOVERNOR
(*signature*:) Camillo Serafini

Der Deutsche Kommandant
Generalmajor S T A H E L

Obige Angaben werden bestätigt, deutschen Wehrmachtsangehörigen ist der Zutritt strengstens verboten.

Der deutsche Kommandant
Gez S t a h e l
Generalmajor

Für die Richtigkeit
(*signature and stamp in ink*) (von Veltheim)
Oberst u. Verbindungsoffizier
des deutschen Reichsbevoll-
mächtigten für Italien

* * * * *

Doc. R. III,7

APIBR K-6-B (I-3)
Translated from the Italian

16 October [194]3.

(*at the bottom of the first page:*)
His Most Rev. Eminence
Cardinal Luigi Maglione
Secretary of State to His Holiness
    Vatican City

Most Eminent Prince

I think it my duty to report to Your Most Reverend Eminence immediately what happened here this morning.

About 11.45 5 German soldiers, under the orders of an "S.S." officer and ignoring the protestations of the doorkeeper to the effect that they were not allowed to enter the Institute, asked to be taken directly to the room of a certain Salvatore di Capua. Di Capua had been a manservant at the Institute over a year ago; he is Jewish by birth, but became a convert to the Catholic religion some twenty years ago; he had left the Institute in September 1942 and is now in some other religious community, also as manservant. So the doorkeeper, not being able to comply with the request, and not knowing German himself, took 4 of them to my room, while the officer along with another person stayed just inside the door. I immediately asked what they wanted, and one repeated that they were looking for [2] di Capua. I replied that di Capua was not in the house any more and added straightaway that, in any case, they had no right to enter the house. "But why?" "Because it is the property of the Holy See. Are you under the Commander General Stahel's orders?" "Yes, but we are from the police". "Read this document then", and I gave him the exemption statement countersigned by General Stahel. Having read the exemption statement, the man I spoke to said he had to show it to his chief who had stayed at the front-door. So I went with him to the officer who straightaway repeated that they were looking for di Capua. I replied saying that he was no longer in the house and asked that he take cognizance of the document, and seeing that the officer was from the "SS" I asked in a formal tone: "Are you under General Stahel?" He, somewhat embarrassed, answered: "Yes, in a way" ("ja, in gewisser Hinsicht"). I replied: "Then you have no right to enter this house". The officer, a bit put out, apologized: "Sorry, sir, we are not used to Rome and we do not know all these details". I answered: "I understand that, but", I added with a smile, "I hope this will be the last time you come here". He answered: "Be sure of that" and took his leave along with his soldier-policemen.

The officer behaved correctly, then, from the moment he was in my presence; but the way in which they got into the house, [3] ignoring the protestation, and, still more, without even wanting to be taken to the Superior, was not right, and had there not been a German Superior, complications might perhaps have arisen. But when they saw that they had to deal with a German who was well informed about the situation, they soon gave up. What would have happened if di Capua had been in the house is, however, another question.

I thought it right to inform Your Most Reverend Eminence immediately, not because I thought any further steps ought to be taken over it but only because the case is typical of the way things are done and it could also be repeated elsewhere and also because it seems important to me to note that the "SS" considers itself dependent on Commander General Stahel "in a way", and also that the "police" (I could not find out whether they were from the Gestapo or a department of the "S.S" police), while admitting they were under General Stahel, insists on being called "police".

I bow to kiss the Sacred Purple and humbly ask Your Most Reverend Eminence to accept the expression of the most reverend and grateful obedience, whereby I have the honour of saying that I am

Your Most Reverend Eminence's
very devoted and obedient

Rector of the Pont. Biblical Institute

* * * * *

Doc. R. III,8

APIBR K-23 (II-1)

Letter from Fr. Bea to Fr. Ledókowski. Translated from the Italian

16 November 1939

Very Reverend Father in Christ,
P. Cti

As I mentioned a few days ago, Fr. Calès has now sent a copy of the booklet on the Psalms of which the General Congregation approved and requested the publication. In order that Your Paternity may see whether the projected booklet corresponds or not to the wishes expressed, I take leave to send you the copy with some explanations to go with it.

Fr. Calès is thinking of putting the Vulgate text, as we have it in the Breviary, on the page to the left, and the Latin text translated from the original on the right, corresponding verse by verse and line by line. The Psalms are arranged in the order of the "Psalterium Romanum" and the antiphons were also placed so as to be used simply in reciting the Divine Office. Anyone reading the Vulgate text slowly while keeping an eye on the literal text easily understands what he is reciting, without being disturbed in prayer. In this way the scholastics and young priests will in a very short time be able to arrive at a sufficient understanding of all the Psalms The text is divided into strophes according to the sense and the laws of Hebrew metrics; this division will make it much easier to understand the meaning. Where it seems suitable, as in Psalm 2, the author is thinking of putting in a somewhat longer "preliminary note" to explain the theological importance of the Psalm. The notes could perhaps be a bit shorter. He sometimes adds "Explanations" in which he explains textual variants. It seems to me that these "Explanations" would perhaps be better placed at the end of the booklet (which is what Fr. Zorell did).

The booklet would be a bit more bulky than Fr. Zorell's and the price (in so far as one can calculate it in these uncertain times) for us would be, if 10,000 copies were printed (the Society numbers more than 8,000 scholastics), about 6 Lire (unbound), so the bound copy could be sold for 9 or 10 Lire.

As far as I can see at the moment, Fr. Calès's plan corresponds quite well with what Your Paternity and the General Congregation wanted. I would be grateful if Y. P. would kindly examine the copy, or have it examined and let me have the wishes and criticisms so that they can be given to Fr. Calès before he goes on with his work.

I commend myself to the Holy Sacrifices

Your Paternity's
most devoted servant in Xto

* * * * *

Doc. R. III,9

APIBR B-XIII-Documents
Document drawn up by Fr. Bea. Translated from the Latin

Committee for revising the translation of the Psalter
Session I
Thursday, January 22nd [1941], 18.30 hrs., in "the Provincial's" room

Programme
Discussion of "Rules" and "Procedure"

[2] Committee for revising the translation of the Psalms
Rules to be followed in the revision
(Draft I)

1. The text of the Vulgate is always followed if it faithfully renders the meaning of the original text (even though there may be a better version).

2. If it seems right to depart from the Vulgate text, St. Jerome's "Psalterium iuxta hebraicam veritatem" should be looked at first; if his version provides the necessary answers, it is adopted.

3. If not even the "Psalterium iuxta Hebraeos" is enough, a new translation according to the original text is attempted.

a) If the Hebrew text is clear and certain on critical grounds, it is simply to be translated.

b) If the Hebrew text is doubtful on critical grounds, the translation must follow a text restored according to critical principles and a prudent and sure method, such as is to be found in the works of contemporary Catholic authors (Calès, Knabenbauer, Vaccari, Zorell, Miller, Peters, Rembold).

4. The translation should also pay the greatest attention to rhythm ("smooth running") so that the text can be recited easily.

5. Translations that can be taken as models are to be found in Calès, Les Psaumes; Zorell, Psalterium ex hebraeo latinum; Rembold, Der Davidpsalter des röm. Breviers.

[3] Procedure

I. The Committee consists of six members: Frs. Bea, Köbert, Merk, Semkowski, Vaccari, Zorell. Members of the Committee are held to strict *secrecy*.

II. Frs. Köbert, Semkowski, Bea 1) shall prepare a draft of the revised text, each one containing Psalms equivalent to at least 25 verses, roughly, every week.

2) The draft is polycopied by Br. Hagemann and given to all the members in order that they may examine it and set out their remarks *in writing*.

3) On receiving these observations the author of the Draft examines them and prepares a report for the *session*.

4) A *Session* is held every week at which a) authors of drafts report on the observations, b) a discussion takes place, c) the text to be chosen is decided upon.

5) The author compiles Draft II, corrected in accordance with what was said during the Session and distributes it again to everyone, so that if anything is left to be desired it may be put down *in writing*.

6) Draft II is read out during the Session, is discussed (if need be), approved or sent back to be corrected.

III. After a sizeable part has been finished by us the text will be sent to the Supreme Pontiff so that he can express His opinion.

* * * * *

Doc. R. III,10

APIBR K-1-E

Translated from the Italian

PONTIFICAL BIBLICAL INSTITUTE
PIAZZA PILOTTA, 35
ROME (101)

MOST BLESSED FATHER,

In deference to the revered task received from Your Holiness to prepare a translation of the Psalms more suited to the private recitation of the Breviary, we have diligently started work, trusting in the Lord's help and Your Holiness's blessing. As fruit of our work I am honoured humbly to present Your Holiness with a first sample today, i. e. the translation of Psalms 1-20. Some pages (I-IV) precede the translation itself in which we give an account of the principles and rules that have guided us in doing the translation, especially as regards the text to be translated, the relationship between the new translation and the Vulgate and its Latin language. Then, to illustrate also in particular, how the rules of textual criticism for fixing the text and along with that the meaning in cases where the Masoretic text and the Vulgate differ, I thought it fitting to add some "notes" (pp. 1*-13*) in which the chosen text and the translation given are justified.

As regards the continuation of the work, which after the first experiments may now proceed more quickly, it would be very helpful for us to know whether the method adopted in this first sample in some ways corresponds with Your Holiness's august intentions or whether we ought to change it and how. In our desire to make the understanding of the Psalms easier for the clergy and the daily recitation of the Breviary more fruitful, we shall be grateful for any indication of Your Holiness's wish and shall with all diligence carry out the august orders that Your Holiness will deign to give us in the matter.

Kneeling to kiss the Holy Foot, I humbly implore the Apostolic Blessing on this important work and on all the work of the Institute.

Your Holiness's

Rome, 10 August 1941

Rector of the Pontifical Biblical Institute

* * * * *

Doc. R. III,11

APIBR B-XIII-Documents
Manuscript in Fr. Bea's hand. Translated from the Italian

17-XI-[19]43

Last Saturday the Holy Father asked Fr. Merk how the revision of the Psalms was going and was very pleased to hear that we are at the end. But he added that we should not be too much in a hurry.

He then expressed two wishes, with no little insistence:

1) that we *keep everything in the Vulgate that* clearly renders the meaning of the Vulgate [! *corr.*: of the Hebrew?].

2) that we choose *good* Latin; he did not actually ask for the classical Latin of the encyclicals or Bulls, but not, on the other hand, late and decadent ecclesiastical Latin, either; as an example he gave: non dico etc., *quod* instead of the acc. and inf. [*In the interests of clarity add here*: Do not write *dico quod*] "which is not Latin". Do not insist overly on the same *word*!

We shall therefore, in the final revision, and starting today, have to take these august wishes into account: the 2nd will not cause any difficulty; as for the Vulgate, we shall certainly often have to retrace our steps and put back the Vulgate text where the meaning of the original is correctly expressed, even though we would perhaps choose another word, e.g. *shama'*: Vulg. *exaudire*, which certainly gives the sense, because the Psalmist does not simply want to be "heard", but *listened to*; *resha'îm* Vulg. *peccatores*; we: the wicked; then expressions such as: *in saecula saeculorum* (which are known to everyone from the liturgy) and cause no difficulty in understanding the meaning. I think we ought to be scrupulous on this point, because the Holy Father is probably concerned not to give the impression that he is breaking with the Vulgate, after having spoken so much in favour of the original texts in the Encyclical. So please keep this wish in mind in the definitive revision, and perhaps it would be useful to appoint, as from today, an "*advocate of the Vulgate*", who could actually be Fr. A. Merk, who would then have to speak up whenever he thinks we ought to keep to the Vulgate.

* * * * *

Doc. R. III,12

APIBR B-XII: Z
Typewritten letter with autograph signature. Translated from the Italian

COMM. PROF. ISRAELE ZOLLI
TRIESTE
VIA NICOLÒ NO. 50

Trieste, 27 December 1935

Very Reverend Father Bea
Pontifical Biblical Institute
Rome

Most Reverend Father

I gave two papers at the Congress of Orientalists. The first is of purely Hebrew philological interest; the second concerns the etymology of the word Nazarene. The latter communication had the privilege of being discussed by the very learned Fr. Vaccari and being favourably quoted in the "Osservatore Romano". The contents are briefly as follows: The fact that Nazareth is not mentioned outside the Gospels does not show that the town did not exist in the time of Christ, but even admitting its existence does not explain the word Nazarene in itself nor the diversity of forms in which it occurs in the Gospels. It cannot be a question of a derisive name, as the illustrious Fr. Lagrange admits, in the sense of "provincial" because, if that were so, the disciples would not have continued to call themselves Nazarenes, nor would the announcement of the resurrection have been made with a term of mockery. The fact that Jesus himself, the fiercest enemies, the most fervent admirers and the disciples use the same epithet makes its interpretation very difficult. It cannot have the meaning of Nazarite, that is to say, "abstainer" in the sense of "saint", as Guignebert would have it, although actually he had hardly come out with the theory than he said he was dissatisfied with it. Nor can it, as others have wanted it, be a name given to an earlier sect, the Nazoreans, because the existence of that sect is generally placed in doubt these days. The term arose with Christianity itself, and not before. Guignebert eventually came to perceive that only a term indicating the *profession*, the main action performed by Jesus and his disciples could constitute the real core, the true meaning of the word Nazarene. – I am proposing to derive the term from the Aramaic verb *nçr*, with its possible derivatives: *naçora*, modelled on *amora* (Talmudic teacher) and *naçran*, modelled on *rabban*. These two forms can explain the two typical designations: *Nazoreans* and *Nazarenes*. If my explanation is accepted then all the difficulties vanish. The term in question means "preacher", and it is the preaching that drew the crowds around Jesus, and, above all, it is the preaching that struck and caught up and overcame the masses in an indescribable enthusiasm; at bottom, the preaching is that particular form of Jesus' activity which Guignebert perceives but does not recognize.

Instead of sending summaries (which are often unclear) of both papers for publication in the "Proceedings", I preferred to give the full text of my first paper because, in the few pages allowed each of us, it would not have been possible to include this second contribution, a bit bigger in size. I take the liberty, therefore, to approach Your Reverence to ask you to tell me whether it seems to you to be suitable for "Biblica" and whether perhaps you would be disposed to accept it. In that case I would take it upon myself to send you the manuscript without, of course, implying any a priori commitment on Your Reverence's part. In any case, it would be very advantageous for me to have your very valuable opinion on the question which I have much at heart.

Allow me, most reverend Father, to offer my best wishes for the New Year, along with the expression of my particular high esteem and devotion

I. Zolli

* * * * *

Doc. R. III,13

ARCHIVES OF THE SECRETARIAT OF THE PIB IN ROME

This document, inserted in the register of the deliberations of the Institute's Council of professors, is accompanied by a Latin translation, done by Fr. Ruwet. A typewritten copy of the document is in the APIBR A-11: III-2. Translated from the Italian

Observations made by Fr. Messina at the Professors' conference
at the end of the visitation in the year 1945, March 8th, 1945, 11.00 hrs.

Concerning the recommendation made by Fr. Visitor to provide a more thorough and scholarly education, a recommendation that was made on earlier visitations, Fr. Messina points out:

1) According to the intention of the Institute's founder, Pius X, the Biblical Institute has two main purposes:

a) to train teachers who, with sound learning and adequate instruction, can teach later on in various seminaries and religious institutes;

b) to train scholars as well who, besides teaching, can promote Scripture studies with thoroughness and scholarly precision and by contributing their personal research.

The first purpose has been achieved, and the merit for it goes indisputably in large measure to the Biblical Institute. Its merit is that much greater when one reflects on the fact that it arose at the time of modernism and had to overcome open and hidden hostility.

The second has not yet been sufficiently achieved. Why?

2) Although certain defects and shortcomings can be laid at the door of the professors, the main fault is not theirs but that of the circumstances in which they have to do their teaching.

In fact:

a) the student body is not uniform as regards ability and earlier preparation; eight or ten percent are capable of benefiting from really scholarly education, twenty percent could, after preliminary studies, be suitable for scholarly education; whereas seventy percent will always be unable to do it. Hence a really serious education is impossible for the great majority.

b) the programmes drawn up by the S. Congregation are so full of different subjects that it is impossible for the professor to give a thorough treatment and for the students to do personal study and train themselves for research.

3) If then we wish to avoid the difficulties that have been so often noted, we must make a selection among the students and separate the majority off from those who are capable of being trained seriously for research.

We must then draw up a new study programme for the latter which is of a real and distinctly university character.

But since the selection and the new programme do not depend on us but on the ecclesiastical authorities on which the Institute depends, their approval is necessary. For practical purposes Fr. Messina suggests:

4) that towards the end of the school year Fr. Rector speak to the H. Father in an audience about:

a) the excellent work that the Institute has done in the thirty years of its existence

b) the chance it now has, in view of its being fully equipped and the availability of new and well-trained professors, of providing a training that measures up even better to the extensive requirements of the new encyclical on biblical studies

c) the need there is, in order to achieve this purpose, of making a choice among [2] the students; and to draw up a new programme for those who are to be trained not only to be teachers but also for research to further biblical studies. The opportunity might also be taken to mention the advisability of some changes to the old programme, drawn up for the bulk of the student body – changes suggested not only by experience but also by the possibility of getting those doing that course to go on to the really advanced one, after serious tests and examinations.

d) In the new programme oriental subjects, besides biblical exegesis, ought to occupy the main position. This is in keeping with what was required by the Pope in the latest encyclical that oriental subjects are of great use to biblical studies [;] this is also clear from the fact that the best Catholic and non-Catholic biblicists, ancient or modern, come from the field of oriental studies.

e) The outlines of this new programme should be presented to the Pope at this audience.

If the Pope gives his approval it would then be a matter of drawing up a more detailed programme, asking for it to be approved and putting it straight into practice.

* * * * *

Doc. R. III,14

APIBR K-12-B (II-2)
Letter from Fr. General's Delegate to Fr. Bea. Translated from the Italian

(*at the bottom of the first page:*)
R. P. Augustin Bea
Rect. Pont. Biblical Instit. - Rome

Rome, 26 March 1947

Reverend in Chr. Fr. Rector
P. Chr.

At the end of the visit I paid to the Institute I promised Your Reverence that I would send some directives about the same. I am keeping my word.

First of all I must recognize that the Institute has done much good and made continual progress especially in recent years. It has merited very well of the Church and the Society. It has earned the merit of having kept to perfect orthodoxy in difficult circumstances; it has trained a large number of seminary professors; it has co-operated in the development of biblical studies.

But is all that enough? I do not think so. The Institute enjoys an extraordinary privilege thanks to the Holy See: apart from the Biblical Commission, it has the monopoly of admitting to degrees in Holy Scripture; it has the mission of training not only good professors but also high-quality exegetes, capable of promoting the Scriptures with their writings. By attaining that really necessary end the Institute will be a lighthouse within the Church and outside it for all who devote themselves to the study of Holy Scripture.

Now it seems that the Institute in its way forward has not yet sufficiently reached that ideal. But during the visit I was consoled to find that all the professors wish to move towards it with all their strength. We then tried together to pin down the obstacles that oppose[2]s it. These seemed to us to be the lack of professors and especially the too small number of capable students, their lack of talent and preparation and also time for devoting themselves entirely to these really higher studies. The great majority of the students are not at all suited for doing work that is really scholarly. Since the students who start studies at the Institute are very uneven in talent and preparation, it follows that the professors have to adapt themselves to the less capable in their teaching.

In that state of affairs I, like you, can see only one remedy, i. e. to double up the courses in exegesis. A higher course would be reserved for the pupils, fewer in number, who will be really able to follow it. It is clear that to put this reform into effect it would be necessary to bring in some new and possibly very good professors. That, of course, could only be done gradually. In the meantime it would be useful to study, along with the professors, and keeping the Institute's resources in sight, how a start could be made in that direction.

There is another obstacle in the way of the correct organization of studies at the Biblical Institute, that is to say a certain rigidity in applying the rules and ordinances emanating from the Holy See. The academic program for students coming with a better training could be made lighter. I would therefore advise using all the powers that the Statutes of the Institute confer on the Rector along these lines. It would also be opportune, as I see it, to revise the program of studies at the Institute. The students in the first two years are so weighed down with courses and examinations that one wonders whether it is possible for them to do any really formative work. Their aim is [3] too limited to repeating what the professors said and to make sure they do well in examinations. If I have properly understood what Your Reverence told me about the way in which the school programmes were made, my conclusion is that if you had a little more freedom in putting them together, you would have thought about them differently. I ask you, therefore, to see what improvement could be made in the school program, in consultation with some of the abler ones. When that is done, Your Reverence could ask the Most Reverend Fr. General's permission to discuss it with the S.

C. for Studies. If it is not possible to ask for everything that is wanted, some very useful improvements could be obtained, I think. It seems to me that the time is ripe for taking such a step. The S. Congregation is really well disposed and if necessary Your Reverence would be able to interest the Holy Father in this delicate matter. Among the things to be got would be an increase in the powers of the Rector of the Institute to settle certain particular cases.

There, Reverend Father, you have the directives I thought fit to send you. They have been approved by the Most Reverend Fr. General, who is very insistent on the need to train good exegetes. I entrust everything to your love for the Institute and to your prudence and discretion. I ask the Holy Spirit to enlighten and help you.

I recommend myself to your Holy Sacrifices.

Your Reverence's

Servant in Xt.
N. de Boynes,
S. J.

* * * * *

Doc. R. III,15

APIBR K-12-B (II-2)

A letter from the Fr. Delegate to Fr. Bea. Translated from the Italian

Rome, 3 April 1947

Reverend in Xt. Fr. Rector
P. Xt.

I thank Your Reverence very much for your letter of the 28th of last March and the diligent care with which you immediately followed up the directives I gave you. It was right to consult the professors first and, when they replied, to form a small Committee which, I hope, will be able to propose a satisfactory conclusion [...].

I have spoken to Fr. General about the visit I paid to the Institute and about possibly changing Your Reverence as Rector. Like me, he thinks we ought to wait until the work in the new building and the full installation of the Institute in its new premises are carried out and completed under Your Reverence's direction; he then adds that when a successor has to be sought he should be someone whose ability is sure and capable of continuing the work already well under way and moving it forward in accordance with the directives given. [. . .]

Fr. General is also ready to help you look for new professors of exegesis, able to do really scholarly work. He likewise approves of doing two courses in exegesis in the 1st and 2nd years, one for beginners, the other for the better prepared and abler students who can start straightaway on scholarly work.

Furthermore, he thinks that, if necessary, some improvements in the programme of studies at the Institute could be got from the Holy See.

I have nothing else to say, and I commend myself to the holy Sacrifices.

Your Reverence's
Servant in Xt.
N. de Boynes
S. J.

* * * * *

Doc. R. III,16

APIBR K-26-F (101)
Adjunct to the letter sent on January 20th 1948 by Fr. Janssens to Pius XII.
Translated from the Italian

Clarifications of the Draft
"Additions and changes to the Statutes of the Pontifical Biblical Institute"

The purpose of the changes proposed in this draft is to make it possible for those students of the Biblical Institute who give promise of successful scholarly work in the field of exegesis and biblical theology to concentrate more intensively and effectively on those central subjects. The multiplicity of subjects prescribed in the Statutes may be useful for those students preparing simply to teach in seminaries, giving them a kind of overview of the whole field of biblical studies and an idea of the contribution the various secondary subjects can make to exegesis. But that very multiplicity seems to prevent the more talented from *going fully* into their biblical learning, forcing them to get lost in secondary matters that can be studied easily and in a shorter time in private and which, besides, are largely a matter of memory.

The suggestions we are making fall into *four categories*:

1) Nos. 1 and 2 concern students who have already done part of the Institute's programme *elsewhere* (either by preparing the Doctorate in S. Theology with a thesis on a biblical subject or in [2] oriental studies, or in other similar Institutes). Making them repeat subjects already treated is not only a waste of time but also impedes the study of more important and central matters. It is therefore proposed to recognize what has been done, but keeping open the possibility of an examination in doubtful cases.

2) The 2nd category concerns those students at the Institute who give promise of *very good success in exegesis*, supposing they are given the right training. The Institute will therefore try to give as many courses in exegesis as will make it possible for students to choose in accordance with their training and purpose (no. 3). Moreover, the possibility of exempting them from attendance at one or other secondary (auxiliary) subject which they can easily and without wasting time study privately is being looked into (no. 4). Lastly, in place of the usual oral examination, a written experiment is being planned which would show not only what the candidate knows but also how good he is at personal work and research (no. 5).

3) The 3rd category concerns *the orientation towards exegesis* of not directly biblical subjects, both the auxiliary (no. 6) subjects and the oriental languages (no. 7). In both cases, however, the possibility of giving a more profound and effective training to those intending to specialize in those subjects is also being looked into.

[3] 4) No. 8 would like to make the *"exegetical lesson"* given by candidates for the doctorate more serious. Experience shows that the one hour allowed by the Statutes (art. 72 §2c) for preparing it cannot be enough – even if the candidate knows the books he is presenting very well – to give a proper exegetical lesson lasting one hour on a difficult subject. The rule still in force has been removed from the Pontifical Biblical Commission's programme which, however, prescribes a lesson of only 15 or 20 minutes on a "classical" topic, whereas at the Institute the candidate has to explain fully a difficult text for a whole hour. Not even a well-trained professor would be

content with only one hour's preparation in a difficult subject and in similar circumstances.

Rome, 13 January 1948

* * * * *

Doc. R. III,17

APIBR K-6-B (I-3a)

Unsigned duplicate of a letter from Fr. Bea, to be dated 1948, not 1947.
Translated from the Italian

3 January 1947

Very Reverend Father,

This evening a good opportunity presented itself for me to speak to the Holy Father about our letter and I courageously asked him why he had given orders to stop the press and not publish the document. I did not fail to tell His Holiness that we accepted the measure in that spirit of obedience and trust which we owe to the Vicar of Christ and we are resigned and at peace. The Holy Father readily accepted what I said and explained that he was struck by the phrase "allowing them, within the limits of revealed doctrines, the fullest freedom" (p. 1). To speak of freedom limited only by revealed doctrines seemed to the Holy Father to be too much. "It is also necessary to take Catholic tradition and the rules laid down by the Church's competent authority into account" ... however that may be, the phrase seemed to Him "ambiguous and exposed to the possibility of false and too broad applications["]. I then pointed out that, things being like that, the formula could be determined more accurately, and the Holy Father did not appear to be opposed to the idea of publishing the letter once the change had been made, although he did not say so explicitly. When I remarked that it is not possible for us to go any further as the Secretariat of State had not indicated the reason for the withdrawal of the document. Then [*read*: , then] he authorized, or rather charged, me to tell Your Reverence to explain to Him exactly what is the meaning of the words mentioned above and perhaps to suggest a formula less open to wrong interpretations. I am carrying out the revered task received from the Holy Father with great pleasure and I hope that a way will be found to give the text a tenor that will satisfy the Holy Father.

You will excuse me for involving myself in a matter that does not concern me at all, without having informed you earlier and getting your permission. But I was not to know beforehand that such a good opportunity would present itself. Knowing how much it is in your interest to see the letter published, I considered myself authorized not to let the good opportunity slip.

With renewed good wishes for the New Year and God's blessings

Your Most Reverend Paternity's
very devoted

Very Reverend Father
P. Giacomo-M. VOSTÉ O.P.
Secretary to the Pont. Biblical Comm.

* * * * *

Doc. R. III,18

APIBR B-XXIII-2

An Extract from the record of the deliberations of the community advisory Committee.
Translated from the Italian

May 1ˢᵗ 1954

The Rev. Fr. Rector informs all the Fathers of the Committee here present that a letter is being drawn up for the H. Father to obtain an authentic document in which the enlargement of premises of our Institute, which was completed in 1950, is stated. This document has been expected for some years now through the intermediary of our general Curia and in particular through the good offices of Fr. Marsili who, back in 1952, had informed us that the papal document in question would be delivered for the feast of St. Ignatius and then for the feast of the Assumption of that year. As the said brother died the day after last Easter and the matter has been in abeyance for almost two years, the Rev. Fr. Rector now considers it expedient to approach the H. Father immediately, also because a letter written by him not long ago to Prince Pacelli has so far gone unanswered.

* * * * *

Doc. R. III,19

APIBR K-11-C (II-4-6)

A letter in the handwriting of Fr. A. Décisier, the Lyons Provincial, to Fr. Bea.
Translated from the French

Lyons July 19ᵗʰ 1947

Reverend Father P. C.

In a letter of June 14ᵗʰ, 1947, the Very Reverend Father General asks me two things: 1. to assign Fr. Guillet to the Biblical Institute 2. to get him to do his tertianship immediately so as to send him to Rome for the beginning of next year.

I have no objection to make against the first point. It had in fact been agreed with you that Fr. Guillet would be given to you to occupy Fr. Vaccari's teaching post when the time came. I was only hoping that Fr. Guillet would be left to us for a few more years…

On the second point, I must point out to you a serious difficulty that Fr. Lyonnet will be able to explain to you in detail. For two years Fr. Guillet has been working closely with Fr. Fontoynont, his professor, on completing a very important book: Introduction to Scripture. If their work together stops, the book will not appear; Fr. Fontoynont, at his age, will not be able to finish it on his own. However, a further year of working with Fr. Guillet will make it possible to complete it.

I would therefore earnestly request from you that Fr. Guillet be allowed a year before his tertianship and that, if need be, you ask the V. R. Fr. General about this. The extra year granted to Fr. Guillet will in fact, as Fr. Lyonnet will explain to you, be a year of preparation for teaching the Old Testament.

I recommend myself to your Holy Sacrifices.

In Xo servus

A. Décisier, sj
Prov.

P.S. I consider that the non-appearance of the book planned by Fr. Fontoynont would be a real misfortune.

* * *

Fr. Bea's reply to P. Décisier. Translated from the French

[*at the foot of the first page:*]
Rev. Fr. Aug. Décisier, Prov.
42 Montée St. Barthélemy
LYON 5

Reverend Fr. Provincial
P. Xti.

Please excuse my not having replied to your letter of June 19 informing me of Fr. Guillet's being sent to join our Institute. But the letter arrived just at the time of the examinations and the close of the school year, and I, along with Fr. General, also had to settle the question of letting Fr. Guillet take a year to work with Fr. Fontoynont. Because it was actually Fr. General himself who had said that he was to do his tertianship immediately. Now Fr. General informs me that he has written to you giving permission to keep Fr. Guillet for another year and to get him to work with Fr. Fontoynont on the publication of the book.

So first of all, Reverend Fr. Provincial, please accept the most heartfelt thanks from me and from our Institute for the great favour you have done us in letting us have Fr. Guillet. I am sure God will reward you and your good Province for this sacrifice – I am fully aware of its being a great sacrifice – and that Fr. Guillet will be replaced in the Province by someone else whom the ever-generous Lord will send you. Here at the Institute the Father will have an active life that will be useful and fruitful for the whole Church and, of course, for your Province and your dear country as well. Once again, then, many thanks for your kindness.

I have not yet written to Fr. Guillet, assuming that Your Reverence has informed him of his new posting. I shall be very pleased if, with his help, Fr. Fontoynont's book could appear. If Fr. Guillet still has some free time, [2] he could get ready for studies at the Institute, studying the languages especially. I shall gladly be at his disposal for advice and directions. He will also have the opportunity to speak with Fr. Lyonnet who will soon be coming to Lyons.

Once again, Reverend Fr. Provincial, please accept our most sincere thanks. May the Lord reward you!

I commend myself to your Holy Sacrifices.

Your Reverence's servant in Xt.
[Aug. Bea, S. J.]
Rector.

* * * * *

Doc. R. III,20

APIBR K-1-A
Handwritten letter from Pius XII to Fr. J. Messina. Translated from the Latin

To our beloved Son
Joseph Messina, S. J.
Professor at the Pontifical Biblical Institute

You, whom We have known and esteemed for some time now, have given great pleasure by not hesitating to dedicate and send Us a volume which biblical scholars have been expecting for a long time, which has just been published and is called "*A Persian Diatessaron*", so that We may have a new token of your longstanding devotion to the See of Peter and may, so to speak, have a taste of the first-fruits of your work. To translate that ancient codex of the Harmony of the Gospels from Persian into Italian, to illustrate it with a survey of its history and to provide a commentary required manifold expertise in the subject, which was not lacking to you, seeing that keen observation and pertinacious work that overcomes difficulties in work of that kind were not lacking to you in completing the task you started on.

This excellent new book, therefore, complete in every part, confers great honour and renown upon the Church, the Pontifical Biblical Institute and you who, in a field where very few people sow, expertly reap sheaves of great value. For those who devote themselves to such austere studies you have indeed provided abundant material which will be of very great use and help to them and you shine forth to them with a practical example showing how accurately and minutely research and investigation into matters that really pertain to early Christianity should be done; only in that way and with that method do sound and lasting results, to be approved by all the best people, come about and prosper.

The gift moved Us deeply, therefore, and We thank you for your very kind services and heartily congratulate and praise you for what you have done, while it is Our fervent desire that it may happily result in spreading knowledge of the Gospel. As an auspicious token of divine bounty and of Our particular benevolence We impart the Apostolic Blessing which implores comfort and strength for you to endure further great labours.

From the Vatican, April 4th, 1951
Pope Pius XII

* * * * *

Doc. R. III,21

APIBR K-11-C (II,7)
Letter from Fr. General Janssens to the professors of the Biblical Institute.
Translated from the French

CURIA OF THE SUPERIOR GENERAL
OF THE SOCIETY OF JESUS
ROME

BORGO SANTO SPIRITO, 5
October 3rd, 1955

Reverend Fathers
P.Xti.

After the visit paid to your house in January 1955 by the Reverend Fr. Delegate I realized that some of you are asking questions about the prudence necessary in your research and teaching. I can understand that concern, for the task that is entrusted to you is difficult and carries responsibilities with it. You all, and I too, must wish that the Pontifical Biblical Institute continue to respond fully to the intentions of the holy Pope who founded it. In another connection, I have heard that from outside some unfavourable judgments have been passed about the safety of your teaching in certain sectors. But the precise allegations claiming to back up those judgments seemed, after serious examination, devoid of any foundation. This is not the first time, as you know, that your Institute is the object of such accusations; it will no doubt not be the last. Prudence cannot suffice to prevent, in a situation like yours, there sometimes being accusations of rashness on the part of rigid or fearful people and sometimes of timidity on the part of impatient or adventurous spirits. But it is good that criticisms, even superficial ones, should lead us to examine our activity in the sight of the Lord, so as to adjust our efforts and perfect our work. And in fact the concerns which I first alluded to arise in part from the feeling that some criticisms were directed against you. For my part, I shall take the opportunity arising, on the one hand, from those praiseworthy concerns and, on the other, from criticisms which I consider undeserved, to pass on some reflections on a matter which you have much at heart: true prudence in your work.

I shall not start, Reverend Fathers, by expounding the principles of Catholic hermeneutics as they are found in the dogma of inspiration and the magisterium, which is the authentic interpreter of the sacred Books. Nor shall I repeat the principles of exegesis to be found in the teaching of the Holy See, especially in the three biblical encyclicals: *Providentissimus Deus, Spiritus Paraclitus, Divino afflante Spiritu*, and in the series of replies from the Pontifical Biblical Commission. Lastly, I shall refrain from writing out the passages from the Society's Institute (for example, the ones from the new *Ratio studiorum* [July 31st, 1954: *ARSI* 12 (1951-1956) 520-663, especially nos. 181-185]) that show how our professors must teach exegesis. It is important, of course, that those various rules must be kept in mind and that you work in that spirit. But if I wanted to give an explanation based on quotations I would have to take up a lot of room in this letter. I do not think that that is necessary, because I would be reproducing texts that are known to you, on which you have reflected and which abound plentifully in the books you have at your disposal.

[2] Nor do I propose to apply those rules to the solution of particular questions that are discussed these days, such as the literary genre of such and such a text, sources, the date and author of this or that book, or the meaning of many passages. You give those explanations with the competence that is yours; you also give them – I have no doubt about it, but I do want to stress the importance of it in my eyes – knowing how to help each other with suitable consultations and frank and fraternal exchanges of views. So without talking here about particular problems I shall confine myself to describing the general characteristics of perfect prudence which you must try to reach. This description takes its inspiration entirely from the rules I have mentioned, but adds some clarifications which may guide your steps among disputed questions.

Professors at the Pontifical Biblical Institute, to deserve the great trust that the Holy See grants you, you cannot do less than strive to excel not only in learning but also in prudence. To excel in prudence in exegetical matters, what are we to understand by that? It cannot mean interpreting more strictly than the Church requires with the rules of hermeneutics it inculcates; rather, it expects you to use knowingly the right freedom it grants. It is not a matter of overestimating, for one's personal use, the weight of traditional authorities in favour of certain opinions either; real prudence calls upon us to assess the weight of authorities loyally and objectively. It is, lastly, not a question of avoiding dealing with important questions that are still obscure or as yet unexplored; for prudence must be courageous and necessary tasks have to be accomplished. I want these serious questions to continue to receive their proper place in your teaching and publications.

Excelling in prudence in the study of the Holy Scriptures means first of all excelling in docility to the Church, more precisely in the quality of a docility that is fully impregnated with a spirit of faith and a spirit of sonship; we want to "think in harmony with the Church" [IGNATIUS OF LOYOLA, *Spiritual Exercises*, no. 352], because it is commissioned by the Lord Jesus and aided by the Holy Spirit. In consequence it means being careful not to interpret the Church's directives in any way according to personal tendencies, but rather to bring one's tendencies into line with the directives it gives. It also means being careful not to depart from apparently surer positions except for really grave and seriously pondered reasons. If one adopts a new solution, one does so in a way that is always moderated by the proofs with which one maintains it. We do not wish a priori to be people with avant-garde solutions nor those with old solutions; rather, we strive to love only the truth and promote it by means of methodical research, drawing on the work of others, but above all by having that constant recourse to seeking answers from the documents that extracts their secrets from them. The publications of the heterodox and unbelievers are studied [3] while preserving enough strength of mind not to let oneself be seduced by theories that in part originate from disastrous philosophical or theological principles. It goes without saying that we keep away from any confusion between perfect sincerity, which knows how to be modest and docile, and the tendency to judge rashly and to be obstinate in one's own views. We are careful not to take pleasure in negative criticism, as if we wanted to state our independence and superiority by destroying. We keep to patient and persevering work so as to be able to contribute to discovering the meaning and bearing of newly discovered texts in order to arrive at an opinion based on new hypotheses; in short, at the cost of hard efforts we purchase knowledge that has the merit of being up to date without sacrificing soundness to being up to date. We should never lose sight of the fact that scientific techniques have their limits and that they do not replace – however precious and indispensable they may be – that light that comes from union with Christ and secretly puts the spirit in harmony with the message of Scripture.

Reverend Fathers, the prudence that must inspire your research must also appear on the outside. Immoderate expressions, cutting remarks and any hurtful words must of course be avoided. Let your writings and teaching be technical and critical, as is only right; but let them at the same time show, discreetly and clearly at the same time, the respect with which you study the divine word in the forms of human livery it has put on. If it should happen that your teaching be lacking in balance or respect, it would harm your Institute – you can have no doubt about that – and it would also harm your students. They will be entrusted with an important and delicate mission, more or less like yours. They, too, will need a special kind of prudence, more than the ordinary one, made up of a very harmonious combination of moral and religious dispositions. Where are they to find the concrete, suitable example and, if I can put it this way, the revelation of it except in their masters? You owe them that example at the same time as communicating your knowledge to them. Still, whatever the importance of outward prudence, it is not on that that I want to insist principally. If one were to concern oneself chiefly with that, it would soon degenerate into a kind of cleverness; whereas it must be the expression, no doubt willed but simple and sincere, of an inward attitude.

May this letter, Reverend Fathers, speak to you of the great interest I have in your work! It speaks to you of prudence; but that is in no way, as you will have understood, to get you to relax your efforts or to slow down. [4] The prudence that I shall always be glad to see in you is the one that can conceive great projects and use great diligence in carrying them out. The spiritual, inexhaustible riches contained in the Holy Scriptures, the desire of Catholics today to have the greatest possible access to those riches, the new exegetical problems that are always cropping up and the difficulty and austerity of your task are all made to stimulate your ardour in delving into and explaining the written word of God.

I commend myself, Reverend Fathers, to your holy Sacrifices
Your servant in our Lord.
John Janssens, S. J.

* * * * *

Doc. R. III,22

APIBR K-130-A

Only the first two pages of a 12-page document + 5 attachments written by Fr. Vogt on January 3rd, 1962, are given here. Translated from the Italian

M e m o r a n d u m
on the attacks on the
PONTIFICAL BIBLICAL INSTITUTE

I. Attacks before 1961

1.- [*Ten lines in two paragraphs on the Cohenel affair, not given here*]

2.- In 1954 rumours about the Biblical Institute were going round, which, however, I was unable to grasp. But on January 27th, 1955, the Most Eminent Card. Pizzardo passed on some serious accusations against the Institute to me concerning two of its professors, Fr. Robert Dyson and Fr. Robert North. It was Mgr. Romeo, as he himself later admitted, who drew up these accusations:

> ... some rather risky ideas are going around at the Pontifical Biblical Institute. Even after [sic!] "Divino afflante Spiritu" and "Humani generis" these "advanced" ideas "of modern criticism" of modern times have continued to be patronized and propagated. Since at the Pontifical Biblical Institute ... hypotheses of criticism coming from Protestant liberals are readily adopted ... which do not seem to be easily reconcilable with Catholic ideology. – The ideas favoured by those people would open the way to the exclusion of the whole of the "revealed economy" of the Old Testament, beginning with the two fundamental objects of faith: God, future retribution.

I answered with a detailed memorandum, refuting the exorbitant accusations and openly expounding what was being taught at the Biblical Institute. Mgr. Romeo, regretting that a chance had been given to answer his accusations, then said to a Professor at the Institute that the accusations ought not to have come into our hands but only those of the Holy Office.

[2] I have reason to believe that the Holy Father Pius XII himself has seen that memorandum of mine. However, when I went to see the Most Eminent Card. Pizzardo on May 5th, 1955, to complain that Mgr. Cechetti and Mgr. Romeo were schem-

ing to have the two professors under attack removed, the Most Eminent Cardinal, with great kindness, said to me, word for word: "Don't worry, it's all over, everything is all right. It really is providential that only the day before yesterday I was with the Holy Father and he told me spontaneously that he was very pleased that everything at the Biblical Institute was all right and was going well". Then the Most Eminent Cardinal added: "Those fundamentalists are prejudiced; one [Mgr. Cechetti] knows nothing about it, and the other [Mgr. Romeo] has his own ideas. I shall tell them not to get involved in these matters any more".

3.- That order had little effect, because on January 15th, 1958, I had to write to the Most Eminent Card. Pizzardo to protest about some very serious calumnies spread by Mgr. Romeo against the Biblical Institute in letters which I have at hand. His Eminence reassured me on the telephone immediately, mentioning the reason why Mgr. Romeo's words were not to be taken seriously.

On July 2nd, 1958, on the front page of the "Osservatore Romano" there appeared an aggressive, fundamentalist, anonymous article against the "Introduction to the Bible", vol. I: "Old Testament", a second edition of which was being got ready with the agreement of the Rev. Fr. Bea and the Holy Office. Because of that article a Most Eminent Cardinal wrote, that same July, a letter to the Holy Father Pius XII, calling his attention to the dangers of fundamentalism and to the attacks on the Catholic exegetes who follow the norms of "Divino afflante Spiritu". In the same month, July 28th, 1958, in reply to that letter, as the same Most Eminent Cardinal told a professor from the Biblical Institute, Pius XII sent the "International Catholic Biblical Congress" at Brussels a message in which he praised the strenuous work of the exegetes, encouraging them to go forward and saying that they could be "strong in Our esteem" ("L'Osservatore Romano", August 25-26th, 1958). [. . .]

* * * * *

Doc. R. III,23

APIBR L-130-A (L & Z)
A typewritten page by Fr. Lyonnet. Translated from the French

MEASURES TAKEN AGAINST FRS. LYONNET AND ZERWICK

15.10.61 The Rev. Fr. Rector receives notice from the V. R. Fr. General that the H[oly] O[ffice] requires that Frs. Lyonnet and Zerwick cease teaching exegesis or biblical theology. V.R. Fr. General adds that he is referring the matter to the Holy See; in the meantime the said Fathers should find a pretext for delaying the start of their classes. He hopes to have an answer in about ten days' time.

In fact the wait went on until the end of November.

End of October 1961. The V. R. Fr. General meets with Frs. Rector and Zerwick (Fr. Lyonnet being in "convalescence" at Fiuggi) and explains how things stand. The V. R. Fr. General refused to take the measure. He is asking the HO to take it itself if it thinks it opportune.

22.11.61 Meeting of Cardinals who are members of the HO (Wednesday).

23/11.61 The Rev. Fr. Rector receives notice from the V. R. Fr. General that the Frs. can start their classes (at least for the school year that has started).

Beginning of January 1962. The V. R. Fr. General calls me to the Curia to bring me up to date on the situation.

Here is a summary of the conversation (which lasted fully an hour):

"What are they accusing you of ? – Father, I don't know exactly. – Nor do I. I have not been able to get any details. In those conditions, I replied that I could not take the measure required, I had no right to". The conversation ended with these words: "Father, I have nothing to reproach you with!".

The V. R. Fr. General then explains to me that, at first, thinking the measure was definitive, he had asked at least for a delay to give him time to find replacements for the two professors. In sending him the authorization for the two Fathers to resume their classes, wrong use was made of the offer formerly made by him; he therefore had, in principle, to find replacements for them during the school year 1961-1962! But the V. R. Fr. General hastened to add that, of course, after [the decree: *words crossed out*] the decision of the Holy Office as such, that restriction had no further *raison d'être* and that he would no longer take any account of it. He was probably wrong in thinking that the matter was settled. I had understood that he intended to submit the case to the Holy Father. He does not seem to have done so and others got in first, at least that is what can be concluded from what followed and what I have heard from Fr. Vogt.

Notes taken by the Rev. Fr. Vogt: he is referring to what the Very Rev. Fr. General told him.

11.2.62. Had audience, went well, kept to generalities. Better not to talk about it so as not to annoy those who started the tempest.

18.5.62. Am in touch with the Secretariat of State about LZ. After the reply from the Biblical Commission we'll see what the Holy Father thinks.

25.5.62. I recently sent some information to the Holy Father; am waiting for reactions. On 23.5.62 there was a call from the Secretary of State. The Holy Father is content with the measures taken over LZ. The matter is now in the hands of the Biblical Commission; the Holy Father, not wishing to act brusquely or arbitrarily, seems to want to have a reply from the B. C. before [acting: *word crossed out*] any other action. I am waiting for the decision which is being studied.

26.5.62. Fr. Vogt notes: "From one of the consultors on the B. C. I know that our case was not submitted to the B. C. It is preparing a decree of a general nature".

* * * * *

Doc. R. III,24

APIBR L-130-A (L & Z)
Two typewritten pages, but title handwritten
In italics are the words underlined in red in the text (by Fr. MacKenzie ?).
Most of the brackets are in the original. Translated from the Italian

THE STORY OF THE BAN

On *October 1st, 1961*, the Rev. Fr. Vicar [John J. Swain] called me and told me that Card. Ottaviani and Mgr. Parente requested the replacement of Frs. Lyonnet and Zerwick for the approaching school year in the teaching of exegesis; they could remain at the Institute and teach other subjects; it should not be said that the order came from the H. O. [There were two weeks to go before the beginning of the new school year.]

The R. Fr. General had replied that at the beginning of the year that measure would cause a sensation; if only it were at least during the year. Besides, in the Society no professor is deposed without his being warned beforehand of what he is accused of. Fr. Vicar also indicated to me the "reasons" that had been put forward against our two professors; they were quite futile; (cf. my "Memorandum on the attacks on the P. B. I.", pp. 13-14, under the heading "The crisis becomes acute").

On *October 16th* 1961 Fr. Vicar wrote to me: "Fr. General has prepared a memorandum for the Holy Father on the question of Fr. Zerwick and Fr. Lyonnet. He is waiting these days for a talk with the Secretary of State to present the abovementioned memorandum. He hopes to have an answer within ten days at the latest. In the meantime he has asked me to ask Your Reverence to find a reason why those two Fathers should not start school before there is any answer from the Holy Father. This must be done so as not to annoy Cardinal Ottaviani". – It was done so under plausible pretexts. But because the delay lasted several weeks some people clearly guessed the reason for it.

On *October 23rd* 1961 Fr. General summoned Fr. Delegate [René Arnou], the Rector, Fr. Zerwick and Fr. Lyonnet (who could not come as he was away from Rome) to the Villa Cavaletti. Fr. General suggested proposing to Card. Ottaviani and Mgr. Parente that the two professors accused should declare in a lesson that they did not teach the doctrines attributed to them. – That proposal was made. [I know that the matter was suggested at the meeting of the Consultors of the H. O. on *October 27th* 1961 and at the meeting of the Cardinals of the H. O. on *October 29th* 1961].

On *November 23rd* 1961 Fr. General summoned me and gave me the order from the H. O.: The two professors may teach, – but let them be replaced during the school year. [N. B. I know for sure that the meeting of the Consultors of the H.O. did not find anything against the two Professors and gave it as their opinion that they could teach. They did not know about the order to replace them during the school year. That came, therefore, either from the meeting of the Cardinals or from those in charge at the H. O.].

So the two Professors began to teach. On December 21st I suggested to Fr. General that Fr. Zerwick finish his exegesis at the end of the course before Easter. Fr. Lyonnet would interrupt his exegesis at Easter and the remaining weeks would be given to another Professor. Fr. General approved.

[2] On February 11th, 1962, Fr. General informed me: "the audience with the Holy Father was good and, although it was confined to generalities, quite reassuring. It will be better not to talk about it so as not to annoy those responsible for the storm". He spoke to me in March along the same lines.

About the same time I learnt from a reliable source (Mgr. Capovilla to Fr. Danesi and he to Fr. Lyonnet): The Holy Father does not want anything changed. The Holy Father's tactics are in favour of not changing anything; then everyone will see that there was nothing in the charges.

I was convinced that the order from the H. O., that is to say the second part of the order had lapsed. Fr. Lyonnet continued his exegesis even after Easter, while Fr. Zerwick had already finished it. But on *May 17th*, 1961, Fr. General, mentioning the names of Mgr. Parente and the Secretariat of State, told me: It is said that nothing in the Institute was done about the two professors. The order against the two Professors still remains. I replied that in a week's time (May 26th) the school year would end and a drastic measure would change nothing. The replacement would be made for the next school year.

In a letter dated *May 18th, 1962,* Fr. General wrote to me: "I am in contact with the Card. Secretary of State about our two Professors. After the reply from the Biblical Commission we shall see what the mind of the Holy Father is and act if it is desirable".

The reply came before the meeting of the Biblical Commission, because on *May 25th* 1962 Fr. General wrote to me: "I was waiting for the reaction of His Holiness to the information I had sent him recently. Two days ago, I was called to see the Card. Secretary of State: the Pope is pleased with the measures taken over Frs. L. and Z.; the matter is now in the hands of the Biblical Commission. It seems clear to me that we must wait for further news. It appears clear to me that His Holiness, not wishing, in his great charity, to act high-handedly nor to seem arbitrary, wishes to have a reply from the Commission before any other action. Let us leave things to Divine Providence. I would think that the Institute will emerge from the trouble greater and more firmly established".

On May 26th, 1962, I was reliably informed that the Biblical Commission *had not been questioned* about our case. The Consultors would be glad to make a pronouncement about us. But the Commission had to produce a decree on the whole biblical situation in the Church, and in a very short time. The Consultors' meeting was in June and that of the (Cardinal) Members of the Commission on June 22nd, 1962. *We have not heard anything more* about our Professors. The differences within the Commission will then come to light in the Council.

On *June 2nd, 1962, I asked Fr. General* whether, the following year, the two Professors could direct a seminar and Fr. Lyonnet teach biblical Theology, because only teaching exegesis was forbidden them. *Fr. General's answer was in the negative.* In 1962-1963 Fr. Zerwick taught biblical Greek, as had been the case for years, anyway. Fr. Lyonnet did not teach anything in the 1st semester; in the 2nd semester he gave a minor course on the Codex Neofiti to our Students in Jerusalem.

September 21st, 1963

E. Vogt, S. J.

* * * * *

Doc. R. III,25

APIBR L-130-A (L. & Z.)
Copy of a letter from Fr. MacKenzie to Cardinal Ottaviani.
Translated from the Italian

PONTIFICAL
BIBLICAL INSTITUTE
THE RECTOR

22 January 1964

Most Reverend Eminence

I thank Your Eminence once again for the kindness shown to me at the audience on December 16th last. The conversation I had with Your Eminence then and the graciousness towards me encourage me to expound to you in writing the main difficulty I have to confront at present. Before the audience I was already aware – and was even more so after it – that the Supreme Sacred Congregation of the Holy Office had not been satisfied that two of our professors, Fathers Lyonnet and Zerwick, had been prudent enough in their way of setting forth some delicate points of doctrine. I also knew that, for that reason, the Authorities of the Institute had received the order to suspend the said two religious from their posts as professors of biblical exegesis.

That order was carried out, as I can assure Your Eminence. Naturally, that happened not without great sacrifice. Apart from the inevitable personal suffering the two professors felt deeply, while accepting it in the spirit of obedience, the said decision deprived the Institute of two full Professors in the New Testament faculty, a gap which it has not been possible [2] to fill satisfactorily. I therefore entertained the hope, as I mentioned to Your Eminence, that the Supreme Sacred Congregation might allow the two religious to resume their activity now, after two years of suspension.

On this matter I wish to reassure Your Eminence about this in writing, too, that I am fully aware both of the need of absolute fidelity to the teaching of the Church and of the need of the greatest discretion and prudence on the part of the professors of the Institute in dealing with Scripture subjects, and in particular the interpretation of the Gospels. It is my wish to take every precaution for the future so that the work of our Institute should not give Your Most Eminent Reverence or the Supreme Sacred Congregation any cause for concern. In fulfilling the duties pertaining to my office it will be my care to see to it that the professors of the Institute are most faithful to the Church's teaching, especially to all the Encyclicals of the Supreme Pontiffs and to the decrees of competent circles and to their directives, in particular the Sacred Congregation for Seminaries and Universities, on which the Institute is directly dependent. In this way we shall make sure, and we trust in the Lord to succeed in this, that Your Eminence will never have reason to be less satisfied with the Institute for the duration of my term of office.

If, however, there should be any question that may give rise to concern on the part of Your Eminence, may I say – as I have already had the opportunity to point out in the audience granted me – that I shall not be other than profound[3]ly grateful if Your Eminence would do me the honour of drawing my attention to it instantly, in the certainty that I shall use all the means at my disposal to remedy it?

I ask Your Eminence to accept my renewed thanks for the favour of the audience granted to me and to permit me to express the hope that I may be able to return again to this matter in person in the near future.

I bow to embrace the Sacred Purple and take this opportunity to state that I am

Your Most Reverend Eminence's
humble servant in Christ
R. A. F. MacKenzie, S. J.
Rector

Cardinal Alfredo Ottaviani [*added in handwriting*]

* * * * *

Doc. R. III,26

Archives of the Bishops of Namur, Belgium
Mgr. André-Marie Charue Collection
Vatican Council II Documents
"On Revelation". A 134

Letter from Fr. Lyonnet to Mgr. Charue. Copy in APIBR K-1-F.
Translated from the French

PONTIFICAL
BIBLICAL INSTITUTE

Rome (2) 30-1-1965
Via della Pilotta 25

My Lord,

It may seem bold on our part to wish to improve still more a draft the excellence of which everyone rightly praises. However, in view of its exceptional importance, the Bishops of Brazil have insistently asked us to suggest a certain number of amendments, very minor ones for the most part, to propose to the theological Commission and we can hardly refuse them; especially as other amendments along very different lines have already been, or soon will be, proposed, as every one here knows.

It is clear that Your Lordship knows better than anyone whether it is right or not to make changes at the last minute to a text that has been maturely written. Nevertheless we thought that Y. L. would not be annoyed at our passing on to you, just for Your information, the suggestions we thought we would make, once again, not on our own initiative but at the express request of the bishops.

I take this opportunity once again to express to Your Lordship the most sincere thanks of the exegetes for a really liberating draft document, and everyone knows what it owes to you. I admit to having been particularly pleased to read this very morning that Lukas Vischer had declared at a meeting of the full Ecumenical Committee that he considered the draft document on Revelation one of the most promising, especially because of the way it speaks of the Bible in the life of the Church. These proposals of ours are precisely concerned with the writing of that important chapter, of which others would practically want to cancel the effect.

With our renewed thanks, please accept, my Lord, the assurance of my religious respect and entire devotion in our Lord

[signature]
Stanislas Lyonnet, S. J.

* * * * *

Doc. R. III,27

APIBR K-26-D

James SWETNAM, *Some reflections on the History of the "Propaedeutic Year" at the Pontifical Biblical Institute, June 23, 2007*

One mild October evening in the autumn of 1963 Fr. Frank McCool of the New York Province came to me during evening recreation (the U. S. contingent of the community used to walk up and down on the southern side of the cortile after supper, i. e. the side without the colonnade). He said there were some Africans who wanted to do the licentiate at the Biblical Institute but that they were weak in their Greek preparation. He asked me if I could help them. This was the beginning of the Greek half of the "Propaedeutic Year", though at the time neither of us suspected it. Up until that point all the men who came to the Biblical Institute to do the licentiate in Scripture had had classical Greek. It was then just a matter of having a course in which the principal differences between classical Greek and New Testament Greek were set out. Fr. Max Zerwick's *Graecitas biblica* was based on this principle. But now we were beginning to get men (the first woman presented herself in 1965) who had little or no Greek.

McCool knew that I had taught Greek in the U. S. in high school, and this seemed to him an excellent preparation for helping beginners. He was exactly right. I had had two years of classical Greek in high school (St. Louis University High School in St. Louis – I had wanted to take Spanish but my academic advisor changed that to Greek; we were then in the years before the invention of non-directive counselling), and then had had Greek a bit during the novitiate at Florissant, Missouri, with two years of rather intensive Greek during my subsequent "Juniorate" at Florissant, taught by the unforgettable Francis R. Preuss, S. J., whose preparation included a classical tripos degree from Cambridge. During my teaching days at Regis High School in Denver, Colorado, I taught Homeric Greek for three years. I was sufficiently prepared from the standpoint of my knowledge of Greek. But more important, I was sufficiently prepared from the standpoint of pedagogical method. Teaching high school boys for three years had been an invaluable dry run for what I was to do for thirty-six years at the Biblical Institute. (I have never fancied myself a professional classicist; my A. B. from Saint Louis University gave me a major in Greek and minors in Latin and philosophy, but I am innocent of graduate work in either language.) Nor have I ever thought it desirable – much less ever attempted – to produce professional Greek scholars at the Biblical Institute. This would have been impossible, and, in any case, not really necessary. From the very beginning I recognized that what was needed was enough Greek to be able to take the advanced course in Greek (now called "Greek A-B"), i. e., two semesters designed to enable the student to follow explanations of the professors and the arguments based on Greek used in scholarly books and articles.

From the very beginning I had the students write their names on file cards the day the course began. (I have kept all of them, from all thirty-three years.) From that first year, 1963-1964, I have cards for six students. Three of the cards bear the annotation "First semester only", which implies that the course went for the entire year. The three apparently had had Greek and wanted just enough help in class to be able to be admitted officially to the advanced course. (Perhaps they had begun this advanced course in October along with my course.) My course concentrated on morphology and basic syntax.

For the academic year 1964-1965 I had eight students, though one quickly left the course. And two left at the semester. In 1965-1966 I had twenty-two students, of whom two were women. One left the Institute before finishing the licentiate, but the other, Maria Luisa Rigato, went on to obtain the licentiate at the Biblical Institute and a doctorate in Biblical Theology at the Gregorian University and has happily remained much in evidence at the Biblical Institute ever since she entered the Propaedeutic Year. As the numbers indicate, by the beginning of 1965 the Propaedeutic Year was a part of the academic landscape at the Institute. It was never a part of the official curriculum for the licentiate, but more and more it became an unavoidable feature of the lives of an increasingly large number of students. A student could always avoid the Propaedeutic Year by taking the Qualifying examination. I always encouraged students whom I thought qualified to take this route. But most were simply not prepared enough. Some came for a semester in order to freshen their previous knowledge of Greek, but more and more they had nothing to refresh and had to take the entire year.

I determined the material to be taught. It was not too difficult a choice. I took the paradigms of the grammar of Jay and made sure the students knew them well. Reading the text of the New Testament began with Day 1. By March we had finished the memory work of the paradigms and I chose two gospels, Mark and John, for reading in class.

In the United States I had found it advantageous to have the high school students answer a brief quiz on a daily basis. At the outset of my first year of teaching Propaedeutic Greek in Rome I thought that this was an unnecessary discipline for mature students, so I did not resort to it. At the semester exam in January, however, I was dismayed by the low level of what the students had retained. From that time on the daily quiz (eventually it became standardized into seven questions) was a feature of everyday existence. For the year 1966-1967 I began the practice of keeping a record of the grades achieved by each student on every quiz. The grades of such quizzes were not used to calculate the official grade for the course, but they were useful for me and for the students to see just where the student stood in relation to his/her peers and to the subject matter of the course. I have all these records still, from thirty-three years.

There were normally four or five major examinations during the year. Grades were assigned for each semester. Students who failed a major examination could repeat it, of course, but a second repetition was granted only after consideration. In the course of my thirty-six years of teaching I was responsible for forty or fifty students leaving the Institute, usually on the grounds of insufficient ability in languages. I tried as best I could, circumstances permitting, to make sure that the student found a place at another ecclesiastical academy in Rome. Lack of language skill, of course, is not necessarily a sign of a lack of intelligence.

The system of exams which I found most to my liking was one initiated by Fr. Horacio Simian-Yofre when he was dean of the Biblical Faculty: the Propaedeutic Year was an entirely voluntary proposition, and all the examinations were voluntary. Only one thing was essential: the taking of the Qualifying Examination whenever the student felt prepared. At one stroke this removed all need for surveillance of the students, and the responsibility was put squarely on their shoulders. (During his mandate as Dean Fr. Simian-Yofre asked me if I wanted to teach Greek A-B. I replied that I thought I was doing more important work right where I was, in the Propaedeutic Year. The material was not as challenging, but the students were more in need of individual attention. And since I was having qualified success in introducing them to the Biblical Institute, I preferred staying were I was.)

As principles in teaching I adopted two basic sets. One set involved the relation of the student to the teacher. In this set there were three principles: Exposition, Communication, Communion. Exposition involved setting forth as clearly as possible the fundamentals of the Greek morphology and of the Greek syntax of the New Testament. Communication involved making sure that this exposition found a place in the existence of the student. Communion was less tangible. It consists in the relation of the student to the teacher precisely as persons. It can be occasioned but not programmed. It involved an active *cura personalis* by the professor for each student that extended beyond the classroom. (A rather delicate matter, for one had to respect the student's privacy.) It was at this level that I had to decide if a student should be advised not to try to go on at the Institute. More frequently, it involved challenging the student. I recall one student in particular, who, after the first exam in November, got a respectable grade in the mid-eighties, But I thought he could do a bit better and I told him so. He worked like a dog from then on and at the end of the year his grade was in the mid-nineties. Corresponding to this *cura personalis*, of course, was the reaction of the student towards the professor. With approximately 120 classes a year, the student had innumerable opportunities to size the professor up, as a student does in any classroom situation. On the whole I got on well with the majority of my students.

The other set of basic principles involved the way I set forth the material. Early on I set the norm that the goal of the student was to know all the details, not just in general but in particular. Repetition was the key here. It was made clear that the students must master everything in detail, and for the normal person that meant constant repetition. Then, in the final weeks of the course, the knowledge learned by rote the first three-fourths of the course had to be translated into ability to read the Greek text. The ultimate test of the success of the course was the pleasure which the student would take in reading the Greek of the New Testament. (I recall the first day of reading the text in my Hebrew class of 1974-1975. We reached the end of the period and indicated that class was over, but a priest from Nigeria said he wanted to continue. He was so excited by his ability to read the text in the original language that he didn't want to stop. This, of course, was the ultimate goal I had in teaching both languages.)

In the late sixties Fr. Carlo M. Martini, then Dean of the Biblical Faculty, asked me if I would assume the new role of Director of the Propaedeutic Year. The Director would be under the authority of the Dean, of course, but would be responsible for the supervision of the students in both Greek and Hebrew in the Propaedeutic courses. I begged off on the grounds that I was not really capable. Looking back, I think I was too diffident of my own abilities which, by that time, had been honed by five or six years of teaching in the challenging international atmosphere of the Institute. Martini as a result kept the responsibility of such work to himself, but I now regret not accepting his request and lightening his work load. When I came back from my three years at Oxford and had resumed teaching the Greek Propaedeutic Year, Fr. José O'Callaghan, as Dean of the Biblical Faculty, asked me to act as Director, and I accepted.

In the academic year 1972-1973 I came across a new grammar of introductory biblical Hebrew written by Thomas Lambdin. It immediately impressed me as an improvement of the grammar which we were using in the Hebrew Propaedeutic Course. That grammar, Weingreen, was quite good. But I felt that Lambdin would prove more satisfactory for our needs. I asked Fr. Luis Alonso-Schökel, who was responsible for the teaching of Hebrew in the Propaedeutic Year, if I could experiment during the coming academic year with eight students who would volunteer for a course taught in English by me using the new grammar of Lambdin. He agreed, and thus I began the academic year 1973-1974 with eight students who had volunteered. One left in the course of the year for personal reasons unrelated to the course, but the rest persevered. And all seven passed the final examination, which was administered by Fr. Alonso-Schökel himself. The final examination in the Hebrew section of the Propaedeutic Year was a formidable thing, and justly feared by the students. But all seven passed. (To celebrate the end of the year they invited me to have supper with them in a sidewalk trattoria on the Viale San Gregorio VII. It was the very evening of the day on which the examination had been held: they chose that day so that none of them would be burdened with the realization that he or she had failed the exam. At that time about a third of the students failed the examination on the first try. I recall that one of the men was about to propose a toast at the end of the meal, but I interrupted, saying that the professor had the right to call for the toast. I then proposed a toast to the entire group, each member of which had passed the examination that morning. [Fr. Alonso was curious about the results, and had corrected the exams immediately.] For a moment there was the silence of disbelief, and then a tremendous shout of joy and relief. I am sure some of the passers-by were bemused by this show of exuberance by this strange assortment of foreigners [three Americans, a Canadian, a Thai, a Malaysian, and an Indian]. This was one of the undoubted high-points of my teaching at the level of the Propaedeutic Year. The following academic year, 1974-1975, Lambdin was adopted as the grammar for the Propaedeutic Year, and I was assigned to teach the English-language section. Lambdin has been in use as the text ever since. But, having succeeded in introducing a more useful textbook, I retired from the Hebrew field of battle after the academic year 1974-1975 and continued in the teaching of Greek.

In the early years of the course Latin was the vehicle of communication. Then, in the early seventies, when it was clear that Latin was not going to continue as a viable vehicle of instruction, an attempt was made by some of us to introduce French as well as English as the common languages of the Institute. For a couple of years I tried to teach the same class using Latin, English and French. But when it was decided that Italian was going to replace Latin, the Propaedeutic Year switched to the practice of sections in Italian and English. (Soon a Spanish section was added to the menu for the Hebrew part of the Propaedeutic Year, but was never thought necessary for the Greek half: the number of students in the Hebrew section was always notably greater than that of the Greek section, and since a third section was deemed expedient because of the need to reduce the size of the classes, Spanish was chosen as the language to be used.)

For the early eighties I taught both sections of the Propaedeutic Year, Italian and English, until administrative duties made the dropping of the Italian section advisable. (I was appointed Dean of the Biblical Faculty in 1986.)

With regard to my work as teacher in the Greek section of the Propaedeutic Year one more thing deserves mention. As the years went on I developed a system of mimeographed notes to help the students, a system which reached fairly definitive form in 1981. Around the year 1988 a Spanish priest presented himself as a student and did remarkably well in the qualifying Examination in Greek. When I asked him how he knew Greek so well he produced a picture of himself in the uniform of the Spanish army. He was on a high hill, and in the background was the Rock of Gibraltar. He was reading something. When I asked him what he was reading, he replied, "Your Greek notes". That was the final stimulus for putting my notes into printed form. Using a Macintosh I composed the first edition of my grammar, which was published in 1991. Unfortunately it had a plethora of typographical mistakes. I was able to redo the grammar and this second edition was published in 1998. Translations of the first or second edition have appeared in Italian, Ukraine, Korean, Spanish and Brazilian Portuguese. Other translations are contemplated. The reviews I have read were not too complimentary. A common complaint was that the grammar expected mastery of the language in far too much detail. All I can say in reply is that the grammar was written for the level of Greek mastery expected at the Biblical Institute. (Here may be a good place to remark that I do not think that the level of mastery of Greek now among the students of the Biblical Institute is as high as it was when I was a student, in the sixties, and understandably so. It is simply impossible in the span of two years, even with an intensive Propaedeutic Year, to give the students anything like the four or five years of classical Greek we had when we arrived at the Institute. On the other hand, I think the level of the mastery of Hebrew is notably higher than it was when I was a student).

During the course of these decades the Biblical Institute has been fortunate to have the assistance of a number of men and women for the teaching of Propaedeutic Year courses. Their names may be found in the *Acta* of the Institute.

I probably can be considered to be the father of the Propaedeutic Year for the Greek half, while the late Fr. Alonso-Schökel merits that title for the Hebrew half. Together with the late William Moran, in the late fifties, Alonso began a program of "Lectio Cursiva" in Hebrew. This program, as I understand it, was based on Moran's experience of Hebrew Lectio Cursiva under Professor William Foxwell Albright at Johns Hopkins in the United States, where Moran obtained a doctorate in Biblical studies before going on for a doctorate in ancient Near Eastern Studies at the University of Chicago.

This sketch is not meant to gloss over the mistakes and false starts which have attended the Propaedeutic Year from its inception. But it does give in a general way an outline of what took place and why.

In the past forty-five years thousands of students have passed through the Propaedeutic Year, which they attended in whole or in part. Most of the students went on to obtain a Licentiate in Sacred Scripture, while some changed to other programs in Rome, usually ones involving Scripture. I personally have had about fifteen hundred students from eighty-five countries. For me it has been a unique experience. I can't imagine a better assignment in the Society of Jesus, one which came to me without any seeking on my part. The level of the students here at the Institute is remarkably high – intellectually, academically, spiritually. Without these students and their loyal cooperation the Propaedeutic Year would never have achieved whatever success it has.

* * * * *

Doc. R. III,28

APIBR K-26-H: Revising Statutes 3
Report on the purpose of the Institute, compiled on April 30th, 1966
by a committee composed of Frs. Alonso Schökel, de la Potterie, Martini and McCool
The third part is given here. Translated from the Italian

Assessment and synthesis

Bearing in mind the inquiry that has been made and the official documents, the Committee thinks it can briefly draw up the following observations on the purpose of the Institute.

A. The fundamental purpose of the Biblical Institute is to promote higher biblical studies in the Church. But that necessarily implies many aspects so that the overall purpose has to be specified:

1. On the part of the professors, work of real *personal research* is expected, on the purely scholarly level, and also regular publications in that field; the publications of professors at the P. B. I. ought in fact to be of this kind for the most part.

2. *Training teachers* of H. Scripture. But this preparation, too, should always be kept at a scholarly level.

3. On the other hand, there is also need to *promote scholarly work* among the students themselves, and to prepare those of them who can engage on a scholarly career.

N. B. These three aims are closely connected; to be able to *teach* at a scholarly level, a faculty must also be committed to *research*; on the other hand, the teaching at the scholarly level and the research done by the professors directly favour the *calling to be scholars* in the field of biblical studies among the students.

B. As regards the content and direction taken by our *exegetical teaching*, scholarly work in the positive sciences (philology, history, etc.) cannot be separated from the theologico-doctrinal dimension. If we want to be faithful to the clear wish of the H. See (cf. *supra* the official documents), to the ever more prevalent tendency in biblical exegesis these days, to the spirit of the Second Vatican Council and to the wish that has been clearly expressed by the Fathers and Biennists [i. e. the Jesuit students registered at the Institute], we must give a biblico-theological and "salvation history" slant to our exegesis.

This does not belong to the field of pastoral application but to the very essence of scholarly exegesis; the object of study being the Word of God, Revelation, scholarly exegesis cannot be done without directing it towards a biblico-theological understanding, within the general setting of salvation history. When many students today ask for a theological and "pastoral" exegesis, that is what they want, basically. Thus it is not a question of making directly pastoral applications to real life, but of steering the interpretation towards a deeper understanding of God's plan. Done in that way, exegesis will in fact always be pastoral and priestly (cf. the statement by John XXIII).

C. On the question of the monopoly held by the P. B. I., opinions are unanimous on the advisability of not maintaining it. It is thought right that this openness on the part of the Institute to consider the rise of other similar institutions favourably should be made known to the competent authorities in suitable ways, making sure, however, that any future increase in the number of establishments authorized to grant degrees takes place without prejudice to, but rather to the advantage of the seriousness of biblical studies in the Church.

* * * * *

Doc. R. III,29

I S P U G
"Information for Students at the Pontifical Gregorian University"
No. 15 – 5 May 1968, p. 4
Translated from the Italian

Renewal at the Biblical Institute

On Friday, April 26th, the Dean of the biblical faculty assembled the delegates of the various linguistic groups of students and asked them to choose a delegate who will have to take part in the next council of professors and present them with their observations concerning a number of points that would be dealt with at that council.

Thereupon the delegates met among themselves to choose the delegate that had been asked for and to give him their opinion on the points in question.

On the same day the meeting of professors was held at the Biblical Institute under the presidency of Fr. Lyonnet, the Vice-Rector, and with 16 professors, the students' delegate and Fr. Secretary being present.

After some words of welcome to the students' delegate the Vice-Rector called upon the Dean to speak; he briefly recalled the earlier reforms that had been made by the Biblical Institute in recent decades.

The points then submitted to the council were divided into two groups:

1) The professors had, some time earlier, presented some changes in the plan for reforming the programme; these had been duplicated and covered five pages; they had been distributed, along with the plan for reform, to the professors and the various delegates from the student groups.

Three of these changes were submitted for discussion and the council's vote on the Friday evening:

– "baccalaureate": this title, and the examination that goes with it, should be abolished or throroughly changed at the next reform; however, we shall have to wait for the new regulations of the new "*Deus scientiarum Dominus*" [the 1968 "*Normae quaedam*"] concerning the reform of academic degrees;

– as regards the special examination "*ad licentiam*", it will have to be changed (but not yet in the coming year) as follows: it will be possible to take it in June, October or February; if it is done with not one but two professors, the syllabus of eight courses, as envisaged in the future plan, will be reduced, in accordance with the request made by the students' delegate (the special committee for reform will prepare a detailed plan to be discussed at a later council); the result of this final examination will not be diriment for the title of the licentiate, but earlier results will be taken into account;

– the reform plan made provision for the student being able to make his own choice from the courses in the exegetico-theological section in the area of the two

Testaments (six courses in each Testament). It was added: "but all are *strongly recommended*" not to omit a course on the Pentateuch, a Prophet, a wisdom book, a synoptic gospel, St. John or a Pauline letter. There was some discussion about whether this recommendation ought not to be made obligatory to avoid finishing the curriculum at the Institute without having touched one or other of these essential books. The majority seemed inclined to leave the choice to the judgment of the students. The discussion will have to be taken further later on.

2) Some points in the reform plan will be introduced as from the next year 1968-1969:

– semesters will be independent and registration will be for each semester; examinations on the syllabus taught during the semester may be taken either at the end of the session that closes the semester or at the two following sessions, but not beyond;

– all exegesis courses will be reduced to two hours a week;

– the interchangeability of courses in the exegetico-theological section will likewise be applied as from next year according to the indications to be given in the programme;

– a beginning will be made to prepare, on an experimental basis, some courses of an "informative" nature or at choice, and others of a "monographic" nature in the introductory and historico-geographic section;

– a start will be made on increasing the number of seminars offered by setting up another kind of seminar (which will not, however, involve written work) as from next year. The obligation to take the latter seminar, however, will only concern students who will be starting their first year next year;

– the pro-seminar that was introduced this year will be continued as a requirement for starting work on seminars; the forms it will take and the methods to be followed will have to be fixed upon and discussed later on.

Carlo M. MARTINI
Dean
Maurice GILBERT
Students' Delegate

CHAPTER IV

In the wake of the council
1968- 1985

The "*Normae quaedam*" promulgated by Paul VI on May 20th, 1968, were going to lead to a complete overhaul of the statutes of the Biblical Institute. On September 11th, 1972, the Congregation for Catholic Education approved those statutes on an experimental basis. However, on April 15th, 1979, John Paul II signed the Apostolic Constitution "*Sapientia Christiana*" which laid down rules for ecclesiastical academic institutions. The statutes of the Biblical Institute were therefore again revised and, on September 24th, 1981, the Congregation again approved them on an experimental basis, but for three years only. After a last revision by the Biblical Institute those statutes were definitively approved by the Congregation on November 14th, 1985. They govern the academic life of the Institute to this day. As regards the "*Ordinationes*" or particular rules, the Institute reviews them regularly with an eye to how things develop and has to get them approved by the Fr. General, the Grand Vice-Chancellor

This period of long maturation will here be divided into two parts, the year 1978 having been that of the death of Paul VI and the election of John Paul II, after the short pontificate of John Paul I.

I. The last years of Paul VI's pontificate: 1968-1978

Fr. MacKenzie ended his term as rector on October 7th, 1969; he then became general editor of the periodical *Biblica* until 1975, the year of his departure from the Institute. Fr. Carlo M. Martini succeeded him as rector (cf. *Acta PIB* 7, 359) and remained so for nine years. In 1969 Fr. Luis Alonso Schökel was appointed vice-rector and remained so for the whole of Fr. Martini's term as rector; also in 1969, Fr. Albert Vanhoye was elected dean of the biblical faculty. In 1975 Fr. Alonso Schökel succeeded him in that office and Fr. M. Dahood was elected dean of the oriental faculty (cf. *Acta PIB* 8, 104). In 1972

Fr. William A. Ryan took over from Fr. Lessel as Registrar of the Institute and remained so for ten years.

At the Congregation for Catholic Education, Mgr. Francesco Marchisano became Undersecretary in 1969 and remained so until 1988; he had obtained the licentiate in biblical studies at the Institute in 1955; in 2003 this faithful friend was made a cardinal (cf. *Acta PIB* 10, 1209; *DC* 85 [2003] 1089).

1. Applying the "Normae quaedam"

a) 1968-1970

The reform of the Biblical Institute's statutes, already begun in 1966 (cf. *supra*), was the object of many meetings during the academic year 1968-1969. A new committee was set up; it consisted of Frs. Alonso Schökel, de la Potterie and Martini, elected by their colleagues. Each part of the statutes to be worked over was given to a professor, then submitted for discussion and finally put to the vote, including that of the students' delegate. Thus, for example, Fr. Lyonnet prepared the historical preamble and the first part that set out the purpose of the Institute and the means at its disposal to achieve it; Fr. Lohfink did the chapter on the academic staff and Fr. Swetnam did the one on students. In May 1969 the rules to be followed in appointing the rector were drawn up; Fr. MacKenzie's term was coming to an end in the summer of 1969.

This exhausting task ended in June 1969. One last general consultation took place in the form of writing at the beginning of July; the approval of the professors and students' delegates was almost unanimous, so that, on July 19th MacKenzie, the rector, was able to send the Fr. General two cyclostyled copies of the new statutes.

Actually, on June 20th, 1969, the Congregation for Catholic Education had prescribed that the statutes revised in accordance with the "*Normae quaedam*" should be sent to it by September 1st. Fr. General saw to this on August 31st, making some slight changes to bring the Biblical Institute's statutes into line with those of the Gregorian and the Oriental; on October 14th he told the new rector, Fr. Martini, about them by letter, adding that these new statutes could be applied provisionally, pending the Congregation's approval. On November 2nd a new committee was set up to prepare this application; it comprised Frs. Alonso Schökel, MacKenzie, Swetnam and Gilbert; in mid-February 1970 it ceased to exist (cf. *Acta PIB* 7, 266 and 360; APIBR K-26-H).

b) From 1970-1972

In the spring of 1970 the various organs required by the statutes were set up (cf. *Acta PIB* 7, 352-353). These organs began to work out the form that, in the "*Ordinationes*", the final examination "*ad licentiam*" and the new curriculum "*ad doctoratum*" in the biblical faculty would take (*Acta PIB* 7, 360, 444-448 and 452-453).

In the final examination for the licentiate in biblical studies the student could choose either to answer in writing one of the two questions on one of the four courses he will have chosen out of the twelve courses in the exegetico-theological section and take four hours over it (*Typus A*), or to write up some research done on one of the courses from this same section (*Typus B*).

Another "*Ordinatio*" radically changed the preparatory year for the doctorate in biblical studies (cf. *Acta PIB* 7, 502 and 445-446). Henceforth it would cover a full year during which the candidate, on the basis of a programme set up by him with the approval of a director, broadens his knowledge in a field of research, prophetism, for example. It ends either with a public lesson prepared by the student or with an interview with two professors on the subjects appearing on the student's programme.

These decisions, inserted into the "*Ordinationes*", which the Institute could review when it thought fit, were taken during the 1970-1971 academic year.

Meanwhile, on August 13th, 1970, the Congregation for Catholic Education sent Fr. General a letter in which it asked for some slight changes in the statutes and also expressed some doubts about one article or another. The senate at the Institute got some professors to propose some answers which were submitted to all their colleagues; these were asked to give their opinion before Christmas. All things considered, the senate confined itself to removing the doubts on the part of the Congregation which, on September 11th, 1972, approved those statutes *ad experimentum* (APIBR K-26-D).

c) From 1972 to 1976

During this period some texts in the statutes and the "*Ordinationes*" were revised and changed.

In the spring of 1972 the senate reworked the 1969 "*Ordinatio*" which regulated the procedure for appointing the rector. When it was finished on May 8th this procedure was sent to the Fr. General who had asked for it to be revised so as to bring it into line with the one at the Gregorian and the Oriental Institute (APIBR K-26-E). Be that as it may, the choice of the new rector stayed within the competence of the Sovereign Pontiff who decided after hearing the opinion of the Grand Chancellor, to whom the Fr. General had given three names chosen from among the five proposed by the senate at the Institute.

In October 1974, at the instigation of Frs. McCarthy and Ryan, the rector prepared the revision of the "*Ordinatio*" at no. 68 of the statutes concerning the doctoral thesis in the biblical faculty (cf. APIBR K-26-E). It proposed that when the candidate handed in the subject of his thesis at the Registrar's office the rector should appoint a second professor who, along with the director of the thesis, should follow its full development. On February 17th, 1976, the senate at the Institute approved the new text of this "*Ordinatio*" (cf. *Acta PIB* 8, 106 and 160-164).

During the academic year 1974-1975 the wording of the fourth paragraph of the "*Ordinatio*" at statute no. 40 was changed. The text, which dated from 1969, stipulated (cf. *Acta PIB* 8, 15):

> If it happens that the students' delegates, at the time of a vote in the faculty council, are unanimous against the majority of voters, three quarters are required for the vote to be valid; and even if three quarters of all the voters are opposed to the unanimous vote of the students' delegates, the latter have the right to have recourse, through an appeal with devolutive effect, to the rector so that the matter be discussed in a joint committee.

This procedure was designed to safeguard students' rights and, in any case, the number of their delegates could not be more than one fifth of the total number of the members of the council. However, when on November 25th, 1974, the students for the first time asked for the application of this paragraph, it was not a matter of refusing to promote Fr. Welch to the grade of full-time professor, because that unpleasant episode on March 18th, 1974, had been the result of a secret vote (cf. the dossier in the Registrar's office at the Institute); instead, it concerned a somewhat trivial matter: normally the examination on a course can be taken at one of the three sessions coming at the end of the course, but what happens when the course is given by a guest professor from abroad? The proposal made to the faculty council was to depart from the rule in this particular case, thereby obliging the students to take the examination straight after the end of the course. The students then asked for the application of the above-mentioned paragraph. The matter took its course and, after some adventures, the senate, at the rector's request, not only confirmed, on April 25th, 1975, that that paragraph did not apply in the case of a vote about persons, but it also proposed a change in the incriminated paragraph which, since then (cf. the third paragraph of the "*Ordinatio*" at article 34b of the 1985 statutes): stipulates:

> Before a vote, if all the students entitled to vote say they think the point has not been sufficiently gone into, the vote is put off until a later meeting. When this vote is taken, an absolute majority of those present and entitled to vote is required. After the vote, there is still the possibility of recourse to the rector within three days, before confirmation.

> [Prima di una votazione, se tutti i delegati degli studenti aventi diritto al voto si dichiarano del parere che il punto non sia stato approfondito abbastanza, la votazione va rinviata ad un'ulteriore sessione. In questa votazione, la maggioranza assoluta dei presenti aventi diritto al voto, sarà richiesta. Dopo la votazione, resta la possibilità di ricorso al Rettore entro tre giorni prima della conferma].

On June 13th the rector passed on the dossier to Fr. General who, on the 24th, confirmed the decision (cf. APIBR K-26-E).

In spite of all the work accomplished, things did not stop there, because the Congregation for Catholic Education was planning to draw up, going beyond the *"Normae quaedam"* of 1968, an apostolic constitution due to replace the one that Pius XI had promulgated in 1931, *"Deus scientiarum Dominus"*. On June 1st, 1975, the Congregation questioned the pontifical universities on a certain number of points. On December 22nd, the rector of the Biblical Institute informed the professors, assistants and students' delegates about this and passed on to them the points that might concern the Biblical Institute. Having received their opinions, Fr. Martini, on May 5th, 1976, sent Cardinal Gabriel M. Garrone, the Prefect of the Congregation, a seven-page detailed response (APIBR K-26-A). The rector insisted on caution and prudence, asking that too strict rules be not laid down, so that each institution might adapt them according to its situation. In this way he, along with almost all the opinions he had received, rejected the obligation whereby the teachers had to have an academic degree conferred by a faculty that was canonically erected and explicitly approved by the Holy See; such an obligation would harm ecumenical relations; besides, an ecclesiastical degree is not necessary for teaching ancient languages. As for promoting a teacher, "a more nuanced general judgment of the professor's activity must be given, without insisting one-sidedly on his publications" ("si debba dare un giudizio globale più sfumato dell'attività del professore, senza insistere in maniera unilaterale sulla bibliographia"). Another point: the length of the cycle for the licentiate at the Biblical Institute is normally three years, as indicated in no. 50 of the 1972 statutes: a period of time to be strictly observed by all the institutions should not be laid down. The same goes for the final examination in the second cycle: the Biblical Institute asks for freedom to decide according to the proper needs of the studies it offers.

Not long after this, Frs. Martini and Vanhoye attended the 2nd international Congress of ecclesiastical Universities and Faculties, organized in Rome by the Congregation from November 23rd to December 3rd, 1976 (*Acta PIB* 8, 177).

So, in about ten years, by reason of the *"Normae quaedam"*, the Biblical Institute had been rejuvenated and had seriously adapted itself to the new situation created by the second Vatican council. It will be noted, lastly, that in May 1973, by means of a letter in Latin, Italian and English, the rector informed the academic and ecclesiastical authorities of the main changes that had taken place at the Biblical Institute (*Acta PIB* 7, 669-673).

2. The students

To go by the data supplied by the *Acta PIB*, one cannot form a precise idea of the development in the number of students at the Biblical Institute. The main reason is that in 1968-1969 those attending the propaedeutic year were explicitly entered in the books (*Acta PIB* 7, 279). As from the following year, the data were changed: henceforth data were provided for both faculties, distinguishing those who were enrolled for the licentiate and those who were doing the preparatory year for the doctorate (*Acta PIB* 7, 385).

Be that as it may, one can see straightaway that the year 1969-1970 marks a high point: in that year there was a total of 380 enrolled students at the Institute, whereas there were 356 the previous year and that as from 1970-1971 their number gradually dropped to reach only 277 in 1977-1978. The main reason for this decline comes from the "*Normae quaedam*" which no longer explicitly required the licentiate in biblical studies for teaching Scripture in faculties and seminaries.

The diminution is seen at the Biblical Institute both in the case of those aiming at the licentiate in biblical studies and those doing the preparatory year for the doctorate. This is especially true for western countries; thus students coming from the United States go from 30 in 1968-1969 to 20 in 1977-1978, the Italians go from 70 to 63, the Spaniards from 58 to 32, the French from 23 to 11, the Germans from 19 to 3 and the Canadians 13 to 2!

On the other hand, between 1968-1969 and 1977-1978, the students from Asia go from 34 to 39 (Indians from 14 to 20), Africans from 14 to 24, Latin Americans from 24 to 31 (Mexicans from 9 to 12) and Eastern Europeans from 10 to 17.

Besides this, for the same period, the nuns go from 3 go 14, while the number of laypeople, men and women, increases slightly.

However, the number of theses defended at the Biblical Institute rose steeply, eighty-one for this period, whereas, during the ten previous years, there were only fifty.

3. The teaching staff

During this period, the Institute had to lament not only the decease of Cardinal Bea, on November 16th, 1968, but also that of two of its older teachers. Fr. Max Zerwick had just finished his thirty-ninth year of teaching biblical Greek when he died at Munich on October 10th, 1975; the previous year he, along with Miss Mary Grosvenor (cf. *infra*), in collaboration with Fathers Welch and Swetnam, had just published *A Grammatical Analysis of the Greek New Testament*; this practical and regularly republished work went back to the one he had published in Latin in 1953 (cf. *Acta PIB* 8, 154-157). Fr. Ludwick Semkowski passed away on the night of August 18th-19th at the Villa Cavalletti, in the Frascati hills; he had served the Institute at Rome, and then in Jerusalem, for half a century (cf. Part Two, chap. II; *Acta PIB* 8, 300-302).

Some new professors were taken on. Among them thirteen Jesuits were numbered. Five of them are already deceased: Fr. Denis J. McCarthy (1924-1983), hailing from Chicago, had obtained the doctorate at the Institut Catholique in Paris in 1962 and his thesis, under the direction of Henri Cazelles, appeared in 1963: *Treaty and Covenant* (AnBib 21); it revealed an exegete of high standing; thus he was called to the Institute in 1969 to succeed Fr. Lohfink in 1969 (cf. *Acta PIB* 8, 780-781); – Fr. Fritzleo Lenzen-Deis (1928-1993), a German, had obtained the doctorate at the Biblical Institute with a thesis on *Die Taufe Jesu nach den Synoptiken*, defended in 1969 and published in Frankfurt in 1970; having been a professor at the Jesuit theological college in that city, he came to the Biblical Institute, at first for one semester a year then, as from 1987, full time, to direct a seminar on the synoptic gospels within the setting of ancient Judaism; he was also the director of many doctoral theses (cf. *Acta PIB* 9, 850-851); – Fr. José O'Callaghan (1922-2001), born at Tortosa in Catalonia, was a doctor of philosophy and literature, from Madrid (1959) and of classical literature, from Milan (1960); he was a specialist in classical Greek and papyrology and was invited to the Biblical Institute for a semester in 1968, then from 1971 to 1992 he taught Greek papyrology full time there; in 1972 he thought he could show that there were some New Testament papyri at Qumrân (*Bib* 53 [1972] 91-100); a theory like that, without sufficient foundation, set off an argument that lasted several years during which he kept his calm; in 1977 he published the *Nuevo Testamento Trilingüe* (Greek, Latin and Spanish; BAC, Madrid); he also published many articles, especially in *Studia papyrologica*, which he had founded in Barcelona in 1962 (cf. *Acta PIB* 10, 974-975); – Fr. John J. Welch (1925-2002), born in Kansas City in Missouri, had obtained the doctorate in classical languages and linguistics in Philadelphia in 1962; then he taught Latin and Greek at the Jesuit University in St. Louis when, in 1972, he was summoned to the Biblical Institute to take over gradually from Fr. Zerwick: thus he taught biblical Greek until 1991 (*Acta PIB* 9, 976); – Fr. William J. Dalton (1916-2004), an Australian, had a doctorate from the Biblical Institute with a thesis on *Christ's Proclamation to the Spirits. A Study of 1Peter 3:18–4;6* (AnBib, 23; Rome, PIB, 1965); from 1968 to 1975 he had been rector of the Jesuit theological college at Parkville, in Australia; from 1975 to 1981 he taught at the Biblical Institute in Rome, while carrying out the task of being superior of the Jesuit community; from 1981 to 1984, he was director of the Jerusalem branch (cf. Part Two, chap. II); on returning to his country he wrote an autobiography entitled *Seeking the Word. Life pilgrimage* (Richmond, Victoria, Jesuit Publications, 1996), in which, pp. 112-158, he describes his time at Rome and Jerusalem (cf. *Acta PIB* 10,1212-1214).

Two Jesuit professors taught at the Institute for only about fifteen years: Fr. Thomas W. Franxman, from the United States, taught ancient Jewish literature there from 1970 to 1986; he published the thesis which he had presented at Oxford in 1975: *Genesis and the «Jewish Antiquities» of Flavius Josephus* (BiOr, 35; Rome, PIB, 1979); – Fr. Dionisio Mínguez, a Spaniard, taught New Testament exegesis from 1972 to 1986, in particular the Acts of the Apostles; his thesis, defended in 1975 and published the following year, was on *Pentecostés. Ensayo de Semiótica narrativa en Hch 2* (AnBib, 75); he later left the Society of Jesus.

Six other Jesuit professors arrived during this period to stay for a long time. In 1971, Fr. Klemens Stock, a German born in 1934, was put in charge of the seminar on methodology; in 1974 he defended his thesis at the Biblical Institute on *Boten aus dem Mit-Ihm-Sein. Das Verhältnis zwischen Jesus und den Zwölf nach Markus*; it appeared in 1975 (AnBib, 70); from 1974 to 1979 he taught the synoptic gospels full time at the Biblical Institute. The 1975-1976 academic year saw the arrival of four others: Fr. K. Plötz, a German born in 1932, had obtained the licentiate in biblical studies in 1973; in 1975 he started his teaching of biblical Hebrew in the propaedeutic course and continued until 2007; – Fr. Maurice Gilbert, a Belgian born in 1934, had defended his thesis in 1972 while he was already teaching at the Catholic University of Louvain; it was on chapters 13–15 of the Wisdom of Solomon (AnBib, 53, 1973); in Rome, as successor to Fr. MacKenzie who left the Institute, he was given charge of the sapiential books of the Old Testament and, from 1975 to 1978, took on the general editorship of the periodical *Biblica*; - Fr. H. Simian Yofre, an Argentinian born in 1936, had obtained a doctorate from the University of Würzburg for a thesis, defended in 1973 and published in 1974, entitled *Die theologische Nachgeschichte der Prophetie Ezechiels. Form- und traditionskritische Untersuchung zu Ez 6; 35; 36* (FzB, 14; Würzburg, Echter Verlag, 1974), 382 p.; called to the Biblical Institute in 1975, he taught the Hebrew propaedeutic course for a year, then, succeeding Fr. Vogt the following year, he was given charge of teaching the prophets; – Fr. W. Mayer, a German born in 1939, had just obtained a doctorate in philosophy from the University of Münster with a thesis on Babylonian exorcism prayers, which he had written under the direction of professor W. von Soden and which he published in 1976 (cf. *infra*). Finally, in 1978, there arrived Fr. Reinhard Neudecker, a German born in 1938; already possessing a doctorate in theology from Innsbruck, he had followed the academic curriculum of the Hebrew Union College – Jewish Institute of Religion in Cincinnati, in the United States, up to the doctorate which he presented at the beginning of 1978 and published with the title of *Frührabbinisches Ehescheidungsrecht. Der Tosefta-Traktat Gittin* (BiOr, 39; Rom, PIB, 1982); in the second semester of the 1977-1978 academic year he began his teaching at the Biblical Institute on rabbinical literature.

In addition, as from the second semester of the 1969-1970 academic year, Fr. Ugo Vanni, an Italian Jesuit born in 1929, a professor at the Jesuit theological college in Naples, then, as from 1974, at the Gregorian, was invited every year to give a seminar and/or a course on the Apocalypse, which he did until 2004, the year of his becoming emeritus; he had defended his doctoral thesis at the Biblical Institute in January 1970 and published it with the title of *La struttura letteraria dell'Apocalisse* (Aloisiana, 8; Roma, Herder, 1971).

Miss Mary D. Grosvenor, coming from a great Scottish family, was a specialist in patristic Greek – she had collaborated for twenty years on the preparation of the *Patristic Greek Lexicon*, edited by G. W. H. Lampe; at the Biblical Institute she worked as a research associate from 1967 until 1985; chiefly in collaboration with Frs. Zerwick, Welch and Swetnam, she prepared the volume *A Grammatical Analysis of the Greek New Testament* (cf. *supra)*; she died in 1991 (cf. *Acta PIB* 9, 618-619).

During these years 1968-1978, there were also several other professors from outside, invited on a stable basis. Here we shall mention only those who cooperated with the Institute for more than five years. Among them two of them have already died: Fr. Luigi Cagni (1929-1998), a Barnabite, with the licentiate in biblical studies from the Institute, taught Akkadian language and Mesopotamian literature in the oriental faculty from 1973 until 1978 (cf. *Acta PIB* 10, 459); – Fr. Jacques Dupont, O.S.B. (1915-1998), a renowned New Testament exegete, taught for a semester each year in the biblical faculty from 1970 to 1980 (cf. *Acta PIB* 10, 575). The others are: Fr. Aelred Cody, O.S.B., who gave a seminar and/or a course on Old Testament exegesis from 1968 to 1979; – Fr. Prosper Grech, O.S.A., who taught mainly biblical hermeneutics from 1969 to 2002 (cf. *Acta PIB* 10, 899-902); – Professor J. Alberto Soggin, from the Waldensian faculty of theology in Rome, who taught mainly the history of the Old Testament in the biblical faculty from 1971 to 1999 (cf. *Acta PIB* 10, 635-638 and 729-737); – Mrs. Cleopatra Basha, of Egyptian origin, who taught Arabic in the oriental faculty from 1971 to 1979.

That is not all. Since 1969 the "*Catholic Biblical Association of America*" has been sending a professor of exegesis for a semester every year, or almost (cf. *Acta PIB* 7, 291). Here is the list of them for the years 1969-1978:

1969-1970: Mgr. Patrick W. Skehan, who gave a course on Ben Sira;
1970-1971: Myles M. Bourke, on the resurrection in the gospels;
1971-1972: Mgr. Jerome D. Quinn, on the letters to Timothy and Titus;
1972-1973: Bruce Vawter, C.M., on the prophet Amos;
1973-1974: Raymond E. Brown, P.S.S., on the gospels of the infancy;
1974-1975: Aelred Cody, O.S.B., on the book of Genesis;
1975-1976: no one;

1976-1977: David L. Dungan, on the synoptic gospels;
1977-1978: John H. Elliot, on the first letter of Peter.

But the Biblical Institute also received three French-speaking professors for a semester:

1974-1975: Henri Cazelles, P.S.S., who gave a course on the Pentateuch;
1974-1975: Mgr. Albert Descamps, on the resurrection in the New Testament;
1975-1976: Mathias Delcor, on the book of Daniel.

The Biblical Institute and especially its rector, Martini, obviously worked hard to enrich the programme offered to the students during these years.

4. *Publications*

At the end of the year 1969, the Institute closed down the periodical *Verbum Domini* which Fr. Zerwick was directing. It had had its day and Latin was no longer the common language of the clergy.

The collection of monographs *Analecta Biblica* went through a period of exceptional growth: between 1968 and 1978 it went from no. 35 to no. 75.

Among the professors' publications, noted every year in the *Acta PIB*, we shall mention here only the more important books that have not yet been indicated in previous pages.

On the whole Bible

L. ALONSO SCHÖKEL (ed.), *Comentarios a la constitución 'Dei Verbum' sobre la divina revelación* (BAC, 284), Madrid, 1969.

L. ALONSO SCHÖKEL, with Juan MATEOS [for the New Testament], *Nueva Biblia Española,* Madrid, Cristiandad, 1975.

On the Old Testament

L. SABOURIN, *The Psalms, their Origin and Meaning*, 2 vols. Staten Island, N. Y., Alba House, 1969.

M. DAHOOD, *Psalms III: 101-150* (AncB, 17A), Garden City, N. Y., Doubleday, 1970.

E. VOGT, *Lexicon aramaicum Veteris Testamenti*, Roma, PIB, 1971.

D. J. MCCARTHY, *Old Testament Covenant. A Survey of Current Opinions*, Oxford, Blackwell, 1972.

ID., *Treaty and Covenant*, new, fully revised edition (AnBib, 21A), Rome, PIB, 1978.

On the New Testament

K. ALAND, M. BLACK, B. M. METZGER, A. WIKGREN, and C. M. MARTINI, *The Greek New Testament*, 2nd ed., Stuttgart, 1968; 3rd ed., 1975.

A. VANHOYE, *Situation du Christ. Hébreux 1–2* (LeDiv, 58), Paris, Cerf, 1969.

S. LYONNET, *Le message de l'épître aux Romains* (LiBi), Paris, Cerf, 1971.

H. QUECKE, *Das Markusevangelium saïdisch. Text der Handschrift PPalau Rib. Inv.-Nr. 182* (Papyrologia Castroctaviana, 4), Barcelona, 1972.

ID., *Das Lukasevangelium saïdisch. Text der Handschrift PPalau Rib. Inv.-Nr. 181 mit den Varianten der Handschrift M 569* (Papyrologica Castroctaviana, 6), Barcelona, 1977.

I. DE LA POTTERIE, *Gesù Verità. Studi di cristologia giovannea*, Torino, Marietti, 1973.

C. M. MARTINI, *Gli Esercizi ignaziani alla luce di S. Giovanni*, Roma, Centrum Ignatianum Spiritualitatis, 1976.

I. DE LA POTTERIE, *La Vérité chez Saint Jean*, 2 vols., (AnBib, 73-74), Rome, PIB, 1977.

On the history of religions:

É. DES PLACES, *La religion grecque*, Paris, Picard, 1969.

L. SABOURIN, *Priesthood. A Comparative Study* (Suppl. to Numen, 25). Leiden, Brill, 1973.

W. MAYER, *Untersuchungen zur Formensprache der babylonischen "Gebetsbeschwörungen"* (StP.SM, 5), Rom, PIB, 1976.

On early Christianity

É. DES PLACES, Eusèbe de Césarée, *Préparation évangélique, I* (SC, 206), Paris, Cerf, 1974; *VII* (SC, 215), 1975; *II-III* (SC, 228), 1976.

J. O'CALLAGHAN, *El cristianismo popular en el antiguo Egipto* (Epifania, 27), Madrid, Cristiandad, 1975.

H. QUECKE, *Die Briefe Pachoms. Griechischer Text...* (Textus Patristici et Liturgici..., 11), Regensburg, Pustet, 1975.

On Greek authors:

É. DES PLACES, *Oracles chaldaïques* (Coll. des Universités de France), Paris, Les Belles Lettres, 1971.

ID., *Numénius. Fragments* (Coll. des Universités de France), Paris, Les Belles Lettres, 1973.

Most of these works are still of great worth.

5. Renovating the premises of the Institute

For more than ten years the number of students had been continually on the increase and, in the library, books were arriving in ever-growing numbers. Yet the building housing the Institute had not been touched since 1949. Within less than a year of entering upon his function, Fr. Martini therefore undertook some work that had become necessary, and which for a long time had even been expected.

In the summer of 1970, a first depot for books and periodicals rarely used because of their antiquity was installed in what had been the refectory of the Jesuit community since 1949 in the south-west corner of the first floor. To do this the flooring was reinforced. Thanks to this operation, the library was not so cluttered. At the time, Fr. Paul Mech (1911-1999), a native of Lyons, had been librarian since 1966 and he remained so until 1973 (*Acta PIB* 7, 363). His successor for less than two years, from June, 1973 to January, 1975, was Fr. M. Joseph Costelloe (1914-2000), from the Wisconsin Province in the United States.

Then, in 1975, the *Aula orientalis* was transferred to new premises in the south-west corner of the second floor; this section for orientalism, kept locked, was better supervised, because of the increased number of thefts (*Acta PIB* 7, 504).

Finally, in 1975, thanks to the generosity of Pope Paul VI, an amphitheatre capable of taking about one hundred persons was installed in the north-west corner of the building. To achieve this, two smaller classrooms had been joined together by replacing the wall that separated them with a long steel girder which could only be brought in through the window! This operation was as impressive as it was dangerous. And on May 23rd the new *Aula Paulina,* so named in honour of the outstanding benefactor, was solemnly inaugurated by Cardinal Gabriel Garrone, the Prefect of the Congregation for Catholic Education and, from that time, Grand Chancellor of the Institute. Besides the professors and a good number of students, also present were Mgr. Giovanni Benelli, Substitute at the Secretariat of State, and Mgr. Giuseppe Caprio, the Secretary of the Administration of the Patrimony of the Apostolic See. Cardinal Jean Villot, the Secretary of State, and the Fr. General of the Society apologized for being unable to take part in the ceremony. A marble slab was placed above the entrance to the hall to recall the Pope's generosity. Lastly, immediately after an address full of gratitude given by the rector, Fr. Dionisio Mínguez defended his doctoral thesis on the story of Pentecost according to chapter 2 of the Acts of the Apostles. It is in this *Aula Paulina* that, ever since, defences of theses at the Institute have in fact taken place (*Acta PIB* 8, 12-13).

Acts of papal largesse also made it possible to put a space in the middle of this same third floor to better use; hitherto, it had served as library for the Jesuit community. It was made into two rooms, one, with room for forty-five places, for classes and the other became the meeting room for the various councils, the *Aula consultationis*. Some twenty years later, the latter became the Registrar's office of the Institute (*Acta PIB* 8,16).

6. *The start of controversies: 1972 and 1975*

a) New Testament fragments at Qumrân?

Bibliography

José O'CALLAGHAN, "¿Papiros neotestamentarios en la cueva 7 de Qumran?" in *Bib* 53 (1972) 91-100. – ID., "¿1 Tim 3,16; 4,1.3 en 7Q4?" in *Bib* 53 (1972), 362-367.

– ID., "Notas sobre 7Q tomadas en el Rockefeller Museum de Jerusalén (Tabulas extra seriem)", in *Bib* 53 (1972) 517-533. – ID., "Les papyrus de la grotte 7 de Qumrân", in *NRT* 95 (1973)188-195. – ID., *Los papiros griegos de la cueva 7 de Qumran* (BAC, 353), Madrid, 1974, viii-100 p. – ID., "The Identification of 7Q", in *Aeg* 56 (1976) 287-294.

Carlo M. MARTINI, "Note sui papiri della grotta 7 di Qumrân", in *Bib* 53 (1972) 101-104. – Pierre BENOIT, O. P., "Note sur les fragments grecs de la grotte 7 de Qumrân" in *RB* 79 (1972) 321-324. – ID., "Nouvelle note sur les fragments grecs de la grotte 7 de Qumrân" in *RB* 80 (1973) 5-12. – Maurice BAILLET, "Les manuscrits de la grotte 7 de Qumrân" in *Bib* 53 (1972) 508-516; 54 (1973) 340-350. – Angel C. URBÁN, "Observaciones sobre ciertos papiros de la cueva 7 de Qumran" in *RQ* 8,2 (1973) 233-251.

Carsten Peter THIEDE, "Eine Rückkehre zu den neutestamentlichen Papyrusfragmenten in der siebten Höhle von Qumran", in *Bib* 65 (1984) 538-559. – ID., *Die älteste Evangelien-Handschrift? Das Markus-Fragment von Qumran und die Anfänge der schriftlichen Überlieferung des Neuen Testaments*, Wuppertal, Brockhaus, 1986 = *Il più antico manoscritto dei Vangeli. Il frammento di Marco di Qumran e gli inizi della tradizione scritta del Nuovo Testamento* (SubBi, 10), Roma, PIB, 1987, 63 p. = *El manuscrito más antiguo de los Evangelios*, Valencia, San Jeronimo, 1989. = *The Earliest Gospel Manuscript?*, London, Paternoster, 1992. – ID., "Greek Qumran Fragment 7Q5: Possibilities and Impossibilities", in *Bib* 75 (1994) 394-398.

Émile PUECH, "Des fragments grecs de la grotte 7 et le Nouveau Testament? 7Q4 et 7Q5 et le Papyrus Magdalen Grec P^{64}", in *RB* 102 (1995) 570-584. – ID., "Note sull'identificazione di 7Q5 con Mc 6,52-53", in *Ho Theologos* 17 (1999), 73-84. – M.- Émile BOISMARD, "À propos de 7Q5 et Mc 6,52-53" in *RB* 102 (1995), 585-588. – Victoria SPOTTORNO, "Can Methodological Limits Be Set in the Debate on the Identification of 7Q5?", in *DSD* 6 (1999) 66-77. – Stefan ENSTE, "Qumran-Fragment 7Q5 ist nicht Markus 6,52-53" in *ZPE* 126 (1999) 189-193 + 1 pl. – ID., *Keine Markustext in Qumran. Eine Untersuchung der These: Qumran-Fragment 7Q5 = Mk 6,52-53* (NTOA, 45), Freiburg-Göttingen, Universitätsverlag-Vandenhoeck & Ruprecht, 2000, viii-163p. + 5pl. – Robert H. GUNDRY, "No *NU* in line 2 of 7Q5: A Final Disidentification of 7Q5 with Mark 6:52-53", in *JBL* 118 (1999), 698-707. – Karl JAROŠ, "Die Qumranfragmente der Höhle 7 (7Q) im Computertest" in *Aeg* 80 (2000) 147-168. – Camille FOCANT, "Un fragment du second évangile à Qumran 7Q5 = Mc 6,52-53?" in ID., *Marc, un évangile étonnant* (BETL, 195), Leuven, Peeters, 2006, 21-29.

This abundant bibliography, although selective, gives some idea of the debate that, over a period of thirty years, a theory put forward in 1972 by Fr. José O'Callaghan, the Biblical Institute's papyrologist, gave rise to. Because, to judge from the titles of his two first publications on the subject in *Biblica*, he was asking questions. In his opinion, some small unidentified fragments which had some Greek letters on them and came from cave 7 in Qumran, might be attributable to some texts in the New Testament; in his eyes, those letters might correspond respectively to texts in Mark 6,52-53 in 7Q5, Mark 4,28 in 7Q6,1, Jas 1,23-24 in 7Q8 and 1 Tim 3,16; 4,1.3 in 7Q4.

These hypotheses went round the world because if the matter were proved, the presence of the New Testament at Qumran would radically change our knowledge of that centre of asceticism on the shores of the Dead Sea; moreover, the dating of the composition of those New Testament writings would probably have to be put back in time.

To be frank, those hypotheses did not convince anyone at the time, not even Fr. Martini, although he was impressed. Objections were not slow in coming, in particular from two Qumran manuscript specialists, Fr. Benoit and M. Baillet. Fr. O'Callaghan defended himself as best he could. Essentially the problem was in fact one of a palaeographical nature: what letters could be read on these fragments of such small dimensions?

In the decade following, the Father found an ally and defender in the person of C. P. Thiede who worked without stinting for the cause. But ten years later, from 1995 to 2000, some renowned epigraphists, É. Puech, M.-É. Boismard, St. Enste and R. H. Gundry definitively proved, it seems, that the readings proposed by Fr. O'Callaghan, especially for 7Q5, were wrong. Today, when the fever has abated, the Jesuit's proposals may be consigned to oblivion.

b) The discovery of the archives at Ebla: 1975

Bibliography

Paolo MATTHIAE, "Ebla nel periodo delle dinastie amorree e della dinastia di Akkad. Scoperte archeologiche recenti a Tell Mardikh", in *Or* 44 (1975) 337-360. – ID., *Ebla. Un impero ritrovato* (Saggi, 586), Torino, Einaudi, 1977, xx-268 p. – Giovanni PETTINATO, "Testi cuneiformi del 3 millennio in paleo-cananeo rinvenuti nella campagna 1974 a Tell Mardikh=Ebla", in *Or* 44 (1975), 361-374. – ID., "Gli archivi reali di Tell Mardikh-Ebla. Riflessioni e prospettive", in *RivB* 25 (1977), 225-243. – ID., *Ebla. Un impero inciso sull'argilla* (Saggi, 126), Milano, Mondadori, 1979, 329 p. = *The Archives of Ebla. An Empire inscribed in Clay, with an Afterword by Mitchell Dahood, S. J.* [pp. 271-321], Garden City, N. Y., Doubleday, 1981, xvii-347 p. – Jean-Louis SKA, "Les découvertes de Tell Mardikh-Ebla et la Bible" in *NRT* 100 (1978), 389-398. – Alfonso ARCHI, "The Epigraphic Evidence from Ebla and the Old Testament", in *Bib* 60 (1979), 556-566.

Mitchell DAHOOD, "Ebla, Ugarit e l'Antico Testamento", in *CC* 129 (1978, II) 328-340. – ID., "I libri profetici e sapienziali dell'Antico Testamento alla luce delle scoperte di Ebla e di Ugarit" in *CC* 129 (1978, II) 547-556. – ID., "Ebla, Ugarit and the Old Testament", in *VTS* 29 (1978), 81-112. – ID., "The Ebla tablets and Old Testament theology", in *Tdig* 27 (1979) 303-311. – ID., "Le scoperte archeologiche di Ebla e la ricerca biblica" in *CC* 131 (1980, II) 319-333. – ID., "Eblaite and Biblical Hebrew", in *CBQ* 44 (1982), 1-24. – ID., "The Minor Prophets and Ebla", in Carrol L. MEYERS (ed.), *The Word of the Lord Shall Go Forth*. FS Freedman (ASOR, Sp. Vol. Ser.1), Winona Lake, IN, Eisenbrauns, 1983, 47-67. – ID., "Hebrew Hapax Legomena in Eblaite", in Luigi CAGNI (ed.), *Il bilinguismo a Ebla* (Ist. Univ. Or., Dep. di Studi Asiatici, Ser. minor, 22), Napoli, 1984, 439-470.

Seventy kilometres south of Aleppo in Syria, the University of Rome has been carrying out archaeological excavations since 1964 on Tell Mardikh which covers the ancient city of Ebla. It was there in 1974 that Professors Paolo Matthiae, the archaeologist, and Giovanni Pettinato, the epigraphist, discovered some tablets with cuneiform writing on them and dating from about 2,300 B. C. According to Professor Pettinato, these texts reveal a northwestern Semitic language. The announcement of the discovery was made at the Biblical Institute by the two protagonists on April 23rd, 1975, and their reports were published in the Institute's periodical *Orientalia*.

That was enough to get Fr. M. Dahood, professor of Ugaritic at the Institute and specialist on the relations between that language and biblical Hebrew, examining the texts from Ebla that had just been discovered. However, when it came to deciphering and transliterating the Eblaite texts, he was dependent on Professor Pettinato, and that quickly led to disputed interpretations. As early as 1979, A. Archi, who had in the meantime become the epigraphist of the Italian mission at Ebla, was disputing whether, for example, the ending of the name *Mi-kà-Yà* could have any connection with biblical Yahwism, because the Eblaite language seems to be more of a Palaeo-Akkadian dialect. The result was that the links suggested by Fr. Dahood between the Ebla texts and the Bible did not hold good; they were abandoned.

7. *The creation of a* Fund Raising *Campaign: 1976*

The Biblical Institute's financial situation, like that of the Gregorian, was becoming disastrous; the Oriental Institute, for its part, was supported by the Vatican Congregation on which it depended.

In 1970 the Fr. General set up the administrative Council for the Roman academic institutions (the CAIAR): every month the Fr. General took part in it, with his Delegate, Fr. Francis J. McCool, the general Treasurer of the Society, Fr. Eugen Hillengass, and the rectors of the Gregorian, the Biblical Institute and the Oriental Institute; all questions of common interest were dealt with at it.

The financial problems were such that from October 1973 to May 1974 several international consultants were called in, in particular Fr. Michael P. Walsh, a former president of Boston College and Fordham University in New York; along with Fr. Charles W. Dullea, he drew up a report complete with figures on the basis of the accounts for the academic year 1972-1973 (APIBR L-96). Although the Jesuit professors do not receive a salary, the Institute was continually making a loss, with school fees and help received from the General not being enough. The idea then took shape of forming a *Fund Raising Campaign* to collect interest-earning funds of which the interest would cover the deficit each year.

At the 32nd General Congregration of the Society of Jesus the question was not on the table but, in January 1975, a group of delegates, which included Fr. Martini, gave support to Fr. Walsh's conclusions (APIBR L-99-B: document dated March 5th, signed by Fr. A. Costes, the French Provincial).

Whereupon, on December 8th, 1976, Fr. General renewed the administrative Council of the international institutions in Rome which was summoned to meet every year (*ARSI* 16, 981-982). It comprised, apart from the Fr. General, Fr. Simon Decloux, his Delegate at the time, and the three rectors concerned, the Provincials or Presidents of conferences of the Provincials of Germany, northern Latin America, Spain, the United States, France and India. This Council was henceforth also to concern itself with the finances of the three Roman academic institutions.

Then, on December 31st of the same year, the Fr. General, to set up this *Fund Raising Campaign*, established an office in Rome and put Fr. Patrick G. Malone and Fr. John E. Blewett in charge of it (*ARSI* 16, 1063).

Paul VI had just heard about the plan when he sent a first gift. Fr. General and all the Provinces of the Society, including the less fortunate ones, made their contribution. From October 10th to the 14th, 1977 Fr. General called upon the superiors general of men's and women's religious orders to contribute to this fund in their turn; in five days, each in a different language, German, English, Italian, Spanish and French, he explained the reasons for this *Fund Raising Campaign* and its purpose: like the Gregorian, the Biblical Institute trains a good number of their young recruits; why not support those institutions financially? (cf. Doc. R. IV,1). Some professors from the Biblical Institute took part in those meetings: Fathers Lentzen-Deis, McCarthy, Welch, Martini, Alonso Schökel and Gilbert. Then the bishops and potential lay benefactors were addressed. In 1978, for the 50th anniversary of the PUG-PIB-PIO Consortium created by Pius XI, the operation was well launched.

Looking back over Fr. Martini's rectorate (1969-1978)

When he became rector of the Biblical Institute at the age of 42, Fr. Martini inherited a situation that was calm and by then open to a profound *aggiornamento*. He had what it takes to carry on the work with discernment, creativity and, let us say it with Brother Sándor Ritz, with consummate art. For nine years, the rector, putting his reputation to good use, led the renewal of the institution both in Rome and in Jerusalem (cf. Part Two, chaps. II and III). Thanks not only to the new, democratically established statutes and to the alterations he planned and put into effect in both buildings, but also to the arrival of young Jesuit professors, to the invitation sent to a good number of other teachers, especially thanks to the *Catholic Biblical Association of America* and a new academic programme created conjointly by the Biblical Institute and the Hebrew University of Jerusalem. This investment and broadness of vision on several fronts could not but be good for the institution, despite the drop in the number of students.

For the benefit of the Institute, the rector put in a lot of time and effort into outside activities. His published writings were numerous during these years. Firstly in the scholarly domain that was his, textual criticism, in which he was a past master; he was a member of the international and ecumenical committee that edited *The Greek New Testament*, [2]1968, [3]1975, [4]1993, and he gave some papers of a high standard at international congresses. Then, trained at first to teach fundamental theology, he showed great interest in the influence of Scripture in the life of the Church; to him we owe several commentaries on chapter VI of the Vatican II constitution *"Dei Verbum"*. As a Jesuit he had it at heart to link biblical texts with the *Spiritual Exercises* of Ignatius of Loyola; he was sowing the seeds of a great future.

His rectorate took place during the most mature years of the generalate of Fr. Arrupe whose full confidence he possessed. Paul VI, too, greatly appreciated him; he received him in private audience several times to find out about the Biblical Institute, which he did not fail to encourage and even support financially (cf. *Acta PIB* 7, 359-360, 478 or 500, 509-510; 8, 104). In June 1972, being invited to Cracow for the congress of Polish biblical scholars, he was the guest of Cardinal Karol Wojtyła, who was not to lose sight of him!

The rector's openness also showed itself in his ecumenical relations; he it was who, in 1970, invited Professor J. Alberto Soggin to come to teach at the Biblical Institute and he, like Fr. Bea, had friendly contacts with Oscar Cullmann and several personalities from Greek Orthodoxy. In Israel he managed, quite easily as it happened, to bring about academic cooperation with the Hebrew University and several professors from it henceforth considered themselves friends of his, in particular Professors R. J. Zwi Werblowsky and Shemaryahu Talmon.

This great rector, imperturbable and profoundly human, set an example and the Biblical Institute fell into step with him.

II. The first seven years of the pontificate of John Paul II: 1978-1985

Appointed by Paul VI on July 5th, 1978, Fr. Maurice Gilbert succeeded Fr. C. M. Martini on July 26th. The latter left the Biblical Institute in September to take up the charge of rector of the Gregorian University until, at the end of December 1979, John Paul II appoints him archbishop of Milan. Fr. Albert Vanhoye became rector of the Biblical Institute on June 29th 1984 and Fr. Gilbert left for Jerusalem.

Paul VI died on August 6th, 1978; on that day the announcement of the papal appointments of Fathers Martini and Gilbert appeared in *L'Osservatore Romano*, but it took some time for the Vatican to send them official notification of their appointment, which was necessary for the Italian State to take due notice.

John Paul I was elected on August 26th, 1978, but died on September 28th. John Paul II was elected on October 16th, 1978. On May 13th, 1981, he underwent an attempted assassination in St. Peter's Square. In 1980 he had appointed Cardinal William W. Baum Prefect of the Congregation for Catholic Education; for ten years he thus succeeded Cardinal Garrone and thereby became Grand Chancellor of the Biblical Institute.

On August 7th, 1981, Fr. Arrupe fell victim to a serious cerebral attack (he died on February 5th, 1991); on October 5th, 1981, John Paul II appointed Fr. Paolo Dezza Papal Delegate for the Society of Jesus with the powers of a General; Fr. Dezza became *ipso facto* Vice-Grand Chancellor of the Biblical Institute. On September 13th, 1983, Fr. Peter-Hans Kolvenbach was elected General by the 33rd General Congregation of the Society. Shortly after his election the Fr. General appointed Fr. Carlos Soltero as his delegate for the international Roman houses of the Society; he succeeded Fr. Simon Decloux who had fulfilled that function since 1975.

At the Biblical Institute, Fr. Francis J. McCool was named vice-rector in November 1978; on November 8th, 1984, Fr. James Swetnam succeeded him. On October 28th, 1981, Fr. Dionisio Mínguez was elected dean of the biblical faculty but resigned for health reasons sixteen months later and Fr. José O'Callaghan succeeded him on March 1st, 1983. In the oriental faculty, Fr. Richard I. Caplice was elected dean in November 1978. On November 1st, 1982, Fr. John R. Crocker became registrar of the Institute.

1. *Revising the statutes after the constitution* "Sapientia Christiana": *1979-1985*

a) From 1979 to 1981: the statutes

On April 15th, 1979, Pope John Paul II promulgates the Apostolic Constitution "*Sapientia Christiana*" which was henceforth to govern ecclesiastical universities and faculties. On the 29th, the Congregation for Catholic education published the "*Ordinationes*" which were to be observed in the application of the constitution. The statutes of the Biblical Institute, approved *ad experimentum* in 1972 were therefore revised.

On May 31st, Fr. Arrupe in his twofold capacity of Superior General of the Society of Jesus, and by that token, of Vice-Grand Chancellor of the Institute, in a letter addressed to the rector and the members of the senate of the Institute, pointed out some "directives on the procedure to be followed and on certain guidelines in the statutory reform". Being also responsible for the Gregorian University and the Oriental Institute, he also asked that in the three institutions a "sufficiently uniform procedure" be adopted. He also asked that in each of those institutions "a technical Committee to prepare the work of revision that the senate will have to do" be formed; the senate would then be presented with the dossier after the Committee has finished its work and, when the senate has finished its work, the rector will give the General the new statutes; the latter, perhaps after asking for some changes, will submit them to the Congregation for approval. As regards general guidelines, Fr. Arrupe started out from the principle that "authority must be on the same footing as real responsibility". He therefore asked that the jurisdiction of the various authorities at the Institute be defined in this way, but he also stressed the fact that people depend first of all on their religious superiors and that, as regards finances, it is the Society that is charged with providing them; the Institute can manage them, not get them for itself. Lastly, the Fr. General called for restraint and clarity in the statutes (cf. APIBR K.7-A).

Following these guidelines, the technical Committee was set up on June 21st. It consisted of Fr. General's Delegate, Fr. Simon Decloux, the rector, the vice-rector, the deans of both faculties, the registrar and the previous dean of the biblical faculty, Fr. Vanhoye. This Committee's work was put off until the next academic year; it was busy with it from October 1979 until the beginning of March 1980; it then handed in a "*textus retractatus*", a revised text of the statutes, comprising twenty-eight pages.

At the request of the Committee, this text was subjected to a wide-ranging discussion during an informal meeting of the teaching staff who were joined by the two senators who were students' delegates; this was on the 19th and 20th of March at the Villa Rufinella in the Frascati Hills. A twenty-two page report brought together the observations made by those taking part; the rector made a fourteen-page synthesis of the proposed amendments to the Committee's plan. The latter got back to work. On May 3rd it finished drawing up new proposi-tions which were then formally discussed by both faculties. Their opinions were integrated into a new version of the planned statutes which the rector submitted to the senators of the Institute on May 9th. The senate is actually the only organ at the Institute that is qualified to propose changes in the statutes to the authorities. At that time it consisted of ten persons: the rector and vice-rector, the deans of the two faculties, two full professors, one for each faculty and elected by their colleagues, two other professors or teachers likewise chosen by their colleagues, and two student delegates.

At the senate, the rector pointed out that several stipulations in that ver-sion of the projected statutes had not received the approval of the faculties and that, in other cases, the Committee or the biblical faculty was suggesting that they be referred back to the "*Ordinationes*". The senate therefore had its work cut out. It acquitted itself so well of its task that on June 27th the pro-jected new statutes could be submitted to the Fr. General. He approved them on December 10th and passed them on to the Congregation for Catholic education which, on September 24th, 1981, approved them *ad experimentum* for three years.

The whole Institute played its part in the operation and Fr. General's orders had been followed, especially as regards defining the jurisdiction of the authorities, both personal and collective. Let us note here some other changes brought about by these new statutes:

- it was in May 1980 that a new definition of the purposes of the Institute came out (art. 3): scholarly research first of all, then, secondly, training students in research and teaching and, lastly, service offered to the Church community; the priority given to research is an original aspect and characteristic of the Institute (cf. *Acta PIB* 8, 394);

- back in March 1980 it had been decided that the only permanent people are the full and associate professors and research fellows; from now on ten are needed in the biblical faculty and five in the oriental faculty;

- in May 1980 it was decided that in the case of an accusation brought against a permanent professor, the statute gives him the right to defend himself first, even in public; only after the accusation is shown to be well-founded should the authorities of the Institute take action;

- finally, in March 1980 the draft statutes included an article on the preparatory year for the doctorate in the biblical faculty and another, more detailed one on the procedure to be followed for the doctorate; it was then that it was decided that the final judgment passed on the thesis itself would be reserved to its director and to the second professor who had followed its development;

- only in June 1980 was it decided that the senate would increase from ten to twelve members.

b) From 1980 on, the "Ordinationes"

Revising, or rather renewing the "*Ordinationes*" was a long and exacting task.

It started with an informal meeting of the teaching staff on October 22nd to the 24th, 1980 at the Villa Campitelli in Frascati. An eleven-page report emerged. The views exchanged were about requirements for admission to the curriculum (knowledge of Latin, propaedeutic course and qualifying examinations), about the curriculum for the licentiate (content, teaching method and examinations) as well as about the preparatory year for the doctorate (requirements for admission and final examination). Nothing had been settled, but it had become clearer where the questions to be answered lay.

The technical Committee resumed work on February 15th, 1981, and went on until January 9th, 1982. Besides the report on the meeting at the Villa Campitelli, several proposals made by some professors were submitted to it. Once its work was over, the dossier went to the faculties. In the biblical faculty, where the discussions about the curriculum leading to the licentiate were endless, it was unanimously decided on April 27th, 1983, to put off reaching agreement: the *"Ordinatio"* on the licentiate therefore remained very sobre (*ad art. 60*), since the earlier practice was adhered to. Neither was any change made to the preparatory year for the doctorate. On procedure for the doctorate and the publication of the thesis, the earlier text was given further precision, taking into account the difficulties that occurred in practice.

At the instigation of Fr. M. Dahood, the school fees were tripled by a decision of the senate taken on April 15th, 1980, because income had to cover actual expenses, as far as possible (cf. *Acta PIB* 8, 509); article 76 of the statutes established the principle and the corresponding *"Ordinatio"* stated who would fix the amount of these fees, adding that in certain conditions a reduction, and even a dispensation, could be granted.

On May 25th, 1984, the rector was able to bring together in a single text the *"Ordinationes"* that had been up to that date approved by the senate.

c) Final revision of Statutes

On June 10, 1984, the rector sent Fr. General Kolvenbach the text of the statutes that had been revised by the senate of the Institute at the request of the Congregation for Catholic education. The rector pointed out that the senate had revised the text "between November 1981 and May 1982, and then from March to May 1984"; he then indicated, point by point, what changes had been made "with a very large majority, often in fact with a unanimous one, or almost", and the requests made by the Congregation for which the senate had not thought it necessary to change the text.

On January 14th, 1985, the Fr. General sent the new rector, Fr. A. Vanhoye, a list of changes he asked to be made to the statutes. On the 23rd they were unanimously accepted by the senate except for one which required that the election of a dean take place on presentation of two candidates. The next day, the rector explained by letter to the Fr. General that the request had not received the majority of votes in the senate because "1) it is often difficult to find two really capable and available candidates; 2) requiring two candidates looks like a lack of confidence in the Council of the Faculty, judged incapable of making a choice". The Fr. General did not insist.

On the other hand, the Fr. General did ask, on April 28th, that the Institute state, in article 27 of the statutes, the age at which people became emeritus, a request he had already expressed on January 14th, but the senate had referred this matter to the *"Ordinationes"*. This time the article was changed as follows: a full professor becomes emeritus at the age of seventy but, up to the age of seventy-five, he may continue to cooperate with the faculty provided he has the rector's approval (the ability of an elderly professor is not discussed in council!); it should be noted that until 1982 the age at which people become emeritus was sixty-five; is that a sign that, for the Society of Jesus, renewing the teaching staff was becoming more difficult?

On April 3rd, 1985, the Fr. General passed on the duly revised statutes to the Congregation and on November 14th Cardinal Baum approved them definitively. So, after almost two decades a reform of statutes willed by Vatican II came to a close. The dossier covering the years 1979-1985 is in the APIBR K-26-L.

2. *The Students*

The total number enrolled at the Institute gradually began to climb the slope: from 274 in 1978-1979 it was 304 in 1984-1985. This return to growth was to become more marked in the years following.

For the period under review here, the slow increase was mainly the effect of the arrival of students in greater numbers from non-western countries, including Eastern Europe still under Soviet rule. As early as 1980-1981, they represented more than half of the total number: 65 from Asia, 38 Latin Americans, 27 Africans and 23 Eastern Europeans, that is to say a total of 153 out of 285 enrolled. This trend was going to be even more pronounced because, in 1984-1985, while the western countries that in the past had been the great suppliers of students were hardly better represented – 55 Italians, 21 from the United States, 15 Spaniards – the big non-western countries had an ever-higher number of students enrolled at the Biblical Institute: 32 Indians, 17 Mexicans, 13 Filipinos, 12 Brazilians, 10 Nigerians and 15 Poles.

For the Institute, this posed the problem of their linguistic and cultural preparation. Since 1975 the Biblical Institute had been offering the propaedeutic Hebrew course in three languages, in English (given by Fr. K. Plötz), in Spanish and Italian. In 1980 Fr. Swetnam divided his propaedeutic Greek course into two, English and Italian. This expansion meant that several teachers of these ancient languages were taken on by the Institute.

In another context, in exegesis, account also had to be taken, as far as possible, of the emergence of the non-western world. Thus it was that in the second semester of the year 1983-1984 Fr. George Soarez Prabhu, S. J., a renowned Indian exegete, gave a course and a seminar at the Institute.

During this seven-year period, the number of doctoral theses defended at the Institute came to forty-nine, which represents a slight decline when compared with the previous period, 1968-1978, during which the number of students enrolled had begun to decline. Of these forty-nine theses defended, five were the work of young biblical scholars from India.

3. *The teaching staff*

Between 1980 and 1985 the Biblical Institute had a hard time: in five years it lost its first research associate and seven of its professors, two of whom were fully active. Fr. G. Patti (1903-1980) had taught Iranian languages until 1978 (cf. *Acta PIB* 8, 458-459); – Fr. P. Nober (1912-1980), a research fellow, had compiled the *Elenchus Bibliographicus Biblicus* until 1979 (cf. *Acta PIB* 8, 531-533); – Fr. K. Prümm (1890-1981) had taught Pauline exegesis and the history of religions until 1966 (cf. *Acta PIB* 8, 610-612); – Fr. M. Dahood (1922-1982), professor of Ugaritic, died suddenly in the chapel of the *Madonna del Pozzo* in the *S. Maria in Via* church in the centre of Rome (cf. *Acta PIB* 8, 612-614); – and Fr. D. J. McCarthy (1924-1983), professor of Old Testament exegesis, was found dead in his room during the international congress of the "Society of Biblical Literature" and of the "Organization for the Study of the Old Testament" which was held at Salamanca and at which he had given a paper (cf. *Acta PIB* 8, 780-781); – Fr. E. Vogt (1903-1984), professor of Old Testament exegesis, in particular the prophetic works, until 1975, and a former rector of the Institute (cf. *Acta PIB* 8, 781-782); – Fr. V. Pavlovský (1911-1984), professor of the history of the Old Testament and Semitic languages until 1983 (cf. *Acta PIB* 8, 783-784); – Fr. A. Massart (1906-1985), professor of Egyptology until 1980, a former dean of the oriental faculty and a former editor of the review *Orientalia* (cf. *Acta PIB* 9, 67-68).

Four other Jesuit professors at the Institute became emeritus during this same period: in 1982 Frs. St. Lyonnet and É. des Places (cf. *Acta PIB* 8, 638-639), Fr. R. Köbert in 1983 and Fr. P. Boccaccio in 1985.

An appeal for reinforcements had to be made. Younger Jesuit professors were brought into the Institute. In the biblical faculty Fr. Jean-Noël Aletti, a Frenchman born in 1942, arrived in 1980 to teach exegesis, especially that of the Pauline corpus, during the first semester; as from 1982 he did it full time, thereby succeeding Fr. Lyonnet; he had defended his doctoral thesis in 1980 and published it in 1982 with the title *Colossiens 1,15-20. Genre et exégèse du texte. Fonction de la thématique sapientielle* (AnBib, 91); – Fr. Frederick E. Brenk, from the United States, born in 1929, arrived in 1982 to take over from Fr. des Places on the relations between the New Testament and the ancient Greek world; a specialist on Plutarch, he taught until 2004 (cf. *Acta PIB* 11, 19-20); – Fr. Pietro Bovati, an Italian born in 1940, also came in 1982 to teach the exegesis and theology of the Old Testament; in 1985 he defended his doctoral thesis which he published two years later; it had as title: *Ristabilire la giustizia. Procedure, vocabolario, orientamenti* (AnBib, 110); – Fr. Stephen Pisano, from the United States and born in 1946, also arrived in 1982 to replace Fr. Martini in textual criticism and, after the death of Fr. McCarthy, to teach the exegesis of the historical books of the Old Testament as well; he was a doctor in theology from the University of Fribourg in Switzerland where, under the direction of Fr. D. Barthélemy, O. P., he had written a thesis with the title of *Additions or Omissions in the Books of Samuel* (OBO, 57); – in 1983, in his turn, Fr. Jean-Louis Ska, a Belgian born in 1946, arrived to teach the exegesis of the Pentateuch; he defended his doctoral thesis at the Biblical Institute in 1984 and published it 1986; it was entitled *Le passage de la mer. Étude de la construction du style et de la symbolique d'Ex 14,1-31* (AnBib, 109). In this way a younger team of exegetes moved into place for a long time. However, in 1979, Fr. K. Stock was summoned to the faculty of theology at the University of Innsbruck, giving only one course a semester at the Biblical Institute on the synoptic gospels, and that until 1987, when he came back full time to the Institute.

The oriental faculty took on two new Jesuit teachers: Fr. Leo Arnold, from England, born in 1929, who had spent a long time in Beirut, came to the Biblical Institute to teach Arabic there; Fr. Christian Sturtewagen, a Belgian, was to take the place of Fr. Massart in teaching Egyptian, which he did from 1980 until 1991, the year in which he left the Institute and later the Society of Jesus. From 1979 Fr. René Lavenant, from the Université Saint Joseph in Beirut and then the Oriental Institute in Rome, was invited to give the course on Syriac.

In the biblical faculty again, gradually to replace Fr. Boccaccio in the teaching of biblical Hebrew and Aramaic, Fr. Fabrizio Foresti, O. C. D. (1944-1987), an Italian, was taken on for Hebrew as from the second semester of the academic year 1979-1980 but in 1986 he had to retire for health reasons (cf. *Acta PIB* 8, 317). The Biblical Institute also relied on Fr. Robert B. Lawton, S. J., from the United States and born in 1947, who arrived in 1982 but, two years later, called upon for university administrative functions in his own country, left the Institute. Don Ambrogio Spreafico, an Italian, who was teaching the propaedeutic Hebrew course, took over from 1984 to 1991; he later became rector of the Pontifical Urbaniana University in Rome.

The "*Catholic Biblical Association of America*" continued to send an exegete to the Institute for a semester every year, or almost:
  1978-1979: John L. Topel, S. J., who gave a course on the gospel of Luke;
  1979-1980: Mgr. Jerome D. Quinn, on 1-2 Timothy and Titus;
  1980-1981: John R. Donahue, S. J., on the accounts of the resurrection in the gospels;
  1981-1982: Neil J. McEleney, C. S. P., on Matthew 5–7;
  1982-1983: no one;
  1983-1984: Charles Homer Giblin, S. J., on the gospel of Luke;
  1984-1985: William Wuellner, on rhetoric in the New Testament.

4. *Publications*

In 1978 Fr. Vanhoye became general editor of the review *Biblica* and, in 1984, Fr. H. Simian Yofre succeeded him. In 1981 Fr. R. I. Caplice took on the general editorship of the review *Orientalia*. As regards the collection *Analecta biblica*, it continued to flourish, publishing thirty-one volumes during this period. In 1983 the Institute celebrated the the 100th volume to come off the press, the one by Angelo Tosato, *Il matrimonio israelitico. Una teoria generale* (cf. *Acta PIB* 8, 640-641).

In 1980, as a tribute to its former rector, the Biblical Institute published a collection of scholarly articles by Fr. C. M. Martini, with the title *La Parola di Dio alle Origini della Chiesa* (AnBib, 93; cf. the presentation of the collection by M. Gilbert in *CC* 132 [1981, I] 462-469). In 1984 Fr. Boccaccio at last published the introductory fascicule (15* p.) and the concluding indices (pp. 913-1005) of the *Lexicon hebraicum Veteris Testamenti quod aliis collaborantibus edidit* Franciscus ZORELL.

Among the publications of the professors of the Institute, apart from those already mentioned, let us chiefly note the following:

on the Old Testament

M. GILBERT (éd.), *La Sagesse de l'Ancien Testament* (BETL, 51), Leuven, Peeters, 1979.

L. ALONSO SCHÖKEL et al., *Profetas. Comentario teologico y literario*. 2 vols., Madrid, Cristiandad, 1980.

L. ALONSO SCHÖKEL, *Treinta Salmos. Poesia y oración*, Madrid, Cristiandad, 1981.

L. ALONSO SCHÖKEL et al., *Job. Comentario teologico y literario*. Madrid, Cristiandad, 1983.

L. ALONSO SCHÖKEL et al., *Proverbios. Comentario teologico y literario*. Madrid, Cristiandad, 1984.

E. VOGT, *Untersuchungen zum Buch Ezechiel*. (AnBib, 95), Rom, 1981.

J.-N. ALETTI et J. TRUBLET, *Approche poétique et théologique des Psaumes. Analyses et méthodes*. Paris, Cerf, 1983.

on the New Testament

L. SABOURIN, *L'évangile selon Saint Matthieu et ses parallèles*, Rome, PIB, 1978.

A. VANHOYE, *Prêtres anciens, Prêtres nouveaux, selon le Nouveau Testament*, Paris, Seuil, 1980.

J. A. SWETNAM, *Jesus and Isaac. A Study of the Epistle to the Hebrews in the Light of the Aqedah* (AnBib, 94), Rome, PIB, 1981 [this was his PhD thesis at Oxford University].

F. LENTZEN-DEIS, *Las imagines de Jesús y la actual investigación bíblica*, Mexico City, 1984.

H. QUECKE, *Das Johannesevangelium saïdisch. Text der Handschrift PPalau Rib. Inv.-Nr. 183 mit varianten der Handschriften 813 und 814 der Chester Beatty Library und der Handschrift M 569* (Papyrologica Castroctaviana, 11) Barcelona, 1984.

on oriental studies

M. DAHOOD, "Ugaritic-Hebrew Parallel Pairs", in L. R. FISHER (ed.), *Ras Shamra Parallels. The Texts from Ugarit and the Hebrew Bible.* I (AnOr, 49), Rome, PIB, 1972, pp. 71-382 (in collaboration with T. Penar); and in St. RUMMEL (ed.), *Ras Shamra Parallels. The Texts from Ugarit and the Hebrew Bible*, III (AnOr, 51), Rome, PIB, 1981, pp. 1-206.

R. I. CAPLICE, *Introduction to Akkadian* (StP.SM, 9), Rome, PIB,1980.

on early Christianity

É. DES PLACES, Eusèbe de Césarée, *Préparation évangélique*, IV-V,17 (SC, 262), Paris, Cerf, 1979; V,18-36-VI (SC, 266), 1980; XI (with G. Favrelle; SC, 292), 1982; XII-XIII (SC, 307), 1983.

ID., *Eusèbe de Césarée commentateur. Platonisme et Écriture Sainte* (Théologie historique, 63), Paris, Beauchesne, 1982.

on the Greek world

É. DES PLACES, *Études platoniciennes (1929-1979)*, Leiden, Brill, 1981.

ID., Porphyre, *Vie de Pythagore. Lettre à Marcella* (Collection des Universités de France), Paris, Les Belles Lettres, 1982.

5. A programme of continuing education offered to former students: 1980-1984

As from 1980, the Biblical Institute, over a period of four academic years, offered a programme of *continuing biblical education*, chiefly designed for its former students. Fr. Dionisio Mínguez took charge of it in his capacity as director of the *"Office of Public Relations"*. This programme began in English during the 1980-1981 academic year and took two trimesters, one in Rome, from November to January, and the other in Jerusalem from March to May. In Rome, two professors, one for the Old Testament, Fr. McCarthy, and the other for the New, Fr. Dalton, were helped by two colleagues from the Gregorian University, Frs. Édouard Hamel and William Van Roo; interdisciplinarity was therefore to be the mark of this offer. At Jerusalem, just one professor from the Institute, Fr. Lentzen-Deis, was in charge of the programme, but many visits to biblical sites were also offered, under the guidance of Fr. José Espinosa (cf. *Acta PIB* 8, 480-481). In 1981-1982 a similar programme was organized, but in French, by Fr. Vanhoye, in collaboration with Fr. Louis Ligier, from the PUG, and by Fr. de la Potterie with Fr. Gilles Pelland from the PUG, while at Jerusalem Fr. Le Déaut directed the seminar, completed with visits to biblical sites under the guidance of Fr. Francesco Rossi de Gasperis (cf. *Bib* 62 [1981] 144; *Acta PIB* 8, 559). In 1982-1983 it was the turn of Spanish, but it consisted of only one big course given by two professors from the Institute,

Frs. Alonso Schökel and Mínguez and a colleague teaching dogmatic theology at the Gregorian University, Fr. Juan Alfaro; complementary to this was a series of lectures given by various professors from the Institute which brought people up to date with recent research in different exegetical fields (cf. *Bib* 63 [1982] 144-145; *Acta PIB* 8, 642). In 1983-1984 the Institute announced a programme of this kind in Italian (cf. *Bib* 64 [1983] 286); but there were so few signed up that it was cancelled or rather commuted into courses or seminars to be chosen from the normal programme for the licentiate, and that no longer corresponded with what was originally intended (cf. *Acta PIB* 8, 729; cf. also Part Two, chap. II), and the initiative stopped there.

6. *Alterations in the building of the Institute continue: 1981-1984*

The work that had been started in Fr. Martini's rectorate had to be carried on. There were two reasons for this. The first was that the library was crammed: it urgently needed to be given room. The second reason was linked with the decision taken to unite the two publishing establishments, the one at the Gregorian and the other at the Biblical Institute, and to have only one bookshop for the two institutions. The publications department would be established on the ground floor of the Biblical Institute, while the bookshop would be at the Gregorian, which would also agree to provide depots for books published by the Biblical Institute.

At the Institute, Fr. Saverio Corradino (1920-1997), who was from Udine and had a degree from the *Scuola Normale Superiore* at Pisa, had been librarian since 1975 and, from 1981 to 1984, the publications department at the Biblical Institute was run by Fr. José Antonio Esquivel, of Cuban origin, who was also the bursar at the Biblical Institute. Without them and without the architect, Mario Leonardi, this work that had become necessary would never have been brought to a successful conclusion in just over three years, from 1981 to 1984 (cf. APIBR L-83: final report by Fr. Esquivel).

To carry out this overall plan, the Institute wanted to remove the staircase that had been put there in 1910-1911 and which, facing the main entrance, led up to the library, situated on the second floor only. There was then a misunderstanding. It was thought at the Institute, in all good faith, that in principle authorization from the Holy See, the owner of the premises, was given, so that, during the summer of 1981, the staircase disappeared. But when the rector returned at the end of August from a stay in the United States there was a letter from the Vatican dated August 25th waiting for him that rejected any idea of demolishing the said staircase (APIBR L-83). On being consulted by the rector, Fr. Paolo Dezza advised going to explain things to the Vatican offices, which the rector did immediately. The chief engineer first gave him the reasons for the refusal – the staircase dated from the beginning of the 20th century and ought to considered part of the heritage – but when he finally learned of its demolition he was perplexed. The matter was settled thanks to Mgr. Paul Marcinkus, pro-president of the Pontifical Commission for the State of the Holy See. Being convinced of the good faith on the part of the Biblical Institute, he considered that the quite relative antiquity of the staircase was not a decisive argument. The Institute could therefore go ahead and, in the place of the staircase, it gained three extra spaces, on the ground floor and on the two first floors.

On the ground floor, the rooms that had been used since 1949 as depots for books published by the Institute were emptied; these rooms are situated mainly in the south-west of the building; the offices of the new administrative unit for the publications of the Gregorian and the Biblical Institute were installed there. The work went to considerable lengths: in an interior wall, a two-metre long tree-trunk was found, at a metre below ground level; this technique, designed to reinforce a wall, must have dated several centuries back!

To the east of the building, the situation was more complex. In Fr. Martini's rectorate, for financial reasons, the Institute had let out to an Italian bank the big hall where the statue of Pius X is, the adjacent rooms and the fine hall on the floor above them which is adorned with frescoes dating from the 17th century; the bank used them for recreational purposes for its staff. The lease was terminated.

But on the same first floor, on the south-eastern side, there was the biblical museum which no one had visited for a long time; even the keys to it had been lost!

> Among other things, this museum contained some tablets with cuneiform texts on them: cf. Luigi Cagni, "La collezione del Pontificio Istituto Biblico – Roma" (Materiali per il Vocabolario Neosumerico, 4), Roma, Multigrafica, 1976, pp. 9-22 + plates. – Werner R. Mayer, "Die altbabylonischen Keilschrifttexte in der Sammlung des Päpstlichen Bibelinstituts (Tab. XXVIII-XXXIX)", in Or 74 (2005), pp. 317-351.

Fr. Pierre Proulx spent the whole summer of 1981 making an inventory of the contents of this museum with a view to offering it to the Vatican Museums, which had said they were interested. On January 19th, 1982, the Institute's senate agreed to the transfer and Fr. Dezza, who had become Vice-Grand Chancellor of the Institute, expressed his approval of the senate's wish so that, in April, agreement was reached with the Vatican Museums who took away the whole content of our museum. In that way, all the eastern part of the building, on the ground floor (the Pius X Hall) and on the first floor, was free (*Acta PIB* 8, 559-561).

Still on the first floor, but on the other side of the building, to the west, it was decided to enlarge the depot for old books which Fr. Martini had already set up. Two other adjacent rooms were propped up to take the weight of all the volumes, books and periodicals which, given their age, were rarely consulted. Since 1976, Fr. Corradino had been withdrawing all books previous to the 19th century from that part of the library open to the public; they went into the new depot.

On the second floor and in the big hall with four levels of metallic framework, built in 1911, space was therefore freed. Fr. Corradino also decided that, while keeping the division into different sections, books of the same height would henceforth be placed on the same shelf of a stack, thereby saving a lot of space, certainly for about twenty years. That exhausting and courageous work called forth the admiration of a former director of the Bibliothèque Nationale de Paris whom Fr. Dezza had called in for consultation.

On the first floor, on the eastern side, it was decided to occupy all the space at last freed with a part of the library henceforth reserved for students in the early stages of their course. Important encyclopaedias, dictionaries and a selection of books and some periodicals – all of them duplicates – were therefore placed there. The Pius X Hall gradually became the refuge of those doing doctorates; there they found some beautiful oak tables, presented by the Gregorian. As for the hall with the frescoes, it was closed, pending restoration.

So, on three levels, the premises of the Institute had been radically refurbished with an eye to the future. The Holy See had seen to the payment of half the cost of the work.

7. The 75th anniversary of the Biblical Institute: 1984

On December 15th, 1979, Pope John Paul II had been received in the atrium of the Gregorian University by the authorities, the professors and other staff, as well as a large number of men and women students from the three Roman university institutions of the Society, the Gregorian, the Biblical Institute and the Oriental Institute; in his speech the Pope expressed his satisfaction at the work done at the Biblical Institute, which was in fact celebrating its seventieth anniversary that year. Then, at the rector's invitation, the Pope paid a visit to the Jesuit community at the Biblical Institute. It was a private visit during which the pontiff spoke freely for one hour with each one in the recreation room; in reply to the tribute paid by the rector, his only words, full of humour, were that he did not feel capable of coming to study at such a school! Two things struck him: the simplicity of the place, if not its poverty, and the number of young African and Asian Jesuits studying at the Institute. Meanwhile, a group of students from the Institute was at prayer in the chapel of the Institute (cf. *Acta PIB* 8, 405-406). At the beginning of 1980 the press at the Gregorian published a 32-page booklet in several languages entitled *John Paul II at the Gregorian University and at the Biblical Institute*; this booklet, commemorating the event, and including many photos, reports the speeches of welcome delivered by the rector of the Gregorian, Fr. C. M. Martini, and the rector of the Biblical Institute, as well as the Pope's speech.

To mark the 75th anniversary, the celebrations were in two stages. On May 7th, 1984, there was a concelebrated Mass in the church of the Holy Apostles, and the homily was given by Fr. Alonso Schökel. Then in the main lecture hall of the Institute the academic session took place in the course of which the rector, then Fr. General Kolvenbach and, finally, Cardinal William W. Baum, the Grand Chancellor of the Institute, spoke. Ten days later, on May 17th, the whole Institute, which was joined by a group of benefactors from the United States, was received by the Pope in the Clementine hall for a good half an hour (the Pope shortened the audience because of a Polish group that was waiting for him in the next room); the Pope made a speech before conversing briefly with some of the people present.

In his homily, Fr. Alonso Schökel, with originality and in depth, developed these themes: man does not live on words and bread alone; we at the Institute "live on bread and the Word, the Bread and the Word". The rector drew a picture of what had been achieved at the Institute since its 50th anniversary. Fr. Kolvenbach spoke of the involvement of the Society of Jesus, since its origin, in the study and teaching of Scripture; he stressed how much the Society had always wanted that the task received from the Holy See be performed as well as possible; he added that the present time required interdisciplinary, pastoral and ecumenical openness, an openness also to African and Asian cultures. Cardinal Baum went over the main statements of the constitution "Dei Verbum" of Vatican II; recalling the work of the best teachers at the Institute, now deceased, from Fr. Zorell to Fr. D. J. McCarthy, he encouraged his listeners to follow the same track, assuring them of the trust and hope of the Holy See.

The Pope reminded all, especially the students, of their responsibility towards the Church; he insisted on the personal and sincere reception of Scripture and putting its message into practice, a message which everyone reads and seeks to understand better; the study of the sacred books also calls for prudence, discretion and moderation so as to remain truly faithful to them; being a service to the Church, exegesis, which is at once a work of science and faith, must in our time pervade the whole of theology and all pastoral activity, ecumenism and dialogue with Judaism; it must also help the Church to get the treasures of the Bible to permeate all the cultures represented today in the Institute; lastly, Pope John Paul II renewed the mandate given by Pius X to the service of the Church, "in unwavering loyalty to its living Magisterium" (cf. *Acta PIB* 8, 713-723; *Bib* 65 [1984] 429-437).

8. *A co-operation agreement between the Biblical Institute*
   and the École Biblique de Jérusalem: 1982-1984

It is well known that at the beginning of the Institute, especially at Jerusalem (cf. Part Two, chap. I), and until the death of Fr. Lagrange in 1938, there were serious tensions between the Biblical Institute and the École Biblique of the Dominican Fathers in Jerusalem. An attempt had to be made to put right an unpleasant past. Now, as far back as 1966, the Institute was considering that its monopoly ought not to be maintained: it did not want to be alone in offering instruction leading to academic degrees in biblical studies (cf. Chap. III, § V,5). In 1983 the teaching staff of the biblical faculty adopted the same position. The following are the circumstances in which it did.

In April 1982, Fr. François Refoulé, O. P., had been elected director of the École Biblique et Archéologique Française in Jerusalem but he took up his post only on September 25th. Now, in mid-September, Fr. Gilbert, the rector of the Biblical Institute, being in the Holy City for a while, paid a visit to the École, as he usually did. During dinner, some professors at the École, Fathers Raymond Jacques Tournay, who had just finished his term as director, Pierre Benoit and M.-Émile Boismard, expressed their concern to him about the very small number of their students, only about ten. The rector answered them point-blank and without any forethought that they should blame themselves for that. The Dominican Fathers asked him why. "Because you do not offer any recognized diploma, with the result that no bishop or religious superior sends you, or will send you, any students". The answer was direct but in no way aggressive. That evening, the rector was called back to the École to speak about the matter again: to survive, the École ought to obtain authorization from the Holy See to grant official academic degrees. The Dominican Fathers explained that in 1972 there had been some question of granting the École the right to confer only the doctorate in biblical studies because it did not have the facilities to cover all the subjects required for a programme for the licentiate; on being consulted by Fathers Benoit and Tournay, Cardinal Garrone, then Prefect of the Congregation for Catholic education, had been definitely favourable, as was Cardinal Seper, Prefect of the Congregation for the doctrine of the faith and, in that capacity, President of the new Pontifical Biblical Commission, but the proposal hung fire for a long time, with the École hesitating to go ahead for fear of administrative checks and harassments. In 1982 the matter was to be taken up again.

On December 9th, on a visit to Rome, Fr. Refoulé came to discuss it with the rector of the Biblical Institute. The solution could only come from the Pope in person and could only be valid for the École Biblique de Jérusalem. To get this result an official request from Fr. Vincent de Couesnongle, the Master of the Order of Preachers, was first of all necessary; it was drawn up on February 18th, 1983, and sent to Cardinal Baum. It was then necessary to obtain the support of the Biblical Institute and the Biblical Commission, which also granted degrees in biblical studies but without providing instruction. At the Institute the rector consulted the professors of the biblical faculty who, on February 16th, gave their unanimous approval, and on March 2nd the rector informed Fr. Dezza, the Institute's Vice-Grand Chancellor, of this. At the Biblical Commission, Mr Henri Cazelles, secretary and chargé d'affaires, had known since October 1982 that Cardinal Ratzinger, the successor of Cardinal Seper, was favourable. It would then be a matter of writing a short memorandum that could be brought to the Holy Father's attention. Mr Cazelles and Fr. Gilbert worked on this and signed it on February 21st, 1983 (Doc. R. IV,2).

On March 4th, the two signatories gave their document to Cardinal Baum and, on the 7th, to Cardinal Ratzinger. Cardinal Baum asked Fr. Dezza for confirmation; he sent it to him on the 7th. On April 13th, Cardinal Ratzinger submitted the document to the Biblical Commission, at which Fr. Benoit became advocate of the cause; approval was almost unanimous, with one vote against.

The Pope gave his approval some days later; Cardinal Baum told the rector of the Biblical Institute about it, but at the Vatican it still had to be decided from whom the decree emanated. This was done on June 29th with a decree signed by Cardinal Baum *"de speciali mandato Summi Pontificis"*. On July 13th, thinking that Fr. Refoulé had already been informed, the rector of the Biblical Institute congratulated the École and suggested, as the last paragraph of the document of February 21st gave one to understand, that an agreement similar to the one the Institute had concluded with the Hebrew University of Jerusalem (cf. Part Two, chap. III) be reached between the École and the Institute. In fact, Fr. Refoulé had not received any news; the decree only reached him in August! Those vital documents in the history of the Biblical Institute are in its Roman archives (K-4-B: 4).

The agreement that had been wished for was finally signed on December 23rd, 1984 (cf. *Acta PIB* 9, 95-96; cf. also Part Two, chap. III). Furthermore, as from 1984, Fr. Gilbert, residing for some of the time in Jerusalem, was invited every year to give a course on the sapiential books of the Old Testament.

Conclusion

In seventeen years the Biblical Institute was thoroughly renewed.

Of course, the number of men and women students at first dropped noticeably, then there was a slow recovery, but what marks this period out was the arrival in ever-growing numbers of students from non-western countries. In addition, the student body, through its delegates, was henceforth cooperating in the academic management of the Institute.

The teaching staff was rejuvenated. In 1985, only ten professors of the previous team were still there: three in exegesis, Fathers Alonso Schökel, de la Potterie and Vanhoye, three in orientalism, Fathers Caplice and Quecke, along with Prof. van Dijk, and four others, Fathers Le Déaut, North, Proulx and Swetnam. The Society had made a big investment in personel.

The premises, both in Rome and in Jerusalem (cf. Part Two, chap. II), were renovated and made better adapted to academic needs. In Rome in particular it was possible to enlarge and reorganize the library; the *Aula Paulina* made it easier to find room for courses and became a more suitable place for the defence of theses.

On the level of administration, the bodies set up by the Father General let in some fresh air, especially through the creation of *Fund Raising*; the house's financial situation definitely improved, more especially as the Holy See had itself also given some help.

Through agreements reached with the *Catholic Biblical Association of America*, and then with the Hebrew University of Jerusalem (cf. Part Two, chap. II) and finally with the École Biblique et Archéologique Française, the Institute opened itself up to inter-university cooperation for the benefit of the students.

Lastly and above all, this period was marked by the renewal of the statutes and regulations of the institution. A slow process of democratically guided maturation has made it possible to arrive at rules that are clear and adapted to the post-Vatican II era; a quarter of a century later they are still governing the house.

Doc. R. IV,1

APIBR L-96

Some reflections on the Pontifical Institutions in Rome
entrusted to the Society of Jesus

A talk given by Father Pedro Arrupe, S. J., on October 11th, 1977,
on the occasion of a meeting with the members of the IUSG

Please excuse me for not having been with you from the beginning. With the Synod in session, there are so many people to meet, so much to do and there is never enough time. Let me begin by thanking each of you for taking time to come to this meeting and for being willing to hear our reports on the Gregorian University and its sister institutions, the Biblical Institute and the Institute of Oriental (Eastern-rite) Studies. You have already heard much from Fathers Carrier and Martini about the work that goes on in those institutions, about their potential, their needs and so forth. Perhaps I will repeat some of what you have already heard. If so, please forgive me.

From my earliest years as a Jesuit in Spain and then in Holland, the United States and Japan, I had some understanding of the importance of the Gregorian, the Biblical, and Oriental Institutes. Most of the textbooks we used in philosophy, theology, and scripture were written by their professors, while many of the men who taught me had studied at one of these institutions. But, after being elected in 1965 to my present position, I came to see them through the eyes of others such as, for example, the bishops at the last session of the Second Vatican Council. One after another, individually or in small groups, the bishops urged the Society of Jesus, and therefore myself, to devote more men and more resources to the study of the major human and theological questions which they were meeting in their parts of the world. "We must have more light for our pastoral work, especially after the Council", they would say, "but we do not have the scholarly resources that we need to help provide the light".

What the bishops said at that time, now twelve years ago, I have since heard repeated hundreds of times in almost every part of the world. Partially because of such repeated requests, I thought it right to propose to the whole Society of Jesus in 1970, at our congregation of procurators, that theological reflection on the major issues of humankind today be our highest priority. The Society has taken up this challenge in many ways.

[2] From this point of view, we can more easily understand the great importance of the three Roman institutions about which you have heard Fathers Carrier and Martini speak. Of all the missions entrusted by the Holy See to the Society, that of the Gregorian and its sister institutions is, in my judgment, the most important. We may close

schools or universities – or better still, turn them over to groups of well-prepared lay people – but we cannot even think of closing down the Gregorian – unless the Holy Father himself were to command it!

All of the Popes of this century have strongly insisted on the central importance of the Gregorian. I have personal experience of that, for almost every time I see Pope Paul he will ask about the work of the Gregorian or comment on a recently published book from its press or indicate that he is pleased – or displeased – with some aspect of its work.

The Holy See has so strongly backed the Gregorian and its sister institutions because they educate so many promising young men from all over the world to become priests. (I do not say that they are educated to become bishops! But almost 20% of the bishops of the world have done much or part of their studies at the Gregorian.)

Let me comment on this point a little. It has always been important for the Church that bishops feel together, think along the same lines, and in general be united among themselves and with the Holy Father. It is just as important today. But perhaps today it is psychologically more difficult, since the Church itself is stressing inculturation and bishops are so keenly aware of the importance of the particular or local Church. So you can see how important it is that in their early manhood future bishops come to know one another, to esteem one another, and to become friends. The Gregorian then is not only a centre for study and research but it is also a foyer for friendship and mutual understanding.

The Holy See has other reasons for wanting the Gregorian to be strong. For a sizeable number of its professors work, quietly and in unpublicized ways, for the different Congregations and other offices of the Vatican. From my own experience I know how important it is to have qualified thinkers and writers [3] nearby on whom I can call for assistance. How much more important this is for the Holy See engaged in leading the entire Church!

So you see the situation. The Holy Father, bishops at the Council, bishops and lay people in different parts of the world keep underlining how essential it is for the Church to have theological powerhouses. Then I look at the Gregorian, the Biblicum and the Oriental. I see good men there, excellent men, but their average age goes higher and higher. So I ask myself how can we make the institutions more attractive for talented young Jesuits from different countries. I do not say "more comfortable or softer". No, more attractive, in the sense that young men may come to Rome and find here some of the assistance they would have in their home countries for carrying on research, publishing books, planning high-level seminars on burning issues, joining in debate with their peers in other countries on the major issues of the world community.

My heart sinks at this point, for I know that the total budget of these three institutions, which educate over 2,000 students (and close to 70% of them at graduate level), is about the same as that of a good secondary school in Germany, Belgium or the United States! Gregorian professors resemble somewhat the Hebrews in ancient Egypt ordered to make bricks without straw. Lacking adequate secretarial help, they type out the draft and the final copy of a manuscript. Instead of having research assistants to check references for them or work up material for an essay, they must do this themselves. Men – and women – can become holy in such conditions, of course, but it is difficult to become the scholar, the thinker, the writer which the Church so badly needs today.

So you see the challenge that faces the Society of Jesus and myself personally; we must enable the Gregorian to have a second spring by attracting young and talented professors from different countries. Jesuits first and foremost, since the Holy See – and we ourselves – see this as important, but also religious from other congregations and lay men and women, too. To do this, we must strengthen the financial underpinning of the institutions.

Sometimes people say to me, "But, Father Arrupe, why don't you give a man an order under obedience to come here to teach and work?" Such questions, you may be sure, do not come from [4] other generals or from religious superiors, for we know – it is our common experience – that before giving an order, it is important to be sure that the human conditions for its acceptance are present. When they are present, yes, then we can give an order.

So, what was to be done? We sought the advice of experts: a Dutch university professor well versed in questions of university administration – a layman; a Jesuit, formerly the president of Boston College and Fordham University; then, a management consulting firm from New York. They made many recommendations, many, many. They were unanimous that the financial situation of the institutions must be improved.

We have tried to keep expenses down, and we will continue to do so. We have raised the fees paid by the students until now they are the highest of any ecclesiastical institution in Rome. Even so, they cover less than 50% of a budget which is already much too small.

Facing this situation, I decided to take a leaf from the book of St. Ignatius: namely, to seek financial help from different quarters. I have some embarrassment, perhaps, in doing this, but no hesitation, because the beneficiary is not the Jesuit Order so much as the Church. (Of the total enrollment of the three institutions, less than 8% is from the Society.) So, with the help of advisers, we have begun a campaign to raise funds from at least four different sources: the Society of Jesus itself; other religious congregations; conferences of bishops; the lay world.

Our strategy is very simple – not at all Jesuitical! We are asking all of the Jesuit Provinces to contribute money and thus show their solidarity with, and confidence in, the Gregorian. Then, we put the facts before other religious congregations, asking them to come to learn more about these works and to see if they can help them at this critical time. With assistance from these two sources, it is easier to go to bishops and gently to remind them of the way in which their dioceses have been served over the centuries by the Gregorian. Finally, with help from these three ecclesiastical pockets, we are in a very strong position to solicit help from lay groups: friends, foundations, individuals and organizations.

[5] Already the work has begun. Some $3 million of the target of $20 has been collected or promised – 50% collected, 50% promised firmly. We have explained our case to some religious congregations already; in fact, our meeting here today grew out of an invitation from some mothers-general who were at a previous meeting on this subject. Father Malone is now in the States to contact different groups of the laity, while we have opened discussions with lay groups in Germany and Holland.

There are, of course, some who might object to what we are doing, for any of several reasons.

For example, some say that theological centres in other parts of the world should be strengthened and that the Gregorian should wither away. I certainly agree with the first part of this contention, but I totally reject the second part. Indeed, I have worked very hard to support theological centres in the heart of major cities in the world: Frankfurt, London, Madrid, New Delhi, Tokyo, Washington, Berkeley, etc. But the stronger such centres become, the more they have need of an outstanding theological centre in Rome. Let us not think of it as the "periphery" and the "centre", but rather as knots in a net, all linked together or as cities sitting on different hills!

Others may say that it is not evangelical to build up an endowment, that we should trust in Providence, etc. Indeed, we should trust in Providence. (We would not dare to start such a campaign if we did not trust Providence!) We can answer such objections in different ways, but for me one of the strongest arguments is the encouragement we have received from the Holy Father himself to build up a fund – encouragement both in words and in a sizeable gift which he sent to us when he was informed of our hopes. Further, the example of St. Ignatius in legislating that, so far as possible, all of our educational works should be endowed. This says more for me than pages of theoretical arguments, for Ignatius wanted to be poor with Christ poor, wanted to love Lady Poverty as a mother, etc. Frugality, even austerity in the personal life of the Jesuit – fine; but in apostolic work we are to use the ordinary means to help us to achieve the very best!

[6] Now I have spoken at some length, and in my poor English. You must excuse my Spanish pronunciation. My mouth has not been fully inculturated in English, you see!

Perhaps now there may be some questions. I will try to answer if I can.

* * * * *

Doc. R. IV,2

APIBR K-4-B: 4

*A typewritten document handed to Cardinals J. Ratzinger and W. W. Baum
in March 1983*

Rome, February 21st1983

Several moves were made in 1972 to make it possible for the École Biblique de Jérusalem to be granted by the Sacred Congregation for Catholic Education the right to grant the Doctorate in Biblical Studies to students who would already have obtained the Licentiate in Biblical Studies either at the Pontifical Biblical Commission or from the Pontifical Biblical Institute. These moves having had no effect, it seemed urgent to Mr Henri Cazelles, Chargé d'affaires at the Pontifical Biblical Commission, and to Fr. Maurice Gilbert, Rector of the Pontifical Biblical Institute, to submit the matter once again to the competent authorities, His Eminence Cardinal Baum, Prefect of the Sacred Congregation for Catholic Education, and His Eminence Cardinal Ratzinger, President of the Pontifical Biblical Commission.

These are the reasons:

1. The École Biblique has given and still gives such service to the Church that it seems reasonable and just that the activities of the the École Biblique be able to continue. Now, for the very reason that it does not confer academic degrees recognized by the Holy See, the École Biblique has been in trouble for several years for lack of students.

2. The École Biblique has acquired international renown thanks to the prestige of masters such as the Reverend Fathers Lagrange, Vincent, de Vaux, to mention only some of those deceased. The publications of the École Biblique, especially the Revue Biblique and the collection Études Bibliques have contributed greatly to the recognition of the worth of Catholic exegesis in our age. But scholarly university circles are surprised that no degree from the École Biblique is recognized by the Holy See.

3. Moreover, this school is recognized as the École Archéologique Française by the French State. The latter would surely appreciate it if the Holy See were to recognize the merits of the almost century-old institution

4. Situated as it is in the Holy Land, at the gates of the Holy City, offering one of the really best libraries in the world in biblical subjects and carrying out archaeological excavations of exceptional renown, at Qumrân for example, the École Biblique represents an incomparable research instrument for use by those doing Doctorates in Biblical Studies.

5. For generations, and this is still the case today, the Pontifical Biblical Institute, along with the Pontifical Biblical Commission, has not wanted to have a monopoly in academic degrees in Biblical Studies. On this level, pluralism can only be beneficial in the Church. Another thing is that while the École Biblique is short of students, the Biblical Institute, by the very fact that it confers academic degrees, sees the number of its students exceeding 350.

6. The École Biblique, as it name indicates, is a highly specialized institution in biblical studies and, as such, has nothing parallel to it except for the Biblical Institute. It would be desirable that these two institutions should collaborate more on an equal footing. The Holy See and the whole Church could only gain by it.

Henri Cazelles, P. S. S.
(*signature*)

Maurice Gilbert, S. J.
(*signature*)

* * * * *

CHAPTER V

The last quarter of the first century
1985-2009

At this early stage it is obviously difficult to tell the story of the Pontifical Biblical Institute in Rome in the proper perspective during the period that occupies our attention here. We shall have to be content with pointing out some objective facts, thereby hoping to provide a correct view of what has happened at it.

I. Up to the Institute's 90th anniversary: 1985-1999

In 1990, Mgr. Pio Laghi became Pro-prefect of the Congregation for Catholic Education and therefore Grand-Chancellor of the Institute; the year following he was made a cardinal and at that time took on the title of Prefect of that Congregation. He retained it until November 1999.

Fr. Albert Vanhoye completed his rectorate in 1990. Fr. Klemens Stock succeeded him for six years. In 1996 Fr. Robert F. O'Toole took over.

In 1986, Fr. James Swetnam became dean of the Biblical faculty. Fr. Klemens Stock succeeded him in 1989, but, a year later, it was the turn of Fr. Jean-Noël Aletti to take on the function; however, after three years, he handed over to Fr. H. Simian Yofre. In 1996 Fr. Stephen F. Pisano was, in his turn, elected dean of that faculty.

In the oriental faculty, Fr. Richard I. Caplice was replaced as dean by Fr. Werner Mayer in 1987. Actually, Fr. Caplice was to leave the Institute in 1989 to devote himself to the direct apostolate in the State of New York. As the faculty did not now have a sufficient number of permanent professors, Fr. Mayer was in fact "pro-dean" as from 1990. In 1996 Fr. James H. Swetnam succeeded him in that office, then, in 1998, Fr. Klemens Stock did.

The charge of Rector was thus fulfilled normally during this period, but the office of dean in both faculties passed too often from one holder to another, to the detriment of continuity in management. Fr. Mayer alone ran his faculty for nine consecutive years.

Finally, in June 1991, Fr. Swetnam succeeded Fr. Crocker as Registrar of the Institute and remained so until October 1997. On November 1st of that year 1997, Mr Carlo Valentino took over; he had obtained the licentiate in biblical studies at the Institute in 1979 and then became assistant to the Registrar for eighteen years.

1. *Students*

During this period of fourteen academic years the number of students enrolled at the Biblical Institute increased regularly. From 301 in 1985-1986, they were 378 in 1998-1999. The year 1997-1998, however, marked a new peak: then, for the first time, the number of enrolled students came to 403 of whom 341 were for the licentiate in the biblical faculty. These figures confirm the observations already made for the year 1980-1981; students from non-western countries were coming in numbers to the Institute; thus, to mention only the larger contingents, in 1997-1998 there were 13 Argentinians, 15 Brazilians, 9 Colombians, 12 from Congo Kinshasa, 12 Filipinos, 41 Indians, 25 Mexicans, 11 Nigerians, 40 Poles, 9 Romanians. Only two western countries continued to send a good number of students to the Biblical Institute: Spain provided 12 enrolled students and especially Italy, which numbered 83!

The number of doctoral theses defended at the Institute during this period went up to seventy, i. e. an average of five per year.

2. *The teaching staff*

During this period the Institute was saddened by the decease of eleven of its members.

Six of them were already emeriti: Fr. Stanislas Lyonnet (1902-1986), who had taught mainly the Pauline corpus from 1942 to 1982, died in the peace of the Lord at Rome (cf. *Acta PIB* 9, 144-145, 166-170); – Fr. Raimund Köbert (1903-1987), a professor of Semitic languages from 1939 to 1983, also died in Rome (cf. *Acta PIB* 9, 316; *Or* 57 [1988] 212-217); – Fr. Francis J. McCool (1913-1996), a professor of New Testament from 1955-1985, passed away in New York (cf. *Acta PIB* 10, 220-221); – Fr. Johannes J. A. van Dijk (1915-1996), a professor of Sumerian from 1968 to 1987, died at Amsterdam (cf. *Acta PIB* 10, 333-336) – Fr. Hans Quecke (1928-1998), a professor of Coptic from 1965 to 1997, died at Münster (cf. *Acta PIB* 10, 715-720); – Fr. Luis Alonso Schökel (1920-1998), a professor of biblical hermeneutics and theology from 1957 to 1995, died at Salamanca (cf. *Acta PIB* 10, 569-574). They had been active witnesses of a great period at the Institute.

Five others died before their time: Fr. Fabrizio Foresti, O.C.D. (1944-1987), taught Hebrew from 1980-1986 (cf. *Acta PIB* 9, 317); – Sister Cecilia Carniti, Helpers of the Holy Souls (1946-1992), with a doctorate from the

Biblical Institute with a thesis on Psalm 68, had taught mainly Aramaic and Hebrew from 1985 to 1991 (cf. *Acta PIB* 9, 726); – Fr. Fritzleo Lentzen-Deis (1928-1993) had directed seminars and theses on the New Testament from 1972 to 1992 (cf. *Acta PIB* 9, 850-851;– Fr. Pierre Proulx (1926-1993), a professor of patristic exegesis from 1961-1991, died in Rome (cf. *Acta PIB* 9, 962); – Fr. Angelo Tosato (1938-1999), with a doctorate in biblical studies from the Institute for his thesis on *Il matrimonio israelitico. Una teoria generale* (AnBib, 100), and a professor at the Lateran University, gave a course, from 1986 until his sudden death, on the history of Israelite institutions (cf. *Acta PIB* 10, 565). Their departures were a serious blow to the Institute that had been counting on them.

Four others, who had reached the age limit, left the Institute; they were: Fr. John J. Welch, who had taught biblical Greek from 1972 to 1991 (he died in Rome in 2002; cf. *Acta PIB* 10, 976); – Fr. José O'Callaghan, a professor of papyrology from 1971 to 1992 (he died at Barcelona in 2001; cf. *Acta PIB* 10, 974-975); – Fr. Roger Le Déaut, a Holy Ghost Father, professor of Targumic literature from 1964 to 1994 (he died at Chevilly in France in the year 2000; cf. *Acta PIB* 10, 868-870); – J. Alberto Soggin, a professor of biblical history from 1971 to 1999 (cf. *Acta PIB* 10, 635-638). Four others, also having reached the age limit, remained at the Institute all the same: Fr. Pietro Boccaccio (1910-2006) in 1985 concluded his teaching of biblical Hebrew and Aramaic that he had started in 1949; – Fr. Ignace de la Potterie in 1989 finished his teaching of the New Testament that had started in 1960 (cf. *Acta PIB* 9, 499-450); – Fr. Robert North in 1989 put an end to his teaching of biblical archaeology that had started in 1951, but he continued to edit the *Elenchus Bibliographicus Biblicus* until the volume covering the year 1995/2 which appeared in 1999 (cf. *Acta PIB* 9, 645-647); – on his part, in 1998, Fr. Albert Vanhoye concluded his teaching on the New Testament that had begun in 1963 (cf. *Acta PIB* 10, 497-499).

Lastly, three professors left the Institute well before becoming emeriti: Fr. Richard I. Caplice, born in 1931, who had taught Akkadian since 1966, returned to his country in 1989, as has been said; Fr. Ambrogio Spreafico, who had taught Hebrew since 1977, withdrew in 1991; – Fr. Silvano P. Votto, born in 1942, who taught Sumerian, and then biblical Greek, from 1985, returned to California in 1999.

Some new professors were therefore taken on.

In exegesis, the succession had been provided by a younger team of Jesuits during the previous period; in particular, Fr. Klemens Stock came back to the Biblical Institute for good in 1987; meanwhile, from 1993 to 1999, Fr. Maurice Gilbert was rector of the university Faculties of Notre Dame de la Paix at Namur, Belgium. In addition to that, Fr. de la Potterie's becoming emeritus in 1989, Fr. Lentzen-Deis finishing his work at the Institute in 1992 for health reasons, Fr. Alonso Schökel becoming emeritus in 1995 and Fr. Vanhoye in 1998 meant finding full time new Jesuit fellow-workers for the Institute. With the Society of Jesus being unable to offer the Biblical Institute any young recruits, there was nothing for it but to take on some well-qualified professors: Fr. John J. Kilgallen, born in 1934, who left Loyola University of Chicago to come back to the Biblical Institute in 1985; he was a doctor in biblical studies from the Institute with a thesis on *The Stephen Speech. A Literary and Redactional Study of Acts 7,2-53* (AnBib, 67), 1976; – Fr. Jesús Luzarraga, born in 1937, leaving the University of Deusto in Bilbao, to come back to the Biblical Institute in 1988, particularly for the exegesis of the Johannine writings; he also was a doctor in biblical studies from the Institute with a thesis on *Las tradiciones de la nube en la Bíblia y en el Judaismo primitivo* (AnBib, 54, 1973); – Fr. Robert F. O'Toole, born in 1936, who came back to the Biblical Institute in 1991, leaving the Jesuit University of St. Louis, in the United States, a doctor in biblical studies from the Institute with a thesis on *Acts 26. The Christological Climax of Paul's Defense (Ac 22:1–26:32)* (AnBib, 78), 1978, in 1992 he became vice-rector of the Institute before becoming its rector in 1996; – Fr. Jan Lambrecht, born in 1926, who came to the Biblical Institute when he had become emeritus at the Katholieke Universiteit te Leuven; a doctor in biblical studies from the Institute with a thesis on *Die Redaktion der Markus-Apokalypse. Literarische Analyse und Strukturuntersuchung* (AnBib, 82), 1967, he had published a lot; notable in particular is *Once more Astonished. The Parables of Jesus* (New York, Crossroad, 1981); at the Biblical Institute he taught from 1996 to 2001. The exegesis of the New Testament in particular was strengthened by them.

This support did not seem to be enough; another five stalwarts in exegesis were also invited; they were: first of all, Fr. Nobert Lohfink, for the Old Testament, 1989-1990, 1993 and 1999; – Fr. José Luis Sicre Díaz, born in 1940, a doctor in biblical studies from the Institute with a thesis on *Los dioses olvidados. Poder y riqueza en los profetas preexilicos* (Madrid, Cristiandad, 1979) and a professor in the faculty of theology at Granada, to teach prophetism in 1992, 1994 and 1996; – Fr. Hans-Winfried Jüngling, born in 1938, a professor in the Jesuit theological college at Frankfurt, to replace Fr. M. Gilbert temporarily in 1993-1994 and in 1996; he was a doctor in biblical studies from the Institute with a thesis on *Richter 19 – Ein Plädoyer für das Königtum. Stilistische Analyse der Tendenzerzählung Ri 19,1-30a;21,25* (AnBib, 84), 1981; – Fr. Yves Simoens, born in 1942, a professor at the Brussels Institute of theological studies, then at the Paris Centre Sèvres, was invited to take the Johannine corpus in 1996-1997 and in 1998-1999; he, too, was a doctor in biblical studies from the Institute, and his thesis had appeared with the title of *La gloire d'aimer. Structures stylistiques et interprétatives dans le Discours de la Cène (Jn 13–17)* (AnBib, 90), 1981; he was later to come back to the

Biblical Institute every other year for a semester; – Fr. Willem Beuken, born in 1931, from the Netherlands and an emeritus professor of the Katholieke Universiteit te Leuven, also taught the prophetic corpus in 1998-1999. With them, it was mainly Old Testament exegesis that received some help.

Still in exegesis, only towards the end of this period, a young, non-Jesuit professor was taken on, Fr. Luca Mazzinghi, from the faculty of theology in Florence who, from 1997-1998, gave a course on the sapiential books of the Old Testament; he had been brilliantly successful in obtaining the doctorate at the Biblical Institute in 1995 with a thesis on the *Notte di paura e di luce. Esegesi di Sap 17,1– 18,4* (AnBib, 134).

For ancient languages, the Society was able to provide the Biblical Institute with six professors, namely, Fr. Santiago Bretón, born in 1940, a doctor in biblical studies from the Institute with a thesis on *Vocación y misión: formulario profético* (AnBib, 111), 1987, had already started teaching Hebrew at the Institute, which he continued until 1994; – Fr. Silvano P. Votto taught Sumerian and Greek from 1985-1999 (cf. *supra*); – Fr. Agustinus Gianto, from Indonesia and born in 1951, taught Ugaritic and biblical Hebrew from 1987; he was already a doctor from Harvard University with a thesis, submitted in 1987, on *Word Order Variation in the Akkadian of Byblos* (Studia Pohl, series Minor, 17), 1990; – Fr. Robert Althann, born in 1939, with the licentiate in biblical studies from the Institute and a doctorate from the University of Zimbabwe with a thesis he defended in 1979 and published under the title *A Philological Analysis of Jeremiah 4–6 in the Light of Northwest Semitic* (BiOr, 38, 1983); in 1989 he started by giving some courses and seminars on the Old Testament but very soon moved on to teaching biblical Aramaic and Hebrew before succeeding Fr. North in 1995 as editor of the *Elenchus of Biblica*; – Fr. Anthony J. Forte, born in 1951, a doctor in classical languages from the University of California, began his teaching of biblical Greek in 1991; – lastly, Fr. Paul V. Mankowski, born in 1953, a doctor from Harvard University with a thesis on *Akkadian Loanwords in Biblical Hebrew* (Harvard Semitic Studies, 47), 2000, began his teaching of Biblical Hebrew in 1991. The field of Semitic and biblical languages was thus well covered.

For the other subjects, colleagues from outside were invited. In this way, apart from Sister Cecilia Carniti, who died in the course of this period (cf. *supra*), the following were called to the biblical faculty: Fr. Guido Innocenzo Gargano, O.S.B. Camald., who taught the history of patristic exegesis, which he had already started doing in 1984, which he then did in 1986, then every year as from 1988; – Professor Antonio Pitta, from the faculty of theology in Naples, who held the pro-seminar in methodology in the biblical faculty between 1986-2000; a doctor from the Biblical Institute, his thesis appeared in 1992 under the title *Disposizione e messaggio della Lettera ai*

Galati (AnBib, 131): – Professor Lorenzo Viganò, a priest from Pavia, who, for seven academic years, between 1986 and 1996, taught mainly the near-eastern background to the Old Testament; he was a doctor from the Biblical Institute and his dissertation entitled *Nomi e titolo di YHWH alla luce del semitico del Nord-ovest* (BiOr, 31) appeared in 1976; – Fr. Carlo Buzetti, S.D.B., from the Salesian University in Rome, with the licentiate in biblical studies from the Biblical Institute; in association with the World Bible Alliance, he offered a seminar on Bible translation techniques every other year between 1987 and 2008; – Fr. Michele Piccirillo, O.F.M., from the Studium Biblicum Franciscanum in Jerusalem, who taught Palestinian archaeology from 1990 to 2000; – Fr. Joseph Sievers, from the Focolarini, who taught ancient Judaism from 1991; a doctor from Harvard University in 1981, he had just published *The Hasmoneans and Their Supporters. From Mattathias to the Death of John Hyrcanus* (Atlanta, Scholars Press, 1990); in 1996 he became an assistant professor in the biblical faculty; – Mrs. Corinne Bonnet, from the *Academia Belgica* in Rome, who, from 1993-2003, taught both ancient Near Eastern history and the Syro-Palestinian background to the Old Testament; – Fr. Don McMahon, O.M.I., who, since 1994, has been teaching Hebrew in the propaedeutic course; – Fr. Jesús García Recio, from Madrid, with the licentiate in biblical studies from the Institute in 1989, who, since 1996, has been giving classes on the relations between Mesopotamia and the Old Testament.

In the oriental faculty, the following were invited: Professor Massimiliano Marazzi, at the time a professor at the "La Sapienza" University in Rome, who, since 1986, has been teaching Hittite language and literature at the Institute.; – Fr. Craig E. Morrison, O. Carm., a doctor in biblical studies from the Institute with a thesis defended in 1995 and published in 2001 under the title *The Character of the Syriac Version of the First Book of Samuel* (Monographs of the Peshitta Institute Leiden, 11); since 1991 he has been teaching Targumic Aramaic and Syriac at the Institute; – Mrs. Loredana Sist, from "La Sapienza" University, who taught Egyptian language at the Institute from 1997 to 2004; – also starting in 1997, Fr. Philip Luisier, S. J., a professor at the Pontifical Oriental Institute, has been giving the course in Coptic at the Biblical Institute.

These long lists, in which only the names of those who had taught at the Institute over a long period have been given, give pause for thought. On the one hand, it seems that the Society of Jesus is concerned to keep the chairs of biblical exegesis and theology, but it has not succeeded in calling young recruits to the Institute to cover those fields; their future is therefore already at risk. On the other hand, for the other subjects taught, the Institute has not hesitated to call upon colleagues from outside; in doing so, it was entering further and more concretely into the fabric of Roman university life.

Almost every year, the *Catholic Biblical Association of America* continued to send the Biblical Institute a professor for one semester; here is the list for this period:

- George E. Mendenhall, in 1985-1986, who dealt with the historical theology of the Old Testament;
- Paula J. Bowes, in 1987-1988, who taught Hebrew;
- Jerome H. Neyrey, S. J., in 1988-1989, who gave a course of introduction to the New Testament;
- Lawrence E. Frizzel, in 1989-1990, who commented on the prophet Zecharia;
- Richard J. Clifford, S. J., in 1990-1991, who spoke on the Pentateuch;
- Brendan Byrne, S. J., in 1992-1993, who commented on Romans 5–8;
- Francis Moloney, S. D. B., in 1993-1994, who studied John 5–8;
- John F. O'Grady, in 1994-1995, who went over the story of the Passion in John;
- Joseph Blenkinsopp, in 1997-1998, who commented on Isaiah 56–66.

Moreover, as from 1990, during the first half of the second semester, another professor was kindly invited to the Biblical Institute thanks to the "*Joseph Gregory McCarthy Professorship*"; they were:

in 1990, Michele Piccirillo, O.F.M., from the Studium Biblicum Franciscanum in Jerusalem, who gave a course on Palestinology;

in 1991, M.-Émile Boismard, O.P., from the École Biblique de Jérusalem, on the meaning of the resurrection;

in 1992, Rolf Rendtorff, from Heidelberg, on the theology of the Old Testament;

in 1993, Daniel Marguerat, from Lausanne, on the figure of Paul in the Acts of the Apostles;

in 1994, Eduard Lohse, on Pauline ethics;

in 1995, Francolino Gonçalves, O.P., also from the École Biblique, who spoke of the book of Isaiah as a whole;

in 1996, Martin Hengel, from Tübingen, who looked into what Paul's activities between the Damascus episode and his arrival in Antioch might have been;

in 1997, Adrien Schenker, O.P., from Fribourg, who studied the legislation in the Pentateuch;

in 1998, Savas Agourides, from Athens, who concentrated on Matthew's gospel;

in 1999, Hermann Spieckermann, from Hamburg, who studied the Psalms.

Last but not least, in 1988-1989, Fr. Raymond Brown, P. S. S., of worldwide renown, gave a course on *The Death of the Messiah*, which attracted so many students that a big amphitheatre in the Gregorian had to be used.

These last two lists show how much the Institute benefited from the generous support of those benefactors thanks to whom exegetes known throughout the world, and from different cultures, were able to pass on their knowledge to our students. On the whole, despite the endangered recruitment of Jesuits, our academic programmes remained rich and varied.

3. Publications

In 1989, Fr. Werner Mayer succeeded Fr. Caplice as chief editor of the periodical *Orientalia*. As for the *Elenchus of Biblica*, Fr. Robert Althann became editor as from the first part of volume 11, covering the year 1996; it came out in 1998.

As a tribute to three of its masters recently deceased, the Institute published:

D. J. McCarthy, *Institutions and Narratives*. Collected Essays (AnBib, 108), 1985;

E. Vogt, *Der Aufstand Hiskias und die Belagerung Jerusalem 701 v. Chr.* (AnBib, 106), 1986;

St. Lyonnet, *Études sur l'Épître aux Romains* (AnBib, 120), 1989.

Among the books published by the professors of the Institute, apart from those already noted and without counting the many scholarly articles that are not mentioned here, these books are especially to be recalled:

The whole Bible:

J.-N. Aletti et al., *Le monde contemporain et la Bible* (Bible de tous les temps, 8), Paris, Beauchesne, 1985;

L. Alonso Schökel, *Hermenéutica de la Palabra. I. Hermenéutica bíblica. II. Interpretación literaria de textos bíblicos. III. Interpretación teológica de textos bíblicos*, Madrid, Cristiandad, 1987, 1987, 1991;

G. J. Norton – S. Pisano (eds.), *Tradition of the Text. Studies offered to Dominique Barthélemy in Celebration of his 70th Birthday* (OBO, 109), Freiburg Schweiz – Göttingen, Universitätsverlag – Vandenhoeck & Ruprecht, 1991;

P. Laghi – M. Gilbert – A. Vanhoye, *Chiesa e Sacra Scrittura. Un secolo di magistero ecclesiastico e studi biblici* (SubBi, 17), Roma, PIB, 1994.

Old Testament:

– basic manuals and introductions:

P. Joüon – T. Muraoka, *A Grammar of Biblical Hebrew* (SubBi, 14), 2 vols., 1991;

L. Alonso Schökel et al., *Diccionario Bíblico Hebreo-Español*, Madrid, Trotta, 1994;

Id., *Manual de poética ebrea*, Madrid, Cristiandad, 1987;

Id, *Antología de poesía ebrea*, Zaragossa, Fundación Teresa de Jesús, 1992;

J.-L. SKA, *"Our Fathers Have Told Us"*, Introduction to the Analysis of Hebrew Narratives (SubBi, 13), Rome, PIB, 1990;

ID., *Introduzione al Pentateuco. Chiavi per l'interpretazione dei primi cinque libri della Bibbia.* Roma, Dehoniane, 1998;

H. SIMIAN-YOFRE (ed.), *Metodologia dell'Antico Testamento* (Studi Biblici, 25), Bologna, Dehoniane, 1995.

– commentaries:

L. ALONSO SCHÖKEL – C. CARNITI, *Salmos, I-II*, Estella, Navarra, Verbo Divino, 1992, 1993;

P. BOVATI – R. MEYNET, *Le livre du prophète Amos*, Paris, Cerf, 1994 = *Il libro del profeta Amos*, Roma, Dehoniane, 1995;

H. SIMIAN-YOFRE, *Testi isaiani dell'Avvento. Esegesi e liturgia* (Studi Biblici, 29), Bologna, Dehoniane, 1996.

– exegetical studies:

L. ALONSO SCHÖKEL, *¿Donde està tu hermano? Textos de fraternidad en el Genesis*, Valencia, Institución S. Jeronimo, 1985;

ID., *El cantar de los cantares o la dignidad del amor*, Estella, Verbo Divino, 1990;

ID., *Símbolos matrimoniales en la Bíblia*, Estella, Verbo Divino, 1997;

H. SIMIAN-YOFRE, *El desierto de los dioses. Teología e historia en el libro de Oseas*, Cordoba, El Almendro, 1993;

ID., *La Chiesa dell'Antico Testamento. Costituzione, crisi e speranza della comunità credente dell'Antico Testamento,* Bologna, Dehoniane, 1997;

M. GILBERT, *Il a parlé par les prophètes. Thèmes et figures bibliques*, Bruxelles, Lessius, 1998.

New Testament:

– edition and grammar:

J. O'CALLAGHAN, *Nuevo Testamento Trilingüe* (BAC, 400), Madrid, 1988;

J. H. SWETNAM, *An Introduction to the Study of New Testament Greek* (SubBi, 16), 2 vols., Rome, PIB, 1992, [2]1998;

– commentary:

J.-N. ALETTI, *Épître aux Colossiens. Introduction, traduction et commentaire* (EB n. s., 20), Paris, Gabalda, 1993.

– exegetical studies:

I. DE LA POTTERIE, *La passion de Jésus selon l'évangile de Jean.* Texte et esprit (LiBi, 73), Paris, Cerf, 1986;

ID., *Marie dans le mystère de l'Alliance* (Jésus et Jésus Christ, 34), Paris, Desclée, 1988;

ID., *La prière de Jésus: le Messie, le Serviteur de Dieu, le Fils unique du Père*, Paris, Desclée, 1990;

Kl. STOCK, *Jesus der Sohn Gottes. Betrachtungen zum Johannesevangelium*, Innsbruck, Tyrolia Verlag, 1987;

J.-N. ALETTI, *L'art de raconter Jésus Christ. L'écriture narrative de l'évangile de Luc* (Parole de Dieu), Paris, Seuil, 1989;

ID., *Comment Dieu est-il juste? Clefs pour interpréter l'épître aux Romains* (Parole de Dieu), Paris, Seuil, 1989;

ID., *Jésus Christ fait-il l'unité du Nouveau Testament?* (Jésus et Jésus Christ, 61), Paris, Desclée, 1994;

ID., *Quand Luc raconte. Le récit comme théologie*, Paris, Cerf, 1998;

A. VANHOYE, *Structure and Message of the Epistle to the Hebrews* (SubBi, 11), Rome, PIB, 1989.

Greek and Latin world:

Éd. DES PLACES, *Jamblique, Protreptique. Texte établi et traduit* (Collection des Universités de France), Paris, Les Belles Lettres, 1989;

F. E. BRENK, *Relighting the Souls. Studies in Plutarch, in Greek Literature, Religion, and Philosophy, and in the New Testament Background*, Stuttgart, Steiner, 1998;

ID., *Clothed in Purple Light. Studies in Vergil and in Latin Literature, Including Aspects of Philosophy, Religion, Magic, Judaism, and the New Testament Background*, Stuttgart, Steiner, 1999.

Patristics:

J. O'CALLAGHAN, Basili de Cesarea, *Sobre l'Esperit Sant*, Barcelona, Proa, 1991.

Semitic world:

R. ALTHANN, *Studies in Northwest Semitic* (BiOr, 45), Rome, PIB, 1997.

Judaism and Christianity:

R. NEUDECKER, *Die vielen Gesichter des einen Gottes. Christen und Juden im Gespräch*, Munich, Kaiser, 1989.

Alongside these scholarly works, several professors at the Institute also published books of meditation and *lectio divina;* this was the case mainly of Frs. L. Alonso Schökel, Kl. Stock and A. Vanhoye. The list of them can be found each year in the *Acta PIB*.

4. *The Institute library*

In June 1989, the oriental section of the library was enriched with a large stock of Egyptian and Coptic books that had belonged to the late Fr. Pierre du Bourguet, S. J. (1910-1988), who had been director of those departments at the Louvre Museum (*Acta PIB* 9, 355).

Under the direction of Fr. Bertels, the library had some radical renovation work done on it that led to closing the library to the public from July 1990 to December 1991. Thus it was that, among other things, a staircase linking the first floor to the second could be placed, behind the Institute chapel; the idea came from Fr. Alfredo Villanueva, a Filipino, bursar at the Institute at the time; henceforth every reader had necessarily to come in on the ground floor, and the checking process was thereby improved. In addition, thanks to some American benefactors, the reserve for precious and rare books could be better arranged.

In 1992, a start was made on the computerized catalogue, so that as from June 1995, the card catalogue ceased to be brought up to date. The library was moving smoothly into the age of computers.

5. *The 80th and 90th anniversaries of the Institute; 1989 and 1999*

In 1984, the Institute had worthily and modestly celebrated its 75th anniversary. In 1989, at the persistent request of the students, Fr. Vanhoye, the rector, considered that it was actually useful to rekindle the flame by celebrating the 80th anniversary very simply; professors and students would feel firmly tied to the Institute. With May 7th, the date of the foundation, falling on a Sunday, Wednesday, April 19th, was reserved. At 9.00 a. m., Fr. General Kolvenbach, the Vice-Grand Chancellor of the Institute, presided at a concelebrated Mass in the church of St. Bonaventure, near the Biblical Institute. In his homily he said, among other things: "The checkered history of biblical exegesis, in which the Biblical Institute takes part in a special way, does not in fact hide the work and indispensable suffering to keep reviving the letter, while bringing the Spirit of the Lord into it". One can hardly say more in so few words. *Intelligenti pauca!*

Then over to the main lecture hall at the Institute to attend an original academic session that lasted about two hours and at which the rector presided. Its theme was: "The Biblical Institute: past, present and future". The first to speak were Frs. Swetnam, dean of the biblical faculty, and Mayer, dean of the oriental faculty. Then, three veterans of the professorial staff spoke: Frs. Alonso Schökel, for the Old Testament, North, for archaeology, and de la Potterie, for the New Testament. Lastly, two students for the licentiate in biblical studies spoke: Fr. Francesco Vannini, an Italian from La Spezia, and Sister Núria Calduch Benages, from Catalonia and a future professor at the Gregorian University.

Nothing was published of these addresses, except that Fr. de la Potterie shortly afterwards wrote an article in *La Civiltà Cattolica* (140 [1989, IV] 166-172) entitled: "L'Istituto Biblico negli ottant'anni della storia", in which it is perhaps possible to guess the essential part of what he said.

In the afternoon, Cardinal C. M. Martini, the archbishop of Milan, a former student, professor, dean and rector of the Institute gave a talk on "The pastoral use of the Bible" and everyone knows his competence in that matter. He emphasized, for instance, all the benefit that he was drawing in his biblical apostolate from the research and teaching experience he had gained at the Institute.

That day, in its simplicity and diversity, had what it takes to get each and everyone thinking (cf. *Acta PIB* 9, 347-348 and 441-443).

For its 90th anniversary, the Institute wanted to do things on a grand scale, but also to mark time just before the big jubilee of the year 2000. Fr. H. Simian-Yofre and Mr C. Valentino were therefore deputed to organize a great international gathering of scholars to which such a great number of people came that the University of St. Thomas, the Angelicum, had to be asked for permission to use their large amphitheatre (*Acta PIB* 10, 490-494 and *Vinea electa* 0 [1999] 2-6; Carlo VALENTINO, "90° anniversario del Pontificio Istituto Biblico", *RivBib* 47 [1999] 491-494).

BIBLIOGRAPHY, in order of the lectures given:

Mario LIVERANI, "Nuovi sviluppi nello studio della storia dell'Israele biblico", in *Bib* 80 (1999) 488-505. – Hermann SPIECKERMANN, "God's Steadfast Love: Towards a New Conception of Old Testament Theology", in *Bib* 81 (2000) 305-327. – Joseph A. FITZMYER, "Melchizedek in the MT, LXX, and the NT", in *Bib* 81 (2000) 63-69. – Florentino GARCÍA MARTÍNEZ, "Las tradiciones sobre Melquisedec en los manuscritos de Qumrán", in *Bib* 81 (2000) 70-80. – Martin MCNAMARA, "Melchizedek: Gen 14,17-20 in the Targums, in Rabbinic and Early Christian Literature", in *Bib* 81 (2000) 1-31. – John P. MEIER, "The Present State of the 'Third Quest' for the Historical Jesus: Loss and Gain", in *Bib* 80 (1999) 459-487. – Vittorio FUSCO, "Passato e futuro nella 'ricerca del Gesù storico'", in *Acta PIB* 10, 605-613.– Paul BEAUCHAMP "Lecture christique de l'Ancien Testament", in *Bib* 81 (2000) 105-115. – Norbert LOHFINK, "La morte di Mosé e la struttura del canone biblico", in *CC* 150 (1999, III) 213-222. – Romano PENNA, "Appunti sul come e perché il Nuovo Testamento si rapporta all'Antico", in *Bib* 81 (2000) 94-104. – Giacomo MARTINA, "A novant'anni dalla fondazione del Pontificio Istituto Biblico", in *AHP* 37 (1999) 129-160; reproduced in an abridged form in the *Acta PIB* 10, 738-766.

The congress lasted three days. On the 6th and 7th there were two lectures in the morning and a round table in the afternoon. The discussion was about where things stood on certain fundamental questions concerning both the Old and New Testament, while also suggesting new approaches.

May 6th was devoted to the Old Testament. Professor Liverani, from the "La Sapienza" University in Rome, showed what the methodological principles at stake were, formerly and at present, in establishing a history of biblical Israel. Professor Spieckermann, from the University of Göttingen, explained how God's steadfast love could serve as a foundation for an overall theology of the Old Testament read by a Christian. The round table in the afternoon gave Fr. Fitzmyer, from Washington, D. C., Prof. García Martínez, from Groningen, and Prof. McNamara, from Dublin, the chance to show how the figure of Melchizedek was understood from the time of the Hebrew Masoretic text until the Jewish and Christian traditions in Antiquity.

On the morning of May 7th, Prof. Meier, from the University of Notre Dame, in the United States, and Mgr. Vittorio Fusco, who was to die two months later, explained the state of recent research into the historical Jesus. In the afternoon, the round table was devoted to the relation between the two Testaments; Fr. Beauchamp, from the Centre Sèvres in Paris, concentrated on the principles leading to a Christ-centred reading of the Old Testament, while Mgr. Romano Penna, from the Lateran University in Rome, showed that faith in Jesus recognized as Messiah is the fundamental hermeneutic criterion that explains the relation between the New and Old Testaments. For his part, Fr. Lohfink, from Frankfurt, showed how the story of the death of Moses at the end of Deuteronomy has its part to play in the structure of the canon.

On May 8th, after a Mass said in the Church of St. Ignatius, at which Mgr. Jorge M. Mejía, a former student at the Biblical Institute and librarian-archivist at the Vatican, presided, Fr. Martina, from the Gregorian, sketched out the history of the Biblical Institute since its origins, without overlooking the enigmatic personalities of the rectors Fonck and Bea. The afternoon was given over to festivities and gave four former students the chance to give their recollections of their time at the Institute: they were Fr. Giacomo Danesi, a student between 1946-1949, Mgr. Wilhelm Egger, bishop of Bolsano, a student between 1966 and 1970, Fr. Ambrogio Spreafico, from the Urbaniana University in Rome, a student between 1974 and 1976, and lastly Miss Maria Luisa Rigato, a student between 1965 and 1968, and again in 1973-1974 (*Acta PIB* 10, 492-493, note 1).

Those eventful three days went off smoothly. The lectures had gone to the heart of the main methodological problems facing exegesis, a tradition at the Institute. The last day laid the historical reality the Biblical Institute had itself gone through before everyone. Never had the Institute marked any of its anniversaries so earnestly and profitably.

6. The creation of the "Ex-alunni/e of the P.I.B. Association": 1999

a) Antecedents

In 1934, on the occasion of the Institute's 25th anniversary, a complete list of its former students had been established (cf. *supra* chap. II, § III,3); it consisted of 911 names with some notes on their curriculum and their address at the time.

A first initiative was taken by Fr. Georgius Novotný (1921-2001) when he was registrar at the Institute (1959-1966); he had two news bulletins about the Institute printed for the benefit of its former students; a third one appeared in Fr. Lessel's time. The title of each of these bulletins was *Qere – Ketiv* (Hebrew words in the margins of the Hebrew Bible often indicating what the Masoretes proposed should be *read* instead of what is *written*). A generous plan, but one that did not last long (cf. APIBR A-14 and K-28-D).

It took until September 1976 for the first *Elenco degli ex alumni del Pontificio Istituto Biblico dall'anno 1909 all'anno 1976 (stesura provvisoria)* to be printed thanks to the "Office for the Development of the Institute and for Public Relations" of which Fr. William J. Dalton was in charge. The volume comprised 124 pages. In his preface, Fr. Martini, the rector, underlined the purpose of this initiative: to strengthen the links between the Institute and its former students and to encourage contacts between them. He also announced that a definitive edition would be published with corrections; for this purpose, he asked those interested for their cooperation, which was forthcoming, because in December a first list of corrections and additions was already published.

In September 1978 the new rector, M. Gilbert, wrote the preface to the definitive edition that had been announced. He thanked the former students for their cooperation and financial support. This second edition, compiled by Mr Sergio Bucaioni, who had been assistant to the general registrar at the Institute from 1966 to 1977, now contained 159 pages and the list of professors and others working along with them at the Institute, as well as of all those who, since 1909, had taught and worked at the Institute, both in Rome and Jerusalem, had been added at the beginning (pp. I-IX). Mr Bucaioni pointed out, for the first time, that in 1978 the Institute numbered about 4,000 former students still living and 600 deceased. In March, 1979, a new list of additions and corrections, covering seven pages, was drawn up.

Regularly since then, thanks above all to Mr Bucaioni, the man in charge who had known so many students, the Institute re-edited its constantly updated *Elenco*. In 1984, on the occasion of the Institute's 75th anniversary, a third edition came from the press; about 5,200 names of former students, along with addresses, were then listed (cf. *Acta PIB* 8, 729). Thereafter, every five years, it has been the custom to publish an updated edition. In 1989, compiling the fourth edition was facilitated by the use of the computer. In his preface the rector, Fr. Vanhoye, took up the subjects Fr. Martini had developed in the 1976 edition (cf. *Acta PIB* 9, 355). The 1994 fifth edition comprised about 6,300 names of former students and gave some statistics confirming what had been known since 1981, namely that students coming from western countries, very much in the majority until 1965, had since given way to students coming especially from Africa, Latin America and Asia (cf. *Acta PIB* 9, 890).

Alongside this initiative concerning the *Elenco*, let us recall that between 1980 and 1984 the Institute offered a refresher programme in Rome and Jerusalem mainly reserved for its former students (cf. *supra* chap. IV, § II,5).

b) Creating the Association

New ways had to be found to tighten links between the Institute and its former students. A certain number of them wanted this. On September 25th, 1998, Fr. O'Toole, the rector, sent a letter to all the former students in which he suggested setting up an *"Association of former students of the PIB"*. Over 600 replied positively so that on May 8th, 1999, at the close of the celebrations for the 90th anniversary, the rector officially announced the creation of that association. At the suggestion of the general registrar, Mr Carlo Valentino, and after consulting the Senate at the Institute, the rector had just appointed Fr. Swetnam director of the Association.

The statutes of the latter appeared in the *Acta PIB* 10, on pages 494-496. The rector was its president, and Mr Sergio Bucaioni, alongside the director, took the post of secretary, with three advisers, Fr. Denis Chukwudi Isizoh, from Nigeria (for two years), Miss Maria Luisa Rigato (for three years), and Fr. Rúben Tierrablanca, O.F.M., from Mexico (for four years), all of them recipients of diplomas from the Institute.

The main purpose of the Association is expressed in these terms: "To consolidate relations between the Pontifical Biblical Institute and its former students, as well as relations between former students among themselves who, as such, take part in achieving the aim of the Institute, that is to say getting the Bible better known and spreading that knowledge throughout the whole world".

In 1999 the annual membership fee came to 35 US dollars; in 2000 it went down to 20, in 2002, to 16 dollars or 16 euros; in 2007, because of the fall of the dollar, people were asked to pay either 16 euros or 20 U. S. dollars. Membership fees actually covered a bit more than office expenses and those of the *Elenco* and one Association newsletter.

The Association in fact announced that every year it would publish a newsletter giving news items about the Institute and its former students; this newsletter was to be sent – and was sent – to all who would enroll in the Association. Moreover, the latter would undertake to publish the *Elenco* of former students of the Institute at suitable intervals.

The first annual bulletin appeared in November 1999; it bore the title *Vinea electa*, Choice Vine; the expression comes from Jeremiah 2,21 and those two words open Pius X's letter whereby, on May 7th, 1909, he created the Biblical

Institute in Rome. That first issue bore the number 0 and number 1 appeared two years later, in October 2001; later, an issue was published faithfully ever year. The contents of *Vinea electa* correspond with the project: to inform people about what goes on in the Institute, both in Rome and in Jerusalem, and to pass on news about former students. This publication, the work of Mr Carlo Valentino, the registrar at the Institute, is carefully produced, practical and adorned with colour photos.

In 1999, the Association already numbered nearly 700 members; in 2007 it had 1,037. So it was a success.

Lastly, in March 1999 the sixth *Elenco degli ex-alunni* of the Institute came out; the seventh appeared in 2004 and the eighth is expected for the centenary in 2009. In the 1999 *Elenco* are to be found the name and some further details, including the address, of 4,926 former students still active, out of about 6,850 enrolled at the Institute since 1909; also to be found there was the list of the 1,380 deceased former students whose names were recovered. At the beginning of the volume, among the statistics, it says that the Institute had granted 3,255 licentiate diplomas and 285 doctorates over a period of ninety years.

7. An internal and external assessment: 1995-1999

At the time of the 34th General Congregation of the Society of Jesus, held in Rome from January 5th until March 22nd, 1995, a committee studied the situation of the Roman academic institutions entrusted to the Society by the Holy See. It heard from, among others, Fr. Stock, the rector of the Biblical Institute (*Acta PIB* 10, 28-29).

Ultimately, with its decree no. 22, the General Congregation instructed Fr. General to "bring about an in-depth assessment" of those institutions. "This assessment, while bearing in mind the specific nature and autonomy" of each of those institutions, "is to include policies, academic programmes, recruitment and development of the teaching staff, financial management and responsibilities [...]". The Congregation warmly recommended "entrusting the task of conducting this assessment to a group of persons with experience and ability who are involved in those activities; this group ought to include representatives of those institutions and people from outside, with Fr. General's Delegate taking part [...]. On the basis of this group's recommendations, Fr. General is to take the necessary steps to reinforce those institutions significantly and secure their future" (no. 464; *ARSI* 21 [1995] 875).

This kind of assessment began to become quite usual, at least in European universities.

In Fr. O'Toole's term as rector an internal assessment, or "self-assessment" was arranged at the Biblical Institute during the 1996-1997 academic year. Right from the start of that year, the new rector had noted that "the main purpose of this self-assessment was the recruitment of new professors" and he called upon each and everyone to cooperate and feel actively involved in the process (*Acta PIB* 10, 260-261). Both faculties therefore got to work on this task and devoted several meetings to it. The dean of the biblical faculty, Fr. Stephen F. Pisano, who had assumed office in December 1996, even thought it suitable to question former students, asking them, among other things, what in their opinion were the strong and weak points in the training they had received at the Institute (*Acta PIB* 10, 260-261).

It was only in December 1998 that the rector submitted the final report on this internal assessment to the Fr. General (*Acta PIB* 10, 380-383). Here are the main points in it. Two principle factors determine the conduct and quality of activity at the Biblical Institute: effective recruitment of good professors and more financial resources; in particular "without a sufficient number of resident Jesuits, it is becoming a problem to run the Institute" and a budget needs to be drawn up for bringing the premises into line with security regulations and paying the salaries of non-Jesuit professors at the recently fixed rate. In Rome the rector and the two deans need people to help them, and professors need assistants so that all of them can devote themselves more to research and publishing. In Jerusalem, where the agreements reached with the Hebrew University and the École Biblique must be adhered to, it is desirable that the number of resident Jesuits be increased. Seeing that it is not a good thing that the biblical faculty should absorb the oriental faculty, for the independent status of the latter offers distinct advantages to the professors, "it is necessary to define more clearly the relation between the two purposes of the Institute, scholarly research and training students", for, among the latter, a great difference at the level of culture and of ability to learn languages is more and more noticeable. In the oriental faculty the ideal would be to have five regular professors. In the biblical faculty, apart from the fact that new professors will have to be taken on within the next ten years – and this is urgent in some sectors – the enquiry conducted among the professors shows that the academic programmes must be reviewed, especially the one for the preparatory year for the doctorate.

Meanwhile, the Fr. General had set up the committee that was to carry out the external assessment; it was composed of four former students of the Institute, Fr. Charles Conroy, M.S.C., from Ireland, a professor of Old Testament at the Gregorian, Mgr. Giuseppe Ghiberti, New Testament professor at the Milan faculty of theology, Fr. Jan Lambrecht, S.J., an emeritus professor of New Testament at the Katholieke Universiteit te Leuven and, at the time, a visiting professor at the Biblical Institute, and Fr. Norbert Lohfink, S.J., professor of Old Testament at the Sankt Georgen faculty in Fankfurt. The committee met in Rome from September 19th to the 24th, 1998, then, as from October 9th, it came to the Biblical Institute to meet "the members of the various sectors in the Institute" (*Acta PIB* 10, 488). On November 24th, it submitted its 26-page report to the Fr. General (APIBR K-26-I) who passed it on to the rector of the Biblical Institute for it to be examined by the various councils there.

The committee mainly considered the biblical faculty, for which it envisaged three possible options: 1. To go back to the first purpose of the Institute, research and the training of qualified candidates able to obtain the doctorate; the training of future seminary professors would be left to the biblical departments of the many theological faculties; the committee preferred this option. 2. At the other end of the scale, the Biblical Institute would concentrate on training these future professors, at the cost of its scholarly purpose and would become the "Roman model" for that kind of training, especially for the third world. 3. To achieve a stable reconciliation of the Institute's scholarly character with the training of those future professors.

The first option justified having the library and would lighten the present professors' work but, with a maximum of 150 students, there was sure to be a financial problem. The second option did not correspond with the Institute's purpose, and it could be doubted whether the Holy See would accept it; the library would be superfluous, as would the oriental faculty; lastly, the academic programme would have to be reviewed and new professors taken on, even non-Jesuits, so that the integration of the Biblical Institute into the Gregorian might be envisaged! The third option would suppose an even greater number of professors than in the second option and the Society could hardly provide them; moreover, this option ought to lead to the Gregorian closing down its biblical theology department (*Acta PIB* 10, 505-507).

That was clear, logical but radical. The Biblical Institute must have been astonished by it, without getting anything out of it. It devoted many sessions to analyzing this far-reaching report, until the Holy See intervened. The Fr. General had passed on this report to Cardinal Pio Laghi, the Grand Chancellor of the Institute, in his capacity as Prefect of the Congregation for Catholic Education, and the cardinal, in a letter addressed to Fr. General on May 24th, 1999, reckoned that only the third hypothesis was compatible with the nature of the Institute, provided that, however, prospective students be better chosen. On the 31st, the council of the biblical faculty took note of the cardinal's opinion all right and promised to study the more important questions in the dossier during the next academic year (*Acta PIB* 10, 507).

In another connection, the 34th General Congregation of the Society had also given Fr. General the mandate to set up a permanent international Committee (CIP), "composed of representatives of the Major [Jesuit] Superiors' Conferences and including experienced educators and administrators", to help him and his Delegate in the ordinary running of the interprovincial houses and operations of the Society in Rome (no. 466; *ARSI* 21 [1995] 875). On February 22nd, 1999, for the first time, this committee went to the Biblical Institute to make a first contact, mainly an informative one (*Acta PIB* 10, 505-507).

II. The ten years preceding the centenary: 1999-2009

In November, 1999, Pope John Paul II appointed Cardinal Zenon Grocholewski Prefect of the Congregation for Catholic Education, who, thereupon, became Grand Chancellor of the Biblical Institute On June 12th, 2002, the Pope appointed Fr. Stephen F. Pisano rector of the Institute and the latter, succeeding Fr. O'Toole, entered upon that function on September 17th (cf. *Acta PIB* 10, 1020).

On November 1st of the same year, Fr. Jean-Noël Aletti was named dean of the biblical faculty by Fr. General Kolvenbach (cf. *Acta PIB* 10, 1021). On November 18th Fr. Kolvenbach appointed Fr. Agustinus Gianto pro-dean of the oriental faculty.

On June 1st, 2002, Fr. James L. Dugan, a Jesuit from the New York Province, born in 1943, succeeded Fr. Henry J. Bertels as librarian at the Institute. The latter, after nineteen years of good and loyal service, went back to New York.

Succeeding Fr. Peter-Hans Kolvenbach who had resigned, Fr. Adolfo Nicolás was elected Superior General of the Society of Jesus on January 19th, 2008, and with that title, became Vice-Grand Chancellor of the Institute. On March 1st, Fr. General chose as Delegate for the international Roman houses Fr. Joseph P. Daoust, at the time President of the *Jesuit School of Theology* in Berkeley, California: he came into office in the October of the same year; he thus succeeded Fr. Ignacio Echarte Oñate, from Loyola, who had held the post since June, 2004.

On 17 September 2008, Fr. José Maria Abrego de Lacy, a Spanish Jesuit born in 1945, succeeded Fr. Pisano as rector of the Institute. He obtained his Doctorate in Sacred Scripture from the Biblical Institute in 1983. His dissertation was entitled *Jeremías y el final del reino. Lectura sincrónica de Jer 36-45* (Estudios del Antiguo Testamento 3; Institución San Jerónimo, Valencia 1983). From 1996 to 2003 he was rector of the University of Deusto in Bilbao.

In November 2008 Fr. Nicolás appointed Fr. Pietro Bovati dean of the biblical faculty.

1. *The outcome of the assessment: 1999-2003*

During the 1999-2000 academic year the various councils and the senate at the Institute examined the questions raised by the double assessment, internal and external, as well as by the letter from Cardinal Laghi. In the biblical faculty, the one that was more affected, the academic council, on which no student sits, met almost every Monday from November 1999 to May 2000 to set out what the Institute had to offer on three points concerning that faculty only: requirements for admission of students, the curriculum for the licentiate and the preparatory year for the doctorate (*Acta PIB* 10, 642-647).

To start on the curriculum for the licentiate in biblical studies, a candidate must not only pass the examination, called the "qualifying" examination, in biblical Hebrew and Greek but also – and this is new, but Fr. Prat had made allowance for it in his 1903 project (cf. Doc. R. I,1: V,2) – show by means of an examination that he has an "adequate" general knowledge of the Bible; the syllabus for this difficult examination has been spelt out every year since 2000 in the booklet that describes courses and seminars at the Institute; in fact a student can only pass an examination like this if he has really worked at the biblical subjects during his baccalaureate in theology. In addition, sufficient knowledge of Latin and Italian is required; as regards German, English and French, which are languages in which the largest amount of exegetical litera-ture is produced, the student must show knowledge of one of these languages during the first semester of his licentiate curriculum, and knowledge of a second one during the third semester at the latest. With these decisions the faculty attempted to do something about the deficiencies that had been noticed for a long time in many students.

The licentiate curriculum was not changed, but structured better. The al-ready long-standing practice of not allowing a student to follow more than seven courses a semester was confirmed. It was again recommended to the student to take at least one course or seminar on each corpus in the Bible (Pentateuch, historical books, prophets, sapiential books and Psalms in the Old Testament and, in the New, synoptic gospels and Acts of the Apostles, the Johannine corpus, letters of Paul). What is new is that normally the first year is entirely devoted to biblical languages, general introductions (archae-ology-geography, history of both Testaments, textual criticism and hermeneu-tics), as well as special introductions to the Old and New Testaments. Lastly, the student can only enrol in a course of biblical theology in one or other Testament if he has already followed two courses in the exegesis of the corresponding Testament. As regards the final examination for the licentiate in biblical studies, it henceforth consists only of a written paper of a schol-arly standard.

The programme for the preparatory year was modified, too. Only those may be admitted to it who have obtained the licentiate degree in biblical studies at the "*magna cum laude*" level. To avoid – what had happened more than once – this year being unduly extended, the candidate, under the guid-ance of the professor of his choice, must, three months after his enrolment, draw up a plan for work in a precise field; then, at the end of a maximum of twelve months, he is to present the results of a study researched at a scholarly level, covering about thirty periodical-size pages; this study is to be given orally and in public by the candidate to a panel of three professors who will discuss it with him for an hour; the committee will decide finally whether the candidate may go on for the doctorate or not. This reform was put into effect *ad experimentum* for three years; on May 19th, 2003, it was approved definitively, by means of some secondary adjustments.

Still, not everything was settled, far from it. In February 2002, the permanent interprovincial Committee (the CIP; cf. *supra*) had come to the Biblical Institute to meet the Jesuit authorities and professors. The discussions with the latter were very frank; the professors were convinced that, unless the Society sent them young colleagues quickly, it might soon no longer be able to continue its commitment to the Institute! In its reaction, the CIP thought that, given this shortage of professors, the Biblical Institute ought to draw up a "strategic plan" and, on May 8th, the Fr. General proposed that a committee be formed for that purpose. Summoned by the rector to a plenary session, the professors considered that such a committee was useless because, on the one hand, the problem is well known and, on the other, it would be enough if the rector, the vice-rector and the deans together formulated concrete proposals, which was done.

In February 2003, with Fr. Pisano having become rector, the CIP asked the Institute "to identify the posts in the biblical faculty for which a resident professor was requested and, among those posts, which were the ones which ought preferably to be filled by Jesuits" (*Acta PIB* 10, 1025-1026). So it was not just a question of employing Jesuits only. The whole subject was then wide open and future prospects were more encouraging.

2. *The students*

The fall in the number of students that had begun the previous year went on inexorably. However, it was contained during the five first years of this decade, from 1999 to 2004, the total number of those enrolled at the Institute going from 387 to 370 and the number of those enrolled for the licentiate in the biblical faculty, from 333 to 296. Yet, between 2004 and 2009, the fall was impressive: for the year 2004-2005, no more than 309 were enrolled at the Institute, of whom only 242 were for the licentiate in the biblical faculty; another fall was observed for the year 2007-2008 for which there was a total of 296 people enrolled at the Institute and 230 for the licentiate in the biblical faculty.

Without going into too many details, it is observable that, for the academic year 2005-2006 as compared with that of 1997-1998, the number of students coming from non-western countries drops in free fall, except for Korea, whereas western countries continue to send us roughly the same number of students, especially Spain and Italy.

Moreover, if the number of doctoral theses defended at the Institute during this period is almost the same as that in the previous period, it is clear that the number of those enrolled for the preparatory year for that doctorate is clearly declining: there is a drop from 30 enrolled in 1999-2000 to 24 in 2004-2005 and to 9 in 2007-2008.

Analysing this phenomenon, which is so close to us in time, is risky, of course. Still, it is possible to put forward the hypothesis that a decline like that may have been the consequence of the recent creation of a department of Holy Scripture in several theological faculties in ecclesiastical university institutions in Rome. In itself, the creation of these departments had been provided for by the "*Normae quaedam*" promulgated by Paul VI in 1968, but their growth in the same city, in this case Rome, was certainly felt at the Biblical Institute as competition that was a cause of concern. Was not there a risk of seeing two categories of exegetes coming into existence, at the service of the Church and local churches? One of them continues to be really trained in scholarly methods, with the other not getting such an exacting training, without, however, any doubt being cast, of course, on the genuine theological dimension of the exegesis offered to both.

3. *The teaching staff*

All honour to whom honour is due! Fr. Albert Vanhoye, a professor emeritus of the Institute since 1998 already, was made cardinal by Pope Benedict XVI on March 24th, 2006 (cf. *Acta PIB* 11, 133-134, with photo).

In another connection, during this decade nine professors who had reached the age limit became emeriti; they were: Fr. Jan Lambrecht who, in 2001, after five years of teaching the New Testament, returned to Heverlee, just outside Louvain (cf. *Acta PIB* 10, 790-792); – Fr. Prosper Grech, O.S.A., who in 2002 concluded his thirty-two years of teaching biblical hermeneutics (cf. *Acta PIB* 10, 899-902); – Fr. James H. Swetnam, who, in 2004, ended his teaching of Greek in the propaedeutic year which he had created in 1963 (cf. *Acta PIB* 10, 1137-1139); – Fr. Frederick E. Brenk, who also finished his teaching in 2004, which he had begun in 1982, on the relations between the New Testament and the Graeco-Roman world (cf. *Acta PIB* 11, 19-20); – Fr. Ugo Vanni, who, also in 2004, concluded his teaching of the Apocalypse which he had commenced in 1969 (cf. *Acta PIB* 11, 21); – Fr. Karl Plötz who, after thirty-two years, stopped teaching propaedeutic Hebrew in 2007. During the Institute's centenary year, three other professors will reach the stage of emeritus: Fr. John J. Kilgallen, whose teaching of the New Testament at the Institute had started in 1985; – Fr. Maurice Gilbert, who had arrived in 1975 to occupy the chair of the sapiential books; – and Fr. Klemens Stock, who had begun teaching methodology in 1971 and then, in 1974, the exegesis of the synoptic gospels.

Besides this, Fr. Robert F. O'Toole, a professor of New Testament exegesis, was temporarily taken from the Biblical Institute in 2003 to become president of the "*Gregorian University Foundation*" which has its main office in
New York. In December 2007 Fr. Jesús Luzarraga, on reaching the age of
seventy, put an end to his teaching of the exegesis of the Johannine corpus,
which he had started in 1988, and returned to Spain.

On the other hand, in exegesis, the biblical faculty could then count upon
five new professors: Fr. Johannes Beutler, S. J., born in 1933, having finished
his time at the Jesuit theological school in Frankfurt, and later at the Gregorian, came to the Biblical Institute, from 2000 to 2007, to teach New Testament
exegesis, in particular the Johannine corpus, and to direct a good number of
doctoral theses there; he was a doctor in theology from the Gregorian University (cf. *Acta PIB* 10, 790); – Fr. Gianguerrino Barbiero, S.D.B., born in 1944,
began teaching the Psalms at the Institute in 2002; in 2004, he became a full
professor in the biblical faculty (cf. *Acta PIB* 10, 1139); with a doctorate in
theology from the Sankt Georgen Faculty in Frankfurt, he published his thesis
with the title of *L'asino del nemico. Rinuncia alla vendetta e amore del nemico nella legislazione dell'Antico Testamento* (AnBib, 128), 1991; – Fr. Dean
P. Béchard, S. J., born in 1959, moved from Fordham University, New York,
to the Biblical Institute in 2005 to teach the synoptic gospels and the Acts of
the Apostles there: at last a younger generation of exegetes was auguring well
for the Institute; in the year 2000 he had published a study called: *Paul Outside the Walls. A Study of Luke's Socio-geographical Universalism in Acts
14:8-20* (AnBib, 143); – Professor Giancarlo Biguzzi, from the Urbaniana
University in Rome, has been giving a course on the Apocalypse since 2006;
– Fr. Peter Dubovský, from Slovakia, born in 1965, who gave a course in
2006 on 2 Kings 15–21; with a doctorate from Harvard University, he published his thesis in 2006 called *Hezechiah and the Assyrian Spies. Reconstruc-
tion of the Neo-Assyrian Intelligence Service and its Significance for 2 Kings
18-19* (BiOr, 49); in 2008 he came to the Institute on a permanent basis.

In addition, Fr. José Luis Sicre Díaz continues to come every other year to
give a course on Old Testament exegesis, most often on the book of Judges;
as from the 2002-2003 academic year, Fr. Yves Simoens also comes every
other year to give a course on John's gospel.

In 2007, Fr. John F. Gavin, born in Boston in 1968, began giving his higher
course in biblical Greek; he is a doctor in patrology from the "Augustin-
ianum" with a thesis on Maximus the Confessor (cf. *supra*).

The biblical faculty also invited several professors from outside to occupy
some vacant posts; here are their names: Fr. Stanisław Bazyliński, O.F.M.
Conv., a professor at the St. Bonaventure theological faculty in Rome, took
over the pro-seminar in methodology as from 2001-2002, for which he published *A Guide to Biblical Research. Introductory Notes* (SubBi, 28); a doctor

in biblical studies from the Institute he had published his thesis with the title *I salmi 20–21 nel contesto delle preghiere regali* (Miscellanea Francescana) in 1999; – Professor Lorenzo Nigro, research director at the "La Sapienza" University in Rome, taught biblical archaeology and geography from 2001 to 2006 (cf. *Acta PIB* 10, 793); – in 2007 Mrs. Ida Oggiano, from the *Centro Nazionale della Ricerca* succeeded him; – Fr. Roman Lebiedziuk, C.R., of Polish origin, has been teaching Greek in the propaedeutic course since 2003; he has the licentiate in biblical studies from the Institute; – Professor Paolo Merlo, from the Lateran University, has been teaching the Syro-Palestinian background to the Old Testament since 2003; – he thus takes it in turns with Professor Francesco Pomponio, from Messina University, who has been teaching Sumerian and Babylo-Assyrian religion likewise every other year since 2004; – lastly, since 2007, Fr. Helmut Engel, S. J., born in 1940, from the Germano-Hungarian College in Rome, was invited to teach the Greek of the Septuagint; in 1979 he had obtained the doctorate in biblical studies at the Institute with a thesis on *Die Vorfahren Israels in Ägypten* (FThSt, 27), then he had taught at the Sankt Georgen Faculty in Frankfurt until becoming emeritus.

Some Jesuit biblical scholars were also invited to give a course occasionally for a semester: Frs. H. W. Jüngling, in 2000, on the Psalms, N. Lohfink, in 2002, on Deuteronomy; Willem Beuken, in 2006, on Isaiah, Ansgar Wucherpfenning, born in 1965, a professor at the Sankt Georgen Faculty in Frankfurt, in 2006 and 2009, on the gospels.

The *Catholic Biblical Association of America* continued with its generous support of the Biblical Institute by sending it a professor every year; here is the list of them for this decade:

in 2000, John F. O'Grady, who gave a course on John 1–2;
in 2001, Charles Talbert, on Matthew 5–7;
in 2002, John C. Endres, S. J., on 1-2 Chronicles;
in 2002-2003, Charles C. Carter, on the Old Testament and sociology;
in 2004, Mark S. Smith, on Israelite religion;
in 2004-2005, Richard J. Dillon, on Luke's gospel;
in 2006, David L. Dungan, on the synoptic problem;
in 2007, Michael Dick, on Nahum, Zephaniah, Micah and Jonas;
in 2008, Richard E. DeMaris, on the rituals in the New Testament;
in 2009, Joan E. Cook, on the prophet Malachi.

For its part, the "*Joseph Gregory McCarthy Professorship*" again made it possible for the Institute to invite the professors whose names follow:

in 2000, Jacob Kremer, from Vienna, who gave a course on the Easter message;

in 2001, Alexander Rofé, from the Hebrew University in Jerusalem, on the historical books;

in 2002, Joseph A. Fitzmyer, S. J., from Washington, D. C., on the 1st letter to the Corinthians;

in 2003, Erhard Blum, from the University of Tübingen, on Exodus 19–34;

in 2004, Hans Dieter Betz, from Chicago University, on "*Paul and Ritual*";

in 2005, Christoph Dohmen, from Regensburg University, on Exodus 19–40;

in 2006, Karl P. Donfried, from Smith College, Northampton, U.S.A., on Paul, the Jew;

in 2007, James L. Crenshaw, from Duke University, on Qohelet;

in 2008, Yann Redalié, from the Waldensian faculty of theology in Rome, on the pastoral epistles;

in 2009, Hugh Williamson, from Oxford, on Isaiah 6–9.

All in all, in the biblical faculty, in spite of the departure of a certain number of professors who had been teaching for a long time, it was possible to continue to offer a full programme covering all the subjects; however, in exegesis, the Institute and the Society of Jesus ought straightaway to bring more young professors able to occupy the posts for the future.

In the oriental faculty, Fr. Vincent P.-M. Laisney, O.S.B., was taken on as professor of Egyptian language and literature, in 2004; he had just defended his doctoral thesis on the teaching of Amenemope at the free University of Berlin (cf. *infra*); he had earlier obtained the licentiate in biblical studies at the Institute in 1997. Besides this, since 2007, Professor Stefano Seminara, from "La Sapienza" University, has been invited to teach Sumerian language every other year.

4. *Publications*

Among the books published by the professors, one of whom is of the first generation, the following are the chief ones:

Basic manuals:

J. J. KILGALLEN, *Guida alla Terra Santa seguendo il Nuovo Testamento*, Roma, PIB, 2000;

J.-N. ALETTI – M. GILBERT – J.-L. SKA – S. DE VULPILLIÈRES, *Vocabulaire raisonné de l'exégèse biblique. Les mots, les approches, les auteurs*, Paris, Cerf, 2005, ²2008 (corrected edition);

P. JOÜON – T. MURAOKA, *A Grammar of Biblical Hebrew* (SubBi, 27), revised edition in one volume, PIB, 2006.

Collected essays:

V. COLLADO BERTOMEU (ed.), *Palabra, prodigio, poesia. In memoriam P. Luis Alonso Schökel, S. J.* (AnBib, 151), 2003;

A. GIANTO, (ed.), *Biblical and Oriental Essays in memory of William L. Moran* (BiOr, 48), 2005;

J. E. AGUILAR CHIU et al. (eds.), *"Il Verbo di Dio è vivo". Studi sul Nuovo Testamento in onore del Cardinale Albert Vanhoye, S. J.* (AnBib, 165), 2007.

Old Testament:

– commentaries:

H. SIMIAN-YOFRE, *Amos, Nuova versione, introduzione e commento* (I libri biblici, A.T., 15), Milano, Paoline, 2002;

G. BARBIERO, *Cantico dei Cantici* (I libri biblici, A.T., 24), Milano, Paoline, 2004;

J. LUZARRAGA, *Cantar de los Cantares. Sendas del amor*, Estella, Verbo Divino, 2005.

– studies:

R. NORTH, *Medicine in the Biblical Background and Other Essays on the Origins of Hebrew* (AnBib, 142), 2000;

ID., *The Biblical Jubilee ... After Fifty Years* (AnBib, 145), 2000;

J.-L. SKA, *La Parola di Dio nei racconti degli uomini*, Assisi, Cittadella, 1999 = *Les énigmes du passé. Histoire d'Israël et récit biblique* (Le livre et le rouleau, 14), Bruxelles, Lessius, 2001;

ID., *Abraham et ses hôtes. Le patriarche et les croyants au Dieu unique* (L'Autre et les autres, 3), Bruxelles, Lessius, 2002;

ID., *Il libro sigillato et il libro aperto*, Bologna, Dehoniane, 2004;

ID., *Una goccia d'inchiostro. Finestre sul panorama biblico*, Bologna, Dehoniane, 2008;

M. GILBERT, *Les cinq livres des sages. Proverbes – Job – Qohélèt – Ben Sira – Sagesse* (LiBi, 129), Paris, Cerf, 2003;

H. SIMIAN-YOFRE, *Sofferenza dell'uomo e silenzio di Dio nell'Antico Testamento e nella letteratura del Vicino Oriente Antico*, Roma, Città Nuova, 2005.

P. BOVATI, *«Così parla il Signore». Studi sul profetismo biblico*, EDB, Bologna 2008.

New Testament

– commentaries

A. VANHOYE, *Lettera ai Galati. Nuova versione, introduzione e commento* (I libri biblici, N.T., 8), Milano, Paoline, 2000;

J.-N. ALETTI, *Saint Paul. Épître aux Éphésiens. Introduction, traduction e commentaire* (EB, n. s., 42), Paris, Gabalda, 2001;

ID., *Saint Paul. Épître aux Philippiens. Introduction, traduction et commentaire* (EB n. s., 55), Paris, Gabalda, 2005;

J. LUZARRAGA, *El* Padrenuestro *desde el arameo* (AnBib, 171), Roma PIB, 2008.

– studies:

Kl. STOCK, *Maria, Mutter des Herrn, im Neuen Testament*, Vienna, Rosenkranz-Sühnekreuzzeug, 1999;

J. LAMBRECHT, *Collected Studies on Pauline Literature and on the Book of Revelation* (AnBib, 147), 2001;

A. VANHOYE, *La lettre aux Hébreux. Jésus-Christ, médiateur d'une alliance nouvelle* (Jésus et Jésus Christ, 84), Paris, Desclée, 2002;

R. F. O'TOOLE, *Luke's Presentation of Jesus. A Christology* (SubBi, 25), 2004;

J. BEUTLER, *L'Ebraismo e gli Ebrei nel vangelo di Giovanni* (SubBi, 29), 2006 = *Judaism and the Jews in the Gospel of John* (SubBi, 30), 2006;

J. J. KILGALLEN, *Twenty Precious Parables in the Gospel of Luke* (SubBi, 32, Rome), 2008.

J. LUZARRAGA, *El Evangelio de Juan en las versiones siríacas* (SubBi 33), 2008.

Patrology

J. F. GAVIN, *'They are like the angels in the heavens. Angelology and Anthropology in the Thought of Maximus the Confessor* (SEAug), Rome, in the press.

Judaism:

J. SIEVERS, *Synopsis of the Greek Sources for the Hasmonean Period: 1-2 Maccabees and Josephus, War I and Antiquities 12-14* (SubBi, 20), 2001;

R. NEUDECKER, *The Voice of God on Mount Sinai. Rabbinic Commentaries on Exodus 20 in the Light of Sufi and Zen-Buddhist Texts* (SubBi, 23), 2002, [2]2006, [3]2008;

J. SIEVERS et al., *Chiesa e Ebraismo oggi. Percorsi fatti, questioni aperte*, Roma, Pont. Università Gregoriana, 2005;

J. SIEVERS – G. LEMBI, *Josephus and Jewish History in Flavian Rome and Beyond* (JSJ Suppl., 104), Leiden, Brill, 2005.

Ancient Near East

V. P.-M. LAISNEY, *L'Enseignement d'Aménémopé* (StP.SM, 19), 2007.

The Greek World:

F. E. BRENK, *With Unperfumed Voice. Studies in Plutarch, in Greek Literature, Religion and Philosophy, and in the New Testament Background* (Potsdamer Altertumswissenschaftliche Beiträge, 21), Stuttgart, 2007.

5. *The library at the Institute*

The computerization of the library went ahead unremittingly during this period, with the purpose of providing readers, especially professors, with all the help that modern means make available. In the year 2000, a "multimedia" room was installed on the first floor of the library; in March 2003 it became a room with computerized teaching aids. The computerized catalogue was completed in the course of the academic year 2000-2001.

On June 2nd, 2002, Fr. James L. Dugan succeeded Fr. Bertels as librarian. It was under his direction that in 2007 some important work was undertaken, including the replacement of windows to reduce noise and variations in temperature; work was also started on cleaning the books themselves by means of a special machine.

In 2007, the library contained 165,000 volumes and the computerized catalogue contained 117,000 entries.

6. The "Bologna Process" and the Biblical Institute

On June 19th, 1999, in the former Jesuit Church of *Santa Lucia* in Bologna, which became the main lecture hall of the University, the "Bologna Declaration" was proclaimed in the name of about thirty European ministers of education coming from countries as far apart as Finland and Portugal and Iceland and Greece. It was about harmonizing the academic programmes of all European countries: they ought to comprise a first cycle lasting *three* years, called a baccalaureate, a second cycle of *two* years, called a "master's", followed by a cycle of research work for the doctorate. An amazing project, and a sign of the desire for European unity.

At the same time and in the same place, but almost independently, the two-yearly meeting of the Conference of European Rectors (the CRE) was held. The author of this book represented the rectors of the French-speaking universities in Belgium at it and, in that capacity, was present at the ministers' declaration. For the rectors, it really was a matter of harmonizing, that is to say making compatible, not identical, the university programmes of Europe with the aim of facilitating the mobility of students, graduates, professors and researchers throughout the whole of Europe. As regards students, the 3+2 principle, baccalaureate and "master's", was gradually adopted, with a semester-based system of credits transferable from one university to another according to the student's possible future moves; this is the ECTS (*European Credits Transfer System*); there also became operational a "*Supplement*" diploma which described in terms common to all European universities the real content of the diploma granted by the university in question and thus made it possible for it to be recognized everywhere in Europe.

In 2003 the Holy See joined this "Bologna Process". For the Biblical Institute, as well as for some other pontifical university institutions in Rome, problems arose. This is the case for the biblical faculty of the Institute. The present licentiate in biblical studies actually takes three years, while the "master's" allows for only two, and the final reason is that this licentiate requires more credits than does the "Bologna Process". Add to this the fact that the course of study offered by that biblical faculty has nothing that really corresponds to it in any European university, and that limits the students' mobility quite seriously. We are therefore faced with an impasse. Still, the fact remains that the *"Supplement"* to the diploma would make it possible for the diploma to be recognized in all European countries, a definite advantage for those who have obtained degrees at the Institute; the problem had already been raised by Fr. Fonck in June 1914 (cf. *supra*, chap. II, I, 2,a)! The future will tell whether a solution may be found.

Conclusion

The heyday of this period comes around the year 1999. The internal and external assessment, mainly of the biblical faculty, was over and the consequences were being drawn; what it had to offer in the academic field was spelt out without anything being changed in the statutes. This long process, called for in 1995, was concluded in 2003. Besides, the year 1999, which marked the Institute's 90th anniversary and was on the threshold of the second millennium, was the occasion for getting up to date on some important questions in exegesis; the congress organized at the Institute saw to that. It was also the year in which the Association of former students of the Institute was created and in which the review *Vinea electa* was inaugurated for them: it strengthened the links between the Institute and its former students.

Students continued to come to the Biblical Institute regularly and, there again, a peak was reached towards the middle of that period: in 1997-1998, a little over four hundred students were enrolled – something never seen before – but a decline was soon observed, so that in 2008 there is a return to the three hundred figure, which was the 1985 one. This decline will certainly pose problems in the future: what, today, do the ecclesiastical authorities really want from the Biblical Institute and is the young generation still capable of making a serious investment in ancient and modern languages without doing so to the detriment of a thorough exegesis of the biblical texts themselves? All the same, the Biblical Institute still trains some good, and even very good, exegetes. And then what will happen at the Biblical Institute under the *"Bologna Process"*?

The teaching staff has aged and the Society of Jesus, thanks to Fr. Pisano's persevering efforts, is again beginning to send the Biblical Institute some valuable young recruits, especially in exegesis. The dark period seems to be indeed over, especially as some non-Jesuit exegetes have been engaged. On the level of exegetical methods, without imposing any, and believing, on the contrary, that plurality can only be good for the students, the use of narrative and rhetorical analyses of the biblical texts, both from the Old Testament, with Fr. J.-L. Ska, and from the New, with Fr. J.-N. Aletti, is noticeable. In its 1993 document on *The Interpretation of the Bible in the Church*, the Pontifical Biblical Commission, under the guidance of Fr. A. Vanhoye, its secretary, did not fail to stress the interest these methods have as complement to the historical critical approach to the texts.

Lastly, the computer has invaded all sectors of life, including the scientific one. At the Biblical Institute, it is there for all to see in the library now, but also when it comes to doing theses for the doctorate or licentiate and for publications; since 1998 the periodical *Biblica* can be read "*on line*".

CONCLUSION TO PART ONE

Brought into being by the wish of Pius X expressed in his letter *"Vinea electa"* of May 7th, 1909, the Pontifical Biblical Institute, of which the main centre is in Rome, was entrusted to the Society of Jesus. One hundred years later it is still there. That is not much as university institutions go, but its destiny has been tied to the story of biblical exegesis in the course of the century.

This account, which is coming to an end and has to be completed by the one about the Jerusalem branch (cf. Part Two), has been put together on the basis of the official statutes that have governed the Institute from its origin to this day. The *"Leges"* of 1909 held true until the statutes of 1934, and the latter were still in force in 1968, when, just after the second Vatican Council, a long period of maturation gradually led to new rules, the 1985 statutes.

In the course of this history, the Popes, at least up to the start of the pontificate of John Paul II, as well as the Council itself, have had a profound effect on the direction taken by the Institute and on its activities. Likewise, the attention given to the Institute by the Fathers General of the Society of Jesus and their concern for it, especially up to the time of Fr. Arrupe, have helped the Biblical Institute to overcome many difficulties.

When the Institute was born, the Church was still going through the acute phase of the modernist crisis. Biblical exegesis is muzzled and Fr. Fonck, though a genius at organization, is the ferocious guardian of that tendency shown by the decrees of the Pontifical Biblical Commission. While being dependent on the latter, the Institute tried in vain to free itself, at the instigation of the same Fr. Fonck. After Benedict XV, who took steps that only made things worse, it took the authority of Pius XI for the Biblical Institute to find its independence at last in 1928. O'Rourke, the rector, had a lot to do with it, too.

Pius XI, whose scholarly reputation was merited, imposed the reform of ecclesiastical faculties and universities in 1931. Under Fr. Bea's guidance the Institute acquired new statutes in 1934, which applied to both the biblical faculty and the faculty for studies of the ancient east, erected in 1932. Fr. Bea, who was a prudent and reticent man when facing any new theory in exegesis, led the Biblical Institute with an iron hand in a velvet glove and, if Pius XII's encyclical "*Divino afflante Spiritu*" in 1943 was immediately perceived as a liberation from the yoke of the consequences of modernism and as the promotion of scholarly exegesis, the pontifical document probably owes little to the rector of the Biblical Institute. Meanwhile, the Institute was publishing for the most part first-class scholarly works, critical editions, grammars, and dictionaries of biblical and oriental languages.

It took the arrival of Fr. Vogt in 1949 for exegesis to get off the ground. The creation of the monograph series "Analecta Biblica" in 1952 was the first sign of this. But very soon the Biblical Institute was faced with bitter and unjust criticism which lasted until the first session of Vatican II was on. From this crisis which nearly cost it its life, the Biblical Institute emerged unscathed and, with men of the calibre of Frs. Lyonnet, Alonso Schökel or de la Potterie, it had an influence that had never been equalled before and which it still maintained.

The twenty years that followed the council were a time of renewal; the statutes were revised, the premises better adapted, and the teaching staff rejuvenated for a long time to come, while the number of students kept growing. Martini, the rector, had left his mark. Since 1985, the Institute has gone peacefully on its way, even if the Society of Jesus was hard put to it, until a few years ago, to send it really good young professors, mainly in exegesis. Shortly before celebrating the centenary of its foundation the Biblical Institute can look to the future with confidence, even if problems are sure to arise.

The main one, about which nothing has been said so far, is about the suspicion that has been questioning scholarly exegesis for the past thirty years or so. Increasingly judged as being inaccessible, accused of being cut off from ancient tradition and of being itself historical, in the sense that, tied to its time, it has had its day, historico-critical exegesis, even when complemented by other more recent methods, still has some aces to play. At a time when so many researchers throughout the world are working on biblical texts to extract their secrets, how could the Institute not discuss things with them? Biblical hermeneutics have made much progress. But the Biblical Institute above all takes the intervention of the Word of God in our history seriously; people of flesh and blood like us wrote it and passed it on to us. It is up to us to hear it in all its purity. This conviction is also an act of faith therefore and the message of the Bible, which the Second Vatican Council wished so much to be spread, remains the key to theology, pastoral activity, and the spiritual life of every believer. In this case, too, for forty years the Biblical Institute has not failed to reply to the best of its ability to this call from the Church by transmitting the best of its research in terms accessible to all.

PART TWO

THE JERUSALEM BRANCH
OF THE PONTIFICAL BIBLICAL INSTITUTE

To understand the history of the Biblical Institute in Jerusalem one has to remember the main events that marked the situation of the Holy City in the twentieth century.

Until December 1917, the Holy City and Palestine were part of the Ottoman Empire. On the 11th of December that year Allenby, the British general, entered Jerusalem. Palestine then came under the control of the British who kept it until May 14th, 1948.

On that day David Ben Gurion proclaimed the State of Israel which took in the western part of Jerusalem where the Pontifical Biblical Institute is.

From 1948 until June 1967, to go from one sector of Jerusalem to the other one had to go through the "Mandelbaum Gate", located to the north of the École Biblique et Archéologique Française.

At the end of the Six-Day War in June 1967 the eastern part of Jerusalem and West Bank came under Israeli control.

Here now is the list of successive Directors and, occasionally, Vice-directors, of the Pontifical Biblical Institute in Jerusalem:

1927-1934:   Fr. Alexis MALLON (died in April 1934 at Bethlehem),
1934-1939:   Fr. Marcel LOBIGNAC (died in 1965),
1939-1947:   Fr. Andrés FERNÁNDEZ TRUYOLS (died in 1961),
1947-1949:   Fr. John J. O'ROURKE (died in 1958),
1949-1954:   Fr. Ludvik SEMKOWSKI (see below),
1955-1956:   Fr. Francis X. PEIRCE (died in 1980),
1956-1959:   Fr. Robert NORTH (died in 2007),
1959-1972:   Fr. Ludvik SEMKOWSKI (died in 1977),
1972-1974:   Fr. Samuel R. PITTS (died in 1982),
1974-1981:   Fr. Francis P. FURLONG (died in 1990),
1981-1984:   Fr. William J. DALTON (died in 2004),
1984-1992:   Fr. Maurice GILBERT,
1986-1989:   Fr. D. Thomas HUGHSON, Vice-director,
1989-1992:   Fr. Carlos SOLTERO, Vice-director,
1992-1995:   Fr. Carlos SOLTERO,
1995-1998:   Fr. John R. CROCKER,
1998-2007:   Fr. Thomas J. FITZPATRICK,
2007-2008:   Fr. Maurice GILBERT,
2008- ... : Fr. Joseph NGUYÊN CÔNG ĐOAN.

CHAPTER I

The project and its fulfilment: from 1909 to 1927

I. In Pius X's time: from 1909 to 1914

The establishment of a branch of the Biblical Institute in the Levant had not been provided for in Pius X's letter "*Vinea electa*", dated May 7th, 1909. The idea grew only gradually. Some quite incredible vicissitudes were, however, to bring about its implementation some fifteen years later.

Today it is permissible to explain calmly this troubled history by means of documents from archives. The tensions it reveals have by now given way to academic cooperation between the Institute and the École Biblique of Jerusalem, founded by Fr. Lagrange in 1890.

1. *1909-1910*

The Biblical Institute in Rome had not yet opened its doors when, on August 13th, 1909, Fr. Lagrange wrote to Fr. Cormier, the Master general of the Order of Preachers: "I have been assured [...] that Fr. Fonck is arranging for scholarships to send students to the Orient" (B. Montagnes, *Exégèse et obéisance*, Paris, 1989, p. 241). It seems that the information was given him by "several Jesuit friends" to whom he refers two lines above in the same letter.

However, at the end of 1909 or the beginning of 1910, Fr. Ladislaw Szczepański, a professor at the Biblical Institute at the time, in a three-page report in Latin (APIBR B-VI [VI-1A]) suggested transferring to Rome the oriental faculty of the University of St. Joseph that the Society had opened in Beirut in 1902. Along with the biblical parts of its museum and the oriental Library it would be united with the Institute.

Formed at the end of the 19th century, this oriental Library actually had a biblical stock. As regards the oriental faculty, it had been offering, since the academic year 1906-1907, besides courses in oriental languages, two courses in exegesis, one for the Old Testament and one for the New Testament (cf. S. Ronzevalle, in *Mélanges de la Faculté Orientale*, 3/2 [1909]

100*). This important innovation, of which Fr. Lagrange was informed in 1907 (cf. his *Souvenirs personnels*, pp. 173-174, 352-353), was to upset him in 1909 (cf. Montagnes, *Ex.-ob.*, p. 241); obviously he may have seen unfair competition in it.

Fr. Szczepański had done his doctorate at this oriental faculty in Beirut. The outcome of his action was that, on June 3rd, 1910, the Father General of the Society, F. X. Wernz, decreed that a way should be sought to unite the Biblical Institute with that faculty (*ARSI* 1910, 50).

2. *1911*

On January 19th, 1911, Fr. Fonck, the Institute's president, wrote a note in French (cf. Doc. J. I,2) in which he suggests the following points to Fr. Antoine Foujols, the rector of Saint Joseph's University in Beirut, as well as to Fr. S. Ronzevalle, a professor at the oriental faculty: courses in special subjects would be given in Beirut by the oriental faculty to students from the Biblical Institute; this programme would start at the beginning of November and finish at the end of March; the rest of the year would be kept mainly for excursions; lastly, there would be an exchange of professors between the Institute and the faculty.

It is obvious that the proposal was essentially aimed at the training of students from the Institute. As Fr. Mallon explains (cf. Doc. J. I,1, pp. 1-4), it must have been about those students who, in the summer of 1911, would have finished the two-year cycle at the Institute. The need was felt to give them the opportunity to get to know the Near East directly at last. While in practice setting aside Szczepański's proposal, Fr. Fonck was providing a first response to Fr. General's request.

Five months later, on June 21st, 1911, the same Fr. Fonck draws up a "*Promemoria de relatione inter Pontificium Institutum Biblicum et Orientem stabilienda*" (APIBR B-VI [VI-1A]). He offered this six-page document in Latin that same day to Pius X and gave it to Cardinal Merry del Val, the Secretary of State; both approved it, as Fr. Fonck notes at the head of the document; on June 26th he gave a copy to Fr. Freddi, the General's Assistant for Italy. In this important document Fr. Fonck explains that students and professors at the Institute need to get to know the East and get training in history, geography, eastern epigraphy, etc. Moreover, for the honour of Catholicism, the Institute ought to undertake archaeological excavations in biblical lands. The oriental faculty in Beirut would favour the Institute if it co-operated, along with the oriental Library, with the Institute through an exchange of professors and common publications. To do this it would be necessary: 1) that the oriental faculty no longer depend on the Jesuit Lyons Province but from the Fr. General through the intermediary of the rector of the Biblical Institute; 2) that a subsidiary establishment of the Institute be created in Palestine, preferably on

Mount Carmel "ad vitandam … omnem offensam". Fr. Fonck adds that this plan has the consent, if not the explicit approval, of Fr. General and his Assistants and that it has the agreement of the Lyons Provincial, Fr. Chauvin, and of Fulcran Vigouroux, the secretary of the pontifical biblical Commission. Furthermore, the necessary money to carry out the plan, one million (gold) francs, i. e. more than six million euros at the end of 2008, is available. The official approval from Fr. General and the Holy See was still needed, with the latter recommending the enterprise especially to the Latin Patriarch of Jerusalem, Mgr. Camassei. Lastly, to get things started a journey to the Near-East of one month may be enough.

Once the agreements were obtained Fr. Fonck left in September 1911. On the 11th of September he took part in a meeting in Beirut with the Superior of the Mission in Syria, Fr. Paul Mattern, who drew up a five-page report in French (cf. Doc J. I,3), Fr. Antoine Foujols, the rector of St. Joseph's University, and Fr. Lucien Cattin, the chancellor of the faculty of medicine at the same university. All four gave a favourable opinion on various points of which the following are the main ones: 1) in matters academic the oriental faculty would depend in future on Fr. General and the rector of the Biblical Institute; 2) practical courses would be given there in languages, history, geography, archaeology, epigraphy, etc., as a complement to the elementary and theoretical courses given in Rome by the Institute, but it would also have its own publications in non-biblical sciences; the students would be those whom the Institute would send or admit; 3) the oriental Library would remain at the university with the Institute covering only running costs.

But before this was agreed upon according to his plans Fr. Fonck had gone to Mount Carmel to carry out the other part of the plan. The Holy See had decided that a branch of the Biblical Institute should be located there. The Holy City was avoided "so as not to arouse the sensitivities of other religious establishments in Jerusalem", Fr. Fonck wrote with delicacy (letter to Mgr. Camassei, Memoir dated 14th of October, 1912; Doc. J. I,8); he meant the École Biblique.

After being well received by the Carmelite Fathers he went to the German Consul in Haifa with them. Thanks to him a building on the upper reaches of Mount Carmel was taken into consideration – to the satisfaction of the Carmelites, adds Fr. Fonck.

What he does not know is that on the following day (H. Vincent, *Vie du P. Lagrange*, p. 204), the Superior of the Carmelites on Mount Carmel hurries off to give the details of Fr. Fonck's visit to Fr. Lagrange. This Superior had all the same told the Jesuit that he had no power to let the Biblical Institute have any land or house belonging to them and that that was their Fr. General's preserve; finally, having raised the problem of competition with the École Biblique in Jerusalem, he got the reply: "the one run by Fr. Lagrange, the disseminator of the worst kind of modernism; I'll break him!'". This is doubtless the origin, or at least one of the earliest manifestations of an unfortunate expression often repeated by the one who first uttered it so as to become all too well known. All was not set fair, then, between Fonck and the Carmelites. He was soon to be shown proof of it.

Finally, Fr. Fonck went to Jerusalem where he arrived on Wednesday, September 13th. He stayed with the White Fathers at St. Anne's and, on the evening of his arrival, the Superior, Fr. Féderlin, told him of his conviction that Jerusalem was the place to locate the branch of the Institute. The details of Fr. Fonck's stay in Jerusalem are known from a letter that Fr. Féderlin wrote on the 15th to Fr. Cattin, S. J. (cf. Doc. J. I,4). The day after, Fonck, having been to see the Custodian, went to see Fr. Lagrange. The next day, the latter wrote to Fr. Cormier (Montagnes, *Ex.-ob.*, p. 316): "Yesterday, he [Fonck] informed me officially that he was going to found what he called a *pied-à-terre* in Galilee but in a place where people could stay in summer! When I objected that the [Jesuit] Fathers had Beirut, he pointed out to me that that was not in the Holy Land enough" (cf. again Lagrange's *Souvenirs personnels*, pp.198-199).

On the afternoon of that same Thursday, September 14th, Fr. Féderlin showed Fonck some land still available on the western slope of the Mount of Olives, and then to the north-east and west of the Holy City. "The Father will be able to reflect and inform his Superiors", writes Fr. Féderlin.

At the end of the afternoon Fr. Fonck was received by the Latin Patriarch, Mgr. Camassei, to whom he hands a letter from Cardinal Merry del Val, the secretary of State to Pius X (cf. Doc. J. I,7). Here is the translation of the original written in Italian:

From the Vatican, August 26th, 1911

Your Excellency,

The purpose of the Pontifical Biblical Institute, founded by His Holiness Pope Pius X, makes it almost indispensable to found a subsidiary house of the same Institute on the soil of Palestine and, thanks to the generosity of some outstanding benefactors, the means necessary for such a foundation are already to hand.

However, having considered all the circumstances, it has been decided, for prudential reasons, to make Mount Carmel the location of the above-mentioned subsidiary house, while, however, leaving open the possibility of a better choice.

For this purpose, the Rev. Prof. Leopold Fonck, S. J., President of the said Biblical Institute, is going, with the approval of the Holy See, to prepare the inauguration of the new house in Palestine.

I am therefore introducing him to Your Excellency and warmly recommend him to you so that you may kindly support him with your efficacious protection and, as far as possible, facilitate this so laudable undertaking which corresponds in a particular way to the wishes and desires of the Holy Father.

Thanking you in advance …

This letter calls for some comments. First of all, there is no question of the Society of Jesus, but of the Pontifical Institute founded by Pius X. 2) It is a question of a subsidiary house of the Institute; there was soon to be talk of a "branch". 3) The financial means for this foundation are available; on June 4th, 1919, Fr. Fonck was to point out (cf. J. Doc. J. I,11) that one million francs had been received from Miss Jeanne du Coëtlosquet; the francs in question must be gold francs, and at the end of 2008 this sum corresponds, as we have seen, to more than six million euros; this sum comes on top of the gift from the same Coëtsloquet family to Pius X starting in December 1909 to provide for the foundation of the Biblical Institute in Rome. 4) The choice of Mount Carmel was necessitated by prudential reasons, probably so as not to arouse the sensitivities of the École Biblique and its director, but this choice could always be changed, which means that coming one day to Jerusalem was not excluded. 5) The foundation of this subsidiary house explicitly corresponds to the wishes of Pius X and Fr. Fonck's mission has pontifical approval.

The next day, September 15th, Fr. Lagrange went to see the Patriarch to find out more about Fr. Fonck's plans. Lagrange, as we have said, already knows that there is talk of Carmel, which Fonck had not told him, but he has two questions to ask. On the one hand, what is coming after Carmel? Because he already suspects the choice of Jerusalem and he himself knows the embarrassing situation the Carmelites are in. On the other hand, has Fr. Fonck the approval of the Holy See? "The approval is quite clear", the Patriarch answers him. Lagrange obviously had not seen the letter from the Secretary of State, which he had only unofficially been informed of at his own request.

On September 16th Fr. Fonck takes ship again at Jaffa, thinking his mission accomplished. He is back in Rome on September 26th.

Now, "some weeks later" (Doc. J. I,8; his Memoir for 14th October 1912, no. 5-6), so still in 1911, two disappointments await him. Because he met only the German consul at Haifa during his journey, he, being German, was accused of wanting to place the house being planned on Mount Carmel under the German protectorate, whereas France is normally the protector of Catholic establishments in the Holy Land. Such a suspicion is unfounded because so far there is no question of looking for a protectorate, but it points up the tension between France and Germany that was to lead to the first world war.

It is certain that, on September 27th, 1911, the French Consul in Jerusalem sent a long note to his Foreign Minister, published by B. Montagnes (*Marie-Joseph Lagrange. Une biographie critique*, Paris, Cerf, 2004, pp. 347-350), in which he informs him of Fr. Fonck's activities and the École Biblique's fears. In his letter to Fr. Cormier, dated November 12th, 1912, and published by Montagnes (*Ex.-ob.*, pp. 378-379), Fr. Lagrange says that he had learned at the Quai d'Orsay that the French government had approached Fr. Wernz who had replied that the matter was one between Fr. Fonck and the Vatican alone.

The other set-back was just as bad. Fonck did not understand the reservations of the Carmelites at the time of his visit to Haifa, and now, in Rome, he gets an official delegation coming in the name of the Fr. General of the Carmelites; the General's assistant, Fr. Clément, and the Vicar Provincial of Mount Carmel, Fr. Cyrille, who had been away at the time of Fonck's visit, urge him to give up the choice of Mount Carmel for the branch – now the word appears – of the Biblical Institute.

Meanwhile, false rumours are circulating: Lagrange writes on October 15th, 1911, to Cormier, the Master general (Montagnes, *Ex.-ob.*, p. 320): "I have heard it said by Mgr. the Patriarch that Fr. Fonck really has acquired something on Carmel, above the Carmelites. A visiting Jesuit Father boasted to the [French] Consul that it was going to be on a very large scale, a kind of headquarters for the administration of the Jesuits in Syria"!

In fact, at the end of 1911, it still was not known where to set up this branch.

3. *1912*

The months go by, giving time for reflection, for, given the opposition from the Carmelites, plans have to be changed.

On May 22nd, 1912, Fr. Fonck sends a crucial letter to Fr. Cré, one of the White Fathers at St. Anne's in Jerusalem. And this letter, Fr. Fonck "had promised and thought it over for a long time", which leads one to think that its contents must have been fixed upon in outline perhaps as far back as April or even March, 1912.

Now this letter contains the following items: (cf. Doc. J. I,5): 1) Its contents must remain "sub secreto". 2) Fonck is writing on an express order from Pius X. 3) The Pope has decided to locate the branch of the Biblical Institute in Jerusalem. 4) Fonck is authorized to purchase two plots of land; one is situated on the fork between the two paths that, starting at Gethsemane, go up the Mount of Olives to the east and north-east; the other, on which the branch of the Institute would be built, is near the plot of land on which France plans to build its new consulate. 5) Fonck appends to his letter the sketch of a plan for this branch on a site of 4,000 square metres. 6) This house will be placed under French protectorate.

It was soon to become known (letter from Fonck to Féderlin, June 25th, 1912: ASAJ) that the triangular-shaped site on the Mount of Olives would be used for archaeological excavations. As regards the other, the one to the west, its dimensions have to be mentioned: the property envisaged is smaller than the one the Institute has had since 1925 (5,000 m^2) and the number of rooms planned for by Fr. Fonck comes to about thirty, i. e. roughly as in the present house. Hence it really is a question of a branch, at least at that date.

On May 29th, 1912, Fr. Fonck draws up a "Pro-memoria" about the branch of the institute to be built in Palestine and he sends this 8-page Latin text to Fr. General, to his Assistant for France, Fr. Fine, to the Lyons Provincial, Fr. Chauvin, and to the Superior of the Mission in Syria. This text has been published in part by B. Montagnes (*Marie-Joseph Lagrange*, pp. 350-355). Fr. Fonck now asks Fr. General, who has already indicated his agreement, for a swift decision and the means to carry it out. As regards the content of the new proposal, these are the essential points: 1) the refusal by the Carmelites has led to choosing Jerusalem to counterbalance the École Biblique, the influence of which is qualified as "modernist" (p. 3); certain persons in the public eye, including F. Vigouroux, cardinals Vives, Gotti e Rampolla, Mgr. Camassei, the Latin Patriarch of Jerusalem, are of this opinion; besides, Pius X has decided in this way: he wants everything to be put in place as soon as possible to further biblical studies in the Holy Land and the influence of the École Biblique to cease; moreover, that school was soon to leave Jerusalem and the Institute's subsidiary house would take its place; 2) to do this the oriental faculty in Beirut is to come to Jerusalem to unite with the Institute and depend henceforth on the Fr. General and the Rector of the Institute; as for the oriental Library, it was to stay in Beirut.

So, from 1912 until 1919 (cf. *infra*), when there was to be a question of the branch of the Biblical Institute in Jerusalem, people would almost automatically come round to talking about the École Biblique to criticize or defend its exegetical stance. For not all Jesuits thought like Fr. Fonck: on the 4th of April, 1914, Fr. Mallon, who had got wind of the letter of May 29th, 1912, sent by Fr. Fonck to Fr. General, wrote to the latter earnestly requesting him to destroy it, for, he said, it can only do us harm if it were to become known! Fr. Wernz did no such thing.

Fr. Fonck is known to be one of Fr. Lagrange's fiercest opponents. Now, in a letter of June 25th, 1912, to Fr. Féderlin, Fr. Fonck, while recommending "the strictest secrecy" about the negotiations to be undertaken at Jerusalem, states that in the eyes of Pius X and Cardinal Merry del Val neither the approval of Fr. Cormier, the Master general of the Dominicans should be requested, nor, if one understands correctly, should discussions with the École Biblique be entered upon. : "the opposition [...] will not last long", he concludes. He must know that four days later, on June 29th, "several of Fr. Lagrange's writings" were to be censured by the consistorial Congregation with the approval of Pius X; the text appeared in the *AAS* for August 16th, 1912, and at his express request, Fr.Lagrange was to leave Jerusalem on September 5th, only to return there, with Pius X's approval, in the July of the following year.

Let us return to Fr. Fonck's letter to Fr. General dated May 29th, 1912. Fr. General's reply to this new plan took its time. Fr. Chauvin was actually coming to the end of his term of office as provincial in Lyons and Fr. Claude

Chanteur, much more reserved, as we shall see, succeeded him on August 26th, 1912. What really was causing a problem was not the establishment of the Institute in Jerusalem, because that seems to have been already decided in May 1912, but what concerns the oriental faculty and the oriental Library in Beirut.

However, in the meantime from St. Joseph's University Fr. Foujols, on June 15th and Fr. Cattin on the 17th suggested the following changes to Fr. Fonck's plan: 1) once it was attached to the Biblical Institute in Jerusalem, the oriental faculty would no longer be part of St. Joseph's University; 2) the oriental Library would become the property of the branch of the Institute and would be transferred to Jerusalem.

Fr. Cattin also insists that it be clearly stated that this foundation in Jerusalem is being imposed on the Society by the Holy See. If it were a foundation of the Society the École Biblique would see a declaration of war in it. If it is the Holy See that is doing the founding the Foreign Minister in Paris, already warned by the École – in reality by the French Consul in Jerusalem (cf. *supra*) – would end up accepting, especially if this foundation were placed under the French protectorate.

In the meantime, Fr. Cré answered F. Fonck. The latter receives the letter on June 26th and adds the abbreviated contents of it to the letter which he had started the day before and so dated the 25th and had addressed to Fr. Féderlin. Fr. Cré's reply contains two points concerning the acquisition of two plots of land requested by Fr. Fonck on May 22nd. The plot next to the one France reserved for its new consulate is not at present up for sale, and this for administrative reasons: the "Society of the Holy Sepulchre", the owner, refuses to renounce its rights so as to transfer them especially to the Greek Orthodox Patriarch of Jerusalem, as the government in Constantinople wished; this difficulty would not exist in 1925 when the Institute was to buy the plot it has occupied ever since from this Patriarch. As for the site on the Mount of Olives only the lower triangular-shape part is for sale for 70,000 francs but, to acquire it it was necessary to find an Ottoman subject who would lend his name and become the legal purchaser of the land.

Fr. Fonck goes on in his letter to Fr. Féderlin and assures him that he is going to find such a person and, as regards the place in which to establish the branch itself, he asks his correspondent's advice. Moreover, this same letter of June 25th-26th contains another element already known from Fr. Fonck's letter of May 22nd but which becomes explicit (no. 5): Fr. Fonck therein declares himself authorized by the Holy See to enter into negotiations unofficially with the French Consul General in Jerusalem with a view to obtaining from the Paris government the protectorate of France over the future branch of the Institute: this is, he says, "the Sovereign Pontiff's very particular wish".

When the summer was over, Fr. Fonck sent a long letter to the Latin Patriarch, followed by a "Memoir on the construction of a branch of the Pontifical Biblical Institute in Palestine" (APLJ Q/89: cf. Doc. J. I,8). The letter contains the following points: 1) After the refusal by the Carmelites, Pius X decided that the branch of the Institute be erected "in the name of the Holy See" in Jerusalem. 2) For this purpose the Holy See wishes to request primarily the protectorate of France. 3) In June Pius X had already authorized Fr. Fonck to contact the French Consul General in Jerusalem for this purpose at the right time and through the mediation of the Latin Patriarch. The day before this letter, October 13th, Pius X confirmed that authorization and even ordered Fr. Fonck to write to the Patriarch along these lines. 5) "It is therefore the will of the Holy Father that Your Excellency ask the French Consul General in Jerusalem whether the French government is willing to take the future branch of the Pontifical Biblical Institute under its protection, providing the efficient execution of the protectorate" (text translated from the Italian).

The "Memoir", in French, gives the history of the matter, relating in particular the mishap of the Mount Carmel project. More interesting are the reasons given for the erection of this branch, first in Palestine, then specifically in Jerusalem. Three reasons are given for the choice of Palestine: 1) Present and future teachers will there make contact with the country and its people in its natural, social and religious situation; they will be able to perfect their knowledge of oriental languages in a practical way. 2) Students from the Institute will find there the necessary assistance for travelling or staying in the Holy Land. 3) The Institute needs this branch for its scholarly research and for carrying out archaeological excavations. The "Memoir" further adds that, "as a Pontifical Institute", the Biblicum "cannot [...] remain dependent on any other religious establishment already set up in the Holy Land" and, lastly, that Pius X fully approves these reasons.

The reasons given for the choice of Jerusalem after the failure of the Mount Carmel plan are, on the one hand, the central position of the Holy City and, on the other, "the need for the Institute to enter into living and immediate contact with the scholarly movement at the centre of the biblical lands".

The Patriarch complied and, on November 26th, 1912, the French Consul General, G. Gueyrand, informed him in a simple note that the French Ambassador in Constantinople was having him transmit the agreement of the government of the Republic to the Patriarch (cf. Doc. J. I,9). The Patriarch immediately informed the Vatican of this, and Fr. Fonck the next day.

But between the request made on October 14th and its acceptance shortly before November 26th some revealing events occurred.

Some days before November 5th, Fr. Paul Dudon, S. J., was received at the Quai d'Orsay in Paris by the one in charge of matters concerning the protectorate in the Levant, probably Pierre de Margerie, one of the sub-directors dealing, among others, with the East. The latter, a Catholic, manifested his concern to him over the creation of an annex of the Biblical Institute in Jerusalem; this will result in "difficulties with Congregations already there in the Holy City": meaning especially the École Biblique; and for the first time there arises on the French side the idea that its protectorate would presuppose that the superior of this annex be French (*AHP* 18 [1999] 155).

On November 5th, the French Consul General in Jerusalem sends a dispatch to the Foreign Minister in Paris. He points out to him that the Prior of St. Stephen's suggests that the Minister inform Fr. Lagrange, then exiled in Paris, of the request for protectorate. The Consul thinks that Fr. Fonck has received only an authorization of a purely oral kind from the Pope (text in the Centre for Diplomatic Archives in Nantes). Fr. Lagrange, on being informed, was received at the Quai d'Orsay by the same Pierre Margerie (Montagnes, *Ex.-ob.*, p. 374). He recounts in 1926 "that it was not for him to get him [P. de Margerie] to see that the Pope, being a sovereign, would not agree to raising any flag other than his own over his pontifical institute. Besides, he goes on, the idea of having recourse to the French government to gainsay a wish of the Holy Father never occurred to me" (*Souvenirs personnels*, p. 199). This passage shows that Lagrange is convinced that the request for the French protectorate comes from Fonck and not from the Pope, but also, and this is contradictory, that the Institute's annex in Jerusalem will really be pontifical!

On November 12th (Montagnes, *Ex.-ob.*, pp. 378-379), Fr. Lagrange is back at the Quai d'Orsay where Mr. Jean Gout, the other sub-director, receives him. The latter tells him that the French government had informed the Society at the end of 1911 that the plan to found the Biblical Institute's branch on Mount Carmel was against its wishes but that the general of the Jesuits, Fr. Wernz, had replied that the plan was not his but the Pope's (cf. *supra*). At present, Mr Gout went on to explain, France will not refuse its protectorate in order to avoid Germany's; however, France is not favourable to this establishment and Mr. Gout can see only one way of counteracting it: an approach made to the Pope by the Fathers General of the main Orders and Congregations already established in Jerusalem, especially as the pontifical authorization to found the Institute's annex in the Holy City is not expressly public. Lagrange concluded from this that this foundation plan has as its origin the intrigues of Fr. Fonck.

A little later, it is the turn of Fr. Chanteur, S. J., the Provincial of Lyons and in charge of the Jesuits in the Levant, to meet Mr. Gout at the Quai d'Orsay. Mr. Gout, a Protestant, Fr. Chanteur points out, told him of the bad impression left on him by Fr. Lagrange; the vehemence shown by the latter had put him off; opposed at first to the Institute's foundation in Jerusalem, Mr. Gout showed himself favourable when Fr. Chanteur explained to him that it was only a question of an annex of the Institute in Rome. Mr. Gout "asked only, so as not to make any inroads into France's traditional rights, that official protection be reserved to it and that the ecclesiastical superior of the house be French" (MS by Fr. Chanteur kept in the APIBJ and written out by Fr. Senès in his unpublished account, p. 11). Fr. Chanteur adds that this last request was granted by the Superiors of the Society. But in 1952 Fr. Senès enquired about any written document that confirmed this agreement and Fr. Prešeren, Assistant to Fr. General J. Janssens, replied to him in a letter dated 21st July, 1952, that no such document existed, either at the Biblical Institute or at the Society's General Curia or at the Vatican or at the French General Consulate in Jerusalem (cf. Fr. Senès' account, p. 11). The fact remains that the Quai d'Orsay had twice raised this question orally and that in any case, agreement or no agreement, the first two Superiors of the Institute's branch in Jerusalem, from 1927 to 1939, were French.

In 1912 there was still the unsettled question of someone who would lend their name and who, according to Fr. Fonck's letter to Fr. Cré dated June 26th, 1912 (ASAJ), would agree to sign the contract of purchase of the site on the Mount of Olives. Fr. Fonck wrote on August 26th to Fr. Féderlin that he had himself asked Fr. Cattin in Beirut to find him this person. On November 5th next Fr. Sébastien Ronzevalle announces in a letter from Beirut to Fr. Féderlin that is was to be Mr. Émile Eddé. The latter (1884-1949), a Maronite, was a leading figure in the political life of the Lebanon. Being opposed to the Ottoman domination he went into exile in Alexandria; he was to return to the Lebanon only in 1920, after the fall of the Ottoman empire. He was subsequently to be Prime Minister and then President of the Lebanese Republic. Hence it was from exile in Alexandria that he wrote to Fr. Ronzevalle on December 28th, 1912: he cannot leave Alexandria – as can be understood – but he can arrange by proxy for the purchase to be made in his name. This matter is thus not settled at the end of 1912.

The only concrete achievement that year was that of obtaining France's protectorate over an annex of the Biblical Institute in Jerusalem, but the Institute had no land for this annex: for one thing, it still did not have the legal means and, for another, it had not made its choice.

The close of this year 1912 brought another positive element. A storm had arisen in the French press over this plan for an annex to the Institute in Jerusalem. On September 7th the *Journal des débats* had apparently opened the argument with an article that caused a great stir. Written in fact by Maurice Pernot (cf. Montagnes, *Ex.-ob.*, p. 356, n. 45) this article, with an abundance of details that actually seem to be genuine but many of which are not, criticizes this plan of the Institute, seeing in it a German ruse against French influence in the Holy Land. Fr. Lagrange's withdrawal from the École Biblique would be the presage of the closure of the school he had founded. This nationalistic interpretation reveals the climate at the time: less than two years later there was to be war between France and Germany. Now if Fr. Fonck may perhaps have something to do with the censorship of several of Fr. Lagrange's writings by means of the decree of June 29th, 1912, it is wrong to say that because of that Fr. Lagrange had to give up being prior of St. Stephen's and leave the school; he himself took a stand against that interpretation (*Souvenirs personnels*, p. 204). It is also incorrect to say that Fr. Fonck came to the school in 1908: it was perhaps in 1907. He had come for the first time in 1896 and came back in 1911 (Lagrange, *Souvenirs personnels*, pp. 70-71). And so on. Yet this article was echoed in other newspapers (Montagnes, *Ex.-ob.*, p. 375, n. 46) and at the beginning of December, 1912, it was the request for the protectorate of France over the Institute's annex that stirred up the controversy: France ought not to grant it. The newspapers did not know that it had already been bestowed at the end of November and, finally, *La Croix* for December 12th set the record straight, with the approval of the Quai d'Orsay (*AHP* 18 [1999] 155: a document by Fr. Dudon). The storm calmed down.

4. *1913*

On January 13th Fr. Fonck, who was silent for a long time because he was ill, resumed correspondence with Fr. Féderlin. On August 26th of the previous year, then on September 18th, he had sent the sum total of 30,000 francs to the Superior of the White Fathers in Jerusalem to cover the cost of the purchase of the land on the Mount of Olives. Still concerned with secrecy he had asked Fr. Féderlin on September 16th, 1912, to contact him, in case of difficulties, through the Jesuit college at Alexandria, using the cryptogram "Biro", meaning "Biblicum Rome". So on January 13th, 1913, he informs his correspondent that he is sending a further 40,000 francs, again through the Deutsche Bank in Berlin. These amounts were to be used to purchase houses that the Muslim owners of the land on the Mount of Olives were asking in exchange for their land. The matter is, however, far from being settled.

In this same letter of January 13th Fr. Fonck also replies to a difficulty reported to him by F. Féderlin, namely that along with the land being sought to the west the Jesuits would be making their entry into Jerusalem. "Those are ideas thought up by our adversaries", writes Fonck "and I most willingly authorize you to state that it is the Biblical Institute alone that is purchasing both sites for the purpose of founding the branch. We have nothing else in mind". The last part of the letter shows that no decision had yet been made on the choice of a site or of an available building to the north or west of the ramparts.

On February 27th Fr. General Wernz authorizes Fr. Fonck to go to Jerusalem to make the choice of this site. For the benefit of his correspondent he then adds some recommendations about prudence and reserve in his words; he also orders him to observe secrecy about the negotiations; lastly he asks him to keep the Lyons Provincial and the Superior of the Mission in Syria informed of the matter.

On March 6th then Fonck announces his arrival in Jerusalem to Féderlin; he was to be there on Holy Thursday, March 20th and leave on the 30th. He will have to decide on the spot about the choice of a plot of land to be bought to the west of the city; of the three or four suitable plots or buildings, one (which it is impossible to identify today) "suits all the preferences both of ourselves and the Superiors". In spite of these good intentions, Fr. Fonck was not to decide anything in the course of this journey.

However, he was also bringing with him a second letter from Pius X's Secretary of State, Cardinal Merry del Val, addressed on March 8th to the Latin Patriarch, Mgr. Camassei (Doc. J. I,10). The cardinal reminds him that in 1911 he informed him of the Pope's wish that a subsidiary house of the Biblical Institute be founded in Palestine. Now that the possibility of Mount Carmel had been ruled out, "the Holy Father now thinks it fitting to build that house in Jerusalem". Consequently, let the Patriarch offer his assistance to Fr. Fonck in the realization of this task. The Pope's approval is therefore explicit.

Although he had not concluded anything, Fr. Fonck did not go back to Rome empty-handed. He had fixed his sights on a huge site two kilometers to the west of the Old City in the Katamone quarter. That Greek word means solitude and it was there that the Greek orthodox Patriarch owned a villa.

In April there was a bolt from the blue brought about by Fr. Chanteur; he gave a written account of it in August 1944; this document is in the archives of the Institute in Jerusalem (cf. also the account by Fr. Senès, p. 12, whose additions are placed here in brackets):

Meanwhile, Fr. Chanteur, having gone to Rome, had the honour of a private audience with Pius X. At the end of the audience, he asked the Holy Father's permission to put a question to him about the Jerusalem project. (And the Pope consented. Here are the sentences reported by Fr. Chanteur:) Most Holy Father, I would like to know your thinking on two points concerning the foundation of the annex in Jerusalem. Is it true that you want an establishment rivaling the Institute in Rome in importance, and, secondly, that you want the Library of the Oriental Faculty in Beirut to be moved to Jerusalem [?] R. Yes, I want an annex for the Rome Biblical Institute, but the size and organization pertain to your superiors. As regards the two points you indicate to me: Hoc non est in mente Patris vestri Generalis. Ergo non debet esse in mente patris Fonck. Ergo non debet esse in mente Patris Universalis Ecclesiae.

On leaving the audience Fr. Chanteur went to the V. R. Father General Wernz's residence to give him an account of the visit. "I am happy at this clarification", his Paternity said, "the case has been heard".

Fr. (Chanteur) went next to Fr. Fonck and repeated His Holiness Pius X's formula to him. ([...]. The clear reply that Fr. Chanteur reported to him was, for Fr. Fonck, the thunderbolt that destroyed his great plans worked out for such a long time.) A thump of the fist on the table marked out his unhappiness at the step taken and its result (and he exclaimed: "You are the first to resist me").

However, Fr. Fonck did not give up. On June 6th, 1913, Fr. General, in answer to one of his letters, fully approves the choice of the site that Fr. Fonck and the majority of his advisers at the Institute preferred. The choice fell on two sites. One might be unhealthy and may be the one occupied by the Institute today; there were fears of the bad effects of the Mamilla reservoir that was quite near and the hesitation was to return in 1924 (cf. the report by Fr. Senès, p. 15). The other plot, of which Fr. General approves the immediate purchase, would certainly cost more, and the fact that it was two kilometres from the Old City was yet a point that counted against it; however, the opinion of Fr. Fonck and his advisers won the day.

In that same letter Fr. Wernz asks Fr. Fonck that two Jesuit Fathers and one Jesuit brother reside at Notre-Dame de France in Jerusalem to work on this whole matter of the foundation. He also proposes some names for the direction of the first "caravan" of Biblicum students (cf. *infra*, chapter III). Actually, it was Fr. Alexis Mallon who was finally chosen both to lead the caravan and to work in Jerusalem on the foundation.

Meanwhile the latter left Rome about fifteen days before the caravan.

On August 25th, 1913, Fr. Senès writes in his report (p. 12), Fr. Mallon, passing through Constantinople to meet up with the Biblical Institute's first caravan at Beirut, went to visit the French ambassador, accompanied by Fr. Riondel. There he only found Mr Mathieu, in charge of religious matters, who was just about to go to the Sublime Porte with the list of establishments placed under the French protectorate in the Ottoman empire.

Thanks to that timely visit he added the Pontifical Biblical Institute to that list; in this way he was able to gain for it the enormous privileges which the old establishments then enjoyed.

Fr. Mallon himself recounted this episode (cf. Doc.J. I,1, pp. 14-15) the result of which was that the Biblical Institute in Jerusalem was, with the title "Convent and Biblical Seminary of the Jesuit Fathers in Jerusalem", on the list of agreements reached on December 18th, 1913, between Turkey and France. On December 24th Mallon informs Fr. Wernz by letter about this.

In November, the "caravan" having embarked at Alexandria to return to Italy, Fr. Mallon came back to Jerusalem and settled down at Notre-Dame de France. On December 3rd he writes to Fr. Féderlin (ASAJ). He notes first of all "that the properties we are acquiring will not be owned by the Society [of Jesus], but by the Holy See for the Biblical Institute. That is the wish of the Benefactors and Superiors". This spells out what Fr. Fonck had written to the same Fr. Féderlin on January 13th. Then Mallon comes back briefly to Mr. Eddé's role in the purchase of the land on the Mount of Olives: nothing is settled so far. Lastly, Mallon clearly states his preference for another site to the west of the Old City: "it is closer to the city than everything that has been suggested to us elsewhere"; this site is perhaps the one the present Institute occupies and Mallon adds: "To tell the truth, the places concerning which Fr. Fonck is engaged in discussion are so distant that I would prefer yours on a bigger scale". That casts uncertainty on the approval given to Fr. Fonck by Fr. General Wernz.

Three days later Fr. Mallon again contacts Fr. Féderlin to put him on his guard against a Maronite monk by the name of Louis Ubaid whose reliability he questions (ASAJ). Now that person had been chosen by Fr. Fonck who, on December 21st, 1924, hence a long time after the events, came to his defence in a letter addressed to Cardinal Tacci, the Secretary of the Congregation for the oriental Church (APIBR B-VI [VI-1A]). Fr. Fonck states in it that Ubaid had been contacted by him with the approval of Pius X and his Secretary of State to help him in acquiring land on which to set up the Institute in Jerusalem. In fact, it is thanks to that monk that the vast site was acquired in 1914, but let us not anticipate. We shall simply note this second point of friction between Fonck and Mallon. The latter was also going to put Fr. General Wernz on his guard, too, in his letter of April 4th, 1914 (p. 2), even adding: "Quidquid de hoc homine scio, jam R. P. Fonck scripsi a longo tempore sed Rev^{dus} P. de litteris meis non curat" (p. 2 recto).

Thus ended this year 1913. The only positive fact was the Holy See's explicit desire to found the branch of the Biblical Institute in Jerusalem. For the rest, nothing was settled and serious divergences appeared between Fr. Fonck and Fr. Mallon.

5. *1914*

This is the year of the purchase of plots in Jerusalem for the Biblical Institute. Let us say first of all, however, that after the 1914-1918 war the Institute was to give up all these properties! Fr. Mallon's report (cf. Doc. J. I,1, pp. 19-29) gives the essentials. What is added here comes from various archive sources.

Fr. General Wernz did not wait for Fr. Mallon's letter of April 4th, 1914, to warn Fr. Fonck about Ubaid, the monk; the letter he wrote on March 2nd to Fr. Fonck is especially a call for prudence (APIBR K-11-A [II-1: 1911-1914]). It is essentially a matter of the terms of purchase of the land recommended by Fr. Fonck. The Holy See's right of ownership must be clearly indicated; this is in connection with the two plots acquired on the 4th and 6th of February. As regards the other plots, Fr. General considers that the property acquired is already very extensive and he only gives permission to buy land that seems "revera necessaria vel valde utilis". With regard to building the house, he asks that it be thought over carefully before starting on it, because the place is far from the city and with no communication routes;

before building a house of any size, will permission be obtained to put access routes in place and at what cost? Concerning Fr. Mallon, he could leave Jerusalem to resume his studies; if there are no more Jesuits in Jerusalem the secrecy of the negotiations will be that much better kept! A radical way of reducing disagreements!

All this about the land to the west. As regards the other, on the Mount of Olives, Mr. Eddé eventually agreed to the purchase in his name and from Alexandria sent a proxy in good and due form to Brother Louis Fournier who, at the White Fathers' place at St. Anne's, was conducting the negotiation (ASAJ). With this proxy four houses in Jerusalem were bought before March, 15th, 1914, two being in the Old City, near Saint Saviour's; three of these houses were to be in exchange for the land being sought on the Mount of Olives (cf. Fr. Fonck's accounts in ASAJ). But for the exchange to have legal value it had to be registered officially and that operation could not be done straight away. The year ended without it being achieved.

In the meantime, despite Fr. General's reservations, Fr. Fonck went ahead. Here one should quote the description which, in his report (pp. 13-14), Fr. Senès left of the building project thought up by Fr. Fonck:

Before the purchases were completed, Fr. Fonck was already drawing up a grandiose plan for the building to be put up on the site in Jerusalem. All the halls were arranged around four sides of a large central cloister. The whole measured about 60 metres by 60 metres.

This plan was redone by the architect Astorri from Rome who envisaged a magnificent irregular block, a kind of oriental style fortress with buttresses, windows scattered on the outside. It had two floors over a ground floor, two inner courtyards, a small dome and a tower. It measured 70 metres by 45 metres between the outer façades, i. e. more than four times, including the inner courtyards, the area of the present edifice built in 1927.

The smaller of these inner courtyards, which followed on from the entrance hall, was of Arab style with a circular pond in the middle. This was the establishment's crossroads.

The large inner courtyard, forming a 16-metre square, was flanked with a cloister on three sides while the chapel took up the fourth side. On to the cloister opened the classrooms, one quite large hall for meetings and the stairwell built into the base of the tower, with walls two metres thick.

The vast proportions of this building give rise to the suspicion that Fr. Fonck had not ceased hoping that the Jerusalem Biblical Institute would end up giving its students a full education in Holy Scripture.

150 metres from this building, on the same site, there was going to be another construction, 40 metres long and varying in width from 14 to 17 metres. It seems that they wanted to place a garage, workshops, lodgings for servants and even students there.

Negotiations for purchase resumed in the summer and on August 9th, 1914, everything, except for two plots to the south of the site, was acquired and legally registered.

In the interests of clarity, let us say that these plots of land were just to the west of the present residence of the President of the State of Israel. Altogether it formed a great horseshoe, a rectangle unfinished on the south, of more than ten hectares. To the west it descended to the road to Gaza; to the north it began at the crossroads in front of the main entrance to the convent or Foyer Saint-Antoine, now belonging to the Franciscan missionaries of the Immaculate Heart of Mary. It had all been bought for just over 200,000 gold francs which, at the end of 2008, is worth about 1,200,000 euros.

The First World War broke out in August, 1914, and in December, being French, Fr. Mallon was expelled from Palestine by the Turks. He went back to Rome.

Thus the year ended in uncertainty, not only because of the ups and downs of the fighting but also because the lands acquired to the east and west of the Old City of Jerusalem were not to be without creating problems. There was no legal registration of the land on the Mount of Olives and, as regards the land to the west, was Fr. Fonck going to be followed in his grandiose plans, clearly going beyond what he himself had proposed in 1912?

II. An official decision by Benedict XV: 1918-1919

In 1915 Fr. Wlodimir Ledóchowski succeeded Fr. Wernz as General of the Society of Jesus. On January 9th, 1918, writing from Switzerland where he took refuge he replies to a communication from Fr. Andrés Fernández, Vice-Rector of the Biblical Institute. During the war, in fact, Fr. Fonck had also taken refuge in Switzerland. One month earlier, on December 10th, 1917, Fr. Fernández had sent Fr. General a "promemoria" from Fr. Mallon. The latter was in fact advising a change of site to the west of the Old City of Jerusalem, the big property bought in 1914. The Vice-Rector was hesitating. The General consulted Fr. Fonck who considered that Fr. Mallon's arguments were exaggerated, especially as they had already been discussed before acquiring that land. The General concluded that, given the situation, it is better not to change anything. He also consulted Fr. Fine, his Assistant for France, who shared Fr. Fonck's opinion. This letter poses a problem: what was at the back of Fr. Fonck's mind? Did he still want to establish a complete Biblical Institute on this site, not just a branch of the one in Rome?

The months go by. On October 4th, before the armistice of November 11th therefore, Fr. Lagrange, who had been in France during the war, is in Rome; he sought and obtained permission to return to Jerusalem from the British, henceforth masters in Palestine. On that day he was received by Cardinal van Rossum, the President of the Biblical Commission, who left an account of the interview (published by Fr. Turvasi, *Giovanni Genocchi e la controversia modernista*, Rome 1974, pp. 363-365). Here is a translation of the beginning: Fr. Lagrange "told me he had heard that the Jesuit Fathers at the Biblical Institute intended to set up a dependent school in Jerusalem and added that, should they do so, they (the Dominicans [at the École Biblique]) could leave; it would be school against school, "altar against altar" [Augustine, *c. Crescon.*, 2,2, who adds: "in the same city": PL 43, 468; the expression has passed into Italian usage]; there would not be enough to keep both alive, given the restricted number of students coming to it. I replied that one could not stop a branch [of the Institute] being built and it is only a natural consequence, a development of the Biblical Institute". The rest of the conversation dealt with reproaches made against the École Biblique and its journal *Revue biblique*.

In his unpublished account of the history of the Institute in Jerusalem, Fr. Senès (p. 14) speaks of the step taken by Fr. Lagrange in 1918 (Senès mistakenly writes: 1919): "He went to visit two influential cardinals at the Curia; he expounded his arguments [about the Institute's plan] with some insistence to them. He was told in reply that nothing could be done to satisfy him on this point, because that was the Pope's wish. One of the cardinals suggested to Benedict XV that he publish a letter aimed at putting an end to all possible opposition from this Dominican over this. That is the origin of the letter of June 29th, 1919, addressed by Benedict XV to the President of the Biblical Institute, the Rev. Fr. Fernández". Fr. Senès does not mention his sources. It will be seen that what he says is on the whole correct, but also that other people had a hand in this affair.

Indeed, on May 11th, 1919, the Master general of the Dominicans, Fr. Theissling, wrote to Mgr. Bonaventura Cerretti, the then Secretary for extraordinary ecclesiastical affairs at the Vatican Secretariat of State (cf. Doc. J. I,12). Now from among the points submitted by Fr. Theissling to his correspondent the second should especially be brought out: "It is important to know whether the Holy Father Pius X has given the Fathers of the Society of Jesus written permission authorizing them to found a house of their Order in Jerusalem, as well as the extent of that permission". The third is also revealing since it suspects: "We have been told that it is simply a matter of building a home for students of the Society or the Biblical Institute in Rome who, on finishing their studies, would come to round off their training in Palestine; there would be no question of a College or a house of studies or anything of the kind. But then, why want to insist on setting up in Jerusalem? [...] By setting up elsewhere the Fathers of the Society will avoid the reproaches of those who would see in their foundation just a College in disguise which would be revealed in more propitious times".

This is, first of all, what the excessive use of secrecy has led to. The Master general of the Order of Preachers does not know that it is the Holy See's project, not the Society's, even if it is the Society that runs the Biblical Institute and the negotiations in Jerusalem. Moreover, Fr. Fonck's grandiose plan, although not overtly confessed, is suspected in Fr. Theissling's third remark; he also sees its purpose, because his sixth remark begins with: "To us it does not seem useful to hasten the destruction of a biblical School that ...".

This letter from the Master general caused a commotion. A letter from Fr. Fonck, sent to Fr. Fernández, who had become Rector of the Biblical Institute, from Zurich on the following 4th of June makes it quite clear that Cardinal van Rossum was informed about this matter (cf. Doc. J. I,11). He asked for Fr. Fernández's opinion and the latter informed Fr. Fonck in a letter dated May 26th. We have already spoken above about this letter from Fr. Fonck. It closes with these words, here translated from the Italian: "I hope His Eminence Cardinal van Rossum will understand the importance of the question and will come to our defence". Earlier in this four-page letter Fr. Fonck had summarized the story of the Jerusalem project, the two letters from Cardinal Merry del Val, dating to 1911 and 1913, and why there had been a change from Carmel to Jerusalem. Then he says that he was received by Benedict XV in September 1914 who asked him for explanations because the Pope had heard it said that, with this house in Jerusalem, "we wanted to erect a 'counter-altar' against the École Biblique". Fonck goes on to say that he briefly expounded to the Pope the reasons why Pius X had decided on this foundation. Benedict XV approved of them and concluded "by telling me explicitly: 'Yes, I want it, too'". We have no other witness to this pontifical audience. As for the reasons Fr. Fonck gives in his letter it is difficult to believe that they really are those he gave to Benedict XV; they seem rather like those meant for Cardinal van Rossum who was asking for an opinion. Because one of the last reasons, with its novelty, makes a break with earlier statements; Fonck writes: "If, in the future, as I hope, to the theoretical part of our teaching there is also added a section on *practical interpretation* [underlined in the text] of Sacred Scripture for the clergy of all the Church and for preaching, and for biblical instruction in primary and secondary schools, an indispensable complement, even for such practical instruction, will be a stay in Jerusalem along with suitable excursions; and this cannot be done without our house". It may honestly be doubted whether this reason was given to Benedict XV in 1914 as justifying Pius X's decision. In October 1919 Fr. Fonck was to make himself more explicit and, in particular, more concrete.

Fr. Fernández had therefore written to Fr. Fonck on May 26th, 1919. Was it really to ask him for his opinion? It may be doubted, for on the same day Fr. Fernández wrote to Cardinal van Rossum to let him have his own opinion as Rector of the Institute (cf. Doc. J. I,13). Now this opinion is diametrically opposed to Fr. Fonck's. According to the Rector, the house in Jerusalem, explicitly desired by Pius X, was, according to the original, and still valid, intention, to be only a complement or annex to the Rome Institute and only geography and archaeology, perhaps also spoken Arabic and Semitic epigraphy, were to be taught there; lectures on these subjects would also be given, at least if the fathers thought fit. In fact everything was to be done under the direction of the Rome Institute. Lastly, the house was to be used for housing people going on the caravans. There were no plans, therefore, for a complete institute along the same lines as other schools (meaning the École Biblique). Then, on June 6[th,] Fr. Fernández wrote directly to Benedict XV to ask his blessing on implementing the plan for a branch of the Institute in Jerusalem (cf. Doc. J. I,14).

On June 29th, 1919, Benedict XV answers Fr. Fernández in a letter published in the *AAS* on August 1st, the main parts of which, translated from the Latin, are as follows (APIBR K-1-A and *Acta PIB* 3, pp 4-5):

> From your letter, we have learnt that you were just going to carry out the mandate our predecessor of holy memory, Pius X, had given you when the war prevented you from carrying it out hitherto, namely that of opening a house in Jerusalem for the study of the Sacred books. That house would not be, strictly speaking, a school where all subjects dealing with the Bible were taught, but would be a kind of annex and as it were a complement to the Roman Institute and only special subjects such as geography, archaeology and Semitic epigraphy would be taught there. To be sure, those giving themselves entirely to biblical studies, having learnt Hebrew and Greek and being sufficiently versed in exegesis, biblical history and like matters – things which are excellently done in Rome under your presidency – must go and spend some time in Palestine [...]. We therefore highly praise your project and we pray God to grant it a successful outcome [...].

This document, seen in the context that led to its composition, should have put an end to the concern felt by the École Biblique and answered the two questions put by the Master general Theissling: founding a house of the Biblical Institute in Jerusalem is, in origin, a "mandatum" of Pius X and Benedict XV approves this "consilium", this plan; but this house was not to give a complete training in Scripture; only secondary subjects which are better assimilated in the Holy Land than in Rome were to be taught. This letter of Benedict XV is still the rule at the Institute.

Yet Fr. Fonck did not admit complete defeat. On October 19th, 1919, he returned to the charge to justify his grandiose plan: in his "Observationes de constructione domus hierosolymitanae" (APIBR B-VI [VI-1-A]), he advised against building only a part of the great building he had imagined and, as a reason, explained that, for this house, apart from offices and outhouses, a minimum of forty-two rooms and even more were needed if his idea of a two-year course in the practical interpretation of Scripture were to become a reality. Building only part of his plan, postponing a more extensive construction "ad kalendas graecas", would be against the purpose of that house in Jerusalem, the intentions of the Holy See, everyone's expectations and the dignity of a pontifical institute! Clearly, Fr. Fonck really had changed since his first plan on June 25th, 1912.

On December 4th, 1919, Fr. Mallon went back to Jerusalem.

Conclusion

What are we to make of all this distressing story? Why did this tension with the École Biblique arise, as well as that between Fr. Fonck and Fr. Mallon? The first cause of tension between the École and the Institute has to be the modernist crisis. It set Fr. Fonck and Fr. Lagrange radically at odds at least as early as 1905, that is to say well before the foundation of the Biblicum in Rome. Both men are irreconcilable although both are honestly convinced that they are working for the Church and Scripture. However, from the Society's point of view, it is known that other Jesuits support Fr. Lagrange's exegesis. The modernist crisis did not put all the Jesuits on the same side.

The second cause, perceived by the French newspapers that aggravate it in 1912, and by Fr. Lagrange, is the conflict setting France against Germany. It appears back in 1911 with Fr. Fonck's visit to the German Consul in Haifa. However, it does not seen to have been the Jesuits' doing, nor in particular Fr. Fonck's; he writes French impeccably.

Besides these main causes there were others just as disastrous. The principal one could have been the secrecy that shrouded the negotiations conducted by the Institute. It was the source of concern, false rumours and misunderstandings. Still, it is quite frightening that in 1919 the Master general of the Order of Preachers does not know that it was Pius X that, in 1913 (six years earlier!), had decided on founding a branch of the Biblical Institute in Jerusalem. On top of this comes a confusion of the Biblical Institute with the Society of Jesus: it is not, however, the latter that does the founding in Jerusalem but the Institute acting on behalf of the Holy See. Of the damage done by secrecy Fr. Mallon complains and speaks openly to Fr. Wernz in April,1914. And back in January, 1913, Fr. Fonck authorizes Fr. Féderlin to state that the Institute is not the Society; in December the same year Fr. Mallon, writing to Fr. Féderlin, is even clearer: the Holy See is acquiring (the land). But in 1919 Master general Theissling is still making the confusion.

Moreover, there is Fr. Fonck's temperament. If his gifts as organizer succeeded in Rome, there was failure in Jerusalem. The intemperance of his language already earned him the rebuke of Fr. General Wernz in February, 1913. In April, 1914, Fr. Mallon complains to the Fr. General that Fr. Fonck takes no account of his advice. Later documents prove that Fr. Fonck does not accept Fr. Mallon's objection: he clings tightly to his grand edifice, even after Benedict XV's letter. Lastly, and this goes hand in hand with this authoritarian way of acting, Fr. Fonck misuses papal authority by speaking to the Patriarch Camassei, for instance, in a cavalier way, to say the least: in the letter he sent him on October 14th, 1912, it is the will of the Pope, he writes, that you ask France for its protectorate for the foundation of the Institute in Jerusalem.

In contrast, Fr. Mallon is much more prudent and reserved in his words and his report for these years (cf. Doc. J. I,1) is pacificatory. It was to leave a very good impression behind, even at the École Biblique (cf. Montagnes, *Ex.-ob.* p. 427, n. 25). It is only through the documents in the archives that one becomes aware of the difficulties he must have met and of which he warned his Superiors.

Finally Benedict XV's letter of June 29th, 1919, was intended to put an end to a long dispute by making Pius X's decisions public – decisions approved by his successor. Yet everything was still only a plan. Putting it into action would have to wait several years but at last things were henceforth clear: this plan to found a branch of the Institute in Jerusalem was officially drawn up.

III. Deciding and building: from 1919 to 1927

When Fr. Mallon got back to Jerusalem on December 4th, 1919, the situation was quite changed. It was two years since the British had taken control of the city and the country; Fr. A. Fernández had succeeded Fr. Fonck a year earlier as Rector of the Institute; lastly, it was six months, or almost, since Benedict XV had officially made clear what the future branch of the Institute was to be.

To be sure, Fr. Mallon found the things he had left behind at Notre-Dame de France in their pre-war state but, as regards the two plots of land acquired in 1914, the one on the Mount of Olives and the other at Katamone, the big plot, their situation, and even that of the Institute, still had to be regularized with the British authorities

Fr. Mallon resumed residence at Notre Dame de France and the Sisters of Marie Réparatrice again lent him the big room he had occupied earlier on. But in September 1920, with the payment for board and lodging at Notre Dame de France costing too much, he found somewhere to live with the Fathers of Our Lady of Sion at their college of Saint Peter of Ratisbonne; the Fathers also made two or three rooms for guests available to him. That was where he settled in until the day in July, 1927, when the Institute's branch was opened.

Fr. Mallon's main task was to regularize the situation of the two sites. In his handwritten report he recounted in detail the ins and outs of these operations (cf. Doc. J. I,1, pp. 29 ff.); we will confine ourselves here to mentioning the main episodes.

In August, 1920, the British Government in Palestine published a "correction of registers" of property order. As the land on the Mount of Olives had been acquired in the name of Mr. Eddé and the land at Katamone in the name of Fr. Ubaid, it was above all necessary that these two persons who had lent their names agree to transfer the two plots to the Pontifical Biblical Institute and that the latter be officially recognized by the British.

From Rome Fr. Fernández dealt with the last-mentioned matter through the mediation of the British Minister in Rome, Count de Salis, and on April 27th, 1921, Fr. Mallon in Jerusalem without any difficulty received the deeds of ownership of the large property at Katamone, made out to the "Pontifical Bible Institute. Jesuit Fathers", recognized as a moral person entitled to be an owner (cf. Doc. J. I,1, pp. 30-32 and Fr. Senès' account, p. 14). To be successful this move meant that, as a preliminary, Fr. Ubaid grant the Institute that extensive plot of land acquired in his name. This, too, was done in Rome without any problem (cf. Fr. Senès' report, p.14).

As regards the land on the Mount of Olives, however, everything concluded in 1914 had to be regularized. In his account (Doc. J. I,1, pp. 58-66), Fr. Mallon relates in detail the difficulties raised by the Muslim authorities, the land in question being a religious endowment, a *waqf*. On December 24th, 1920, a new proxy from Mr Eddé arrived allowing the exchange of the land in question for the four houses that had been bought but the Muslim authorities put up the price of the land. In September 1921, faced with the impossibility of reaching an agreement, Fr. Mallon gave up that land and, on December 12th, had the four houses that had been bought in 1914 registered in the name of the Institute. Being henceforth of no use to the Institute, these houses were sold, two in 1922, one in 1923 and the last, situated outside the walls in the Musrara quarter, in 1929.

The fact remains that at the end of October, 1923, Fr. Mallon returned to Rome with the VIth caravan (cf. chapter III) and stayed there for three months. "On February 6th, 1924", he writes in his report (cf. Doc. J. I,1, p. 42) "I was back in Jerusalem. It has been decided that I should lodge at St. Peter's again. For the moment it does not suit us to open a house of our own. We do not need it. Two or three rooms are kept at our disposal at St. Peter's. That is quite enough". In fact, on December 13th, 1923, the Advisory Committee of the Professors at the Institute – the minutes are kept in the Registrar's office – had decided to postpone the construction of the Jerusalem branch: there was neither money, nor were there available professors, nor interested students! But then, what about that great plot of land at Katamone and the grandiose plan drawn up by Fr. Fonck? The clash between Fonck and Mallon was below the surface and Fr. Fernández, the Rector, who had already come out in favour of Fr. Mallon, did not intervene.

Everything changes as from July, 1924, when Fr. John J. O'Rourke succeeds Fr. Fernández as Rector of the Institute. "He was", writes Fr. Senès in his account (p. 23) "a more decisive and pugnacious character". Fr. Mallon, who probably thinks that he now has a freer hand, sends a report to his new Rector in which he explains his preference for a smaller and, especially, closer plot of land, than the one Fr. Fonck had chosen back in 1913, that great plot at Katamone which had become the Institute's property officially in 1921.

O'Rourke agreed with this all right and asked for Fr. General's agreement but Fonck threw a spanner in the works, still sticking to his grandiose plans, in spite of Benedict XV's letter in 1919. The General then wanted an independent opinion. He got Fr. Norbert de Boynes, his Assistant for France who was already in the Near East where he was making the official visit of the missions in Syria and Egypt, to go up to Jerusalem, see the lands that were being talked about and make a report to him about them. Fr. de Boynes came to Jerusalem from February 7th until 12th, 1925, and on the last day of his visit drew up the report requested. His manuscript is in the archives of the Institute in Rome (cf. Doc. J. I,15). In his fine handwriting he manages to advise strongly against Fr. Fonck's big plot of land for the building of the Institute's branch because, in his opinion, it is too far from the city and besides, he concludes, "it seems that there is no place for an establishment for biblical education on a large scale in Jerusalem, but only for an annex where people could come to find a special complement to studies done in Rome". So Benedict XV's letter, six years later, or almost, was still being contested by Fr. Fonck!

On the other hand, Fr. de Boynes was giving his preference to the plot suggested by Fr. Mallon, the one the Institute now owns, but the Greek Orthodox who were the owners were not selling it at the time. Thus there was only the land that had already been bought by France possibly for the construction of its Consulate and which, for reasons of economy it was said, its government wanted to sell. Let it be bought as soon as possible, advised Fr. de Boynes. On March 22nd, 1925, the order is given to Fr. Mallon to buy this land from France but at the beginning of May the Consulate told him that it was not actually for sale. And in fact France built its Consulate, our neighbours, there in 1930.

Thereupon, on May 13th, Fr. O'Rourke, after consulting Fr. de Boynes, told Fr. Mallon by letter to buy the land the latter had suggested. On August 22nd this was done and the legal registration was signed on October 5th. Thus on Sunday, October 18th, 1925, on the feast of St. Luke at 4.00 p. m. the first stone was blessed and laid by the Latin Patriarch, Mgr. Barlassina, in the presence of the British governor of Jerusalem, the consuls of France, Italy and Spain, the Fr. Custodian and the parish priest of Saint Saviour's, the Superiors of religious communities, many Jerusalem Christians and students on the VIth caravan. The École Biblique was represented by the Prior of the convent of St. Stephen, Fr. Savignac, because all the Dominican community was on retreat. Fr. Luis Gonzaga da Fonseca, a professor at the Institute accompanying the VIth caravan had helped Fr. Mallon to draw up in Latin the parchment text inserted in the stone. This is how it reads:

IN NOMINE SANCTISSIMAE ET INDIVIDUAE TRINITATIS. AMEN
QUOD SS. CORDE JESU AUSPICE ET AUCTORE FELIX FAUSTUMQUE SIT.
ANNO JUBILAEI MCMXXV DIE XVIII OCTOBRIS.

PIO XI PONTIFICE MAXIMO ANNO III FELICITER REGNANTE, P. JOHANNE-
JOS. O'ROURKE PONTIFICII INSTITUTI BIBLICI PRAESIDE, CIRCUMS-
TANTE CORONA PROFESSORUM ET ALUMNORUM EIUSDEM INSTITUTI
SEXTUM ITER PALAESTINENSE PERAGENTIUM, EXCMUS DD. ALOYSIUS
BARLASSINA, PATRIARCHA HIEROSOLYMITANUS, LAPIDEM AUSPICALEM
DOMUS AUXILIARIS PONTIFICII INSTITUTI BIBLICI, INVOCATO VIRGINIS
DEIPARAE ET SANCTORUM SUFFRAGIO, BENEDIXIT ET POSUIT.

To this parchment were added four medals, one, in silver, of the Holy Year, offered by the Patriarch, one of the Sacred Heart and Our Lady, one of St. Ignatius, and lastly one of Saint Teresa of Lisieux whom Pius XI had just canonized the previous month of May. Fr. Mallon made a brief speech and the minutes of the ceremony were signed by, among others, Fr. Savignac, as he himself notes in the diary of the École Biblique. Since 1927 the foundation stone has been inside the building, at the entrance to the kitchen. As a token of gratitude after so many difficulties Fr. Mallon went and placed an ex-voto in honour of Our Lady in the church consecrated to her on the hill of the Ark of the Covenant at Kyriat Yearim; the plaque is still very visible at the left entrance to the chancel.

The construction took just under two years. From January, 1926, to May, 1928, Fr. Giuseppe Marini of the Venice province and minister-bursar of the Institute in Rome stayed in Jerusalem to draw up plans for the building, supervise their execution which had been entrusted to the Farro firm in Jerusalem and see to the finishing touches when possession was taken. Money for paying bills was often lacking because the million gold francs available in 1911 had evaporated with the war. Fr. Marini then used to send telegrams to Fr. O'Rourke who, in turn, sent telegrams to Mrs Catherine Simpson in the United States and she would reply positively in the same way: she thus gave about £15,000, a fine sum in those days but she always wanted to remain anonymous. It is Fr. Senès who mentions her in his account (p. 27) lest she be forgotten.

Fr. Marini's plans, drawn up in March, 1926, were accepted by Rome in April on condition that more space be provided for the library. On May 11th Fr. Mallon obtained an official declaration from the British Governor in Palestine recognizing that the Institute had a right to be exempt from taxes and import duty. (Doc. J. I,1, p. 51).

Finally, on July 1st, 1927, Fr. Mallon and those working with him took possession of the house. But what neither Fr. Mallon nor Fr. Senès mention in their respective accounts is that there was a serious earthquake in the Holy Land at about 2.30 p. m. on July 11th; its epicentre was at Nablus, which was largely destroyed; in Jerusalem it shook the Holy Sepulchre, which was propped up with steel girders, and a wing of the Carmel on the Mount of Olives collapsed, whereas many cracks only slightly damaged the Institute's new building.

DOCUMENTS FOR CHAPTER I

Doc. J. I,1

APIBJ

Fr. Mallon's report translated from the French
(There is a second copy of this manuscript going up to 4 October, 1914.)

I
Pontifical Biblical Institute
House in Jerusalem. Short history
The foundation. 1914

1. The Choice of Jerusalem. 1913

The Pontifical Biblical Institute, initiated at Rome in 1909 by Pope Pius X, was now finally established with its own premises, professional staff and regular courses. The first students had reached the diploma stage and were about to leave us when the need for a branch in the Middle East, to facilitate practical study of the land where the sacred events had taken place, became glaringly obvious for the first time.

Three years of lectures at Rome, highly specialized professors, a well-stocked library put together as if by magic and a wide variety of conferences, all provided a solid basis for furnishing the memory, opening horizons on different branches of oriental studies and providing the breadth of the knowledge indispensable [2] today to anyone wishing to deal authoritatively with biblical questions. All this is no longer a project. It is a reality. Yet, in one way, it still remains at the level of theory, not yet fully in application.

Can a young man, with his newly acquired doctorate and scarcely out of the library, seriously deal with the interpretation of Books written in the East by Orientals, can he be sure enough of himself to grasp their true spirit, so complex and different from ours, can he hope to resolve the problems of history, topography, archaeology, literature and of the other matters that make up the very texture of the sacred narrative?

It is common knowledge today that the great struggle between belief and unbelief is taking place in the field of positivism and that it is on the basis of facts and in the area of self-evident realities that our opponents hope to make their breakthrough against the traditional doctrine of the Church.

Now, the Biblical Institute has not been [3] founded solely to form professors capable of taking a repetition in a seminary. An essential part of its aim and programme is the formation of masters in their field, well equipped to fend off attacks and write with competence and success in biblical matters. Undoubtedly, after only four years in existence, it would be unbecoming of the new School to vaunt its achievements but the onus remains to keep the focus fixed firmly on the ideal, something beautiful and great, with all energies employed on making it a reality.

Travelling and residing in the East today poses so little difficulty and given the enormous advantages that this provides, it would be inexcusable to neglect such an indispensable addition to the formation of our students.

To let a dozen young priests go on their own each year [4] into a country completely unknown to them would be unthinkable, let alone to entrust them to others for a period of two to three months or even a year. Having initiated their formation, the Institute owes it to itself to complete it. This is a responsibility to be carried to the end.

Moreover, the merit of the decision was not ours. When consulted, the Sovereign Pontiff expressed clearly his own wish that a branch of the Biblical Institute be set up in the East. Will of the Pope, will of God, we had only to obey.

Under what form and in which location this branch should be established were the two questions requiring serious examination and formed the object of prolonged deliberations.

[5] In 1902, the Lyons Province had founded at Beirut a Faculty for teaching oriental languages and sciences. It was in this Faculty that a number of the professors of the Biblical Institute had been formed. The operation there was running smoothly, it was directed by men of recognised merit, possessed an excellent library and as a result of its publications had acquired a high reputation in scholarly circles.

Both schools were run by the Society so was the solution not obvious? Why not come together and work towards the same aim; if, at least, the Oriental Faculty, without giving up its own proper activity, could provide the young Doctors of the Biblical Institute with the additional practical formation which can only be acquired in the Orient, would that not be an immense advantage for the Institute?

[6] Was not this the desired branch, with the bonus of saving on personnel, time and money? Union is strength. The two establishments could provide mutual support, the professors would move from one to the other where needed, the Faculty would be guaranteed a large number of students in advance: three years of Holy Scripture at Rome and one year of Oriental studies at Beirut, was, it seemed, a happy solution.

In fact, negotiations were already taking place among Superiors with a view to implementing the project, a number of preparatory measures had already been taken and the union between the two schools already envisaged in general terms.

And yet - time brings its own counsel - on reflection, after careful scrutiny, and after some months of respite in the negotiations, it became apparent that the project, so attractive at first, contained a number of defects and that, all things considered [7] and weighed carefully, it would not guarantee the real interests of either the Faculty or the Institute.

The candidates sent to Rome, young priest graduates, after three years of specialized studies of Holy Scripture and also in oriental studies, could not be students at the Faculty. They could not be expected to sit again on a school bench; what they come for is a practical knowledge of the country, its customs, people, and artifacts, something acquired by personal effort, not in a class-room but out in the fresh air.

It would be difficult for the doctors from Rome to fit in with undergraduates at the Faculty, mainly beginners needing classes. It would have proved too heavy a burden for the Faculty.

But the biggest defect of the project was Beirut itself, certainly an oriental city, but without special interest for a professor of Holy Scripture.

[8] The proper milieu for our young people is to be sought in Palestine, not in Syria. It is Palestine, its towns and monuments that they must study, the Holy Land itself that they must see so that later they would have a proper context for their teaching. Undoubtedly, near Beirut, there is Damascus, an eminently biblical city, which we will be sure to visit in our outings but it is not our primary focus.

In Palestine, especially at Jerusalem, every voyage, walk, even the stay itself, provides both gain and profit; not an instant of time is lost. A host of things, effortlessly, imprint themselves in the memory, the imagination, from which, one day, a light long sought will burst forth. In Syria, there is nothing similar. It was therefore decided that we would establish ourselves in Palestine.

[9] One could envisage, at least in theory, a compromise solution, that would retain something of the original project.

Beirut was not suitable for the Institute, but if the Oriental Faculty were to move to the Holy Land with its professors and library, the principal obstacle would disappear and the union of the two schools be realized.

It is not hard to see how this would have been disastrous for the Faculty. It would have been torn from its natural milieu, St Joseph's University, where it was born and grew up, and whence it draws its resources of personnel and students. It would not find these anywhere else. It would have been uprooted and, consequently, destroyed. The idea was resolutely rejected.

There was nothing else to do but to build a branch in Palestine from scratch.

[10] Here, there was still some doubt about the location. Opting immediately for Jerusalem could have indicated a lack of sensitivity, given that Galilee, especially Carmel, seemed to have much to offer.

In the Autumn of 1912 [*error*: 1911], Rev. Fr. Fonck, Rector of the Biblical Institute, during a visit to Palestine studied the project on the ground and made enquiries about setting things in motion. Unseen developments caused delays. In the meantime, a number of men with long experience of the Middle East, unconnected with the Pontifical Institute but genuinely concerned for the Pontifical work, judged that our place was not in Galilee, but in Judea, at Jerusalem, the centre of Palestinian life and science. The main merit for this considered and disinterested advice is due to Rev. Fr. Féderlin, Superior of the Seminary of St Anne. Fr. Féderlin communicated his opinion to Rev. Fr. Cattin at Beirut, and he, in turn, [11] convinced by the idea, passed it on to Rome.

It was attractive, clear and in accord with what the best interests and dignity of the Institute required. Our only fear was that it might not be opportune. The matter was submitted to the Sovereign Pontiff. The Pope did not hesitate for an instant. In substance his answer was: "Yes, go to Jerusalem, it is my will, I order you to do it."

This put an end to all our hesitations.

Without delay, negotiations were set in motion in Jerusalem for the choice of a site and the purchase of land. During a short visit in spring, 1913, Rev. Fr. Fonck visited a number of possible locations without, however, coming to any conclusion.

A very important point was the protectorate of the new house. This decision belonged exclusively to the Holy See. For his own part, the Sovereign Pontiff wished that an approach be made [12] to France, already the authorised secular protector of

Christians and religious communities in the Middle East. The request was made through the good offices of the Patriarch of Jerusalem and the French Embassy in Constantinople. Through the same channel, the Government replied that it would be happy to assume the Pontifical Biblical Institute under its protectorate. This put an end to all difficulties.

The end of the school year was approaching with its full complement of examinations. It was the first time, after four years in existence (1909-1913), that the Institute was authorized by the Holy See to grant officially recognised degrees.

A number of candidates urged us to organise a trip in Palestine. As all questions of right had been resolved there was no reason to put it off any longer. It was an ideal opportunity for inaugurating [13] our archaeological expeditions in the Middle East. The voyage was decided. First class material was ordered, tents, litters, saddles and cooking equipment which reached Beirut just in the nick of time.

II. *First Voyage of the Institute in the Middle East: August-November 1913*

Travellers:

Alexis Mallon, S.J.	Prov. Lugd. ⎫ Director
Andreas Fernández, S.J.	Prov. Arag. ⎬
Sandalio Diego, S.J.	Prov. Cast.
Karl Meyer, S.J.	Prov. Germ.
[Antonio] Biondini	Conventual
[Joseph] Patsch	C.SS.R
[Johannes] Schaumberger	C.SS.R
[Raffaele] Tramontano, S.J.	Prov. Neap.
Ernesto Ruffini	dioec. Mantov.
Gustavo Testa	.. Bergam.
Petrus Pous, Spaniard	

[14] Father Louis Heidet, from the Patriarchate of Jerusalem, chaplain at Tantur, was happy to be our guide beginning at Tabgha.

We do not intend to give a detailed account of the voyage except in so far as it is related to the foundation.

In August, fifteen days before the caravan, I left [Rome] for Beirut. At Constantinople, during a short stop, I got the idea of going to the Embassy. Rev. Fr. Riondel wished to come with me. To be honest, I had very little idea what I was going to say. My main aim was to commend our work in Jerusalem. The whole staff was at Therapia, the country residence of the Embassy. By an extraordinary coincidence, better described as providential, there was only one secretary in town and this was precisely the one responsible for religious affairs, Mr Mathieu, former chancellor of the Consulate [15] at Jerusalem. This meant that our work interested him from two points of view. He wanted to know all about it; what we were doing, where we planned to build, which was more that I knew myself. After some discussion he said to me all of a sudden: You come just in time. Here in my drawer I have a list of all the establishments placed under the French Protectorate in the Ottoman Empire which we are going to have approved by the Government of the Sublime Porte.

At present you do not yet exist in Jerusalem but that makes no difference. I will place you on the list and you will be approved with the others. I have taken care to make clear all the privileges that these establishments enjoy. They are immense. Indeed it is unlikely that future foundations will obtain the like.

This was the official recognition of our house, given in advance. Providence had arranged everything.

[16] Our voyage in Palestine, since it was the first of the Institute, was particularly important. How would we be received? Would it be with indifference, coldness or on the other hand sympathy and good-will? After the odious press campaign against the Institute the previous year there was reason, humanly speaking, for a certain amount of apprehension. We can say right away that there was no need for apprehension. During the whole voyage, the "biblical caravan" was received everywhere with a graciousness beyond anything we were entitled to expect. At Beirut, the French Consulate attended to all our requests with the utmost courtesy.

I had written to the Rev. Fr. President, acting Custodian of the Holy Land - the Custodian, the Very Rev. Fr. Carcaterra was in Italy at the time - to inform him of our arrival and to request hospitality in the *Casa Nova* of Galilee. Some days later, I received the following telegram: "Father Mallon. Catholic University [17], Beirut. Caravan Biblical Institute will be very welcome. Orders have been sent to Nazareth and other places. Custodial President."

This was not a mere formality. At Tiberias and Nazareth we were welcomed with open arms. We were feted at Mount Tabor, a mountain abounding in game. Together, we proposed toasts to the Pope, the Institute.

The Lazarist Fathers at Tabgha and the Carmelite Fathers at Carmel also offered us the warmest hospitality.

On reaching Jerusalem, our first visit was to the Patriarch. His Beatitude showed an interest in every one of the travellers and spoke very encouragingly to us.

On leaving the Patriarchate, we went directly to the Custody. It was already 11.20. "It is too late" the *kawas* said to us. "The community dines at 11.15". In any case I gave [18] him my card. He took it and went up the stairs. A few moments later he came down again and invited us into the divan [drawing-room]. We had hardly entered when the Most Rev. President Custodian, accompanied by the Rev. Fr. Vicar arrived. In very good French, they made us welcome, asked for news of our voyage, enquired after our health and insisted again that it was a pleasure for them to help us in any way possible. We thanked them profusely, apologizing for any inconvenience we had caused.

Two or three days later the Most Rev. Father, wishing to reciprocate our visit and to meet with us, sent his *kawas* to N.D. de France. We were on an outing at the time. The next time the *kawas* came we were at home. The whole caravan gathered to receive our eminent visitor who came shortly afterwards.

On the eve of our departure for Egypt, the Rev. Fr. Vicar came to bring the good wishes of the Custodial President. He brought a Pilgrims' [19] Diploma of the Holy Land for each of us and a delightful little package containing souvenirs, a crucifix, rosaries in olive wood, images and oil of Gethsemane. Everywhere, in all the establishments where the caravan turned up, we were treated with the utmost courtesy.

The Lord guides everything. He prepared the moral foundation necessary for our establishment in Jerusalem.

III. *The purchases*

To the south-west of the city stretch waste-ground and delightful hills planted with olive trees, each slope suitable for cultivation and at the top, stone eminently suitable for building purposes. This was where we should buy and build. In fact, for a long time, this had been our aim.

Starting from the city the lay-out of the properties was [20] as follows: the Convent of the Greek Orthodox, an Englishwoman, another part of the Greek Convent and then a number of individual owners. Our plan of campaign was very simple; go for the four positions at the same time and should more than one become available to us, pick the most advantageous; in all this, anonymity was an indispensable condition of success. Fortunately, to confuse any unwelcome attempts at discovery, at the same time we also expressed interest, with a just the least whiff of mystery, in properties situated on the other side of Jerusalem and in different locations. This was enough to baffle the most curious.

Two intermediaries gave us invaluable help, Father Louis Heidet of the Latin Patriarchate and the Honorable [*effendi*] Bechara Habib, a Greek Catholic and Secretary-Interpreter of the Governor. Without them, the whole thing would have been impossible and our efforts in vain. Through his high position and his influence in official circles, Mr Bechara Habib was the best-placed [21] person to overcome difficulties. It was he, and he alone, who finalized all the contracts with the Government.

The first of the Greek properties, an immense olive-grove facing east, would have been an ideal location for a house of studies. It stretched from the Jewish colony of Montefiore right to the top of the hill and from the city to the railway station. It is there that the Ottoman Government wishes to relocate their Hall [*serai*] and France has bought a site for its Consulate. Unfortunately, it became clear early on that our efforts would be in vain. Besides the fact that the asking price was extremely high, at least 20 francs per square metre, it would have meant an interminable delay before a meeting of the Council could give its consent. Over such a period, how would it be possible to keep the matter secret?

The adjoining property, that of the English woman, a beautiful [22] rocky place of 8 hectares, with slopes to both east and south, was in no way inferior to those of her neighbours. But... this good lady, already aged, living in London, apparently in no financial need, was inflexible in her demand for the exorbitant sum of 25,000 pounds sterling.

We had to forget about the second Greek property for a number of reasons.

That left Number 4, a group of four properties linked together on a ridge with slopes north and south and a plateau in the middle, forming an absolutely ideal setting for a grand house in Jerusalem. As things were turning out, we were now situated a good half hour from the Holy Sepulchre, to take one important landmark. However, not having been sent to Jerusalem for the purposes of ministries or teaching, this inconvenience was not, in fact, of any great consequence to us. It had the added bonus of nearness to the railway station and being an excellent site.

[23] On the northern slope was Mrs Bagarry, the mother of Alphonse Bagarry, our alumnus from Beirut; to the south, a Greek Archimandrite called Joachim, the south-west a property in liquidation as a result of the bankruptcy of a German banker called

Frutiger; all the summit belonged singly to four individuals, an Englishman, an Armenian, a Latin from Jerusalem called Selim Méo and an American named Clark.

(*The other MS. adds*: This gives an idea of the speculation going on in this cosmopolitan country.)

Without the special assistance of Divine Providence, finalizing all purchases would have been impossible, especially as there were so many interested parties. Our work is that of the Pope, that is to say of God. The first condition for success is confidence.

Archimandrite Joachim wished to sell and we came to an agreement right away; he was in more of a hurry than we were. One of the joint-owners of the summit, an Englishman called Edwards jumped at the opportunity of [24] turning into cash a property that was not bringing him in anything. Mrs Bagarry was also ready to sell. As hers was the largest plot, four and a half hectares, there was a long discussion over the price. One unexpected event helped us. Rev. Fr. Fonck, Rector of the Biblical Institute, had chosen a Rome-based Maronite monk and Ottoman subject, Louis Ubaid as the legal owner in order to facilitate the purchase. The time had come to present the contracts to the Government. Archimandrite Joachim, who owned the best of all the properties, was getting impatient and threatened to withdraw. Fr. Louis Ubaid was therefore sent to Jerusalem. He saw Mrs Bagarry and as a Maronite, managed to get a reduction from her.

Everything was ready and on 4 February, 1914 Mr Bechara Habib brought the employees of Tabo - Tribunal of Sales - to the Convent of Archimandrite Joachim and the contract was legal-[25]ly passed. In order to avert suspicion, the Maronite monk was not present. This first purchase was inscribed in his name without difficulty. From that time on, it would be the same for all the others.

After leaving the Convent, everyone went to Mrs Bagarry's place for the same operation.

The following day it was the turn of the property of Edwards, the Englishman.

The day after that, Friday, 6 February, the civil servants went to the Tribunal, when everything was closed down and inscribed the contracts in the official registers and that same evening brought the title-deeds of the properties (*kouchans*) to Mr Bechara Habib.

For a number of reasons, the other negotiations were interrupted. The lot of the Armenian, co-owner of the summit, was acquired on July 23. The two last [26] co-owners, Méo and Clark had made it clear from the beginning that they did not wish to sell. This refusal was not perhaps definitive but even if it were, this would not have impeded our establishment. The important thing for us was to sink roots, obtain whatever was necessary and try to grow afterwards.

More important than that of Méo and Clark was the land involved in Frutiger's liquidation.

In June, the negotiations were nearing completion when the liquidator died. We had to wait for the nomination of his successor which depended on the German Consulate. After a few weeks he was named, the Chancellor of the German Consulate at Jaffa. A new difficulty arose which could only be dealt with in Jerusalem. It was necessary to get the signature of some Jew, who was linked in some way, about which I know nothing, in the liquidation.

One day, towards the end of July, Mr Bechara Habib [27] told me that everything would be completed that evening. In fact, that evening, all the interested parties turned up at the Tribunal, the German Consul, the Chancellor of Jaffa and the Jew.

The President opened his large book. [and: *crossed out*] We were surprised to learn that there was an irregularity with regard to the property in question, since it had already been sold ten years earlier to/with another and he had not paid the tax. Everything came to a halt. Before all sales, the arrears of tax must be paid, evidently by the former owners. Forthwith they were valued at 3,000 francs. As the property has to be sold, these gentlemen must deal with it. Settling the legal situation of the property required another preliminary operation. For this, the law required a deliberation of the municipal council. This would have passed without problem but that Ramadan, the month of fasting, arrived in the middle of everything when all work ceases, facilitating the official penance.

Thanks to the influence and dexterity of Mr Bechara Habib, all the Council members, [28] when contacted in their homes, responded favourably and the relevant requirements were finally satisfied.

On Monday, August 3rd, the Chancellor went back to Jaffa. Everything was ready when, at 3 p.m. the order for general mobilisation arrived at both French and German Consulates. This thunderbolt caused universal astonishment and shock. With the halt to all financial operations, the German bank to which Rome had sent the money in the name of the intermediary announced that it could not pay. This new delay, the most dangerous and perhaps permanent, threatened stalemate and perhaps the loss of our capital. And yet, there was no ill-will on any side. Everyone wanted a resolution of the affair as soon as possible. Finally, the principal sellers, in order not to discredit the German bank, were content with a paper settlement. It was simply a question of finding 6,000 francs for the immediate expenses. The Crédit Lyonnais could provide this and on Saturday, August 8, after [29] sundown, because of the Jew, everyone met at the house of the Honorable Bechara and the contract was signed. The following Sunday morning, the employees of Tabo brought us the title-deeds of the property (*kouchan*).

At that date, the total of the properties acquired formed a unit of a little more than 10 hectares. To complete the rectangle, we still need the parts that belong to Méo and Clark. There is reason to believe that after the crisis we will make that acquisition. In the meantime, we move to the legal partition.

Jerusalem, 4 October 1914

Alexis Mallon S.J.

Returning to Jerusalem after the war, on 4 December 1919, I found things just as I had left them at the time of our expulsion in December, 1914. The travelling material remained intact and had not suffered much damage. There is some [30] damage to Talbieh, the property near the railway station. The vineyard and trees which were on the south side have been rooted up and there is no sign of them. Two ancient tombs used by the Turks for a munitions dump have been bombed by the English after the occupation of the city. A tramway, constructed during the war for military purposes, crosses the south-west corner of the property. After making a loop over the hill, it then crosses the north-west corner. Since this line is no longer used and the rails taken up, the cloister wall that we have erected around the property cuts right across it. The central part is still occupied by the co-owners. The Tabo - office of property transactions - has not yet reopened. The new plan for the city envisages a large boulevard which will take up nearly the whole central part. We have no interest in buying the whole lot.

9 May 1920

Having set about rectifying all the registers of properties, [31] in August 1920, the new Government published an ordinance called "correction of registers". This ordinance makes it possible to register in the name of the real owner of a property, whether society, institute, school or convent, properties acquired in the time of the Turks and placed in the name of a third party. This was our situation as with most of the religious communities.

After having received from Rome the necessary procuration, I submitted the request for rectification to the Director of "Land Registries". He acknowledged right away the bona fides of our case and, anticipating no difficulties, told me that the rectification would be made. This proved correct. A few days afterwards, I received a dossier from him with the order to register, inviting me to come along to finalize the matter. On 27 April, 1921, I received the *"kouchans"* (title deeds to the property) in the name of the Pontifical Biblical Institute. The *"kouchans"* were written in Arabic but the registration in English under the title: "Pontifical Biblical Institute. Jesuit Fathers". I had only to pay [32] the chancellery fees, totalling 230 piastres. However, they took the opportunity of requesting the taxes (*werko*) that were outstanding since 1918, amounting to 377 piastres a year. In the whole affair, the English directors with whom I had to deal, were very friendly and did not bring up the least objection. This is evidence of the protection of the Sacred Heart who wishes that His Institute be established in Jerusalem.

29 April 1921

Note. The procuration made by Rev. Fr. Ubaid, former legal owner, to Fr. Nicolas, is in Tabo in the dossier of the Institute with the old *"kouchans"*.

[We now translate pp. 58-66 of the MS. The handwriting in the first part, dated May 9th, 1920, is that of a tired man; the ink is different, too.]

[58] Land on the Mount of Olives

During their voyage in 1912 [*should be* 1913] Rev. Fr. Fonck and Rev. Fr. Coët-losquet, former rector of the College of Boulogne and currently residing in Cairo, decided to buy a piece of ground situated on the west slope of the Mount of Olives, between the two paths that rise from the bridge of Gethsemane. A number of reasons swayed them. The other piece of ground, to the west of the city, was ideal for building purposes but it had no special sacred connotation. Since God had sent us to Jerusalem for His glory, it was in line with our devotion, and almost a duty, to acquire a place sanctified by the footsteps of Our Lord.

The Mount of Olives is one of the most sacred places of the Holy Land. Our Lord moved there in every sense. He rested there frequently with his apostles, just opposite the great city. And it is there that he instructed them and opened his Heart to them in intimate effusions.

[59] It was also Fr. Féderlin who encouraged Fr. Fonck to acquire the property about which we have spoken. He knew that the owners would sell willingly, in return for cash [*these last four words crossed out in pencil*]. The owners were Moslems. This was an added reason for taking away from infidels this patch of land so dear to our faith. Moreover, we learn from pilgrims [authors: *word crossed out*] of former times that the Mount of Olives was once covered with monasteries and convents and

that there was good reason to believe that on this hill we would [have: *crossed out*] find some precious shrine.

The purchase was therefore decided and the matter entrusted to the White Fathers at St Anne's. It was Brother Louis, well versed in such operations for a long time, who took the matter in hand.

There was a big problem. The land was a *waqf*, i.e. something sacred to the mosque, for the use of a Moslem family. Now, *waqf* land is inalienable. The law, however, permits an exchange with another equivalent property. It was up to us to buy the new property and then make the legal exchange.

The tenants of the *waqf* land asked for three houses in the city. After many difficulties, [60] three houses were bought in the name of Mr Emile Eddé of Beirut. He subsequently effected a regular procuration which he passed on to Brother Louis.

Everything was ready and it only remained to register the exchange legally when the war broke out. As a result, everything came to a halt.

After the war, things were at the same stage. However, we made use of the land as if it were our own and the owners did likewise with the houses.

A fourth house, bought in addition because of the complexities of such negotiations, will remain our property.

9 May 1920

As the Land Law was not published until October 1920, the affair could not be dealt with before that time. From the beginning the owners and the employees of the Tribunal declared that the former conditions could not be maintained because of the changes in the economic life of the country. They demanded the fourth house and pointed out that [61] the expenses and fees were very high. Should we give up because of a question of money? We thought not. The Sacred Heart who had given us all would repay us. I renewed the order to continue the operations. A new procuration by Mr Emile Eddé of Beirut was needed. It did not come until December 24. Everything was ready. The official request for exchange was drawn up in proper and due form by the Cadi and sent to the Government. After the new law, a written order from the Government was necessary for all transactions involving real estate.

All authorization required for proceeding with the affair was duly granted. The beneficiaries accepted our conditions. All that remained was the approbation regularizing the exchange. According to Moslem law, this approbation is given by the Cadi on receipt of a favourable report of a commission. A commission composed of ten members was appointed. It visited the places, [62] examined the houses and the site.

Under a number of influences which, in fact, amounted to nothing other than sheer blackmail, the majority of the Commission arrived at an over-valuation of the land, reaching 7,000 Egyptian pounds. We learned later that these gentlemen, if offered a good tip, would have been willing to alter their estimate and approve the exchange. The amount asked was however too much and Rev. Fr. Burtin preferred to bring a complaint to the Ministry of Justice.

The commission was dissolved and the Cadi was ordered to establish a new one. A number of new members were recommended to serve on this second commission. This was labour in vain since the Cadi (who in fact pulls all the strings), now humiliated, demanded that the new commission sustain the decision of the original one. He himself went around with the commission as they reassessed the estimates. In the publication of the report the value of the land was raised to 24,000 pounds against 8,000 for the houses. Some members of greater integrity refused to sign but the majority gave their approval.

[63] It became clear that there would be no end to the affair and that the Cadi, the real master of the situation, would not give in.

Time resolves many problems, especially in the East. We wait.

May 1921

1 September. As the end of the Muslim year was approaching (2 September), I decided to take up the matter with a view to bringing it to an end, one way or another. I asked the Cadi through one of his friends, Mr Bechara Habib, if he really wished to complete the exchange. At the same time, I had a letter to the same effect sent to him by the Secretariat of Justice. The Cadi replied in two ways, public and private, indicating that he was willing to approve the exchange on condition that we offer a new house in compensation for the surplus in the former estimates. He went so far as to say that he was prepared to inflate the price of the new house in order to arrive at a balance.

I pointed out that the four houses [64] that we offered were worth much more than the land. The houses brought in £200 a year while the land scarcely £15. These gentlemen agreed on that point, but said that the land had a historic value that had to be taken into account, - obviously a subterfuge. The nub of the question is that the Cadi is afraid of Muslim public opinion and, therefore, unwilling to back down on his original position.

In this situation I decided that it was not worth pursuing the affair. In agreement with the White Fathers we returned the land to the beneficiary, Denef, and we took possession of the houses for the new year (3 September). One problem is that Denef has already collected a part of the rent for the year. We will have to make him return it, if possible.

It only remained to regularize the situation with the houses. Armed with a regular procuration (in the name of Brother Louis) from Mr Emile Eddé of Beirut, I asked for a correction of the register in [65] favour of the Biblical Institute. My request was received at Tabo and sent, according to law, to the Courts. There, it was officially approved and I paid the correction fee, 1/2 per cent (T. P. 1,585). The documents will be sent to Tabo for registration.

12 December 1921. The documents have been returned to Tabo. I still had to pay taxes outstanding for three and half years (T. P. 4,983.5), otherwise the registration would have been put off indefinitely. The four houses were registered in the name of the Pontifical Biblical Institute. Of these four houses, one is outside the walls, near the Damascus Gate, opposite the Italian hospital and the three others are within the walls. All the documents of the transaction are at Tabo under number 996 (1921)

30 May 1922. One of the houses within the city has been sold. The other two are rented out.

[66] 15 September 1922. A second house has been sold. The third which is inside is rented out as is the one outside the walls.

20 January 1923. The house situated within the walls has been sold.

Ministries

While on a journey to Rome in Spring, 1920, Mgr. Louis Barlassina, Patriarch of Jerusalem, easily obtained written authorisation from Propaganda to bring Fathers of the Society of Jesus into his diocese for apostolic ministries. Very Rev. Fr. General agreed willingly to send at least one missionary immediately. This was a contribution to [33] the projected house. Moreover, in the original plan for this foundation, the presence of a missionary provided by the Lyons Province had been positively envisaged and hoped for. For, if the first aim of the annex at Jerusalem is to provide students from Rome with a practical complement to their biblical formation and to allow the Institute to have more ease of access to Palestinian sciences, a sacred ministry in a land where the Society had never before existed was never excluded from our horizons. Especially as we have always had in view the implementation of the project of St Ignatius himself to remain in Jerusalem and preach the Gospel.

And all of a sudden, these desires of our Blessed Founder seemed possible to achieve much sooner than we had thought and in an unexpected way.

In October, 1920, a missionary (Fr. Kozah) was sent from Beirut to Jerusalem and came to join me at St Peter of Zion. The Patriarch confided to him the spiritual direction of the Sisters of the Rosary, a small diocesan congregation for [34] for [*sic*] primary schools. During Lent, 1921 he was sent into Transjordan for the missions to Christian groups in that region.

20 August, 1921. Fr. Kozah left for Syria where he would stay until the end of September. At my request, during the last days of June, Fr. Bovier-Lapierre came to Jerusalem to begin organizing the Palestinian museum that we wished to found. Our research that year focused mainly on prehistory. Our aim was to explore the neighbourhood of Jerusalem and the surrounding regions that could be reached without carrying tents. Thanks to the experience and tenacity of Fr. Bovier-Lapierre, the results went far beyond my expectations. In two short months of exploration, we had gathered an abundant harvest of flint and discovered a number of stations as yet entirely unknown. This collection of flint will look very well in the museum and form the nucleus of the section on prehistory. The results of the campaign will, I hope, form the basis of a publication. [35] Besides the area immediately around Jerusalem, we have done research at Tantur, Bethlehem, Ramallah and El-Bireh, Djifneh, Abu-Gosh, and Koubeibe. All these places yielded their contribution of flint.

Fr. Bovier-Lapierre left for Cairo on 18 August, with the community of the College.

[We shall not translate here what goes from the end of this page 35 in the MS to the bottom of page 43 and which concerns the caravans, from the second to the fifth. However, we shall translate the following passages from pages 38 and 42.]

[38] During the summer months [1922] we continued, with Fr. Bovier-Lapierre, our research on prehistory in Palestine. We quickly visited Cremizan, Beit Djemal, Hebron, Taiebeh, Nablus and Nazareth. In all these places we discovered sites from the stone-age, hitherto unknown.

[42] This year [1924], I joined the [4th] caravan as far as Rome. I stayed three months at the Biblical Institute. On 6 February, I returned to Jerusalem. It had been decided that I would stay again at St Peter [of Ratisbonne]. For the moment, it was not appropriate to open a house of our own as there was no need of one. At St Peter's, the two or three rooms placed at our disposal were totally sufficient.

[44] 1925

Purchase of the new property for the construction of the house.

As the old property bought before the war was too far away from the city (2 km), there was no other alternative but to replace it with one closer. This entailed a double operation, choosing and buying a new site and selling the old one.

In July, 1924, Rev. Fr. O'Rourke was appointed Rector of the Biblical Institute at Rome. In August, I sent him a report on the situation and submitted the project. Fr. O'Rourke approved it, made it his own and immediately set about seeking the official approval of the Major Superiors, i.e. Fr. General. But before long he ran into multiple difficulties, the details of which, he alone knows.

V.R.Fr. General was on a journey to Spain at the time. When informed of the project, Rev. Fr. Vicar preferred to await the return of His Paternity.

On his return, Fr. General found quite [45] a complicated situation as a consequence of opposition surfacing against the project. He also judged it prudent to find out more about the Jerusalem situation.

At that period, October 1924, Rev. Fr. de Boynes, Assistant for France, was sent as Visitor to the Missions of Syria and Egypt. V.R.Fr. General asked him to go to Jerusalem and to bring him a report on the situation.

After his visit to Syria, Rev. Fr. de Boynes reached Jerusalem on 7 February, 1925 and stayed there until 12 February. Together we visited a number of sites.

I had already proposed to Rome the purchase of a plot of ground at Nikephorieh East, facing the Jaffa Gate in a plantation of olive trees belonging to the Greek Patriarch. Opposition to this choice arose at Rome.

After examining everything, Fr. de Boynes sent a detailed report to Rome. He, himself, approved entirely of the location chosen. However he proposed as a first option, the land at the Consulate of France that we had reason to believe was for sale and secondly, the contiguous site that I had chosen.

A letter from Fr. O'Rourke, dated March 22, informed me that the project had been approved and ordered me to buy the land from the French Consulate. I opened negotiations right away, through our intermediaries, in order not to compromise anything.

The request was received favourably at Jerusalem and transmitted to Paris. But in May, the Consulate informed us that the land was not for sale. Whatever the motive for this change of attitude, there was no point in insisting.

There was nothing for it now but to return to the contiguous property, located between the Consulate and the road to the railway station.

This land belonged to the Greek Orthodox Patriarchate [46] and could be acquired under slightly better conditions. Although it is less isolated, it is higher up. The location is the same. We could have the surface when we want. When made aware of what was happening, Fr. O'Rourke, after consulting Fr. de Boynes, agreed to the purchase of the property. We would take 9,000 pics. The order to buy was given to me in a letter dated 13 May, 1925. Negotiations were broached right away.

Towards the middle of June we reached an agreement. The price of the land, 9,000 square pics [*a pic is about 75 cm*], was fixed at £E 10,000 (ten thousand Egyptian pounds). At the time, the Greek Patriarch undertook a voyage to London for the festivities to commemorate the Council of Nicea. This held things up. On his return, the Financial Commission of the Patriarchate asked him to sign the act of sale. After further delays, the Patriarch signed on 22 August, the Octave of the Assumption. The establishment of the plan for the property occasioned other delays.

[47] A projected boulevard would run along the south side of the land. It was important to obtain from the Municipality and the Town Planning Commission an assurance that the boulevard would not be enlarged to our detriment.

At the same time as the purchase of the new place at Nikephorieh, I received the order from Rome to negotiate the sale of the old one bought before the war on the Malha road. After long and careful reflection, this property was considered to be unsuited to our purposes because it was too far away from the city (2 km from the Jaffa Gate). As a matter of fact, both for visiting monuments and celebrating Masses at the shrines, it is necessary that our house be as close to the Walls as possible. We have to make it easy for our young people who come to Jerusalem, not to study in their rooms but to examine the Holy Places and biblical sites up close.

Several offers were made by Jews, but I was not permitted to sell to them. Finally, towards the end of August, a Christian from Jerusalem made us [48] an offer as attractive as that of the Jews, 10 Egyptian piastres per square pic. I had been looking for eleven piastres for six months without success. As Rome agreed to the price offered, I concluded a contract with the buyer. The terms were that the sale and the payment must be made within at least a year from the signature of the contract.

This provisional contract was signed on 17 September.

5 October. As all the preparatory formalities had been fulfilled and the plan of the new property signed by all the neighbours, on 5 October, I signed the act of purchase in the name of the Pontifical Biblical Institute, after having paid the registration fee (3%) and paid the rest of the purchase (£E. 10,000) i.e. ten thousand Egyptian pounds.

On 18 October, the Feast of St Luke, Evangelist, Mgr. Barlassina, Latin Patriarch of Jerusalem, solemnly blessed and laid the first stone.

[49] The Governor of Jerusalem, Sir Ronald Storrs, and the Catholic Consuls attended the ceremony in the presence of representatives of all the communities and many Christians from the city. The ceremony was as follows: I gave a short talk while all present remained standing, "Veni Creator" intoned by the Patriarch, Litany of the Saints (during this time the witnesses signed the parchment), blessing of the stone, insertion of the parchment and medals in the stone. At the end, refreshments were served. I inserted the following medals: a silver medal of the Jubilee offered by Mgr. the Patriarch, a medal of the Sacred Heart and the Blessed Virgin, a medal of St Ignatius and a medal of St Theresa of the Child Jesus.

[added in smaller handwriting] The text of the formula on the parchment, inserted in the stone, is preserved in the archives.

6th caravan

The 6th caravan, leaving Beirut on 23 September, followed the traditional route, except for a few minor modifications, dictated by [50] circumstances. It re-embarked on 3 November at Alexandria on the "Lotus" of Messageries Maritimes. The group comprised:

- Rev. Fr. L. de Gonzague da Fonseca, S.J. Prof. at the Biblical Institute
- Fr. Joseph Pijoan, S.J.   Prov. Arag.
- Dr. Joseph Lengle   Rector Gymnasii, Freiburg

– .. Albert Bickel	Parochus ad S. Martinum
– .. Peter Ketter	Prof. of Holy Scripture at Trier
– .. Enrico Foschiani	Prof. of Holy Scripture at Udine
– Mr Henri Dubuc	Dir. Venezuelan Seminary
– .. Felix Henao, from Colombia	Law student at Rome.

I availed myself of the presence of the caravan for the blessing of the first stone. On that occasion Fr. da Fonseca was an invaluable help to me, placing his insights and dedication at my disposal. It was he who composed the Latin text written on the parchment and inserted in the stone.

On 29 December 1925 work began on the cistern in the new property.

[51] *1926*

January 26 1926, Rev. Fr. Marini, Minister-Procurator of the Biblical Institute, arrived in Jerusalem to finalize preparations, the plan and contract, for the building of the new house and to oversee the work.

Monday 22 March, I signed the official sale of the first plot of the old property and lodged the proceeds.

April 8, as the plan and the outright price had been approved by Rome, we entrusted the work to the architect-builders of the Farro firm.

April 24, work began with the levelling of the ground. The builders hope that the construction will be finished by January or February, 1927.

May 4, I sent a request to the Government, recommended by Mgr. Kean, V.G., in order to obtain an official declaration recognising that we are entitled to the usual privileges of religious houses (especially, exemption from taxes and customs duties). This declaration from the General Secretariat was sent to me on 11 May following. It is now in the archives.

[Pages 52 and 53, about the 7ᵗʰ caravan and some guests, will not be translated here.]

[54] 1ˢᵗ July [1927]. First Friday of the month. Under the auspices of the Sacred Heart, we took up definitive residence in the new house. It will be dedicated to St Ignatius in memory of the voyage to Jerusalem of our Blessed Father and his vow to remain here. The chapel will also be dedicated to St Ignatius. This is our wish but in order that the dedication should be made definitive we need the approbation of Rome. In the meantime, we wait.

16 July. This evening three new guests arrive, Fr. Arconada, Prov. Legion., Fr. Willmering, Prov. [Missour.] and Fr. Francis Keenan, professor of Holy Scripture at the diocesan seminary at Boston.

15 August. Fr. Al. Mallon, appointed Superior of the house at Jerusalem by a decree of V.R.Fr. General on 30 July, took up his post on this day.

[The MS does not mention the earthquake of July 11ᵗʰ, 1927. The end of page 54 in the MS and page 55 concerning the 8ᵗʰ caravan will not be translated here, nor will the beginning of page 56.]

[56] Project for the Renting of the House by the Government (August-December 1927)

Towards the end of August, 1927, the Governor of Jerusalem, Mr Edward Keith-Roach, accompanied by his assistant, Ruhi-bey Abd-ul-Hadi, came to the house and asked if would be possible to rent the building to the Government for the Residence of the High Commission, until such times as a special edifice should be built for that purpose. The old residence, the palace of the Empress Augusta-Victoria at Scopus, had been rendered uninhabitable by the earthquake in July and no other habitation suitable for the needs of the High Commission could be found.

[57] The renting of our house was presented as a public service that we might render to the country. We expressed our objections, showing that we needed the house for our work. They replied that it would be possible for us to continue our work in another smaller location for a short period of two or three years and as they insisted on the necessity of finding accommodation for the High Commission, we told them that the matter would have to be referred to Rome. In the meantime, Lord and Lady Plumer visited the house.

Satisfied with his visit, Lord Plumer sent us a personally written request and sent a similar request to V.R.Fr. General and to Rev. Fr. Rector. Because of the pontifical dimension of the house, the request was forwarded to the Holy See. By a letter dated 14 October 1927, Cardinal Gasparri replied that the Sovereign Pontiff willingly gave permission for Lord Plumer to rent the Biblical Institute at Jerusalem.

So negotiations for the contract began. Naturally the conditions of this contract fixed at Jerusalem had to be sent to Rome and could not be accepted until given definitive approval there. It was necessary to allow for delays.

(Continues on p. 68.)

[68] (Continuation of page 57)

At the same time, it was necessary to send the outline of the principal modifications to be made on the house. It was now mid-November. Winter was approaching and the Government of Jerusalem was anxious to complete the negotiations in order to prepare for the installation of the High Commission before the rains. They insisted on having the contract signed right away at Jerusalem without recourse to Rome. But the orders were clear-cut and nothing happened. After losing another ten days or so, the Governor decided to send the sought-for requirements to Rome, indicating his wish to have an immediate reply by telegram. Rome waited for advice from Jerusalem, which contained a number of restrictions and required a new formula for the contract. The one sent to Rome by the Government had been drawn up without our approval and was not acceptable to us. We wanted, above all, to insist on the clause that the rent would only be for two years, in conformity with the decision of Rome.

[69] All this was communicated to the Government at Jerusalem by Rev. Fr. Rector. It was now mid-December. It was then that the Government sent a final telegram to Rome. This indicated that as they were under pressure to find a residence right away for the High Commission they were giving up renting the house and consequently were withdrawing their request. At Jerusalem, the break-up happened without incident. Negotiations had, in fact, been suspended since the middle of November.

*   *   *   *   *

Doc. J. I,2

APIBR B-VI (VI-1A)

(Manuscript page in Fr. Fonck's handwriting, translated from the French)

+

Orient fac.   19.1.[19]11   R. P. Foujols (and Séb. Ronzevalle)

1) The or. fac. will continue with its courses, its publications and promoting candidates to the degree of doctor in or. lang.

2) The lectures will give higher and complementary instruction to the instruction at the Biblical Institute, especially in the following subjects: a) literary Arabic; b) colloquial Ar.; c) orient. geog. and top.; d) special questions in hist. and orient. arch.; e) Sem. epigr.; f) bibl. natural sciences; g) or. ethnol. (with study of customs etc.). The programme could be deleveped and completed later on.

3) A programme for these courses will be published in time for the year 1911/12.

4) The lectures will go from the beginning of Nov. to the end of March. The rest of the school year is set aside for voy., the pract. st. of the country and the prep. for exams.

5). The conditions for obtaining the OF dipl. will be set down later, studies done by candidates at the B. I. being taken into account. But it remains understood that other candidates, who have not attended any lectures at the BI., may also be admitted.

6) The exchange of prof. between the OF and the BI will be mutual, so that the OF and the BI help each other according to need, both for courses and for journeys.

7) As regards publications, too, cooperation will be mutual, keeping the biblical character of the scient. publ. of the BI in first place and directly and the orient. char. of those of the OF in first place and directly; indirectly, there will always be for the other complementary element [*sic*].

These are, in outline, the two great common institutions. It seems to me that the two complement each other well and each will gain by them A. M. D. G.

* * * * *

Doc. J. I,3

APIBR B-VI (VI-1)

(Five typewritten, unsigned pages, translated from the French)

Beirut Oriental Faculty

On September 11th, 1911, the Rev. Fr. Superior of the Mission in Syria, the Rev. Fr. Rector of St. Joseph's University in Beirut, the Rev. Fr. Fonck, Rector of the Biblical Institute in Rome, and Fr. Cattin, Chancellor of the Medical Faculty in Beirut met to examine certain points concerning the oriental Faculty and expressed a favourable opinion on the following points:

1. Organization of the Oriental Faculty

1° As regards common life, meals, recreation, spiritual duties, it would be part of St. Joseph's University and would follow its regulations.

2° As regards religious discipline it would be placed under the Authority of the Rev. Fr. Rector of the University, the Rev. Fr. Superior of the Mission of Syria and the Rev. Fr. Provincial of the Lyons Province.

3° The price that each member of the faculty would have to pay to the University would be 1,000 francs a year. (If by common agreement the Rev. Fr. Provincial of the Lyons Province and the Rev. Fr. Rector of the Biblical Institute judged that, circumstances having changed, the cost of bed and board had to be raised, it could be raised.) – Stamps for letters and parcels of books sent by the Faculty would be debited to the Biblical Institute as would office supplies and journeys.

3° bis Students at the Faculty not belonging to the Society would also pay 1,000 francs for bed and board at the University which, however, would not have to clothe them.

4° The financial administration of the Faculty would in no way depend on the Rector of the University or the Superior of the Mission, but it would depend on the Rev. Fr. General Treasurer of the Society who would do it on the spot by a local proxy of the Faculty.

5° Directing studies, teaching, academic work and publications would depend directly on the Very Reverend Fr. General of the Society and the Rector of the Biblical Institute.

6° The Faculty would have its Minister, distinct from the University's Minister, and its Librarian, distinct from the University's Librarian, chosen from the staff of the Oriental Faculty.

7° The Students of the Oriental Faculty would have their refectory apart, and, as far as possible, on the premises of the Faculty.

II. Its buildings

1° Situation [a plan of the University campus is drawn in ink here]

2° Plan A, which consists in buying the Tabets' house with the courtyard and setting up the Oriental Faculty there would be preferable and should be adopted if this house and courtyard do not cost too much.

3° Project C, that is to say, buying the Tabets' house with or without the courtyard and transferring the Arts and Crafts department there and building the Faculty on site C, would come second. The Faculty would be nearer the Press.

4° Plan B, that is to say buying the Tabets' house, installing the Arts and Crafts there and building the Oriental Faculty's premises on B, does not seem favourable.

III. Academic work

1° Purpose: to pursue oriental linguistic, historical, geographical, archaeological, epigraphic studies, etc., and, by means of practical courses (to the exclusion of theoretical courses) and by directing studies and the preparation of theses, to provide a complement to the somewhat elementary and theoretical instruction at the Biblical Institute.

2° Means: a) practical courses, in conformity with higher education, on special questions noted above in N° 1.

b. Guidance given to students especially in the preparation of a learned thesis and in their personal work.

c. Co-operation with the Biblical Institute's publications.

d. Scholarly research and journeys in the country; directing excavations.

e. Learned oriental publications (as distinct from biblical publications reserved to the Institute).

f. Public lectures.

N. B. Al-Mashriq would not deal with higher theoretical learning but only with the practical fields of learning and with popularizing them.

3° Students. a) Students sent by the Biblical Institute (the Biennists) to complement their studies.

b) Other students asking to do special tasks or to further their knowledge in the subjects mentioned.

N. B. Never accept beginners.

c) Beginners must be referred to the Biblical Institute in Rome.

4° Admission (Conditions of admission)

The following will be admitted: a) All those presented by the Biblical Institute.

b) An official certificate from a University accompanying a particular letter of introduction from a Professor of some standing and the approval of the local bishop.

c) Lay students will not be admitted as boarders.

N.B. Whether non-catholics could be admitted will have to be discussed: the Committee did not give a firm and unanimous opinion on this matter.

Oriental library

1° Ownership of the or. Library rests entirely with the University. - 2° Access to the Library and using the books that are there will have to be made as easy as possible both for the Fathers at the University and to the Fathers at the Oriental Faculty. – 3° The library will be installed in the new building of the oriental Faculty. (The Rector of the University believes that, 'without great inconvenience', it could stay on the premises of the University itself, to which it belongs. He prefers this course.)

4° Library expenses will be covered by the Biblical Institute.

5° All contributions made to this library will be the property of the University.

[*signed*] Paul Mattern S. J.
[*Superior of the Mission in Syria*]

* * * * *

Doc. J. I,4

ASAJ
(*Translated from the French*)

Africa Missions
(White Fathers)
St. Anne's in Jerusalem
[*added in pencil*:] to Fr. Cattin

Jerusalem, 15.9.1911
Confidential

Very Reverend and Dear Father,

Although I am fairly busy I think that I will be doing something you will like by hastily sending a few words about Fr. Fonck and his very rapid visit. The Father leaves for Egypt tomorrow morning, Saturday, on Lloyds.

Having arrived on the evening of Wednesday, the 13th he went to Mgr. Camassei's residence on Thursday morning. Very well received by His Excellency. Mgr. Camassei, busy with the priests' conference, gave him an appointment in the evening so that he could see him for longer. – The Father then went to see the Custodian – a tame reception according to what the Father told me. – From there the Father went to St. Stephen's where he met Fr. Lagrange. Altogether things went well. – I do not think I am lacking in discretion in giving you this small summary which I believe to be true.

On the Wednesday evening I thought fit [2] to tell the Father straight that an establishment here was necessary as soon as possible in the interest of the Biblical Institute. – I offered to accompany him around Jerusalem in the afternoon so that he could have at least a general idea of the places that might be suitable. – I pointed out and showed him round the plots of land still available on the western slope of the Mount of Olives, then we turned north-east and west. – The Father will be able to think it over and inform his superiors.

I accompanied the Father as far as the door of the Patriarchate where the Father was kept until 7[h] ½. In the morning the Father was able to say mass at the Holy Sepulchre, in spite of the presence of the pilgrims from [*two illegible words*]. Today the Father did some shopping and paid some visits. About 5[h] Mgr. the Patriarch came to St. Anne's to see the Father and hand him some letters for the Holy Father and the Card. Secret. of State. Mgr. Camassei told me that during the day Fr. Lagrange had gone to see him. Fr. Lagrange very categorical-[3]ly asked some questions of which the purpose was to inform him [to be: *word crossed out and corrected*] about the plans for the establishment. – Fr. Fonck had never spoken about Carmel in his visit to St. Stephen's. – Fr. Lagrange guessed about Carmel. – He really wanted to know what would come after Carmel. Mgr. Camassei, who knew no more about it, left Fr. Lagrange to his suppositions. The Prior of St. Stephen's having asked whether the Holy See approved, the Patriarch said that the approval was clear.

Fr. Fonck met Mgr. Camassei when he was coming back from St. Anne's and the Patriarch told him about the interview with Fr. Lagrange.

For my part, I did not think I had to be on my guard with Mgr. the Patriarch and, without revealing anything, I told Mgr. Camassei that in my opinion there was need of an annex for the Biblical Institute in Jerusalem. Fr. Fonck is very pleased with his relations with the excellent Mgr. Camassei.

Fr. Fonck is leaving tomorrow morning; as the Patriarch said, he will have passed like a flash of lightening. – I expect Fr. Lagrange will pay a visit to Fr. Fonck … when the latter will be in Jaffa. I also expect that [4] Fr. Lagrange is trying to find out something; he will have all his trouble for nothing.

In my humble opinion the Society of Jesus has been entrusted with an extraordinarily important institution for the good of the Church. This institution really needs a complementary one in Jerusalem if it is not to find itself in a state of inadequacy with regard to the purpose to be achieved. It is not a question of similar institutions arising from the initiative of two religious Societies and hence there is no reason for taking sensitivities into account which, if given too much prominence, would to a great extent be likely to paralyse an institution that concerns the whole Church. – An establishment in Jerusalem will be just as unwelcome to the Dominican School in two or three years as it would be today. Better not delay, then, and not run the risk of having intrigues formed which would make an establishment needed right now difficult later on: the Pontifical Institute.

You will forgive me, Very Reverend and Dear Father, for the disconnected nature of a letter, written at night and in a hurry. If I can be of [*in the left margin*:] any use to your Fathers, you know that you can count on my entire devotion.

Please say some prayers for me,

Ever yours most affectionately in our Lord,

L[ouis]. Féderlin

* * * * *

Doc. J. I,5

ASAJ

(*Translated from the French*)

Istituto Biblico Pontificio
Piazza Pilotta
Roma
22 May 1912

Sub Secreto

Reverend and Dear Father [*added in pencil*:] (Cré)

Pax Christi

At last I can send you the letter that has been promised and thought over for so long. Please pardon me if my silence has been too long.

The Reverend Fr. Puretin [*correction in pencil*: Burtin], your Procurator General here, has just informed me that the Reverend Fr. Féderlin cannot yet return to Jerusalem due to the state of his health. I am therefore having recourse to your charity and to that of your excellent Brother Louis [Fournier] to ask for your help in a matter of the greatest importance which absolutely requires the greatest discretion. I come to you in the name of the Holy Father himself and at his express command. The Sovereign Pontiff is himself as interested as possible in the complete success of this matter. He regards it as having supreme importance for the whole Church. I do not therefore have to give you any motives for calling forth your charity.

It is a question of finding and acquiring the necessary and useful land in Jerusalem for the branch of this Pontifical Biblical Institute. It is now a thing decided on and willed by the Sovereign Pontiff. I also already have all the funds ready for the purchase. And I am glad to be able to tell you that I am authorized to buy two plots of land: one on the Mount of Olives, which you know; the other in the district near the railway station and the new French Consulate. The latter seemed to the competent judges to be more suitable for the construction of the building for the branch; but the former is of such exceptional importance that it seems very useful to gain possession of it for the Institute.

You will no doubt ask to know how big the plots of land to be bought should be. I think that will depend somewhat on the right [2] opportunity that presents itself and on the needs of our branch. If it is possible to have all the land on the Mount of Olives lying between the two paths I would prefer to purchase the whole upper and lower part. As for the other plot in the district of the railway station, this, it seems to me, should be taken into consideration: we need 1° land for building a suitable house for about thirty people on, with a chapel, possibly open to the public, dining room, library, museum, hall for meetings and lectures, enough private rooms and places for general use; 2° a suitable and large enough garden; 3° possibly two courtyards with cloisters inside.

To give you a clearer idea of my thinking, I am adding a small, quite simple and rough sketch. Supposing that the land is rectangular, it seems we would need about 4,000 square metres on which we could build our house, either along the general lines of the plan in the sketch (the rooms would all be on the first floor; the library above the chapel, no second floor), or in some other way. If the land is not regular in shape it would be necessary to adapt the building to conditions on the site.

The house would be called "Sacred Heart House"; it would be placed under French protectorate. But on all these matters we must, for the moment, until everything is finished, keep the strictest secrecy. Please tell me if my presence in Jerusalem is necessary for the conclusion of this matter. As regards sending the needed funds, I think I could do it perfectly safely through the Crédit Lyonnais, addressed to you. Hoping that the month of the Sacred Heart will crown your efforts with every success. Give my kind regards to the excellent Brother Louis. [*handwritten addition:*] In caritate X^t Yours sincerely

L. Fonck, S. J.

[As an attachment, the sketch of the plan, drawn by L. Fonck: a plot 80 m. × 50 m., the façade of the building fronting the street being 60 m. long, the chapel being in the centre; cf. following page]

* * * * *

Doc. J. I,6

ASAJ
(Translated from the French)

Istituto Biblico Pontificio

Reverend and Dear Father Superior [Féderlin]

P. X.

Very many thanks for all you have done and are doing.

Yes, I shall be coming myself, and soon. In accordance with V. R. Fr. General's decision I shall be leaving from Naples on Friday, March 14th, and I hope to be in Jerusalem on Holy Thursday the 20th, in the evening. To avoid unnecessary difficulties as far as possible I will stay with the Director of the Austrian Catholic Hospice, from which I will not have far to go to get to St. Anne's. I will stay until the 30th of March, so we will have enough time to discuss and decide on necessary matters. I will be bringing a new letter from the Holy See with me to recommend the matter to the authorities.

From among the 10 or 12 sites our choice will stay limited to n°s 1, 2 and 10: perhaps n° 5 (and 11: Former German Catholic hospice ?) will not be altogether beyond consideration. N° 2 is also generally preferred by us and our Superiors. But it needs to be looked at closer and decided on the spot.

If you have anything to communicate to me before my arrival you could write to me at Alexandria, St. Francis Xavier's College where I will be passing through on the

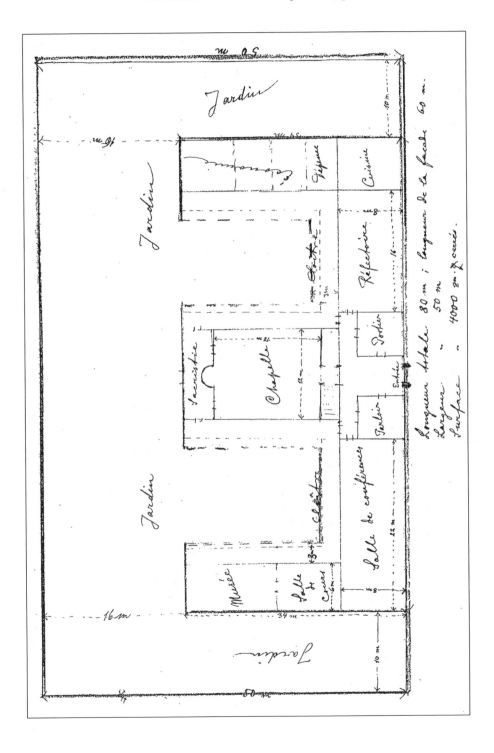

Monday of Holy Week. I will try to see Mr Eddé to get him to come to Jerusalem when it is time to transform [correction for transfer] provisional to permanent ownership.

I hope you received the dispatch of the remaining sum that was to reach you from Berlin, immediately after your telegram.

See you soon! United in prayer and holy sacrifices
in caritate X^i

R. V. infimus servus
Leop. Fonck, S. J.

6 March [19]13

* * * * *

Doc. J. I,7

APIBR B-VI (VI-1A)

(Copy in Fr. Fonck's handwriting, translated from the Italian)

Secretariate of State
of His Holiness

From the Vatican 26 August 1911

n° 52353

Most Rev. Excellency

The purpose of the Pontifical Biblical Institute, founded by His Holiness Pope Pius X, makes it almost indispensable to found a subsidiary house of the same Institute in Palestinian territory, and through the generosity of outstanding benefactors the means necessary for this foundation are already to hand.

Considering, therefore, all the circumstances, Mount Carmel has, for reasons of prudence, been fixed upon as the site of the abovementioned subsidiary House, but with the possibility of a better choice always being left open.

To this end the Rev. Prof. Leopold Fonck, S. J., President of the aforementioned Biblical Institute, is going there, with the approval of the Holy See, to prepare the inauguration of the new House in Palestine.

I am therefore introducing him to Your Excellency and warmly recommend him to you so that you will kindly favour him with your effective protection and facilitate, as far as you can, such a praiseworthy undertaking for him, which corresponds in a particular way with the wishes and desires of the Holy Father.

Thanking you in anticipation for this, I take the opportunity of the meeting to reaffirm my feelings of sincere esteem
for Your Most Rev. Excellence

Servitor vero
/pr.p./R. Card. Merry del Val

Mons. Filippo Camassei
Patriarch of Jerusalem

* * * * *

Doc. J. I,8

ALPJ (Q/89)

(The letter is here translated from the Italian, and the Memoir from the French.)

Pontifical Biblical Institute
Piazza Pilotta
Rome

Very Reverend Excellency
14 Oct. [19]12

When last year I had the honour of conveying a letter to Your Excellency from the Most Eminent Cardinal Secretary of State of His Holiness, relating to the foundation of a branch of this Institute, the Holy See's intention was primarily centered on Mount Carmel as the place of that foundation. As is known to Your Excellency, I, for my part, made every possible effort to carry out the Holy See's project in the said place.

For reasons entirely independent of my will or by disposition of the Holy See I have had to give up that plan at the request of the Reverend Carmelite Fathers. The Supreme Pontiff, after this necessary change in the plan, has decided and arranged that the branch of the Pontifical Biblical Institute be erected, in the name of the Holy See, in Jerusalem.

Having now, by express order of the Supreme Pontiff, to prepare the erection of this branch, I have begun negotiations for the purchase of a suitable plot of land. So in order more securely to obtain the fruit and achieve the aim the Holy See expects from a foundation like this it needs to be placed right from the beginning under the protection of one the great western powers.

To this end the Holy See is turning its eyes to France in the first place. If the representatives of the French government wish to assume, in an effective way, the protection of the new enterprise which has to take shape in Jerusalem, it will be placed right from the beginning under the protectorate of France.

Last June His Holiness, Our Lord Pius X, with the agreement of His Eminence the Cardinal Secretary of State, had authorized me, at the right time and through Your Excellency's mediation, to approach the French Consul General in Jerusalem with a view to asking him if his government wished to take the branch of the Pontifical Biblical Institute, to be built in Jerusalem, under its protection, providing effective implementation of the protectorate.

At yesterday's audience His Holiness again confirmed this authorization on me and ordered me to write to Your Excellency with this in mind. It is therefore the will of the Holy Father that Your Excellency ask the French Consul General in Jerusalem whether the French government wishes to take the future branch of the Pontifical Biblical Institute under its protection, providing effective implementation of the protectorate.

In an enclosed aide-mémoire I briefly expound the reasons why the Holy See has decided to found this branch.

Indicating to Y. E. the Supreme Pontiff's revered orders I am very pleased to take the opportunity to restate that I am

Your Most Rev[nd] Excellency's humble servant in X[t]

Leop. Fonck, S. J.

MEMOIR ON THE ERECTION OF A BRANCH OF
THE PONTIFICAL BIBLICAL INSTITUTE IN PALESTINE

1. The aim sought by the Holy See in the foundation of the Pontifical Biblical Institute in Rome requires the erection of a branch of the Institute in Palestine as a necessary complement.

Here are three decisive reasons for it: a) First of all professors at the Institute and those preparing to be professors later on must find a post in the Holy Land for making immediate contact with the countries and people of the East and its natural, social and religious conditions, and to round off their practical knowledge of oriental languages. - b) Students at the Institute must then have all the desirable facilities and the necessary facilities for a journey to, or a prolonged stay in the Holy Land, as provided for in the Institute's program. - c) Lastly, the Institute must have a central post in the biblical lands for the scholarly research and excavations to be undertaken.

For these reasons the Institute must necessarily try to found a branch house in Palestine. As a Pontifical Institute it cannot, to implement the essential points of its program, be dependent on any other religious establishment already set up in the Holy Land.

2. The Sovereign Pontiff, fully approving of these reasons, has charged the President of the Institute with preparing the erection of a Palestinian branch of the Institute to be done in the name of the Holy See.

Obeying the orders of His Holiness and bearing a letter from the Most Eminent Cardinal Secretary of State to His Excellency the Latin Patriarch of Jerusalem, the President of the Institute went in September 1911 to Palestine to look for the necessary information there on the spot. In accordance with the intentions of the Holy See, he first looked for a place for the branch on Mount Carmel, so as not to arouse the sensitivities of the other religious establishments in Jerusalem. Following the advice of the Rev. Fr. Brocard, a French Carmelite, and of his brethren on Mount Carmel, and accompanied by the Rev. Fr. Corbinien from the same convent, he visited the German Consul in Haifa who had already been pointed out to him by the Rev. Carmelite Fathers as the only person capable of giving him the necessary information about a house being considered as the branch.

All the Carmelite Fathers he met either at the monastery on Mount Carmel or in the Carmelite convent in the city of Haifa were not only very kind but also very glad and delighted at the establishment of the branch that was planned for the neighbourhood of the monastery on the heights of Mount Carmel.

3. With this impression and regarding the establishment of the branch on Mount Carmel as very likely and almost certain, the President of the Institute then visited Beirut and Jerusalem, where he handed the letter from His Eminence the Cardinal Secretary of State to Mgr. the Patriarch Camassei. He also communicated the plan for the erection of a branch of the Pontifical Biblical Institute to the Most Reverend Father Custodian of the Holy Land as well as to the Very Reverend Father Lagrange at St. Stephen's.

4. Returning to Rome on September 26th, 1911, he gave an account of his journey to the Sovereign Pontiff and the Cardinal Secretary of State, still considering the location of the projected branch on Mount Carmel as practically certain.

5. It was a real and very great surprise to him when he was informed some weeks later first of all of a complaint made against him because of his visit to the German

Consul at Haifa – in his very rapid passage in the Orient he had not had the pleasure of seeing any other Consul – as if he had wanted to place the branch of the Institute under German protectorate. However the reply to this accusation was very simple: it was an absolutely gratuitous invention without the slightest objective foundation in reality. The question of the protectorate for the branch of a Pontifical Institute to be established in the name of the Holy See depended exclusively on the Holy See itself, and in 1911 the President of the Institute had not received the slightest instruction on this point.

6. The other point, no less surprising but more serious, was the request presented to the President of the Institute in an official visit, in the name of their Very Rev. Father General, from two Carmelite Fathers, Rev. Fr. Cyrille, then Vicar Provincial of Mount Carmel – who had been away from Carmel at the time of the visit in September 1911 – and the Rev. Fr. Clément, the Order's Assistant in Rome, who entreated the President to be so good as not to insist on the choice of Mount Carmel as the place to put the Institute's planned branch.

But this request, too, left no doubt about the answer to be given: one could barely think about an establishment on Mount Carmel against the so officially expressed will of the Rev. Carmelite Fathers. The first plan had to be abandoned and one had to go elsewhere.

7. But where was one to choose another spot? After collecting suitable information from many sides, from the most competent persons in different religious orders and the secular clergy, and after long deliberations the Holy See decided to choose Jerusalem as the new place for the Biblical Institute's branch. The decisive reasons for this choice were especially the central position of the Holy City and the need for the Institute to enter into living and immediate contact with the scholarly movement in the centre of the biblical lands.

8. As for the question of the protectorate, the Holy See wanted to take the French protectorate into consideration first of all, if the French government actually wishes to grant the new Establishment its protection and guarantee its effective implementation.

Rome, 14 October 1912

[*sign.*] Leopold Fonck, S. J.
President of the Pontifical Biblical Institute

*   *   *   *   *

Doc. J. I,9

APIBR B-VI (VI-1A)
(*Translated from the French*)

French General Consul
In Palestine
Jerusalem, 26 November 1912

Monsignor,

In a telegram bearing today's date which I have just received the Ambassador instructs me to let Your Excellency know that the Government of the Republic has decided to grant its protection to the future Pontifical Biblical Institute.

I hasten to inform Your Excellency of this, being pleased to tell you again that, while I assure you of my great esteem, I am,
Yours sincerely,

G. Gueyrand

* * * * *

Doc. J. I,10

APIBR B-VI (VI-1A)

(*Translated from the Italian*)

To His Most Rev. Excellency
Monsignor Filippo Camassei
Patriarch of Jerusalem

Secretary of State
to His Holiness

From the Vatican 8 March 1913

n° 62922

Most Reverend Excellency

Your Most Rev. Excellency will recall how in 1911, on the occasion of the visit that the Very Rev. Leopold Fonck, S. J., President of the Pontifical Biblical Institute, paid to the Holy Land, on sheet N. 52353 I informed you that the Holy Father had expressed the wish that a Subsidiary House of the same Institute be founded within the confines of Palestine.

Mount Carmel had been taken into consideration as a possibility, as being a suitable place for that House.

But, the accomplishment of that plan not being possible, on Carmel, the Holy Father now considers that it is fitting to erect the said House in Jerusalem where, for the purpose of necessary preparations, the abovementioned President is again going, with the consent of the Holy See.

In keeping with the above, your Excellency will kindly be so good as to give the Rev. Father Fonck your effective assistance so as to facilitate his work there, as far as is possible for you.

I very gladly take this opportunity to assure you once again of the high esteem with which I renew my being
           Your Most Rev. Excellency's
                   Servant

/*sign.*/ R. Card. Merry del Val

Copy made at
Alexandria 18-3-1913
L. Fonck, S. J.

* * * * *

Doc. J. I,11

APIBR B-VI (VI-1A)

(*Translated from the Italian*)

Rev. and Dear Father Rector [A. Fernández]

P. X.

Thank you for the letter of May 26th.

1. With regard to the house in Jerusalem, here are a few points. Pope Pius X, to his great consolation, accepted the foundation for the said house that was made by Miss Jeanne du Coëtlosquet with a million francs; moreover, the same Sovereign Pontiff, in 1911 and 1913, gave me one of his letters, signed by the Most Eminent Card. Secretary of State, addressed to the Most Illustrious and Most Rev. Patriarch of Jerusalem, Filippo Camassei, in which letters the Holy Father warmly recommended the foundation of our house to the said Patriarch, for the building of which house on Mount Carmel efforts were made in 1911 and then, given the opposition of the Rev. Carmelite Fathers, by the Pope's decision it was proposed [decided : *word crossed out*] to build in Jerusalem. Of these two letters I have made a copy, with a typewriter, and those copies should be among my papers. The one from 1913 would be the more important.

2. When His Holiness Pope Benedict XV received me in audience the first time, in September 1914, he asked me for information about the house in Jerusalem, saying that others had told him that we wanted to erect a "counter-altar" against the École Biblique at St. Stephen's. I briefly expounded to His Holiness the reasons why Pius X had decided on our foundation and the purpose of that house. And His Holiness deigned fully to approve of those reasons and that purpose, telling me expressly: "Yes, I, too, want that".

3. Among these reasons the following seem to me more important: a) The Pontifical Biblical Institute must have a residence of its own in Jerusalem for its Professors and for Students when they are on study tours or when they want to stay for some time in the centre of the Holy Land to do research or special studies. It is practically almost impossible to achieve the purpose of these journeys and this stay in the country without a proper residence, which is also fitting for the dignity of the Institute and is necessary to secure the purity and integrity of our students' learning. – b) For our study tours and our scholarly research we need a modest library and all the necessary equipment, which we cannot leave in anyone else's house. – c) Our study tours form an indispensable complement to the theoretical teaching given to the students at the Institute. We cannot entrust that complement to the care of others, nor can we depend on others to provide that complement. – d) Back in 1909 or 1910, immediately after the foundation of the Institute, a journal opposed to us (in Belgium) wrote that the Biblical Institute in Rome would always be inferior to the biblical schools in the Holy Land because it does not have living, close and permanent contact with the Holy Land. [*sic*: the number of that journal is also among my papers.] – e) If it may be hoped that the future, in Palestine, will give greater freedom for excavations, etc., our Institute must not be excluded from taking an active and effective part in such work, given the <u>primary</u> purpose of the Institute, and the supreme authority in the scholarly world that is generally acquired with such work. – f) If in the future, as I hope, there is also added to the theoretical part of our teaching a section on the <u>practical interpreta-</u>

tion of Holy Scripture for the benefit of the Clergy of the whole Church, for preaching and biblical teaching in primary and secondary schools, an indispensable complement to this practical teaching will also be a stay in Jerusalem with the right kind of excursions; and it cannot be done without our house.

I hope that His Eminence Card. van Rossum will understand the importance of the question and will come to our defence.

Your Reverence will have received the article and my last postcard, sent on the 23rd and 24th of May.

At least as far as I know, the post is now accepting <u>direct</u> correspondence from Rome for Germany and Austria, so they can write without going through me.

I commend myself to your holy sacrifices. In caritate X^i

Zurich 1 Leonhardstr.12   Your humble servant in X°
4 May [*sic, for*: June 19]19   L. Fonck, S. J.

* * * * *

Doc. J. I,12

ASEJ

(*Extract from* H. VINCENT, *Le T. R. P. Marie-Joseph Lagrange, sa vie, son œuvre. Manuscript, towards the end of chapter VI: The return and the World War. Translated from the French*)

Rome, May 11th, 1919 – To his Excellency Mgr. Bonv. CERRETTI. –
Excellency, To satisfy the request that Your Excellency made of me at the time of the interview that was granted me last Saturday, May 10th, I take leave to submit the following remarks concerning our École Biblique in JERUSALEM.

1°) – I wish first of all, in the name of the whole Order of St. Dominic, to state our full submission to all the decisions that the Holy Father will think good to have to take.

2°) – It is important to know whether the Holy Father Pius X has granted the Fathers of the Society of Jesus permission in writing allowing them to found a house of their Order in the city of JERUSALEM, and the extent of this permission.

3°) – We are told that it is only a matter of a hostel to be built for students of the Society or of the Biblical Institute in ROME who, after finishing their studies, would come to round them off in Palestine itself; there would be no question of a College or a house of studies or anything similar. But why insist on settling in JERUSALEM, then? Anywhere else in Palestine is good for that and even better. By setting up elsewhere the Fathers of the Society will avoid the reproaches of those who would see in the foundation just a College in disguise which would reveal itself in more propitious times.

4°) – The Society of Jesus would incur no financial loss by selling the land already bought in JERUSALEM; people who know about these matters assure us that quite the contrary would happen.

5°) – It is of the greatest importance to avoid dissensions between religious Orders in the East; the prestige of the Catholic Church when compared with Eastern Christian bodies would suffer considerably by it, the Roman Church being the only example of the most perfect unity there.

6°) – It does not seem useful to us to hasten the ruin of a biblical School that has been alone in the Catholic world for a long time and which has been able to earn the esteem of all the learned circles in the Catholic world and elsewhere. If any person there could be displeasing to the Holy See we are ready to withdraw him.

It does not seem to us, however, to be out of place to note here the esteem that Fr. LAGRANGE has been able to acquire with his most recent works, in which nothing blameworthy has been pointed out, and to insist on the other hand on the well-founded suspicions that several competent and serious people have not ceased to have in the campaign launched against Fr. LAGRANGE, namely that too many prejudiced and personal motives come into play.

Your Lordship's devoted and obedient servant,

Br. Louis THEISSLING, O. P. Master General

* * * * *

Doc. J. I,13

APIBR B-VI (VI-1A)
(Copy with its errors, translated from the Italian)

EMINENCE (Card. G. van Rossum) [: *addition in Fr. Fernández's handwriting*]

This is what it seems to me I can say coram Domino about the house to be constructed by the Biblical Institute in Jerusalem.

1. His Holiness Pope Pius X gave not only permission but encouragement and desired its foundation. His Holiness wanted a Maronite religious, the Very Rev. P. Ubaid, Abbot Procurator General of the Congregation of St. Isaiah, to go and buy the land at Jerusalem as he did in the early months of 1914. On returning to Rome he had an audience with Pius X in which he informed His Holines of the transaction. (The said Rev. Fr. Ubaid will be able to inform). – The H. Father wanted Mgr. Camassei, Patr. of Jerusalem, to make a request of the French Government for the Protectorate for the abovementioned house. (His Em. Card. Merry del Val and the same Mgr. Patriarch could provide information). – Pius X, knowing that certain people did not look kindly on this foundation, none the less insisted that it go ahead. (H. Em. Card. Merry del Val knows this).

2. The intention from the beginning was – as is now – not to build a second P. Biblical Institute in Jerusalem, but rather a complement for putting the finishing touches on the spot, i. e. the East, especially in Palestine, to studies done in the West. Consequently, there is no intention of giving, in Jerusalem, classes in Hebrew and Greek, general or special introduction, exegesis, history of exegesis . . .; subjects that are, and will continue to be dealt with exclusively at the Bibl. Inst. in Rome. In Jerusalem, however, there will only be studies of geography and archaeology and perhaps also spoken Arabic and Semitic epigraphy; these studies will, naturally, be pursued under the guidance and direction of some Professor or Professors from the P. Bibl. Inst. in Rome.

In connection with the abovementioned subjects, lectures will also be held, if considered fitting by the Fathers.

A purpose of the said house is also to take in the caravan that the Bibl. Inst. will direct in Palestine every year. Those who are not students at the Institute are also admitted to form part of this caravan, as was done for the first journey; the same also applies, naturally, to residing normally in the said house in Jerusalem, if the priests or the Very Rev. Bishops, as some have already expressed the wish, ask for it.

From all this it is easy to see that it is not a question of founding an Institute parallel to other schools where all biblical sciences are taught, but solely and exclusively a complement or annex to the Pontifical Biblical Institute in Rome.

Kneeling to kiss the Sacred Purple
    Your Very Rev. Eminence's
        humble servant in Xto.
[*handwritten addition:*] Rome 26 May 1919   A. Fernández, S. J.

* * * * *

Doc. J. I,14

APIBR B-VI (VI-1A)

(Handwritten copy with additions in pencil – in italics here – by Fr. Fernández.
Translated from the Italian)

Most Blessed Father (*Benedict XV*)

6.6.19

Now that social conditions have improved somewhat with the dawn of peace, and that the difficulties hindering the work of the Pontifical Biblical Institute have hence been largely removed, relying on the Lord's help we are getting ready to put into action the plan entrusted to us and warmly recommended by the most Blessed Father Pius X of glorious memory: namely, to found in Jerusalem, on ground already purchased for that purpose several years ago, a house to be a help and complement to this Roman Institute.

Mindful in the meantime of Your Holiness's very great interest, demonstrated to us a number of times, and especially on the occurrence of the 25th anniversary of the Encyclical "Providentissimus Deus" in which [you deigned: *word crossed out*] you were pleased, in your fatherly goodness, to encourage and bless our modest efforts for useful and solid biblical education in the Capital of the Catholic world, we make so bold as once again to implore the apostolic blessing on the new foundation which opens up for us in the holy city a fruitful field of studies of the mysteries of our redemption.

From the blessing of the Vicar of Jesus we shall draw energy and strength, together with sure hope of the faithful and happy completion of the plan entrusted to us by this Apostolic See.

Andr. Fernández

Rome 6 – 1st Friday – June 1919

* * * * *

Doc. J. I, 15

APIBR B-VI (VI-1 1928)

Report by Fr. N. de Boynes on the plot of land to be chosen in Jerusalem.
Original handwritten text in French.

(In a note there is reference to six documents, four of which have been found and are
in the archives.)

+

Report on the land owned by the Biblical Institute and on new sites which it has been suggested be bought with a view to building a new annex in Jerusalem.

I. *The site owned by the Biblical Institute*

This is situated to the west of Jerusalem in the direction of the Greek Patriarch's villa.

Surface area: 189,000 pics – one pic = a square of 75 × 75 cms.; so 109,000^{m2} is about 27 acres.

Cost of purchase about 200,000 gold francs or £7,800 (Egyptian pounds). At present the price of the site would be at its lowest and an average of ten piastres a pic hence about £18,000.

Since the site was bought it has more than doubled in value. But to make a correct assessment of this financial transaction one has to allow for interest lost on this capital which has been tied up at least since 1914 and for the expenses.

The rapid increase in the value of the site is due to the war and its consequences. At the moment there is something of a drop in the price of plots of land except in places near the city which are much sought after.

To make it easier to find this site on a [2] map a traced outline representing it and the other sites suggested by Fr. Mallon may be useful. It is enough to place it over the map of the environs of Jerusalem in Badieher [*corr*: Baedeker] p. 68, French edition 1912.

Advantages

1. It is a huge area, quite open on several sides, with a pleasant view.

On the raised part of the site there is a flat area big enough for building the house on. There is a quite noticeable slope towards the north, steeper towards the south and west.

2. The terrain is rocky and contains good stone – very useful for building.

3. Completely isolated and far from other human habitation; a house of studies would find silence and perfect peace there.

Disadvantages

1. It is very far from Jerusalem. I think it is about two kilometres as the crow flies from this site to the Jaffa Gate, which is the nearest.

2. Moreover, the site is difficult to get at [3] being at about a 400 metres walk whether coming from the north (the shortest way) or from the south (the long way round). This part of the way is encumbered with stones and rocks. Walking there is difficult for pedestrians; at night it would be a real death-trap. I think vehicles and cars would hesitate to take that way. On the other hand it must be said that the local council would agree to make a suitable road largely at our expense.

There is a plan for a boulevard constructed by the local council to link the city to the Greek Patriarch's villa more directly. It would cut our property in two. A beginning has already been made with this road, but the plan is in abeyance.

3. Would the relative proximity of a leper colony be seen as an obstacle?

4. The rocky soil, together with the lack of water in the district and the poor quality of the soil will make any cultivation, for use or pleasure, difficult and costly.

5. Keeping the house supplied with provisions would be difficult.

Conclusion. Given time, this site will become more approachable, but it will always be far from Jerusalem.

[4] II. *Site suggested by Fr. Mallon in September, 1924*

This site is situated to the west of Jerusalem. It is a small part of the huge area planted with olives of Nikephorieh belonging to the schismatic Greeks. For a long time now they have not wanted to sell, especially to Latins. As a result of financial difficulties they have had to show themselves more amenable.

They therefore agreed to sell part of it to Fr. Mallon.

The exact location of this site can be seen on the Plan of Jerusalem. It is marked with a cross + and shown by an arrow starting in the margin.

Another plan in pencil shows it more fully.

Area = 7,000 pics, i. e. 4,000 square metres.

Price = when Fr. Mallon suggested the purchase to Rome he could have clinched it at 90 piastres a pic, i. e. £6,300.

[5] *Advantages.*

1. The site is near the city; just over 300 metres as the crow flies.

2. It is easily accessible on foot and by car. The road that joins the road going along by the city to the boulevard on the west side of the property has not yet been paved. It will be ten metres wide.

3. Height above sea-level is 772^m. This is the height of the Jaffa Gate (at the foot of the walls). The house will overlook the houses that may be built between the site and Jerusalem because of the slope which gets very steep, whereas the property is on a plateau that rises fairly gently towards the west.

4. The house would not be near the boulevard and so would be partly free from one of the scourges of the country - dust.

5. The site has stone for building.

6. The site is fertile enough for olives to grow.

7. The orientation of the site is excellent. It will make it possible to build the main façade towards the south, which is important in Jerusalem.

[6] *Disadvantages*

1. A serious disadvantage: the high cost of the site. When Fr. Mallon wrote to Rome he could have had the site for 90 piastres a pic. Now the Greeks are talking of not parting with it for less than a pound and a half. We might get it for a pound and a quarter.

2. New difficulties are now obstructing the purchase. Since September a new factor has appeared. The Greeks have debts; the government has sequestered their possessions. A committee made up of people from the government on the one hand and Greeks on the other is dealing with the sale of the land. But a conflict has arisen between the committee and the Greek Patriarch. The result is that sale of land has been halted for a while. But they will soon have to sell because the government is pressing them.

3. It has been said that this property was in a low-lying part of the city and its environs. There are, of course, higher parts in and around Jerusalem. But this site is at a height of 770^m. This is the height of the base of the walls of the city on the [7] west side. But between the walls and the hill opposite on which the site stands there is a deep ditch which is at height 74° opposite the Jaffa Gate. A look at the map where the elevation is marked will easily show the geographical position of the site.

4. It has been said that this district is unhealthy. Obviously not on the hill, otherwise land there would not be so expensive, and the French Consul would not have thought of settling there. To make sure, I have had a doctor who lives at the very bottom of the valley asked for his opinion.

5. People have spoken of marshes. In winter I have seen no trace of them. The bottom of the valley is either inhabited or cultivated. As for the proposed site itself, quite a rocky place, it would be desirable that it were better watered and not so dry.

6. One may point out the disadvantage of being near a hotel planned near the boulevard.

7. The site is perhaps too small: 4,000 square metres.

Conclusion. This site is near Jerusalem and easily accessible. It is expensive but it will be difficult to find anything cheaper near [8] the city. Should it be impossible to find an available property now it would be good to bear this plan in mind.

III. *The French consulate's plot of land.*

The French consulate's plot of land is adjacent to the site just studied. It is almost rectangular in shape. It can be seen on the general plan marked 83a and indicated by an arrow which starts in the margin.

Area: 9,000 pics, i. e. 5,000 square metres

Price: at a minimum of £1 or 100 piastres a pic, i. e. £9,000 all told. The Consul has tried to sell this plot at £1¼ a pic [:] he has not found a buyer. He will have to lower his price.

Advantages

1. The property is for immediate sale. The Consul is selling this property because he needs money & because the French government is making spending cuts.

2. The plot is bigger than the one before [:] 1,000 square metres bigger.

[9] 3. The property is nearer the city and further away from the boulevard and the dust. The altitude is the same 770 metres. The kind of soil is identical.

4. The land will be even more open on the eastern side.

5. The orientation.of the site is identical with that of the other site, hence very advantageous.

All these advantages have already been explained above.

Disadvantages.

1. The very high cost of the site

2. The area may perhaps be found to be too small. The extent of the property is certainly useful, in this case, for isolating oneself from the neighbours and for building later on. Much greater use is made here of well-made and well-orientated terraces

than of gardens of which the maintenance is difficult and expensive due to the lack of water.

3. The objection about being too low-lying and unhealthy is no more applicable to this site than the previous one for the same reasons.

[10] *Conclusion.* A site very near Jerusalem, and accessible. Expensive, more so than the previous one at the price offered last September, probably not at the present price. According to the latest information it is available now. If it is decided to buy it should be done soon, otherwise a good opportunity may be lost or the prices may go up again.

Other sites or houses have been looked into. All have been set aside for obvious reasons. Only one plan would merit attention if possible, it is inside the city the Austrian Hospice on the map n. 69 – D – 5. This would be very good. I have been told that steps had already been taken at Rome and that the reply had been that the house was not for sale. It is no doubt better also to build our house according to a plan worked out by us in conformity with our own purpose and needs.

Mgr. Barlassina's plans would take us far from Jerusalem; they therefore do not deserve to be taken seriously. There is reason for wondering whether he wants us near the city.

[11] *Remarks by Fr. Visitor* [Fr. de Boynes].

1. It certainly seems that the differences of opinion on the respective advantages and disadvantages of the sites being considered come from different ways of conceiving [*sic*] the work of the Biblical Institute in Jerusalem.

2. It is clear that any establishment far from the city will not give satisfaction to those who will be in Jerusalem permanently or temporarily. If it were set up in these conditions it would immediately give cause for complaint on the part of those who would have to live there. We would end up preferring to send the Fathers here for short stays to the Casanova or Notre-Dame de France.

I believe I can state that quite definitely.

3. A well-situated establishment will necessarily be expensive and even very expensive. The longer we wait the more likely prices will rise.

4. It is time the Society carried out the plans announced and got a foothold in Jerusalem, without doing it on a large scale and attracting attention to itself.

[12] 5. It seems that in Jerusalem there is no room for a large-scale institution for teaching the Bible, but simply for an annex where people can come to seek something special to complement studies done in Rome.

Jerusalem, 12 February 1925
N. de Boynes

CHAPTER II

History of the branch from 1927 to 2009

The details of the history of the Institute in Jerusalem are mainly known through the house diary which goes on faithfully until June 25th, 1974. It ends with this wish: "May God help us!" However, for all the period that goes from 1927 to 1974, as for what follows, we also have the archives of the Institute at Jerusalem and Rome, as also short notices appearing regularly in the *Acta PIB*. This chapter, covering a long period, will dwell on certain episodes, often unknown, which caused some interest. Everything directly concerning academic life and the means used for setting it up will be kept for a later chapter.

I. Unsuccessful plan to lease to the British Government: 1927

The house could lodge twenty-five people but, at the time of its inauguration at the beginning of July 1927, only Frs. Mallon, Marini and Sutcliffe, a student at the Institute, and a Brother, who was cook, came to live there, with three domestic servants. The first three guests arrived on July 16th as scouts for the VIIIth caravan (cf. chapter III).

On July 30th Fr. General appointed Fr. Mallon superior of the house, in dependence on the rector of the Institute in Rome. As from that time, the superior is in charge not only of the Jesuit community living in the house but also of the academic activities of this branch of the Institute. The fact is that this fine Venetian style house, only just opened, was largely unoccupied during its first three months. It was only with the arrival of the VIIIth caravan at full strength that it was really full throughout the whole month of October. Among the twenty-five people in this caravan were Frs. Ludwik Semkowski and Robert Koeppel who were to return to Jerusalem later for long-term activities.

Now, the British High Commissioner, Lord Herbert C.O. Plumer, had seen his residence on Mount Scopus seriously damaged by the earthquake on July 11th. He had to find other lodgings. The Institute's only just finished building seemed to fit the bill. He had good taste, Pius XI was soon to remark. On

August 21st Lord Plumer, who had just visited the house, wrote to Fr. Mallon to let him know his wish, making it clear to him that he was also writing to the rector of the Institute, Fr. J. J. O'Rourke, and to Fr. General. His request got as far as the Pope, who quickly gave his consent. Fr. Mallon was informed without delay by the rector and a letter from Fr. General, dated September 13th, confirmed it for him, adding the Pope's witticism cited above, but the Fr. General asked that the Institute could keep "some small rooms". However, when it came to drawing up a contract in correct and due form, the British set aside for the Institute no more than only one of the large corner rooms and the corridor on the mezzanine for depositing everything belonging to the Institute. The matter got bogged down in procedural matters, yet important ones for the Institute and finally, in mid-December, in a hurry because of the approaching winter, Lord Plumer courteously withdrew his request, as Fr. Mallon recounts in his report (cf. Doc. J. I,1, pp. 56-57 and 68-69).

In the meantime Fr. Mallon, Vice-President of the *Palestine Oriental Society* in 1927, was elected its President for the year 1928.

II. Organizing excavations at Teleilat Ghassul: 1929-1938

It was in January, 1929 that Fr. Mallon for the first time inspected the site at Teleilat Ghassul, 6 km. to the north-east of the mouth of the Jordan in the Dead Sea. The main points in the story of the excavations at this site will be found in chapter III. In this chapter, however, we shall dwell on certain episodes more concerned with the organization of these excavations than with what happened during them and the discoveries they made.

Fr. O'Rourke, the rector of the Institute, had very quickly agreed that Fr. Mallon should, on March 1st, 1929, obtain official authorization to carry out excavations on this site. He was clearly in a hurry because the permit, signed by George Horsfeld, the Director of Government Antiquities in Transjordan, allowed for the excavations to be done in April and May, 1929, whereas they were to start only in the November of that year. Be that as it may, the permit was renewed every year until 1938. Although the war prevented the excavations from continuing, the Institute did not renounce resuming them once the war was over; this was the explicit opinion of Fr. Bea who had become rector of the Institute in 1930; in a letter dated December 26, 1941, he begged Fr. Fernández, the then Director of the Institute in Jerusalem, to inform the Transjordan Antiquities Department of this and Fr. Fernández did so by letter on April 3rd, 1942. However, one had to wait until 1959 for the Institute to return to excavate at Ghassul.

At the end of his first preliminary report published as the first item in the first issue of *Biblica* in 1930, Fr. Mallon suggested that the Ghassul site might, in his opinion, be in the Pentapolis of which Gen 19 spoke. On May 3rd he even published an article in the Paris *La Croix* in which he wrote: "Do we have there the ruins of Sodom (or of Sodom and Gomorrah together)? There are, in fact, many reasons for believing so and proofs to support this thesis are not lacking …". Such statements were, to say the least, premature. It is important to point out, however, that, on June 6th, 1930, Fr. General sent Fr. Mallon a letter, which is kept in the archives of the Institute in Jerusalem, in which he called for greater prudence. Here are the General's precise words:

> I must first of all congratulate you on the zeal you and the other Fathers helping you have shown on the excavations at Teleilât Ghassul. God has blessed your researches, too, and the discoveries made are surely most comforting for you.
>
> But, as you know, this is a very delicate area and that is why I think it well to recommend great reserve in this matter to you, whether you have to speak about it or still more write about it. Before passing judgment it is better, I think, to wait until agreement is reached among the specialists in the field, so as to avoid any premature statement liable to leave room for attacks. You know in fact that we are not without our enemies who spy on everything we do and who will not spare us if they can find fault with us.
>
> I must also add, to be precise, that even among our friends there are some who find that you perhaps jump to conclusions and that you went too far in your article in *La Croix*.
>
> This is why I wanted to recommend very great prudence to you and all the Fathers there. This attitude is in fact particularly enjoined on us out of regard for the Holy See of which the honour is in some way at stake, since the excavations are directed by the Pontifical Institute.

Unfortunately for the Institute, these recommendations had hardly any effect. An unpleasant controversy between the Biblical Institute and the École Biblique could have been avoided if the General had been listened to.

A month after the dispatch of this letter Fr. Bea was installed as rector of the Institute. On July 26th, 1930, he was received by Pius XI who showed him his interest in the excavations at Ghassul; the Pope insisted that the most advanced scientific methods be practised there and, by way of support, emptied his wallet into the hands of Fr. Bea so as to share in the cost of the excavations in this way. Fr. Bea recounted this audience in detail in a letter to Fr. Mallon, dated June 29th. So there is nothing surprising in the fact that Fr. Bea twice, in July, 1931, then in March, 1932, sent the Pope a report of barely a few pages on the discoveries made at Ghassul, The first report adopts, without the slightest hesitation, the very risky hypotheses put forward by Fr. Mallon, who thought he had discovered the Pentapolis of Gen 19! The second report presents the Pope with the two paintings of the star and of the bird discovered at Ghassul, but dating them to the time of Abraham! As for the Pontiff's financial aid, an undated and unsigned note in Latin, which seems to be written by Fr. Mallon in 1932, points out that the expenses for the first three years of the excavations came to £1,180, of which 400 were covered by an American benefactor and the rest by the Pope.

As from the school year 1931-1932, the *Acta PIB* gives the title of Director to the academic authority of the Jerusalem Institute, a title that he bears today. From this detail it is obvious that the new rector is a man with clear ideas.

On November 6th, 1932, when he had already come to Jerusalem from October 7th to the 12th, 1930 – he was to come back with the caravan in 1934 – Fr. Bea put his signature in Rome to an "Instruction on the way to carry out excavations undertaken by the Pontifical Biblical Institute", a document which the General approved that same day. This six-page Latin document has eight paragraphs, of which here are the contents in brief:

1. The excavations and the publications concerning them should be of quality; the reputation of the Institute is involved in them.

2. The rector of the Institute has the ultimate responsibility; he should be consulted in every important matter.

3. Those working on the excavations should form a "common council" in which the excavation director is the "primus inter pares" who carries out the orders of the Institute's authorities and the decisions of this council with charity and fraternal co-operation, keeping each one's expertise in mind. In particular:

   a. before every excavation campaign the plan of work should be discussed and fixed upon in Jerusalem;

   b. each week the council should discuss the work accomplished, the questions it raises and the program for the next week; – the excavations Secretary, appointed by the Superiors, shall draw up the Minutes of the meetings mentioned in a and b and shall send them regularly to the rector;

   c. when an important discovery is made, all the collaborators should be notified of it and should give their opinion with due regard for scientific laws.

4. Excavations should be begun in an orderly way, according to the scientific method, without making much of the discoveries, but with the purpose of contributing to a better knowledge of such an important period in the history of Israel. This is why:

   a. the Secretary shall make a report about every more important object, noting the place and nature of the find, using photography as well;

   b. each team member on the dig shall have some workmen according to need and shall direct them, showing them how to proceed, how to use such and such an instrument etc.;

   c. care will be taken in the preparation and maintenance of scientific instruments and of the hut [a wooden shed 14 ms by 13] where work can be done conveniently;

   d. photographs and designs or plans shall be at everyone's disposal; for each ceramic object a card shall be made out with all the necessary particulars, but the object shall not be removed from its site before the card has been compiled nor before everyone has been able to discuss it and the Secretary make a report on it.

5. Each worker is answerable, in his own field, to the rector of the Institute, except when it is a matter of the "common council" (nn. 3-4) and publications (n. 6).

6. Every publication about the excavations, before being sent to Rome for review, shall be read by all the workers, and each shall send his comments to the rector. Preliminary reports shall be short and only indicate what is obvious, leaving aside doubtful or hypothetical points to be kept for the final report.

7. Comparison with other excavations and other experts is to be favoured. This is why:
   a. these experts are to be graciously received and, if necessary, a second hut shall be built;
   b. those working on our excavations may visit others and personally get to know other excavation specialists in action;
   c. when the interpretation of a discovery is difficult, experts from different countries should be consulted [at that time there were German, American. British and French experts in Jerusalem]. Who to invite will be seen during the "common council" indicated in 3, a and b. If need be, the rector will be asked to consult the professors of the Institute about this.

8. These principles will be applied at the "common councils" in reciprocal co-operation for the honour of the Church, the good of the Institute and the progress of biblical science.

Such is, in summary form, the content of Fr. Bea's Instruction, but he not being an archaeologist, it may be surmised that Fr. Mallon had a hand in drawing it up. It will be noted that, as the rector points out, the idea of a "common council" derives from the practice of the Bollandists, just as the request to make out a card for every ceramic object derives from the practice adopted by the excavations at Megiddo. The fact remains that the Instruction came after three excavation campaigns at Ghassul and just before the start of the fourth. But its effect was of short duration in fact, because in April, 1934, at the end of the fifth campaign, Fr. Mallon died. On September 30th, 1934, Fr. Marcel Lobignac became director of the Institute in Jerusalem. A sixth excavation campaign at Ghassul was possible only in February and March, 1936, being different from the previous ones in that Fr. Lobignac was not an archaeologist and that directing the excavations was entrusted to Fr. R. Koeppel who until then had been helping Fr. Mallon. Things did not go well, especially since the team now included some rather enterprising and very independent young Jesuit scholastics.

To settle the problems posed by the new team, Fr. Bea came to Jerusalem from December 21st, 1936 to January 7th, 1937, and as a result of that visit he rewrote his Instruction which he sent from Rome to those concerned on February 5th, 1937. Now this second Instruction was certainly prepared by a dialogue between Fr. Bea and Fr. Lobignac. The handwritten documents referred to here are neither dated or signed but are relevant to this matter and were drawn up by these two Fathers.

The first document is by Fr. Lobignac. He notes some difficulties arising out of the application in 1936 of the Instruction of 1932. The main one is that the "common council" in no. 3 and the deliberations in no. 3b do not work properly any more; these proceedings have become, he says, "a constant battle between divergent opinions whose propounders are unwilling to give way on anything, only seeking to bring the others round to their own point of view in the discussion". To get out of this impasse Fr. Lobignac considers that "either the excavation director or the director of the Institute *must* have the deciding vote and give a final decision on what is to be done".

Fr. Lobignac then draws up a second document including proposals on three points: the primordial role of the director of the Institute at Jerusalem, the role of the excavation director, who should work in agreement with the Director of the Institute and may not take over the whole life of the Institute and, lastly, apropos of the publications, the distinct roles of the excavation director, competent in scientific matters, and the Director of the Institute, the established authority.

Thereupon Fr. Bea writes out a synthesis, in pencil and in Latin, of Fr. Lobignac's proposals: 1. The Director of the Institute is responsible for the scientific work done by the Institute in Jerusalem; he has to promote, direct and co-ordinate everyone's activities. 2. These principles also apply to the excavations at Ghassul; henceforth the director of excavations bears responsibility in scientific matters in the sight of the civil authority, but also in the sight of the Institute and the Holy See, both represented by the Director of the Institute; if there is any disagreement among those working on the excavations, it is the Director of the Institute who decides, and if the problem is more serious, the latter shall refer it to the rector. 3. Likewise for publications, if there is no agreement among the team members the Director of the Institute shall decide the matter or refer it to the rector.

These documents were preparing for the new Instruction of February, 1937. In it (cf. Doc. J. I,1) the main changes are the replacement, pure and simple, of the "common council" which had recently caused so many difficulties, with clear and precise statements on the central role of the Superior-Director of the Institute at Jerusalem, on the restructured role of the excavation director, not just still "primus inter pares" but also dependent on the authorities of the Institute. Understanding and collaboration among all those working on the excavations is insisted upon. Lastly, as Fr.Lobignac had asked in his first document, no. 4b of the first Instruction disappears in the 1937 one.

During the same stay in Jerusalem the rector, on January 5th, 1937, also sets out in writing the plan of volume II of the final report on the excavations at Teleilat Ghassul over the period from 1932 to 1936. Still in the same spirit he reserves the Preface and Introduction ("de ratione et historia effossionum etc.") for Fr. Lobignac, as well as the first chapter "de methodo et modo procedendi", which Fr. Lobignac was to have written with Fr. Henri Senès. But when the volume finally appeared in 1940 these two items were not in it. Fr. Lobignac had left Jerusalem in 1939.

Thus, during the first years of his long time as rector (1930-1949) Fr. Bea gave much attention to his men working at Ghassul. Of course, he could, at the beginning, have been more reserved over the interpretation of the facts of the excavations, but he had this work of the Institute at heart and when the trouble came in Fr. Lobignac's time (1934-1939) he took the situation fully in hand. On the one hand he trusted the one who depended on him and a number of his letters to Fr. Lobignac reveal the heart of a father who never fails to support the discouraged Director who lacked resources. On the other, he came out to try in a concrete way to set things right again. His second Instruction proves this and seems to have brought peace at the time of the seventh excavation campaign at Ghassul, from January to March, 1938. Moreover, from January 1937 on, the people working on them knew that the final report on the excavations over the period going from 1932 to 1936 was expected from them.

Finally, it was once again Fr. Bea who got the young Jesuit Jacques Guillet to spend two years in Jerusalem and who got hold of Br. Joseph Šira to be photographer at Ghassul; the latter lived at Jerusalem from 1937 to 1973.

III. A lecture in Jerusalem by Fr. Pierre Teilhard de Chardin?

It is only a matter of a plan that was not carried out, but it seems useful to speak about it, with documents in support (Doc. J. II,2-5), the figure of Fr. Teilhard de Chardin being such an outstanding one among 20th-century Jesuits. What characterizes this unfulfilled plan is that it goes right to the top of the Society where it was approved, but with some reservations.

It was Mr. René Neuville, the chancellor of the French Consulate at Jerusalem, who took the initiative, probably at the beginning of March, 1935. He had taken part in the Teleilat Ghassul excavations in the company of Fr. Mallon, his friend, and was known for his work on prehistory in Palestine and elsewhere.

As the French Consulate was next to the Institute, it is likely that instead of sending a letter to the Director of the Institute, Fr. Lobignac, Mr. Neuville came to the Institute in person. With the Director in France, the chancellor approached Frs. Fernández and Koeppel and told them about his idea. He said he knew that Fr. Teilhard de Chardin was to be in Jerusalem in June. Teilhard was in Beijing at the time and great had been his reputation since his discovery of sinanthropus in 1929. Neuville must have thought that, en route for Paris, Teilhard would stop in Jerusalem, being interested in the research into prehistory that was being conducted there. So why not invite the famous palaeontologist to the "Palestine Oriental Society"? He would give a lecture on sinanthropus and on prehistoric research in China. This lecture would be of the greatest interest for a milieu that had a passion for prehistory and, as the Institute shared that interest with its excavations at Ghassul, it was normal that it should take part in the project, especially as Fr. Teilhard was a Jesuit. So Neuville proposed that Teilhard give his lecture at the Institute, but under the auspices of the "Palestine Oriental Society". It seemed in any case more fitting that Teilhard the Jesuit should speak in a house of his Order than at the École Biblique or at the American School, the "Palestine Oriental Society" not having premises of its own.

Whereupon, Frs. Koeppel and Fernández wrote, each on his own account, to Fr. Lobignac, the former to support the plan and the latter to show himself somewhat afraid of it. For a long time Fr. Teilhard had actually been worrying the Roman authorities. In 1930, for example, because of the suspicion hanging over him, he had had to suspend publication of his book, *Le Milieu Divin*, the manuscript of which continued to circulate undercover, however, among theologians for several decades until its publication.

Fr. Lobignac, for his part, showed himself favourable to the project on condition that Teilhard confined himself to the domain of facts and methods in prehistory. This was actually the sole purpose of the project and, being given at the Institute, the lecture would be aimed at a learned society that was not concerned either with philosophy or theology. If it was accepted, it would be proved that, while being pontifical, the Institute really was open to the problems of prehistory. Lastly, it would be an excellent start – for Lobignac did not doubt its success – for a series of public lectures at the Institute, which would affirm its standing in Jerusalem. It would also be the occasion for adapting the big hall in the house into a lecture room. That, in short, was what Fr. Lobignac wrote to the rector, Bea, on March 22nd, 1935.

On receipt of the letter, the latter judged it necessary to refer it to Fr. General, given the importance of the matter, but he was convinced that Fr. General would give his consent. Actually, Fr. Ledóchowski wanted to answer Fr. Lobignac himself. First of all he drew up for him some fundamental principles, traditional in the Society, then, reminding him of his responsibility as Director of the Institute with regard to the Holy See and the Society, he agreed to Fr. Teilhard's giving his lecture at the Institute on the twofold condition that the Father should keep to the field of scientific prehistory and that his script be duly reviewed by censorship, as provided for in the Society's law.

Two days later, on March 29th, Fr. Bea, who knew Fr. General's position, wanted the lecture to be a success but made Fr. General's second condition stricter, for he asked Fr. Lobignac to make a careful "and somewhat severe" revision of Teilhard's script. He also suggests that, from the outset, the lecturer exonerate the Institute from all responsibility by saying that he was not a member of the Institute's teaching staff and that he would therefore be speaking on his own behalf. In this way, adds Bea, any wrong interpretation will be avoided.

On April 4th Fr. Lobignac replied to Fr. Bea from Lyons, assuring him that all precautions will be taken and that Fr. General's instructions will be carried out, but he especially informs his correspondent that things were getting complicated: not only had Mr. Neuville not sent him any letter about the plan, but also that he had just heard that Teilhard had to be in Paris as early as May.

Finally, on May 8th, Fr. Bea, replying to several letters from Fr. Lobignac, of which the last was dated May 1st, tells him: "As for Fr. Teilhard, Fr. General is very pleased to know that all will be arranged according to his prescriptions". Thus, at the beginning of May, 1935, a lecture by Teilhard in Jerusalem was still being considered.

The dossier ends there. Nothing shows that Teilhard came through Jerusalem; no mention in the house diary. In 1985, the then Director, M. Gilbert, through the intermediary of Fr. Pierre Wittouck, of the Catholic University of Louvain, inquired of the Teilhard de Chardin Foundation, whose headquarters are in Paris, and on July 8th the general secretary of the Foundation, Mrs S. Clair-Michot, replied that the Foundation's archives made no mention of any lecture by the Father in Jerusalem between April and June, 1935; on April 10th Teilhard was still in Beijing and on June 23rd was certainly in Paris, for two of his letters confirm those dates. Would he even have been invited?

IV. The Institute partly occupied: 1941-1948

Fr. Henri Senès, from January 1936 to October, 1964 – he died on November 7th, 1964 – kept a precise record of the occupation of rooms at the Institute at Jerusalem. Now between January 1936 and the outbreak of the second world war it must be admitted that more often than not the house was half empty, if not two-thirds empty. Only during the summer of 1937, from July to September, were almost all the rooms occupied.

At the beginning of November 1938, with the situation in Palestine deteriorating once again, there were more and more British in the country. The idea occurred to them to requisition the Institute for billeting their men. On the 9th, Fr. Bea told the Vatican Secretariat of State about it and on the 12th the Apostolic Delegate, Mgr. Gustavo Testa, telegraphed from Rome to the Institute saying that the Holy See was asking the British Minister (to the Holy See, it may be supposed) that the military authority apply directly to the Apostolic Delegate, seeing that the Institute was the property of the Holy Father. Back in Cairo, on the 19th he renewed his instructions in a letter he sent to Fr. Lobignac and the matter was not followed up, at least not immediately.

For at the end of August 1941, with the war raging, the manager of St. Julian's Hotel, near the Institute, was short of rooms. This hotel was on the then Julian's Way, now King David Street, on the corner facing the Hebrew Union College. The manager came to ask Fr. Fernández if the Institute could not serve as an annex to his hotel. On August 28th Fr. Fernández, not being able to contact Rome, asked the Apostolic Delegate for his permission and the latter granted it to him the same day (cf. Doc. J. II,6-7). Thus it is that from September 5th, 1941, to March 15th, 1942, the first floor of the house was occupied by British officers. The hotel paid rent and took charge of the upkeep (meals and other services) of the four Jesuits remaining at the Institute.

But from March 15th, 1942, the government took the place of the hotel to set up the "Food Control" at the Institute. The British even tried to relodge the four Jesuits at the Institute elsewhere at government expense. When that move failed, the "Food Control" occupied, as from June, 1942, the western half of the second floor of the house as well. In August, 1946, the "Food Control" gave up the second floor rooms to the "Town Planning". Two months later this new occupant, being short of room, suggested building, at government expense, a large workroom as an extension to the garage, situated on the northwestern corner of the property. Contacted by Fr. Fernández, whom Fr. Senès supported, Fr. Bea telegraphed his approval from Rome.

However, at the end of 1946 the contract between the Institute and the government had expired and had not been renewed. So, on a secondary matter, Fr. Bea sent Fr. O'Rourke, the new Director, a letter stating perfectly clearly the illegality of the British occupation of our house (cf. Doc. J. II,8). Nothing happened, so on January 27th, 1948, Fr. Bea wrote directly to Pius XII and, on February 4th, he sent on to Fr. O'Rourke the very firm reply of the Pope: the latter "requires", wrote Fr. Bea, "that the building shall be returned to the Holy See immediately after the departure of the British authorities" (cf. Doc. J. II,9). In confirmation, Mgr. G. B. Montini, the future Pope Paul VI, then Substitute at the Secretariat of State, on March 24th, 1948, put out an official document, which the British recognized, stipulating that the buildings of the Institute at Jerusalem were the property of the Holy See (cf. Doc. J. II,10). The future was safe. In mid-March, 1948, however, the "Price Controller" came to join the "Town Planning", but at the end of April, with the war of Israel's independence raging, all the British departments occupying the house stopped functioning and withdrew, leaving behind an important part of their archives which the State of Israel, proclaimed on May 14th, 1948, came to collect in June 1949. The Institute in Jerusalem at last found its complete freedom again.

We have here wanted to note only the most remarkable events of this difficult period. The Institute's archives in Jerusalem preserve a number of documents about the development of the situation. It is noticeable in them that, on the one hand, the Institute always stayed on good terms with the civil and military authorities, as with the other religious leaders in Jerusalem and that, on the other, the concern shown by Fr. Bea, the rector in Rome, was constant and full of prudence. Everyone can imagine the very real risks run by the few Jesuits who, throughout those years of great tension in Jerusalem, kept their cool. They saved the main thing. The war had completely changed the situation in the country. From the British mandate that had ended in chaos, the passage was made to the State of Israel, but the latter, although internationally recognized, was still to experience a lot of difficulties. Now, since May, 1948, the Institute was in Israel, cut off for a long time from the Old City.

V. Surviving as best one can: 1949-1972

From May to December, 1948, the battle had raged in Jerusalem. In the Institute diary Fr. Senès day by day recorded in detail the operations and their effect on the house. As the Institute adjoined the French Consulate and relations were close between the two houses, on May 26th, 1948, a breach in the wall separating them had been made to facilitate passing from one to the other. Several people from the Consulate actually lodged in the Institute then, the Consulate drew supplies of water from the cistern in our garden and the children of René Neuville, the Consul, made use of our garden. This gate was to be blocked up on July 6th, 1950. However, at the time of the Suez affair at the beginning of November 1956, the Consulate opened it again but, faced with objections from the Institute, closed it again immediately. The outline of this passageway in the wall separating the Institute from the Consulate can still be seen today.

The United Nations, having decided in 1948 on the partition of Palestine between Jews and Arabs, Count Folke Bernadotte was sent to Jerusalem as mediator but on September 17th was assassinated, along with one of his aides. Their bodies were placed in the YMCA, near the Institute, and at the request of the French Consul Fr. Senès went to bow in prayer before their bodies and recommend them to the divine mercy.

Mentally exhausted by so many worries, Fr. O'Rourke had a cerebral attack on March 12th, 1949, from which he recovered in a few days without any consequences, except that he had to take care of his health. Having rested, he went back to Rome on July 21st.

The situation in the country was now fixed for almost twenty years. The Institute, like the French Consulate, was now in the territory of Israel. A "demarcation zone", a no man's land separating us from the Old City started just at the end of our street. In October 1948 that street had received the name of Paul-Émile Botta; an archaeologist and Assyriologist, Botta had published five volumes on Nineveh, between the years 1846 and 1850, while being French Consul in Jerusalem.

The Semkowski era was beginning for the Institute in Jerusalem. At the end of his studies in Rome Fr. Ludvik Semkowski had come to the Holy Land for the first time in 1923 with the 4th caravan, then again in 1927 with the 8th. He had been seen again in Jerusalem for short stays in 1928 and 1929, then in 1939. A Hebrew scholar at heart, he had been teaching Hebrew, Aramaic and Semitic epigraphy at the Institute in Rome since 1925. He it was who had finished the publication of the Hebrew-Latin dictionary by Fr. F. Zorell, who died in 1947.

In 1949 his life took quite a different turn. Appointed Director of the Institute in Jerusalem, as replacement for Fr. O'Rourke, now too weak to keep the post, Fr. Semkowski occupied it until 1972, apart from an interim period spent as rector of the Pontifical Polish College in Rome from 1955 to 1959. During his absence his place was taken firstly by Fr. Francis X. Peirce (1894-1980); at the end of his studies at the Institute in Rome Fr. Peirce took part in the 14th caravan in the summer of 1931, then taught Old Testament at the Jesuit theologate at Woodstock in Maryland; apart from English, he spoke Spanish and French; in fact he was Director of the Institute in Jerusalem for only a year and a half, from February 1955 to August 1956, his health, too, being so weak. Then came Fr. Robert North, from 1956 to 1959, who then resumed the excavations at Ghassul.

Altogether, Fr. Semkowski was to spend eighteen years as Director of the Institute in Jerusalem. While being modest and reserved and possessing delicate courtesy, he concealed great learning. Being a polyglot, more so than most of the Jesuits living in Jerusalem at the time, and thanks to his knowledge of biblical Hebrew which he gave the impression of speaking better than modern Hebrew, he had many regular contacts with many people, particularly with Israeli university people. As the library of the Hebrew University situated on Mount Scopus was inaccessible because of the division of Jerusalem, the Father opened the Institute's library to Israeli researchers. Abraham Malamat, for example, and several other masters in the Hebrew University did their work there, doctoral theses, among other things, and professed profound gratitude to Fr. Semkowski. For years he was even on the Israeli board for the young people's competition, checking their knowledge of biblical Hebrew.

As for the academic life of the Institute at Jerusalem during Fr. Semkowski's first term in office, as during Fr. Peirce's short stay, it was practically non-existent. To be sure, the entire building had been recovered, which actually needed to be put in order again, but with a community of four or five Jesuits the house was empty; in 1952 the caravans had made their way to the Near East again but they only stopped at the Institute for a few days, for instance, from July 25th to the 28th, 1952; besides, before 1957, no student from the Biblicum came to Jerusalem to follow part of the academic program offered by the Institute there (cf. chapter III).

With the arrival of Fr. North as Director on August 6th, 1956, the situation at the Institute in Jerusalem was to improve notably. Some students from Rome came again in the second semester of their third year of study, so that the house was half full each year, or almost, from March to June. Still, Fr. North rightly considered that, in spite of everything, the house continued to be desperately empty. He considerably enriched the library, he marketed a series of colour slides of the Holy Land and neighbouring countries which he and Br. Šira had made and his relations with the Israelis, authorities and university people, were excellent. On the other hand, with the Rector in Rome, Fr. Vogt, as with the Jesuit community in the house, it was quite a different matter, so much so that after a period of three years he asked to be relieved and Fr. Semkowski, who was free at the time, was sent back to Jerusalem as Director. He arrived on October 13th, 1959. Fr. North then resumed excavations at Ghassul, then again guided three caravans in 1960, at Easter, in the summer and in September. On September 27th, 1960, he left by plane for the United States.

Fr. Semkowski's second term (1959-1972) may be divided into two periods, before and after the Six-Day War in June, 1967. Before that date Jerusalem was cut in two and it was not always easy to pass from one sector to the other. In any case the holy places in Jerusalem were on the other side, hence less interest for biblical scholars also wishing to be pilgrims to come to the Institute, although Galilee and the lake were in Israel. Add to this the fact that the house did not have an archaeologist any more after Fr. North's departure. Fr. Léopold Sabourin had been sent to Jerusalem to replace him but archaeology was not his thing and his stay was not a long one; having arrived on June 9th, 1964, he left on May 28th, 1967. Consequently, still the same problem of a building empty from October to February, half full from March to June and full in summer. But whereas Fr. North had been able to get financial help from American benefactors, Fr. Semkowski did not have that charism, so that until 1964 he complained regularly to Fr. General John Janssens about the lack of money for the house he ruled. Besides, he also had to see to the management of the house, which did not prevent him from offering many courses in Hebrew, biblical and modern.

It was during these years that two veterans of the Institute died. On March 21st, 1963, Br. Antonio Vives passed away in his sleep; he "leaves an impression of holiness everywhere", notes Fr. Senès in the house diary. Born in 1889 in the small village of Maldà near Lerida in Spain, he had arrived in Jerusalem on July 10th, 1929, after a short stay at the Roman Institute, and stayed in the Holy Land for thirty-four years uninterruptedly. He had taken part in all the Institute's excavations at Teleilat Ghassul, including the one Fr. North organized in 1959-1960 (cf. chapter III). A practical and very calm person, he restored and classified the pieces of pottery discovered on the site (cf. *Bib* 44 [1963] 396-397). And on November 7th, 1964, Fr. Henri Senès died. An architect by training, born in Marseilles in 1897, he had arrived in Jerusalem on August 9th, 1935, twenty-nine years earlier. As designer and surveyor at Ghassul he drew the maps and precision plans; the last pages of the second volume of the final report on the excavations that appeared in 1940 are his work. Being a painter at times, he did the great mural fresco on the terrace in those days; in it he painted the panorama of Bethlehem as seen from Ramat Rachel. In addition, he was for years interested in the excavations situated below the convent of the Sisters of Nazareth at Nazareth; in that place he saw the house of the Holy Family and the museum in that convent still recalls his work today (cf. *Bib* 46 [1965] 112-116).

Lastly, this period ended with new prospects. On January 16th, 1967, Fr. Semkowski wrote to Fr. Francis J. McCool, the General's Delegate, about how he viewed the future of the Institute in Jerusalem (cf. Doc. J II,11). While voices were being raised (in Rome?) saying that that house ought to be closed, the Director vigorously defends its preservation as a branch of the Roman Institute. He lists its basic traditional academic activities: third year students during the second semester, caravans, archaeological excavations etc. But to carry out this program there not only a Father to deal with the management would be needed in Jerusalem but also two professors of archaeology, geography and philology, one of them being Director. Then, once again stressing the precarious financial state of the house, he points out that it has been possible to install running water (cold only) in the rooms and even electricity from the mains in them for warming up the occupants in that way. However, he adds, all the inside of the house would have to be repainted, which had not been done for about fifteen years, and, finally, a lift would have to be installed; two of the Jesuits were already suffering from weak hearts.

On April 26th, 1967, at the end of his canonical visitation, Fr. McCool asked Fr. Semkowski what institutions in Israeli Jerusalem, including the Hebrew University, could take our students. On May 17th the Director, analyzing the various possibilities, considered that the Hebrew University would be the most suitable. This idea was to take shape.

The Six-Day War, from June 5th to the 10th, 1967, might have been tragic for the Institute, being situated almost on the front line. Windows shattered, two shells ended up in the library but on the whole the Institute was spared. Some people living in the house took refuge in the cellar under the stone staircase. They were sheltered there, and as that cellar served as a store for food and drink, they held out. Fr. Semkowski, Brs. Šira and Decher, and perhaps one or two other people at the most were there. Some guests of the house had found refuge elsewhere "for", as Fr. Semkowski notes in the diary, "it is so not comfortable, and some people snore [at night]"! For his part, Fr. John J. Kilgallen slept in his room on the first floor.

When the alert was over, everything was different in Jerusalem. A new era opened – the one of the unified city with free access on both sides. Fr. Semkowski then thought it was the time to step down. But a year later, in June, 1968, then in January, 1969, despite several attempts to find the needed successor, Fr. McCool was still without anyone; Fr. Semkowski had to hold on until August 22nd, 1972.

In spite of his age, he still displayed astonishing activity. In 1967 the Institute in Rome decided to offer a one-year preparatory course in biblical Greek and Hebrew in Jerusalem, starting in autumn, 1968 (cf. chapter III). Fr. Richard M. Mackowski took charge of the Greek; Fr. Semkowski took the first semester of Hebrew on himself and Fr. John F. Sheehan the second. But as from the following year it was only half successful. However, thanks to that program the house was fuller, with guests taking advantage of the new situation in Jerusalem also being greater in number.

Even before June 1967, as we have seen, Fr. Semkowski was concerned about the renovation of the building. Now on January 16th, 1968, writing to Fr. McCool, he adds the installation of an oil-fired central heating system to the plans. He comes back to this several times until June 3rd, 1969, but its implementation is postponed each time.

Finally, in 1971, Fr. Carlo Maria Martini, who had become rector of the Institute in the summer of 1969, took things in hand. At the end of long negotiations Fr. Samuel R. Pitts (1911-1982) succeeded Fr. Semkowski on August 22nd, 1972. Fr. Pitts had studied philosophy at Eegenhoven-Louvain in the days of Fr. Joseph Maréchal, then theology at Woodstock; spirituality being then his field, he had taught theology at Georgetown University D. C.; he knew the Institute at Jerusalem, having lived there from August 18th, 1964, until January 5th, 1965, and had left very good recollections of himself there; when he was called there as Director he was directing the students from Georgetown who were living at Fribourg in Switzerland. As he could get leave of absence from his University only for two years, he ended his term of office at Jerusalem at the end of July, 1974.

Fr. Semkowski only left Jerusalem for Rome on June 24th, 1973; he had had serious health problems. He fell asleep in the Lord on August, 18th, 1977, at the Villa Cavalletti near Grottaferrata in the "castelli romani".

VI. **The big changes: 1972-1974**

No rector of the Institute involved himself in the problems of the house in Jerusalem as much as Fr. Martini, especially when one considers that, at the same time, he was also taken up with the important work going on at the premises in Rome (cf. *Acta PIB* 7, 512-513).

In Jerusalem two problems had to be solved at the same time, the renovation of the house and setting up an academic program that would attract students and justify the branch's existence by their being present in greater numbers.

For the thorough renovation of the house Fr. Martini could count on the effective co-operation of the Director, Fr. Pitts, with whom he was in constant touch, both by letter and telephone. As regards setting up a new program, he did it on his own initiative. The two problems were connected, but quite distinct.

Let us start with the one about the academic program (cf. chapter III). It will be recalled that in May, 1967, Fr. Semkowski had already recommended to Fr. McCool that co-operating with the Hebrew University of Jerusalem be envisaged.

On August 28th, 1972, Fr. Martini flew to Los Angeles. During his stay he had the opportunity to meet Professor Shlomo Morag, the eminent specialist in biblical Hebrew at the Hebrew University, He asked him whether the university could not, during the summer from June to September, offer students from the Biblicum a more attractive program of modern Hebrew than the one they had been following until then. The person addressed promised to contact the department running the Ulpan at the University and to make concrete proposals. On September 11th, on his return, the rector informed Fr. Pitts about this. But on October 18th he only got an evasive answer; he could approach the person in charge of the Ulpan Centre in Rome. That line was therefore abandoned.

On March 10th, 1973, Fr. Martini came to spend just over three weeks in Jerusalem. At the end of the month, through the kind offices of Professor Moshe Goshen-Gottstein who went with him, Fr. Martini was received by the President of the Hebrew University, Dr. Avraham Harman. The latter immediately understood the importance of the rector of the Biblicum's visit. Fr. Martini asked what the university could offer his students. At Dr. Harman's request, Fr. Martini gives the details of his plan in a letter dated July 16th and after the summer vacation the President still answers him favourably on September 10th, suggesting contacts between representatives of the two institutions (cf. Doc. J. II,12). On September 13th Goshen-Gottstein tells Fr. Martini that several members of the university met at his initiative, with President Harman's approval, and that all had shown themselves favourable with the proposal from the rector of the Biblicum. But the matter dragged on, due to the Yom Kippur war in October, 1973.

On January 25th, 1974, Fr. Martini once again met President Harman in Jerusalem, in the company of Professor H. M. Daleski, Principal of the School for Overseas Students; during this meeting a program covering the second academic semester and the summer was envisaged for the first time. On February 13th President Harman tells the rector that Professor Shemaryahu Talmon has agreed to be the academic director of students from the Institute. On March 20th Fr. Martini, during a brief stay in Jerusalem, receives a detailed plan for a program from Professor Talmon; it would go from February 15th until September 15th. On May 24th Talmon leaves Rome where he had come to meet the rector, the professors and the students to put the project before them and Fr. Martini thanked him warmly on June 28th. Professor Talmon showed himself very well informed about the Institute's academic level and the serious nature of what it wanted. At all events, the two institutions reached agreement for, on June 21st, Talmon sends Fr. Martini the definite program and the description of the courses, so that in July the Registrar's office at the Institute issues a written description of the project (cf. Doc. J. II,13).

Finally, on August 15th, Professor Daleski informs Fr. Martini that the senate of the Hebrew University has approved the inauguration of a special program offered to students from the Biblicum, The cost of this program for each student remains to be fixed, 250 or 300 dollars. To put the finishing touches to the program Talmon visited Rome again from January 5th to the 6th, 1975. At the beginning of February twenty-three students arrived at the completely renovated Institute in Jerusalem and they stayed there until mid-September, following the courses at the Hebrew University (for the details cf. *Acta PIB* 8, pp. 17 and 58-59).

On the academic level a great step had just been taken. This program proved its worth in the long run because thirty years later it is still working overall, to the general satisfaction of the Institute and the Hebrew University (cf. chapter III). Fr. Martini, for his part, thought that a long stay by the students from the Biblicum in the Israeli university milieu could only be beneficial for Jewish and Christian relations in the course of time.

Let us now come to the second problem, the one about renovating the building at the Jerusalem Institute. It was solved at the same time as the first, the academic problem. It will be remembered that between 1967 and 1969 Fr. Semkowski had given attention to it, but without success. Now Fr. Pitts, who had only just been installed, discovers that the house is not connected to the city's sewage system. It is using a septic tank that is no longer suitable: it overflows and hence the plants in the garden are in danger. And the Father is astonished that the house works with no budget, without any regular financial income. On November 6th he draws up a calculated plan for the restoration of the whole building. That gets things going. By the end of the month a tidy sum is already in reserve in Rome credited to the account of the Jerusalem branch. Fr. Eugen Hillengass, the general treasurer of the Society, and Fr. Charles W. Dullea, in charge of the Institute's investment funds in Rome, are involved, and promise to get friends and foundations interested. On March 9th, 1973, through the good offices of Fr. Martini, who was one of those mainly concerned and about to leave for Jerusalem, Fr. General Arrupe sends Fr. Pitts quite an adequate cheque for immediate purposes. At the beginning of April, on Fr. Martini's return, the decision is taken to set about the complete renovation of the house in Jerusalem and, consequently, to close it to all other activity during the academic year 1973-1974. On June 5th, in a letter to Fr. Pitts, Fr. Martini lists the main tasks to be done; this is the fruit of much consultation. Apart from linking up the sewer, being seen to by the city, he mentions above all the central heating to be installed throughout the house, constructing eight small rooms on the covered terrace on the second floor (and Fr. Senès's fresco in fact has to go), the extension of the library and, possibly, moving the museum. Everything is there except the lift called for by Fr. Semkowski earlier on (cf. Doc. J. II,14). Br. Ermenegiglio Consonno, from Milan, was to direct the work; he was to be seen in Jerusalem therefore from June 10th, 1973 until November 2nd, 1974, when the restoration was over. He gave a daily account of the work in the house diary. Some specialized Jesuit Brothers also took part in the work.

Then, on July 11th, Fr. Martini, along with Fr. Dullea, drew up the calculated plan of the work envisaged and on the 14th, after discussions with Fr. Hillengass and Fr. Snoeck, who had succeeded Fr. McCool as Fr. General's Delegate, the plan, amended once again, was sent by Fr. Martini to the higher authorities of the Society for approval. Three days later, on the 17th, Fr. Arrupe gave his approval and has the sum of fifty thousand dollars, set aside for installing central heating and constructing the eight small rooms on the terrace, paid into the account of the Institute in Jerusalem.

Work started on the drains in the middle of May, 1973, then at the end of October the work on the Institute building, and when Fr. Pitts handed over to Fr. Francis Furlong on July 31st, 1974, the post of Director, it was three-quarters complete. The bulk of the work would be finished at the end of October and Br. Consonno could then return to Italy; it would then be only a matter of cleaning up and putting the house back in order so as to receive its guests in mid-February. The work programme would have been carried out, except for the library, the extension of which is postponed until later.

This renovation would only have been possible thanks to the generosity of the German bishops who, alone, covered half of the expenses, thanks to the gifts from Fr. General and the North Belgian Province, to which Fr. Snoeck belonged, and thanks, lastly, to some other benefactors. If the library was left out, the Cologne Catholic agency "Adam Schall von Bell" did offer to settle all bills for books coming from German-speaking countries until May, 1991.

During this period another veteran of the Jerusalem Institute went back to Europe, Br. Joseph Šira. Born in eastern Moravia, now in Slovakia, in 1904, he had arrived in Jerusalem on July 12th, 1937, and left there for Rome in December 1973. A tailor by training, he was intelligent, methodical and determined; he was first of all photographer for the seventh excavation campaign at Teleilat Ghassul in 1938; he had charge of the archaeological collections, drew up a model catalogue of the Institute's collection of coins, received visitors to the museum and kept an eye on the library. After being intitiated into the history and geography of the Holy Land by Fr. A. Fernández, he was a competent guide for students and pilgrims. To be of greater help to everyone, he had learnt Italian, French and English. He died peacefully on December 6th, 1974, at the Biblical Institute in Rome (cf. *Biblica* 56 [1975] 149).

VII. **New enterprises: 1975-1989**

This period closes with a change in the status of the community of Jesuits in Jerusalem that was decided upon by Fr. General Peter-Hans Kolvenbach on October 31st, 1989 (cf. *infra*).

Getting the Jerusalem Institute back on the road again was fortunate. Of course, it was more than once necessary to revise the program offered by the Hebrew University, while keeping the essentials. Students from the Biblicum in Rome most often came in large numbers. A new opportunity of coming to Jerusalem for a semester was offered to other students from the Biblicum (cf. chapter III). Other programs were thus created that attracted former students of the Biblicum and Jesuits, which was good for the house during the second academic semester. Lastly, some work inside the Institute building that had been envisaged, requested or even planned but had not yet been done was completed.

Directing the Institute was first entrusted to Fr. Furlong. No more that Fr. Pitts, he was neither exegete nor archaeologist, but he had received training as a moral theologian. In fact the Society had made a superior out of him mainly: he had been one in the United States at St. Mary's College, Kansas, then in Rome at the Society's international houses, the Bellarmino, then at the Gesù and then it was that he was sent to Jerusalem; after seven years spent in the Holy City, he was again rector of the House of Writers back in Rome. A man of easy-going and pleasant tact, he had many fruitful contacts in Jerusalem with civil and religious authorities and with officials of the Hebrew University who, on his departure in 1981, offered him the University Medal in token of gratitude.

As soon as he took charge of the Jerusalem Institute on July 31st, 1974, he took on the onerous and tedious task of concluding the work undertaken in Fr. Pitts's time; he did it excellently. In particular, it was he who, in the last months of 1974, called upon Fr. William J. Fulco to move the former museum to the hall at the entry to the house (cf. chapter III). Later, with the Israeli architect Dan Ben Dor, who became a friend of the Institute, he had the railings on the terrace and balcony redone; back in 1963 Fr. Senès had recorded in his report, still in manuscript (p. 27), that they had been made with "really bad cement that crumbles a lot under the action of rain and sun". Fr. Furlong was not a creative person but a parcimonious administrator, in loyal relations with Fr. Martini then, as from July 26th, 1978, with the latter's successor, Fr. M. Gilbert. Yet it was Fr. Furlong who carried out the long and minute restoration of the Egyptian mummy in the Institute's museum (cf. chapter III).

In 1981 Fr. Furlong had to stand down for personal reasons. Fr. William J. Dalton agreed to succeed him for three years. He was teaching exegesis of the New Testament at the Roman Institute and since 1976 he had succeeded Fr. Dullea as the one in charge of the Institute's investment funds and as superior of the Jesuit community in that house. More outgoing than his predecessor, he was close to the students and very well received at the Hebrew University, but he did not like this stay in Jerusalem too much. The theft of coins from our museum did not help (cf. chapter III) and in the summer of 1984 he went back to Australia, his home country, without any regrets.

A rather strange period was now entered upon in which people in charge at the Institute overlap and succeed each other, but also a period of creativity in which some never solved problems at last found solutions.

Fr. Carlos Soltero, a Mexican who was then Fr. General's Delegate, did not manage to find a successor to Fr. Dalton, but in Rome in June, 1984, Fr. Albert Vanhoye had just assumed the post of rector of the Institute. Fr. Gilbert was thus free; he offered to stand in at Jerusalem for a period of six months, which was renewed for another semester, then for a second year. So he was Director *ad interim* for two years, from August 15th, 1984 to September 26th, 1986.

Fr. Delegate then got Fr. D. Thomas Hughson, from the Jesuit Marquette University in Milwaukee in the United States who, although not a biblical scholar, agreed to come to Jerusalem. For him it was an opportunity to finish a big task in theology. A year after his arrival he published the following work: D. Thomas HUGHSON (ed.), *Matthias Scheeben on Faith. The Doctoral Dissertation of John Courtney Murray* (Toronto Studies in Theology, 29), Lewiston/Queenston, Edwin Mellen Press, 1987, 274 p. It was an important work because it made Fr. Murray's thesis known; he was famous in the United States for his writings on morality in politics and, at Vatican II, for what he said about religious freedom, apart from the fact that Murray had studied Scheeben, the great 19th century theologian. The introduction to the book (pp. 1-54) was by Fr. Hughson and the preface ends with a mention of the Biblical Institute in Jerusalem.

Fr. Hughson took up his post on September 27th, 1986, and left for the United States on July 20th, 1989. However, he was just Vice-Director, with Fr. Gilbert remaining as Director. Hence the latter used to return to the Roman Institute regularly to give a course in exegesis that did not last the whole of each semester, and that continued until 1992.

Meanwhile, Fr. Soltero had been replaced by Fr. Giuseppe Pittau as Fr. General's Delegate. He came to Jerusalem to succeed Fr. Hughson as Vice-Director of the Institute. He held that office there from 1989 until June 2nd, 1992, then becoming Director for three years. At Rome, in the summer of 1990, Fr. Vanhoye had been replaced as rector by Fr. Klemens Stock.

Now on October 31st, 1989, Fr. General, after a discussion in Jerusalem between the rector, the director and the Vice-Director, changed the status of the house: the Jesuit community would no longer depend on the rector in Rome but became independent, whereas, as regards the Jerusalem Institute's being a branch of the one in Rome, nothing was changed (cf. Doc. J. II,15). The house in Jerusalem thereby gained autonomy but it lost the real and concrete support of the mother house in Rome. At the Institute in Rome the majority took no further interest in the Jerusalem branch, so much so that one of the later rectors coming to Jerusalem went so far as to say: "I am no more than a guest here!".

Fr. Gilbert had been afraid of that for some years. Giving an account of the situation of the house in Jerusalem in a letter addressed to Fr. General on January 15th, 1986, he wrote:

We depend entirely on the Biblical Institute in Rome. The programs followed here are decided upon and judged by the PBI in Rome which sometimes makes choices with immediate effect upon us (and negative effect), without consulting us, sometimes even without knowing exactly what it is about (that happened again a few weeks ago). In fact there are too many periods of silence between the two houses of the Biblical Institute and we do not feel any interest or attention, on the part of the Roman one, for ours. We look for some simple means to increase contacts but we also feel that the Biblical Institute in Rome (and especially the authorities there who are also ours) ought to be more aware of their responsibilities and act accordingly. Do the people at the PBI in Rome realize our dependence and isolation? Every decision, or lack of decision (for example about the renewal programs for exegetes and theologians) has a bearing on our work and even on what our financial situation will permit. If the PBI in Rome does not really do something to send us students we lose part of our raison d'être and must face serious financial problems, without benefiting from the Consortium's Fund Raising [which brings together the Gregorian University and the two Institutes – the Biblical and the Oriental]; […]. One of our people who is away this year wrote to me recently this year about this: 'the Biblicum in Rome needs Jerusalem; it really does; otherwise exegesis such as this (without Jerusalem) is likely to be carried on without history and, in practice, on the moon!' There is a point there for us that worries us, too.

In reply Fr. General wrote on January 23rd:

> Your report gave me a better understanding not only of the truly special situation of our presence in Jerusalem but also of the need for a much deeper and more organic relationship with the Biblicum in Rome and with the Provincials, especially in Europe, with regard to the various programs for permanent education and renewal. […] Your remarks will be passed on to the various people responsible, while observing secrecy about the sources, and I hope that at least some urgent problems will be studied and solved.

But before these new statutes in 1989 the Institute in Jerusalem was able to go ahead with several matters that had become necessary or opportune, in agreement with the Roman house.

The first was the agreement reached between the Institute and the École Biblique et Archéologique Française run by the Dominicans in Jerusalem. The origin of this agreement has been described in Part One of this book. It was signed on December 24th, 1984 (cf. *Acta PIB* 9, pp. 95-96) and in February, 1986, the first students from the Biblicum came to pass the second semester at the École (cf. chapter III). This agreement had the added advantage that several of these students were lodged at the Institute.

Two other programs were also arranged. The first, run by the Institute's two houses, offered exegetes and theologians – former students at the Biblicum – the opportunity to follow a renewal program in Jerusalem after one term of three months in Rome. Thus it was that from March 1st until May 31st, 1981, thirteen people, mainly priests, took part in a session directed by Fr. Fritzleo Lentzen-Deis, a professor at the Institute in Rome, which had "Jesus-Texts in the Gospels" as subject. From February 25th until May 31st, 1982, Fr. Roger Le Déaut, CSSp, also a professor at the Roman Institute, offered nine other persons a similar program on the following subject: "Jewish Tradition and New Testament" (cf. *Acta PIB* 8, pp. 480-481, 559). However, the experiment was not taken further, mainly because no other professor in Rome was available.

A second program was more successful. It was offered by the Institute to about fifteen Italian Jesuit priests. This "corso biblico-ignaziano", arranged by Fr. Francesco Rossi de Gasperis along with some helpers, began on March 1st and finished at the end of May, over a period of ten years, from 1984 to 1995. In addition, a similar program, confined to the month of September, was offered to thirteen Italian Jesuit laybrothers in 1989.

These various programs also meant that the house was full at times when, in the past, it was too often empty.

Finally, during this period some work on the building in Jerusalem was done. In the spring of 1985, with Ben Dor the architect, the big hall of the library was divided into two floors so that ten thousand books could be placed on the new floor and in this way clear up the ground floor for a while. As for the depot of the former museum in the north-east corner of the house, it was emptied, not only by putting the fresco with the star of Ghassul in the new museum set up in 1974, but especially by placing all the material from the depot, including the museum's archives, on another level in the form of a mezzanine, and thereby the former museum became a large living room.

To the north of our property there was some waste ground that was bought by the Hebrew Union College that wanted to expand. But first the ground had to be dug to a depth of several metres. It was hard rock that had to be blown apart bit by bit with dynamite. These explosions, which occurred almost daily in the evenings, went on for almost two years and damaged our building: the inside water-tank in the house was cracked and emptied, while many cracks appeared on all floors of the house. When the excavation was over agreement was reached on June 19th, 1986, with those responsible for the damage who took charge of the cost of repairs. At that time the dean of the Hebrew Union College was Professor Michael L. Klein. In 1980 he had published two volumes in the Roman Institute's *Analecta Biblica* collection (no. 76) entitled: *The Fragment-Targums of the Pentateuch* and we had good relations with him. Our architect, Ben Dor, also did his part to see that the repairs were well done.

There was still the lift that Fr. Semkowski had asked for in January 1967. Only on May 10th, 1988, did Fr. General take the decision to install it and he asked Fr. Hillengass, the General Treasurer for a goodly sum to cover the costs. The installation was done in the spring and summer of the following year.

Thus the period from 1975 to 1989 was a fruitful one for the Jerusalem Institute and may be regarded as one of the most splendid in its existence. The house was most often working full time and rendered good and loyal service to budding biblical scholars, as well as to fully-trained ones. Moreover, the house had really benefited from some work that had become necessary.

VIII. **Difficulties, then successful modernization: 1989-2009**

Fr. Soltero's first three years in Jerusalem (1989-1992) were marked mainly by the change in the status of the house (cf. *supra*) and by the Gulf War. For some years the number of students registered for the program offered by the Hebrew University had already been decreasing and the situation had got worse by reason of the first Palestinian "Intifada" which broke out in December 1987, but it improved noticeably during the subsequent period in which Fr. Soltero was Director (1992-1995).

About 2 o'clock in the morning on January 17th, 1991, the Gulf War broke out. Fr. Soltero was in Rome and stayed there for a while. Exams at the Hebrew University had been brought forward as a precautionary measure and the semester was consequently shortened. Most of the students had left Israel in good time. Only five of them stayed, despite the risks. Two rooms on the second floor had to be got ready which, in case of an alert, were to be used as a shelter because, it was said, the Iraqi missiles contained poison gas that would gather at ground level, especially as it rained so much those days. In case of danger, then, it was better to be at the highest part of the house. Once the inhabitants assembled in two minutes (sic!) the two rooms were hermetically sealed. Seats and blankets, food and drink had been placed there, should it be necessary to hold out for several hours.

With fear in the pit of the stomach, people prayed. The siren sounded most often at night, sometimes even four times on the night of Friday to Saturday, the sabbath! At least three loud explosions were heard in the distance; each time it was a "Patriot" missile that had just made a direct hit on an Iraqi missile. The radio used to broadcast reassuring messages in several languages, clearly indicating when one could leave the shelters once the danger had passed. By day, not knowing what might happen the next night, some excellent meals were taken and, above all, work was done. It was in this context that the writer of these lines wrote about thirty pages on charity, according to the writings and witness of the life of Fr. M.-J. Lagrange. The Hebrew University also took care of us: Professor Aaron Singer, in charge of our students' program, regularly came to see how we were getting on, asking if there was anything we needed.

Fr. John J. Crocker succeeded Fr. Soltero at the end of August 1995 and the latter returned to Mexico. Fr. Crocker knew the house in Jerusalem, having been registrar at the Institute from 1982 to 1991. In Jerusalem, where he stayed for three years, not only did the number of students again increase until the house was practically full, but also, from 1996 to 1999, in March and April Fr. Juan Manuel Martín-Moreno offered a biblical-ignatian renewal course to some Spanish Jesuits who came in growing numbers each year: 15 in 1996 and 22 in 1999, but this offer was discontinued. Meanwhile, in summer, 1996, Fr. Robert F. O'Toole had succeeded Fr. Stock as rector of the Institute

Then again, Fr. Crocker resumed the modernization of the house. In particular, he embellished and put the ground floor of the library in order, where the students could henceforth be more at ease while working; with the help of Fr. William J. Fulco, the only one who knew the museum well, he reorganized and modernized the hall of the museum and installed an anti-theft security device in it as well (cf. chapter III).

On October 1st, 1998 Fr. Thomas J. Fitzpatrick succeeded him, while remaining superior of the Jesuits in Amman, where he went for a week about once a month, until 2004. He had been given the task of continuing the modernization of the Institute in Jerusalem. He did it with good taste and perseverance. Today the Institute is certainly more attractive and practical for academic activity. Thus it was that he solved the by now urgent problem of a classroom. Until then classes were held, for example, in a room on the first floor in Fr. Semkowski's time, then, after the work done in 1974, on the ground floor in the small hall in the south-west corner of the building, and more recently in the library. Now, in 1927 in the north-east corner of the property a small building had been put up in which they were thinking of installing an electricity-generating plant, which proved to be useless. This building had become a lumber-room. In 2002 it was made into an attractive classroom. In the same year the central building was linked to the internet. In the spring of 2004 the precious reserved section in the library was completely renovated. In 2005, being again short of room, this was given the western part of the ground-floor corridor. The cost of these and other equally important operations which did not concern academic life, could be borne by the house, some benefactors having generously covered one quarter of the costs.

After nine years Fr. Fitzpatrick finished his term of office on October 3rd, 2007, and left the Institute on the 7th to return to Boston. Fr. Maurice Gilbert took his place for a year, pending the appointment of a Director to serve for a full term. During this interlude, the archives in the museum were rearranged; in particular, thanks to Fr. Jean-Michel Tarragon, O.P., from the École Biblique et Archéologique Française, the many glass negatives of photos taken during the excavations at Teleilat Ghassul – several hundreds – were scanned and placed on DVD's; as a safety precaution, a copy of those DVD's was deposited in the archives of the Biblical Institute in Rome. In addition, all the other documents about the excavations at Elephantine that were found in the archives of the Biblical Institute, both in Rome and in Jerusalem, were also photocopied so that Fr. W. P. Fulco can write a book about those excavations which are still of interest today to several researchers.

Lastly, in November 2008, Fr. Joseph Nguyên Công Đoan, from Vietnam, became Director of the Jerusalem branch of the Institute. He was familiar with the house, having followed a programme in it during the academic year of 1972-1973; besides modern Hebrew, this programme included biblical languages as well as the geography, history and archaeology of the country; in 1975 he had gained the licentiate in biblical studies; he had been a consultor and assistant to the Father General in Eastern Asian matters since 2003.

On the academic level, there were several significant events. In the year 2000 the program offered by the Hebrew University reached the twenty-fifth year of its existence. On January 17th the university organized a symposium.

On behalf of the Institute, Fr. Jean-Louis Ska who in the past had given some courses in Jerusalem, and Fr. Gilbert, who had come back as "academic adviser" (Fr. General had asked that there be a professor of exegesis at least for half of the time in Jerusalem) addressed it and the university was represented by Professor Avi Hurvitz, who had taught our students since 1975, and Professor Yair Zakowitz, the dean of the faculty. An academic session followed at which the origin and meaning of this program were recalled. Professor Talmon described his recollections. A warm message from Cardinal C. M. Martini, Archbishop of Milan since 1980, was read.

In the months of June and July, 2000, on the occasion of the jubilee year, five congresses in succession were held at the Jerusalem Institute for Jesuits working in various sectors of the apostolate (cf. *Acta PIB* 10, p. 642). Another congress, on the situation of "Christians in the Holy Land" in July, 2001, in the same place brought twenty-five Jesuits together; Fr. David Neuhaus was the main organizer, along with Fr. Peter DuBrul, a Jesuit professor at the University of Bethlehem since 1975 (*Acta PIB* 10, p. 908).

In addition, as from September, 2000, a new program in biblical history and geography in Italian is offered yearly to about thirty students from the Biblicum by the *Studium Biblicum Franciscanum* (cf. chapter III).

Finally, from October 2002 until March 2008, Cardinal Martini, a former professor and rector of the Institute, came to stay at the Jerusalem Institute. The emeritus Archbishop of Milan quietly slipped back into editing and researching the history of biblical manuscripts, while carrying on a spiritual ministry (cf. chap. III).

As can be seen, this recent period was full of pleasant surprises. The Institute in Jerusalem is still very much alive and one can only wish for an ever more fruitful co-operation with the house in Rome, to the benefit of both places.

Conclusion

Can one draw conclusions from a story that is not yet finished? After eighty years of good and loyal service the Biblical Institute's branch in Jerusalem faces the future calmly, and with no illusions about the difficulties awaiting it, either. Such is life.

Only the major events in this story have been recounted in these pages, while care has been taken to keep to the thread running through it. Each period has thrown up very different situations that never repeat themselves in exactly the same way and yet the intention remains the same: to be the Jerusalem branch of the Pontifical Biblical Institute of which the main seat is in Rome.

Problems have not been lacking, and they will not cease to be lacking. The main one is the involvement of the Society of Jesus, to which the Holy See entrusted the Institute, in sending qualified Jesuit staff to ensure the welfare of the house in Jerusalem on the academic as well as the administrative level. The second problem, notwithstanding greater participation in the activities of the scholarly biblical world in Jerusalem, will still be attracting many students at the Roman centre to come to Jerusalem to study one of the programs offered there by several institutions with which the Institute has entered into agreement. It is up to the house in Rome not to forget this!

Doc. J. II,1

APIBJ

*The Two Instructions from Fr. Bea about how to carry out excavations
Comparison of the two versions of n° 3 in them, translated from the Latin*

The 1932 Instruction:

3. – Work on excavations by Fathers who are appointed by Superiors to work on them is done by *common council*. The person who "directs the excavations" is a *"primus inter pares"*, as happens in certain other scholarly work undertaken by the Society, e. g, the work done by the Bollandists, and it is first of all incumbent upon him to insure that things prescribed either by the Authorities of the Institute or decided upon by Fathers working on the excavations in common consultation and council be done.

Everything should, however, be done with that spirit of charity, mutual trust and fraternal help that is proper to sons of the Society and which has borne such great fruit in the history of the Society, and care should be taken that everyone, according to his own special knowledge, contribute as much as possible to the success of the work and help the others as far as he can.

The 1937 Instruction:

III.- Work on excavations should be carried out with really fraternal co-operation by those who are appointed by Superiors to do it.

1) Besides the supervision of religious life, which is to be observed also during excavations, the general preparation for and organization of excavations, financial administration and representation of the Institute to the outside world even in matters concerning the excavations and the direction of the consultations that will take place in his presence pertain to the Fr. Superior (in so far as he is Director of the Jerusalem house of the Institute).

2) He who *"directs the excavations"* is answerable in scientific matters to the civil authorities as regards the procedure and method followed in excavating. In actually carrying out the work, however, he is a *"primus inter pares"*, as is also the case in other scientific work undertaken by the Society; it is his duty to supervise the methodical and scientific method in carrying out what is prescribed by the civil Authority or laid down by the Governors of the Institute or agreed upon in common consultation by the Fathers actually engaged in the excavations.

3) *The Father Superior and the Director of the excavations* should collaborate very carefully in doing the work, discuss together what is to be done and co-ordinate in

common consent between them the work of all concerned. If agreement between them about anything of minor importance cannot be reached, the Fr. Superior, as vicegerent of the Rector of the Institute, must decide; in more serious matters the reasons for and against must be drawn up and recourse be had to the Rector.

4) Lastly, *all* those engaged on the work of excavations should be united in that spirit of charity, mutual trust and fraternal assistance which is proper to sons of the Society and which has borne such great fruit in the Society. All, according to their own particular knowledge, should contribute to the successful outcome of the work and help each other as much as they can.

* * * * *

Doc. J. II,2

APIBR B-VI (VI-1 19 1935-1938)

A letter from Fr. Lobignac about a lecture by Fr. Teilhard, translated from the French

+M

Séminaire des Missions de Syrie
4, Montée de Fourvière
Lyon

March 22nd, 1935

Reverend and dear Fr. Rector,

P. C.

Thank you for the booklets "ad montem Sinai". I have had two letters these days, one from Fr. Fernández, the other from Fr. Koeppel, concerning the following plan. Fr. Teilhard de Chardin has to stop off in Jerusalem in June. Mr Neuville had the idea of getting him to give a lecture on sinanthropus and prehistoric research in China, under the patronage of the "Palestine Oriental Society". Mr Neuville would like to have this lecture given at our place, instead of the Dominican École biblique or the American archaeological school. Fr. Koeppel is urging me in that direction, Fr. Fernández is a bit afraid. Here is my opinion, and you will tell me what you think expedient.

I would be quite pleased to start public lectures at the Institute. It would strengthen our situation at Jerusalem a bit more. Besides, Fr. Teilhard has a very high reputation among prehistorians. His lecture is sure to be a great success.

The difficulty is the stance taken by the Father on certain problems. He has a tendency, despite all the remarks that have been made to him, to make philosophical or theological syntheses which have alarmed the authorities more than once. I could tell him to confine himself exclusively to the scientific field. On the other hand, as people from the "Palestine Oriental Society" are not specifically Catholic, a certain freedom of speech causes less trouble than it would in a lecture held at an ecclesiastical educational establishment or in front of a Roman public.

All things considered, I think it is better that the proposed lecture be given at our place rather than elsewhere. The importance that questions of prehistory in Palestine assume justifies a lecture on the subject. I shall use my influence to keep the lecturer on the level of facts and methods. If any persons were to be surprised in Rome that the Biblical Institute should open its doors to Fr. T. de Ch., it would have to be said that at Jerusalem we cannot remain indifferent to these questions which are being asked every moment, and that you are leaving me with the responsibility for this initiative. In specialist circles, however, our attitude will make a good impression and stop it being said that Rome closes its eyes to certain problems (people could criticize the fact that a Jesuit speaking in Jerusalem was forced to ask protestant Americans, or the École biblique for asylum, which could thus appear to be more open scientifically than ours). Rely on me to see to it that there are no more problems. I shall write to Fr. Teilhard de Chardin as soon as I receive your answer. He will understand that at the Biblical Institute one cannot not take certain matters of prudence into account. At Rome itself it would seem to me better not to say anything *ante factum*, so as not to give rise to any comments.

This lecture may also provide the opportunity to "set up" our big salon a bit and to make it suitable for public lectures. If this first event succeeds, I may invite Fr. Poidebard next winter to talk on his method of archaeological research by air. We could then perhaps invite officers from the "Royal Air Force" and the High Commissioner himself. [...]

In union with your Holy Sacrifices, yours very devotedly in Our Lord,

M. Lobignac, S. J.

* * * * *

Doc. J. II,3

APIBJ

Letter from Fr. General to Fr. Lobignac, translated from the French

Rome, March 27th, 1935

Dear Reverend Father,

P. C.

Fr. Bea has passed on to me the part of one of your letters where there is a question of a *lecture by Father Teilhard de Chardin in Jerusalem*.

This is the directive I think I should give you: first of all no Father can give a lecture in a city where there is a house of the Society without the authorization of the Superior of that house. So if you judge it inopportune that Father Teilhard give that lecture at the Biblical Institute, he could not give it elsewhere without your permission.

It seems impossible to let Father Teilhard give this lecture in a Protestant place or at the place belonging to the Dominicans who, if there were problems afterwards, might complain that we compromised them.

There remains thus only one solution, which is to agree that the Father give his lecture in our house in Jerusalem, but on two conditions, namely that he keep strictly to the scientific field and that his lecture be duly checked as is required by the Epitome n. 685.

This reply will be of use to you as a directive in other similar cases; be aware that you are answerable to the Holy See and the Society for everything that a Father of the Society does in Jerusalem.

I recommend myself, Reverend Father, to your Holy Sacrifices.

Your servant in Our Lord

Wl Ledóchowsky

* * * * *

Doc. J. II,4

APIBJ

Reply from Fr. Bea to Fr. Lobignac, translated from the Italian

Pontificio Istituto Biblico

Rome, March 29th, 1935

Reverend Fr. Superior,

P.Xti

By now you will have at hand the letter from V. R. Fr. General with which he himself wished to reply to the question about Fr. Teilhard de Chardin's lecture. The matter seemed to me too important to reply to without informing Fr. General of it – besides, I was fairly sure that he would in this case give an affirmative answer, as he in fact did. It only remains for me to hope, therefore, that the lecture enjoys the greatest success and to ask you make an accurate and rather strict check on it before the event. It is clear that on this occasion other people will pay great attention to what is said, and should Fr. Teilhard say anything not quite correct or too risky you can be certain that it will be said that that is the teaching of the Pont. Biblical Institute. It will therefore perhaps be opportune that the Father say right at the beginning that he thanks the Institute for the "hospitality that it has kindly given someone who does not belong to its teaching staff and who cannot speak in the name of the Institute but only in his own name". In this way any wrong interpretations are cut short right at the start.

For the rest, I am very happy that in this way we can hope to inaugurate the series of lectures to be held at our Institute, and I wish the enterprise all success. Would it not also be possible to invite Mr Neuville, too, to give a report there after the campaign at Ḳafze? [...]

That's all for now! With every best wish in union with your holy sacrifices.

Augustin Bea, S. J.

* * * * *

Doc. J. II,5

APIBR B-VI (VI-1 1938-1935)

Extract from a letter from Fr. Lobignac to Fr. Bea, translated from the French

+M

April 4th, 1935

Séminaire des Missions de Syrie
4, Montée de Fourvière
Lyon

Reverend Father Rector, P. C.

[...] I have received the letter from V. R. Fr. General, the contents of which you already know. I have not yet replied to his Paternity because I am waiting for a letter from Mr Neuville, who is the promoter of the lecture. The latter is to be given under the auspices of the Palestine Oriental Society (which shows very clearly at this stage that we are not taking the initiative in it, and that we are *lending* our hall, as the

American School or the École Biblique do in similar cases). Also, the Rev. Fr. de Bonneville tells me that Fr. Teilhard is to come to Paris in May. I do not yet see very clearly how things are going to be arranged. In any case the necessary precautions will be taken and V. R. Fr. General's instructions will be carefully carried out. On the spot, experience will instruct us about what must be tried in the category of "lectures".

Kind regards to everyone. In union with your Holy Sacrifices, yours sincerely in our Lord.

M. Lobignac, S. J

* * * * *

Doc. J. II,6

APIBJ

Translated from the Italian

Pontifical Biblical Institute
P.O.B. 497
Jerusalem (Palestine)

August 28th, 1941

To His Excellency Monsignor Gustavo Testa, Apostolic Delegate

Excellency:

Y. E. recalls that, with Your full approval, the British government was informed that the Pont. Biblical Inst. was ready to receive some British officers; this we did, in addition to doing a favour to the public authority, to avoid the threat of having to receive, unwillingly, whole families, as happens in some religious houses – a threat that still exists and will probably cease only with the end of the war. On the other hand, having so many free rooms, it is embarrassing for us to give a negative answer to those who ask us for hospitality, which is what we cannot grant conveniently.

Now an opportunity has presented itself to us which may in some way solve these difficulties, and to a certain extent to our advantage.

This would be to grant our first floor for the use of British officers – excluding families – along with the kitchen and dining room, and we would not have to worry about anything, everything would be looked after by a certain Mr (Hadad) who owns a hotel not far from us. I have made the necessary enquiries about him and I have been told in many quarters that he is a good Catholic and a reliable, honest man; the impression he made on me is a good one.

We would withdraw to the second floor, with the gallery, more than enough room for our small Community and some guests. A small partition would be built so that the part reserved for us would be completely separated and independent.

As regards conditions, they would pay for water, electricity, telephone, servant; they will also give free board to the four of us in the Community, and then 600 P. P. a year. In the critical conditions in which we find ourselves this, too, seems to be an advantage to be considered.

Now, drawing up this contract is obviously beyond my capabilities and I would certainly have to have recourse to Rome. But, as such recourse is impossible now, I take leave to approach Y. E. as the Representative of the Holy See, submitting the aforesaid suggestion to Your esteemed judgment, and most ready to do what, in the present conditions, well known to Y. E., Y. E. will judge more suitable and convenient.

Reverently kissing the ring

please believe me Your Most Reverend Excellency's humble servant in Xto.

Andrés Fernández, S. J.

* * * * *

Doc. J.II,7

APIBJ

Translated from the Italian

Delegatio Apostolica
Palestinae

Jerusalem (Mons Sion) August 28th, 1941

Very Reverend and dear Father,

I have given most careful attention to what you submitted for my advice on the proposal to grant British officers a certain part of the Biblical Institute for use as lodging, according to what you wrote to me in your letter with today's date.

Taking into full consideration the prudent reasons adopted by you, I think it is fitting, with so great a shortage of accommodation in Jerusalem, to offer the officers of the British Army the possibility of finding lodgings in the Biblical Institute. I am sure that the Secretariat of State will have no objections and I take full responsibility in the matter.

With all good wishes I remain, Most Reverend Father, yours sincerely,

+ G. Testa
Ap. D.

Very Rev. Father A. Fernández
Rector of the Pont. Biblical Institute
Jerusalem

* * * * *

Doc. J. II,8

APIBJ

Translated from the Italian

Pontifical Biblical Institute

Rome (101) August 13th, 1947
Piazza della Pilotta, 35

Reverend Fr. Director,

We have received the letter dated August 7th in which Y. R. reports that by the "Food Control Office" the proposal has been made to connect the drains at our house to the main sewers and you ask what our contribution to this work might be.

We are very sorry not to be able to enter into negotiations in this matter before the legal situation of the Food Control Office with regard to the house of our Institute is fully clarified and settled by mutual agreement. When the contract expired, the Chairman of the "District Housing Committee" informed us on December 27th, 1946, that "Government is unable to release hiring Nr. 716, Jerusalem, owing to the absence of any other accommodation". In response to this unilateral declaration we protested on February 4th, 1947, in a letter passed to the competent British authorities, saying that our house is the property of the Holy See, that is, of *another State*, and as such cannot be requisitioned, as if it were a private house, without the consent of the owner, i. e. the Government of the Vatican City State. Not having so far received a reply to this protest, we cannot enter into any negotiations concerning our house before the "Government" has settled the question of the rent and put an end to a situation which we must consider illegal and contrary to international law.

We could not therefore give our consent to the drainage work which is being discussed, even if the Government were willing to pay for it themselves, without a contribution from us.

Please inform the competent British authorities of this reply of ours.

With kind regards

Office of the Director of the Pontifical Biblical Institute
Augustin Bea
Rector

Rev. John J. O'Rourke
Director of the Pontifical Biblical Institute, Jerusalem
Jerusalem – Palestine

* * * * *

Doc. J. II,9

APIBJ

Translated from the French

PONTIFICIO
ISTITUTO BIBLICO

Rome, February 4th, 1948

Rev. Fr. John J. O'Rourke, Direct.
Pont. Inst. Bibl.
P.O.B. 497 Jerusalem

Dear Fr. Director,

The Rector of the Pontifical Biblical Institute, in a letter dated January 27th, explained to His Holiness Pope Pius XII the present situation of the house of the Biblical Institute in Jerusalem, which belongs to the Holy See, and Pius XII has decided that his Secretariat of State should negotiate this matter with the British government. The Holy See's point of view is as follows: it insists that the relations be regulated by contract but in a way that it should not lay down unilaterally what is to be left to us, but also do justice to the needs and wishes of the Institute. However, this contract will only be made with the present "Palestine Government" and that for as long as the

British Administration is still there, and will be no longer valid once the British Authorities have left the house. The Holy See reserves full freedom of action *vis-à-vis* a future Government of Palestine, and requires that the building be returned to the Holy See immediately after the departure of the British authorities.

Meanwhile neither the Director of the house nor the Rector of the Institute are authorized to settle the future use of the house, but it is the Secretariat of the Papal State that reserves all this matter to itself. Should any suggestion be made to Your Reverence, therefore, please request that it be made in writing and then kindly send it to me immediately, adding what you think of it so that I can forward the document to the Holy See.

I ask you to explain this situation in a suitable manner to the British authorities, if it would be useful.

Yours very devotedly.

Augustin Bea, S. J.
Rector

* * * * *

Doc. J. II,10

APIBJ

Secretariat of State
of His Holiness

From the Vatican, March 24th, 1948

N° 142148

The undersigned Substitute of the Secretariat of State of His Holiness certifies that the buildings of the Pontifical Biblical Institute in Jerusalem entrusted to the direction of the Fathers of the Society of Jesus, are the property of the Holy See, and may not be handed over to anybody under any title without the express consent of the Holy See.

GB Montini

I hereby certify that the
above is the signature of H. E.
Monsignor G. B. Montini,
Substitute of the Secretariat of State
of His Holiness.

(*Seal of*) HIS BRITANNIC
MAJESTY'S LEGATION
TO THE HOLY SEE.
(*with signature of*) J S Somers Cocks
for H. M. Minister
April 3rd 1948

* * * * *

Doc. J. II,11

APIBJ

Translated from the Italian

Pontifical Biblical Institute
3, Paul Emile Botta St.
POB 497
Jerusalem (Israel)

16 January 1967

Very Reverend Father Delegate [Francis J. McCool], P. Ch

I suppose that the deliberations at your consultations are carried on in Italian, so I take the liberty to write this reply of mine to your letter of the 7th inst. in the same language.

There being certain rumours going round that the house in Jerusalem should be closed, I, however, reply that it should be kept. Because if we give it up (which we could not do without the consent of the Holy See), the Holy See will look for another Community instead of us. For the prestige of the Institute and the convenience of our students and of so many Jesuits, who pass through Palestine in ever-increasing numbers, we must have a *pied-à-terre* in Jerusalem; we have one in Jewish Jerusalem, but it would be very useful to have a proxy in the Arab one.

The house must not develop into an Institute independent of the Roman one but must be its branch in the Holy Land.

What must be done? I think what has been done in these recent years, that is to say the second semester of the third year and giving those who wish the chance to study modern and ancient Hebrew during the summer.

Holding public lectures from time to time on subjects in the field of biblical and Palestinian archaeology, geography and philology.

Writing articles and books on these subjects in collaboration with the journals of the Biblicum in Rome and others.

Helping with writing reviews for those journals.

And any other things of that kind pertaining to our work, which do not come to mind at present.

To accomplish all these tasks there is need of two competent men in archaeology, geography and philology, resident in Jerusalem throughout the year or who could teach one semester in Rome, another in Jerusalem.

A Fr. Minister would also be needed who, if he did not teach, would at least be well versed enough in knowledge of the Country to be able to give advice to those who need it, such as visiting it or even accompanying pilgrims on their visits.

As regards financial resources, with the small income we get from the foundation, along with Mass stipends, if we have enough (so far, for the almost eight years I have been here and for five years before that, we have always had enough of them, sometimes modest ones, sometimes more substantial ones), from the sale of slides, from the board and lodging fees of guests and students, from assistance given to pilgrims, from some one-off contributions, we have been able to get by so as to be able to install running water (cold only) at last and mains electricity for heating rooms.

Hanging over us is a debt of more than 12,000 I. L., owed to the City Cleansing Department to which we have paid nothing for about twelve years. The calculation seems exaggerated, however, so we are not in a hurry to pay.

There are still some things to be done in the house, such as whitewashing many rooms, painting window-frames, which have not been whitewashed or painted for about fifteen years, redoing the gate at the entrance to the courtyard – all this will need several thousand dollars.

And lastly it would be necessary to install a lift, so that some elderly people or those with weak hearts could also live on the upper floors. (Fr. Senès lived for many years in the garage in the garden and Br. Šira lives on the ground floor, precisely because both had to avoid any strain on the heart.)

Fr. Sabourin, during his last visit to Rome last year, gave V. Rev. Fr. General a memorandum with more extensive plans. He wanted to bring to Jerusalem some Catholic (or perhaps even Protestant) students who would stay here for some weeks in summer to initiate themselves on the spot into a knowledge of the Country.

But since at that period (June-September) our house is usually occupied by our students who come to study at the ulpan, the other group would have to live elsewhere, and another place outside our house would have to be found for classes, too, because our lounge would have to remain at the disposal of our visitors. That room n° 3, which we use for our own classes, would perhaps be too small, if there were quite a number of those students (especially American or Canadian). And what would happen if women came to these classes, too?

To sum up, in my modest opinion, we need to keep the house in Jerusalem, especially for the use of our students from Rome and of so many Jesuits passing through the Holy Land who would otherwise have to go to non-Christian hotels and go without the guidance which we can give them.

As permanently resident staff in charge, there would be need for a Fr. Minister and two good professors, one of whom would be Superior, who would be willing to do work of a scholarly nature and be able to acquire authority in the sight of people outside.

With renewed good wishes to Your Paternity and all the members of the Council for a Happy New Year

> your humble servant in Chr.

Ludovic Semkowski

Very Reverend Father
Francis McCool
Delegate for the interprovincial houses.

* * * * *

Doc. J. II,12

APIBR K-32-A(32/8A)

Pontifical Biblical Institute
The Rector

16/7/73

Prof. Dr. A. Harman
President of
The Hebrew University of Jerusalem
JERUSALEM – ISRAEL

Dear Professor Harman,

I hope you will recall my visit at the end of March to your office, at the University, with Prof. Goshen-Gottstein. We discussed the possibility of having a one-year program for Hebrew, archaeology and history, which could meet the needs of our students of the Bible. The main lines of the plan were:

– July-September: modern Hebrew, to give the students the possibility to follow courses at the University
– October-June: Biblical Hebrew (elementary grammar, historical grammar, reading of the Hebrew Bible; biblical archaeology with excursions, biblical history).

Your first reaction to this idea was very favourable and you told me to write to you after some months to give you the time to make a first tentative inquiry about the feasibility of such a program, which should begin in the academic year 1974-1975.

We have in the meantime studied a plan for the renovation of our house of the Pontifical Biblical Institute in Jerusalem to provide accommodation for a first group of 20 students.

At this time it would be important for us to know whether you still see the possibility for the University to offer such a program for our students, and what should be done in order to explore further this possibility and to arrive at a detailed program.

With gratitude for your kindness and cooperation

Carlo M. Martini, S. J.

THE HEBREW UNIVERSITY OF JERUSALEM
OFFICE OF THE PRESIDENT
Jerusalem, September 10, 1973

Professor Carlo M. Martini, S. J., Rector
Pontificio Istituto Biblico
I – Roma
Via della Pilotta, 25
ITALY

Dear Rector Martini,

After receiving your letter, I have consulted with my colleagues here. There has been some delay, owing to the fact that some of my colleagues have been away for the Summer Vacation.

After consultation, I find that it would be possible for us to offer a program for your students along the lines discussed between us and referred to in your letter of July 16, 1973.

I would suggest that a convenient next step might be either for one of your representatives to come here to discuss the matter with our people, or for one of our colleagues to proceed to Rome to discuss the matter with you. During such discussions, the specifics of the curriculum could be worked out that would accord with your requirements.

I feel that this could be done in time for the academic year 1974/1975. To make this possible, the contacts suggested should take place between now and the end of 1973.

I look forward to hearing from you, so that we can set the matter in train.

Sincerely yours,
Avraham Harman
President

* * * * *

Doc. J. II,13

APIBR K-32-B (32/4)

There is also an Italian version of this document

PONTIFICIO ISTITUTO BIBLICO
00187 ROMA
Via della Pilotta, 25

Projected Program of Studies for the Preparatory Year at Jerusalem
February 15 – September 15, 1975

During the coming academic year (1974-1975) the Pontifical Biblical Institute, jointly with the Hebrew University of Jerusalem, will inaugurate a new program of studies. This program will be integrated with the degree program of the Biblical Faculty of the Pontifical Biblical Institute in Rome.

The program will consist of three terms, the first of which will be spent at Rome, and the last two at Jerusalem. During the Term I, the regular October-February semester at Rome, candidates for the program will follow the course in propaedeutic Hebrew and, if need be, in propaedeutic Greek. Toward the end of the semester, prospective students will be offered an intensive course (25 hours a week for 2-3 weeks) in Colloquial Hebrew, to prepare them for their work at Jerusalem where Hebrew will be the language of instruction at the University. This course will be offered in collaboration with the Hebrew University. Those students who pass the examination in propaedeutic Hebrew and, if necessary, in propaedeutic Greek *with the grade of 8* will be eligible to continue the program at Jerusalem. beginning on or about February 15.

The Program at Jerusalem: Terms II and III will each last 12-13 weeks – Term II from mid-February to the end of May, Term III from mid-June to mid-September. Courses will be given both at the Hebrew University and at the Biblical Institute. At the University there will be 12-14 class hours per week, about 170 hours by term, a total of 320-340 hours. At the Biblical Institute classes will be held for 12 weeks at 3 hours per week (the equivalent of the second semester at Rome).

Courses at the Hebrew University

1. *Colloquial Hebrew*: the aim of this course is to give, through the use of the living language, a knowledge of Hebrew lexicography which will facilitate the students' approach to the Hebrew Bible.

2. *Biblical Hebrew*: on the basis of the elementary Hebrew grammar already studied in the propaedeutic courses during Term I at Rome, this course aims to give a deeper knowledge of Biblical Hebrew, especially with regard to morphology, primitive forms, etc., corresponding to the course entitled "Hebrew A-B" given at the Biblical Institute in Rome.

3. *Reading of Biblical Texts* (with philological and lexicographical treatment): texts to be read in Term II will be chosen from narration; in Term III from poetry.

4. *Introduction to Archaeology and Historical Geography*: these courses will cover the matter corresponding to the following courses given at Rome: Biblical Archaeology, Biblical Geography, History of the Old Testament, History of the New Testament. Students will participate in tours and in historical sight-seeing; they will take part in an archaeological excavation for one week. (The tours and excavation work together will satisfy the requirement for the *Seminar without Paper* at Rome.)

Courses at the Biblical Institute

Propaedeutic Greek: second semester. The number of classes will be equivalent to a semester of 12 weeks at five hours per week. Class period will be so allocated as to allow an intensive study of Biblical Hebrew during the first part of the program.

Seminar in Biblical Methodology: optional

NOTES

1. Although candidates of any language will be eligible for the program, it is recommended that they know English or Italian well. As noted above, classes at the Hebrew University will be conducted in Hebrew.

2. Students will be housed at the Pontifical Biblical Institute, 3, Rehov Paul Emile Botta, B. P. 497, Jerusalem, Israel.

3. A Director of the Biblical Institute in Jerusalem will act as coordinator with the Hebrew University.

4. The cost of board and lodging at the Biblical Institute and of tuition at the Hebrew University are not immediately available. Every effort will be made to keep them at a level commensurate with the cost of a similar program at Rome.

For further information write

      The Secretary
      Pontificio Istituto Biblico
      00187 Roma
      Via della Pilotta, 25

July 1974

* * * * *

Doc. J. II,14

APIBJ
Translated from the Italian

PONTIFICIO ISTITUTO BIBLICO

I -00187 Rome 5/6/73

The Rector

Rev. Fr. Samuel Pitts, S. J.
Pontifical Biblical Institute
P. O. Box 497
91000 JERUSALEM

Dear Father Pitts,

Along with this letter of mine I am sending you my greetings and those of all the Community, passing them on to you through Br. Consonno. I spoke with him today about the problems concerning the work to be planned in Jerusalem, on the basis of the points you raised in your letter of November 6th, 1972, and the conversations I had with you during my visit in March.

I spoke to him in particular about the following items concerning construction and brickwork:

1. The problem of canalization, to be assessed within the various possible solutions and the cost it may incur, taking into account the municipality of Jerusalem's plans for the city's canalization.

2. Problems of heating. The Brother tells me that we should carefully consider whether in fact a central heating system is not more suitable, once certain savings have been achieved in the way it is set up.

3. Renovation of bathrooms and toilets.

4. Extension of the Library (for which a German donation of 2 or 3 million lire is very likely), and, if necessary, the extension or relocating of the Museum.

5. Possibility of building small rooms on the covered terrace.

6. Painting rooms and corridors.

7. Possible repairs to parts of the building (balconies, cracks where found etc.).

These seemed to me the main problems for which it would be important to have, as soon as possible, a plan and budget for deciding to do them, possibly using some help from coadjutor Brothers who may be given us by some Provinces.

I also spoke to the Brother about whether it would be useful to explore whether through some religious communities, such as the Salesians, the Passionists or the Franciscans, it would be possible to use their carpentry equipment, for carrying out work on window-frames, etc.

[*handwritten:*] You will see that the Brother is very competent and obliging. We are expecting Fr. Semkowski before the end of June. Would it not be possible to send him back with Br. Consonno on June 24th? […]

Kind regards to everyone. Yours in Xt.

Carlo M. Martini, S. J.

* * * * *

Doc. J. II,15

APIBJ

STATUTES OF SAINT IGNATIUS HOUSE
JERUSALEM
Extracts concerning the Institute

1. The Jesuit Community called "St. Ignatius House" which is established in the building of the Pontifical Biblical Institute in Jerusalem has depended juridically on the Rector of the Pontifical Biblical Institute (PBI) in Rome as well for its religious life and for its service of the PBI. From now on it becomes immediately dependent on the Delegate for the International Roman Houses and is governed by the present statutes.

2. This adjustment in the religious government of the community leaves undisturbed the juridical situation and the specific work of the "sedes hierosolymitana" of the PBI which continues to be governed by the PBI Statutes approved in 1985 (cf. Arts. 73, 74).

3. The specific activities of the PBI in Jerusalem remain the principle task of St. Ignatius House and continue to be under a Director who, according to the PBI Statutes (Art. 14, b), will be appointed by the Vice-Chancellor of the PBI and in the exercise of his office depends on the Rector of the PBI in Rome. When the Director is absent, the administration of the PBI in Jerusalem depends on the Vice-Director, who is, at the same time, the religious Superior of the Jesuit Community of St. Ignatius House. [...]

6. In order to contribute to the Biblical formation of priests, religious and laity who request lodging, St. Ignatius House also devotes itself, as far as possible, to serving as a residence community for visitors and guests. This is a principal apostolic activity of St. Ignatius House according to the Statutes of the PBI.

7. It belongs to the Superior to accept or refuse such requests according to the following order of precedence: a) professors and students of the PBI in Rome; b) priests and religious who engage in biblical/spiritual formation-renewal; d) laity who take up biblical studies. [...]

14. The PBI of Rome with the help of the Gregorian Consortium (PUG, PBI and PIO): a) will support the annual cost of library purchases and subscriptions and the salary of the assistant librarian; b) will also pay the usual stipend for accredited courses given to PBI students by members of the community, and c) will subsidize the difference between the fees for PBI students and the fees for other guests.

APPROVED: October 31, 1989
EFFECTIVE: November 1, 1989
          Feast of All Saints

                                   Peter-Hans Kolvenbach, S. J.
                                   Superior General

CHAPTER III

The academic life and the means it uses

In this last chapter a systematic account will be given of how, at the Biblical Institute in Jerusalem, academic activities have developed; it will also be shown what were and still are the means used to start them off.

I. Students and programs

The first aim, expressed by A. Mallon going back to before the First World War, was to have a house in Jerusalem from which students from the Institute could see the biblical land with their own eyes and go through it. It was more a question of guided excursions than of studying in one's room. It was also supposed that those students had already completed the course of biblical studies at Rome (cf. Doc. J. I,1, pp. 1-4).

The letter that Benedict XV wrote on June 29th, 1919, to the rector of the Institute, A. Fernández, made it clear that the future house of the Institute would not give a complete training in exegesis but would confine itself to connected subjects such as biblical geography and archaeology and Semitic epigraphy. This house would be complementary to the one in Rome (cf. *Acta PIB* 2, pp. 4-5).

1. *From 1927 to 1934.*

Faithful to this papal decision, in 1927 the Institute sent some professors, competent in these subjects; they were five in 1927, but were no more than three in 1933. It does not seem that a real academic program had been put in place during that period. The important thing was to visit the country. Lectures given by professors on the spot would prepare the visits or extend them.

As to the number of students coming from the Institute in this first period we only have some scarce and fragmentary facts, as if the Institute had not officially made any provision in that matter. An example: the Jerusalem house diary for August 28th, 1930, notes that Johannes Simons, S. J., passed the examination in biblical geography with Fathers Mallon and Fernández as examiners, receiving the grade of "bene probatus"; now Fr. Simons obtained the licentiate in Rome only at the end of the academic year 1930-1931.

2. From 1935 to 1968

The Institute obviously had to offer its students something more coherent. This came with the new statutes in 1934. In them (*Acta PIB* 4, p. 23) 3rd-year students were offered the opportunity of spending the second semester in Jerusalem to study the antiquities of biblical lands there, i. e. geography, archaeology, history and other similar subjects (*ibid.*, p. 12).

Despite the institutional good will, this program had little success and in fact hung fire. In 1935, 8 out of 26 students took advantage of it, but none in 1936; there were only 3 in 1937 and 4 in 1938.

The political situation then made it impossible to run this program. From 1939 to 1955 no student registered for it. As from 1941, the restriction on the offer made to students was even added, up to 1955: "si per conditiones publicas licebit" (*Acta PIB* 4, p. 270, for instance).

In 1957, with the situation calmer, some 3rd-year students made their way to Jerusalem in February. There were not many of them, however: from 2 in 1961-1962 to 8 in 1962-1963. In all, from 1957 to 1967 there were only 56, no student coming forward in 1965-1966.

On the other hand, the intensive study of modern Hebrew in an "Ulpan", the one of Etzion, from the summer of 1957 on, attracted other students. There were even 17 of them in 1964.

3. From 1968 to 1974

It was then understood that the program offered to the students at Jerusalem had to be radically changed. Announced in 1967, the new program henceforth no longer concerns students coming to the end of the licentiate but candidates doing the curriculum for it; to prepare them for the entrance exam, called "qualification", in biblical Hebrew and Greek, the Institute had, for some years, been offering a one-year course called "propaedeutic" in Rome. It was thought that offering the same course in Jerusalem would attract candidates; the latter would also have the opportunity of following an "Ulpan" and especially of spending an academic year in the Holy Land. However, the problem was to convince future students (and their Superiors!) to go to Jerusalem first before coming to Rome. As a matter of fact that new program survived for only five years, from 1968-1969, with 11 students, until 1972-1973, with 8 or 9 students (*Acta PIB* 7, pp. 509 and 555). For each of the intervening years there were only 3 students.

Work on the renovation of the house in Jerusalem was planned, by installing in it, among other things, central heating and especially by constructing eight rooms on the big covered terrace on the second floor. The house now had not just twenty-five rooms but thirty-five. How were they going to be occupied? C. M. Martini, rector at the time, had in fact decided to ask for the collaboration of the Hebrew University of Jerusalem. Through the mediation of Prof. Shemaryahu Talmon, academic Director of the "School for Overseas Students" (now the "Rothberg International School") on Mount Scopus and a renowned biblical scholar, the University agreed and even suggested a precise program without waiting any more.

4. Since 1975, collaboration with the Hebrew University of Jerusalem

The plan was brilliant. It was putting the spirit of the Second Vatican Council to work and anticipating what the European Union was later to organize under the name of program "Erasmus": students from the Institute were going to spend at least one academic semester at the Hebrew University and the results achieved during this semester would be validated by the Institute.

The fact that over half a thousand Catholic exegetes have so far received part of their training at the Hebrew University is not without its importance when the Church and Judaism are intensifying their relations. Right from the beginning the Hebrew University has invested considerably in the project. It has got its best professors to take part in it. For its part, the Institute was convinced that it was bringing down a barrier, for the good of both sides. It was also solving the nagging problem posed by the house in Jerusalem. Because the "Ulpan" had been attracting students for twenty years, and since the subjects taught, which Benedict XV had limited to what was neither exegesis nor biblical theology, gained by being acquired at the beginning of the licentiate curriculum rather than at the end – this was the weakness in the 1934 program – there was a good chance that the new project would prove workable. It did.

Still, without altering its worth or bearing, this program underwent some changes in the course of the years.

The first group of 23 students came to Jerusalem from February to September, 1975. Twenty of these students had just finished a semester of "propaedeutic" courses in Rome. In Jerusalem, the Hebrew University gave them a semester of intensive modern Hebrew and the second semester, in the summer, was mainly devoted to archaeology and historical geography; biblical Hebrew was taught throughout both semesters; this program at the Hebrew University was given in modern Hebrew, while a professor at the Institute gave the continuation in English of the "propaedeutic" course in biblical Greek in the house.

The first change soon took place: henceforth the students would come to Jerusalem only after successfully completing all the "propaedeutic" year in

Rome: from July, 1976, to February, 1977, there were 17 of them. Giving the classes in modern Hebrew at the Hebrew University was also dropped and English was adopted.

As from 1979, the Institute took on the task of introducing the students to Christian sites in the Holy Land and those connected with the New Testament, especially in Galilee. As from 1980-1981, the two-week excavation on an archaeological site was also given up, as several students could not bear such physical effort. Lastly, as from 1986-1987, the course in modern Hebrew, given in summer, became optional, which did not stop some students registering for it before starting the full academic semester offered by the Hebrew University.

Taken together, from 1975 until 1985-1986, 169 students followed this new program. From 1986-1987 until 2008-2009, there were 354 and about 100 of them did the modern Hebrew course during the summer. Had tension in the Middle East not been so high, the numbers taking this joint Biblical Institute – Hebrew University program would have been still greater.

5. *Since 1986, working along with the* École Biblique et Archéologique Française

In December, 1984, an agreement was reached between the Institute and the Jerusalem École Biblique (cf. *Acta PIB* 9, p. 95). As from 1986 about ten students from the Institute could, every year, go to the École Biblique during the second semester in the second year of their licentiate course at the Institute. The École Biblique would offer them courses in biblical Aramaic, exegesis and biblical theology, as well as archaeology. The students would take examinations at the École Biblique in the courses taken and the results would be validated by the Institute. The language of instruction would normally be French and the students could live at the Institute's house in Jerusalem, the École Biblique giving priority to its own students.

This program was limited to about ten students, because the École Biblique only enrolls a small number every year; those from the Institute in the second semester were not to become the majority!

This collaboration, which marked a turning-point in the history of the often tense relations between the two institutions, was made possible by the fact that in 1983 the Holy See had authorized the École Biblique to confer the doctorate in biblical studies, just like the Institute and the Biblical Commission. The *a fortiori* principle was followed: the École Biblique had not wished to ask for authorization to confer the licentiate in biblical studies, because it could not provide instruction in all the subjects leading to that diploma, but the courses it offered were at that level. Students from the Institute could therefore fit some of them into their licentiate curriculum and, among these courses, exegesis and biblical theology took pride of place. In fact the limitation placed on the Institute by Benedict XV did not concern the École Biblique, especially since the doctorate conferred by it had received papal endorsement.

So since 1986, every year, except in 1991 because of the first Gulf war, students from the Institute enrolled at the École Biblique for the second semester, from February until June. Their numbers vary from 10 to 12 in 1989, 1990, 1994, 1996 and 1998, from 7 to 8 in 1988, 1992, 1993 1995, 1999 and 2000; they diminish when the political situation deteriorates.

6. *Since 2000: working along with the* Studium Biblicum Franciscanum

It is normal that a biblical scholar should be acquainted with the Holy Land. As the two one-semester programs offered both by the Hebrew University and by the École Biblique involve costs that not every student at the Institute can always face and, on the other hand, it is cheaper to come to Jerusalem during studies at the Institute, a third joint program has been arranged since the year 2000 in collaboration with the *Studium Biblicum Franciscanum,* situated in the Old City of Jerusalem (cf. *Acta PIB* 10, p. 797). This program takes place in the month of September; under the direction of two professors at the *Studium,* Frs. E. Alliati and P. Kaswalder, O. F. M., it comprises courses in biblical geography and history, as well as visits to the main Old and New Testament sites.

The course is planned to take a maximum number of 35 students. At the request of the biblical theology department in the faculty of theology at the Gregorian University, five places are reserved for students from this faculty. The students live at the Institute's house where the classes are given them in Italian and where they do the final examination, which is validated by the Institute.

The Institute has by now reached agreements with the three main academic institutions in Jerusalem concerned with the Bible. Each of these institutions offers a different program and in a different language. So much so that about three quarters of the students at the Institute can henceforth join one of these programs, at least when the situation allows it. It also follows that the Institute's house in Jerusalem fulfils its academic function as branch of the Rome one more normally.

II. The Caravans

From 1913 until 1978 the Biblical Institute has organized sixty-four "caravans". This term, in use since 1913, designates a journey for making contact with and finding out about biblical lands.

The story of these caravans comprises two quite distinct periods. Each of them has received the stamp of a master who prepares and accompanies the caravan.

1. *From 1913 to 1938*

In twenty-five years the Institute organized twenty-two caravans, mainly for its students at the end of their academic course. The First World War stopped the experience that had just begun successfully. We had to wait until 1921 to organize the second one. The trouble in the Holy Land in 1936 caused an interruption. After the caravan in the spring of 1938, the first symptoms of the conflict that was to lead to the Second World War and to its consequences in the Middle East, far beyond the declaration of the independence of the State of Israel in May, 1948, caused a long interruption: there was no caravan before the summer of 1952.

The main character behind the caravans in this first period was undoubtedly Fr. Alexis Mallon. Even after his unexpected death on April 7th, 1934, those who, from Jerusalem, took charge of the following ones until the spring of 1938, Frs. Marcel Lobignac, Andrés Fernández and Robert Köppel, followed his program with hardly any changes to it.

However, the idea of starting up these journeys in fact came from the first students at the Institute about to finish their biblical studies in Rome (cf. Mallon, Doc. I,1, p. 12). This must have been about April-May, 1913. But who was to take on the preparation of this journey and see it through? The surprising thing is that no one thought of Fr. Mallon. When consulted by the Rector L. Fonck, Fr. General Fr.-X.Wernz, on June 6th, 1913, replied that he preferred Fr. Szczepański as guide and Fr. Fernández as Superior of the group. The former in fact did not come and it was Fr. Mallon who took on the work of guide. He was thirty-eight and had had a long spell in Lebanon; he spoke French, his mother tongue, English and Arabic.

Fr. Fonck ordered the necessary equipment in Germany, tents, bedding, kitchen-ware and saddles for horses (cf. Mallon Doc. J. I,1, p. 13; Senès, MS p. 19). It was all in Beyrouth when the small group on the first caravan arrived there. Fr. Mallon had preceded them by fifteen days. Having left Naples by boat on September 6th, 1913, the group re-embarked on November 12th at Alexandria. In the meantime it visited Athens, Smyrna and Constantinople before landing at Beyrouth; from there it went on to Byblos and Tripoli, then Homs, Baalbek and Damascus before visiting the Holy Land in a more leisurely way, from Galilee to Judea, not omitting Jericho. It then embarked at Jaffa for Port Said whence it went to Cairo and on to Upper Egypt towards Luxor, Aswan and Elephantine. From there it came back to Cairo and took the boat at Alexandria.

One of those on this first caravan, Fr. Rafaele Tramontano, S. J., who had not studied at the Biblical Institute, published an account of this journey under the title *Un viaggio in Oriente* (Lecce 1914, 48 p.). Fr. Mallon, for his part (cf. Doc. I,1, pp. 16-19), stressed the favourable reception received everywhere. However, when giving an account of the journey to Fr. General Fr.-X. Wernz on December 24th, 1913, he notes that some Dominicans at St. Stephen's in Jerusalem, especially Fr. Lagrange, had clearly denied the group of travellers the marks of ordinary courtesy, fleeing from them like the plague, whereas the group omitted nothing that might favour peace and concord (translation from the Latin text).

The countries visited by the first caravan were part either of the Ottoman Empire, then in full decline (Lebanon, Syria and Palestine) or of an independent State (Egypt), though occupied by the British. But it does not seem that that situation caused any particular problems.

When the caravans were resumed in 1921, the Middle East had changed face. The Ottoman Empire had disappeared from the map; only Turkey remained. Lebanon and Syria came under French influence, while the British ruled in Palestine and in Transjordan, as well as in Egypt.

The second caravan, the one in 1921, thus avoided Greece and Turkey. Several articles in *Verbum Domini* 2 (1922) can be read in which some of those on this second caravan recount its various stages. But as from the following year the road to Athens and Constantinople was taken again, so as to follow almost the same route as in 1913. Apart from 1923, they pushed on to Amman and thereafter Transjordan, with Madaba, Mount Nebo and Petra, was on the itinerary. The accompanying table gives the day-by-day details of the route taken by the VIIIth caravan in 1927 (*VD* 7 [1927] 350-351).

OCTAVUM ITER PALAESTINENSE

September

20 v. Byblos
21   Baalbeck, Damascus
22   Damascus
23   Iter in Galilaeam: Cesarea Philippi (Bânyás), Heptapegon (Tabgha)
24   Littus maris Tiberiadis
25 m. Capharnaum, Corozain
    v. Iter ad Nazareth, in via: Magdala, Tiberias, Kefr Kenna (Cana)
26   Nazareth
27   Iter ad Carmelum; in via: Meggiddo, "locus sacrificii"
28 m. Missae in sanctuario Carmeli; Nazareth
    v. Scythopolis (Beisân), Thabor
29 m. Missae in sanctuario Transfigurationis, Nazareth
    v. Sepphoris

30 m. *Vacat*
   v. Iter in "Flaviam Neapolim"; in via: Dothain, Samaria (Sebastieh)

October

1 m. Sichem, puteus Iacob, sepulcrum Ioseph
   v. Iter in JERUSALEM; in via: Lebbona, Silo
2 m. SS. Sepulcrum
   v. Caenaculum, Sanctuarium Dormitionis B. Mariae V., Sanct. S. Iacobi
3 m. Moschea Omar
   v. Mons Oliveti: Ascensionis locus, Bethphage, Bethania
4 m. *Vacat*
   v. Ophel (Ierusalem primitiva), Siloe, vallis Hinnom
5 m. Sanctuarium Sanctae Annae, "Ecce Homo", Sanctuarium S. Stephani, "sepulchra regum"
   v. Bethlehem
6   Bethlehem, Beit Sahur
7 m. Reditus Ierusalem; *Vacat*
   v. Via Crucis, "murus ploratus"
8 m. Synagoga, exemplaria Templi
   v. Ain Karem
9 m. *Vacat*
   v. Getsemani
10 Hebron, ad "quercum Mambre", Beit Djebrîn, Beit Djemal
11 *Vacat*
12, 13, 14 Iter ad desertum Cades Barnea: Bersabee, Asludj, El-Audja, El-Qeseimeh, Ain Qedeis, Ain Qudeirat, Tell Beit Mirsim (Qiryat Sepher?)
15 *Vacat*
16 *Vacat*
17 m. Iericho, Mare Mortuum
   v. *Vacat*
18 Nebi Samuil, Kubeibeh
19 *Vacat*
20-25 Gerasa (Djerasch), Amman, Petra, Kerak, Madaba, Hesebon, Nebo
26 *Vacat*
27 Bethel, Ai, Tell en-Nasbeh (Maspha?)
28 m. *Vacat*
   v. Via Crucis, ad S. Petrum in Gallicantu
29 Nicopolis (Amwas), Ramleh, Lydda, Ioppe, Cariathiarim
30 *Vacat*
31 Iter in Aegyptum

November

1 m. Musaeum aegyptiacum
   v. Heliopolis nova
2 m. *Vacat*
   v. Monumenta Saqqara, Memphis
3 m. Matarieh, Heliopolis antiqua

v. Pyramides
4 m. Monumenta urbis, musaeum (ad libitum)
v. Iter in Aegyptum superiorem
5 m. Templum Luxor
v. Magnum Templum, Karnak
6 m. Sepulcra regum
v. *Vacat*
7 m. Iter ad Assuan
v. Elephantine
8 m. Insula Philae et circa
v. *Vacat*
9 Reditus Luxor
10 m. *Vacat*
v. Reditus Cairum
11 m. Cairi, *vacat*
v. Iter Alexandriam
12 m. hora undecima navis conscenditur

As from 1928, Tarsus, in Turkey, was also visited. We have the account given by Fr. Galileo Venturini, S. J., of this IXth caravan, *Viaggio in Oriente*: I. *Da Roma a Gerusalemme*, II. *Gerusalemme* (Roma 1933 and 1938, 410 and 454 p.). Of the XIIth caravan, Fr. Gustave Lambert, who was on it, left a written account, *Voyage en Palestine de juin à octobre 1930*, which is at Brussels in the archives of the French-speaking Belgian Jesuits. In 1931 Palmyra and Aleppo were added for Syria. Two years later Sinai was also on the route. Finally, the 1937 caravan seems the high point of this program: disembarking at Haifa on July 11th, the small group, having settled in at the Institute in Jerusalem, first of all visited Jerusalem and the centre of Palestine; on the 12th and 13th of August it went into Transjordan and from the 16th until the 21st of August into Galilee; on September 6th it left for Syria whence it returned on the 15th; on the 6th and 7th of October it visited Qadesh, in the north of the Negev then, on the 10th, it left by train for Cairo, intending to see Sinai as well. Despite the outline of the impressive program published in *Verbum Domini* 18 (1938) 250-251, the reality as provided by the diary of the Institute in Jerusalem is much more modest: one gets no sense of any real guidance of the group, and the latter is not properly constituted; out of six members at the start, it consists of no more than three on October 10th; as it went along, others joined the group and, finally, two had to be hospitalized in Jerusalem for several weeks!

We also find that from 1913 to 1929 the caravans last two months, most often at the end of summer and the beginning of autumn. As from 1930, those going on them do so most often during the first two weeks of July and the caravan lasts longer: in 1931, for example, from July 3rd to October 23rd.

Did such an investment meet with real success? Even taking into account the still restricted number of students at the Institute, it has to be admitted that apart from the VIIIth caravan, the one in 1927, which numbered 24 people, not including Fr. Mallon and two other professors from the Institute, the caravans numbered only a small number of young biblical scholars, a dozen at the most, often far fewer.

2. *From 1952 to 1978*

In just over a quarter of a century the Institute organized forty-one caravans, from the XXIIIrd to the LXIVth, during this second period. The Second World War and its consequences had profoundly changed the situation, especially in the Middle East. Since May, 1948, the State of Israel had been proclaimed, with the West Bank passing into the control of the Kingdom of Jordan, also independent. Jerusalem was divided: the East, with the Old City, on the Jordanian side, and the West, where the Institute's house is, on the Israeli side. An inaccessible and mined "no man's land" separated the two zones. The only passage from one side to the other was through the "Mandelbaum Gate", to the north of the École Biblique. Such a situation did not make the movements of the caravans easy: Galilee was in Israel, while Bethlehem, the Old City of Jerusalem and Qumran were under Jordanian control. The "Six Day War" at the beginning of June, 1967, put an end to this division, with Israel having conquered the West Bank up to the Jordan.

The main organizer of the caravans in this second period was Fr. Robert North. He came to the Biblicum in 1951. He was thirty-five years old. He was professor of biblical geography and archaeology, and resumed the regular caravans from 1952 to 1960, then from 1974 to 1978. Between 1960 and 1967 he organized only two, in 1962 and 1965, whereas from Christmas 1967 to the summer of 1973 eleven caravans were guided by Fr. Richard M. Macowski. Altogether Fr. North organized thirty. These last overall figures are explained by the fact that apart from the summer caravans, taking in several countries in the Middle East over a period of about two months, the two guides just mentioned organized others with a shorter itinerary and centred on the Holy Land, and even Sinai, either at Easter, in September or at Christmas.

At Jerusalem, the Institute's house as far as possible served as a *pied-à-terre*. Fr. North was in fact Director there from 1956 to 1959 and Fr. Mackowski was living there as a professor when he took over.

As regards the number of people on the caravans of this second period, it was clearly greater than during the first period: from 1952 to 1959 there were between twenty-five and thirty-two of them on the summer caravans. The number even rose to fifty in the summer of 1965 and for the two weeks at Easter in 1976 and 1977; the record was reached at Easter in 1975: there were sixty-five.

Four accounts of the caravans of this period have been published. Fr. Gaetano M. Savoca, who was on the XXVth caravan, from July 7th to August 18th, 1953, between 1954 and 1959 published a series of articles amounting to some 140 pages in the review *Palestro del Clero*. Fr. Luis Alonso Schökel, who was on the XXVIth, from June 20th until August 10th, 1954, published *Viaje al país del Antiguo Testamento* (Santander 1956, 384 p.), an account as well as a description of the great moments of ancient biblical history; the book was translated into English by J. Drury under the title *Journey through the Bible Lands* (Milwaukee 1964). Alberto Vidal Cruañas was also on this XXVIth caravan and published his *Viaje a Tierra Santa. Egipto, Sinai, Líbano. Siria, Jordania, Israel* (Barcelona 1957, 318 p.). Mauro Rodriguez Estrada was on the XXXth caravan in the summer of 1957 and published an account of it: *La Biblia en su cuna. Diario de un viaje por Grecia, Turquía, Israel, Reino del Jordán, Siria, Libano y Egipto* (Mexico 1958, 202 p.).

In addition, Fr. James H. Swetnam, who had been teaching biblical Greek in the "propaedeutic" course at the Institute in Rome for over ten years, wrote a long account, still in manuscript, of the two summer caravans he was on: the one in 1975, the LVIIIth, which went to Egypt, Jordan, Lebanon and Syria, as well as the one in the summer of 1976, the LXIst, which visited Turkey and Mesopotamia, which is shared between Iraq and Iran. This 1976 caravan was a very trying one for Fr. North: at the end of October he spent two days in hospital in Baghdad, but he was then able to resume it and complete it. Having recovered, he was still able to organize three more, two in 1977 and one in 1978, at Easter. The long tradition of the Institute's caravans was coming to an end. The new rector, M. Gilbert, who had just taken over in 1978, decided, in agreement with Fr. North, then aged sixty-two, and Fr. Swetnam, who had witnessed Fr. North's setback, to put a definite end to the Institute's caravans. The Institute did not have a young and vigorous specialist able to take charge of such expeditions, especially as, at that time, cultural tourism had already developed and travel agents were arranging them themselves.

Every caravan experienced some memorable ups and downs that remain engraved on the memory of those who went through them. Only two episodes will be recalled here; one was tragic, the other nearly was.

The XXVth caravan, the one in summer 1953, numbered thirty-two members. In the diary of the house in Jerusalem, under the date of Tuesday, August 11th, 1953, we read the following, written by Fr. Senès:

Departure of the caravan, by coach, for Jaffa where it will spend the night. Departure is at 8.00 hrs. The coach is from the Egged Company.
In the afternoon, Rev. Fr. Semkowski [the Director of the Institute at Jerusalem] is going to spend some hours in Tel Aviv.

Towards 17.30, at Jaffa, most of those on our biblical caravan, who are bathing at the beach, are in danger because the water pulling back from the coast is dragging them to the open sea. At least three members cannot get back to the beach alone. Fr. Lelandais who is also in danger but swims well dies suddenly during his exertions. Fr. Zerwick who is a good swimmer was able to save two or three of the bathers.

The person in question is Fr. Maurice Le Landais, a French Jesuit, born at Lons le Saunier in the Jura on July 8th, 1916. He had just finished three years of his studies at the Biblical Institute in Rome.

Then, in the same diary for Wednesday 12th we read:

At 16.00 hrs., at Nazareth, the whole caravan and Fr. Senès met at the Annunciation around the coffin of Fr. Lelandais that had been brought from Jaffa in the car belonging to the Brothers. The burial takes place in the small cemetery to the east of Our lady of the Fright [near the present monastery of the Poor Clares at Nazareth]. Fr. Lelandais is the first Jesuit buried in Nazareth. The caravan split up for the night, some going to the Franciscans, others to the Betharam Fathers […].

In 1970 the remains of the Father were moved into the crypt of the new church, a few metres away from the cemetery that had to be deconsecrated so as to construct a new building in its place.

The surprising thing is that the *Acta Pontificii Instituti Biblici* made no mention of this tragedy. A silence that deserved to be broken here.

The other episode, in the summer of 1959, involved Fr. Carlo Maria Martini, S. J., who had just published his doctoral thesis in theology at the Gregorian University. He was one of the twenty-nine young biblical students making up the XXXVIth caravan. This is how, in 2002, at the end of his episcopal mission at Milan, he tells what happened:

On this journey I also had – I do not remember the precise day – an experience of death. A simple, very ordinary experience.
We were visiting the wells of El Gib (the former Gabaon), the site of Solomon's dream, the dream in which he asks the Lord for the gift of wisdom (cf. I Kings). I was reflecting on the fact that Gabaon is again mentioned in the Book of Joshua (9–10) in connection with the special alliance artfully obtained by the Gabaonites, just as in 2 Sam 21 in connection with the cruel hanging of some of Saul's sons, a hanging granted by David to please the people who were asking for it so as to avoid the divine wrath.
Around the big, deep wells made of bricks – probably of the time of Solomon – the building material from the excavations had accumulated and, to take a photograph, you had to go up and lean over. We queued up (about thirty people) and when my turn came to take a photo, the heap of sand and stones began to give way, perhaps because it had been trodden on too much; so I began to slide down.
I saw myself dead already, buried in the rubble, but suddenly a thought came to me – which I consider a real grace for the moment which has never been repeated: how marvellous it is to die in this land! I felt tranquil, serene, content with what

was happening. I even think it is probable that it is that absolute tranquility that saved me; in fact, being in peace, as I tumbled down I instinctively dug my hands into the mass of sand mingled with stones and managed to stop myself just when I was going to fall to the bottom.

This experience of death close at hand [...] has remained engraved on my heart (C. M. Martini, *Verso Gerusalemme*, Milano 2002, pp. 27-28, translated from the Italian).

III. The archaeological excavations

It is obvious that the main archaeological excavations carried out by the branch of the Institute at Jerusalem were the ones at Teleilat Ghassul. In speaking of them we shall here confine ourselves to their scientific aspect. The problems concerning their management have in fact been explained in the previous chapter. However, in order not to disperse what has to be said about this archaeological matter, we shall speak first of all about the excavations carried out by the Institute at Elephantine during the First World War.

1. *Excavations at Elephantine in 1918*

Bibliography

A. STRAZZULLI, P. BOVIER-LAPIERRE, Séb. RONZEVALLE, "Rapport sur les fouilles à Éléphantine de l'Institut Biblique Pontifical", *Annales du Service des Antiquités de l'Égypte* 18 (1918) 1-7.

On the present state of research at Elephantine, cf. W. KAISER, "Elephantine", E. M. MEYERS (ed.), *The Oxford Encyclopedia of Archaeology in the Near East*, 2, New York - Oxford, Oxford University Press, 1997, pp. 234-236, with recent bibliography – W. KAISER, "Elephantine", K. A. BARD, S. B. SHUBERT (eds.), *Encyclopedia of the Archaeology of Ancient Egypt*, London – New York, Routledge, 1999, pp. 283-289, with plans of the site at successive periods.

A short campaign of archaeological excavation was carried out in 1918 in the name of the Institute on the site at Elephantine, the island in the Nile on a level with the town of Aswan. It started on January 23rd and ended on March 16th. A seven-page preliminary report, the only one to be published, allows one to form an idea of the work undertaken and of the precise location of these excavations. They were never followed up and the complete report on them, although promised, never appeared.

The published report is dated Cairo, April 17th, 1918 and it is signed by three Jesuits. The first, A. Strazzulli (1883-1956) had been at the Institute in Rome for just a year, 1915-1916; it was he who had received permission to excavate in the southern part of the island; it was he who also took charge of the administration and supervision of the work. The second, P. Bovier-Lapierre (1873-1950), a specialist in prehistory, dealt with "the minute scrutiny of the loose earth and [with] establishing the archaeological, mineralogical and natural series that constituted the spoils of the excavation", says the Report (p. 5). As for the third, Séb. Ronzevalle (1865-1937), a specialist in Semitic epigraphy, he belonged to St. Joseph's University in Beirut and had taught for only a year, in 1910-1911, at the Institute in Rome; it was he who provided the scientific direction of the expedition. Despite what Fr. H. Senès says (p. 25 of his report), Fr. Mallon does not seem to have taken part in these excavations.

The German and French excavations in the first decade of the XXth c. had above all made it possible to discover and recover the famous papyri. The 1918 expedition meant to clear away, going down to virgin soil, some parts of the site that the predecessors had left intact. However, these areas were then covered with the rubble of earlier excavations, which in any case had not gone down deeper than the layer of the Persian period. The work of clearing away was an exhausting job, especially as everything went through the sieve. About fifty, perhaps even about a hundred local workmen, as is shown in some photographs, facilitated the work. The results were modest. A lot of small objects were recovered, either complete or in fragments, which in part are now either in the Egyptian Museum in Cairo, or in part in the Museum of the Institute in Jerusalem, where some more significant pieces are on show, others, along with photographic and manuscript documentation, being kept in the reserve section.

The most interesting piece, if it really does come from the 1918 excavation – which unfortunately cannot be proved – is a potsherd on which an Aramaic alphabet can be read. A. Lemaire and H. Lozachmeur made it the object of a learned publication in 1977 (cf. *infra*).

The report that appeared in 1918, too short as it is, arouses curiosity. How did they manage to carry out those excavations, and, especially, why were they not followed up at all? Some documents kept in the archives of the Institute in Rome make it possible to answer these two questions.

Fr. Ronzevalle sent Fr. Fernández, then Vice-Rector of the Institute, a long report that he had drawn up in Cairo and in Alexandria on the 15th and 19th of April, 1918 (cf. Doc. J. III,1). In it he explains that he had visited Elephantine in 1915 and that he had been convinced that there was still a lot to be excavated after the German and French expeditions. Probably at the beginning of October, 1917, he met Fr. Strazzulli in Alexandria and told him he was prepared to resume the excavations on the site on condition that he received 10,000 francs! Fr. Strazzulli contacted Fr. P. Tacchi Venturi, then Secretary of the Society at the general headquarters in Rome. Rather than ask the Vatican for funds, as Fr. Strazzulli suggested, Fr. Tacchi Venturi spoke to Fr. General Ledóchowski, who consulted Fr. Fonck, still Rector of the Institute but resident in Zurich because of the war. The latter signalled his agreement with the project, the expenses of which would be covered by the Institute; this was in mid-October, 1917. On December 20th permission from the Department of Antiquities of Egypt was granted. On January 5th, 1918, the three Jesuits mentioned above were at Aswan, but they spent two weeks getting some indispensable shovels and sieves from the Management of the Dam. What interested Fr. Ronzevalle first and foremost was to find the site of the Jewish temple of Yaho, and perhaps even its genizah with its sacred books.

So much for the origin of this excavation project. But why did the first campaign not have any outcome other than the short seven-page report? In the long account given to Fr. Fernández, written on the 15th and 19th of April, 1918, almost a month after the close of the excavations, Fr. Ronzevalle asks Fr. Fonck's advice on two points (p. 5): should we publish, in addition to the administrative Report by the *Annales du Service des Antiquités de l'Égypte*, an introduction to the full report on the excavations, and can we envisage a second campaign? It was then that things got complicated.

Fr. Ronzevalle mentions to Fr. Fernández that he is favourable to continuing the excavations but that his two Jesuit co-workers, for various reasons, will not be taking part in them (p. 5). And then there is the question of finances which, in the case of the first campaign, did not exceed the budget, but would be notably greater, double or even treble, for a second campaign. On May 6th, 1918, Fr. General again asks Fr. Fonck's opinion on a second campaign and a specialist to join Fr. Ronzevalle. On July 11th and 17th Fonck replied to the General that he is in favour of resuming the excavations straight away in the winter of 1918-1919 and that Fr. Mallon, whose health is too poor, should be left out. On July 23rd Fr. General informs Fr. Fonck of his agreement with an immediate second campaign. Thereupon Fonck lets Fr. Fernández know that resuming the excavations has been decided upon and that nothing more should be published for the time being.

Meanwhile, Fr. Strazzulli had, on June 19th, 1918, already suggested to Fr. Tacchi Venturi to postpone resuming the excavations for a year and in fact Fr. Ronzevalle, on November 22nd, is explaining to Mr Lacau, the general Director of the Antiquities Department, that, for health reasons, he is not going on a second campaign in the winter of 1918-1919, but he asks that that be permitted during the next season, 1919-1920. On April 29th, 1919, Mr Lacau gives his agreement.

At Rome in the meantime, on December 9th, 1918, Fr. Fernández succeeded Fr. Fonck as Rector of the Institute. In the early months of 1919 he consults Frs. E. Power, J. J. O'Rourke and A. Vaccari on the suitability of resuming the excavations at Elephantine and the answer is unanimously in the negative for the following reasons: the first campaign had brought in nothing, or hardly anything, and a new outlay of funds, just after the war that had considerably diminished the Institute's reserves, was not justified, especially as the hope of making a real discovery was slender. On March 31st, 1919, Fr. Fernández told

Fr. Ronzevalle that these excavations were to be given up. But Fr. Ronzevalle made representations to the Fr. General, who in reply to him confirmed Fr. Fernández's decision, the Institute's financial difficulties being serious. On July 15th, 1919, when informing Fr. Fernández of Fr. General's reply, Fr. Ronzevalle explains to the Rector that he cannot envisage the writing of the full report of the 1918 excavations at Elephantine in under two years and calls upon the Rector to write to Mr Lacau to inform him of the Institute's definitive withdrawal, which Fr. Fernández did by letter on August 28th, 1919. Henceforth Fr. Ronzevalle no longer busied himself with Elephantine and the full report on the excavations never appeared.

The site at Elephantine stills draws tourists, and researchers even more so. A German and Swiss team has been at work on the excavations there since 1969 (cf. W. Kaiser). But no traces of the Jewish temple of Yaho have yet been found.

2. Discovery and excavations at Teleilat Ghassul

Bibliography

The preliminary reports on the excavations carried out by the Institute first appeared under the name of A. Mallon in *Biblica* 11 (1930) 3-22, 129-148; 12 (1931) 257-270; 13 (1932) 273-283; 14 (1933) 294-302; then under the name of R. Koeppel in *Biblica* 16 (1935) 241-256; 17 (1936) 393-406; 19 (1938) 260-266.

The final reports appeared in three volumes: A. MALLON, R. KOEPPEL, R. NEUVILLE, *Teleilat Ghassul, I. Compte rendu des fouilles de l'Institut Biblique Pontifical, 1929-1932*, Rome, 1934, XVIII-193 p. + 72 pl. – R. KOEPPEL, H. SENÈS, J. W. MURPHY, G. S. MAHAN, *Teleilat Ghassul, II. Compte rendu des fouilles de l'Institut Biblique Pontifical, 1932-1936*, Rome, Pontifical Biblical Institute, 1940, VIII-140 p. + 113 plates and 2 plans – R. NORTH, *Ghassul 1960. Excavation Report*. Analecta Biblica 14, Rome, Pontificio Istituto Biblico, 1961, XIII-88 p. + 12 pl. and 19 ill.

On the excavations that followed, cf. J. B. HENNESSY, "Preliminary Report on a First Season of Excavations at Teleilat Ghassul", *Levant* 1 (1969) 1-24 + 16 pl. – J. B. HENNESSY, *Teleilat Ghassul. An Interim Report*, Sydney 1977. – S. BOURKE et al., "Preliminary Report of the First Season of Renewed Excavations at Teleilat Ghassul by the University of Sydney", *Annual of the Department of Antiquities of Jordan* 39 (1994) 31-64. – S. BOURKE et al., "A Second and Third Season of Renewed Excavation at Tulaylat al-Ghassul (1995-1997)", ibid., 44 (2000) 37-89.

For a recent overall description see J. B. HENNESSY, "Ghassul, Tuleilat el", *The Anchor Bible Dictionary*, II, 1992, pp. 1003-1006. – T. E. LEVY, "Ghassul, Tuleilat el-", *The New Encyclopedia of Archaeological Excavations in the Holy Land*, 2, Jerusalem, Israel Exploration Society, 1993, pp. 506-511.

The main studies, in chronological order, are those by: H. VINCENT, "Les fouilles de Teleilat Ghassoul", *Revue Biblique* 44 (1935), 69-104, 220-244. – J. SIMONS, *Opgravingen in Palestina Tot aan de Ballingschap (586 v. Chr.)*, Roermond-Maasiek, Romen & Zonen, 1935, pp. 108-143 and *passim*. – A. BEA, "Die Bedeutung der

Ausgrabungen von Telelat Ghassul für die Frühgeschichte Palästinas", *Beihefte zur Zeitschrift für die alttestamentliche Wissenschaft* 66, 1936, pp. 1-12. – R. NORTH, "'Ghassulian' in Palestine Chronological Nomenclature", *Biblica* 40 (1959) 541-555 = *Studia Biblica et Orientalia*, I. *Vetus Testamentum*, Analecta Biblica 10, Rome, Pontificio Istituto Biblico, 1959, pp. 407-421. – ID., "A Unique New Palestine Art-Form", FS A. Fernández, *Estudios Bíblicos* 35 (1960) 381-390. – J. R. LEE, *Chalcolithic Ghassul. New Aspects and Master Typology.* A thesis presented at the Hebrew University of Jerusalem, 1973, XIV-470 p. + summary in Hebrew, pp. A-I. – Carolyn ELLIOTT, "The Religious Beliefs of the Ghassulians", c. 4000-3100 B. C.", *Palestine Exploration Quarterly* 109 (1977) 3-25. – Carolyn ELLIOTT, "The Ghassulian Culture in Palestine: Origins, Influences and Abandonment", *Levant* 10 (1978) 37-54. – Dorothy O. CAMERON, *The Ghassulian Wall Painting*, London, Kenyon-Deane Ltd, 1981, 35 p. + 38 ill. – J. B. HENNESSY, "Teleilat Ghassul: Its place in the Archaeology of Jordan", *Studies in the History and Archaeology of Jordan"*, I, Amman, Department of Antiquities, 1982, pp. 55-58. – R. NORTH, "The Ghassulian Lacuna at Jericho", ibid., pp. 59-66. – S. J. BOURKE, "The Urbanisation Process in the South Jordan Valley: Renewed Excavations at Tulaylat al-Ghassul 1994/1995", *Studies in the History and Archaeology of Jordan, VI*, Amman, Department of Antiquities, 1997, pp. 249-259. – S. BOURKE, "The 'Pre-Ghassulian' Sequence at Teleilat Ghassul", H.-G. GEBEL et al., eds., *The Prehistory of Jordan, II: Perspectives from 1997*, Berlin, 1997, pp. 395-417.

On the controversy about Ghassul and the Pentapolis, cf. on one side, E. POWER, "The Site of the Pentapolis", *Biblica* 11 (1930), 23-62, 149-182. – R. KOEPPEL, "Uferstudien am Toten Meer. Naturwissenschaftliches zur Lage der Pentapolis und zur Deutung von Tell Ghassul", *Biblica* 13 (1932) 6-27. – A. MALLON "Les fouilles de l'Institut Biblique Pontifical dans la vallée du Jourdain. Villes du temps d'Abraham et question de la Pentapole", *Recherches de Science Religieuse* 22 (1932) 409-436. – and on the other: F.-M. ABEL, "Exploration du Sud-Est de la Vallée du Jourdain", *Revue Biblique* 40 (1931), esp. pp. 388-400: "VIII. Histoire d'une controverse". – M.-J. LAGRANGE, "Le site de Sodome d'après les textes", *Revue Biblique* 41 (1932) 489-514. – H. VINCENT, "Les fouilles de Teleilat Ghassoul" (cf. *supra)*, esp. pp. 235-244: "III – Ghassoul et la Pentapole biblique".

In an article that appeared in *Biblica* 10 (1929) and dated March 1929 (p. 232), Fr. Alexis Mallon mentions that on January 17th (p. 214) he had gone down by car (p. 215) to the eastern part of the valley of the Jordan, a few kilometres from where it flows into the Dead Sea. This excursion was designed to prepare the article in question. Fr. Mallon did the expedition again on January 20th and February 19th, as noted in the diary of the Institute in Jerusalem. Among the sites visited was the one at Teleilat Ghassul (pp. 217-218), situated about 6 km. to the north-east of the mouth of the Jordan. The site had already been mentioned in the *Survey of Eastern Palestine* by the British (p. 217, n. 1).

Fr. Mallon first of all mentions the name of the site according to the Bedouin: Teleilat Ghassul, i. e. "The small tells of Ghassul"; he notices about twelve of them in fact. It is only later, in *Biblica* 11 (1930), p. 3 and especially 129, that he was to explain the meaning of the term "Ghassul": it was a plant, the "salsola" that grows on the site and which, once dried and made into powder, is used for washing clothes. As for the term "Teleilat", from 1960 on, with Fr. R. North, it was also to be vocalized "Tulaylat". Recent authors give other vocalizations but without changing the meaning of this plural.

Now what Fr. Mallon recalls from his first inspections of the site is first of all "that the ground is covered with very fragmentary red potsherds, pieces of cut flint, fragments of pink sandstone, pieces of basalt and limestone mill-stones ..." (p. 217). He dates the site to "the period of transition between the stone age and the bronze age" (p. 218), hence between the neolithic and the chalcolithic, and more precisely "about 2500 B. C." (p. 217). Finally, Fr. Mallon writes (p. 218) further, "We shall come back to it, if God wills".

Fr. Mallon had flair. He had just discovered one of the most famous prehistoric sites in biblical territory, with work still going on there and the name "Ghassulian" acting as a term of reference to an epoch that left its mark throughout the country (cf. R. North, *Ghassul 1960*, pp. 37-70).

Fr. Mallon had trained in prehistory, in particular in collecting and studying flint, mainly with Fr. Bovier-Lapierre. In 1921, from the end of June and mid-August they had together visited a number of prehistoric sites around Jerusalem, including the one at Mount Scopus. In 1922, again during the summer, they had visited Cremizan, Beit Jemal, Hebron, Taybeh, Nablus and Nazareth for the same purpose. In February, 1923, Fr. Mallon was in Jaffa and, in September, 1924, at Shuqba, on the way down to Lydda (Lod). From each station he brought back flints still kept today in the Museum of the Institute in Jerusalem. He made these discoveries of sites unknown before his time the subject of an article ("Quelques stations préhistoriques en Palestine", *Mélanges de l'Université Saint-Joseph* 10 (1925), 181-214 + 8 pl.). Lastly, in October, 1927, along with the "caravan" from the Institute, he visited the site of Qeșeimeh in the Negev and brought back a collection of flints from it which he describes in *Biblica* 8 (1927) 251-252.

With that said, let us return to Ghassul. Here we will give the main facts about the excavations that were carried out there by the Institute between 1929 and 1938, then during the winter of 1959-1960.

From 1929 to 1934 Fr. Mallon directed five excavation campaigns at Ghassul and gave an account of them in yearly preliminary reports that appeared in *Biblica*, except for the last one because death prevented him from doing so. In this period the excavations began in November; they were broken off in January and February because of the rain; they were resumed in March, except in 1934, because of the exhaustion suffered by Fr. Mallon, who was to succumb to an attack of malaria and who died on April 7th, 1934, at the French Hospital in Bethlehem. The first four campaigns finished at the end of March or the beginning of April.

Thereafter, there were only three campaigns at Ghassul. The first two were directed by Fr. R. Koeppel from February 3rd until March 19th, 1936, and from January 3rd to March 1st, 1938. Trouble in the Holy Land, then the Second World War with its consequences, including the creation of the State of Israel along with its first troubled early years, explain why we had to wait twenty-one years before Fr. R. North could lead the last excavation campaign on the site on behalf of the Institute: this was from December 4th, 1959, until February 20th, 1960.

The first definitive report appeared in 1934. With a preface by Fr. A. Bea, then Rector of the Institute, it was written mainly by Fr. Mallon, with the co-operation of Fr. Koeppel and Mr René Neuville, a specialist in prehistory and at that time chancellor of the French Consulate in Jerusalem. This report puts together the results of the excavations carried out from 1929 to 1932 and is confined to what concerns Tell 1 in the south-east of the site.

The second definitive report appeared in 1940. It covered the excavation period from 1932 to 1936 and is written by Frs. R. Koeppel, J. W. Murphy and G. S. Mahan, each having an almost equal share, and the two latter dealing respectively with the ceramics and stonework discovered at the site. This time it deals with the upper levels, IV A and IV B (cf. *infra*), of Tell 3, situated in the north-west of the site and separated from Tell 1 by a little over a hundred metres.

Only two Tells had been excavated from 1929 to 1938. When Fr. R. North resumed the excavations in 1959-1960 he confined himself to taking soundings in a long cross-section partly adjacent to the two tells previously excavated. His aim was to solve some problems concerning the four successive settlements already known about.

Meanwhile, a detailed report of the seventh excavation campaign, the one in 1938, was still not available. Just a few pages by Fr. Koeppel that appeared in *Biblica* 19 (1938) 260-266 provided a brief preliminary report. Thanks to J. Lee's 1973 thesis the ceramic and stone material discovered during this campaign has now been identified, catalogued and analysed (pp. 168-243, 282-283). This material comes from layers II and III at Tell 3, further down than layer IV, the results from which had appeared in the final report for 1940.

In 1929 the excavators tackled Tells 1 and 3 in particular. But it was only in the course of the next campaign, in the winter of 1930-1931, that they realized that the uncovered ruins showed four successive human settlements, separated from each other by a layer of ashes that was proof of a devastating fire.

In the course of the third campaign, in the winter of 1931-1932, the first traces of paintings were discovered at Tell 3, in particular the painting of a bird. Still at Tell 3 and during the next campaign, the famous painting of the star and the masks was discovered: it was December 19th, 1932. In another connection, the winter campaign of 1933-1934 made it possible to discern two distinct layers at the upper level: here we have two successive phases of the most recent settlement, not far removed in time from each other, namely levels IV A and IV B.

Let us stop for a moment, because the death of Fr. Mallon necessitated a break: there were no excavations in the winter of 1934-1935.

In his first preliminary report, Fr. Mallon wondered whether the discovery of Ghassul did not lead to identifying the site region with biblical Pentapolis (cf. Gen 19) to which Sodom and Gomorrah belonged, and therefore connected with the time of Abraham. The following year, 1931, he could see quite well that the discoveries meant that Ghassul is situated in time both before and at the beginning of the bronze age, but he considered that the bronze age extended from 2500 to 1900 BC. Lastly, for the archaeologist, the final destruction of Ghassul would have been caused by a catastrophe of which he did not yet state the nature (cf. *Biblica* 12 [1931] 263). Soon after, in *Recherches de Science Religieuse* 22 (1932) 414, Fr. Mallon was more precise, but more audacious as well: the final destruction of Ghassul would have been about 2000 or 1900 BC, i. e. in Abraham's time and, as Fr. E. Power put forward in *Biblica*, the Pentapolis should be located, not to the south of the Dead Sea but to the north and henceforth Ghassul may have belonged to it.

These statements, not always made with sufficient reservation, set off several controversies. First of all, concerning the dating of Ghassul, W. F. Albright rejected the one suggested by Fr. Mallon and put back the date of the last settlement by a millennium. Fr. Mallon held to his position in his article entitled "Les dernières phases de l'âge de la pierre et les premiers temps historiques en Palestine", which appeared in *Biblica* 14 (1933) 199-211. However, as the work on the excavations went on, such a late dating was eventually abandoned. Today it is thought that Ghassul was occupied from 4500 to 3500 BC, i. e. for a millennium.

Then the thesis on the geographical location of the Pentapolis also came under fire in 1931, 1932 and 1935 from three Dominicans at the École Biblique in Jerusalem, Fathers Abel, Lagrange and Vincent. No one spoke about it again.

Lastly, Fr. R. North, in 1960, could state that as a result of his own investigations on the site at Ghassul (cf. *Ghassul 1960*, p. 37) in fact there were four successive periods of occupation of the site, each period lengthening in duration, but that the end of Ghassul had not been caused by a "universal catastrophe".

Meanwhile the excavations directed by Fr. North brought two new frescoes. The first, found at Tell 3, like the earlier ones, seems to represent a tiger at rest or being ambushed, unless it is a case of a man standing and holding a mask at arm's length, as D. O. Cameron suggested later. The second fresco, found this time at Tell 1, is of a geometrical design; Fr. North described it in the Festschrift A. Fernández.

All the objects found at Ghassul at the time of the excavations organized by the Institute are in the Institute's museum and the documents concerning them are kept in the depot.

IV. The museum

Bibliography

Ruth AMIRAN, with the assistance of Pirhiya Beck and Uzza Zebulun, *Ancient Pottery of the Holy Land from its Beginning in the Neolithic Period to the End of the Iron Age*, Jerusalem, Massada Press, 1969, esp. pp. 9, 120-121; 158-159. – Shua AMORAI-STARK, *Engraved Gems and Seals from Two Collections in Jerusalem: the Studium Biblicum Franciscanum Museum Gem Collection and the Pontifical Biblical Institute Gem Collection* (Studium Biblicum Franciscanum Museum, 11), Jerusalem, Franciscan Printing Press, 1993, pp. 127-173 + pl. 42-54. – Walter E. AUFRECHT, *A Corpus of Ammonite Inscriptions* (Ancient Near Eastern Texts and Studies, 4), Lewiston-Queenston-Lampeter, Edwin Mellen, 1989, esp. pp. 133-134 + pl. XVI, p. 480. – Nahman AVIGAD, "Some Unpublished Ancient Seals", *Bulletin of the Israel Exploration Society* 25 (1961) 241, n. 3, pl. 5,3 (in Hebrew). – William J. FULCO "A *YHD* Stamp from Battir", *Orientalia* 47 (1978) 265. – Leo KADMAN, *Corpus Nummorum Palestinensium: I-IV*, Jerusalem-Tel Aviv, 1956-1961. – John Robert LEE, *Chalcolithic Ghassul: New Aspects and Master Typology*. Ph. D. Dissertation, Hebrew University of Jerusalem, 1973, XIV-470 p. + A-I (in Hebrew). – André LEMAIRE and Hélène LOZACHMEUR, "Deux inscriptions araméennes du Ve siècle avant J.-C.", *Semitica* 27 (1977) 99-104 + pl. XII. – Stanislao LOFFREDA, *Lucerne bizantine in Terra Santa con iscrizioni in greco* (Studium Biblicum Franciscanum Collectio Maior, 35), Jerusalem, Franciscan Printing Press, 1989, esp. pp. 31, 87-88, 115-116, 122 + pl. – Alexis MALLON, "Une hache égyptienne trouvée en Syrie", *Mélanges de l'Université Saint-Joseph* 10/2 (1925) 51-54 + 1 pl. – ID., "Quelques stations préhistoriques en Palestine", *Mélanges de l'Université Saint-Joseph* 10 (1925) 181-214 + 8 pl. – ID., "Note sur les silex [collected at Qeṣeimeh in the Negev], *Biblica* 8 (1927) 251-252. – ID., "Quelques ostraca coptes de Thèbes", *Revue de l'Égypte ancienne* 1 (1927) 152-156. – ID., "Nouvelle série d'ostraca ETMOYLON", *Revue de l'Égypte ancienne* 2 (1928) 89-96. – ID., "Une nouvelle peinture murale trouvée dans les fouilles de Teleilat Ghassul", *Biblica* 15 (1934) 1-7 + 1 pl. – ID., "Le disque étoilé en Canaan au troisième millénaire avant Jésus-Christ", *Mélanges Maspero, I, Mémoires de l'Institut Français* 71 (1934) 55-59 + 1 pl. – Ya'akov MESHORER, *Jewish Coins of the Second Temple Period"*, translated from the Hebrew by I. H. Levine, Tel Aviv, Hassefer, 1967, esp. pp. 144 (n. 108 + pl. XV), 167-168 (n. 211A + pl. XXVIII), 171 (n. 221A + pl. XXIX). – René NEUVILLE, "Additions à la liste des stations préhistoriques de la Palestine et Transjordanie", *Journal of the Palestine Oriental Society* 9 (1929) 114-121. – ID., "L'industrie lithique de Teleilat Ghassoul", *Bulletins et Mé-*

moires de la Société d'Anthropologie de Paris, 1931, 12 p. + 9 pl. – Alan ROWE, *A Catalogue of Egyptian Scarabs, Scaraboids, Seals and Amulets in the Palestine Archaeological Museum*, Cairo, 1936, pp. 283-289: "Addendum A. Axe-Head of the Royal Boat-Crew of Cheops (Or, Sahew-Ra (?)) Plate XXXVI". – Sandra A. SHAM, "Shiqmim's Violin-Shaped Figurines and Ghassul Bone Artifacts", *Biblical Archaeologist* 60/2 (1997) 108. – Sandra A. SHAM and Yosef GARFINKEL, "Perforated Rods. A New Chalcolithic Ivory Type", *Bulletin of the American School of Oriental Research* 319, August 2000, pp. 1-5. – H. SENÈS, "Trois poteries de Ghassul trouvées aux fouilles de 1938 et reconstituées", *Biblica* 29 (1948) 411-413 + 2 pl. – Eythan SHANY, "A New Unpublished 'beq'a' Weight in the Collection of the Pontifical Biblical Institute, Jerusalem, Israel", *Palestine Exploration Quarterly* 99 (1967) 54-55 + 1 pl. – Ephraim STERN, *Material Culture of the Land of the Bible in the Persian Period 538-332 B. C.*, Warminster, Aris and Phillips, 1982, esp. p. 128. – S. P. VLEEMING, *Ostraka Varia. Tax Receipts and Legal Documents on Demotic, Greek, and Greek-Demotic Ostraka, Chiefly of the Early Ptolemaic Period, From Various Collections [Ostr. Varia 1-60]* (Studia Demotica 5), Leiden, Brill, 1994, XII-167 p. + 18 pl. (pieces from the Museum of the Pontifical Biblical Institute in Jerusalem, numbered 1, 2-5, 7-11, 14, 39, 42, 51 and 55).

The idea of having a museum at the Institute in Jerusalem appears for the first time in a letter from Fr. Fonck to Fr. Cré, a White Father at St. Anne's in Jerusalem, and that letter is dated May 22nd, 1912 (cf. Doc. J. I,5). In the summer of 1913, Fr. Mallon was chosen to carry out the plan to establish the Institute and it was he also who directed the first "caravan". With the latter having re-embarked at Alexandria for Italy on November 12th, Fr. Mallon returned to Jerusalem. Before the end of the year he received from Rome the sum of 3,500 gold francs, i. e. a little over twenty thousand euros at the end of 2008, "for purchasing a collection of antiquities; this probably represents the majority of the objects other than those from Ghassul that fill out the glass cases of our museum", writes Fr. H. Senès in his account of the origins of the Institute in Jerusalem (p.16). He adds the total amount of expense from January to July, 1914, on purchases of old coins, namely a total of about 900 gold francs.

At the time, Fr. Mallon was residing at Notre-Dame de France, but the Marie Réparatrice Sisters, whose convent, until its destruction in 1967, was just opposite the Hospital of St. Louis, gave him a big room with two windows where the Father stored books and antiquities destined for the future Institute. However, in September, 1914, the whole of this depot was moved to Notre-Dame de France and placed under the seal of the Holy See (p. 21 of the report by Fr. Senès). So the Turks did not touch it and, just after the war, on Fr. Mallon's return to Jerusalem on December 4th, 1919, he got it all back, or most of it, and moved back into the room lent by the Réparatrice nuns and stayed there until the summer of 1927 when the Institute building was inaugurated. It was in this same room that Fr. Mallon deposited the few pieces coming from the excavations at Elephantine in 1918 and the flints brought back from his expeditions between 1921 and 1924 and mentioned above.

Thanks to an article by Fr. William H. McClellan "The Biblical Institute in Jerusalem" that appeared in *The Woodstock Letters* 58,1 (1928) 1-23, we learn what the museum at the Institute was a year after its inauguration. According to the house diary Fr. McClellan actually arrived at Jerusalem on June 5th, 1928, and left on September 12th, having gone on the IXth "caravan".

In the big hall to the left as you go in, which served as a lounge, you saw at the far end a large cupboard containing a stuffed vulture. This had been a gift from Pius X given at the beginning of 1914 for which Fr. Mallon had had this showcase made in the March of the same year. This vulture had been shot, it was said, in the desert of Judah. It sat proudly enthroned in that great hall, later to be surrounded by some other, smaller, animals, also stuffed, until, in 1996, they were all, in a deteriorating state, permanently lent to the Jerusalem Natural History Museum which saw to their restoration.

The museum in the strict sense did not yet occupy a particular place. Its items were on show in the library, which actually only possessed just over a thousand volumes. There, then, were to be found the collections of flints brought together by Fr. Mallon, as well as a rich collection of ancient pottery, including several hundred ceramic lamps from the Roman and Byzantine periods. Perhaps also some items brought back from Elephantine, but Fr. McClellan says nothing about them, no more than he does about the collection of ancient coins.

The situation changed with the excavations at Ghassul. The amount of material discovered and the precise account of all the items, along with a description of the work accomplished at the site, required some space. The room in the north-east of the house was taken over. Having been a linen-room, it became the museum; the material discovered, together with the card-indexes and dossiers, were stored in it; it was also possible to work there. In 1941 and 1942 Frs. Fernández and Senès put some order into the collections; to make some room in the library the collections of flint were exposed in a dozen glass cupboards placed along the walls of the corridor on the second floor. That was still the situation in 1967.

From November 1974 to January 1975, in bitterly cold weather, these cupboards, the content of which was henceforth centred on the objects discovered at Ghassul or acquired elsewhere were brought down and ranged along the walls of the lounge and in the reception area at the entrance to the building. It was Fr. William J. Fulco, an archaeologist and then visiting professor at the École Biblique, who took charge of the operation. The treasures of the museum were then put to good effect. The coin collection also took its place in this lounge. From that time on, visitors came in greater numbers, especially children from the schools, to whom Fr. Juan Esquivias, from 1985 to 1994, explained the contents of the cupboards in modern Hebrew. So much so that, in 1985 the Ghassul star and the Egyptian mummy left the former museum for the lounge; this former museum was emptied, the material belonging to it in the depot and all the documentation moved to the mezzanine floor and into a depot fitted out for the purpose; the former museum became a lounge and living room. Finally, in 1996, wishing to protect and at the same time display our best items better, Fr. J. Crocker, with the help of Fr. Fulco, the one who knew our museum best, reorganized the layout; the small room in the south-west of the house was joined on to the former lounge that had become a more accessible museum in 1974: the mummy was placed in the middle of it. Un-fortunately, since the death of Fr. Esquivias in 1995 there has not been anyone in the house to guide the occasional visitors,

Items from our museum have often been, and still are, lent for exhibitions, sometimes even for several years; in particular, some were lent, before 1948, to the Palestinian Museum that, after 1967, took the name of the Rockefeller Museum, as well as to the Israel Museum, these two museums being, one to the east of the city of Jerusalem, the other to the west.

As ill-luck would have it, one night, about the 9th or 10th of December, 1981, thieves got into our museum and made off with quite a lot, about a third, of our collection of ancient coins. Thanks to Prof. Yaakov Meshorer, a numismatist at the Israel Museum, and to Fr. Fulco, at the end of a police enquiry and a trial, we got back about fifty of the stolen coins, i. e. about a quarter of the booty, on October 3rd, 1985. Since then, as a precautionary measure, we have not displayed what remains of that collection.

The bibliography given above proves that many rare objects in our mu-seum, even the coins, have been the subject of learned publications. By way of example, one could mention an axe bearing an inscription in hieroglyphics making it possible to date it to the time of the Pharaoh Cheops; it was found in Syria in 1911.

But what draws the visitors most is the Egyptian mummy. It is the only one in Israel. Its origin cannot be documented. If the description of the house given by Fr. W. McClellan in 1928 is to be believed, the mummy had not yet reached us by that time. On the other hand, Fr. Ed. Decher states in a letter of October 5th, 1985, that on his arrival in Jerusalem on October 23rd, 1933, the mummy was there all right. The rest is oral tradition: it may have come from the college of the Jesuits in Alexandria who offered it as a tribute to Fr. Mal-lon and it would have come through diplomatic channels, i. e. French ones. In any case a photo from 1934 shows it in a corner of the lounge at that time.

The mummy is in good condition. Still enveloped in wrappings it rests in a wooden sarcophagus. The head and chest are covered in a bound and coloured mask and breastplate. On the cover of the sarcophagus some texts in hiero-glyphics can be read. Prof. Joseph Leibovitch, from Jerusalem, suggested an interpretation of them in 1960: "The text is from a late period", he wrote to Br. Šira, "even from the Roman period, at a time when [hieroglyphic texts] were copied without being understood; all the mythology [used in the two columns of the text] seems in disorder. The middle column gives the title and name of the person; the other columns are a version of chapter CXXVI of the Book of the Dead". And here is his reading of the central text: "Proxyneme to Osiris, Lord of Abydos, the priest of Akhmîm *Hrysst3* (of) the Mother of the god, *îr.t-Hr-r-w*….. son of the person with the same title … born of the lady….. of Akhmîm, *Na-menkh-imen-djed*".

So it was already known back in 1960 that the mummy was of a young man from a priestly family; however, everyone in the house affectionately called him "Cleopatra", thereby denoting a woman of the Roman era. Confirmation of the male sex came in the course of a restoration done by the Israel Museum: after being in the Biblical Institute for half a century, the mummy was deteriorating.

The initiative for the restoration is to be credited to Prof. Raphael Giveon, an Egyptologist at the University of Tel Aviv. In March, 1976, he suggested doing an analysis of the mummy in the laboratory of the Israel Museum. It was he who, in the December of the same year, wrote to the Mayor of Jerusalem, Teddy Kollek, to ask for financial assistance for the restoration of this mummy, a jewel in Israel and more particularly in Jerusalem. The cost was then estimated at 12,000 Israeli pounds. In May, 1977, the mayor, having approached the *Jerusalem Foundation*, granted the sum of 18,000 Israeli pounds; in March, 1979, with the cost ever increasing, the *Jerusalem Foundation* actually granted a total of 28,500 Israeli pounds, i. e. 2,000 US dollars. In the meantime, in April 1977, there was a question of sending the mummy to Paris to restore it there, but two months later Fr. Pierre du Bourguet, S. J., from the Louvre Museum, concluded an exchange of letters with Fr. Furlong in the negative: too many technical, financial and diplomatic problems made the Paris hypothesis impracticable.

Restoring the mummy could then start in Jerusalem. When examined with X-rays at the Hadassah Medical School, the mummy indeed proved to be that of a young man. Restoring, in the strict sense, was done at the specialized laboratory at the Israel Museum; it took a long time. It was only in June, 1978, that the mummy returned to the Institute, now with a protective Plexiglas cover to it. However, the restoration of the mask paintings, the breastplate and especially the lid of the sarcophagus was only finished in the summer of 1982. Now completely restored, our mummy was exhibited in the Rockefeller Museum in 1984 and its breastplate in colour was at the top of the bill. It only came back to the Institute a year later.

Just one more word about the big fresco with the star from Ghassul, of which it is the greatest discovery. In *Biblica* 15 (1934), pp. 1-3, Fr. Mallon told how it had been discovered on December 19th, 1932, and how it had been partly but sufficiently recuperated. A 1936 photo shows that at that time the big reproduction on oilskin, executed by Miss Tirsa Ettinger (cf. *ibid.*, p. 3 in the note), hung on the wall at the end of the lounge; some recently discovered objects were also displayed on tables along the walls.

In 1938 the fresco was lent "permanently", it was thought (cf. *Acta PIB*, 4, p. 94), to the Palestine Museum; it returned to the Institute at an unknown date. It was then placed in the room used as a museum at the time in the north-east of the house until, in 1985, it resumed its place in the former lounge that had become a museum eleven years earlier.

Here is a short description of this faithful reproduction of the fresco. Three concentric stars with eight points take up most of the tableau. The starry part measures 1 metre, 84 in diameter. Three colours were used, white, black and red, forming a varied, harmonious whole. On the left a stylized bee can be discerned above, then two masks. The interpretation of the other elements depicted remains hypothetical. The main question is to know whether this fresco has a religious significance. Back in 1934 Fr. Mallon noticed that eight-point stars are often found "in later times as a symbol of Ishtar" (*ibid.*, p. 7).

Let us conclude. Small in size, but rich in its original and diverse content the museum at the Jerusalem Institute deserves its reputation. It shows some items of great worth coming from prehistoric times, especially with its Ghas-sulian collection, but also with its flint pieces. It contains some good items from Mesopotamia, Pharaonic Egypt, and the Persian, Greek, Roman and Byzantine periods.

All of it comes from purchases, gifts and archaeological discoveries, over a period stretching from 1913 to 1960, the date of the Institute's last excava-tions at Ghassul. Nothing has been acquired since.

V. The library

Any academic institution worthy of the name must have a library special-ized in its field. The one at the Biblical Institute in Jerusalem can only be that of a branch of the Institute in Rome. It will therefore be a modest one, but answering the needs of this dependency that concerns itself with the Bible and everything in the Holy Land that can cast light on it: the country, its history, its geography, its near-eastern setting and the ancient languages that were used in it. In addition, because of the Ghassul excavations, links with other archaeological excavations carried out all over the Near East are not over-looked. Lastly, importance is given to what is needed for work such as dic-tionaries, encyclopaedias, critical editions of the literary sources as well as collections of monographs and the more important periodicals. In another connection, since in this Catholic institution there are resident priests, a section on theology is not lacking, no more than is another on Judaism; the Institute is in Israel.

This library, too, has a history. Back in the autumn of 1913, Fr. Mallon had received eleven boxes of books from the Rome Institute (cf. Fr. Senès's report, p. 16): these were to be the first to find a place in the library of the building inaugurated in July, 1927.

The definitive plan of the house had, however, been changed. On February 17th, 1926, in fact, the Rector of the Institute, Fr. O'Rourke, writing to Fr. Marini about the plans for the house that the latter had submitted to Rome, noted that Fr. General thought that the space devoted to the library was "quite insufficient" and that the library had to be bigger. The remark was taken into account. Yet as the years went by, the library, even when enlarged, was constantly proving to be too small.

In 1967 there was hardly enough room to put the new accessions. The corridor on the mezzanine that extends from west to east in the middle of the house began to be invaded by books and, since 1979, has been completely occupied by the periodicals and collections of monographs. In the south-east of this corridor a depot was installed, and renovated in 2004; in it were placed some rare books or books that were too old to be in current use. In 1985 the original room of the library was cut in two by a platform covered in shelves able to take ten thousand volumes; then, to gain some room all the sections were reorganized by ranging the books according to size – a move to save space that ten years earlier had been successfully tried in the Institute in Rome. But twenty years later more space had to be given to the library again: in 2005 it also engulfed the ground floor corridor that separated it from the museum. It is therefore very likely that in about 2025 library space will have to be increased.

Thus the accumulation of books took place progressively. From 1928 to 1931 accessions were regular: 400 books in 1928, about a thousand in 1929. Later on, from 1932 to 1955, because of the world financial crisis, then the war with its consequences, few books were acquired each year. Between 1956 and 1959, with Fr. North as director, 1,122 books or periodicals came in; Fr. North gave details about them regularly in a duplicated bulletin called "Jerusalem Pontifical Library News-Flash". The total number of books at the end of 1945 was 5,633. Twenty years later, in September 1966, they numbered 9,657 and in 1975, 11,395. A decade later, in 1985, when the first big extension with the platform was undertaken, it was calculated that the library contained about 16,000 volumes (cf. *Acta PIB*, 9/1, p. 19). During the next two decades, from 1985 to 2005, there were about 7,900 new entries. At that ever-increasing rate, by about 2025 there will be around 35,000 volumes in this library. It does not of course bear comparison with the one in the Institute in Rome, nor with the one at the École Biblique of the Dominicans in Jerusalem, but it does answer the immediate needs of the house, its permanent residents and students.

Among the rarities this modest library possesses let us mention a hundred and fifty books in the fields of geology and prehistory: this batch came from Fr. R. Koeppel when he was excavating at Ghassul. More precious and in perfect condition and purchased cheaply – 350 dollars – by Fr. North in 1959 when he was director of the house, is the famous *Description de l'Égypte*, luxuriously produced between the years 1809 and 1828 by the scientists accompanying Napoleon Bonaparte on his expedition in 1798: twelve huge volumes consisting of engravings, some in colour, and seven volumes of learned explanations.

VI. Publications

Bibliography

Andrés FERNÁNDEZ, *Problemas de topografía palestinense* (Colectánea Bíblica 1), Barcelona, Ed Litúrgica Española, 1936, 220 p. + maps. – ID., *Commentarius in Librum Iosue* (Cursus Scripturae Sacrae II, 5), Paris, Lethielleux, 1938, XVIII-291 p. – ID., *Florilegio Bíblico*, Jerusalem, Imprenta de los Franciscanos, 1940 (13 monographs). – ID., *Vida de Nuestro Señor Jesu Cristo* (Colectánea Bíblica 3), Madrid, Editorial Catolica, 1948, LXVI-612 p. + 7 maps. – ID., *Comentario a los libros de Esdras y Nehemías* (Colectánea Bíblica 4), Madrid, Consejo Superior de Investigaciones Cientificas, 1950, XXI-459 p. – ID., *Geografía Bíblica (El País de Jesús)*, Barcelona, Vilamala, 1951, XXI-151 p. + map – Robert KOEPPEL, *Palästina. Die Landschaft in Karten und Bilden*. Tübingen, Mohr, 1930, V-174 p. – ID., *Praelectiones geologiae et praehistoriae ad usum theologorum accomodatae, I, 3: Tabulae cum explicatione*, Rome, PIB, 1933, 33 p. + 9 illustrations. – ID., *Zur Urgeschichte Palästinas. Ein Übersicht aus Geologie, Prähistorie und Archäologie* (Scripta PIB), Rome, PIB, 1937, VII-65 p. + 14 indexes and 9 illustrations. – Alexis MALLON, *Les Hébreux en Égypte* (Orientalia 3), Rome, PIB, 1921, 213 p. – ID., *Grammaire copte avec bibliographie, chrestomathie et vocabulaire*, Beyrouth, Imprimerie Catholique, [3]1926, XVIII-325-192 p. – Donatien MOLLAT, *Saint Jean Maître spirituel* (Bibliothèque de Spiritualité 10), Paris, Beauchesne, 1976, 175 p. – ID., avec Jacques GUILLET, *Apprendre à prier à l'école de Saint Paul et des évangélistes* (Renouveau 6), Paris, Feu Nouveau, 1977, pp. 39-138 (on the gospels). – Alain MARCHADOUR and David NEUHAUS, *La Terre, la Bible et l'histoire. Lecture chrétienne*, Paris, Bayard, 2006, 237 p. English version: *"The Land that I will show you...". Land, Bible, History: A Christian Approach*, New York, Fordham University, 2006. – Francesco ROSSI DE GASPERIS, *La roccia che ci ha generato. Un pellegrinaggio nella Terra Santa come esercizio spirituale* (Bibbia e Preghiera 20), Rome, Apostolato della Preghiera, 1994, 178 p. – ID., *Maria di Nazareth, icona di Israele e della Chiesa*, Bose, Qiqajôn, 1997, 142 p. – ID., *Cominciando da Gerusalemme. La sorgente della fede e dell'esistenza cristiana*. Casale, Piemme, 1997, 588 p. – ID., *Sentieri di vita. La dinamica degli Esercizi ignaziani nell'itinerario delle Scritture*, 4 vols., Milan, Ed. Paoline, 2005-... (Vol. 1: 501 p.) – Card. Carlo Maria MARTINI, *Beati Petri Apostoli Epistolae Ex*

Papyro Bodmeriana VIII Transcriptae (Bibliotheca Apostolica Vaticana, Bodmer VIII). *Introductio, Textus et Apparatus*, Bibliotheca Apostolica Vaticana – Madrid, Testimonio Compañía Editorial, 2003, XLIX-73 p. + 10 facsimiles (English translation by St. Pisano published in 2006 by the same publishers). – Pino DI LUCCIO, *The Quelle and the Targums. Righteousness in the Sermon on the Mount/Plain* (AnBib, 175), Rome PIB, 2008.

Even in the branch of a scholarly institution, professors and others working along with them, whether still active or retired, publish the results of their research. There is no worthwhile teaching that does not presuppose or give rise to research. This is why it is not surprising to discover that the resident Jesuits at the Institute in Jerusalem have, for the most part, published some important works. Several of these have already been mentioned when dealing with the Ghassul excavations or the treasures in the Institute's museum: they are books and articles by Frs. Mallon, Koeppel, Simons, Senès and North. The first two mentioned, and the last, also published other articles concerning their activity in the Holy Land, but in order not to add too many tedious references, only the books by these authors and their colleagues and successors are noted here.

Now one thing one finds is that no generation considered itself dispensed from publishing, at least when the staff on the spot had trained in biblical sciences or when there were enough of them not to be totally immerged in the immediate problems of management.

In any case, the example set by the founder, Fr. Mallon, is eloquent. Setting aside Coptic, in which he was a past master, he delved into biblical history during the First World War: it was mainly in Cairo that he wrote his study on *les Hébreux en Égypte*. Afterwards it was Ghassul that occupied our archaeologists from 1929 to 1940 and again from 1959-1960. In the meantime, in 1930, Fr. Koeppel published a work on the relief maps of the Holy Land and Jerusalem that he had made with plaster in 1927; some examples are to be found in various places, mainly at the Biblical Institute, both in Rome and in Jerusalem. Fr. Mallon, for his part, also published many articles, especially in *Biblica*, in which his competence as an archaeologist comes out.

Yet the one who published most among the Jesuits of the first generation in Jerusalem was undoubtedly Fr. A. Fernández, six of whose books are noted here. He arrived in the Holy City in 1929 and left in 1947. All his books are redolent of his stay in the land of the Bible. Two of them, on the geography and topology of the Holy Land, are directly in line with the purpose of the house, as defined by Benedict XV, which was actually what the Father suggested when he was rector of the Institute, as we have seen. Fr. Fernández was primarily an exegete: his commentaries prove it, while benefiting from the author's contact with the land in which the events related in these biblical books took place. However, it should be borne in mind that Fr. Fernández had in fact already written an earlier commentary on the book of Ezra at the beginning of the thirties, but his manuscript, of which he had not kept a copy, went up in flames in Madrid in 1936 during the revolution. Finally, his 1948 Life of Jesus was a success in the book-shops, so much so that in 1950 he put out an abridged popular edition; in 1954 he published a second edition of his 1948 work, even more fully developed than the first one; in 1960 this second edition was translated into Italian and published at the Vatican!

The torch was taken up by Fr. D. Mollat. When he reached the age of re-tirement at the Pontifical Gregorian University in Rome he withdrew to Jeru-salem and it was there that he wrote those pages of a highly spiritual nature on St. John, then on some passages in the gospels. But he did not see the publica-tion of these second commentaries, since his peaceful and lonely demise took place on the night of Easter Monday to Tuesday in 1977.

He was replaced by Fr. Rossi de Gasperis, also a theologian at the Gre-gorian, but fully active. A disciple of Fr. Lonergan, he took his reflection on the theological and spiritual relation which links Israel and the Church fur-ther while commenting on Scripture in the light of that land in which it was written.

Finally, when Cardinal Martini, a former rector of the Institute and emeri-tus archbishop of Milan, retired, like Fr. Mollat, he withdrew to the Institute in Jerusalem and when, having got back into textual criticism there, he came out with a new edition of the two letters of Peter from the Bodmer papyrus in 2003, a new generation arose. In collaboration with Fr. A. Marchadour, an Assumptionist in Jerusalem, Fr. D Neuhaus in 2006 published a study on the Bible, the land and the history. Fr. Pino di Luccio, for his part, published a doctoral thesis in 2008 presented at the Hebrew University of Jerusalem; it is about some relations between the Sermon on the Mount (Matt) or on the Plain (Luke) and the Targums.

That is enough to prove that, apart from many articles and other publica-tions, by the writings of its members the Jerusalem Institute never ceased, and still does not cease to take part in the concert of biblical sciences.

Conclusion

Since its foundation in Rome in 1909 and especially since the opening of its branch in Jerusalem in 1927, the pontifical biblical Institute has been pre-sent in the Near East to achieve an important part of its mission there, mainly in Jerusalem. Even before the establishment in the Holy City, the "caravans" provided biblicists with services that no one else could offer throughout the Near East on that scale, but the Institute had to give up that service in 1979 for lack of practical means and experienced guides. For the same reasons it also gave up archaeological excavations, first of all at Elephantine, given the poor quality of the first results in 1918, then at Ghassul in 1960. On the other hand, its museum is better laid out, its study programs have definitely been improved and diversified, while its library continues to grow, responding to ever-growing needs. Lastly, the Jesuits who were and still are resident in the house in Jerusalem, each in his own field, have not failed to publish important works in which their presence in Jerusalem is easily felt.

Doc. J. III,1

APIBR B-VI-4 (VI-3)

Report by Fr. Ronzevalle on the excavations at Elephantine[1]
Translated from the French

+ Cairo April 15th 1918.[2]

Reverend Father Vice-Rector [A. Fernández],[3]

P. C.

As I mentioned in my last letter to you from Aswan (dated the 6th inst.)[4] I am sending enclosed herewith an exact copy of the Report – purely administrative – which, in accordance with the *New Law on the Antiquities of Egypt*, 1912, ministerial Decree, n° 52, article 14, we had to submit to the Director General of the Antiquities Office. This report contains a plan of our first and chief excavation site and a complete list of all the objects discovered. We added some similar items found which we had bought at Aswan and Elephantine.

As you will see from the closing lines of this report, we have kept the full and detailed publication of our discoveries for the Biblical Institute. The Report could be published by the Antiquities Office in its *Annales*: they have the right, if they think fit: but no other publication can be released by it without our consent.

The full and detailed academic publication, mentioned above, can only be undertaken by the Biblical Institute after a thorough study of the objects from antiquity discovered, especially the inscriptions, papyri and ostraca, which are very numerous. This publication could therefore not appear earlier than a year or two, in any case before the end of the war. But does the Biblical Institute at present want to publish a

---

[1] The manuscript has additional notes in the margin, some of them are in red concerning photos sent with the manuscript; those photos are in the photo collections in the APIBR and APIBJ; the additional notes in red ink will not be given here, with one exception.

[2] *Additional note in right-hand margin*: Documents attached to this report:
1. Administrative report to the Antiquities Office
2. Plan of the extensive excavation, with legend
3. List of objects found
4. 32 various photos with notes on the back
5. 2 plans: 1st and 2nd permit from Office

[3] *Note in left-hand margin*: Please send me word by telegram on receipt of this report in its full form: "Ronzevalle Jesuits Alexandria. Received. Fernández".

[4] *Note in margin*: refers to April 24th.

general introductory booklet dealing with the history of the campaign and a description of the main results achieved? If the answer is yes, I would be grateful if you could let me know as soon as possible, as well as details about this publication (illustrated or not, and to what extent? In Rome or in Egypt? &c., &c).[5]

[2] At this moment, too, the Rev. Fr. Rector must decide, yes or no, whether he wants the excavations to resume in autumn. Our request, made several times already, has already been granted in principle by the Directorate of the Office. On the other hand, it does not commit us; so that if we decide not to resume our research it will be enough to inform the authorities without delay. Later on in this report you will find the archaeological reasons in favour of a second campaign. I only want to touch on one point here, the question of funds. In his letter[6] in reply to the question asked by Fr. Tacchi Venturi, Rev. Fr. Rector had rightly discovered - as the facts show - that 10,000 francs would not be enough to produce a result worthy of the Institute; he added that, if necessary, he would go as far as doubling or trebling that sum. On our part, however, we did not think it wise to go beyond the first figure in the first campaign, a somewhat improvised one because of the difficulty in communications and, consequently, begun too late, given the excessively hot climate. So if Rev. Fr. Rector wants there to be a second campaign and wants it to start at the right time, i. e. at the beginning of November, will he please let us know as soon as possible and see to it that the funds reach us at the beginning of September at the latest? Any plan not taking this overriding need into account is to be rejected in advance. You should not be unaware of the fact[7] that out of the 10,000 francs for the first campaign, the bursar's office of the house in Cairo, which has generously made all the loans, has so far only received the first cheque for 5,000, with a loss in the exchange of more than 400 francs. It would be impossible for us to operate again on such a footing. Thus, to summarize the question of funds, if a second campaign is to take place in November, the sum granted us (10,000 or 20,000) will have to reach us in Cairo at the beginning of September.

Why in September again? Because experience shows that, despite the advantages of hospitality in a religious house, the Catholic Church where we stayed is much too far from the excavation site. This house is at the *northern* end of the town of Aswan and the site to be dug up is at the *southern* end of the island of Elephantine. Hence the considerable waste of [3] time and money which it was obviously impossible for us to avoid in our first campaign but which it is easy to stop if we have enough time to set ourselves up on the island itself. On foot, from the Catholic Mission to the ferry opposite the excavation site takes a quarter of an hour, and much longer at the hottest times of the day. By boat, with a good wind, a quarter of an hour is enough, but when the wind is against you, the crossing sometimes takes three quarters of an hour. As to costs, they really have been heavy, even though we have been content with a third-class boat and a small tent just big enough to take a small table and our ordinary equipment at night-time. So if the resumption of work is decided upon and if the funds are to be sent to us we must be able to get to Elephantine several weeks before the beginning of the excavations, find a habitable small house in the village there, get

---

[5] *Note in red in margin*: I have a large number of photographs taken at Aswan and Elephantine. I can have some more made (in Cairo) of the objects which it would be good to publish.

[6] *Note in margin*: October 14th, 1917.

[7] *In the margin*: If need be, ask Fr. Tacchi Venturi.

our indispensable (hired) furniture moved in and, finally, make sure that we are set up for three or four months. Some people are advising us to have a wooden hut made on our own, as our predecessors did, or a small house in rough brick. That is something, to be sure, which must be settled as soon as possible otherwise we are likely either to undergo the drawbacks of our first construction, or to fall ill and put the outcome of a campaign much more important than the earlier one at risk.

Once these material conditions of time and money have been settled, we can turn to the technical reasons favouring the resumption of the excavations. As you can easily gather from our report and all the supplementary information which I am appending to it, we have taken on a methodical task that leaves nothing to chance and can amply reward the Biblical Institute even in the *very possible* case where the "supreme" goal of our expedition would never be achieved. We have excavated and will continue to excavate at Elephantine (and even at Aswan, as our second permit allows us to) to discover Jewish documents of direct interest to biblical studies; but we cannot imitate our predecessors who too easily sacrificed the rest in the interests of a purpose that they no more achieved than we did, despite the *hundreds of thousands* of francs which they set aside for it. I have already informed you that in the very last days of our searches we brought to light a small fragment of a *lapidary* Jewish inscription which is worth ten times its weight in gold and is enough to justify a new campaign, longer and more patient. It is thanks to our painstaking method that this revealing fragment was discovered and to find other fragments of the same monument or of its like it will not be going too far to explore the whole hill where [4] it was found and of which we have not excavated one tenth. I have calculated that to clear the whole of this hill, so rich in Aramaic and other ostraca and in various relics of several periods, would cost us about 6,000 francs, not including, of course, our housing and maintenance costs. It was this too high a cost that prevented us from limiting ourselves to clearing this part of the ancient site; we would have begun without being able to finish, and others, especially the fellahin and the Sabakhin, would have deprived us of the benefit of our efforts and expenditure. If the sum made available to us is not greater than what we had in hand (i. e. 9,000 francs instead of 10,000) we will not get off the island and it is very likely that we will not be able to complete the examination of all that remains to be excavated in the district. So I cannot insist too much that Rev. Fr. Rector keep to his promise, if he can, to treble the first payment. Especially now that we have our essential equipment (except for pickaxes and sieves that had been lent to us by the Management of the Dam), our technical instruments and our personal equipment, a sum of 20,000 frs., even if reduced to 18,000 by the exchange transaction, would make it possible to examine all those places at Elephantine itself where there is still something to be done and, once that job is done, to move for a month to Aswan itself where there was once another colony of Jews and Semites. The second campaign would last four months (November 1918 – February 1919), it would be exhaustive, and if the Jews of the Persian period or earlier really did leave books or other sacred documents here the chances of finding them would be doubled or trebled. To complete the picture, I would add that study concerning the site of the Jewish temple will require special efforts. This study, already started and well in hand, cannot be brought to a successful conclusion, from the scientific point of view, if we do not have the time and funds needed. The secret store or genizah, which I got people to look for over a period of ten days (see the Report to the Office) has not been found; but we have not excavated a tenth of the places where the Jews may have buried the books not in use which they were by no means allowed to destroy. To give up just this study, when so many sacrifices have already been borne with a view to making a discovery that could revolutionize biblical studies, would not make sense, even in these critical times we are passing through. One could also add that it is thanks to present circumstances that we found the ground completely free, not only at Elephantine, but also at Aswan. After the war, conditions could change considerably, even if the high cost of living, which is [5] so high at present, were to come down. In short, if there is to be a resumption, it is in November that it has the chance of being most fruitful for the Biblical Institute.

On the economic side, it is fitting to point out another change, due to take place in the organization of the campaign, to you. There were three of us during the first one, but Fr. Strazzulli will not be in the second one, and Fr. Bovier-Lapierre does not think he will be able to join me for the second time, having found that our archeological work kept him on the spot, without being able to explore the country with its prehistory in mind. Thus I will be on my own, which will greatly reduce the cost of lodging and maintenance. One lay-brother will be enough, if that kind[8] of help can be given me, or a kind of hired major-domo who would not cost much more than the other companion. I will say Mass daily at Elephantine in a small chapel that we shall reserve for the purpose in the house hired or built by us quite near the excavation site. There would be no waste of time and there will be a considerable saving of money.

It goes without saying that if I offer to continue the work begun it is on the express condition that the Rev. Fr. Chanteur[9] agrees. I wrote to him towards the middle of March saying that the second campaign seemed to me so necessary and so worthy of the Biblical Institute that I willingly give up my journey to Rome to carry it out. I have not yet received any answer[10], but I think the Rev. Fr. [Chanteur] must have written directly to those concerned to say that he was putting me at the disposal of the Institute for the resumption of the excavations. If I am not available the Institute should not give up the project but itself look for a substitute as Director of the second campaign. Personalities must step aside here, given the importance of the end being sought.

To summarize all that has gone before, I ask you to find out as soon as possible what the Rev. Fr. Rector thinks about

1°/ the introductory publication mentioned above (p.1)

2°/ the second campaign and the means for carrying it out.

As soon as you have decided this, please send me the answers in a telegram
ad primum: "no publication", or "publication decided on, instructions follow".
ad 2um: "resumption decided on", or "we're not resuming".

I will thus know without delay what to do and will get down to work immedia-[6]tely, if that is what is to be done.

---

[8] *In the margin*: Fr. Mallon, as Egyptologist, would be very useful. The climate is "just right" for the lungs. But it will not be comfortable for him.

[9] Provincial of the Lyons province on which the Syrian Mission, to which Fr. Ronzevalle belonged, depended.

[10] *In the margin*: The reply has just reached me from Alexandria; it is dated March 24th and quite *affirmative*, even as regards Fr. Bovier-Lapierre, if he were of any assistance.

Now here are some further items of information on the work done; they are meant to inform you about the past and help you to understand the future.[11]

It was in the course of a conversation with Fr. Strazzulli that my idea to excavate at Elephantine took shape. I had told him that if I had 10,000 francs at my disposal I would not hesitate to devote them to this work. I had seen the site in 1915, a few weeks after leaving Rome, and I had been struck by what still remained to be done, despite the huge amount of excavation, duplicated in part, done in the years 1906-1909. Fr. Strazzulli went out of his way to get funds from the Vatican. For this purpose he addressed Fr. Vaccari, asking him to pass on his request to the Fr. Secretary [Fr. Tacchi Venturi]. The latter did not want to approach the Vatican without having consulted the authorities. Our Father [General Ledóchowski] asked the Rev. Fr. Rector, who "seized the opportunity". I can tell you that if I had been able to suppose for a moment that the Rev. Fr. Rector would so easily agree to this expedition I would not have hesitated to write to him myself back in 1915. Be that as it may, the answer from the Rev. Fr., dated, as I said above (p. 2), October 14th, 1917, was passed on to us by Fr. Tacchi Venturi. It was already unfortunately quite late when it reached us,[12] and I for my part was about to leave for Rome. This journey being optional, it could in any case have been put off until much later, I thought it over and found that at least a start could be made with research into a first campaign. Rev. Fr. Rector was offering us not just 10,000 francs, but even 20,000 and 30,000, if necessary. He was appointing me as director of the enterprise, with Fr. Bovier-Lapierre as assistant. Fr. Strazzulli, although not appointed by him, could and even ought to come with us; this was suitable since it was thanks to him that the expedition was taking place; it was very useful for his training; it was very advantageous for us who found in him a thrifty bursar, we who were to lodge in an Italian house. We even thought it necessary to have the concession from the Antiquities Department put in his personal name,[13] as a former alumnus of the Biblical Institute. He readily agreed, and after making inquiries from this end from the Antiquities Department, all three of us went to Cairo and got permission to excavate (20th of December). This authorization, valid for a year, starting from November 15th (the official date for excavation "seasons") granted us the whole of the Kôm at Elephantine[14] and, on the opposite bank of the Nile, (to the west) a vast stretch of land where we could search the necropolis of the Elephantine and Aswan Semites .

[7] When Fr. Bovier-Lapierre and I, having finished all our preparations at Cairo, arrived at Aswan, Fr. Strazzulli had already got everything ready to receive us. This was the 5th of January of this year. We had allowed for excavation tools, which we did not find on the spot (just three pickaxes and two shovels), and we had to wait two long weeks before getting shovels and sieves[15] from the Management of the Dam. On January 23rd we were ready and we started. It was already very late, and our expenses were already very heavy; our material and technical preparations had taken almost 2,000 francs, our housing had been costly, our sustenance, in a run-down house which

---

[11] *In the margin*: Alexandria, April 19th.

[12] *In the margin*: (mid-November).

[13] *In the margin*: acting *in the name of the Institute*: this is spelt out in full in the official documents.

[14] *In the margin*: and even a bit more, to the NNE, but cultivated fields prevent any extensive soundings beyond the exact due north.

[15] *In the margin*: kindly lent, along with a lever.

was short of many things, was to be even more so. It was easy to calculate that, out of a first payment of 10,000 francs over a period of two months, only a relatively modest sum would be left for us to spend on the excavation in the real sense. So we resolved to do things on a small scale and with as few workmen as possible so as not to add to the cost of supervision, itself a tricky business when done by locals. This method worked, thank God, and we can say that, in all the places dug by us, nothing important could escape our attention, nothing could be stolen from us by our workmen.

Our first blow with the pickaxe fell near the point marked *a* on our plan. Very shortly after we found on the granite the statue, or rather a piece of the statue in wood from the Old Empire, which is a remarkable work of art and a very rare piece. As we went gradually towards points f and h we found some Semitic remains, then, when we got to sector x, we saw the first fragments of papyrus appear. We had to dig very deep in this sector, sometimes to more that 7 metres. (Cf. the report sent to the Department). The number of our workmen had gradually increased; it never went beyond 98, including children and guards. We were lucky enough to find workmen far from Aswan and Elephantine and at a very advantageous low price (1^f to 1^f25 per day for men and 0^f50 to 0,75 for children, removing loose earth); moreover, these workmen were generally honest. Several made real discoveries themselves, and most of them will come back to us if we resume work in the autumn; this will be very valuable, given the delicate nature of excavations in this field.

Looking for the site of the Jewish shrine had occupied me from the beginning. I did not want to give any details in the report to the Department; [8] but the signs (traces of fire and locating the streets indicated in the Cowley papyri which I had picked up[)] convinced me that it really was at the place indicated by Maspéro and Clermont-Ganneau that the temple of Yaho was to be found. To find a genizah, there is no point in looking elsewhere, and that is why one should not, as far as possible, give up this quest, even if one gives up everything else. One should have no illusions, of course, and *expect, unfailingly*, to make a similar discovery; the genizah may have existed, but may have later disappeared, or remain undiscoverable despite all efforts.[16] It may also be that it never existed; the Elephantine colony, the military style one, could not have possessed or used up a really large number of sacred books. I am greatly stressing the negative side of the search to forestall possible, and even probable, disappointment. The role of the Biblical Institute in an expedition of this kind is one of final rescue; if there is still anything important at Elephantine we will get it, provided that we put the necessary time and money into it; we have all facilities for four or even five campaigns if necessary, as we have been given to understand at the Museum, *but on condition that we continue uninterruptedly*. If, however, we do not find anything which we all hope so fervently for, we must not blame ourselves and consider that the expense allowed us has been wasted. A small Egypto-semitic museum, quite an original one, will certainly result from the excavations on which 30,000 fr. will have been spent, to say nothing of the various publications that will follow.

The enclosed photographs and the explanations accompanying them will give you a sufficiently concrete idea of our work and of a small part of our spoils. Our ostraca,

---

[16] *In the margin*: According to the rule, it is not permitted to destroy the walls of existing buildings, and perhaps it is under a wall, in the foundations, that the genizah was placed when the temple was reconstructed, if that is what happened, or when some important repairs were made.

including the small fragments and those which we able to buy at Elephantine and Aswan, amount to more than 500. All this will be published by the Institute, if we find the necessary specialists. Unfortunately, the Regulations forbid the exportation of documents other than papyri – of course for the part that will be taken by the Museum.[17] According to this Regulation, the Museum is entitled to keep *half of the spoils*; in practice the apportionment is done on a friendly basis and the Museum only keeps what it does not have at all in any form, and in other cases makes compensation if necessary. I will probably return to Cairo when the cases arrive there and when the apportionment is due to take place. In the meantime you can rest assured; the full publication is reserved for us and we will get moulds of everything that will do credit to the Biblical Institute and which will have to go to the Museum in Cairo.

I beg you, please tackle the somewhat tedious task, [9] tedious but necessary, required by the careful reading of the report, the plan and the list of things found. Make a summary of them for the Rev. Fr. Rector[18] and let him have your personal opinion on the advisability of starting work again in the conditions just mentioned. For my part, I am of the opinion that it is a matter of honour for the Institute to continue until there is nothing left at the Kôm at Elephantine. Apart from the area next to the village, for which we are going to need 6,000 frs., there is still the temple to study and a big area to be cleared away to the south of the site. This part has not been cleared away by earlier excavators for two reasons:[19] firstly because there is a small modern cemetery to be moved elsewhere; then, because the area did not seem promising enough. The first reason has been set aside because we have got permission to move the small cemetery a short distance; besides, there is very little to do. The second is not quite well-founded. The height to be cleared away is considerable and we even have some chance of coming across some Semitic, Aramaic, Jewish or even Babylonian monuments. This point of the island, situated facing ancient Aswan, has been inhabited at all times and the Semites there were certainly mingled with the Egyptians, as in the rest of the locality.

There remain the soundings to be made at Aswan itself. This is how we got this addition to the concession. As you have [read] above, our original concession included Elephantine and a very extensive area on the west bank of the river. We had not yet started our dig when the central office of the Department informed us that a mistake had been made by granting us the necropolis to the west. That necropolis had been granted to Mr Schiaparelli (the Italian archaeologist) who had interrupted his work at the beginning of the war but with the intention of resuming it in better times; in 1915 he reminded the Department that he maintained his rights. This was forgotten by the Department, and it was after granting us everything that Mr Daressy, the Secretary General, noticed the mistake that had been made. He wrote to us on the 16th of January to let us know, with his apologies. Instead of complaining, we made the best of a bad job and took the opportunity to ask to excavate at Aswan also, if time permitted. We were only asking for a permit just to make soundings which, fortunately, was immediately granted us (letter and new concession dated January 29th). We therefore

---

[17] *In the margin*: so that some antiquities will have to be studied in Cairo, or be photographed to be studied in Rome.

[18] *In the margin*: unless he has time to read it all for himself, which would be desirable.

[19] *In the margin*: cf. the account in Z. f. Ägypt. T. 46. One needs to have this account and the plans that go with it before one's eyes to follow and locate our own work properly.

have some real chance to discover some Semitic remains there as well; the Elephantine papyri speak constantly of Jews and [10] other Semites living at Aswan.

I shall say no more, leaving it to you and the Rev. Fr. Rector to reflect and decide. Naturally, or rather, physically speaking, I would prefer not to return to those parts, where I suffered a lot as regards health; but I am ready to suffer three times as much for the honour of the Institute and the Church. I await your answer as soon as possible.

To end with, here is a summary of the state of our finances:[20]
[11]

Grand total on April 11th, 1918. £.E.341,32
i. e. at a rate of 26^f to the £Egyptian pound: 8.882^f

With an overall loss in the exchange amounting to more than 800^f, there are about 200f. still in hand, which will be enough for the return of the antiquities to the house [the College of the Holy Family] in Cairo (after the apportionment),[21] as well as when further minor costs of transport, correspondence, etc. are made.

It is evident that if, for the second campaign, I stay at Ele-[12]phantine itself, alone or with just one companion, I will make a saving of nearly 2,5000^f for 4 months. Some expenses will also disappear, such as technical instruments, personal equipment, trunks, etc., implements, etc. So that out of 10,000$^{fr.}$ we will be able to use about 6,5000 (perhaps 7,000) on work on the dig, and out of 20,000, nearly 17,000, *if there is no loss in the exchange.*

Yours sincerely in our Lord,
Rae Vae servus in Xo infimus
Commendo me SSRV
Séb. Ronzevalle SJ

P.S. 1°/ If resumption of the dig is decided upon, it is much better not to publish anything about it before the end of the second campaign. This second campaign, which will *certainly* be more fruitful than the first in many respects, will make it possible for me to give an overall description of the results obtained, much more comprehensive and worthier of the Institute, pending the big final volume. In this case, the report sent to the Department will be enough and, despite its purely administrative character, may be considered as the first official publication by the Institute. If the Department does not intend publishing our Report we could publish it ourselves with some interim illustrations.

2°/ It would be very fitting to send an official letter of thanks for the very liberal help he has given us to the Rev. Fr. Dalléry, Rector of the College of the Holy Family.

---

[20] *The details of these accounts, which cover almost two manuscript pages, are omitted here; however, the following notes are found in the margin*: Note that, as regards the second campaign, the railways are going to raise their prices by 50%. – As regards the second campaign, note that the cost of food, wine, etc. will be higher, but that we will be able to cut down a bit and have our meals cooked by a local or by a hotel in Aswan. – As regards the second campaign, it will be a case of buying indispensable equipment such as *pickaxes* and *sieves*. We cannot go back to the Management of the Dam a second time. – *Only the sum total of the expenses in the manuscript are given here.*

[21] *In the margin*: Rev. Fr. Dalléry agrees to boxes of antiquities being left, until the Biblical Institute in Rome orders their tranference to Rome, no doubt after the war.

In these critical times we are living in, the loan he made us constitutes an act of disinterestedness and fraternal charity beyond all praise. I even have good reason to think that if the second cheque for 5,000 fr. is not cashed by the bursar's office in Cairo before the end of June the house will be worse off.

Please see, along with the Rev. Fr. Rector, whether it would be possible to present the College in Cairo with some of the Institute's publications and, before sending them to it, to ask the Rev. Fr. Dalléry whether, for greater security, he prefers to receive them after the war.

3°/ Fr. Strazzulli is taking steps to get permission to go to Jerusalem. That is one of the reasons why he is not thinking of taking part in the second campaign. There is another, of which he makes no secret, namely the disappointment which the first one caused him. Like many others, he expected sensational discoveries which would have made the Biblical Institute and its excavators suddenly famous. That we have to lower our sights, even after a second campaign, is something I cannot stress enough. We can only discover what really exists, and by dint of persevering manfully in our scheme. If the Biblical Institute and its authorities share these feelings of disappointment, we absolutely must give up any further research and I should be informed of this immediately.

CONCLUSION TO PART TWO

The beginnings of the story of the Pontifical Biblical Institute in Jerusalem, or more precisely the plan to set it up were indisputably an unfortunate adventure. It had become necessary and above all possible clearly and faithfully to reveal its vicissitudes. From that point of view, the later course of events was a happier one. Today there is peace where discord used to reign.

Still, this century-long history bears the stamp of uncertainty. Not only because of the political situations through which the Holy Land and the Holy City have been passing for a century, but also because of their consequences which make themselves felt both in the recruitment of the Jesuits who have charge of this house and in the number of people the land of the Bible can draw to the Institute in Jerusalem.

What saves this branch is firstly the fact that it depends on a highly renowned academic institution situated in Rome, far from the Near East and its manifold tensions, but also, and more probably because this institution is a pontifical one. The Holy See never loses interest in this land in which Jesus of Nazareth was born and in which the Church had its first witnesses. Since the Apostolic See has been normalizing its relations with Judaism and the State of Israel, the branch of the Institute can only gain thereby in security and hope for continued existence.

There are, it seems, two conditions for the survival of this modest institution. The first is that it continue and even accentuate its concrete involvement in the land that is its own. The second is that its links with the Institute in Rome do not loosen, but that on the contrary they grow stronger. Being isolated would be fatal for it.

GENERAL CONCLUSION

A specialized university institution of the second and third cycles, to be of any worth, must meet certain requirements. The first is to have a teaching staff large enough to cover all aspects of what it specializes in; the professors must devote themselves just as much to research, and publishing results, as to teaching. To do this the institution must have a specialized library that is kept up to date and is as complete as possible. Students entering upon the second cycle of the special subject offered by the institution must be both capable and determined; they will therefore be very select. Their number will depend on the quality of the curriculum offered them and on the real needs of the society to which the institution wishes to bring the light of its learning. If the object of research and teaching requires it, the institution will have an affiliated branch in the country which needs to be known if the institution is to fulfil its purpose. Lastly, the institution will make its work known by means of publications, periodicals, monographs and other things needed to make sure that it is well known in the scholarly world.

The Pontifical Biblical Institute, of which the Society of Jesus is in charge, complies with all that. In the biblical faculty, it has thirty-three professors: eleven permanent professors and eight other professors brought in to teach the exegesis of the Old or New Testament, five professors of biblical Greek or Hebrew, eight professors of allied subjects from history to hermeneutics, by way of textual criticism and patristic exegesis, and finally two professors specialized in ancient Judaism. In the faculty of studies of the ancient East, in which the biblical world figures, there are six permanent professors and three others from outside; together they cover the whole field of ancient Semitic languages, as well as the Hittite, Egyptian and Coptic world; besides their own research, those professors provide courses for students in the biblical faculty, each in his own special field.

The Institute's library is one of the best in the world in its twofold domain, biblical and oriental; it possesses at least one hundred and eighty thousand volumes; even its stock of old books is very extensive. Access to books and periodicals is direct, except for old books, and the catalogue is fully computerized.

Students preparing the licentiate in biblical studies, which the Institute alone in the world can bestow, in 2008 number two hundred and thirty, and those working for the licentiate in oriental studies are only four. In the biblical faculty, only those are admitted to the curriculum for the licentiate who have passed the entrance examinations in biblical languages and basic knowledge of the Bible; to prepare them for these, the faculty offers them a propaedeutic course in Greek and Hebrew. The training offered by the Institute aims at being scholarly, with a view to a better understanding of Holy Scripture and only about a tenth of those with licentiates go on to get doctorates. People with licentiates and doctorates in biblical studies then help the local Church, especially in seminaries and ecclesiastical faculties.

To avoid making their training entirely bookish, the Institute offers them, in the course of their studies, the chance of a long stay in biblical lands. For this purpose, the Jerusalem house can take in about twenty-five people, mainly men and women students; they can choose between two programmes, each of one semester: one at the Hebrew University of Jerusalem and the other at the École Biblique et Archéologique Française de Jérusalem. In addition, a programme of biblical history and archaeology is offered in September to students from the Institute by the *Studium Biblicum Franciscanum* in Jerusalem.

Lastly, the Jesuits at the Institute in Rome have their own publishing firm; this publishes two periodicals at present: *Biblica* and *Orientalia*, an exhaustive annual bibliography, the *Elenchus of Biblica*, and four series of monographs: *Analecta Biblica, Subsidia Biblica, Biblica et Orientalia* and *Studia Pohl*.

What was the situation a century ago when the Institute opened its doors? Ten Jesuit professors, only two of whom were for exegesis, but three orientalists, including Fr. Anton Deimel, a genius at Sumerology. Forty-seven students, all ecclesiastics, who could aim at academic degrees, but only at the Pontifical Biblical Commission, on which, since 1908, Fr. Fonck sat as consultor, he being a fierce opponent of anything smacking of Modernism. An embryonic library, with six thousand volumes and over three hundred periodicals already. But no proper building and a precarious financial situation. Still, Leo XIII's wish is taking shape thanks to Pius X's desire and Fr. Fonck's ingenuity.

The situation was going to stabilize within a few years. In 1910 the Vatican acquired the former Muti Papazzuri palace which, once it had been quickly adapted, became the seat of the Institute for good in the centre of Rome in 1912. That was only possible through the generosity of the Coëtlosquet family, from Nancy, which put all its fortune into it and from now on, it was thought, the Biblical Institute could go ahead. The teaching staff was increased with the arrival in 1912 of Fr. Alberto Vaccari, a historian of exegesis; he and Fr. Deimel were to leave their mark on the Institute for many decades. The question of academic degrees had been asked back in 1914 by Fr. Fonck, but without any answer. Exegesis was marking time; the obsession with Modernism was everywhere in Rome, and so in the Institute as well. For Fr. Fonck the *bête noire* was Fr. Lagrange, the founder of the Dominican Fathers' École Biblique in Jerusalem in 1890. So much so that when in 1910 the need of an establishment in the Middle East was felt, things did not go at all well. Finally, the Biblical Institute was soon to publish its first books, but it still did not have a periodical of its own, although it had given it some thought in 1911.

The comparison of the situation at the Institute in 1909 with that of 2009 brings out some great differences. What happened in between? It seems to me that in the course of the hundred years there were two key periods which, up to a point, break with the past and open up new prospects. The first goes from 1927 to 1932 and the second from 1962 to 1965, the period of the second Vatican council. Let us look at this more closely.

During the first two decades of its existence, the Institute did not go through any major episodes. To be sure, the 1914-1918 war seriously cut down the teaching staff, students became fewer and fewer and the cashbox emptied! The first "Caravan" to the Near East had been organized in 1913 all right, but they were only started up again in 1921. Yet Fr. Paul Joüon was at the Institute from 1915 to 1925 to prepare his famous *Grammaire de l'hébreu biblique* there, published by the Institute in 1923. In 1918, archaeological excavations were undertaken on the island of Elephantine in the name of the Institute, but without much success. In 1919, Benedict XV restricted the academic field of a future branch of the Institute in Jerusalem so as to avoid any competition with the École Biblique; he put an end to any unwarranted clashes. The first fascicule of the periodical *Biblica* appeared in 1920, as did the first monograph in the series *Orientalia*. The Pontifical Biblical Commission kept control over academic degrees, the licentiate and doctorate in biblical studies to which students at the Institute aspired, and the latter claimed its autonomy in vain. The situation was gradually deteriorating in other respects.

The first pivotal point lasts from 1927 to 1932. The branch of the Institute in Jerusalem opened in 1927; the master of works there was Fr. Alexis Mallon. In Rome, the teaching staff was enriched in 1928 by the arrival of four aces, Frs. Augustin Merk, to whom we owe the critical edition of the New Testament in Greek and Latin, Giuseppe Messina, a librarian and specialist in Iranian languages, Alfred Pohl, a master of Akkadian, and Franz Zorell, who compiled the Latin version of dictionaries of biblical Greek and Hebrew; their learning was universally recognized. Still in 1928, thanks to the tenacity of

Fr. General Ledóchowski and the rector, J. J. O'Rourke, Pius XI created the *Consortium* of the Gregorian University, the Biblical Institute and the Oriental Institute and, thereby indirectly, the Biblical Institute obtained its complete autonomy from the Pontifical Biblical Commission. Pius XI also named Fr. Vaccari one of its consultors in 1928 as well as Fr. Bea in 1931; the latter had become rector of the Biblical Institute the year before. In 1929, Fr. Mallon discovered the prehistoric site of Teleilat Ghassul, to the north of the Dead Sea and, in the name of the Institute, started on excavations that produced a rare wealth of archaeological finds. In 1931, the periodical *Orientalia* saw the light of day, as did the monograph collection "Analecta Orientalia" the following year. Also in 1932, the Institute henceforth comprised two faculties, the biblical faculty and the faculty of ancient Orient studies; Pius XI had patronized the initiative.

All is now in place. A new era is opening which the 1934 statutes will codify. But exegesis is vegetating; despite Pius XI's opening things up, we still have not yet finished with Modernism, or rather anti-Modernism.

The long period going from 1934 to 1962 was a difficult one.

In Jerusalem, the only positive point was that the excavations at Teleilat Ghassul went on until 1938. As did the "caravans". Then the tensions in the Middle East, the Second World War and the war of independence of Israel with its consequences meant that the house was almost empty; from 1941 until 1948 it was even occupied by the authorities of the British mandate. For the students, the 1934 statutes had not provided anything really serious, so that until 1938 there were only a few individuals; they only came back as from 1952, but mainly to take courses in modern Hebrew. The "caravans" also took the road to the Near East again in 1952.

In Rome, the year 1949 marked a turning point. The Jesuit community moved into the former College of St. Bonaventure and thereby the Institute was more at ease in its original building; that same year, Fr. Bea stood down in favour of Fr. Vogt. During Fr. Bea's long term as rector the Biblical Institute had already had to suffer the first serious criticisms, which were not endorsed by Pius XI or by Pius XII; they even led to the latter publishing his encyclical "*Divino afflante Spiritu*" in 1943; it was a document that granted freedom and promoted modern exegesis of the Old Testament. Yet it was only with Vogt, the rector, that exegesis sprang into action at the Biblical Institute; in 1952 the first volumes of the monograph series "Analecta Biblica" appeared, and it was during that decade that Fr. Stanislas Lyonnet produced his best work on Pauline exegesis. In 1954, attacks on the Biblical Institute started up again, ever more virulent: the scholarly exegesis of the New Testament was now the target, and that lasted until the first session of Vatican II was on, from October until December, 1962. The critics were so successful that in 1962 the Holy Office obliged Frs. St. Lyonnet and Max Zerwick to interrupt their teaching of exegesis. The Institute was seriously threatened.

But the Biblical Institute got the upper hand in the council. It defended itself before the council fathers and the latter consulted them; Fr. Lyonnet, in particular, was listened to with great attention. The dogmatic constitution "*Dei Verbum*", promulgated in 1965 marked a new era for exegesis in its work for the church. The Biblical Institute could go on its way, especially as, in 1964, Frs. Lyonnet and Zerwick had been reinstated as teachers of exegesis. Vatican II was the second milestone in the hundred year history of the Biblical Institute.

The post-conciliar period, from 1966 to the present day, was marked mainly by an overhaul of the statutes of the Institute. It was a slow process of maturation desired by the council and then by John Paul II; it went on from 1965-1985.

In Jerusalem, after several unsuccessful attempts to attract students, the rector, Carlo Maria Martini, caused a surprise by suggesting to the Hebrew University of Jerusalem that it offer a group of students from the Biblical Institute a specific programme lasting one semester every year; it was a success: so far, more than five hundred young Catholic exegetes from all over the world have followed that programme, to the satisfaction of both parties. In 1984, an agreement was also reached between the Biblical Institute and the École Biblique of the Dominican Fathers in Jerusalem, putting an end to formerly tense relations; since then, almost one hundred and twenty students from the Biblical Institute have been at the École for a semester. On the other hand, the Institute discontinued the "caravans" in 1978.

In Rome, during the council period and immediately after it, some professors made a considerable impact: they were Frs. St. Lyonnet and Ignace de la Potterie for the New Testament, Frs. Luis Alonso Schökel and Denis J. McCarthy for the Old, Fr. Mitchell Dahood for Ugaritic and biblical Hebrew. Between 1974 and 1983 the teaching staff was to a large extent rejuvenated by the arrival of young Jesuits; most are still there. Later on, with the Society of Jesus no longer being able to offer other than already experienced professors over a period of twenty years, the Institute continued to take on some teachers from outside also, as it had already started doing; these were either from among its former students or from Roman university circles.

In 1972 Paul VI changed the statutes of the Pontifical Biblical Commission and summoned the following to join it, henceforth as members: Frs. Lyonnet (1973-1979), de la Potterie (1973-1984) and Martini (1974-1980). In 1985 Fr. Albert Vanhoye became a member of it and, in 1990, its secretary until 2001. The following year, Fr. Klemens Stock was called upon to succeed him, while Fr. Jean-Noël Aletti was appointed a member of that Commission.

As from the end of the council, the number of students in the biblical faculty began to increase. The first women students were admitted in 1965 and, as from 1980, students coming from Africa, Latin America, Asia and eastern Europe were in the majority. The service provided by the Biblical Institute was now on a truly universal scale.

Between 1970 and 1984, thanks to the support of the Holy See, which owns the place, the premises of the Institute were reorganized in two stages, to the advantage of the library, which got more room. In 1975, Fr. Arrupe, by setting up a *Fund Raising Scheme*, found a solution to the Institute's financial problems once and for all.

Closer to our own time, the year 1999 was significant, on the threshold of the second millennium. The Institute celebrated its 90th anniversary that year with an imposing three-day congress and the creation of the Association of Former Students. The internal and external assessments ended that same year and the consequences were later drawn from it by giving some details about the programmes offered to students by the biblical faculty, but without changing them radically.

Such were the major events in the history of the Pontifical Biblical Institute throughout the century. Since its foundation in 1909 it has evolved to a great extent. Two key periods have helped it on, the first between 1927 and 1932 and the second, during Vatican II.

At the moment, it can look forward with serenity. It relies on the trust and hope of the Holy See, as Cardinal Baum had already assured it of them in 1984. It knows that the Society of Jesus is keeping an eye on things. For its part, it intends "to penetrate and expound the meaning of Holy Scripture more profoundly so that, through [its] somewhat preparatory studies, the Church's judgment may mature" ("*Dei Verbum*" 12). Lastly, to take up an expression from the same conciliar source, one which our predecessors had suggested to the council in 1965, it is thoroughly convinced that "Holy Scripture must be read and interpreted in the light of the same Spirit who caused it to be written". Science and faith are on an equal footing.

"*Verbum Domini manet in aeternum*"; this sentence from the book of Isaiah (40,8), repeated in the first letter of Peter (1,25), has been our house's motto since 1909.

ABBREVIATIONS

AAS	*Acta Apostolicae Sedis*
Acta PIB	*Acta Pontificii Instituti Biblici*
Aeg	*Aegyptus*
AfO	*Archiv für Orientforschung*
AHP	*Archivum Historiae Pontificiae*
AnBib	Analecta Biblica
AncB	Anchor Bible
AnGr	Analecta Gregoriana
AnOr	Analecta Orientalia
APIBJ	Archivum Pontificii Instituti Biblici Jerusalem
APIBR	Archivum Pontificii Instituti Biblici Romae
APLJ	Archives du Patriarcat Latin de Jérusalem
ARSI	Archivum Romanum Societatis Iesu
ARSI	*Acta Romana Societatis Iesu*
ASAJ	Archives de Sainte-Anne à Jérusalem (Pères Blancs)
ASEJ	Archives de Saint-Étienne à Jérusalem (Dominicains)
ASOR	American Schools of Oriental Research
BAC	Biblioteca de Autores Cristianos
BETL	Bibliotheca Ephemeridum Theologicarum Lovaniensium
Bib	*Biblica*
BiOr	Biblica et Orientalia
BMus	Bibliothèque du *Muséon*
CBQ	*The Catholic Biblical Quarterly*
CC	*La Civiltà Cattolica*
CrSt	*Cristianesimo nella Storia*
DBS	Supplément au Dictionnaire de la Bible
DC	*La Documentation Catholique*
DHCJ	Diccionario Histórico de la Compañía de Jesús, 4 vol., Roma-Madrid, 2001
DHGE	Dictionnaire d'Histoire et de Géographie Ecclésiastiques
Doc. J.	Document about the PIB in Jerusalem
Doc. R.	Document about the PIB in Rome
DSD	*Dead Sea Discoveries*
DV	Vatican II's dogmatic Constitution *Dei Verbum*

EB	*Enchiridion Biblicum. Documenta ecclesiastica Sacram Scripturam spectantia*, [4]1961
EB	Études Bibliques
ETL	*Ephemerides Theologicarum Lovaniensium*
FThSt	Frankfurter theologische Studien
FzB	Forschung zur Bibel
JBL	*Journal of Biblical Literature*
JSJ Suppl	Supplements to the *Journal for the Study of Judaism*
LeDiv	Lectio divina
LiBi	Lire la Bible
MD	*La Maison-Dieu*
NRT	*Nouvelle Revue Théologique*
n.s.	new series
NTOA	Novum Testamentum et Orbis Antiquus
OBO	Orbis Biblicus et Orientalis
OCA	Orientalia Christiana Analecta
Or	*Orientalia*
OR	*L'Osservatore Romano*
PIB	Pontificio Istituto Bblico
PIO	Pontifico Istituto Orientale
PUG	Pontificia Università Gregoriana
RB	*Revue Biblique*
RHE	*Revue d'Histoire Ecclésiastique*
RivBib	*Rivista Biblica*
RQ	*Revue de Qumrân*
RSR	*Recherches de Science Religieuse*
SC	Sources Chrétiennes
ScC	*La Scuola Cattolica*
SEAug	Studia Ephemeridis 'Augustinianum'
SN	Studia Neotestamentaria
S.O.	Santo Ufficio
StP.SM	Studia Pohl. Series Maior
SubBi	Subsidia Biblica
TDig	*Theology Digest*
UCL	Université Catholique de Louvain
VTS	*Vetus Testamentum, Supplements*
ZPE	*Zeitschrift für Papyrologie und Epigraphik*

INDEX OF NAMES

An asterisk in front of a name means that the DHCJ has an article about that person

PHOTOGRAPH CAPTIONS

1. The Pontifical Biblical Institute in Rome

Page 1. Above, obverse and reverse of the medal commemorating the foundation of the Institute; it was struck in 1912 and represents Pius X on the obverse and Moses and Saint Peter on the reverse, with the Institute in the background; this rough sketch of the reverse does not bear any inscription; cf. p. 56. APIBR.

Below, left, Caroline du Coëtlosquet; cf. p. 50; right, Fr. Leopold Fonck about 1908. APIBR.

Page 2. Above, The *Aula Magna* in 1912; cf. p. 55. APIBR. Below, the same hall in 2008; cf. pp. 264-265; photo by Paolo Bizzari.

Page 3. Above, the museum at the Institute as it was about 1960; cf. pp. 89 and 266. APIBR. Below, the same room in 2008; cf. p. 266.

Page 4. Above, the staircase erected in 1910; cf. p. 55; the photo seems to date from January 1922, at the time of the death of Benedict XV. APIBR.

Below, left, Fr. Paul Joüon about 1910; cf. p. 58; photo by courtesy of the Oriental Library at the Université Saint-Joseph in Beirut; on the right, Frs. Andrés Fernández, the rector, (on the left) and Leopold Fonck (on the right) on either side of Fr. Franz Ehrle who had just been made a cardinal in December 1922; cf. p. 65. APIBR.

Page 5. The teaching staff at the Institute in 1937. From left to right, seated: Fathers Maurus Witzel, O.F.M. (cf. p. 79), John J. O'Rourke, Anton Deimel, Augustin Bea, the rector, Alberto Vaccari, Augustin Merk, Luis Gonzaga da Fonseca; standing: Frs. Ludwik Semkowski, Jean Simon, Giuseppe Messina, Robert Koeppel, Franz Zorell, Urban Holzmeister, Robert A. Dyson, Alfred Pohl, Alfredo Vitti (?) and one unidentified person. APIBR.

Page 6. Defence of doctoral thesis by Fr. Benjamin Wambacq, a Premonstratensian, on November 24th, 1938, at the Vatican in the presence of Pius XI. In the foreground, Fr. Wlodimir Ledóchowski; cf. p. 120. APIBR.

Page 7. Above, Fr. Augustin Merk and the bust of Pius XII in February 1945.

Below, Fr. John Janssens at the Biblical Institute on December 16th, 1954; cf. p. 158; on the right, Fr. Augustin Bea in his room shortly before becoming cardinal in December 1959. APIBR.

Page 8. In the centre on the left, the construction of the *Aula Magna* in 1947; cf. p. 142; above, on the left in the photo, the Church of the Holy Apostles; on the right, the façade of the Institute; photo by Mario Leonardi, the architect. APIBR.

Page 9. The teaching staff on May 6th 1959; cf. p. 176. From left to right, seated: Frs. Raimund Köbert, Édouard des Places, Luis Gonzaga da Fonseca, Augustin Bea, Alfred Pohl, Ludwik Semkowski (cf. p. 388), Ernst Vogt, the rector, Alberto Vaccari, Stanislas Lyonnet, Jean Simon, Gioacchino Patti; standing: Frs. Viliam Pavlovský, Pietro Boccaccio, Karl Prümm, Adhémar Massart, William L. Moran, Francis J. McCool, Stjepan Schmidt, the registrar, Luis Alonso Schökel, Joseph P. Smith, Malachi F. Martin, Max Zerwick and Eugen Bergmann. APIBR.

Page 10. Above, the *cortile* of the former College of Saint Bonaventure (cf. pp. 142 and 143), which became the residence of the Institute's Jesuit community in 1949; in the background on the left above the arcades, the *Aula Magna* of the Institute; photo taken about 1950. APIBR.

Below, at the audience in the Vatican on February 17th, 1960, John XXIII with Frs. Ernst Vogt, the rector, and, in profile, Karl Prümm; cf. p. 177. APIBR.

Page 11. Above, left, Fr. Stanislas Lyonnet about 1970; right, Fr. Karl Prümm about 1975.

Below, left, Fr. Pedro Arrupe at the Biblical Institute in 1972; right, Fr. Peter Nober about 1970. APIBR.

Page 12. Above, Paul VI and Fr. Carlo Maria Martini in the Vatican, at the time of the meeting of the Pontifical Biblical Commission in April 1978. APIBR.

Below, left, Fr. Luis Alonso Schökel in 1984; right, Fr. Édouard des Places in 1986. APIBR.

Page 13. Above, John Paul II chats with Fr. Mitchell Dahood at the Biblical Institute on December 15th, 1979; in profile, Fr. Saverio Corradino; cf. p. 267. APIBR.

Below, Miss Mary Grosvenor in 1984; cf. p. 247. APIBR.

Page 14. Above, Fr. Ignace de la Potterie during his last lesson on December 15, 1989, in the *Aula Magna* of the Institute.

Below, left, Fr. Robert North in 1986; right, Fr. Hans Quecke in 1984. APIBR.

Page 15. Above, Cardinal Joseph Ratzinger with Frs. Albert Vanhoye (left) and Klemens Stock (right); photo taken in the Jesuit community refectory at the Biblical Institute in April 2002 or 2003, on the occasion of a meeting between the community and the Pontifical Biblical Commission; photo by Frederick E. Brenk; cf. p. 469.

Below, Fr. James H. Swetnam during his last lesson at the Institute, November 5th, 2003, in the Institute's *Aula Magna*; cf. p. 300. APIBR.

Page 16. The teaching staff at the Institute, January 13th 2009. An asterisk in front of a person's name means he is a permanent professor. From left to right, seated (all are Jesuits): Karl Plötz, *Reinhard Neudecker, *Klemens Stock, *Stephen F. Pisano (vice rector), *José M. Abrego de Lacy (rector), *Pietro Bovati (dean of the biblical faculty), *Agustinus Gianto (pro-dean of the oriental faculty), *Robert Althann, *Horacio Simian Yofre and *Maurice Gilbert.

Second row, from left to right: Leo Arnold, S.J.; Yves Simoens, S.J.; *Gianguerrino Barbiero, S.D.B.; Giancarlo Biguzzi; *Jean-Louis Ska, S.J.; Don McMahon,

O.M.I.; Vincent Laisney, O.S.B.; Philippe Luisier, S.J.; Edmond Farahian, S.J.; Paul V. Mankowski, S.J.; and Carlo Valentino (registrar).

Third row, from left to right: Stanisłas Bazyliński, O.F.M.Conv.; John F. Gavin, S.J.; Roman Lebiedziuk, C.R.; Yvan Hruša, O.Carm.; *Joseph Sievers; Marc Rastoin, S.J.; Innocenzo Gargano, O.S.B.Cam.; *Craig Morrison, O.Carm.; Paolo Merlo, *Jean-Noël Aletti, S.J.; and J.M. Granados, S.J. Photo taken by Przemysław Adam Wisniewski, O.F.M.Conv., in the *Aula Paulina*. Some professors are absent: *Dean P. Béchard, S.J.; Peter Dubovský, S.J.; Anthony J. Forte, S.J.; *John J. Kilgallen, S.J.; *Werner Mayer, S.J. and Luca Mazzinghi.

2. The Pontifical Biblical Institute in Jerusalem

Page 1: Above, the 1913 caravan: from left to right, *seated*: Johannes Schaumberger, Andrés Fernández, Alexis Mallon, Louis Heidet, Jozef Patsch, Raffaele Tramontano; *standing*: Gustavo Testa, Antonio Biondini, Sanalius Diego, Pedro Pous, Ernesto Ruffini; cf. pp. 344 and 425-427. APIBJ.

Below, laying the first stone of the Biblical Institute building, October 18th, 1925; on the right, Mgr. Luigi Barlassina, Latin Patriarch of Jerusalem; on the left, Fr. Alexis Mallon making his speech; cf. pp. 338-339 and 354. APIBJ.

Page 2: Above, Fr. Alexis Mallon in his workshop at Ghassul, in December 1933, APIBJ.

Below, left, Fr. Robert Koeppel, March 5th 1939; on the right, Brother Josef Šira, about 1940. APIBJ.

Page 3: Above, the community, February 2nd 1936: from right to left, front row, Andrés Fernández, Marcel Lobignac, Henri Senès, Robert Koeppel; second row: Joseph W. Murphy, George S. Mahan, Antonio Vives, and Eduard Decher; cf. pp. 381-383 and 432. APIBJ.

Below, left, Fr. Andrés Fernández, June 29th 1939; on the right, Fr. Henri Senès, February 12th 1942. APIBJ

Page 4: Above, the terrace on the second floor with Fr. Henri Senès' fresco, November 30th 1942; cf. pp. 390 and 394. APIBJ.

Below, on the left, Br. Antonio Vives, May 11th 1939; on the right, Fr. John J. O'Rourke, January 8th 1948; cf. pp. 386 and 389, 390. APIBJ.

Page 5: Above, the community, July 14th 1944: from left to right, Br. Antonio Vives, Br. Josef Sira, Fr. Andrés Fernández (*seated*) and Fr. Henri Senès. APIBJ.

Below, the community in 1950: from right to left: Br. Antonio Vives, Fr. Ludwik Semkowski (seated), Br. Eduard Decher, Fr. Henri Senès, (*seated*) and Br. Josef Sira. APIBJ.

Page 6: Above, a summer 1967 group: from left to right, *seated*: Gérard Lajeunesse, Josef Sira, J. Ganuzza, Ludwig Semkowski, G. S. Petros, Piero Ferraboschi, Maurice Gilbert; *standing*: John J. Kilgallen, Thomas J. Fitzpatrick, John R. Lee, Aloysius Fitzgerald, Robert A. Hagan, Antonio Ammasari, Michael Spiteri, Pierre Gibert; cf. pp. 390. APIBJ.

Below, right, Fr. Ludwik Semkowski, in front of the house, February 6th 1950, in 50 cms. of snow; left, Fr. Francis P. Furlong in the museum, about 1980; cf. pp. 394-396. APIBJ.

Page 7: Above, Fr. William J. Fulco and Fr. Juan Esquivias holding the facial mask of our mummy in 1988; cf. pp. 443 and 444. APIBJ

Below, left, Fr. Pino Di Luccio in 2009; cf. pp. 449 and 450; on th right, the new classroom since 2002 cf. p. 401. Photos by Piergiacomo Zanetti, S. J.

Page 8: Above, Cardinal Carlo Maria Martini saying Mass in St. Jerome's Cave in Bethlehem on December 25th, 2003; photo by Françoise Mies.

Below, the community, December 26th 2008; from left to right: Peter B. DuBrul, Piergiacomo Zanetti (in the foreground), Francisco Javier Leandro, Flavio Gillio, Joseph Nguyên Công Đoan (director), David Neuhaus, Francesco Rossi de Gasperis; photo by Fr. Zanetti in Bethlehem. Cf. pp. 402 et 448.

TABLE OF CONTENTS

PART TWO
THE JERUSALEM BRANCH
OF THE PONTIFICAL BIBLICAL INSTITUTE

Commemorative medal for the foundation of the Institute (obverse)

Commemorative medal for the foundation of the Institute (reverse)

Caroline du Coëtlosquet

Fr. Leopold Fonck (about 1908)

The Aula Magna in 1912

The same hall in 2008

The Institute's museum about 1960

The same room in 2008

Staircase at entrance built in 1910 and demolished in 1981

Fr. Paul Joüon   *Fathers Andrés Fernández, Frans Ehrle and Leopold Fonck*

The teaching staff at the Institute in 1937 (cf. names on p. 485)

Fr. Benjamin Wambacq defends his doctoral thesis in the presence of Pius XI

Fr. Augustinus Merk and bust of Pius XII

Fr. John Janssens   *Fr. Augustin Bea in 1959*

Building the Aula Magna in 1947

The teaching staff at the Institute in 1959 (cf. names on p. 486)

The cortile *of the former College of Saint Bonaventure*

John XXIII with Fathers Ernst Vogt, the rector, and Karl Prümm (17.02.1960)

Fr. Stanislas Lyonnet about 1970

Fr. Karl Prümm about 1975

Fr. Pedro Arrupe in 1972

Fr. Peter Nober about 1970

THE PONTIFICAL BIBLICAL INSTITUTE IN ROME [photos, page 12]

Paul VI and Fr. Carlo M. Martini in 1978

Fr. Luis Alonso Schökel in 1984

Fr. Édouard des Places in 1986

John Paul II and Fr. Mitchell Dahood (15.12.1979)

Miss Mary Grosvenor in 1984

Fr. Ignace de la Potterie in 1984

Fr. Robert North in 1986   *Fr. Hans Quecke in 1984*

Fr. Albert Vanhoye, Card. Joseph Ratzinger and Fr. Klemens Stock (2002)

Fr. James H. Swetnam (05.12.2003)

Fr. Henry J. Bertels in 1984

The teaching staff at the Institute in 2008-2009 (cf. names on p. 486-487)

The 1913 caravan (cf. names on p. 487)

Laying the first stone of the Institute's building in Jerusalem (18.10.1925)

Fr. Alexis Mallon (December 1933)

Fr. Robert Koeppel (05.03.1939)   *Br. Josef Šira about 1940*

The community (02.02.1936; cf. names on p. 487)

Fr. Andrés Fernández (29.06.1939)   *Fr. Henri Senès (12.02.1942)*

The second floor terrace with Fr. Senès' fresco (30.11.1942)

Br. Antonio Vives (11.05.1939)   *Fr. John J. O'Rourke (08.01.1948)*

The community in 1944 (cf. names on p. 487)

The community in 1950 (cf. names on page 487)

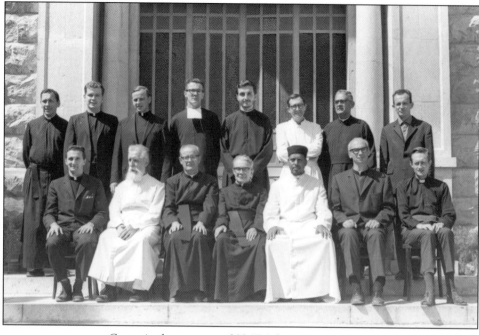

Group in the summer of 1967 (cf. names on p. 487)

Fr. Ludwik Semkowski (06.02.1950)

Fr. Francis P. Furlong about 1980

Fathers William J. Fulco and Juan Esquivias in 1988

Fr. Pino Di Luccio in 2009   *The new lecture room set up in 2002*

Card. Carlo Maria Martini at St. Jerome's Cave at Bethlehem (25.12.2003)

The Community in 2008-2009 (cf. names on p. 488)